WORKSHOPS IN COMPUTING
Series edited by C. J. van Rijsbergen

Also in this series

continued on back page...

Geoffrey Burn, Simon Gay and Mark Ryan (Eds.)

Theory and Formal Methods 1993

Proceedings of the First Imperial College
Department of Computing Workshop on
Theory and Formal Methods,
Isle of Thorns Conference Centre,
Chelwood Gate, Sussex, UK,
29–31 March 1993

Published in collaboration with the
British Computer Society

Springer-Verlag
London Berlin Heidelberg New York
Paris Tokyo Hong Kong
Barcelona Budapest

Geoffrey Burn, BSc (Hons), PhD, DIC

Simon Gay, BA (Hons), DipCompSci

Mark Ryan, MA, PhD

Department of Computing
Imperial College of Science, Technology and Medicine,
180 Queen's Gate
London, SW7 2BZ, UK

Some of the diagrams in this proceedings were drawn using the diagrams macro package designed and written by Paul Taylor.

ISBN 978-3-540-19842-0   ISBN 978-1-4471-3503-6 (eBook)
DOI 10.1007/978-1-4471-3503-6

British Library Cataloguing in Publication Data
A catalogue record for this book is available from the British Library

Library of Congress Cataloging-in-Publication Data
Imperial College Department of Computing Workshop on Theory and Formal Methods
(1st : 1993 : Chelwood Gate, England)
    Theory and formal methods : proceedings of the First Imperial College Department of
Computing Workshop on Theory and Formal Methods, Isle of Thorns Conference Centre,
Chelwood Gate, Sussex, UK, 29–31 March 1993 / Geoffrey Burn, Simon Gay, and Mark
Ryan, eds.
        p.   cm. – (Workshops in computing)
    "Published in collaboration with the British Computer Society."
    Includes bibliographical references and index.
    ISBN 978-3-540-19842-0
    1. Electronic digital computers–Programming–Congresses. I. Burn, Geoffrey,
1960– . II. Gay, Simon, 1969– . III. Ryan, Mark, 1962– . IV. Imperial
College of Science, Technology, and Medicine (Great Britain). Dept. of
Computing. V. British Computer Society. VI. Title. VII. Series.
QA76.6.I4457 193   93–25444
005.1'01'5113–dc20   CIP

Typesetting: Camera ready by contributors

34/3830-543210 Printed on acid-free paper

Preface

This volume contains the proceedings of the first workshop held by the Theory and Formal Methods Section of the Imperial College Department of Computing. It contains papers from almost every member of the Section, from our long-term academic visitors, and from those who have recently left us.

The papers fall into four broad areas:

- semantics
- concurrency
- logic
- specification

with some papers spanning a number of disciplines.

The subject material varies from work on mathematical foundations to practical applications of this theory, expressing the Section's commitment to both the foundations of computer science, and the application of theory to real computing problems.

In preparing the workshop and these proceedings, care was taken to ensure that there were papers overviewing a field, as well as ones whose primary aim was to present new scientific results. This had a dual purpose: to bring our Section members up to speed in some of the areas being worked on by the Section; and to provide the reader of the proceedings not only with a good introduction to many of the specific areas being investigated by the Section, but also with details of some of our latest results.

All the papers presented at the workshop were revised following comments made by the workshop participants, and all were subsequently reviewed by at least two people before producing the final versions contained in this volume.

We envisage that future workshops will occur at intervals of eighteen months, so that the next workshop will take place in September 1994.

Imperial College
June 1993

The Programme Committee:
Geoffrey Burn
Simon Gay
Mark Ryan
Paul Taylor

Contents

Part 1: Overview and Introductory Papers

The Abstract Interpretation of Functional Languages

Geoffrey Burn

glb@doc.ic.ac.uk
Department of Computing, Imperial College
180 Queen's Gate, London SW7 2BZ, United Kingdom

Abstract

Abstract interpretation is a methodology for developing provably correct program analyses. Uses of such analyses include optimising compilers and program verification.

In this introductory paper, we introduce key issues in the abstract interpretation of higher-order languages, including some open problems. Intuitions, examples and open problems are given instead of a list of theorems.

1   Introduction

Most compilers contain data flow analyses to help generate more efficient code. *Abstract interpretation* is a generic term used to describe any such analysis *which has been proved correct* against the semantics of the language being compiled. Many of the flow analyses of the 'dragon book' [3] can be reformulated as abstract interpretations.

The purpose of this paper is to introduce the main ideas and issues concerning the abstract interpretation of higher-order functional languages.

We will focus on denotationally-based program analysis techniques, in the style of [6, 29][1], rather than the operationally-based ones of the Cousot school [11], but we will return to the latter in Section 3, the final section of this paper.

Six key issues in the abstract interpretation of higher-order functional languages, including some open problems, are discussed in Section 2. The presentation will be by way of giving intuitions, examples and open problems rather than by theorems.

A (mono-)typed lambda-calculus with fixed points and constants is defined in Figure 1, and will be used as the example language in this paper. In the language definition, the term $\mathbf{k}_\sigma$ stands for an arbitrary constant of some type σ, $\mathbf{if}_{bool \rightarrow \sigma \rightarrow \sigma \rightarrow \sigma}$ or $\mathbf{plus}_{int \rightarrow int \rightarrow int}$ for example, and x^σ and x^τ are different variables if σ is not equal to τ.

---

[1]Due to space restrictions, we have adopted a policy of citing only the most recent paper by an author which deals with a particular topic. Other papers, including many seminal works, can be found by following the references in the cited paper.

The set T of types is the least set defined by:

$$\{bool, int\} \subseteq T$$
$$\sigma, \tau \in T \Rightarrow (\sigma \rightarrow \tau) \in T$$
$$\sigma, \tau \in T \Rightarrow (\sigma \times \tau) \in T$$

The type system of Λ_T

(1) $\quad x^\sigma \ : \ \sigma$
$\qquad\qquad$
(2) $\quad \mathbf{k}_\sigma \ : \ \sigma$

(3) $\quad \dfrac{E_1 \ : \ \sigma \rightarrow \tau, \ E_2 \ : \ \sigma}{(E_1 \ E_2) \ : \ \tau}$
$\qquad$
(4) $\quad \dfrac{E \ : \ \tau}{(\lambda x^\sigma.E) \ : \ \sigma \rightarrow \tau}$

(5) $\quad \dfrac{E_1 \ : \ \sigma, \ E_2 \ : \ \tau}{(E_1, E_2) \ : \ \sigma \times \tau}$
$\qquad$
(6) $\quad \dfrac{E \ : \ \sigma \rightarrow \sigma}{\mathbf{fix}_\sigma \ E \ : \ \sigma}$

Abstract Syntax of Λ_T

Figure 1: Definition of the Language Λ_T

2 Six Key Issues in Abstract Interpretation

2.1 Interpretations

Giving a (denotational) semantics to a language can be done in two stages: firstly translating programs into a semantic meta-language; and then giving an interpretation to the meta-language (see [29] for example). Different meanings, or *interpretations* can be given to a programming language by varying the meaning of the semantic meta-language.

In practice, it is only necessary to do this two-stage process for the parts of the language which change from interpretation to interpretation. An example of such an interpretation is given in Figure 2. There the function type constructor is always interpreted as giving a domain of continuous functions, whereas the interpretation of $\times$ has not been fixed. Because of these choices, the interpretations of a lambda-abstraction and an application are always a function and an application respectively, whereas the interpretation of the pairing constructor is expressed using a meta-language constant, whose meaning depends on the interpretation given to the product type. The meanings of programming language constants depends on the interpretation given to the types.

Example 2.1 We give three example interpretations.

- The *standard interpretation* is defined by giving the usual interpretations for $\mathbf{M}_{int}$, $\mathbf{M}_{bool}$ and the constants, and defining $\mathbf{M}(\times)$ to be product, so that $\mathbf{pair}_\mathbf{M}(v, w)$ is (v, w).

- In a *strictness interpretation*, the property we are interested in at base types is if the value is definitely bottom. Therefore we set $\mathbf{S}_{int} = \mathbf{2} = \{0, 1\}$ with $0 \sqsubseteq 1$, where 0 'represents'[2] $\perp_{\mathbf{M}_{int}}$ and 1 'represents' $\mathbf{M}_{int}$. Similarly for

---

[2] We formalise the notion of 'represents' in the section on correctness.

$$\mathbf{I}_B \quad = \quad \text{some domain for the base type } B$$
$$\mathbf{I}_{\sigma \to \tau} \quad = \quad \mathbf{I}_\sigma \to \mathbf{I}_\tau \qquad \text{(domain of continuous functions)}$$
$$\mathbf{I}_{\sigma \times \tau} \quad = \quad \mathbf{I}(\times)\,(\mathbf{I}_\sigma, \mathbf{I}_\tau)$$

Semantics of the Types

$$\mathbf{I} \llbracket x^\sigma \rrbracket \, \rho^{\mathbf{I}} = \rho^{\mathbf{I}} \, x^\sigma$$
$$\mathbf{I} \llbracket k_\sigma \rrbracket \, \rho^{\mathbf{I}} = \mathbf{K}^{\mathbf{I}} \llbracket k_\sigma \rrbracket$$
$$\mathbf{I} \llbracket E_1\,E_2 \rrbracket \, \rho^{\mathbf{I}} = \mathbf{I} \llbracket E_1 \rrbracket \, \rho^{\mathbf{I}}\,(\mathbf{I} \llbracket E_2 \rrbracket \, \rho^{\mathbf{I}})$$
$$\mathbf{I} \llbracket \lambda x^\sigma.E \rrbracket \, \rho^{\mathbf{I}} = \lambda d \epsilon \mathbf{I}_\sigma . \mathbf{I} \llbracket E \rrbracket \, \rho^{\mathbf{I}}[d/x^\sigma]$$
$$\mathbf{I} \llbracket (E_1, E_2) \rrbracket \, \rho^{\mathbf{I}} = \mathbf{pair}_{\mathbf{I}}\,(\mathbf{I} \llbracket E_1 \rrbracket \, \rho^{\mathbf{I}}, \mathbf{I} \llbracket E_2 \rrbracket \, \rho^{\mathbf{I}})$$
$$\mathbf{I} \llbracket \mathbf{fix}_\sigma\,E \rrbracket \, \rho^{\mathbf{I}} = \bigsqcup_{i \geq 0}(\mathbf{I} \llbracket E \rrbracket \, \rho^{\mathbf{I}})^i \perp_{\mathbf{I}_\sigma}$$

Semantics of the Language Terms

Figure 2: A Parameterised Semantics of Λ_T

$\mathbf{S}_{bool}$. Set

$$\mathbf{K}^{\mathbf{S}} \llbracket \mathbf{plus} \rrbracket = \lambda x \epsilon 2 . \lambda y \epsilon 2 . x \sqcap y; \text{ and}$$
$$\mathbf{K}^{\mathbf{S}} \llbracket \mathbf{if}_{bool \to \sigma \to \sigma \to \sigma} \rrbracket = \lambda x \epsilon 2 . \lambda y \epsilon \mathbf{S}_\sigma . \lambda z \epsilon \mathbf{S}_\sigma . \begin{cases} \perp_{\mathbf{S}_\sigma} & \text{if } x = 0 \\ y \sqcup z & \text{otherwise} \end{cases}$$

Intuitively, as **plus** is strict in both of its arguments, the abstract interpretation has to return 0 if either of its arguments are 0. If the first argument to **if** is undefined, then it returns the bottom of the appropriate type, giving the first case in the abstract interpretation of **if**. Otherwise, the abstract interpretation has to capture the fact that the conditional may return either its second or third argument, so it uses $\sqcup$ to capture the information about both arguments. We will leave discussing the interpretation of $\times$ in an abstract interpretation until Section 2.2.2.

This abstract interpretation will be used as an example throughout the rest of the paper.

♦ In a *binding time analysis* we want to know which expressions can be evaluated at compile-time (are *static*), and which can only be evaluated at run-time (are *dynamic*). Set $\mathbf{B}_{int} = 2 = \{\mathcal{S}, \mathcal{D}\}$ with $\mathcal{S} \sqsubseteq \mathcal{D}$, so that $\mathcal{S}$ represents the property of being static, and $\mathcal{D}$ for dynamic. The following interpretations of two constants are intuitively obvious.

$$\mathbf{K}^{\mathbf{B}} \llbracket \mathbf{plus} \rrbracket = \lambda x \epsilon 2 . \lambda y \epsilon 2 . x \sqcup y; \text{ and}$$
$$\mathbf{K}^{\mathbf{B}} \llbracket \mathbf{if}_{bool \to \sigma \to \sigma \to \sigma} \rrbracket = \lambda x \epsilon 2 . \lambda y \epsilon \mathbf{B}_\sigma . \lambda z \epsilon \mathbf{B}_\sigma . \begin{cases} \top_{\mathbf{B}_\sigma} & \text{if } x = \mathcal{D} \\ y \sqcup z & \text{otherwise} \end{cases}$$

■

The last two interpretations are examples of what are commonly called *abstract* interpretations, because they abstract away some of the detail of the standard interpretation in order to study some properties of interest. In the strictness example, we abstract away from the values of objects to focus on how defined they are. In the rest of this paper we will denote an arbitrary abstract interpretation by **A**.

It is often possible to induce suitable abstract interpretations of constants once the interpretations of the types has been fixed (see [6, Section 4.1.2] and [29, Sections 2.5 and 8]).

2.2 Properties

Two important questions that must be asked about an abstract interpretation framework are: what properties can be represented?; and how can they be combined? [8].

2.2.1 What properties can be represented?

The abstract interpretation framework of [6] was developed with a specific application in mind: to determine how functions use their arguments so that the evaluation order of programs could be changed. It was implicit in that work that abstract domain points represented Scott-closed sets, which had a natural fit with the application (see [6, Chapter 5]).

However, some properties cannot be encoded using Scott-closed sets. For example, consider expressing the fact that function is constant, that is, $\forall x, y. f\ x = f\ y$. Using Scott-closed sets, one could only say that $\forall x, f\ x \in S$ for some set S, which is not powerful enough to express constancy in general, because every Scott-closed set has at least bottom in it.

The key insight of Hunt was that the above property is expressing a *relation*[21]. In particular, if ALL is the relation which is satisfied by all pairs, and $x\ ID\ y$ if and only if $x = y$, then f is constant if and only if for all x and y such that $x\ ALL\ y$ we have $(f\ x)\ ID\ (f\ y)$. Another classic example is the property of *head-strictness* [31], which is naturally expressed as a relation, but which cannot be expressed using a finite number of Scott closed sets [23][3].

What sort of relations should be considered? In the examples in the previous paragraph, if u and v are in the relation because they both have the same property, then we should expect that both u is related to v and v is related to u, that is, the relation should be symmetric. Similarly, it can be argued that the relation should also be reflexive and transitive, that is, an equivalence relation. However, there is a problem with saying that properties must be equivalence relations: even if the relations S and T on types σ and τ are equivalence relations, the natural relation $S \Rightarrow T$ on $\sigma \rightarrow \tau$, defined by

$$f\ (S \Rightarrow T)\ f' \text{ if and only if } [s\ S\ s' \text{ implies } (f\ s)\ T\ (f'\ s')],$$

may not be (e.g. $ALL \Rightarrow ID$ contains only constant functions). As Hunt observed, this forces us to consider *partial equivalence relations (pers)*, which are symmetric and transitive, but not necessarily reflexive relations[4] [21]. We

---

[3]It is important that this result of Kamin is not misunderstood. He did not prove that head-strictness cannot be determined by using an abstract interpretation of the form discussed in this paper. In fact, such an interpretation is given in [20, Section 5.3]. The key point is that the appropriate notion of property must be used.

[4]It is easy to see that the relation is reflexive on the elements in the relation, so that a per is an equivalence relation on a subset of the set over which the per is defined.

have seen three examples of pers in this section: *ALL*, *ID*, and *ALL* $\Rightarrow$ *ID*; the first two are *total* pers (or equivalence relations) because all elements of the domain over which the per is defined are in the per, and we have seen that the second is not. Pers can also be used to encode sets: for the set S define $x\ R_S\ y$ if and only if $x \in S$ and $y \in S$.

It would be foolish to suggest that pers are the last word in specifying what a useful notion of property is; after all, everything can be encoded using sets. However, what is clear is that some notions of property are too restrictive to be used in all applications (e.g. Scott-closed sets), or do not fit well with the higher-order nature of the language (e.g. equivalence relations), whilst others may be more general than is needed for a particular application.

2.2.2   How can they be combined?

One of the techniques of abstract interpretation is to define abstract domains for the base types which capture the properties of interest. The constructions used for the abstract interpretation of the type constructors then determine which properties can be represented on constructed types. These issues are discussed more fully in [8, 10, 16, 28].

Example 2.2 Consider the strictness abstract interpretation, and suppose that product is used to interpret $\times$. Then, intuitively, the pair $(0, 1)$ represents $\{(\perp_{\mathbf{M}_{int}}, b)|b \in \mathbf{M}_{int}\}$, and $(1, 0)$ represents $\{(a, \perp_{\mathbf{M}_{int}})|a \in \mathbf{M}_{int}\}$. In order to determine that the function:

$$\lambda c.\lambda x.\mathbf{if}\ c\ (x, 12)\ (5, x)$$

is strict in its second argument, we need to be able to represent the property "either the first element of the pair is bottom or the second element of the pair is bottom", that is, the set $\{(\perp_{\mathbf{M}_{int}}, b)|b \in \mathbf{M}_{int}\} \bigcup \{(a, \perp_{\mathbf{M}_{int}})|a \in \mathbf{M}_{int}\}$? The point in the abstract domain which best approximates this property is $(0, 1) \sqcup (1, 0) = (1, 1)$, but $(1, 1)$ represents $\mathbf{M}_{int} \times \mathbf{M}_{int}$, a safe approximation to the property we wish to represent, but not a very accurate one. However, if the *tensor* product, $\otimes$, is used, then there is an extra point, $0 \otimes 1 \sqcup 1 \otimes 0$, which is not the same as $1 \otimes 1$, and which represents this property. ∎

This example shows that it can be important to have sets of properties which are closed under conjunctions and/or disjunctions, and that interpretation of a type constructor in the abstract interpretation determines how the sets of properties are closed. The following example discusses three possible choices that can be made for products if properties are Scott-closed sets, where conjunction is intersection and disjunction is union.

Example 2.3   ♦ $\mathbf{A}_{\sigma \times \tau} = \mathbf{A}_\sigma \times \mathbf{A}_\tau$ gives a set of properties closed under $\bigcap$;

♦ $\mathbf{A}_{\sigma \times \tau} = \mathbf{A}_\sigma \otimes \mathbf{A}_\tau$ gives a set of properties closed under $\bigcap$ and any unions present in the properties given by $\mathbf{A}_\sigma$ and $\mathbf{A}_\tau$; and

♦ $\mathbf{A}_{\sigma \times \tau} = \mathbf{LC}\ (\mathbf{A}_\sigma \times \mathbf{A}_\tau)$, the set of lower-closed subsets of $\mathbf{A}_\sigma \times \mathbf{A}_\tau$, gives a set of properties closed under all finite intersections and unions.

Note: $\mathbf{A}_{\sigma \to \tau} = \mathbf{A}_\sigma \to \mathbf{A}_\tau$ gives a set of properties closed under intersections. No construction is known which results in a set of properties closed under unions. ∎

Muchnick and Jones introduced the terms *independent attribute* and *relational* to distinguish between an analysis which treated elements of a pair separately, and one which could express relationships between them [26]. The example above shows that this is not a fine enough distinction, for there may be many different levels of relationship that one can, and might want to express in an analysis.

2.2.3 Program Logics

An alternative approach to abstract interpretation is to define a program logic, where a property of a term is expressed by a formula in the logic. Formulae are constructed from a set of logical constants, which are the original set of properties, and logical connectives. A deduction system can be defined, similar to a type deduction system. A model must then be given for the logic, and the deduction system proved correct with respect to the model. A disadvantage of using pers as properties (i.e. a model for the logic), is that the union of two pers is not in general a per. Further details can be found in [22, 5, 7].

2.2.4 Recursive types

What abstract domain should be given for lists of integers, defined by:

$$listint \cong 1 + int \times listint?$$

The problem is that the 'obvious' abstract domain might be infinite. For example, in a strictness analysis we might define:

$$S_{listint} \cong 1 + 2 \times S_{listint},$$

and it is not clear that this is what is needed. There are two approaches we might take:

♦ **fix abstract domains which capture the properties of interest:** For example, if the information is to be used to find out when lists can be evaluated, then the abstract domain should capture the modes of evaluation which are to be implemented. Easily implemented evaluation modes are going to be ones which treat elements of a list in a uniform manner: evaluating a list to weak head normal form (WHNF); or evaluating the structure of a list; or evaluating the structure of a list and each element to WHNF for example. This inspired Wadler to define a four point abstract domain for lists:

$$
\begin{array}{lll}
\bot & \text{representing} & \{\bot_{\mathbf{M}_{listint}}\} \\
\infty & \text{representing} & \{a | a \text{ is not finite}\} \\
\bot_{\in} & \text{representing} & \{a | a \text{ is not total}\} \\
\top_{\in} & \text{representing} & \{a | a \in \mathbf{M}_{listint}\}
\end{array}
$$

with the intuition that all except the last point correspond to the set of values for which one of the modes of evaluation will fail to terminate [32]. The idea is further investigated in [14, 30].

The two essential problems with this approach are that: the fact that a function has a property may depend on some other property not expressed in the analysis, and so it will not be detected; and it is not clear how to generalise the idea to arbitrary data type definitions and analyses.

♦ **allow the abstract interpretation process to fix the set of properties it uses:** For example, the analysis may be allowed to determine the evaluation patterns for lists that are used in a particular program rather than fixing them beforehand (see [17] for example). In fact, it is essential to use this second approach for some analyses, even when considering non-recursive data types; see [11] for further details.

It is still an open problem to find a good way of dealing with a general data type definition in an arbitrary analysis.

2.3 Correctness

So far we have been very loose in our terminology when saying that an abstract point 'represents' some property. Clearly a relationship must be established between the standard and abstract interpretations of a language. There are two standard approaches to this:

♦ define a concretisation function γ from abstract values to properties and show that $(\mathbf{A} \; [\![E]\!] \; \rho^{\mathbf{A}}) = p$ implies $(\mathbf{M} \; [\![E]\!] \; \rho^{\mathbf{M}})$ has the property $(\gamma \; p)$; and

♦ define a *relation* between abstract values and properties, and prove that the standard and abstract interpretations of every term are in the relation.

In the first case it is usual to define the concretisation map on the base types, and then to induce a concretisation map for the constructed types according to the interpretation of the type constructors in the abstract interpretation.

Example 2.4 For the various interpretations of × given in Example 2.2, where properties are Scott-closed sets, we would define γ in the following way:

$\mathbf{A}_{\sigma \times \tau} = \mathbf{A}_\sigma \times \mathbf{A}_\tau$: $\gamma_{\sigma \times \tau} = \gamma_\sigma \times \gamma_\tau$; and

$\mathbf{A}_{\sigma \times \tau} = \mathbf{A}_\sigma \otimes \mathbf{A}_\tau$ *or* $\mathbf{A}_{\sigma \times \tau} = \mathbf{P} \; (\mathbf{A}_\sigma \times \mathbf{A}_\tau)$: $\gamma_{\sigma \times \tau} \; A = \bigcup_{(a,b) \in A} \gamma_{\sigma \times \tau}(a, b)$.

When properties are pers, the concretisation function has to return a per (see [20] for details). ∎

When a relation is being used to expressed correctness, it is usual to define the relation on the base types, and then extend it to higher-types as a logical relation. In general, the relation has to have some properties — the relation must be strict (bottom is related to bottom) and bottom-preserving (only bottom is related to bottom) for a strictness analysis for example — and it must be inductive (if elements of two chains are related, then so are the limits of the chains) in order for fixed points to work. Typically these properties are inherited from the relation on the base types. Details can be found in [1, 29].

Example 2.5 For the various interpretations of × given in Example 2.2, where properties are Scott-closed sets, we would define the relation $\mathbf{R}_{\sigma \times \tau}$ as follows:

$\mathbf{A}_{\sigma \times \tau} = \mathbf{A}_\sigma \times \mathbf{A}_\tau$: $(s_1, s_2) \; \mathbf{R}_{\sigma \times \tau} \; (a_1, a_2)$ if and only if $s_1 \; \mathbf{R}_\sigma \; a_1$ and $s_2 \; \mathbf{R}_\tau \; a_2$; and

$\mathbf{A}_{\sigma \times \tau} = \mathbf{A}_\sigma \otimes \mathbf{A}_\tau$ *or* $\mathbf{A}_{\sigma \times \tau} = \mathbf{P} \; (\mathbf{A}_\sigma \times \mathbf{A}_\tau)$: $(s_1, s_2) \; \mathbf{R}_{\sigma \times \tau} \; A$ if and only if $\exists (a_1, a_2) \in A$ such that $s_1 \; \mathbf{R}_\sigma \; a_1$ and $s_2 \; \mathbf{R}_\tau \; a_2$.

For function types $\mathbf{R}_{\sigma \to \tau}$ is defined by:

$$f \; \mathbf{R}_{\sigma \to \tau} \; f' \text{ if and only if } [s \; \mathbf{R}_\sigma \; s' \text{ implies } (f \; s) \; \mathbf{R}_\tau \; (f' \; s')].$$

When properties are pers, the relation has to be between the abstract value and a per (see [20] for details). ∎

Correctness theorems are typically of the form: if the constants in the language satisfy the correctness condition, then all terms in the language satisfy the condition.

2.4 Computability

Evaluating an abstract interpretation involves the calculation of (safe approximations to) fixed points. There are two basic approaches:

- if all chains in abstract domains are finite, then the fixed point can be calculated exactly; or
- develop a method which guarantees that a safe approximation to the fixed point will be found, whether or not all chains are finite.

Nevertheless, calculating (safe approximations to) fixed points can be a time-consuming process, and good algorithms need to be developed for doing this, which is what we discuss in the next section.

2.5 Finding Fixed Points

Consider the example:

```
cat :: [[int]] -> [int]
cat xss = foldr append xss []
```

If we use **2** for the abstract interpretation of `int`, the four point chain domain **4** for `[int]`, and the six point chain domain **6** for `[[int]]`, then `foldr` is being used at a type where its abstract interpretation is in $((4 \to 4 \to 4) \to 6 \to 4 \to 4)$, and the argument domain (of the uncurried version) of this function contains of the order of 10^6 elements [20, pp.143f]. Such examples are common-place in programs which use higher-order functions seriously. This has two consequences for finding the least fixed point by calculating the chain of approximations: the time to test a new approximation against the last one is expensive; and a large number of iterations might be needed. A number of techniques have been suggested to tackle these problems:

- **use of frontiers:** For a strictness analysis of first-order functions, a line can be drawn across the argument lattice such that at all points on and below the line the function has the value 0, and at all points above the line it has the value 1 [9]. This cuts down the costs of representing and comparing various approximations to a fixed point, but does not change the number of approximations that must be calculated. The idea can be generalised to other abstract interpretations and to higher-order functions [24, 20].

- **use of concrete data structures:** The frontier representation does not give any information about the dependencies between the values of the function at various argument values. Using a variant of Berry and Curien's concrete data structures enables these dependencies to be encoded, cutting down the number of iterations needed to find a fixed point. It has the further advantage that the fixed need only be calculated at the points which are needed [15].

- **doing calculation in a smaller domain:** Hankin and Hunt have shown how a safe approximation to a fixed point can be obtained by mapping the problem into a smaller space, doing the calculation there, and mapping the result back [18] (and see also [4]). Either of the two methods above can be used to calculate the fixed point in the smaller lattice. This can be understood as an example of the more general technique of defining widening and narrowing operators.

♦ **use of widening and narrowing:** Roughly speaking, a *widening* operator traverses the lattice of approximations much more quickly than calculating each approximation to the fixed point, stabilising at a safe approximation to the fixed point, and a *narrowing* operator can be used to move back towards the fixed point, to get a better approximation [11]. It is essential to use this method if abstract domains contain infinite chains. Even when all chains are finite, they may be so long that defining a widening operator and a narrowing operator is the only way of calculating safe approximations to a fixed point in an acceptable amount of time. However, defining such operators is a hard problem in itself.

2.6 Polymorphism

So far we have been dealing with a monomorphically typed language, whereas most functional languages are polymorphically typed. There are three approaches we may take to this:

♦ **translate programs into monomorphic ones:** Holmstrom proved that it is possible to translate polymorphic programs into monomorphic ones [19], so at least programs in a polymorphically typed language can be analysed within the framework. However, this has three drawbacks: firstly it is inelegant to do this when polymorphism has the informal meaning "it behaves the same way at every type"; secondly it means calculating the fixed point of a recursive function at every type at which it is used, and we have seen that calculating a fixed point is an expensive process; and finally, many programs have some properties at every type: the identity function is strict at every type for example.

♦ **find out information true of every monomorphic instance:** The next best thing is if we can prove a theorem which says that if some property holds for some monomorphic instance of a function, then it holds for all instances of that function. Then, if an analysis can show that one instance of a function has that property, we can conclude that all instances have that property. Clearly it is most efficient to try to determine whether the property holds at the smallest monomorphic instance. This approach was pioneered by Abramsky [2].

♦ **determine the abstract interpretation of an expression from its simplest monomorphic instance:** The problem with the previous approach is that it does not give enough information: sometimes an expression is needed for the abstract interpretation of a language term. Two examples of when this is the case are: the abstract interpretation of an expression may be needed in a particular context; and, when separate compilation is used, a representation of the abstract interpretation of each function exported from a module must be available for analysing any other module which uses one of the exported functions. Baraki shows that this expression can be the abstract interpretation of a function at its simplest type, because from this an expression can be determined for the function at any type [4].

Monsuez has suggested that it may be possible to combine polymorphic type inference with the approach of program logics, (Section 2.2.3), all in an abstract interpretation framework, as a different approach to the problem of polymorphism [25].

3 Relationship with the Cousot Framework

This topic is a research area in itself. The simplest observation to make is that our work has focused on denotationally-based analyses, always with higher-order languages in mind, whereas the Cousot school has historically focused on analyses based on operational semantics. Initially all the applications of their framework were for first-order imperative languages, but latterly it has been applied to higher-order languages [11, 12, 13].

The typical methodology of the Cousot school has been to first lift the semantics to a *collecting semantics*, one which works on sets rather than values, and then to develop abstract interpretations of this. Correctness can be proved by exhibiting a Galois connection between the collecting semantics and the abstract interpretation. Latterly they have shown that widening and narrowing can be used to specify and prove analyses correct, rather than just using it as a technique for finding fixed points [11].

Recently the Cousots have developed a new method for giving semantics to programs, from which operational and denotational semantics can be derived, and which can be used as a basis for work on abstract interpretation [12]. In this framework, the denotation of a function is not necessarily a function, and so this seems to overcome the problem with the approach of this paper: that function spaces do seem to admit a notion of disjunction. Another promising approach to this problem can be found in [27].

Acknowledgements

The presentation of this paper has a bias introduced by my own research over a number of years, during which time I have benefited from discussion and collaboration with many people, some of whom were: Samson Abramsky, Lennart Augustsson, David Bevan, Chris Hankin, John Hughes, Sebastian Hunt, Denis Howe, Thomas Jensen, Thomas Johnsson, Raju Karia, David Lester, Daniel Le Metayer, Juarez Muylaert-Filho, Simon Peyton Jones, John Robson, David Sands, and Philip Wadler. The research has been funded over the years by a number of different projects: ESPRIT Project 415 (Parallel Architectures and Languages for AIP – A VLSI-Directed Approach), ESPRIT BRA 3124 (Semantique), ESPRIT Project 3003 (CLICS II), and SERC grant GR/H 17381 (Using the Evaluation Transformer Model to make Lazy Functional Languages more Efficient). David Clark, Patrick Cousot and Chris Hankin made helpful comments about drafts of this paper.

References

[1] S. Abramsky. Abstract interpretation, logical relations and Kan extensions. *Journal of Logic and Computation*, 1(1):5–39, 1990.

[2] S. Abramsky and T.P. Jensen. A relational approach to strictness analysis for higher-order functions. In *Proceedings of the Symposium on Principles of Programming Languages*, pages 49–54, Orlando, Florida, 21–23 January 1991.

[3] A.V. Aho, R. Sethi, and J.D. Ullman. *Compilers: Principles, Techniques and Tools*. Addison-Wesley, Reading, MA, 1986.

[4] G. Baraki. *Abstract Interpretation of Polymorphic Higher-Order Functions*. PhD thesis, Department of Computer Science, University of Glasgow, Lilybank Gardens, Glasgow G12 8QQ, UK, 1993.

[5] P.N. Benton. Strictness logic and polymorphic invariance. In A. Nerode and M. Taitslin, editors, *Proceedings of the International Symposium on Logical Foundations of Computer Science*, pages 33–44, Tver, Russia, 20–24 July 1992. Springer-Verlag LNCS620.

[6] G.L. Burn. *Lazy Functional Languages: Abstract Interpretation and Compilation*. Research Monographs in Parallel and Distributed Computing. Pitman in association with MIT Press, 1991. 238pp.

[7] G.L. Burn. A logical framework for program analysis. In J. Launchbury and P. Sansom, editors, *Proceedings of the 1992 Glasgow Functional Programming Workshop*, pages 30–42. Springer-Verlag Workshops in Computer Science series, 6–8 July 1992.

[8] G.L. Burn. Properties of progam analysis techniques. Technical Report DOC92/19, Imperial College of Science, Technology and Medicine, Department of Computing, June 1992.

[9] C. Clack and S.L. Peyton Jones. Strictness analysis – a practical approach. In J.-P. Jouannaud, editor, *Proceedings of the Functional Programming Languages and Computer Architecture Conference*, pages 35–49. Springer-Verlag LNCS 201, September 1985.

[10] P. Cousot and R. Cousot. Abstract interpretation and application to logic programs. *Journal of Logic Programming*, 13(2–3):103–179, 1992.

[11] P. Cousot and R. Cousot. Comparing the Galois connection and widening/narrowing approaches to abstract interpretation. In M. Bruynooghe and M. Wirsing, editors, *Programming Language Implementation and Logic Programming, Proceedings of the Fourth International Symposium*, pages 269–295. Springer-Verlag LNCS631, Leuven, Belgium, August 1992.

[12] P. Cousot and R. Cousot. Inductive definitions, semantics and abstract interpretation. In *POPL'92*, pages 83–95. ACM, Albuquerque, New Mexico, 19–22 January 1992.

[13] A. Deutsch. An operational model of strictness properties and its abstractions (extended abstract). In R. Heldal, C. Kehler Holst, and P. Wadler, editors, *Proceedings of the 1991 Glasgow Functional Programming Workshop*, 13–15 August 1991.

[14] C. Ernoult and A. Mycroft. Uniform ideals and strictness analysis. In *Proceedings of ICALP'91*. Springer-Verlag Lecture Notes in Computer Science, 1991.

[15] A.B. Ferguson and R.J.M. Huges. Abstract interpretation of higher-order functions using concrete data structures (summary). In J. Launchbury and P. Sansom, editors, *Proceedings of the 1992 Glasgow Functional Programming Workshop*, pages 57–61. Springer-Verlag Workshops in Computer Science series, 6–8 July 1992.

[16] P. Granger. Combinations of semantic analyses. In INRIA, editor, *Proceedings of Informatika 88 (French-Soviet Workshop)*, pages 71–88, Nice, February 1988.

[17] C.V. Hall and D.S. Wise. Generating function versions using rational strictness patters. *Science of Computer Programming*, 12:39–74, 1989.

[18] Chris Hankin and Sebastian Hunt. Approximate fixed points in abstract interpretation. In B. Krieg-Brückner, editor, *ESOP'92*, pages 219–232. Springer-Verlag LNCS 582, 1992.

[19] S. Holmström. *Polymorphic Type Systems and Concurrent Computation in Functional Languages*. PhD thesis, Chalmers Tekniska Högskola, Göteborg, Sweden, 1983.

[20] L.S. Hunt. *Abstract Interpretation of Functional Languages: From Theory to Practice.* PhD thesis, Department of Computing, Imperial College of Science, Technology and Medicine, University of London, 1991.

[21] L.S. Hunt and D. Sands. Binding time analysis: A new PERspective. In *Proceedings of the Symposium on Partial Evaluation and Semantics-Based Program Manipulation (PEPM'91)*, pages 154–165, Yale University, USA, 11–19 June 1991. ACM.

[22] T. P. Jensen. *Abstract Interpretation in Logical Form.* PhD thesis, Imperial College, University of London, November 1992.

[23] S. Kamin. Head-strictness is not a monotonic abstract property. *Information Processing Letters*, 1991. To appear.

[24] C. Martin and C. Hankin. Finding fixed points in finite lattices. In G. Kahn, editor, *Proceedings of the Functional Programming Languages and Computer Architecture Conference*, pages 426–445. Springer-Verlag LNCS 274, September 1987.

[25] B. Monsuez. Type inference by abstract interpretation. Technical report, Laboratoire d'informatique de l'École Polytechnique, 91128 Palaiseau Cedex, France, February 1991.

[26] S.S. Muchnick and N.D. Jones, editors. *Program Flow Analysis: Theory and Applications.* Prentice-Hall Software Series. Prentice-Hall, 1981. ISBN 0-13-729681-9.

[27] J. Muylaert Filho and G.L. Burn. Continuation passing transformation and abstract intrepretation. In this volume.

[28] F. Nielson. Tensor products generalise the relational data flow analysis method. In *Proceedings of the 4th Hungarian Computer Science Conference*, pages 211–225, 1985.

[29] F. Nielson. Two-level semantics and abstract interpretation. *Theoretical Computer Science*, 69:117–242, 1989.

[30] F. Nielson and H. Riis Nielson. The tensor product in Wadler's analysis of lists. In B. Krieg-Brückner, editor, *Proceedings of ESOP'92*, pages 351–370, Rennes, France, February 1992. Springer-Verlag LNCS582. Preliminary version of Chapter 8 of Two-level Functional Languages, CUP, 1992.

[31] P. Wadler and R. J. M. Hughes. Projections for strictness analysis. In G. Kahn, editor, *Proceedings of the Functional Programming Languages and Computer Architecture Conference*, pages 385–407. Springer-Verlag LNCS 274, September 1987.

[32] P.L. Wadler. Strictness analysis on non-flat domains (by abstract interpretation over finite domains). In S. Abramsky and C.L. Hankin, editors, *Abstract Interpretation of Declarative Languages*, chapter 12, pages 266–275. Ellis Horwood Ltd., Chichester, West Sussex, England, 1987.

Deriving Category Theory
from
Type Theory

Roy L. Crole

rlc@doc.ic.ac.uk

Department of Computing, Imperial College
180 Queen's Gate, London SW7 2BZ, United Kingdom

Abstract

This work expounds the notion that (structured) categories are syntax free presentations of type theories, and shows some of the ideas involved in deriving categorical semantics for given type theories. It is intended for someone who has some knowledge of category theory and type theory, but who does not fully understand some of the intimate connections between the two topics. We begin by showing how the concept of a category can be derived from some simple and primitive mechanisms of monadic type theory. We then show how the notion of a category with finite products can model the most fundamental syntactical constructions of (algebraic) type theory. The idea of naturality is shown to capture, in a syntax free manner, the notion of substitution, and therefore provides a syntax free coding of a multiplicity of type theoretical constructs. Using these ideas we give a direct derivation of a cartesian closed category as a very general model of simply typed λ-calculus with binary products and a unit type. This article provides a new presentation of some old ideas. It is intended to be a tutorial paper aimed at audiences interested in elementary categorical type theory. Further details can be found in [5].

1 Introduction

Typed λ-calculus is a subject very well understood by today's computer scientists, being an embodiment of the basic principles which underlie functional programming. In fact the foundations of λ-calculus were laid many years ago by logicians, but this will not concern us here. The interested reader might care to consult [2] and [3]. Many computer scientists are also aware that the λ-calculus has a formal connection with the notion of a cartesian closed category; this idea is due to Lambek [6]. However, experience shows that this connection is often only fully appreciated by those working in very theoretical areas of computer science. We hope that this article will go some way towards bridging this gap, as well as high-lighting some of the more fundamental connections between category theory and type theory. The techniques described here can be used to derive categorical semantics for quite general type theories and similar logical systems.

2 Deriving a Category from Monadic Type Theory

Readers not familiar with type theory will find that [8] is an excellent reference. There are a number of textbooks now available which cover basic category theory; see for example [1] or [9].

Before we embark on our derivation of a category, let us review the traditional set-theoretic semantics which can be given to elementary type theory. The "elementary" type theory which we shall consider is sometime also called *algebraic* type theory. In order to define such a type theory, we shall assume that we are given a *signature Sg* which consists of some *types* and some *function symbols*. Each function symbol f has an *arity* which is a natural number a, and a *sorting* which is a list of $a + 1$ types, usually written $f: \alpha_1, \ldots, \alpha_a \to \beta$, or just $f: \alpha$ in the case that f has arity 0. In the latter case we usually call f a *constant* function symbol. For each type α take a countably infinite set $Var^\alpha \stackrel{\text{def}}{=} \{x_1^\alpha, x_2^\alpha, \ldots\}$ of variables (we assume that such sets of variables are disjoint for different types α) and define the terms of the algebraic type theory by the rules

$$\frac{x \in Var^\alpha}{x: \alpha} \qquad \frac{}{k: \alpha} \qquad \frac{M_1: \alpha_1, \ldots, M_a: \alpha_a}{f(M_1, \ldots, M_a): \beta}$$

where $k: \alpha$ and $f: \alpha_1, \ldots, \alpha_a \to \beta$ are function symbols. A set-theoretic semantics would then be defined by giving a set $[\![\alpha]\!]$ for each type α, an element $[\![k]\!] \in [\![\alpha]\!]$ for each constant $k: \alpha$ and a function of the form $[\![f]\!]: [\![\alpha_1]\!] \times \ldots \times [\![\alpha_n]\!] \to [\![\beta]\!]$ for each function symbol $f: \alpha_1, \ldots, \alpha_n \to \beta$. An environment for the type theory is essentially a function which assigns a meaning to each of the variables. More precisely an environment ρ is a function

$$\rho: \bigcup \{ Var^\alpha \mid \alpha \text{ is a type} \} \to \bigcup \{ [\![\alpha]\!] \mid \alpha \text{ is a type} \}$$

where $\rho(x^\alpha) \in [\![\alpha]\!]$ for $x^\alpha \in Var^\alpha$. Given such an environment ρ, we assign a meaning to the terms by setting $[\![x^\alpha]\!] \stackrel{\text{def}}{=} \rho(x^\alpha)$ and

$$[\![f(M_1, \ldots, M_n)]\!] \stackrel{\text{def}}{=} [\![f]\!]([\![M_1]\!], \ldots, [\![M_n]\!]),$$

so in general if $M: \alpha$ then $[\![M]\!] \in [\![\alpha]\!]$.

There are at least two problems with this approach. The first is that each of the types must be interpreted by non-empty sets and that we must restrict to a set of types. For if any of the $[\![\alpha]\!]$ were empty, or we had a proper class of types, then we would not be able to define the function ρ. The second problem is that the semantics is specified in terms of elements of sets. Of course, we might consider replacing the sets by some mathematical object which has an underlying set-theoretic structure. But we would be in a much stronger position if we could interpret our syntax in a more general setting, such as a category. Categories are very general mathematical structures, and category theory is a powerful organisational tool, but are categories suitable worlds in which to interpret syntactical systems such as algebraic theories? We shall see that categories are in fact tailor made mathematical universes for interpreting type theories.

Let us consider the first problem high-lighted above. We can think of a term as giving rise to a function with the variables of the term taking input data and the effect of the term on such data as the output. With this perspective, we can give a meaning to the types by assigning sets to them, and a meaning to the terms as functions. With due regard for this interpretation of the syntax, we should abandon type tagged variables and present the syntax using terms which have an associated environment of declared variables. We do this using the following three rules

$$\frac{}{\Gamma, x:\alpha, \Gamma' \vdash x:\alpha} \qquad\qquad \frac{}{\Gamma \vdash k:\alpha}\ (k:\alpha)$$

$$\frac{\Gamma \vdash M_1:\alpha_1 \quad\ldots\quad \Gamma \vdash M_a:\alpha_a}{\Gamma \vdash f(M_1,\ldots,M_a):\alpha}\ (f:\alpha_1,\ldots,\alpha_a \to \alpha)$$

along with the usual structural and substitution rules. Here, each Γ is a *context* of (variable, type) pairs in which the *variables are distinct*, and we refer to a judgement of the form $\Gamma \vdash M:\alpha$ as a term-in-context. Thus a term-in-context $x_1:\alpha_1,\ldots,x_n:\alpha_n \vdash M:\beta$ will be modelled by a function $f:A_1 \times \ldots \times A_n \to B$, where we think of the n input variables of M being modelled by an element of the cartesian product $A_1 \times \ldots \times A_n$. We may now (if we wish) interpret types by empty sets: we no longer need to define the environment ρ.

Now let us think about terms M with exactly one variable; thus $x:\alpha \vdash M:\beta$, for example, where x occurs in M. We tacitly assume that we are only dealing with function symbols of arity 1 and will refer to this limited type theory as *monadic*. We shall try to generalise our set-theoretic model using as few assumptions as possible. Suppose we model α and β by "objects" A and B of which we make no assumptions. So we have in mind that A and B are sets, but are not held to this. For the time being the word "object" is just some arbitrary reference. A function is a form of relation; so let us model $x:\alpha \vdash M:\beta$ as a "relation" m between A and B of which we make no assumptions; we write $A \xrightarrow{m} B$ for this. While we are not at this stage being mathematically precise, we will make things more watertight later on. For the time being we are just trying to set up a very general framework in which to model our monadic type theory.

Now let us think about how our syntactic term language is built up. The crucial point is that terms are built up by *substitution*, in the sense that a raw term $f(M)$ is precisely $f(x)[M/x]$. We now think about the process of substitution in general. Suppose that we have terms-in-context $x:\alpha \vdash M:\beta$ and $y:\beta \vdash N:\gamma$. One can prove by induction on the structure of N that there is a derived term-in-context $x:\alpha \vdash N[M/y]:\gamma$—so how should we model this? Let us just say for the moment that whatever models this term depends on how we model $x:\alpha \vdash M:\beta$ and $y:\beta \vdash N:\gamma$. We can write this as

$$\frac{[\![x:\alpha \vdash M:\beta]\!] \stackrel{\mathrm{def}}{=} A \xrightarrow{m} B \qquad [\![y:\beta \vdash N:\gamma]\!] \stackrel{\mathrm{def}}{=} B \xrightarrow{n} C}{[\![x:\alpha \vdash N[M/y]:\gamma]\!] \stackrel{\mathrm{def}}{=} A \xrightarrow{\Box(n,m)} C}$$

where one reads $[\![\xi]\!] \stackrel{\text{def}}{=} \zeta$ to mean that ξ is modelled by ζ, and $\square(n, m)$ is some relation depending on n and m. What about the order of substitution of terms for term variables? Let $z: \gamma \vdash L: \delta$ be a further term-in-context (where we tacitly assume that x, y and z are distinct variables). Well, both of the terms-in-context

$$x: \alpha \vdash (L[N/z])[M/y]: \delta \qquad \text{and} \qquad x: \alpha \vdash L[N[M/y]/z]: \delta$$

are syntactically the same (caution - why is this?). So the relations which model them ought to be the same too, namely $A \xrightarrow{\square(\square(l,n),m)} C$ and $A \xrightarrow{\square(l,\square(n,m))} C$, and we will write $\square(\square(l, n), m) = \square(l, \square(n, m))$ to indicate this.

Now we shall take a step backward and think about how terms-in-context with at most one variable are formed. We will have to model $x: \alpha \vdash x: \alpha$ as a relation $A \xrightarrow{\star_A} A$. If we think about how the substitution of terms for variables is modelled, then we deduce that if $E \xrightarrow{e} A$ and $A \xrightarrow{m} B$ then $\square(\star_A, e) = e$ and $\square(m, \star_A) = m$. This follows from the observation that $E = x[E/x]$ and $M = M[x/x]$. A term-in-context $x: \alpha \vdash f(M): \beta'$, where $f: \beta \to \beta'$ is a function symbol, is the term-in-context $x: \alpha \vdash f(y')[M/y']: \beta'$, and so will be modelled by the relation $A \xrightarrow{\square(r,m)} B'$, where B' models β' and we *specify* that the term-in-context $x: \beta \vdash f(x): \beta'$ is modelled by $B \xrightarrow{r} B'$. The specification of r is just a reflection of the fact that we already have some intended meaning for the function symbol f.

Now we summarise our deductions, writing $n \circ m$ for $\square(n, m)$ and id_A for $\star_A$:

- Types are interpreted by "objects," say $A, B \dots$
- Terms-in-context are interpreted by "relations," say $A \xrightarrow{m} B \dots$
- For each object A there is a relation id_A.
- Given relations $A \xrightarrow{m} B$ and $B \xrightarrow{n} C$, there is a relation $A \xrightarrow{n \circ m} C$.
- Given relations $E \xrightarrow{e} A$ and $A \xrightarrow{m} B$, then we have $id_A \circ e = e$ and $m \circ id_A = m$.
- For any $A \xrightarrow{m} B$, $B \xrightarrow{n} C$ and $C \xrightarrow{l} D$, we have $l \circ (n \circ m) = (l \circ n) \circ m$.

The above summary amounts to the specification of a category! Thus we have deduced, subject to certain primeval assumptions about how to model function symbols and substitution, that we can interpret algebraic type theory in which at most one variable appears in a term, in an arbitrary *category*. In such a category, *the substitution of raw terms for variables will be interpreted by composition of morphisms*; because of the importance of this idea, we give a special summary: see Figure 1.

3   Categories for Algebraic Type Theory

In the previous section we deduced that monadic type theory could be soundly interpreted in an arbitrary category. What happens when we consider full algebraic type theory? In the original model based around sets and functions,

---

— Interpreting Substitution by Composition —

Here, $x: \alpha \vdash M: \beta$ and $x: \gamma \vdash M': \alpha$ are terms of an algebraic type theory, and $[x: \alpha \vdash M: \beta]$ and $[x: \gamma \vdash M': \alpha]$ are morphisms of a category C interpreting the proved terms.

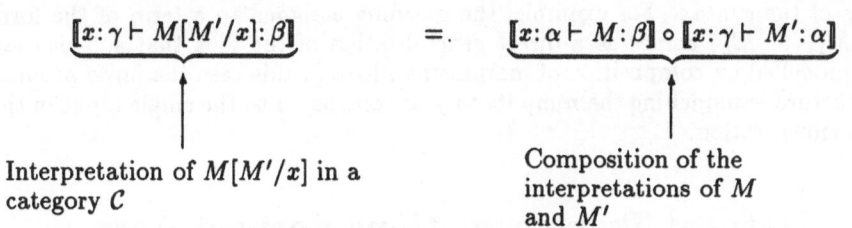

$$[x: \gamma \vdash M[M'/x]: \beta] \qquad =. \qquad [x: \alpha \vdash M: \beta] \circ [x: \gamma \vdash M': \alpha]$$

Interpretation of $M[M'/x]$ in a category C

Composition of the interpretations of M and M'

Figure 1: A Basic Principle of Categorical Type Theory

a term-in-context was modelled by a function which took n arguments. There is nothing in the formal rules for giving an algebraic type theory which will allow us to deduce how to model contexts in the same way that we deduced a framework for modelling substitution. The nearest categorical structure which mimics a set-theoretic function with n arguments is a morphism in a category induced by a finite product.[1] Here we assume that the reader has some knowledge of categories with finite products. The definition can be found in any basic book on category theory, such as [7] or [1]. Using such a category we can give a semantics to algebraic type theory as follows:

Let C be a category with finite products and let Sg be an algebraic signature. A *structure*, **M**, in C for Sg is specified by giving

- for every type α of Sg an object $[\alpha]$ of C,
- for every constant function symbol $k: \alpha$, a morphism $[k]: 1 \to [\alpha]$ where 1 is the terminal object of C, and
- for every function symbol $f: \alpha_1, \ldots, \alpha_n \to \beta$ of Sg a morphism

$$[f]: [\alpha_1] \times \ldots \times [\alpha_n] \to [\beta].$$

Given a context $\Gamma = [x_1: \alpha_1, \ldots, x_n: \alpha_n]$ we set

$$[\Gamma] \stackrel{\text{def}}{=} [\alpha_1] \times \ldots \times [\alpha_n].$$

Then for every proved term $\Gamma \vdash M: \alpha$ we shall specify a morphism

$$[\Gamma \vdash M: \alpha]: [\Gamma] \to [\alpha]$$

in C. The semantics of proved terms is specified inductively using the rules for generating terms-in-context:

---

[1] Apologies to linear categorical logicians; I am just considering one possibility in this article.

♦ $[\Gamma, x\!:\!\alpha, \Gamma' \vdash x\!:\!\alpha] \overset{\text{def}}{=} \pi\!:\![\Gamma] \times [\alpha] \times [\Gamma'] \to [\alpha]$ where π is a projection,

♦ $[\Gamma \vdash k\!:\!\alpha] \overset{\text{def}}{=} [k] \circ !\!:\![\Gamma] \to 1 \to [\alpha]$, and

♦ $[\Gamma \vdash f(M_1, \ldots, M_a)] \overset{\text{def}}{=} [f] \circ \langle [M_1], \ldots, [M_a] \rangle\!:\![\Gamma] \to (\Pi_1^a[\alpha_i]) \to [\alpha]$.

The interpretation given to the terms-in-context models our intended meaning of the syntax. For example, the meaning assigned to a term of the form $f(M_1, \ldots, M_a)$ comes as a direct generalisation of the idea that substitution is modelled by composition of morphisms where in this case the finite product structure is modelling the n inputs to f as contrasted to the single input in the previous section.

4 Natural Transformations derived from Introduction Rules

Let us suppose that we are now working with a general type theory in which the forms of judgement still take the simple form $\Gamma \vdash M\!:\!\alpha$. As in Section 1, types will be modelled by objects in a category; and as a simplifying assumption we shall take all categories to be locally small, that is, the collection of morphisms $A \to B$ (where A and B are objects) can be indexed by a set. This set will be denoted by $\mathcal{C}(A, B)$.

As discussed in Section 2, the interpretation of a term-in-context $\Gamma \vdash M\!:\!\alpha$ is given by a morphism $[\Gamma \vdash M\!:\!\alpha]\!:\![\Gamma] \to [\alpha]$ in $\mathcal{C}$. At the moment we do not know how to define such an interpretation, but by looking at how to soundly interpret the terms and equations of the type theory we will deduce how to do this.

Let us think about the rules of formation of term-in-contexts in general, assuming just one hypothesis. A typical rule looks like

$$\frac{\Gamma \vdash M\!:\!\alpha}{\Gamma \vdash R(M)\!:\!\beta} \quad \text{(R)}$$

where $R(M)$ is a new raw term depending on M. Suppose that $m \overset{\text{def}}{=} [\Gamma \vdash M\!:\!\alpha]$ which is an element of $\mathcal{C}([\Gamma], [\alpha])$. How do we model

$$[\Gamma \vdash R(M)\!:\!\beta] \in \mathcal{C}([\Gamma], [\beta])?$$

All we can say at the moment is that this latter morphism will depend on m, and we can model this idea by having a function

$$\Phi_{[\alpha],[\beta],[\Gamma]} : \mathcal{C}([\Gamma], [\alpha]) \longrightarrow \mathcal{C}([\Gamma], [\beta])$$

and setting $[\Gamma \vdash R(M)\!:\!\beta] \overset{\text{def}}{=} \Phi_{[\alpha],[\beta],[\Gamma]}(m)$. Now think about how the raw terms are formed. The crucial point is that new raw terms are formed from old raw terms by substitution; and we can easily see that a derived rule for our type theory is

$$\frac{x\!:\!\gamma \vdash M\!:\!\alpha \quad y\!:\!\gamma' \vdash N\!:\!\gamma}{y\!:\!\gamma' \vdash M[N/x]\!:\!\alpha} \quad \text{(Sub)}$$

Suppose that $x: \gamma \vdash M: \alpha$ and $y: \gamma' \vdash N: \gamma$ are any two given term-in-contexts. Using our basic assumption that substitution is modelled by composition of morphisms, if $m \stackrel{\text{def}}{=} [x: \gamma \vdash M: \alpha]$ and $n \stackrel{\text{def}}{=} [y: \gamma' \vdash N: \gamma]$ then we must have that $[y: \gamma' \vdash M[N/x]: \alpha] = m \circ n$. Applying each of (Sub) and (R) in turn, we deduce that there are term-in-contexts

$$y: \gamma' \vdash \mathsf{R}(M)[N/x]: \beta \qquad \text{and} \qquad y: \gamma' \vdash \mathsf{R}(M[N/x]): \beta.$$

However, both of the above raw terms should be syntactically identical (by the definition of substitution), and therefore the categorical interpretations should be the same, that is

$$\Phi_{[\alpha],[\beta],[\gamma]}(m) \circ n = \Phi_{[\alpha],[\beta],[\gamma']}(m \circ n). \qquad (*)$$

The reader may notice that $(*)$ looks similar to a naturality condition; in fact we can be certain that it will hold if we demand the following. For every object A and B of $\mathcal{C}$ there is a natural transformation

$$\Phi_{A,B} : \mathcal{C}(-, A) \longrightarrow \mathcal{C}(-, B) : \mathcal{C} \longrightarrow Set.$$

We can summarise these thoughts in the slogan:

— Categorical Modelling of Substitution ——————————————

The sound categorical interpretation of the notion of substitution of syntax amounts to requiring that certain naturality conditions hold in the categorical model.

---

5 How to Model Binary Products and the Unit Type

The categorical semantics given to algebraic theories was strongly motivated by traditional set-theoretic semantics. We shall now show how to derive a semantics for the syntax of binary products and unit. Some readers will know that this syntax can be modelled in categories with finite products. However, we shall present a uniform analysis of the syntax and rules of the unit type and binary product type to discover what, in categorical terms, is the most general interpretation.

Let us recall that the raw syntax of binary products, in a setting which subsumes algebraic type theory. First we specify a collection of *ground types*. The *types* are then given by the grammar $\alpha ::= \gamma \mid unit \mid \alpha \times \alpha$ where γ is any ground type. The *raw terms* are given by

$$M ::= x \mid f(M, \ldots, M) \mid \langle \rangle \mid \mathsf{Fst}(M) \mid \mathsf{Snd}(M) \mid \langle M, N \rangle.$$

The interpretation of a type $\alpha \times \beta$ will depend on the interpretations of α and β. The term-in-contexts will be interpreted by morphisms in a category, and the assumption that the equations-in-context are soundly interpreted will then determine equations which hold between morphisms: this will become clearer later on. In the cases of binary product types, we shall see that the equations between morphisms will determine the objects which model the types up to isomorphism. Finally, recall the basic assumption that all of our syntax is interpreted in a category with (at least) finite products: products are used to model the list of types which appear in contexts.

First we consider the types of Sg. We have to give an object $[\gamma]$ of C to interpret each of the ground types γ, and an object $[unit]$ to interpret $unit$— for the moment we cannot say anything more specific about $[unit]$. We will assume that the interpretation of binary product types $\alpha \times \beta$ depends on the interpretations of α and β. So there should be operation in C which gives an object $A \square B$ for all objects A and B so that we can define

$$[\alpha \times \beta] \stackrel{\mathrm{def}}{=} [\alpha] \square [\beta].$$

Having done this, we can now choose a morphism $[f] : [\alpha_1] \times \ldots \times [\alpha_n] \to [\beta]$ in C for each function symbol $f : \alpha_1 \ldots \alpha_n \to \beta$ of Sg. We will obviously have an intended interpretation of the function symbol f and the choice of the morphism $[f]$ will reflect this.

Let us now think about specific types and terms.

First we deal with the type $unit$. The rules for the unit type are

$$\frac{}{\Gamma \vdash \langle\rangle : unit} \qquad \frac{\Gamma \vdash M : unit}{\Gamma \vdash M = \langle\rangle : unit}$$

To interpret the first rule there must always be a morphism

$$u_0 \stackrel{\mathrm{def}}{=} [\Gamma \vdash \langle\rangle : unit] : [\Gamma] \to [unit].$$

To soundly interpret the equation-in-context, whenever there is a morphism $m \stackrel{\mathrm{def}}{=} [\Gamma \vdash M : unit]$ in C, we must have $m = u_0$. All this amounts to saying that for every object A of C, there must exist a unique morphism $! : A \to [unit]$, that is up to $isomorphism$ $[unit]$ is a terminal object 1 of C.

Recall that the rule for introducing product terms is

$$\frac{\Gamma \vdash M : \alpha \quad \Gamma \vdash N : \beta}{\Gamma \vdash \langle M, N \rangle : \alpha \times \beta}$$

In order to soundly interpret this rule we shall need a natural transformation

$$\Phi_{A,B} : C(-, A) \times C(-, B) \longrightarrow C(-, A \square B)$$

for all objects A and B of C. Now let $m : C \to A$ and $n : C \to B$ be morphisms of C. Applying naturality in C at the morphism $\langle m, n \rangle : C \to A \times B$ we deduce

$$(\Phi_{A,B})_C(\pi_A \langle m, n \rangle, \pi_B \langle m, n \rangle) = (\Phi_{A,B})_{A \square B}(\pi_A, \pi_B) \circ \langle m, n \rangle,$$

that is $(\Phi_{A,B})_C(m,n) = (\Phi_{A,B})_{A \square B}(\pi_A, \pi_B) \circ \langle m, n \rangle$. Now let us define the morphism $q_{A,B} \colon A \times B \to A \square B$ to be $(\Phi_{A,B})_{A \times B}(\pi_A, \pi_B)$. Then we can make the definition

$$[\Gamma \vdash \langle M, N \rangle \colon A \square B] \overset{\text{def}}{=}$$

$$[\Gamma] \xrightarrow{\langle [\Gamma \vdash M \colon \alpha], [\Gamma \vdash N \colon \beta] \rangle} [\alpha] \times [\beta] \xrightarrow{q_{[\alpha],[\beta]}} [\alpha] \square [\beta].$$

Recall one of the rules for eliminating product types

$$\frac{\Gamma \vdash P \colon \alpha \times \beta}{\Gamma \vdash \mathsf{Fst}(M) \colon \beta}$$

Arguing as above, to model this rule we shall need (for each A and B) a natural transformation $\Phi_{A,B} \colon \mathcal{C}(-, A \square B) \longrightarrow \mathcal{C}(-, A)$. So for any object C, and morphisms $m \colon C \to A \square B$ and $\theta \colon C' \to C$ of $\mathcal{C}$, we have

$$(\Phi_{A,B})_C(m) \circ \theta = (\Phi_{A,B})_{C'}(m \circ \theta).$$

By considering the instance of this equation when $m = id_{A \square B}$, we see that in general we have $(\Phi_{A,B})_C(\theta) = p_{A,B} \circ \theta$ where $p_{A,B} \overset{\text{def}}{=} (\Phi_{A,B})_{A \square B}(id_{A \square B})$. So now we can define

$$[\Gamma \vdash \mathsf{Fst}(P) \colon \alpha] \overset{\text{def}}{=} [\Gamma] \xrightarrow{[\Gamma \vdash P \colon \alpha \times \beta]} [\alpha] \square [\beta] \xrightarrow{p_{[\alpha],[\beta]}} [\alpha].$$

Of course we can deduce a semantics for term-in-contexts of the form $\Gamma \vdash \mathsf{Snd}(P) \colon \beta$ in much the same way, involving a morphism $p'_{A,B} \colon A \square B \to B$. Our last task is to see what information we obtain by soundly interpreting the equations-in-context for product types. These are

$$\frac{\Gamma \vdash M \colon \alpha \quad \Gamma \vdash N \colon \beta}{\Gamma \vdash \mathsf{Fst}(\langle M, N \rangle) = M \colon \alpha} \quad (1) \qquad \frac{\Gamma \vdash M \colon \alpha \quad \Gamma \vdash N \colon \beta}{\Gamma \vdash \mathsf{Snd}(\langle M, N \rangle) = N \colon \beta} \quad (2)$$

$$\frac{\Gamma \vdash P \colon \alpha \times \beta}{\Gamma \vdash \langle \mathsf{Fst}(P), \mathsf{Snd}(P) \rangle = P \colon \alpha \times \beta} \quad (3)$$

If we put $h \overset{\text{def}}{=} [\Gamma \vdash P \colon \alpha \times \beta] \colon C \to A \square B$, $m \overset{\text{def}}{=} [\Gamma \vdash M \colon \alpha] \colon C \to A$ and $n \overset{\text{def}}{=} [\Gamma \vdash N \colon \beta] \colon C \to B$, and demand that our categorical interpretation satisfies the equations-in-context, this forces

$$p_{A,B} \circ q_{A,B} \circ \langle m, n \rangle = m \qquad (1)$$
$$p'_{A,B} \circ q_{A,B} \circ \langle m, n \rangle = n \qquad (2)$$
$$q_{A,B} \circ \langle p_{A,B} \circ h, p'_{A,B} \circ h \rangle = h. \qquad (3)$$

At last we are done, because these equations imply that, up to isomorphism, $A \square B$ and $A \times B$ are the same. Thus we may *soundly interpret binary product types by binary categorical product*.

6 How to Model Function Types

Now we shall enrich our type theory so that it contains not only product types but also function types $\alpha \Rightarrow \beta$. The raw terms are the same as in Section 5 but also include the terms $\lambda x{:}\,\alpha.M$ and $M\,N$. To model the type $\alpha \Rightarrow \beta$ we shall need an object $A \lozenge B$ for all pairs of objects A and B of $\mathcal{C}$. To soundly interpret the introduction rule

$$\frac{\Gamma, x{:}\,\alpha \vdash F{:}\,\beta}{\Gamma \vdash \lambda x{:}\,\alpha.F{:}\,\alpha \Rightarrow \beta}$$

we shall need (for every object A and B) a natural transformation

$$\Phi_{A,B}{:}\,\mathcal{C}(- \times A, B) \longrightarrow \mathcal{C}(-, A \lozenge B),$$

and we can then define

$$\llbracket \Gamma \vdash \lambda x{:}\,\alpha.F{:}\,\alpha \Rightarrow \beta \rrbracket \overset{\text{def}}{=} (\Phi_{\llbracket\alpha\rrbracket,\llbracket\beta\rrbracket})_{\llbracket\Gamma\rrbracket}(\llbracket \Gamma, x{:}\,\alpha \vdash F{:}\,\beta \rrbracket) : \llbracket\Gamma\rrbracket \rightarrow (\llbracket\alpha\rrbracket \lozenge \llbracket\beta\rrbracket).$$

To soundly interpret the elimination rule

$$\frac{\Gamma \vdash M{:}\,\alpha \Rightarrow \beta \quad \Gamma \vdash N{:}\,\alpha}{\Gamma \vdash M\,N{:}\,\beta}$$

we shall need a natural transformation

$$\Psi_{A,B}{:}\,\mathcal{C}(-, A \lozenge B) \times \mathcal{C}(-, A) \longrightarrow \mathcal{C}(-, B)$$

for all objects A and B of $\mathcal{C}$. Given any two morphisms $m{:}\,C \rightarrow A \lozenge B$ and $n{:}\,C \rightarrow A$ and applying naturality, we have

$$(\Psi_{A,B})_C(m, n) = (\Psi_{A,B})_{(A\lozenge B)\times A}(\pi, \pi') \circ \langle m, n \rangle$$

where $\pi{:}\,(A \lozenge B) \times A \twoheadrightarrow A \lozenge B$ and $\pi'{:}\,(A \lozenge B) \times A \twoheadrightarrow A$. So if we define the morphism $ev_{A,B} \overset{\text{def}}{=} (\Psi_{A,B})_{(A\lozenge B)\times A}(\pi, \pi')$, we can make the definition

$$\llbracket \Gamma \vdash M\,N{:}\,\beta \rrbracket \overset{\text{def}}{=}$$

$$\llbracket\Gamma\rrbracket \xrightarrow{\langle \llbracket\Gamma \vdash M{:}\,\alpha \Rightarrow \beta\rrbracket, \llbracket\Gamma \vdash N{:}\,\alpha\rrbracket\rangle} (\llbracket\alpha\rrbracket \lozenge \llbracket\beta\rrbracket) \times \llbracket\alpha\rrbracket \xrightarrow{ev_{\llbracket\alpha\rrbracket,\llbracket\beta\rrbracket}} \llbracket\beta\rrbracket.$$

The equations-in-context for the function type are

$$\frac{\Gamma, x{:}\,\alpha \vdash F{:}\,\beta \quad \Gamma \vdash M{:}\,\alpha}{\Gamma \vdash (\lambda x{:}\,\alpha.F)\,M = F[M/x]{:}\,\beta} \quad (4)$$

$$\frac{\Gamma \vdash N{:}\,\alpha \Rightarrow \beta}{\Gamma \vdash \lambda x{:}\,\alpha.(M\,x) = M{:}\,\alpha \Rightarrow \beta} \quad (5)$$

If our categorical interpretation is to satisfy the equation-in-context (4), then we must have $ev_{A,B}\langle(\Phi_{A,B})_C(f), m\rangle = f\langle id, m\rangle$ for all morphisms $f: C \times A \to B$ and $m: C \to A$. Using the naturality of $\Phi_{A,B}$ we can show that this equation holds just in case

$$ev_{A,B}((\Phi_{A,B})_C(f) \times id) = f. \tag{*}$$

Satisfaction of (5) requires that $(\Phi_{A,B})_C(ev_{A,B}(m \times id_A)) = m$ for every morphism $m: C \to A \Diamond B$ and from the naturality of $\Phi_{A,B}$ this holds just in case

$$(\Phi_{A,B})_{A \Diamond B}(ev_{A,B}) = id. \tag{†}$$

Now we come to the crucial point. If we define a natural transformation

$$\theta: \mathcal{C}(- \times A, B) \longrightarrow \mathcal{C}(-, A \Diamond B)$$

by setting $\theta_C(f) \stackrel{\text{def}}{=} ev_{A,B} \circ (f \times id)$ the equations (*) and (†) imply that θ_C is a natural bijection. *Thus, up to isomorphism in the category $\mathcal{C}$, the object $A \Diamond B$ is exactly the exponential $A \Rightarrow B$ and of course $ev_{A,B}: (A \Diamond B) \times A \to B$ is the evaluation morphism, and such categorical structure will soundly interpret function types.*

7 Conclusion and Acknowledgements

By considering some of the underlying principles of set-theoretic models of equational type theory, we have set up a very general framework in which such type theories can be modelled, and shown that such a framework corresponds to the notion of a category. We have also shown that introduction rules can be soundly modelled by suitable natural transformations. This very general framework was then used to find a minimal categorical structure for soundly interpreting a specific elementary type theory, namely simply typed λ-calculus with finite products. The methodology of manipulating naturality and soundness equations to compute general categorical structures can be applied to less well known type theories. Examples can be found in [4].

I would like to thank Andrew Pitts for discussions which threw light on my understanding of the way category-theoretic ideas capture slickly the essence of intricate syntactic constructions. I would also like to thank the Science and Engineering Research Council for providing funding in the form of a Research Fellowship.

References

[1] M. Barr and C. Wells. *Category Theory for Computing Science*. International Series in Computer Science. Prentice Hall, 1990.

[2] A. Church. A formulation of the simple theory of types. *Journal of Symbolic Logic*, 5:56–68, 1940.

[3] A. Church. *The Calculi of Lambda Conversion*. Princeton University Press, 1941.

[4] R.L. Crole. *Programming Metalogics with a Fixpoint Type*. PhD thesis, Computer Laboratory, University of Cambridge, 1991.

[5] R.L. Crole. *Categories for Types*. Cambridge Mathematical Textbooks. Cambridge University Press, 1993. To appear: ISBN 0521 450926 HB.

[6] J. Lambek. From λ-calculus to cartesian closed categories. In J.P. Seldin and J.R. Hindley, editors, *To H.B. Curry: Essays on Combinatory Logic, Lambda Calculus and Formalism*. Academic Press, 1980.

[7] S. Mac Lane. *Categories for the Working Mathematician*, volume 5 of *Graduate Texts in Mathematics*. Springer-Verlag, 1971.

[8] B. Nordström, K. Petersson, and J.M. Smith. *Programming in Martin-Löf's Type Theory*, volume 7 of *Monographs on Computer Science*. Oxford University Press, 1990.

[9] B.C. Pierce. *Basic Category Theory for Computer Scientists*. Foundations of Computing Series. The MIT Press, 1991.

Graph Rewriting Systems and Abstract Interpretation

Chris Hankin

clh@doc.ic.ac.uk
Department of Computing, Imperial College
180 Queen's Gate, London SW7 2BZ, United Kingdom

Abstract

Graph rewriting systems are the generalisation of term rewriting systems from (finite) trees to graphs. They provide the basis for an abstract treatment of graph reduction, a well-established technique for the implementation of declarative languages. Given this last observation, it is sensible to develop tools for the compile-time analysis of graph rewrite programs; it is to be expected that opportunities for optimisation which are difficult to detect in the source program might be exposed at this level. This paper summarises the work that we have done on semantics-based static analysis of programs represented by Term Graph Rewriting Systems.

1 Introduction

Graph *reduction* has emerged as the major approach to implementing lazy functional programming languages. Its use was first proposed by Wadsworth [15] in his thesis but was popularised by Turner [13]. The book [10] is an excellent source for a deeper insight into this aspect of graph rewriting. Meanwhile, since the mid sixties, there has been considerable work on the theory of *graph grammars* [5] and *graph rewriting* [12].

A graph grammar is like a conventional grammar except that productions relate pairs of graphs rather than strings (trees). Much of the work in this area has focussed on the properties of languages generated by such grammars and on applications. Applications have included developmental systems in biology, databases and algebraic specification. Although this is a very rich vein of work we will not pursue it further in this paper.

The work on graph rewriting has emphasised the rôle of graphs in a computational model which may be used to formalise graph reduction. In fact, for functional programming, we only consider a restricted form of graph rewriting, namely *term graph rewriting* (TGR). From now on, we will emphasise TGR.

2 Graph Rewriting Categorically

The definitions in this section are largely derived from [Ken88]. We consider a category whose objects are graphs over some set of symbols, Σ:

Definition 1 (Term Graphs)
A Graph is a triple $G = (N_G, lab_G, succ_G)$ where
$lab_G : N_G \rightarrow \Sigma_\perp$ is a labelling function (variable nodes are labelled $\perp$).
and $succ_G : N_G \rightarrow N_G^*$ is the node successor function.
Multiple instances of a variable all share the same $\perp$-labelled node.

Morphisms consist of pairs. The first component is a mapping between graphs (the obvious notion of mapping nodes to nodes) and the second component identifies the subset of nodes at which the mapping is homomorphic:

Definition 2 $f : G \rightarrow H$ is a *homomorphism* at $s \in N_G$ if either:
$$lab_G(s) = \perp$$
or:
$$lab_H(f(s)) = lab_G(s)$$
$$succ_H(f(s)) = f(succ_G(s))$$

The identity morphism on G is just (id, N_G) and given two morphisms, $(g, T) : H \rightarrow J$ and $(f, S) : G \rightarrow H$ then there composition is defined:

$$(g, T) \circ (f, S) = (g \circ f, S \cap f^{-1}(T))$$

It is useful to define the following "selector" functions:

Definition 3 For $F : G \rightarrow H = (f, S)$ we define:

1. $fun(F) = f - fun(F)$ is the mapping component of the morphism.
2. $mor(F) = S - mor(F)$ is the set at which the mapping is homomorphic.
3. $rew(F) = N_G - mor(F) - rew(F)$ is the set of nodes that are "changed" by the morphism.
4. $ker(F) = \{n \in N_G \mid \exists n' \neq n.f(n) = f(n')\} - ker(F)$ is the set of nodes where sharing is introduced by the morphism.

F is *total* if $rew(F)$ is the empty set and *strict* if it takes empty nodes to empty nodes.

A graph rewrite is just a morphism, $f : L \rightarrow R$ such that:

♦ $fun(f)$ is one-to-one on $mor(f)$
♦ f is strict

Since $mor(f)$ identifies the nodes which are "preserved" by the rewrite, these two requirements prevent a rewrite from coalescing nodes that are to be preserved and also require that variable nodes are preserved. An *occurrence* of the left hand side of a rule in a graph is identified by a total homomorphism. An occurrence may map several nodes from the left hand side of the rule to a single node; if the rewrite does not preserve all of these nodes, we may be left with "dangling" pointers after the rewrite:

Definition 4 An occurrence g of a rewrite f is *admissible* if:
$$ker(g) \subseteq mor(f).$$

The situation we have is as follows:

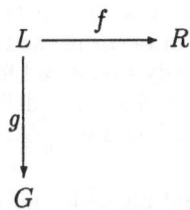

The conditions are sufficient to ensure the existence of a *pushout*, consisting of the two arrows $k : G \rightarrow H$ and $h : R \rightarrow H$ where:

 ◆ h is a total homomorphism
 ◆ k is a graph rewrite such that $rew(k) = g(rew(f))$

The graph H is taken to be the result of the rewrite.

There are a number of observations to be made:

 ◆ the construction is for acyclic graphs
 ◆ for term graph rewriting, $rew(f)$ is a singleton consisting of the root of the graph being rewritten.

The categorical construction is quite elegant; it forms the basis for concise diagrammatic proofs of standard results such as confluence [11, 8]. Future work might involve using this formalism (or a related one) to provide a basis for abstract interpretation. One difficulty from this point of view is that of composing rewrites to build sequences. However, the categorical construction does motivate the details of a more operational model, presented in the next section.

3   A More Operational Account

The first three definitions of this section are based on those in [1]. We work with the same graph objects as before with the addition of a fourth component identifying the root node. Since rewrites only affect the root of the graph, they can be represented by a triple representing the combined graph (left and right hand side of the rule — not rooted) and the roots of the left and right hand sides, (g, n, n'). The notation:

$$g \mid n$$

is used to denote the subgraph of g rooted at n. The process of graph rewriting is a three phase process: *building*, *redirection* and *garbage collection*.

Definition 5 (Build)
H, the result of the build phase on G using (g, n, n') at occurrence $f : g \rightarrow G$ is defined as follows:

$$
\begin{aligned}
N_H &= N_G + (N_{g|n'} - N_{g|n}) \\
lab_H(m) &= lab_G(m) \text{ if } m \in N_G \\
&= lab_g(m) \text{ otherwise} \\
succ_H(m)_i &= succ_G(m)_i \text{ if } m \in N_G \\
&= succ_g(m)_i \text{ if both } m \text{ and } succ_g(m)_i \in N_{g|n'} - N_{g|n} \\
&= f(succ_g(m)_i) \text{ if } m \text{ in } N_{g|n'} - N_{g|n} \\
&\quad \text{and } succ_g(m)_i \text{ in } N_{g|n} \\
r_H &= r_G
\end{aligned}
$$

Thus N_H is the set of nodes that are in G plus the nodes from the right hand side of the rule which do not occur in the left hand side. Nodes that occur in both sides of the rule are already accounted for in G via the occurrence. The definition of lab is as expected and $succ$ is defined to connect the right hand side of the rule to the appropriate nodes in G.

Definition 6 (Redirect)

If H is the result of the build phase for an occurence f and rule (g, n, n'), then the reult of the redirect phase, J, is defined as:

$$J = H[f(n) := f(n')] \text{ if } n' \in g \mid n$$
$$= H[f(n) := n'] \text{ otherwise}$$

where $H[a := b]$ is the term graph $(N_H, lab_H, succ, r)$ with:

$$succ(n)_i = b \text{ if } succ_H(n)_i = a$$
$$= succ_H(n)_i \text{ otherwise}$$
$$r = b \text{ if } r_H = a$$
$$= r_H \text{ otherwise}$$

The subtlety in this definition arises because the root of rewrite graph may be a subgraph of the occurrence (consider selector rules such as $I\ x \rightarrow x$).

The combined effect of these two phases is the construction of the pushout object of the last section. The final phase is necessary for implementation, but as shown in [1] it can be delayed indefinitely:

Definition 7 (Garbage Collect)

K, the result of garbage collection on some graph J, is defined as:

$$J \mid r_J$$

i.e. the nodes reachable from the root of J.

We shall write:

$$tgr(G, r, f)$$

to denote the result of applying these three phases to graph G at occurrence f of rule r.

In the following, let R be a set of rules:

$$R = R_1 \cup R_2 \cup \cdots \cup R_f$$

where each of the R_i defines some operator F_i, i.e. is a set of rules of the form:

$$R_i = \{r_{i,1}, \ldots, r_{i,j_i}\}$$

where $r_{i,k} = (g_{i,k}, n_{i,k}, n'_{i,k})$, $k = 1 \ldots j_i$ and the label on each of the $n_{i,k}$ is F_i. (In the following, we will drop the i index, when the context makes it clear which R_i we are considering). *Constructor symbols*, in contrast to *operators*, are the symbols that do not label the root node of the left hand side of any rule of R (including the δ-rules). We assume that the operators and constructors form disjoint subsets of the set of symbols. The notion of normal form for our operational semantics can now be defined:

Definition 8 (Root Normal Form (rnf))

A term graph G is in *root normal form* whenever $lab_G(r_G)$ is a constructor symbol.

In its most abstract form, the operational semantics is defined in terms of two functions, *Reduce* and *Strategy*. The function *Strategy* has type:

$$Graph \times \wp(Rule) \rightarrow \wp(((Graph \rightarrow Graph) \times Rule)^*)$$

The intention is that, for a given graph and set of rules, *Strategy* returns a set of sequences of (occurrence,rule) pairs which identify possible rewrite sequences from the given graph. The strategy defined by *Strategy* is *deterministic for R* if $Strategy(G, R)$ contains at most one element for every G; it is *one step for R* or a *1-strategy for R* if $Strategy(G, R)$ is a sequence of length 1 for every G. To keep things simple, for the moment we will restrict our attention to deterministic 1-strategies (the *functional* strategy considered later is deterministic but is not a 1-strategy); we abuse notation by identifying a (graph,occurrence) pair with the singleton set containing the pair as a sequence of length 1. *Reduce* is defined as follows:

$Reduce : Graph \times \wp(Rule) \rightarrow Graph$

$$\begin{aligned} Reduce(G, rs) \quad &= \quad G \text{ if } G \text{ is an rnf} \\ &= \quad Reduce(tgr(G, r, f), rs) \text{ otherwise} \\ &\quad \text{where } (f, r) = Strategy(G, rs) \end{aligned}$$

4 Abstract Interpretation

Rather than define an abstract interpretation directly in terms of the standard semantics it is usual to factor the process via a *collecting interpretation* [3]. The collecting interpretation "collects" information about the program's behaviour at certain *program points*. For example, in a flowchart program, the program points might be identified with the arcs and the information collected would record all of the "states" that exist whenever a program point is passed during execution. We claim that a suitable notion of program point for graph rewriting is a rule and the information collected records the Graphs and occurrences that the rule is used to rewrite.

The following definitions generalise those in [6].

Definition 9 (Context Vector)
A *context* for a given rule is a collection of pairs of a graph, g, and an occurrence of the left hand side of the rule (in g). Thus a context is of type $\wp(Graph \times (Graph \rightarrow Graph))$.
A *context vector* associates a context with each rule and is of type $Rule \rightarrow Context$.

One purpose of the collecting interpretation is to compute the context vector associated with an initial (set of) graph(s). The context vector records intensional information; while it is possible to recover extensional information from the context vector, it is often more convenient to compute it directly. Therefore we define the collecting interpretation in two parts, in the following way (where CV is the lattice of context vectors [6]):

$CReduce : \wp(Graph) \times \wp(Rule) \rightarrow CV \times \wp(Graph)$

$$CReduce(\mathcal{G}, rs) \quad = \quad (In(\mathcal{G}, rs), Ex(\mathcal{G}, rs))$$
$$\text{where}$$

$$In(\mathcal{G}, rs) \quad = $$
$$\bigcup_{G \in \mathcal{G}} \{(r, (G, f)) \mid G \text{ not rnf} \wedge (f, r) = Strategy(G, rs)\}$$
$$\cup In(next(\mathcal{G}, rs), rs)$$
$$Ex(\mathcal{G}, rs) \quad = \quad \{G \mid G \in \mathcal{G} \wedge G \text{ is a rnf}\}$$
$$\cup Ex(next(\mathcal{G}, rs), rs)$$
$$next(\mathcal{G}, rs) \quad = $$
$$\bigcup_{G \in \mathcal{G}} \{tgr(G, r, f) \mid G \text{ not rnf} \wedge (f, r) = Strategy(G, rs)\}$$

In order to define an abstract interpretation, our first task is to identify a suitable abstract domain. Depending on whether we are interested in intensional or extensional properties, we will abstract either the context vector or the set of root normal forms. It is standard to relate the abstract domain to the concrete one using a Galois connection [3]. A Galois connection between a pair of complete lattices, L and M, is a pair of monotonic functions $(\alpha : L \rightarrow M, \gamma : M \rightarrow L)$ such that:

$$\alpha \circ \gamma \sqsubseteq id \text{ and } \gamma \circ \alpha \sqsupseteq id$$

There are two properties of the abstract interpretation that are of interest. The first is *safety*. *AReduce*, the abstract interpretation, is safe if:

$$AReduce \sqsupseteq \alpha \circ CReduce^* \circ \gamma$$

where $CReduce^*$ is the appropriate component of the collecting interpretation. The Cousots [3] give local conditions under which safety is guaranteed: providing the basic operators are safe then the complete interpretation will be. In our setting the basic operators are *tgr* and *Strategy*. Safety requires, for example, that:

$$\overline{tgr} \sqsupseteq \alpha \circ tgr^* \circ \gamma$$

where $\overline{tgr}$ is the abstract operator and tgr^* is the operator introduced above, lifted to work on collecting interpretation values.

We will consider these questions in more detail when we consider the specific examples below. The second property is *termination*; this can be guaranteed by chosing a *finite* abstract lattice but this is not always possible and then a more sophisticated approach based on the Cousots' notions of *widenings* and *narrowings* [3] is appropriate. Our two examples illustrate both cases.

5 Examples

5.1 Lock Avoidance

This analysis is a also a naive form of type inference. It is part of a larger data flow analysis proposed by Banach. The objective of the analysis is to determine the set of symbols that can label successors of nodes labelled with a particular symbol. The information collected takes the form of SkT-triples; where S and T are symbols and k is an integer. The meaning of a triple is that, at some point in the computation, a node labelled S had a node labelled T as its k-th successor.

In [6] this analysis is presented as an abstract interpretation of the intensional collecting interpretation. The abstract domain used is the powerset of

SkT-triples ordered by subset inclusion. The original formulation of the analysis was not specific about reduction strategy; in the abstract interpretation we apply the Gross-Knuth strategy which gives a safe (but not necessarily accurate) approximation of any other strategy.

Finiteness of the analyis is guaranteed by considering finitely branching graphs and a finite set of symbols (for example, all integers could be abstracted by a new distinguished symbol *Int*).

5.2 Abstract Reduction

Abstract reduction has been proposed as an alternative to abstract interpretation for the analysis of graph rewriting systems [9]. Its interest lies in the fact that the implemented analysis seems to be considerably more efficient than abstract interpretation. The approach uses the standard notion of rewriting applied to "abstract" graphs. For strictness analysis the abstract graphs are constructed over the same symbol set as concrete graphs, augmented with the new symbols $\{Bot, Top, Union\}$.

To get accurate information from abstract reduction, it is important that the reduction mechanism accurately simulates the real reduction strategy. The functional strategy, which is used to implement lazy evaluation of term graph rewriting, depends on the textual order of the rules; the matching algorithm selects the needed redexes 'from top to bottom, and from left to right'. If $g = F_i(\ldots)$ is the graph to be reduced, the strategy first tries to rewrite it by rule $r_{i,1}$, if not, by $r_{i,2}$, and so on. Then the arguments of $F_i(\ldots)$ are reduced from left to right, in order to match some rule $r_{i,k}$.

We can expand our earlier operational semantics to describe the behaviour of the functional strategy:

$$
\begin{aligned}
Match &: Graph \times Graph \times \wp(Rule) \to \{tt, ff\} \\
Rewrite &: Graph \times \wp(Rule) \to Graph \\
Reduce &: Graph \times \wp(Rule) \to Graph
\end{aligned}
$$

Rewrite and *Match* together implement the strategy. *Rewrite* performs a rewrite step, and *Match* implements the matching algorithm. The functions are defined via the following equations (to be read top to bottom):

$$
\begin{aligned}
Reduce(g, rs) \;=\; & g \\
& \text{if } in\_rnf g \\
=\; & Reduce(Rewrite(g, rs), rs) \\
& \text{otherwise}
\end{aligned}
$$

$$
\begin{aligned}
Match(g, p, rs) \;=\; & tt \\
& \text{if } is\_var(p) \\
=\; & Match(Reduce(g, rs), p) \\
& \text{if } \neg in\_rnf(g) \\
=\; & ff \\
& \text{if } root(g) \neq root(p) \\
=\; & MatchArg(args(g), args(p), rs) \\
& \text{otherwise}
\end{aligned}
$$

$$MatchArg([\,],[\,],rs) \quad = \quad tt$$
$$MatchArg(g:gs,p:ps,rs) \quad = \quad MatchArg(gs,ps,rs)$$
$$\text{if } Match(g,p,rs)$$
$$= \quad ff$$
$$\text{otherwise}$$

$$Rewrite(g,r:rs) \quad = \quad Rewrite(g,rs) \qquad \text{if } root(g) \neq root(r)$$
$$= \quad Rewrite(g,rs)$$
$$\text{if } \neg MatchArg(args(g),args(r),r:rs)$$
$$= \quad tgr(g,r,f) \qquad \text{otherwise}$$
$$\text{where } f = occ(g,r)$$

The abstract interpretation [14] is expressed with respect to the extensional collecting semantics. We abstract a set of graphs by a single abstract graph. Choosing a suitable domain of abstract graphs is a non-trivial task, sharing and the presence of cycles both cause problems. In [4] we present a lattice structure on abstract graphs via unravellings into (infinite) trees; the construction is relatively complex and imposes some apparently arbitrary restrictions on the class of graphs. Recently, in [2], we have proposed an alternative lattice structure where the ordering is defined directly on the graph structure.

Abstract reduction is essentially a syntactic approach to analysis. Termination is therefore a problem. In [14] we justify a number of heuristics for enforcing termination of the reduction, whilst ensuring safety. The following two properties are used extensively in the implementation to force termination of recursive programs. The first result allows the introduction of cycles and is related to the Cousots' widening operations [3]. The second is a result that supports the introduction of Bot (cf. "pending analysis" [7]).

The function $E^{\#\infty}$ effectively computes a "Böhm tree" for the graph. Such a function is necessary because the functional strategy terminates with rnf but, in abstract interpretation, we normally require normal forms. For example, in strictness analysis we may want to test the value of a program against Bot. $E^{\#\infty}$ computes the normal form by a leftmost evaluation of rnfs.

Let $g' = h|n$. Then:

$$g \to^k h, g' \sqsubseteq g \quad \Rightarrow \quad E^{\#\infty}(g) \sqsubseteq E^{\#\infty}(h[n := root(h)])$$
$$g \to^k h, g' \sqsubseteq g,$$
$$g' \text{ is needed in } h \quad \Rightarrow \quad E^{\#\infty}(g) \sqsubseteq Bot$$

The first result says that if g reduces to some graph h which contains a subgraph that approximates g (in the ordering on abstract graphs), then the normal form of g is safely described by the normal form of the cyclic graph. The second result applies in similar circumstances but where we also know that the approximating sub-graph is needed (i.e. will definitely be reduced); in this case the whole graph may be safely replaced by Bot. A more rigorous account of these and other heuristics may be found in [4]. It is still a conjecture whether these results are true for all functions we can define. For the moment, it seems that we can only prove them for certain classes of functions, like the class of mutually tail-recursive functions.

6   Conclusions

We have summarised the work that we have been doing over the last few years on the static analysis of term graph rewriting programs. The work is important because TGR provides a suitable abstraction of graph reduction and is therefore at an intermediate level between functional languages and their implementation. Working on analyses at this intermediate level might expose more opportunities for optimisation than can be determined at the source language level.

Our main achievements have been the definition of a suitable notion of collecting interpretation for TGR and the technical developments that have resulted from our work on demonstrating the correctness of Nöcker's abstract reduction algorithm.

In future, we would like to make better use of the categorical semantics as a basis for abstract interpretation.

Acknowledgements

The author was partially funded by ESPRIT III Working Group 6345 (Sema-Graph II). The author would like to thank Paul Taylor and Ian Mackie for comments on an earlier draft of this paper. This work has benefited considerably from collaboration with David Clark, Eric Goubault, Eric Nöcker and Marko van Eekelen.

References

[1] Barendregt H. P., van Eekelen M., Glauert J., Kennaway J. R., Plasmeijer M. J. and Sleep M. R., *Term Graph Rewriting*, in Proceedings PARLE '87 Volume II, Springer Verlag LNCS 259, pp141-158, 1987.

[2] Clark D. and Hankin C. L., *A Lattice of Abstract Graphs*, to appear in PLILP'93, Estonia, 1993.

[3] Cousot P. and Cousot R., *Abstract Interpretation: A Unified Lattice Model for Static Analysis of Programs by Construction of Approximations of Fixed Points*, 4th POPL, pp238-252, 1977.

[4] Goubault E. and Hankin C. L., *A lattice for the abstract interpretation of term graph rewriting systems*, In [12].

[5] Ehrig H. and Kreowski H.-J. (eds), *Graph Grammars and Their Application to Computer Science*, (Proceedings of the 4th International Workshop, Bremen, Germany, March 1990), Springer-Verlag, LNCS 532.

[6] Hankin C. L., *Static Analysis of Term Graph Rewriting Systems*, In Proceedings PARLE '91 Volume II, Springer Verlag LNCS 506, 1991.

[7] Hudak P. and Young J., *Finding Fixed Points on Function Spaces*, Manuscript,1986.

[8] Kennaway J. R., *On "On Graph Rewritings"*, Theoretical Computer Science, **52**, pp 37-58, 1987.

[9] Nöcker E., *Strictness Analysis based on Abstract Reduction*, In proc. 2nd International Workshop on Implementation of Functional Languages on Parallel Architectures, University of Nijmegen, 1990.

[10] Peyton Jones S. L., *The Implementation of Functional Programming Languages*, Prentice-Hall International, 1987.

[11] Raoult J. C., *On Graph Rewritings*, Theoretical Computer Science, **32**, pp 1-24, 1984.

[12] Sleep M. R., Plasmeijer M. J. and van Eekelen M. C.(eds), *Term Graph Rewriting: Theory and Practice*, John Wiley & Sons Ltd., 1993.

[13] Turner D. A., *A New Implementation Technique for Applicative Languages*, Software Practice and Experience, Vol. 9, January 1979.

[14] van Eekelen M., Goubault E., Hankin C. L. and Nöcker E., *Abstract Reduction: Towards a theory via abstract interpretation*, In [12].

[15] Wadsworth C. P., *Semantics and Pragmatics of the Lambda Calculus*, Chapter 4, PhD thesis, Oxford, 1971.

Geometric Logic in Computer Science

Steve Vickers

sjv@doc.ic.ac.uk

Department of Computing, Imperial College
180 Queen's Gate, London SW7 2BZ, United Kingdom

Abstract

We present an introduction to geometric logic and the mathematical structures associated with it, such as categorical logic and toposes. We also describe some of its applications in computer science including its potential as a logic for specification languages.

1 Introduction

What I shall present here is a personal overview of how—and why—I see geometric logic being used in computer science.

Mark Ryan commented on an earlier, rather different, draft of this paper that he understood the title and thought "Oh, good", but quickly ran into words that made no sense to him. My revised intention therefore is to write a popularization of geometric logic for the benefit of computer scientists. I shan't present any new results, and in fact I shall hardly even present any old ones in any technical details, but I shall try to explain the essential features of the mathematics by explaining them (rather than by leaving the reader to sift them out of a grand formal structure). I shall also try to take stock of the ingredients we have to hand and what roles they should play.

2 Geometric Theories

Although the full mathematical insights come only through category theory, I'm going to start from a very logical point of view because I think in computer science people are more comfortable with that. It is important to realise that the particular properties of geometric logic come as much from its particular definition of *theory* as from its definition of formulas.

Our notion of *vocabulary* is standard in many-sorted logic: it comprises *sorts, predicate symbols* and *function symbols* (representing *total* functions). Remember, of course, that functions and predicate symbols have *arities*, specifying the number and sorts of their arguments and (for functions) the sort of the result, and that term formation has to respect the arities. Function and predicates with no arguments are *constants* and *propositions*.

If there are *no* sorts, then function symbols are impossible because there are no possible result sorts. But propositions are possible, so a theory with no sorts is a propositional theory.

Given a vocabulary, *geometric formulas* are constructed in a way that is completely unsurprising except that a peculiar collection of connectives is used: these are

- ◆ conjunction ($\wedge$ for binary conjunction, **true** for nullary conjunction)
- ◆ disjunction ($\vee$ for binary disjunction, **false** for nullary, and moreover *arbitrary infinitary disjunction* is allowed: $\bigvee_{i \in I} \phi_i$)
- ◆ equality (this is sorted, so in $e_1 = e_2$ the two terms e_i must have the same sort)
- ◆ existential quantification $\exists$

There is also the restriction that a formula may have only finitely many free variables.

Why these connectives? To my mind, the most compelling reason is that they have observational content in a way that the others ($\neg$, $\implies$, $\forall$ and $\bigwedge$) do not. For a detailed discussion, see Vickers [10] or (for the propositional case) [9]; but, briefly, the idea is that the sorts and formulas represent "observational classes" in the real world, each comprising two ingredients:

- ◆ how to "apprehend" elements
- ◆ how to determine that two elements are equal

Moreover, these "how to"s are *positive* (e.g. nothing about determining inequality), *serendipitous* (they merely describe how to know in retrospect when you have succeeded) and *finite* (they don't call on you to do an infinite amount of work). The geometric connectives can then be interpreted as operations on observational classes.

For the rest of the paper, I shall concentrate more on the mathematical consequences of the particular choice of connectives.

The admission of infinitary disjunction may seem alarming. Since the disjuncts will be indexed by a set, a full formal system for geometric logic must include a formal set theory and that is a heavy overhead. But even the *coherent* fragment, in which disjunctions must be finitary, is interesting, and as we shall see it is desirable to go beyond and bring in formal constructions that are geometric but non-coherent. One important example uses a theory of finite sets and a formalism that includes universal quantification bounded over finite sets.

A *geometric theory* comprises a vocabulary and a set of axioms of the form $\phi \vdash_{\mathbf{x}} \psi$ where

- ◆ $\mathbf{x}$ is a set $\{x_1, \ldots, x_n\}$ of sorted variables
- ◆ ϕ and ψ are geometric formulas whose free variables are all taken from $\mathbf{x}$

Such a set $\{\phi_i \vdash_{\mathbf{x}^i} \phi_i : i \in I\}$ of axioms should be thought of as meaning $\bigwedge_i \forall x_1^i, x_2^i, \ldots, x_n^i. (\phi_i \implies \psi_i)$. Now $\forall$, $\implies$ and infinite $\bigwedge$ are not geometric connectives and don't appear in ϕ_i or ψ_i; but just at this one level they are allowed into the geometric theory.

Note that this does not use the standard logical idea that a theory is a vocabulary together with a set of sentences (formulas without free variables). Hence geometric logic may fail to fit assumptions made for a general purpose logic environment. Also, the fact that implication is not internalized in the logic means that Hilbert style presentations of the logic are impossible, and there is no deduction theorem.

Labelled Turnstiles

The label **x** on the turnstile is not peculiar to geometric logic. It is seen in Lambek and Scott's treatment [7] of intuitionistic logic, and its use improves even classical logic. The essential logical point behind it is that the use of the free variables **x** is just as much a hypothesis as the premiss ϕ—it hypothesizes the presence of values **x**. Some arguments are valid only in the presence of values not explicitly mentioned in ϕ or ψ, and such values must be referred to in the set **x**.

In many standard presentations of classical logic, one is allowed to deduce $\forall x.P(x) \vdash \exists x.P(x)$: from $\forall x.P(x)$ we can deduce $P(x)$ by $\forall$-elimination, and then $\exists x.P(x)$ by $\exists$-introduction. The deduction looks natural enough, but of course it is invalid in any model with an empty carrier: $\forall x.P(x)$ will then be true, $\exists x.P(x)$ false. The traditional classical response is to reject empty carriers—after all, what is the point of having the language of predicate logic if there is nothing for it to talk about?—but that approach doesn't work at all well in constructive logic, where "non-emptiness" is a much subtler notion, and even classically it is distinctly problematical in many-sorted logic. The labelled turnstiles allow more careful rules of deduction that are valid even for empty carriers. The example deduction depends not just on the truth of $\forall x.P(x)$, but also on the presence of x. Labelling turnstiles we see that $\forall x.P(x) \vdash_x P(x) \vdash_x \exists x.P(x)$, so we can write $\forall x.P(x) \vdash_x \exists x.P(x)$ meaning that the entailment holds *in the presence of an x*, i.e. if the carrier is inhabited. From that, we should not deduce $\forall x.P(x) \vdash \exists x.P(x)$. This example is not geometric, but similar considerations apply for us. In a sequent calculus formalization, we can reason freely within a context (list of free variables). What we deduce within one context is true also in any bigger context:

$$\frac{\phi \vdash_{\mathbf{x}} \psi}{\phi \vdash_{\mathbf{x},y} \psi}$$

However, contexts can be reduced only in a controlled way using $\exists$-elimination.

$$\exists E : \qquad \frac{\phi \vdash_{\mathbf{x},y} \psi}{\exists y.\phi \vdash_{\mathbf{x}} \psi} \qquad\qquad y \text{ not in } \mathbf{x}, \text{ nor free in } \psi$$

The effect in natural deduction is that we cannot freely invent new free variables (or constants). Some will be given us as the context for the overall problem (e.g. the free variables in the premises and conclusion), and they can also be introduced in a controlled manner for $\exists$-elimination (and, in more standard logics, for $\forall$-introduction); but that is all.

Examples of Geometric Theories

1. Algebraic theories, possibly many sorted. There are too many different meanings for the word "algebraic", but what I mean here is "defined by finitary operators and equational laws". These are geometric theories presented with sorts and functions, but no predicates, and all the axioms are of the form $\vdash_{\mathbf{x}} t_1 = t_2$.

2. Essentially algebraic theories. I mention these explicitly because although they can look difficult to define they share most of the pleasant universal algebraic features of algebraic theories. The big generalization is that the operators can represent operations that are partial, though not in an unrestricted way. The operators are arranged in a well-founded hierarchy, and for each operator its domain of definition is defined by a conjunction of equations involving more primitive operators. The equational laws are interpreted in the sense "if both sides are defined then they are equal". Putting such a description into the form of a geometric theory is not difficult, though of course a partial operator must be expressed as a predicate symbol, not a function.

   A good example is the theory of categories. It has two sorts, for objects and arrows. The most primitive operators (necessarily total) are source, target and identity; and then composition has its domain of definition determined by equality between the target of one arrow and the source of the other.

3. Topological spaces. Let X be a topological space, ΩX its topology (family of open subsets). A corresponding geometric theory can be defined as follows:
   ◆ *no sorts* (it is a propositional theory—hence no functions either)
   ◆ for each open set a, a proposition P_a
   ◆ if $a \subseteq b$ are open sets, then an axiom

$$P_a \vdash P_b$$

   ◆ if S is a family of open sets, then an axiom

$$P_{\cup S} \vdash \bigvee_{a \in S} P_a$$

   ◆ if moreover S is finite, then an axiom

$$\bigwedge_{a \in S} P_a \vdash P_{\cap S}$$

(The converses of the last two axioms follow from the first.)

If $x \in X$, then x gives a model of the theory in which P_a is interpreted as **true** iff $x \in a$. It may be that different points x can give the same model, and that some models do not arise from points in this way. If these pathologies do not happen, and the points are in bijection with the models of the theory, then X is *sober*. If you're familiar at all with locales, you'll understand that generators and relations for a frame give propositions and axioms for a propositional geometric theory (see [9]).

Some Logical Manipulations

I shall not attempt to give a full set of proof rules for the logic—you can find them in Makkai and Reyes[8]. There are no surprises, because (apart from the infinite disjunctions) the logic is a restriction of standard logic.

On a short digression, let me show how to simplify the sequents considerably.

Proposition 1 *Every geometric formula $\phi(\mathbf{x})$ is equivalent to one of the form* $\bigvee_i (E_i \wedge \exists \mathbf{y}^i . \bigwedge_{j=1}^{n_i} P_{ij})$, *where*

1. *The sets $\mathbf{x}$ and $\mathbf{y}^i$ are disjoint.*

2. *Each E_i is a conjunction of non-trivial equations among the free variables* **x**. *(A "trivial" equation is one of the form $x = x$, which can obviously be omitted.)*

3. *Each P_{ij} is either a primitive predicate applied to variables, or is an equation $z = t$ where z is a variable (from* **x** *or* $\mathbf{y}^i$*) and t is a primitive function symbol applied to variables.*

The description of the possible P_{ij}'s doesn't look nice. But it is always possible to present a geometric theory without function symbols, by replacing them by their graphs as predicate symbols, and then each P_{ij} is just a primitive predicate applied to variables.

Proof   I shan't give a detailed proof; after all, I haven't given the full proof rules. Instead, I shall show how to use equivalences that you might reasonably expect geometric logic to have.

First, formulas of this form are (up to equivalence) closed under the geometric connectives. For disjunctions, this is obvious. Next, consider existential quantification $\exists x$ (x in **x**). This should (expected equivalence) distribute over disjunction, and the disjuncts are of the form $\exists x.(E \wedge \exists \mathbf{y}.\bigwedge_{j=1}^{n}P_j)$. If x appears in E, i.e. there is an equation $x = x'$ (or $x' = x$), then our disjunct is equivalent to $(E' \wedge \exists \mathbf{y}.\bigwedge_{j=1}^{n}P_j)[x'/x]$, where E' is obtained from E by omitting all equations $x = x'$ or $x' = x$. If x does not appear in E, then the disjunct is equivalent to $E \wedge \exists x.\exists \mathbf{y}.\bigwedge_{j=1}^{n}P_j$. Finally, consider conjunction. Assuming that conjunction distributes over arbitrary disjunction, we get a disjunction of formulas $(E \wedge \exists \mathbf{y}.\bigwedge_{j=1}^{n}P_j) \wedge (E' \wedge \exists \mathbf{y}'.\bigwedge_{j=1}^{n'}P_j')$. By renaming, we can assume that the sets **y** and **y**$'$ (and **x** too, of course) are disjoint, and then the disjunct is equivalent to $(E \wedge E') \wedge \exists \mathbf{y}, \mathbf{y}'.(\bigwedge_{j=1}^{n}P_j \wedge \bigwedge_{j=1}^{n'}P_j')$.

It remains to be shown that atomic formulas are of this form. An equation between variables is OK. An equation $f(\dots) = g(\dots)$ is equivalent to $\exists z.(z = f(\dots) \wedge z = g(\dots))$, and the only remaining problem is to arrange for predicates and functions to be applied only to variables. This is done using equivalences such as that between $P(f(\dots),\dots)$ and $\exists u.(u = f(\dots) \wedge P(u,\dots))$.   □

Let us note something rather curious. The equations get divided up between "functional" equations, $z = t(\dots)$, which can be replaced by predicates in a transformed theory presentation and are kept amongst the conjuncts, and "structural" equations $x = x'$, which are ineradicable and pushed outside the existential quantification. The structural equations look like atomic formulas, and you might think their natural place is conjoined with P_{ij}'s under the existential quantifications. But there is a good sense in which '$E \wedge \exists \mathbf{y}$' is a single unit, a generalized quantifier. E generates an equivalence relation on **x**; let us then choose a representative from each equivalence class and define a new set **z** of variables comprising these canonical representatives and also **y**. We have an obvious relabelling function $r : \mathbf{x} \longrightarrow \mathbf{z}$, and $E \wedge \exists \mathbf{y}$ is left adjoint to relabelling: $\phi \vdash_{\mathbf{z}} \psi[r(x)/x(x \in \mathbf{x})]$ iff $E \wedge \exists \mathbf{y}.\phi \vdash_{\mathbf{x}} \psi$. (When E is empty, this just reduces to well-known properties of $\exists$.)

The proposition allows a rather drastic simplification of geometric axioms on the left-hand side, using $\vee$-elimination and $\exists$-elimination: for $\bigvee_i(E_i \wedge \exists \mathbf{y}^i.\bigwedge_{j=1}^{n_i}P_{ij}) \vdash_{\mathbf{x}} \psi$ can be replaced by a set (one for each i) of axioms $E \wedge \exists \mathbf{y}.\bigwedge_{j=1}^{n}P_j \vdash_{\mathbf{x}} \psi$, and then each of these can be replaced (after suitable juggling of the variables) by one of the form $\bigwedge_{j=1}^{n} P_j \vdash_{\mathbf{x}} \psi$.

3 Models

If a geometric theory is given, then the models for it are understood in an utterly standard way. First, the vocabulary must be interpreted: sorts as sets (the carriers), predicates as relations (subsets of products of carriers) and functions as functions (each from a product of carriers to a carrier). Once that is done, then every geometric formula can be interpreted as a relation in its free variables; then for an axiom $\phi \vdash_{\mathbf{x}} \psi$, both ϕ and ψ can be interpreted as subsets of the product of carriers for the sorts of the variables in $\mathbf{x}$; and then the interpretation is a model iff for every such axiom, the subset corresponding to ϕ is included in that for ψ.

Homomorphisms

Suppose a geometric theory is given, and we have two models M and N of it. A homomorphism from M to N is a family of carrier functions $\alpha_\sigma : M_\sigma \to N_\sigma$, one for each sort σ, that respect the vocabulary ingredients (the axioms don't enter in here). Specifically, if $f(x, y, z, \ldots)$ and $P(x, y, z, \ldots)$ are function and predicate symbols, then (suppressing sorts)

♦ $f_N(\alpha(x), \alpha(y), \alpha(z), \ldots) = \alpha(f_M(x, y, z, \ldots))$

♦ $P_M(x, y, z, \ldots) \implies P_N(\alpha(x), \alpha(y), \alpha(z), \ldots)$

For algebraic theories, this is exactly the usual definition of homomorphism between algebras. For theories that include predicates, it is worth pointing out the direction ' $\implies$ ' in the second of these conditions. '$\Longleftarrow$' would not be compatible with the algebraic homomorphisms, as you can see if you consider replacing an algebraic operator (say multiplication for monoids) by its graph: $P(x, y, z)$ means '$z = x.y$'. For an arbitrary monoid homomorphism α we have $z = x.y \implies \alpha(z) = \alpha(x).\alpha(y)$, but $\Longleftarrow$ would not be right in general. As an example, for the theory of posets the homomorphisms are the monotone functions.

It is also worth noting that once these two conditions are known for the vocabulary ingredients, they are also true for *all* terms and geometric formulas: this is because of the positivity of geometric logic. Of course, as soon as negation is included, the second condition is destroyed because the implication for $\neg P$ gives us the reverse implication for P. Hence, this notion of homomorphism is one that is not so useful in ordinary logic.

The topological example is interesting. A homomorphism will carry no data, but it still has to obey a non-trivial condition: that for each proposition P_a, if it holds in M then it must hold in N. Let us write $M \sqsubseteq N$ if M and N satisfy this for every P_a, so that there is a (unique) homomorphism from M to N. If M and N correspond to the points x and y, then this says that every open neighbourhood of x also contains y (i.e. meets $\{y\}$), in other words x is in the topological closure of $\{y\}$. This is exactly the specialization preorder on points.

The Category of Models

It is easy to see that under this notion of homomorphism, the models of a theory $\mathbb{T}$ form a category, $\mathrm{Mod}(\mathbb{T})$—though the topological example shows that $\mathrm{Mod}(\mathbb{T})$ can have extra "topological" structure that is not categorical.

In general, this category has little categorical structure, lacking in general most limits and colimits. However, a very important exception is that it has all filtered colimits. I don't want to define these in detail (see, e.g., Johnstone [5]), but they are the categorical generalization of directed joins, and I shall describe two particular cases. There are some general points to remember. First, they are constructed set-theoretically: a filtered colimit of models is carried by the set-theoretic filtered colimits of the carriers. Second, the existence of these colimits is intimately bound up with the geometric restrictions that conjunctions must be finite, and only finitely many free variables are allowed in each formula. Third, although the general filtered colimits may seem arcane, even the special cases are crucial in domain theory, both in finding least fixpoints within domains and in solving domain equations.

The first example of filtered colimit is the ω-colimit, of a diagram

$$ M_0 \xrightarrow{\ \alpha_0\ } M_1 \xrightarrow{\ \alpha_1\ } M_2 \xrightarrow{\ \alpha_2\ } \cdots $$

If $i < j$, let us write α_{ij} for the composite $\alpha_i; \ldots; \alpha_{j-1} : M_i \to M_j$. First, suppose this is a diagram of sets and functions. You can think of progression along the diagram as bringing in more and more elements (insofar as the α_i's are not onto), and making more and more equalities among them (insofar as the α_i's are not 1-1). The elements in the (co-)limit and the equalities between them are exactly those that appear at some finite stage. (If you want to be more formal, first take the disjoint union of the M_i's, then define an equivalence relation by $x \equiv y(x \in M_i, y \in M_j)$ iff $\alpha_{ik}(x) = \alpha_{jk}(y)$ for some k, and then the colimit is the set of equivalence classes.)

Now let us return to the original problem, in which the M_i's are models (of $\mathbb{T}$) and the α_i's are homomorphisms. We can apply the set-theoretic construction to the carriers, but more work is needed to show that we still have a model. If f is a function symbol, then to define $f(x, y, z, \ldots)$ in the limit we find a finite stage at which $x, y, z, \ldots$ all exist (there is such a finite stage *because there are only finitely many variables $x, y, z, \ldots$*) and calculate $f(x, y, z, \ldots)$ there. This gives us a well defined result in the limit, because the homomorphisms α_i preserve the results at the finite stages. Predicates are similar; $P(x, y, z, \ldots)$ holds in the limit iff it holds at some finite stage (and hence at all subsequent ones, from the homomorphism property). Now consider an axiom $\phi \vdash_{\mathbf{x}} \psi$. If ϕ holds in the limit, then it must hold at some finite stage—the finiteness of conjunctions is used here, as well as the finiteness of the set $\mathbf{x}$—, so ψ also holds there, so ψ holds in the limit.

I'll mention one other example, that of splitting idempotents, to dispose of a possible misconception. I said that filtered colimits were the categorical generalization of directed joins, and you know that directed joins are essentially infinite: finite directed joins are trivial. This is not quite the case with filtered colimits. Finding a finite filtered colimit is equivalent to *splitting an idempotent*: that is to say, if we are given a homomorphism $\alpha : M \to M$ such that $\alpha^2 = \alpha$, we seek a diagram $M \underset{e}{\overset{p}{\rightleftarrows}} N$ such that $p; e = \alpha$ and $e; p = \mathrm{Id}_N$. The argument that such colimits exist is similar to that for ω-colimits.

Let me repeat two points that explain why this doesn't look like conventional logic. First, the above definition of homomorphism works well because geometric logic is positive (no negation or implication), and second, the filtered colimits exist because of the finiteness restrictions.

Varying Set Theory

A point of greater importance than you might expect is that if we vary the notion of set, then we vary the notion of *model*; for instance, we could take "set" to mean "object in some given elementary topos", and—suitably interpreted, and provided there are enough infinitary colimits to cope with all the disjunctions—the definition of model still makes perfect sense. We have to be careful to reason constructively about these generalized models, for the logic appropriate to an elementary topos is not classical but intuitionistic. But this is not just a concession to the generalizing ambitions of constructivists. It has key significance in at least three ways.

First, the proof rules of geometric logic (as in [8]) are classically incomplete: that is to say, within a given theory, there may be a sequent that holds in all the classical set-theoretic models but is not provable from the axioms using the proof rules. Even in the propositional case, there are theories that have no models at all, but which are still consistent: you can't prove **true** ⊢ **false**. (This arises from the infinitary disjunctions. When they are banned—i.e. in *coherent* theories—Deligne's theorem proves completeness.)

However, this incompleteness is the fault *not of the proof rules but of the models*. In the classical category S of sets, the constraints imposed by having to satisfy excluded middle and choice sometimes make models impossible. But the proof rules are constructive in nature, and hold for models in non-classical set theories, and it turns out that they are complete as long as you allow your set theory to vary (technically, by taking models in other elementary toposes).

Second, although in general we must allow the set theory to vary to get completeness, *for any given theory* there is a "canonical geometric set theory" that contains a *generic* model—any sequent that holds in the generic model is provable. This set theory is really just made by taking the standard sets and freely adjoining a model of the theory. It will be treated in more detail in the next section, where we shall see how it can be used to understand the idea of interpreting one theory in another.

Finally, you'd often like to think of a theory as being concretely embodied in its class of models, but for an arbitrary geometric theory this can't be done naively because you don't know a priori where the models have to be taken from. I shall try to explain how *topos theory* answers this by providing a language that's designed to make it look as though we have a decent category of models.

4 Interpretations

One very restrictive idea of interpretation (of one theory, $\mathbb{T}$, in another, $\mathbb{T}'$) is a syntactic one: interpret the sorts, predicates and functions of $\mathbb{T}$ as sorts, predicates and functions of $\mathbb{T}'$, and prove that axioms of $\mathbb{T}$ become theorems in $\mathbb{T}'$. We shall be much more liberal, in effect by allowing syntactic interpretations not just in $\mathbb{T}'$ but more generally in theories (or rather theory presentations) equivalent to it.

Equivalence of Presentations

We shall take it that two theories are equivalent if they have the same models (essentially, i.e. up to isomorphism). By incompleteness, it is not enough just to look at classical set-theoretic models; we should give equivalence arguments that are constructively valid and so hold in the more general elementary toposes where the models might be taken. Here are some ways of modifying a theory to get an equivalent one:

♦ Add axioms that are consequences of the given ones.

♦ Replace axioms by logically equivalent ones as outlined above.

♦ For each function symbol $f(x,\ldots)$, replace it by a predicate $P(z,x,\ldots)$ (which is to represent the graph of the function), and add axioms to say that it is total and single-valued:

$$P(z,x,\ldots) = P(z',x,\ldots) \quad \vdash_{z,z',x,\ldots} \quad z = z' \qquad \vdash_{x,\ldots} \quad \exists z.P(z,x,\ldots)$$

Also, eliminate f from formulas by replacing $Q(f(x,\ldots))$ by $\exists u.(P(u,x,\ldots) \wedge Q(u))$ (u new) and similar manoeuvres.

♦ Eliminate the sort structure by replacing sorts σ by unary predicates $S_\sigma(x)$ over a single new sort representing their disjoint union:

$$S_\sigma(x) \wedge S_\tau(x) \quad \vdash_x \quad \textbf{false} \qquad (\sigma \neq \tau)$$
$$\vdash_x \quad \bigvee_\sigma S_\sigma(x)$$

(Note how this works when we start with no sorts at all! The first axiom scheme has no instances, and the second becomes $\vdash_x$ **false**. The x on the turnstile stops this asserting out-and-out inconsistency; instead, the axiom forces the single sort to represent the empty set.)

The sorting discipline shown by the arities of the symbols must also be taken care of. For instance, if $Q(u)$ had arity σ, then there must be a new axiom $Q(x) \vdash_x S_\sigma(x)$. Functions must be replaced by their graphs, so that if $f(u)$, with arity $\sigma \to \tau$, is replaced by $P(v,u)$ with arity $\tau \times \sigma$, then we need axioms

$$\begin{array}{ll}
P(z,x) & \vdash_{z,x} \quad S_\tau(z) \wedge S_\sigma(x) \\
S_\sigma(x) & \vdash_x \quad \exists z.P(z,x) \qquad \text{(modified totality)} \\
P(z,x) \wedge P(z',x) & \vdash_{z,z',x} \quad z = z'
\end{array}$$

♦ Add sorts that can be characterized uniquely up to isomorphism by geometric axioms. For instance, consider products. If σ and τ are existing sorts, extend the presentation by a new sort π with functions $\mathrm{fst} : \pi \to \sigma$, $\mathrm{snd} : \pi \to \tau$, and axioms

$$\vdash_{x:\sigma,y:\tau} \exists z : \pi.(\mathrm{fst}(z) = x \wedge \mathrm{snd}(z) = y)$$

$$\mathrm{fst}(z) = \mathrm{fst}(z') \wedge \mathrm{snd}(z) = \mathrm{snd}(z') \vdash_{z,z'} \quad z = z'$$

In any model, the carrier for π is forced by the axioms to be the product of the carriers for σ and τ: so π is characterized uniquely up to isomorphism by σ and τ. Models for the new theory are essentially the same as those for the old theory, the only difference being that the product $\sigma \times \tau$ is given explicitly instead of implicitly.

Other constructions that can be characterized geometrically include coproducts (disjoint unions—even infinitary ones), equalizers and coequalizers (slightly tricky! You need the infinitary disjunctions): in short, all colimits and finite limits.

♦ Here is an interesting construction that can be characterized geometrically: finite power sets. The finite power set $\mathbb{F}X$ is just the free semilattice over X, and as it happens free things (for finitary algebraic theories) can always be characterized geometrically. Here is a logical presentation.

Let σ be a given sort. We add a new sort π and functions $\{\cdot\} : \sigma \to \pi$ (the singleton embedding), $\emptyset : \pi$ and $\cup : \pi \times \pi \to \pi$; also axioms

$$\vdash_{S,T,U} \quad S \cup (T \cup U) = (S \cup T) \cup U$$

$$\vdash_{S} \quad S \cup \emptyset = S$$

$$\vdash_{S,T} \quad S \cup T = T \cup S$$

$$\vdash_{S} \quad S \cup S = S$$

$$\vdash_{S} \quad \bigvee_{n=0}^{\infty} \exists x_1, \ldots, x_n.S = \{x_1, \ldots, x_n\}$$

$$\{x_1, \ldots, x_m\} \subseteq \{y_1, \ldots, y_n\} \vdash_{\substack{x_1,\ldots,x_m \\ y_1,\ldots,y_n}} \bigwedge_{i=1}^{m} \bigvee_{j=1}^{n} x_i = y_j$$

where

$$\{x_1, \ldots, x_n\} \equiv_{\mathrm{def}} \{x_1\} \cup \cdots \cup \{x_n\}$$

$$\{\} \equiv_{\mathrm{def}} \emptyset$$

$$S \subseteq T \equiv_{\mathrm{def}} S \cup T = T$$

Using this construction, we can see that universal quantification is geometric, *provided that it is bounded over finite sets*. If ϕ is a formula with free variables in $\mathbf{x}$, $x : \sigma$ is one of those variables, and $S : \mathbb{F}\sigma$, then we can define

$$\forall x \in S.\phi \equiv_{\mathrm{def}} \bigvee_{n=0}^{\infty} \exists y_1, \ldots, y_n.(S = \{y_1, \ldots, y_n\} \wedge \bigwedge_{i=1}^{n} \phi[y_i/x])$$

The knowledge that this is possible seems to be folklore, but I know of nowhere where the formal details have been set out.

To show how different equivalent presentations may be, an example in [10] has two of which one has infinitely many sorts and functions but no predicates, while the other has one sort, no functions and infinitely many predicates (all unary).

Giraud Frames

Given a theory $\mathbb{T}$, one fundamental trick of categorical logic is to make a category whose objects are the sorts and predicates, both primitive and derived: a derived sort is one characterizable geometrically, and a derived predicate is just a formula. These are all the things that in models get interpreted as sets, and it is useful to think of them as sets parametrized by the model. For this reason, the category obtained behaves sufficiently like the category of sets to have many nice properties. In particular, by ignoring the parameter, the model, you can generally reason validly as though the objects actually are sets, though of course the reasoning has to be constructive. This category is really the "canonical geometric set theory" for $\mathbb{T}$ referred to earlier; it includes of course the ingredients explicitly presented in $\mathbb{T}$, and these constitute the "generic model".

If the theory is $\mathbb{T}$, then this category is written $S[\mathbb{T}]$: this means S (the category of sets) extended by formally adjoining the ingredients of $\mathbb{T}$ (as indeterminate sets) subject to the axioms. (The notation comes from the notation $R[X]$ for a ring of polynomials.) The category is usually called the "classifying topos" of $\mathbb{T}$, but I shall offer my excuses for not doing so when I discuss toposes. Instead I shall call it the "Giraud frame presented by" $\mathbb{T}$.

In general, a Giraud frame is a category with all colimits and finite limits, satisfying certain other conditions that (i) make the colimits and limits behave like those in S, and (ii) ensure that it can be presented by a small (in the set-theoretic sense) theory presentation. The conditions are exactly those set out for Giraud's theorem in Johnstone [4].

One aspect of Giraud frames being similar to S is that constructive set theory can be interpreted in them, and we can talk about models of a theory $\mathbb{T}$ in a Giraud frame—in fact, a model of $\mathbb{T}$ in $S[\mathbb{T}']$ is just an interpretation of $\mathbb{T}$ in $\mathbb{T}'$. (This is in accordance with what we originally said about interpretations, because $S[\mathbb{T}']$, by being made from *all* sorts geometrically derivable from $\mathbb{T}'$, can be seen as including all the theories equivalent to $\mathbb{T}'$.) Once that is given, then we know—up to isomorphism—how to interpret all the derived types, the objects of $S[\mathbb{T}]$, and in fact we get a functor from $S[\mathbb{T}]$ to $S[\mathbb{T}']$. Moreover, if we have two models and a homomorphism between them, then the homomorphism carrier functions for the primitive sorts extend uniquely to the derived sorts, and categorically we get a natural transformation.

To summarize: if $\mathbb{T}$ is a theory and A is a Giraud frame, then

- Models of $\mathbb{T}$ in A are functors from $S[\mathbb{T}]$ to A that preserve the colimits and finite limits. (We shall call such functors *homomorphisms* between Giraud frames. More correctly, they are adjunctions $f^* \dashv f_*$ for which the left adjoint f^*, which anyway preserves colimits, also preserves finite limits.)

- Homomorphisms between models are natural transformations between the Giraud frame homomorphisms. (Sorry to have the two different kinds of homomorphisms so close together.)

Thus the constructive model theory has been turned into category theory.

Non-geometric Type Constructors

Since the finite power set constructor (which I'm calling $\mathbb{F}$) is geometric, it's natural to ask whether the full power set $\mathbb{P}$ is. The answer is no: it cannot be characterized by geometric axioms. The same also goes for exponentials Y^X (the set of functions from X to Y). The way this is proved is by working in the Giraud frame. As it happens, Giraud frames have $\mathbb{P}$ and exponentials (the categories are elementary toposes, in fact), characterized uniquely but non-geometrically. The functors that correspond to interpretations preserve all the geometric constructions. It is possible with some work to see these categories and functors concretely, and to find examples of interpretation functors that do not preserve $\mathbb{P}$ and exponentials: hence those constructions are not geometric.

There is a parallel here to the way that $\forall$ and $\implies$ come in to a theory at just one level. The predicate and function symbols can be considered to be elements of power type or function type; but this is allowed just at the one level: you can have sorts such as $\mathbb{FFF}X$ for finite sets of finite sets of finite subsets of X, but you can't do this with $\mathbb{P}$.

It is natural to ask whether geometric logic is classical or intuitionistic in nature, though on the face of it the question is meaningless because the prime distinguishing feature—excluded middle—cannot be expressed in the absence of negation. The non-geometric structure of Giraud frames casts some light on this, because using it one can interpret the non-geometric logical connectives and it turns out that excluded middle is not obeyed: hence geometric and intuitionistic logic are intimately associated with one another. On the other hand, the very fact that this extra structure is not preserved by Giraud frame homomorphisms shows a sharp distinction between the two logics.

5 Toposes

I have been somewhat coy so far about the word "topos". If you're at all familiar with the literature, you will know that it generally means "category somewhat like $\mathcal{S}$". There are elementary toposes, and amongst those there are some—in fact exactly what I have called Giraud frames—that are called Grothendieck toposes; and $\mathcal{S}[\mathbb{T}]$ is normally called the classifying topos of $\mathbb{T}$.

I'm going to use the word with a quite different meaning. It would be vain to expect to overturn the established usage, but I'd like to try to show you how the word can convey some different intuitions. These are not new insights of my own. Grothendieck invented the word topos as a back-formation from "topology" (so toposes are "those things of which topology is the study") and said that a topos is a generalized topological space, and topos theorists understand these intuitions perfectly well. However, they have not often expressed them clearly, and I shall try to explain them by enforcing a distinction—between toposes and Giraud frames—that is analogous to that between locales and frames.

Definition 2 *A topos is the space of models (the classifying topos) of a geometric theory. If $\mathbb{T}$ is a geometric theory, then we write $[\mathbb{T}]$ for its classifying topos.*

Definition 3 *Let D and E be toposes. A geometric morphism (or map) from D to E is a continuous transformation of points of D into points of E.*

IMPORTANT! These definitions are mystical. They are intended to convey not the mathematical formalization but the intuitive meaning, and if you try to analyse them compositionally through detailed accounts of the terms "space", "model", "geometric theory" and so on, you will get a false formalization.

- ♦ A "space" is more than an unstructured class of points, for we have already seen that the models form a category. But there is also some mysterious topological structure that we haven't attempted to formalize, so a topos is not just the category of models. One problem in the formalization is how to account for this "topology".

- ♦ Similary, "continuous transformation" is mysterious. Actually, even for topological spaces it is quite mysterious.

- ♦ "Models"—where? It is not enough to consider models in S; they must be allowed in arbitrary Giraud frames. The formalization must allow for this.

- ♦ "Geometric theory presentations" have sets of sorts, predicates, functions and axioms, and sets of disjuncts in a disjunction: so what geometric theories are possible depends on what your underlying set theory is. Each elementary topos leads to its own theory of Grothendieck toposes. We shall assume a fixed underlying category of "the classical sets" S.

Implementation 4 *A topos D is equipped with a Giraud frame SD. If D and E are toposes, then a geometric morphism f from D to E is equipped with a Giraud frame homomorphism Sf (or f^*) from SE to SD (note the reversal of direction!)*

"Implementation" means that this is just a means to an end, a formalization that gives us a mathematical handle on the prior intuitions. Toposes could equally well be implemented as theory presentations—more easily, in fact, though geometric morphisms are then harder to describe.

"Equipped with" has no technical substance—giving a topos is just the same as giving a Giraud frame. But it is intended to dispel ideas that a topos "is" a Giraud frame and "has" objects and morphisms that are those of the Giraud frame. It decouples the language of toposes from that of Giraud frames, and hides the implementational details behind the "S" prefix. Large parts of the traditional language of toposes are designed to reinforce the "space of models" intuitions, and my own opinion is that this can usefully be taken even further. (See the remarks on notation at the end of this section.)

An example of this is in the apparently perverse direction of geometric morphisms. Suppose $f : D \to E$ is a geometric morphism, with $D = [\mathbb{T}]$. A point of D is a model of $\mathbb{T}$, in other words a Giraud frame homomorphism from SD to your favourite Giraud frame A (where you like to look for models). Composing with Sf turns it into a Giraud frame homomorphism from SE to A, and so transforms points x of D into points $f(x)$ of E, in accordance with the conceptual definition and without regard to your choice of A. It is easily checked that this extends to homomorphisms, giving a functor, but as for the topological aspects of continuity we are really defining what continuity means by our implementation.

Note also that if f and g are two geometric morphisms from D to E, and $\alpha : f \to g$ is a natural transformation, then each point x of D gives rise to a homorphism $\alpha_x : f(x) \to g(x)$; and that this is natural with respect to x.

Summary: Suppose we have $[\mathbb{T}] \underset{g}{\overset{f}{\rightrightarrows}} \Downarrow \alpha \; [\mathbb{T}']$ where $\mathbb{T}$ and $\mathbb{T}'$ are geometric theories, f and g are geometric morphisms and α is a natural transformation. Then the *intuitions* are

♦ [T] is the space of models for T. It has category structure using the homomorphisms as arrows (this intuitive category is not S-like, and is quite different from $S[T]$).

♦ f is a continuous transformation of models for T (points of [T]) into models for T'. It is functorial with respect to homomorphisms, and so can be considered a functor.

♦ α is a natural transformation from f to g considered as functors.

As a particularly important example, consider the empty theory $*$ with no vocabulary and no axioms. It has a unique model, and the Giraud frame $S[*]$ it presents is just S. $[*]$ can be thought of as a one-point space. A geometric morphism $f : [*] \to [T]$ intuitively just picks out a model of T; looking at it another way, Sf is a model of T in S. A natural transformation between two geometric morphisms f and g is just a homomorphism. Up to equivalence, there is only one geometric morphism from [T] to $[*]$: intuitively, every point of [T] has to map to the unique point $*$ of $[*]$.

For another example, consider the theories MON and SET of monoids and sets. SET can be interpreted in MON in an obvious way—its only ingredient is a single sort, which is interpreted as the single sort in MON—and this corresponds to a geometric morphism Forget : [MON] → [SET]. On points, it works exactly like the forgetful functor from the category of monoids to that of sets, taking a monoid and returning its carrier, forgetting the multiplicative structure. It is in fact intuitively helpful to think of the classifying toposes [MON] and [SET] as the categories of monoids and sets (in these algebraic examples there is no extra "topological" structure), but this is clearly incompatible with any idea that these toposes *are* their Giraud frames. (For instance, the Giraud frame $S[SET]$ that implements [SET] is most definitely not the Giraud frame S.) That is why I took such care to separate out the notions.

It is also interesting to note that there is a geometric morphism Free : [SET] → [MON] that on points constructs the free monoid over a set. Free is left adjoint to Forget just as one would expect from ordinary categories, though the definition of adjunction here has to be the general one that applies within 2-categories.

The 2-category structure—the natural transformations between geometric morphisms—is important, because it gives real support to our intuition that the individual toposes have the structure of categories (and categories with all filtered colimits, because filtered colimits of natural transformations always exist).

A good example of this is part of Johnstone's discussion [6] of bagtoposes. If D is a topos, then the bagtopos $B_L(D)$ classifies set-indexed families of points of D, and a homomorphism from $(x_i)_{i \in I}$ to $(y_j)_{j \in J}$ is a function $\alpha : I \to J$ together with, for each i, a homomorphism $f_i : x_i \to y_{\alpha(i)}$. If you carried out this construction with a category instead of a topos, you'd be constructing the free category-with-all-coproducts over D. Now a category D has an initial object (nullary coproduct) iff the unique functor from D to 1 has a left adjoint, and it has binary coproducts iff the diagonal functor from D to $D \times D$ has a left adjoint. (These are easy to see as direct expressions of the definition of coproduct.) Hence a category that has both these left adjoints has all finite coproducts; and if it has filtered colimits too then it has all coproducts. So we can reasonably define a topos D to "have all coproducts" iff these two left adjoints both exist, and we just need the 2-categorical structure to be able to define what adjoints are. It then turns out that the two adjoints are equivalent to B_L-algebra structure for D, so for toposes too we can say that $B_L(D)$ is the free topos-with-all-coproducts over D.

Remarks on the Notation

Although the notation $S[\mathbb{T}]$ is standard, its separation into $[\mathbb{T}]$ and SD is not. A happy accident of the notation is that S can stand not only for Sets, but equally well for Sheaves. Locales can be understood as a particular (*localic*) kind of topos, namely those classifying a propositional theory, and for a locale D, SD is the category of sheaves over D. This could be made more general. If a topos D is a generalized space, then I propose that the objects of the corresponding Giraud frame SD should be called *sheaves* over D. Then, just as in [9] a locale has points and opens but not elements, a topos would have points and sheaves but not objects.

6 Three Examples in Computer Science

These are the three examples that I have worked on myself. I should say that applications of elementary toposes—"S-like categories"—are more common; it is specifically the application of geometric logic and Grothendieck toposes that is still quite new.

Geometric Theories and Databases

This is my paper [10]. The applications to database theory are very simplistic—as presented, the theory cannot cope with relations between entities, nor with database update to reflect change in the world (as opposed to improved knowledge in the database). However, it sets out some aspects of the move from propositional geometric logic in computer science—principally localic domain theory—to predicate logic.

First, we have an observational account. The propositional case (Abramsky [1], Vickers [9]) corresponds to observing a single atomic world, though the theories may often be constructed (e.g. for product domains) to allow for components. In the predicate case the components are allowed for in the logic itself: a theory then expresses ideas of (i) how we can "apprehend" components of the world—observe their existence and lay hands on them—, and (ii) how to observe equality between apprehended objects.

Second, the theory of the lower powerdomain is generalized to a "bagdomain" that naturally uses toposes instead of locales. (Johnstone [6] took this much further and also showed how to generalize the upper powerdomain.)

Third, it gave an ilustration of the use of the well known categorical generalization of algebraicity, replacing ideal completions of posets by ind-completions of categories (i.e. free categories-with-all-filtered-colimits—see [5]).

Topical Categories of Domains

This work is still in preparation, though a preliminary account was given in Vickers [11]. It exploits the fact that theories of "information systems" used to present domains (there are various flavours) are geometric: so there are toposes classifying information systems and hence in a sense classifying domains. Where the sense falls down is in the morphisms—homomorphisms between information systems are not at all the same as the continuous maps between the domains, which must be represented by "approximable mappings". However, the theory of approximable mappings is also geometric, so there is a classifying topos for them. Putting these together with the appropriate geometric morphisms gives a "topical category", an internal category in the category of toposes. This means that starting from an ordinary category of domains, its unstructured classes of objects (domains) and arrows (maps) have been made into toposes and hence given categorical and topological structure.

The benefits of doing this are great. First of all, limits needed for finding least fixpoints within domains, and for solving domain equations, exist for free in the filtered colimits. When writing a domain equation $D = F(D)$, it is not possible to express F without it having the necessary continuity and functoriality properties. Because the functoriality is with respect to information system homomorphisms, not continuous maps, the problem of the contravariant argument in the function space construction vanishes—it turns out that for SFP, where function space is expressible, the information systems have so much structure needing to be preserved that homomorphisms correspond to embedding- projection pairs between domains.

It is hoped that this work will lead to an axiomatic account of domain theory.

Geometric Logic as Specification Language

When a software system is specified, an important aspect of it is the way it models the real world. For instance, for a credit account system the computer should be aware that the world contains a class of people (and that people have names, ages, and so on), a subclass comprising creditworthy people, and a subclass of *that* comprising the account holders. In the format of logical theories, we have a sort **person** and functions and predicates (confused with classes)

- ♦ name: **person** → **string**
- ♦ age: **person** → **num**
- ♦ cw, ah: $\mathbb{P}$**person**

We also want an axiom $ah(x) \vdash_x cw(x)$.

There is on the face of it no special reason why the logic should be geometric, but the observational account gives grounds for believing that the restrictions of geometric logic fit natural restrictions of the real world. For instance, compare cw with ah. There are untold numbers of people in the world, of whom untold numbers are creditworthy. The computer is certainly not expected to have a list of them all; rather it needs to know that if you do come across a person there are various procedures for establishing their creditworthiness—get a bank reference, ask their parents, see if they have an honest face, and so on. On the other hand, it really does need a complete list of all account holders, so ah is fundamentally different from cw. In geometric logic this would be reflected by making ah not a predicate of arity **person** ("type $\mathbb{P}$**person**"), but a constant of sort $\mathbb{F}$**person**, and it is only when that is done that useful notions such as the cardinality of ah can be considered. In observational terms, the computer must know how to "apprehend" (i.e. in this case record in its database) individual people and finite sets of them, but not the entire class. The work of Hodges [3] on IZ lends support to this idea that a restricted logic is better for specification.

The equivalences inherent in geometric logic make functions equivalent to their graphs (just as in set theory), and in the observational account functions lose all their computational content and become retrospective checks that the result is correct. This obviously looks like specification as opposed to implementation, and again supports the idea that geometric logic is good for specification (but this time in a negative way, by saying that it is not good for expressing dynamic computational features).

These considerations suggest a program of using geometric logic—or at least a finitary approximation to it, including coherent logic and finite sets and universal quantification bounded over them—as a specification language. The idea is to take existing specificational notation (such as Z) and give it a semantics in geometric logic and toposes: slogan—schemas are geometric theories. The expected benefits are

- ♦ Some existing specificational constructions will have to be dropped, but if the program is soundly based they should be in some sense unrealistic anyway (e.g. replacing $\mathbb{P}$ by $\mathbb{F}$).

- ♦ There is a very precise geometricity criterion to decide when a proposed new construction is legitimate.

- ♦ A "categorical specification theory" (or perhaps "categorical schema calculus") exists in the 2-category of toposes, the category structure being the key to modularization. The reason for this is that the aim of a module is to hide internal workings behind an interface specification of how the module is to relate to all other possible modules, and this is just what a universal property such as that for product or pullback does. It is category structure that makes this possible, by describing through the morphisms how the objects relate to each other. Working in the category of toposes, rather than the opposite category of Giraud frames, aids this through the spatial intuitions: for instance, a product topos is a "space of pairs".

Acknowledgements

There are things that topos theorists know but do not often write down, and it is some of these mysteries that I have tried to express. But I am uncomfortably aware that I am nowhere near having climbed to the shoulders of the giants. I want to thank Peter Johnstone in particular for much of what understanding I do have. By his careful theoretic working [6] of my bagdomain constructions, not only has he shown me how the work ought to be done technically, but he has also given me invaluable insight into the way the toposes have to be seen in order for the results to make sense.

I must also thank Mark Dawson, Reinhold Heckmann and Mark Ryan for their careful reading of earlier drafts. Their many pertinent comments have greatly helped me to improve the exposition. In addition, I am very grateful to Mark Dawson for producing the LaTeX version of the paper.

My own work mentioned here has been and continues to be supported by the UK Science and Engineering Research Council through the "Foundational Structures in Computer Science" project at Imperial College.

References

[1] S. Abramsky, Domain theory in logical form, pp. 1-77 in *Annals of Pure and Applied Logic* vol. 51, 1991.

[2] M.P. Fourman, P.T. Johnstone and A.M. Pitts (eds.), *Applications of Categories in Computer Science*, London Mathematical Society Lecture Note Series vol. 177, Cambridge University Press, 1992.

[3] Wilfrid Hodges, Another Semantics for Z, unpublished notes.

[4] Peter Johnstone, *Topos theory*, Academic Press, London, 1977.

[5] Peter Johnstone, *Stone Spaces*, Cambridge University Press, 1982.

[6] Peter Johnstone, Partial products, bagdomains and hyperlocal toposes, pp. 315-339 in [2].

[7] J. Lambek and P.J. Scott, *Introduction to Higher Order Categorical Logic*, Cambridge University Press, 1986.

[8] Michael Makkai and Gonzalo E. Reyes, *First Order Categorical Logic*, Lecture Notes in Mathematics 611, Springer-Verlag, 1977.

[9] Steven Vickers, *Topology via Logic*, Cambridge University Press, 1989.

[10] Steven Vickers, Geometric theories and databases, pp. 288-314 in [2].

[11] Steven Vickers, Topical categories of domains, pp. 261-274 in Winskel (ed.) Proceedings of the CLICS Workshop 1992, Technical Report DAIMI PB - 397-I, Computer Science Department, Aarhus University, 1992.

Part 2: Research Papers

Interaction Categories

(Extended Abstract)

Samson Abramsky

sa@doc.ic.ac.uk
Department of Computing, Imperial College
180 Queen's Gate, London SW7 2BZ, United Kingdom

1 Introduction

We propose *Interaction Categories* as a new paradigm for the semantics of computation. In place of the standard paradigm for categories *qua* universes for denotational semantics:

Objects	Structured sets
Morphisms	Structure-preserving functions
Composition	Function composition

we propose the Interaction Category paradigm:

Objects	Specifications
Morphisms	Processes
Composition	Interaction

Interaction Categories provide a framework for the unification of a number of hitherto disparate aspects of programming theory:

sequential	vs.	concurrent
functional programming	vs.	communicating processes
propositions-as-types	vs.	program logic
correctness	vs.	efficiency

Potential applications include:

- ♦ A useful type discipline for concurrent programming, integrated with a compositional verification methodology.

- ♦ Foundations for programming languages incorporating both concurrency and higher-order polymorphic constructs.

We do not, as yet, offer definitive axioms for Interaction Categories. More to the point at this stage, we can provide a number of substantive examples (the first with hindsight), in each of which the above paradigm is clearly visible:

1. Concrete Data Structures and Sequential Algorithms [9]
2. Geometry of Interaction Categories [3]
3. Games and Strategies [2]
4. Specifications and Processes (this paper)

The examples (1)–(3) above apply to sequential and/or functional computation. The decisive example needed to make the Interaction Category framework compelling is (4), to encompass concurrency. This was first mooted in [1] which explicitly proposed the Interaction Category paradigm, albeit couched in terms of sequent calculus rather than categories.

2   The Category of Synchronous Processes

This section is the technical core of the paper. We describe an Interaction Category **SProc** (which can be read as "Synchronous Processes" or as "Specifications and Processes") built from the following ingredients:

Objects	Concurrent System Specifications
Morphisms	Synchronisation trees
Composition	Synchronous product + restriction
Identities	Synchronous buffers ("wires" or "relays")

We will show **SProc** to have a very rich structure. Firstly, it provides a model for full (second order) Classical Linear Logic, and hence also, quite automatically, for typed λ-calculi such as System F. It also supports a hierarchy of *delay monads* which express the temporal structure of the category. They allow asynchrony to be built on top of synchrony, as in Milner's original work on SCCS, but in a richer mathematical framework. The delay monads also satisfy distributive laws with respect to the exponentials, relating delay—extension in time—to replication—extension in space.

Much of the familiar process calculus material can be extracted from the structure of **SProc**. *Relabelling* and *restriction* can be described in terms of a subcategory of "embeddings"; *non-determinism* arises from the semi-additive structure of **SProc**; *simulations* appear as 2-cells.

Our development of **SProc** clearly exhibits a view of processes as "relations extended in time". This is made precise by the fact that **SProc** is a *bicategory of relations* in the sense of Carboni and Walters [10]. Finally, we show how the compact closed structure of **SProc** supports a "Multi-Cut" rule which allows general process networks to be described within a typed framework.

Before beginning the detailed development, a few preliminary comments are in order.

♦ The "specifications" considered in this paper are quite rudimentary—just a sort and a set of traces (safety property). A tower of refinements (faithful functors)

$$\mathbf{SProc} \hookleftarrow \mathbf{SProc}_1 \hookleftarrow \cdots \hookleftarrow \mathbf{SProc}_k$$

can be set up, by incorporating progressively more refined specifications, covering behavioural properties such as deadlock-freedom and fairness. All these categories will share a common core structure; in particular, each of the above functors will preserve all the linear type structure. This is covered in detail in the full paper.

♦ We will build on the established process calculus work, in particular on Milner's synchronous calculus SCCS [19]. There are two reasons for choosing a synchronous product for the notion of interaction in **SProc**:

– Our paradigm indicates taking buffers as the identity morphisms. This works well in both the synchronous case, where buffers impose no delay—they behave like hardware wires—and in the "buffered" or "receptive" process case [15], in which processes are insensitive to delay. However, there are problems with the asynchronous concurrency + handshaking communication paradigm of CCS [20] or CSP [15], for which buffers are evidently not identities with respect to restricted parallel composition. (*Note added in proof.* An asynchronous interaction category has just been found as this paper is completed: it makes essential use of *simultaneity*.)

– Synchronous calculi such as SCCS [19] and MEIJE [6] are known to be very expressive; most other concurrent formalisms, including asynchronous calculi such as CCS and CSP, and real-time languages such as ESTEREL [8], can be interpreted as derived calculi in SCCS and MEIJE. So we lose no generality in taking synchronous interaction as the basic notion.

2.1   Preliminaries

We will take labelled transition systems modulo strong bisimulation as our notion of "process", hence of morphism in **SProc**. Since this is such a staple of concurrency theory, it allows immediate comparison with much of the literature. Also, strong bisimulation is the *finest* equivalence usually considered on transition systems. By showing that it suffices to yield all the equations we will need in order to establish the structure of **SProc**, we will automatically obtain the same result for any coarser equivalence. There is one important caveat to this remark. In this paper, we work within the interleaving paradigm, and ignore "true concurrency" issues.

In fact, instead of working explicitly with labelled transition systems quotiented by strong bisimulation, we will take advantage of Peter Aczel's work on non-well-founded sets [4], and work with *synchronisation trees* as canonical representations of strong bisimulation equivalence classes.

We define the synchronisation trees over $\mathcal{L}$ as the largest solution of the set equation

$$\mathsf{ST}_{\mathcal{L}} = \wp(\mathcal{L} \times \mathsf{ST}_{\mathcal{L}}).$$

More precisely , we take $\mathsf{ST}_{\mathcal{L}}$ as the final coalgebra of the functor

$$X \mapsto \wp(\mathcal{L} \times X).$$

The existence of this final coalgebra is guaranteed by Aczel's theory. Moreover, the final coalgebra property supports a method of definition by (non-well-founded, but "guarded") recursion, and a principle of coinduction. See [4] for further details.

Note that a synchronisation tree p yields a labelled transition system. Henceforth, we shall use the term "process" interchangeably with "synchronisation tree".

We will also make a conceptual point about synchronisation trees, in preparation for our subsequent development. The essential way in which computational processes generalise traditional mathematical objects such as functions and relations is that they have extension in time—they are *reactive systems* in Pnueli's apt terminology. Moreover, they evolve over time; their behaviour in future interactions will depend on those which have already taken place. In short, they have state.

For this purpose, we can generalise relations

$$\wp(X \times Y)$$

to "relations extended in time"

$$R = \wp((X \times Y) \times R),$$

and this will give a space of non-deterministic transducers. Note that these will be non-deterministic in two senses: firstly, outputs are not uniquely determined by inputs, and secondly continuations need not be uniquely determined by observable interactions, e.g.

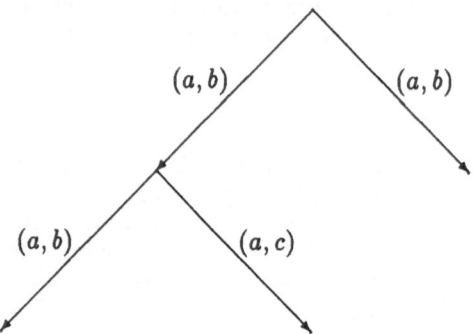

Now note that, taking $\mathcal{L} = X \times Y$, R is precisely $ST_{\mathcal{L}}$. Thus, if we introduce a cartesian product structure on actions, we can regard synchronisation trees as "relations extended in time". This simple idea will guide all our work in this section. It leads to a new way of seeing many familiar things, and brings some quite new structures to light.

Although our underlying computational paradigm of synchronous computation is similar to that of SCCS, we will not use that calculus itself. In particular, we will not assume an Abelian monoid structure on the "actions" (or labels, as we prefer to call them).

In fact, our treatment of labels represents an important conceptual break with the process calculus tradition. Instead of regarding labels as "proper names", which gives process calculus a strongly intensional slant from the outset, we will use our typed framework to take a more structural view. The labels in our framework play a similar rôle to *tokens* in information systems [23, 24]; and we will develop a very expressive set of categorical combinators for process algebra which *never mention labels explicitly* at all; cf. the use of categorical combinators to give variable-free translations of functional programs [11].

It will turn out that all the processes and process operators we will need to construct will be definable from the following four combinators plus guarded recursion:

Prefixing: $\qquad\qquad a : p = \{(a, p)\}$

Sum: $\qquad\qquad\qquad \sum_{i \in I} p_i = \bigcup_{i \in I} p_i$

Synchronous product: $\quad p \times q = \{((a, b), p' \times q') \mid (a, p') \in p, (b, q') \in q\}$

Restricted relabelling: $\quad p[f] = \{(b, q[f]) \mid (a, q) \in p, fa \succ b\}$

where $f : \mathcal{L} \to \mathcal{L}$ is a partial function on the ambient label set, and $fa \succcurlyeq b$ means "fa is defined and equal to b"(cf. [12]). In terms of labelled transitions, these combinators are specified as follows:

$$\frac{}{a : p \xrightarrow{a} p} \qquad \frac{p_i \xrightarrow{a} q}{\sum_{i \in I} p_i \xrightarrow{a} q}$$

$$\frac{p \xrightarrow{a} p' \quad q \xrightarrow{b} q'}{p \times q \xrightarrow{(a,b)} p' \times q'} \qquad \frac{p \xrightarrow{a} q \quad fa \succcurlyeq b}{p[f] \xrightarrow{b} q[f]}$$

Finally, some notation. Given a set X, we write X^* for the free monoid on X. We shall generally treat the canonical injection $X \hookrightarrow X^*$ as an inclusion. If $f : X \to Y$, we write $f^* : X^* \to Y^*$ for the unique homomorphism extending f. If $L \subseteq X^*$, then $L/a = \{s \in X^* \mid as \in L\}$.

2.2 The Category

The objects of **SProc** are defined to be structures

$$A = (\Sigma_A, S_A)$$

where Σ_A is a set of "labels"—the *sort* or *alphabet*, and $S_A \subseteq^{\text{nepref}} \Sigma_A^*$ is a non-empty prefix-closed subset of Σ_A^*, i.e. a set of traces giving the permissible finite behaviours: a *safety specification* [5]. As already explained, these are quite rudimentary specifications. More refined properties will be examined in the full version of the paper.

We will now go through the following hierarchy of definitions to arrive at the definition of morphism in **SProc**. (This hierarchy is typical of interaction categories—cf. [2], [9]). Firstly, we will define a *satisfaction relation* $p \models A$ between processes and specifications. Then we will define linear negation $A^\perp$ and tensor product $A \otimes B$ and hence also

$$A \,\otimes\, B \;=\; (A^\perp \otimes B^\perp)^\perp$$
$$A \multimap B \;=\; A^\perp \,\otimes\, B.$$

Finally, we will define a morphism $p : A \to B$ to be a process p such that $p \models A \multimap B$. (Strictly speaking, p unadorned is a *proto-morphism* in the sense of [12]; the triple (A, p, B) will be a morphism with uniquely defined source and target).

Firstly, given a process $p \in \mathrm{ST}_{\Sigma_A}$, we define

$$\mathrm{traces}(p) = \{s \in \Sigma_A^* \mid \exists q. p \xrightarrow{s} q\}.$$

Now, we define

$$p \models A \equiv p \in ST_{\Sigma_A} \wedge \text{traces}(p) \subseteq S_A$$
$$A^{\perp} = A$$
$$\Sigma_{A \otimes B} = \Sigma_A \times \Sigma_B$$
$$S_{A \otimes B} = \{s \in \Sigma^*_{A \otimes B} \mid \text{fst}^*(s) \in S_A, \text{snd}^*(s) \in S_B\}.$$

Note that $A = A^{\perp}$ implies that $A \multimap B = A \otimes B = A \otimes B$; in particular, **SProc** is *compact closed* [7]. This point is discussed in Section 2.6

Next, we turn to composition in **SProc**. Given $p : A \rightarrow B$, $q : B \rightarrow C$, we define $p; q : A \rightarrow C$ by:

$$p; q \equiv (p \times q)[((a,b),(b,c)) \mapsto (a,c)]. \tag{1}$$

Here and henceforth we specify a partial function on labels using pattern-matching notation. The intention is that the function is defined just on those arguments matching the pattern. In (1) the function is defined on those arguments

$$((a,b),(b',c)) \in (\Sigma_A \times \Sigma_B) \times (\Sigma_B \times \Sigma_C)$$

such that $b = b'$.

Composition can be specified in terms of labelled transitions:

$$\frac{p \xrightarrow{(a,b)} p' \qquad q \xrightarrow{(b,c)} q'}{p; q \xrightarrow{(a,c)} p'; q'}$$

Note that at each step, $p; q$ behaves like the relational composition of p and q. One may say that a process $p : A \rightarrow B$ is a "relation from A to B extended in time". This analogy will recur throughout our work in this section.

For the identities, we define

$$1_A \equiv \Sigma_{a \in S_A}(a, a) : 1_{A/a}$$

where $A/a = (\Sigma_A, S_A/a)$. Thus 1_A is the "identity relation extended in time".

Proposition 2.2.1 *SProc is a category.*

One comment is already in order. Even at this very basic stage, a significant revision of the standard process calculus paradigm has occurred. Following Milner [20] and Hoare [15] all process calculi and algebras separate out the two operations of parallel composition and hiding or restriction. In [18], Milner remarks that perhaps it would be more natural to take the combined operation as the fundamental primitive; his main reason for not doing so is that this combined operation is not associative.

By contrast our typed framework, even with the rudimentary types currently being considered, suffices to guarantee that our composition, built from synchronous product and restriction, *is* associative. The familiar terrain already looks a little different; the map starts to be redrawn.

2.3 The Linear Types

As mentioned previously, **SProc** yields a model of full Classical Linear Logic [14] We now outline the interpretation of the multiplicatives and additives—the exponentials are described in the full paper. The theme of relations extended in time is followed consistently; see [7] for a description of the category of relations as a model of Linear Logic.

2.3.1 Multiplicatives

We have already described the object parts of the multiplicative connectives except for the units I and $\bot = I^\perp = I$, which are defined by

$$I = (\{*\}, \{*^k \mid k \in \omega\}).$$

The action of tensor on morphisms is as follows. Given $p : A \to B$, $q : A' \to B'$ then $p \otimes q : A \otimes A' \to B \otimes B'$ is defined by

$$p \otimes q \equiv p \times q[((a, b), (a', b')) \mapsto ((a, a'), (b, b'))].$$

In terms of labelled transitions:

$$\frac{p \xrightarrow{(a,b)} p' \qquad q \xrightarrow{(a',b')} q'}{p \otimes q \xrightarrow{((a,a'),(b,b'))} p' \otimes q'}.$$

The canonical isomorphism for asssociativity

$$\mathsf{assoc}_{A,B,C} : (A \otimes B) \otimes C \to A \otimes (B \otimes C)$$

is defined by

$$\mathsf{assoc}_{A,B,C} \equiv 1_{(A \otimes B) \otimes C}[(((a, b), c), ((a, b), c)) \mapsto (((a, b), c), (a, (b, c)))].$$

The canonical isomorphisms for unit and symmetry are defined similarly. The application morphisms

$$\mathsf{Ap}_{A,B} : (A \multimap B) \otimes A \to B$$

are defined by

$$\mathsf{Ap}_{A,B} \equiv 1_{A \multimap B}[((a, b), (a, b)) \mapsto (((a, b), a), b)].$$

Given $p : A \otimes B \to C$ we define $\Lambda(p) : A \to (B \multimap C)$ by

$$\Lambda(p) \equiv p[((a, b), c) \mapsto (a, (b, c))].$$

Proposition 2.3.1 **SProc** is a ∗-autonomous category.

2.3.2 Additives

Since **SProc** is self-dual (i.e. **SProc** $\simeq$ **SProc**^{op}), if it has (finite) coproducts then it also has (finite) products. Since moreover $A = A^{\perp}$ in **SProc**, these will actually coincide, i.e. it has biproducts.

The initial object is

$$0 = (\varnothing, \{\epsilon\}).$$

The unique map $0_A : 0 \to A$ is defined by

$$0_A = \varnothing$$

("NIL"). For binary coproducts we define

$$
\begin{aligned}
\Sigma_{A \oplus B} &\equiv \Sigma_A + \Sigma_B \\
S_{A \oplus B} &= \{\text{inl}(^{)}*(s) \mid s \in S_A\} \cup \{\text{inr}(^{)}*(t) \mid t \in S_B\} \\
\text{inl}(_{)}A, B &\equiv 1_A[(a, a) \mapsto (a, \text{inl}((\text{)}a))] \\
\text{inr}(_{)}A, B &\equiv 1_B[(b, b) \mapsto (b, \text{inr}((\text{)}b))] \\
[p, q] &\equiv p[(a, c) \mapsto (\text{inl}((\text{)}a), c)] + q[(b, c) \mapsto (\text{inr}((\text{)}b), c)].
\end{aligned}
$$

These definitions easily extend to arbitrarily set-indexed coproducts $\bigoplus_{i \in I} A_i$.

Proposition 2.3.2 **SProc** has all small biproducts.

2.4 Semi-additivity and Non-determinism

We say that a process $p \in \mathsf{ST}_{\mathcal{L}}$ is *deterministic* if, for all $s \in \mathcal{L}^*$, $p \xrightarrow{s} q$ and $p \xrightarrow{s} r$ implies that $q = r$. The processes arising from the constructions in **SProc** already considered need not be deterministic. For example, even if p and q are deterministic, $p; q$ need not be. In fact, non-determinism is explicitly accounted for by the categorical structure we have already described. It is standard that any category $\mathbb{C}$ with biproducts is *semi-additive* [16, 12]; i.e. each hom-set $\mathbb{C}(A, B)$ has an Abelian monoid structure, and composition is bilinear.

Explicitly, given $f, g : A \to B$, the addition is defined by

$$
\begin{aligned}
f + g &= A \xrightarrow{\Delta_A} A \oplus A \xrightarrow{[f,g]} B \\
&= A \xrightarrow{\langle f,g \rangle} B \oplus B \xrightarrow{\nabla} B
\end{aligned}
$$

where $\Delta_A = \langle 1_A, 1_A \rangle$ is the diagonal and $\nabla_A = [1_A, 1_A]$ is the codiagonal, with unit given by

$$0_{A,B} = A \longrightarrow 1 = 0 \longrightarrow A.$$

Moreover, any functor on $\mathbb{C}$ which preserves products or coproducts is automatically semi-additive.

As we saw in Section 2.3.2, **SProc** has all small biproducts. Applying the general definition, we see that $p + q$ is exactly the standard non-deterministic plus operation, with unit $0_{A,B}$ the standard "NIL" process. Thus we get the equations

$$\begin{aligned}
p + 0 &= p \\
p + q &= q + p \\
(p + q) + r &= p + (q + r) \\
p; \left(\sum_{i \in I} q_i\right) &= \sum_{i \in I}(p; q_i) \\
\left(\sum_{i \in I} p_i\right); q &= \sum_{i \in I}(p_i; q).
\end{aligned}$$

Moreover, since $A \otimes -$ and $- \otimes A$ are left adjoints, they preserve coproducts, so we get the distributivities

$$\begin{aligned}
p \otimes \sum_{i \in I} q_i &= \sum_{i \in I}(p \otimes q_i) \\
\sum_{i \in I} p_i \otimes q &= \sum_{i \in I}(p_i \otimes q).
\end{aligned}$$

Thus we have recovered many familiar process algebra equations, and gained some new ones, from these very general considerations.

2.5 Delay Monads

The linear types play an essential rôle in articulating the process-algebraic aspect of **SProc**. However, they by no means suffice to exploit the rich structure of **SProc**. In particular, they do not reflect the temporal structure of processes. To see this consider the following proposition.

Proposition 2.5.1 The category **Rel** of sets and relations is bireflective in **SProc**. The reflection $R : \textbf{SProc} \longrightarrow \textbf{Rel}$ preserves all the linear category structure.

This means that the linear connectives never take us out of the processes with trivial—one-step only—extension in time, i.e. relations. The moral of this observation is that while Interaction Categories should certainly model the linear types, we should also look for additional structure to reflect the fact that processes can have non-trivial extension in time. This structure should be orthogonal to the "spatial" or distributed structure expressed by the linear types.

This point can be related to the distinction made by Milner in the context of process calculi between "static" and "dynamic" operations [20]. The multiplicatives correspond to static operations (product, restriction); the additive to choice operators giving "one-step dynamics"; and the exponentials combine features of both. But the crucial operation of *prefixing* which alone yields extension in time is nowhere catered for by the linear types. This can be related to the results in [2] showing that the history-free strategies suffice to interpret the linear types.

Our approach to capturing this additional temporal structure in **SProc** is closely related to Milner's work on building asynchrony on top of synchrony in

SCCS [19], but we will make full use of the Interaction Category framework to recast this work in a more conceptual fashion. This will lead us to some remarkable formal properties of these computational notions.

We will consider a hierarchy of three delay operators:

- Unit delay: $\bigcirc A$
- Unbounded delay before the first action: δA
- Propagation of unbounded delays *after* the first action: ΔA

The key role of δ and Δ as process combinators is clear from the SCCS and MEIJE literature. However we will recast these constructions in our framework as *bimonads*, leading to a radically different perspective.

In this extended abstract, we will concentrate on the case of unbounded delay. The other delay operators are dealt with in the full version of the paper.

2.5.1 Unit Delay

The unit delay functor is defined as follows. The action on objects is

$$\begin{aligned} \Sigma_{\bigcirc A} &= 1 + \Sigma_A \\ S_{\bigcirc A} &= \{\epsilon\} \cup \{*s \mid s \in S_A\}. \end{aligned}$$

and the action on morphisms is, for $p : A \to B$,

$$\bigcirc p = (*, *) : p.$$

2.5.2 Unbounded Delay

We consider the unbounded delay monad δ. δA is defined by

$$\begin{aligned} \Sigma_{\delta A} &= 1 + \Sigma_A \\ S_{\delta A} &= \{*^k s \mid k \in \omega, s \in S_A\}. \end{aligned}$$

We will specify the monadic structure of δ using the streamlined presentation of [17]. Firstly, the unit

$$\eta_A : A \to \delta A$$

is defined—as a protomorphism—by

$$\eta_A \equiv 1_A$$

where we exploit the abuse of notation by which $S_A \subseteq S_{\delta A}$. Thus the unit forces the case of zero delay. The multiplication will "add" two nested delays, so that the monadic structure of δ will arise from the monoid $(\mathbb{N}, +, 0)$ seen as the underlying model of discrete future time.

The "Kleisli extension" [17, 21]

$$\frac{A \xrightarrow{p} \delta B}{\delta A \xrightarrow{p^\dagger} \delta B}$$

is defined by the guarded recursion

$$p^\dagger \equiv p + \bigcirc(p^\dagger).$$

The picture is

$p:$	a_1	$\cdots$	a_k	a_{k+1}	$\cdots$
	$*$	$\cdots$	$*$	b_1	$\cdots$

$p^\dagger:$	$*$	$\cdots$	$*$	a_1	$\cdots$	a_k	a_{k+1}	$\cdots$
	$*$	$\cdots$	$*$	$*$	$\cdots$	$*$	b_1	$\cdots$

We can then define, for $p : A \to B$,

$$\delta p \equiv (p; \eta_B)^\dagger,$$

and $\mu_A : \delta\delta A \to \delta A$ by

$$\mu_A \equiv 1^\dagger_{\delta A}.$$

Proposition 2.5.2 (δ, η, μ) is a monad.

2.6 Compact Closure and Multi-Cut

As we have already seen, the linear type structure of **SProc** is quite degenerate, in that $A^\perp = A$, so that $\otimes = \mathbin{\text{\textcolor{black}{$\otimes$}}}$ (**SProc** is compact-closed), $\& = \oplus$ and $! = ?$. In the full version of the paper, we show how to enrich the specifications of **SProc** to stronger behavioural properties. This will have the effect of "sharpening up" the linear type structure so that the degeneracies disappear.

Our point here is that the looser type discipline of **SProc** can actually be *useful* in that it permits the flexible construction of a large class of processes within a typed framework. In particular, compact closure validates a very useful typing rule which we call the *multi-cut*. (This is actually Gentzen's MIX rule [13] but we avoid the use of this term since Girard has used it for quite a different rule in the context of Linear Logic [14].)

The usual Cut Rule

$$\frac{\vdash \Gamma, A \qquad \vdash \Delta, A^\perp}{\vdash \Gamma, \Delta}$$

allows us to plug two modules together by an interface consisting of a single "port" [1]. This allows us to connect processes in a tree structure, but not to construct cyclic interconnection networks such as the Scheduler described in [20]. The problem with building a cycle is at the last step where we have already connected and to connect

$$\alpha \;-\!\!\left(\; p_k \;\right)\!-\beta$$

we must plug both α and β simultaneously into the existing network. This could be done if we had the following "binary" version of the cut rule

$$\frac{\vdash \Gamma, A_1, A_2 \qquad \vdash \Delta, A_1^\perp, A_2^\perp}{\vdash \Gamma, \Delta}$$

or more generally the "multi-cut":

$$\frac{\vdash \Gamma, \Delta \qquad \vdash \Gamma', \Delta^\perp}{\vdash \Gamma, \Gamma'}$$

This rule is not admissible in Linear Logic and cannot in general be interpreted in Linear Categories. However it can always be canonically interpreted in a compact closed category (and hence in particular in **SProc**).

3 Conclusions

As already emphasized we are building on the extensive existing work on concurrency. In particular, much of the formal content of process calculus is reconstituted in **SProc**, but with a radical shift in perspective. The "functorialization" of process calculus changes the conceptual map of the subject, leading to the re-interpretation of much of the familiar material and bringing some quite new structures to light.

Previous work on categorical models for concurrency has invariably modelled processes or concurrent systems by the *objects* of a category with some notion of simulation for the morphisms. This has confined categorical methods to a useful but limited taxonomic role of organizing classes of models into categories and comparing them by adjunctions [25]. There has also been a mismatch, first noted in [22], with standard denotational semantics in which programs are modelled by elements of, or more generally functions between, domains. The Interaction Category framework introduced here finally removes this mismatch; with the immediate dividend that we can model concurrent processes and type theory within the same framework in a uniform and elegant way.

Acknowledgements

I have had useful and enjoyable discussions with Simon Gay, Rajagopal Nagarajan, Charles Matthews, Pierre-Louis Curien, Claudio Hermida and Pino Rosolini. Simon and Raja provided invaluable assistance in getting this paper ready in time. The referees Sebastian Hunt, Michael Huth and François Lamarche provided useful comments. I would particularly like to thank Radha Jagadeesan; I could never have got from [1] to the ideas described in the present paper without the insights gleaned from our joint work on Geometry of Interaction [3] and Game Semantics [2].

References

[1] S. Abramsky. Proofs as processes. Unpublished Lecture Notes, 1991.

[2] S. Abramsky and R. Jagadeesan. Games and full completeness for multiplicative linear logic. Technical Report DoC 92/24, Department of Computing, Imperial College of Science Technology and Medicine, 1992.

[3] S. Abramsky and R. Jagadeesan. New foundations for the geometry of interaction. In *Proceedings, Seventh Annual IEEE Symposium on Logic in Computer Science*, pages 211–222. IEEE Computer Society Press, 1992.

[4] P. Aczel. *Non-well-founded sets*. CSLI Lecture Notes 14. Center for the Study of Language and Information, 1988.

[5] B. Alpern and F. B. Schneider. Defining liveness. *Information Processing Letters*, 21(4):181–185, 1985.

[6] D. Austry and G. Boudol. Algèbres de processus et synchronisations. *Theoretical Computer Science*, 30:91–131, 1984.

[7] M. Barr. *-autonomous categories and linear logic. *Mathematical Structures in Computer Science*, 1(2):159–178, July 1991.

[8] G. Berry, P. Couronné, and G. Gonthier. Synchronous programming of reactive systems: An introduction to ESTEREL. Technical Report 647, INRIA, 1986.

[9] G. Berry and P.-L. Curien. Sequential algorithms on concrete data structures. *Theoretical Computer Science*, 20:265–321, 1982.

[10] A. Carboni and R.F.C.Walters. Cartesian bicategories I. *Annals of Pure and Applied Algebra*, 49:11–32, 1987.

[11] Pierre-Louis Curien. *Categorical Combinators, Sequential Algorithms and Functional Programming*. Research Notes in Theoretical Computer Science. Pitman, 1986.

[12] P. J. Freyd and A. Scedrov. *Categories, Allegories*, volume 39 of *North-Holland Mathematical Library*. North-Holland, 1990.

[13] G. Gentzen. Investigations into logical deduction. In M. E. Szabo, editor, *The Collected Papers of Gerhard Gentzen*. North-Holland, 1969.

[14] J.-Y. Girard. Linear Logic. *Theoretical Computer Science*, 50(1):1–102, 1987.

[15] C.A.R. Hoare. *Communicating Sequential Processes*. Prentice Hall, 1985.

[16] S. Mac Lane. *Categories for the Working Mathematician*. Springer-Verlag, Berlin, 1971.

[17] E. Manes. *Algebraic Theories*, volume 26 of *Graduate Texts in Mathematics*. Springer-Verlag, 1976.

[18] R. Milner. *A Calculus for Communicating Systems*, volume 92 of *Lecture Notes in Computer Science*. Springer-Verlag, Berlin, 1980.

[19] R. Milner. Calculi for synchrony and asynchrony. *Theoretical Computer Science*, 25:267–310, 1983.

[20] R. Milner. *Communication and Concurrency*. Prentice Hall, 1989.

[21] E. Moggi. Computational lambda calculus and monads. In *Proceedings, Fourth Annual Symposium on Logic in Computer Science*. IEEE Computer Society Press, 1989.

[22] M. Nielsen, G. D. Plotkin, and G. Winskel. Petri nets, event structures and domains I. *Theoretical Computer Science*, 13(1):85–108, 1981.

[23] D.S. Scott. Domains for denotational semantics. In M. Nielson and E. M. Schmidt, editors, *Automata, Languages and Programming: Proceedings 1982*. Springer-Verlag, Berlin, 1982. Lecture Notes in Computer Science 140.

[24] G. Winskel. *The Formal Semantics of Programming Languages*. Foundations of Computing. The MIT Press, Cambridge, Massachusetts, 1993.

[25] G. Winskel and M. Nielsen. Models for concurrency. In S. Abramsky, D. Gabbay, and T.S.E. Maibaum, editors, *Handbook of Logic in Computer Science*. Oxford University Press. To appear.

Animating LU

Mark Dawson

md@doc.ic.ac.uk

Department of Computing, Imperial College
180 Queen's Gate, London SW7 2BZ, United Kingdom

Abstract

The logician J.-Y. Girard has proposed the calculus LU that unifies Classical, Intuitionistic and Linear logics in a single proof theoretic presentation. In this paper we show how we have used our logic environment to explore LU. Unlike other 'generic' logic environments, presenting a logic in $ICLE$ preserves the structure, so that proof-theoretic properties can be retained, e.g. cut-elimination and consistency.

1 Introduction

Girard's unified calculus LU combines Linear, Classical and Intuitionistic logics in a single proof theoretic presentation. The combination is intriguing since the "rules of the game" remain the same for each subsystem and the fragments are free to communicate - through cuts. But there is a price to pay for the amalgamation; sequents become 4-tuples and each connective may be defined by up to twenty-seven rules.

We start by showing how a translation, such as Girard's embedding of Classical in Intuitionistic logic, can be represented in our logic environment [1]. Next we explain Girard's calculus LU from translations of its different fragments. Finally, we illustrate the development of different presentations of LU in our logic environment. Unlike other 'generic logic' environments ours is particularly well suited to the natural presentation of sequent style systems which can be encoded in a very direct fashion.

2 Animating translations

Girard's translation of Classical Logic into Intuitionistic Logic helps to set the scene for LU in two respects. Firstly, it contains a translation idea which is also used in LU. Secondly, it provides an example of representing such a translation in our logic environment.

Several translations have been designed for the purpose of encoding Classical sequents in Intuitionistic logic by Gentzen, Kolgomorov and Gödel and these are lucidly given in [3]. The translations take a classical sequent of the form $\Gamma \vdash_c \Delta$ to $\Gamma, \neg(\Delta)^\circ \vdash_i \bot$. Here $(-)^\circ$, due to Gentzen, is defined by cases on the structure of A, where P ranges over atomic propositions:

$$(P)^\circ = \neg\neg P$$
$$(\neg A)^\circ = \neg(A)^\circ \qquad (A \wedge B)^\circ = (A)^\circ \wedge (B)^\circ$$
$$(A \rightarrow B)^\circ = (A)^\circ \supset (B)^\circ \qquad (A \vee B)^\circ = \neg(\neg(A)^\circ \wedge \neg(B)^\circ)$$
$$(\forall x A)^\circ = \forall x (A)^\circ \qquad (\exists x A)^\circ = \neg\forall x \neg(A)^\circ$$

Notice that atoms are double negated which, as pointed out by Girard, makes the translation incompatible with substitution,

$$(A[B/P])^\circ \neq (A)^\circ[(B)^\circ/P]$$

Girard's translation $(-)^g$ improves on this translation with the aid of two *polarities* '+' and '−', and it turns out to be compatible with substitution. The idea is to convert sequents of the form $\Gamma \vdash_c \Delta$ to ones of the form $\Gamma, (\Delta)^g \vdash_i \bot$.

$$(A)^g = \begin{cases} \neg C, & (A)^g = C+ \\ C, & (A)^g = C- \end{cases}$$

The translation $(-)^g$ works by replacing occurrences of classical right-introduction rules with other intuitionistic rules. There are cases for $(A)^g$ depending on the form of the translation obtained for subformulas of the formula A.

Taking the $\vdash\wedge$ rule as an example. Sequents in the proof are transformed from $\Gamma \vdash_c A, \Delta$ and $\Gamma \vdash_c B, \Delta$ to $\Gamma, (\Delta)^g, (A)^g \vdash_i \bot$ and $\Gamma, (\Delta)^g, (B)^g \vdash_i \bot$ respectively. There are four cases to consider depending on the polarity of the translation of $(A)^g$ and $(B)^g$. Suppose $(A)^g = C+$ and $(B)^g = D+$ then the derivation is constructed as follows:

$$\frac{\Gamma \vdash_c A, \Delta}{\Gamma, (\Delta)^g, \neg C \vdash_i \bot}{\scriptstyle (A)^g = C+} \qquad \frac{\Gamma \vdash_c B, \Delta}{\Gamma, (\Delta)^g, \neg D \vdash_i \bot}{\scriptstyle (B)^g = D+}$$

$$\frac{}{\Gamma, (\Delta)^g \vdash_i \neg\neg C} \qquad \frac{}{\Gamma, (\Delta)^g \vdash_i \neg\neg D}$$

$$\frac{\Gamma, (\Delta)^g \vdash_i \neg\neg C \wedge \neg\neg D}{}$$

$$\frac{\Gamma, (\Delta)^g, \neg(\neg\neg C \wedge \neg\neg D) \vdash_i \bot \qquad \qquad \neg(\neg\neg C \wedge \neg\neg D) \vdash_i \neg(C \wedge D)}{\Gamma, (\Delta)^g, \neg(C \wedge D) \vdash_i \bot}$$

$$\frac{}{\Gamma \vdash_c A \wedge B, \Delta}{\scriptstyle (A \wedge B)^g = (C \wedge D)+}$$

When the argument illustrated above for the case of $\vdash\wedge$ is carried out for the other right-introduction rules the system of translation obtained can be summarised in the following table.

$(A)^g$	$(B)^g$	$(A \wedge B)^g$	$(A \vee B)^g$	$(A \rightarrow B)^g$	$(\neg A)^g$	$(\forall x A)^g$	$(\exists x A)^g$
$C+$	$D+$	$(C \wedge D)+$	$(C \vee D)+$	$\neg(C \wedge \neg D)-$	$\neg C-$	$\neg\exists x \neg C-$	$\exists x C+$
$\neg C-$	$D+$	$(\neg C \wedge D)+$	$\neg(\neg C \wedge D)-$	$\neg(C \wedge D)-$	$C+$	$\exists x C+$	$\exists x \neg C+$
$C+$	$\neg D-$	$(C \wedge \neg D)+$	$\neg(C \wedge \neg D)-$	$(C \vee D)+$			
$\neg C-$	$\neg D-$	$\neg(C \vee D)-$	$\neg(C \wedge D)-$	$\neg(\neg C \wedge D)$			

Representation in the logic environment. The language part of the system defines two *judgement* categories, Sequent '⊢' and Translates '⤳'. The main translation $(-)^8$ is expressed by 'apply' rules of the form:

$$\frac{\varphi \rightsquigarrow \psi + \quad \neg\psi, \Gamma \vdash \Delta}{\Gamma \vdash \varphi, \Delta} \qquad \frac{\varphi \rightsquigarrow \neg\psi - \quad \psi, \Gamma \vdash \Delta}{\Gamma \vdash \varphi, \Delta} \qquad \frac{\Gamma \vdash \bot}{\Gamma \vdash}$$

and the subsidiary translation $(-)^9$ can be represented using a collection of rules defining the relation $\varphi \rightsquigarrow \psi+$ or $\varphi \rightsquigarrow \psi-$, i.e. '⤳' takes formulas to their polarised translations.

$$\frac{\varphi \rightsquigarrow \varphi' + \quad \psi \rightsquigarrow \psi' +}{\varphi \wedge \psi \rightsquigarrow \varphi' \wedge \psi' +} \qquad \frac{\varphi \rightsquigarrow \neg\varphi' - \quad \psi \rightsquigarrow \psi' +}{\varphi \wedge \psi \rightsquigarrow (\neg\varphi') \wedge \psi' +}$$

$$\frac{\varphi \rightsquigarrow \varphi' + \quad \psi \rightsquigarrow \neg\psi' -}{\varphi \wedge \psi \rightsquigarrow \varphi' \wedge (\neg\psi') +} \qquad \frac{\varphi \rightsquigarrow \neg\varphi' - \quad \psi \rightsquigarrow \neg\psi' -}{\varphi \wedge \psi \rightsquigarrow \neg(\varphi' \vee \psi') -}$$

and so on for the other connectives. If, in addition to translation of this form, the traditional rules for Intuitionistic logic are present we can construct derivations of propositions using a *strategy* such as:

$$\overbrace{\texttt{[apply]}\,(\texttt{done})}^{\text{construct}}\overbrace{\texttt{<left,right>[BASIC]}}^{\text{prove}}$$

the effect of which is first to apply the rules for '⤳' to obtain a translation for the classical sequent, and then to construct a derivation for the intuitionistic sequent using the Intuitionistic rules. Figure 1 is taken from the presentation in the environment and illustrates the strategy applied to Peirce's Law.

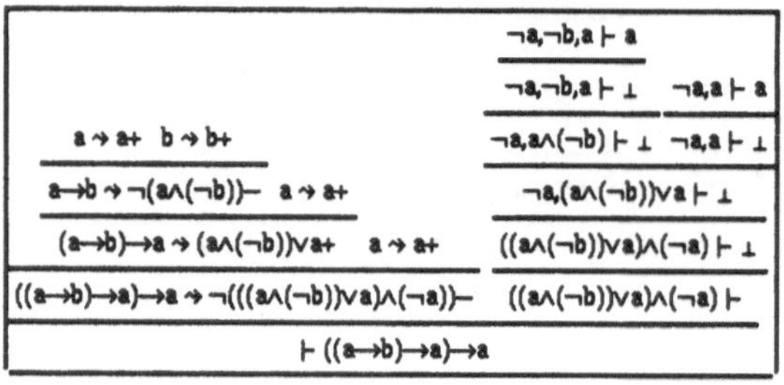

Figure 1: Girard's Translation applied to Peirce's Law

The derivation tree shown in the figure is divided into two parts: on the left is the translation of the classical judgement into an intuitionistic one, and the righthand side gives a derivation of the intuitionistic judgement.

3 The Calculus *LU*

The system *LU* is more complex. Instead of two polarities there are three which leads to many more cases to consider; for disjunction almost 27 rules are required, and it is natural to ask how this system is constructed using the translations of the fragments into polarised LU sequents. The reader may wish to refer to Girard's full presentation of LU in [4]. The LU's judgement is a special form of sequent

$$\Lambda; \Gamma \vdash \Delta; \Theta$$

where Λ, Θ are *bags of signed formulas* and Γ, Δ are *sets of signed formulas*. The inner part of the sequent '$\cdots; - \vdash -; \cdots$' is governed by "classical" structural maintenance—exchange, contraction and weakening—the outer part '$-; \cdots \vdash \cdots; -$' has "linear" maintenance—exchange only.

3.1 Polarities

The system LU assigns signs, or polarities, to formulas in its sequents, but instead of simply expressing some inherited property concerning negation, they also indicate how the formulas interact with the exponentials from Linear Logic, ! and ?. To clarify this further, positive formulas are hereditarily ! 'ed whereas negative formulas are hereditarily ? 'ed. A third, neutral '0', polarity is used for formulas that have no natural exponentiation. Communication between the inner and outer regions of the LU sequent is permitted with 'permeability rules', these allow positive (resp. negative) formulas to pass freely from the inner to the outer region on the left (resp. right). Other formulas can pass to the outer region but they must be decorated with ! on the left (and ? on the right). These polarities allow Girard to extend the same type of translation illustrated in the previous section.

3.2 Logical Rules

The logical rules are divided among the different logical constants in each subsystem.

♦ Linear logic: $\otimes, \oplus, \&, \invamp, !, ?, {}^{\perp}, \top, \bot, 1, 0, \wedge x, \vee x$
♦ Intuitionistic Logic: $\wedge, \vee, \supset, \sim, \mathbf{F}, \forall x, \exists x$
♦ Classical Logic: $\wedge, \vee, \rightarrow, \neg, \forall x, \exists x$

3.3 Linear Logic and LU

A Linear logic sequent may be translated into LU by $(-)^l$ as follows:

$$\Gamma \vdash_l \Delta \quad \longrightarrow \quad \Lambda 0; \Gamma' \vdash \Delta'; \Theta 0$$

where $\Lambda 0, \Gamma' = (\Gamma)^l$ and $\Theta 0, \Delta' = (\Delta)^l$, the translation $(-)^l$ annotates the formula with its polarity:

$$(A)^l = \begin{cases} Bs & \text{if } (A)^s = Bs \\ A0 & \text{otherwise} \end{cases}$$

where $(-)^l$ assigns a neutral polarity to a formula when $(-)^s$ is undefined.

$$(A \otimes B)^s = (C \otimes D)+ \quad \text{if } (A)^s = C+ \qquad (A \wp B)^s = (C \wp D)- \quad \text{if } (A)^s = C-$$
$$\text{and } (B)^s = D+ \qquad\qquad\qquad\qquad \text{and } (B)^s = D-$$
$$(A \oplus B)^s = (A \oplus B)+ \quad \text{if } (A)^s = C+ \qquad (A \& B)^s = (A \& B)- \quad \text{if } (A)^s = C-$$
$$\text{and } (B)^s = D+ \qquad\qquad\qquad\qquad \text{and } (B)^s = D-$$
$$(A^\perp)^s = (A^\perp)+ \quad \text{if } (A)^s = C+ \qquad (A^\perp)^s = (A^\perp)- \quad \text{if } (A)^s = C-$$
$$(A \multimap B)^s = (A \multimap B)- \quad \text{if } (A)^s = C+$$
$$\text{and } (B)^s = D-$$
$$(\wedge x A)^s = (\wedge x A)+ \quad \text{if } (A)^s = C+ \qquad (\vee x A)^s = (\vee x A)- \quad \text{if } (A)^s = C-$$
$$(1)^s = 1+ \qquad\qquad\qquad\qquad\qquad (\perp)^s = \perp -$$
$$(0)^s = 0+ \qquad\qquad\qquad\qquad\qquad (\top)^s = \top -$$
$$(!A)^s = !(A)^s+ \qquad\qquad\qquad\qquad (?A)^s = ?(A)^s -$$

Proofs in Linear Logic are translated into the new calculus as follows:

$$\frac{}{P \vdash_l P} \quad \longrightarrow \quad \frac{}{P0; \vdash ; P0}$$

$$\frac{A, \Gamma \vdash_l \Delta \quad B, \Gamma \vdash_l \Delta}{A \oplus B, \Gamma \vdash_l \Delta} \quad \longrightarrow \quad \frac{A, \Lambda; \Gamma \vdash \Delta; \Theta \quad B, \Lambda; \Gamma \vdash \Delta; \Theta}{A \oplus B, \Lambda; \Gamma \vdash \Delta; \Theta}$$

$$\frac{!\Gamma \vdash_l A, ?\Delta}{!\Gamma \vdash_l !A, ?\Delta} \vdash ! \quad \longrightarrow \quad \frac{;\Gamma+ \vdash \Delta-; A}{;\Gamma+ \vdash \Delta-; !A}$$

and so on for the other linear rules. On the other hand, sequents in LU can be written as $\Lambda; \Gamma+, \Gamma' \vdash \Delta', \Delta-; \Theta$ formulas in each inner region are divided according to their polarities. Those with a positive polarity, $\Gamma+$, and the remaining formulas in Γ'. Such a sequent can be translated into Linear Logic as $\Lambda, \Gamma, !\Gamma' \vdash_l ?\Delta', \Delta, \Theta$. As positive formulas are implicitly !'ed they can be translated without an additional ! mark (and dually for ?). So LU *derivation* can be straightforwardly interpreted in Linear Logic except for rules with restricted contexts, these must be translated using the rules $\vdash !$ or $? \vdash$, e.g.

$$;\Gamma+, \Gamma' \vdash \Delta', \Delta-; A \quad \longrightarrow \quad \Gamma, !\Gamma' \vdash_l ?\Delta', \Delta, A$$

since all the formulas in Γ (resp. Δ) where originally positive (resp. negative) in the original LU sequent they are implicitly !'ed (resp. ?'ed).

The next section considers the encoding of classical logic in LU; for a discussion of the intuitionistic case see [2].

3.4 Representing Classical Logic in LU

The derivation of the 'chimeric' connectives of $\wedge, \vee, \rightarrow, \supset$, *etc* introduced by Girard in [4] is a little unclear. To see their relevance consider the standard translation of Classical Logic to Linear Logic:

$$\Gamma \vdash_c \Delta \quad \longrightarrow \quad !(\Gamma)^{cl} \vdash_l ?(\Delta)^{cr}$$

The translations for the left and righthand sides of the sequent $(-)^{cl}$ and

$(-)^{cr}$ are defined as:

$$
\begin{array}{rcl}
(P)^{cl} & = & P \\
(\neg A)^{cl} & = & (A)^{cr\perp} \\
(A\wedge B)^{cl} & = & (A)^{cl}\&(B)^{cl} \\
(A\vee B)^{cl} & = & !(A)^{cl}\oplus !(B)^{cl} \\
(A\rightarrow B)^{cl} & = & !(A)^{cr\perp}\oplus !(B)^{cl}
\end{array}
\qquad
\begin{array}{rcl}
(P)^{cr} & = & P \\
(\neg A)^{cr} & = & (A)^{cl\perp} \\
(A\wedge B)^{cr} & = & ?(A)^{cr}\&?(B)^{cr} \\
(A\vee B)^{cr} & = & (A)^{cr}\oplus (B)^{cr} \\
(A\rightarrow B)^{cr} & = & (A)^{cl\perp}\oplus (B)^{cr}
\end{array}
$$

The case of $\vdash\wedge$ is interesting because of the merging (multiplicative) contexts. Suppose that we have derivations for the upper sequents $\Gamma_1\vdash_c A,\Delta_1$ and $\Gamma_2\vdash_c B,\Delta_2$ viz $!(\Gamma_1)^{cl}\vdash_l ?(A)^{cr},?(\Delta_2)^{cr}$ and $!(\Gamma_2)^{cl}\vdash_l ?(B)^{cr},?(\Delta_2)^{cr}$ we can proceed as follows:

$$
\cfrac{
\cfrac{!(\Gamma_1)^{cl}\vdash_l ?(A)^{cr},?(\Delta_1)^{cr}}{!(\Gamma_1)^{cl}\vdash_l !\,?(A)^{cr},?(\Delta_1)^{cr}}\;\vdash!
\qquad
\cfrac{!(\Gamma_2)^{cl}\vdash_l ?(B)^{cr},?(\Delta_2)^{cr}}{!(\Gamma_2)^{cl}\vdash_l !\,?(B)^{cr},?(\Delta_2)^{cr}}\;\vdash!
}{
\cfrac{!(\Gamma_1)^{cl},!(\Gamma_2)^{cl}\vdash_l !\,?(A)^{cr}\otimes !\,?(B)^{cr},?(\Delta_1)^{cr},?(\Delta_2)^{cr}}{!(\Gamma_1)^{cl},!(\Gamma_2)^{cl}\vdash_l ?(\,?(A)^{cr}\&?(B)^{cr}),?(\Delta_1)^{cr},?(\Delta_2)^{cr}}\;a
}\;\vdash\otimes
$$

where a follows from cutting with $!A\otimes !B\vdash_l ?(A\&B)$. It is worth remarking that the upper $\vdash !$ rules would not be needed if the translation could be adjusted to provide a positive polarity for the translated $(A)^{cr}$—rather than expecting it to be negative. This insight gives an improvement in the translation that can be obtained and seems to agree with the one used by Girard in LU.

The improved classical translation. In the revised translation, $(-)^c$, polarities are used to indicate the behaviour of the translated formula with respect to the exponentials; this allows a more delicate translation.

$$
\begin{array}{rcllll}
 & & (A)^c = C+ & (A)^c = C- & (A)^c = C+ & (A)^c = C- \\
 & & (B)^c = D+ & (B)^c = D+ & (B)^c = D- & (B)^c = D- \\
(P)^c & = & P+ & P- & & \\
(\neg A)^c & = & C^{\perp}- & C^{\perp}+ & & \\
(A\wedge B)^c & = & (C\otimes D)+ & (!C\otimes D)+ & (C\otimes !D)+ & (C\&D)- \\
(A\vee B)^c & = & (C\oplus D)+ & (C\oplus ?D)+ & (?C\invamp D)- & (C\invamp D)- \\
(A\rightarrow B)^c & = & (C\multimap !D)- & (C^{\perp}\oplus D)+ & (C\multimap D)- & (!C\multimap D)- \\
 & & \cdots & & &
\end{array}
$$

A classical sequent is now translated into LU as follows:

$$\Gamma\vdash_c\Delta \quad\longrightarrow\quad ;\Gamma'+\vdash\Delta'-;$$

where $\Gamma'+ = (\Gamma)^c$ and $\Delta'+ = (\Delta)^c$. The context is positive on the lefthand side and negative on the other. The general form the classical sequent is defined to be:

$$\Lambda-,\Lambda';\Gamma\vdash\Delta;\Theta+,\Theta', \qquad |\Lambda-,\Theta+|\geq 1$$

The translation extends to derivations as follows. Suppose that we have derivations of the upper sequents of $\wedge\vdash$, $\vdash\wedge$ and we wish to paste the derivations together to construct the translation. Knowing that there is a positive formula in Θ_1 and Θ_2 allows us to conclude that all the remaining formulas in the Λs are positive and those remaining in Θs are negative; which satisfies the condition on sequents in the classical fragment.

$$\frac{\dfrac{A+,B+,\Gamma;\Gamma'\vdash\Delta';\Delta}{(A+)\otimes(B+),\Gamma;\Gamma'\vdash\Delta';\Delta}}{(A\otimes B)+,\Gamma;\Gamma'\vdash\Delta';\Delta} \qquad \frac{\dfrac{\Gamma;\Gamma'\vdash\Delta';A+,\Delta \quad \Lambda;\Gamma'\vdash\Delta';B+,\Theta}{\Gamma,\Lambda;\Gamma'\vdash\Delta';A+\otimes B+,\Delta,\Theta}}{\Gamma,\Lambda;\Gamma'\vdash\Delta';(A\otimes B)+,\Delta,\Theta}$$

$$\frac{\dfrac{A-,B+,\Gamma;\Gamma'\vdash\Delta';\Delta}{(!A)+,B+,\Gamma;\Gamma'\vdash\Delta';\Delta}}{(!A\otimes B)+,\Gamma;\Gamma'\vdash\Delta';\Delta} \qquad \frac{\dfrac{\dfrac{;\Gamma'\vdash\Delta';A-}{;\Gamma'\vdash\Delta';(!A)+} \quad \Lambda;\Gamma'\vdash\Delta';B+,\Theta}{\Lambda;\Gamma'\vdash\Delta';(!A)+\otimes B+,\Theta}}{\dfrac{\Lambda;\Gamma'\vdash\Delta';(!A)+\otimes B+,\Theta}{\Lambda;\Gamma'\vdash\Delta';(!A\otimes B)+,\Theta}}$$

A sequent of the form $A-,B-,\Gamma;\Gamma'\vdash\Delta';\Delta$ would violate the condition given above, so there are two possibilities:

$$\frac{A-,\Gamma;\Gamma'\vdash\Delta';\Delta}{(A\&B)-,\Gamma;\Gamma'\vdash\Delta';\Delta} \qquad \frac{B-,\Gamma;\Gamma'\vdash\Delta';\Delta}{(A\&B)-,\Gamma;\Gamma'\vdash\Delta';\Delta}$$

$$\frac{\dfrac{\dfrac{\dfrac{\Gamma;\Gamma'\vdash\Delta';A-,\Delta}{\Gamma;\Gamma'\vdash\Delta';!A+,\Delta} \quad \dfrac{\Lambda;\Gamma'\vdash\Delta';B-,\Theta}{\Lambda;\Gamma'\vdash\Delta';!B+,\Theta}}{\Gamma,\Lambda;\Gamma'\vdash\Delta';(!A)+\otimes(!B)+,\Delta,\Theta}}{\Gamma,\Lambda;\Gamma'\vdash\Delta';(A-)\&(B-),\Delta,\Theta}}{\Gamma;\Gamma'\vdash\Delta';(A\&B)-,\Delta}$$

3.5   The full system

These translations, together with translations for the intuitionistic fragements, are merged to give translations of all the logical connectives which consists of:

♦ identity and cut rules;

♦ structural rules for the inner part of the sequent with classical maintenance: contraction and weakening;

♦ permeability rules which allow any signed formula into a central region, but only appropriately signed formulas out without a penalty;

♦ linear logic rules—restricted to the outer parts of the sequent;

♦ rules encoding connectives from other logics whose translations are summarised in Girard's table repeated below. Each point in the table is responsible for at least two, and in some cases three, introduction rules.

$(A)^\natural$	$(B)^\natural$	$(A{\wedge}B)^\natural$	$(A{\vee}B)^\natural$	$(A{\to}B)^\natural$	$(A{\supset}B)^\natural$	$(\forall x A)^\natural$
$C+$	$D+$	$(C\otimes D)+$	$(C\oplus D)+$	$(C\multimap\,?D)-$	$(C\multimap D)0$	$(\textstyle\bigwedge x\,?C)-$
$C0$	$D+$	$(!C\otimes D)+$	$(!C\oplus D)+$	$(!C^\perp\oplus D)+$	$(!C\multimap D)0$	$(\textstyle\bigwedge x\,?C)-$
$C-$	$D+$	$(!C\otimes D)+$	$(C\,\wp\,?D)-$	$(C^\perp\oplus D)+$	$(!C\multimap D)0$	$(\textstyle\bigwedge x C)-$
$C+$	$D0$	$(C\otimes\,!D)+$	$(C\oplus\,!D)+$	$(C\multimap\,?!D)-$	$(C\multimap D)0$	
$C0$	$D0$	$(C\&D)0$	$(!C\oplus\,!D)+$	$(!C^\perp\oplus\,!D)+$	$(!C\multimap D)0$	
$C-$	$D0$	$(C\&D)0$	$(C\,\wp\,?!D)-$	$(C^\perp\oplus\,!D)+$	$(!C\multimap D)0$	$(\exists x A)^\natural$
$C+$	$D-$	$(C\otimes\,!D)+$	$(?C\,\wp D)-$	$(C\multimap D)-$	$(C\multimap D)-$	$(\textstyle\bigvee x C)+$
$C0$	$D-$	$(C\&D)0$	$(?!C\,\wp D)-$	$(?!C^\perp\wp D)-$	$(!C\multimap D)-$	$(\textstyle\bigvee x\,!C)+$
$C-$	$D-$	$(C\&D)-$	$(C\,\wp D)-$	$(!C\multimap D)-$	$(!C\multimap D)-$	$(\textstyle\bigvee x\,!C)+$

The translations for Classical and Intuitionistic systems are restricted to $\{+,-\}$ and $\{+,0\}$ polarities respectively, so there is an overlap only in the case $(+,+)$. Fortunately the translations almost agree for these polarities:

$(A)^i$	$(B)^i$	$(A{\wedge}B)^i$	$(A{\vee}B)^i$	$(A{\supset}B)^i$
$(A)^c$	$(B)^c$	$(A{\wedge}B)^c$	$(A{\vee}B)^c$	$(A{\to}B)^c$
$C+$	$D+$	$(C\otimes D)+$	$(C\oplus D)+$	$(C\multimap D)0$
$C+$	$D+$	$(C\otimes D)+$	$(C\oplus D)+$	$(C\multimap\,!D)-$

But the encodings disagree for implication, making two connectives necessary to separate the classical and intuitionistic cases. Places where the polarities are not determined allow flexibility of encoding defined by $(-)^\natural$, and other choices are possible.

4 LU and the logic environment

Looking at the rules of LU one might think that the addition of polarities would make the task of formalising these in a logic environment would be too cumbersome, but it turns out to be relatively straightforward. There are several approaches to the formalisation of LU to try in our environment. We start by discussing a *direct* interpretation of Girard's rules.

4.1 A direct approach

The main focus of interest is LU's judgement '$\Gamma;\Gamma' \vdash \Delta';\Delta$' which includes regions with different structural properties. The usual formulas, gathered from each of the fragments, are annotated with polarities. These are formalised in the environment as:

```
a:BagOf(PolarisedFormula) ';' b:SetOf(PolarisedFormula)
 '⊢' c:SetOf(PolarisedFormula) ';' d:BagOf(PolarisedFormula)
 → LU(a,b,c,d):Sequent
a:Formula b:Polarity → PF(a,b):PolarisedFormula
'+' → P:Polarity ; '0' → Z:Polarity ; '-' → N:Polarity
 ...
```

Structural rules pertaining to the central 'SetOf' regions include rules for weakening ($\vdash weak$ and $weak\vdash$). These can be avoided in favour of what might be termed *procrastinated weakening*—by performing all weakening operations on the leaves of the proof. It is easy to show that the rule for identity Id can be changed to include

$$\frac{}{A;\Gamma' \vdash \Delta'; A} \; Id'$$

other leaf rules require similar adjustments: $\vdash 1$, $0\vdash$, $\vdash T$ and $\perp \vdash$. The rules for *permeability* and *contraction* remain explicit however.

Some rules are applicable over a range of polarities, this constraint can be expressed with the introduction of a second judgement called 'Signed':

a:Polarity '$\in$' '{' b:SetOf(Polarity) '}' $\rightarrow$ Sign(a,b):Signed

Now rules that are admissible for a limited number of polarities can now be stated using this judgement. In the following example s ranges over polarities

$$\frac{\psi+, \Lambda; \Gamma, \varphi s \vdash \Delta; \Theta \quad s \in \{-, 0\}}{\varphi \wedge \psi+, \Lambda; \Gamma \vdash \Delta; \Theta}$$

Derivations. This presentation can be used to construct derivations of judgements like those illustrated in figure 2, two derivations are shown: the first in the Classical fragment, the second in the Intuitionistic one.

+:+	+:+	+:+		+:+	+:+	
+:+	+b;⊢+c;+b,−a	+c;⊢+b;+c,−a		+a;⊢+c;+a,−b	+b;⊢+b,−a	+:+
+a;⊢+c;+a,−b	+b;⊢+c;+b;−a	+c;⊢+c,+b;−a		+a;⊢+a,+c;−b	+b;⊢+(bvc),−a	+c;⊢+c,−a
+a;⊢+c,+a;−b	+b;⊢+c;−(avb)	+c;⊢+c;−(avb)		+a;⊢+a;−(bvc)	+b;⊢+(bvc);−a	+c;⊢+(bvc),−a
+a;⊢+c;−(avb)	+b;⊢−((avb)vc)	+c;⊢−((avb)vc)		+a;⊢−(av(bvc))	+b;⊢−(av(bvc))	+c;⊢+(bvc);−a
+a;⊢−((avb)vc)	+b;⊢−((avb)vc);	+c;⊢−((avb)vc);		+a;⊢−(av(bvc));	+b;⊢−(av(bvc));	+c;⊢−(av(bvc))
+a;⊢−((avb)vc);	+(bvc);⊢−((avb)vc);			+(avb);⊢−(av(bvc));	+c;⊢−(av(bvc));	
+(av(bvc));⊢−((avb)vc);				+((avb)vc);⊢−(av(bvc));		
;+(av(bvc))⊢−((avb)vc);				;+((avb)vc)⊢−(av(bvc));		

Figure 2: Associativity of $\vee$

Derived rules. The interpretation of the table can be verified by constructing derived rules. Figure 3 taken from the environment shows this for the derivation of the left and right introduction rules for $A-\!\!\rightarrow B+$. Compare this with the rules $\vdash -\!\!\rightarrow_1 +$, $\vdash -\!\!\rightarrow_2 +$ and $-\!\!\rightarrow +\vdash$ in [4].

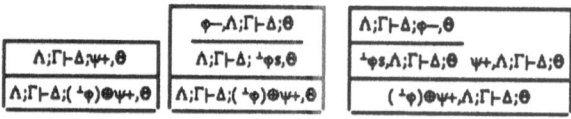

Figure 3: Derived rules

Eliminating permeability rules. In general, a presentation is more effective with respect to proof search when there are fewer applicable rules at any stage in the construction of the proof. The structural rules for *weakening* and *permeability* are good candidates for elimination as these are applicable at every stage. We saw that weakening rules could be avoided by delaying their application until the tips of the derivation. The *permeability* rules can also be avoided by noting where their use is essential and building them into the relevant rules. Recall that permeability rules are used to allow formulas with the correct polarity to pass from the inner part of the sequent outwards. When these rules are interpreted backwards during proof search they can be seen to move formulas inwards. Although they may occur freely in a derivation they commute with all rules with unrestricted outer contexts. The first stage to eliminating these rules is to notice that they can be recast in a more general form using *'modal' patterns*:

$$\frac{\Gamma; A+, \Gamma' \vdash \Delta'; \Delta}{A+, \Gamma; \Gamma' \vdash \Delta'; \Delta} +; \vdash \quad \text{and} \quad \frac{\Gamma; \Gamma' \vdash B-, \Delta'; \Delta}{\Gamma; \Gamma' \vdash \Delta'; B-, \Delta} \vdash; -$$

becomes

$$\frac{\Gamma; \Lambda+, \Gamma' \vdash \Theta-, \Delta'; \Delta}{\Lambda+, \Gamma; \Gamma' \vdash \Delta'; \Theta-, \Delta} perm$$

Now, this more general form can be incorporated in rules with restricted contexts, for example $-\vee+\vdash$ when combined with the new permeability rule:

$$\frac{M, \Gamma; \Gamma' \vdash \Delta'; \Delta \quad ; Q, \Gamma' \vdash \Delta';}{M\vee Q, \Gamma; \Gamma' \vdash \Delta'; \Delta}$$

becomes

$$\frac{M, \Gamma; \Lambda+, \Gamma' \vdash \Theta-, \Delta'; \Delta \quad ; Q, \Lambda+, \Gamma' \vdash \Theta-, \Delta';}{M\vee Q, \Lambda+, \Gamma; \Gamma' \vdash \Delta'; \Theta-, \Delta} -\vee+\vdash,$$

Rules for axioms require similar adjustment. In the derivation of K shown in figure 4, the uppermost rule includes a built-in occurrence of *perm*.

+;+
+b,+a;⊢;+a
+a;⊢;s(b→a)
;⊢z(a→(b→a))

Figure 4: Derivation of K in the Intuitionistic Fragment

4.2 An indirect approach

As we have shown, LU can be thought of as an elaborate encoding of its sublogics into linear logic. Indeed the translation rules for connectives not in the linear core are easily derived from table in section 3.5. So a sequent taken from an appropriate fragment is translated to a sequent in Linear Logic as determined by the polarities. The implementation of this strategy in the environment follows the same pattern as the translation given in the first section; the target logic is Linear rather Intuitionistic and because of the larger number of polarities there are more cases to consider. The translation is expressed using relation '$\rightsquigarrow$' as before.

$$\frac{\varphi \rightsquigarrow \varphi's \quad \psi \rightsquigarrow \psi'+ \quad \{s \vdash 0, -\}}{\varphi \wedge \psi \rightsquigarrow (!\varphi') \otimes \psi'+}$$

$$\frac{\varphi \rightsquigarrow \varphi'+ \quad \psi \rightsquigarrow \psi'0}{\varphi \Rightarrow \psi \rightsquigarrow \varphi' \multimap (?(!\psi'))-} \qquad \frac{\varphi \rightsquigarrow \varphi'- \quad \psi \rightsquigarrow \psi'+}{\varphi \vee \psi \rightsquigarrow \varphi' \otimes (?\psi')-}$$

The judgement $\{s \vdash 0, -\}$ constrains the polarity of s to be non-positive. Figures 5 and 6 show the effect of executing the translation on $a \vee \neg a$ in the Classical fragment and $\sim\sim (\sim a \vee a)$ in the Intuitionistic one.

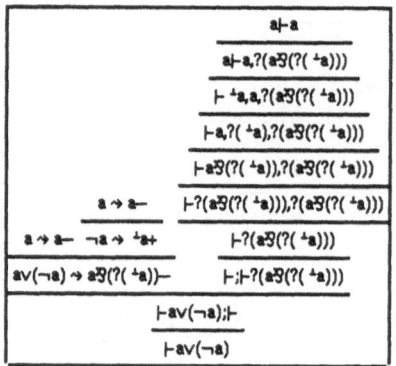

Figure 5: Translation of $a \vee \neg a$ to Linear Logic

5   Concluding remarks

Girard's LU is an interesting almagamation of its constituent fragment logics. The structural properties of the fragments are modelled by the introduction of polarities, but the underlying logic of the LU is Linear Logic which has a very natural translation. Girard claims that the fragments are better as subsystems in LU than they are as isolated systems. Although some technical reasons exist to support this claim it is clear that the amalgamation produces a presentation that is far removed from the simple explanations used to justify presentations of the isolated fragments. Girard hints that the techniques used to produce LU could be extended to a system that does not include exchange such as non-commutative linear logic; one would proceed by adding further polarities, structural regions, and more rules.

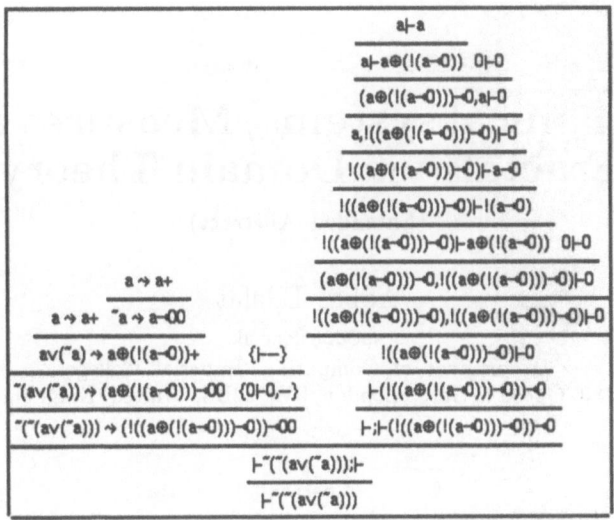

Figure 6: Translation of $\sim\sim$ ($\sim a \vee a$) to Linear Logic

The large number of rules (in excess of 100) makes it much harder to ensure the overall consistency of the logic—because it is more difficult to spot typographical mistakes when there are so many of them. This provides good motivation to enhance the support meta-level reasoning in the enviroment, e.g. cut-elimination, which can be carried-out for simpler systems. Similarly, when a system has a large number of rules strategies become very useful when expressing the approaches discussed above: (i) they can be used to impose control on the construction of the search space, (ii) they can be used to focus on the subset of the rules relevant to a particular fragment. Unfortunately, the large number of rules makes the environment slower to use because the process that internalises rules has more work to do; an incremental approach would be more satisfactory. It is nevertheless satisfying that the environment could cope adequately with a system as unusual as LU.

Acknowledgement. The author would like to acknowledge the support of the UK Science and Engineering Research Council through the "Foundational Models in Computer Science" project.

References

[1] W.M.G. Dawson. *A Generic Logic Environment.* PhD thesis, Imperial College of Science, Technology and Medicine, 1990. Available by ftp from theory.doc.ic.ac.uk.

[2] W.M.G. Dawson. Animating LU. Technical report, Department of Computing, Imperial College, 1993. Available by ftp from theory.doc.ic.ac.uk.

[3] J. Gallier. Constructive logics. part I: A tutorial on proof systems and typed λ-calculi. *Theortical Computer Science*, ?(?), 1993. to appear.

[4] J.-Y. Girard. On the unity of logic. To appear in the proceedings of ALC'90, 1991.

Dynamical systems, Measures and Fractals via Domain Theory

(Extended Abstract)

Abbas Edalat

ae@doc.ic.ac.uk

Department of Computing, Imperial College
180 Queen's Gate, London SW7 2BZ, United Kingdom

Abstract

We introduce domain theory in the computation of dynamical systems, iterated function systems (fractals) and measures. For a discrete dynamical system (X, f), given by the action of a continuous map $f : X \to X$ on a metric space X, we study the extended dynamical systems (VX, Vf) and (UX, Uf) where V is the Vietoris functor and U is the upper space functor. In fact, from the point of view of computing the attractors of (X, f), it is natural to study the other two systems: A compact attractor of (X, f) is a fixed point of (VX, Vf) and a fixed point of (UX, Uf). We show that if (X, f) is chaotic, then so is (UX, Uf). When X is locally compact UX is a continuous bounded complete dcpo. If X is second countable as well, then UX will be ω-continuous and can be given an effective structure. We show how strange attractors, attractors of iterated function systems (fractals) and Julia sets are obtained effectively as fixed points of deterministic functions on UX or fixed points of non-deterministic functions on CUX where C is the convex (Plotkin) power domain. We also establish an interesting link between measure theory and domain theory. We show that the set, $M(X)$, of Borel measures on X can be embedded in PUX, where P is the probabilistic power domain. This provides an effective way of obtaining measures on X. We then prove that the invariant measure of an hyperbolic iterated function system with probabilities can be obtained as the unique fixed point of an associated continuous function on PUX.

1   Introduction

A *discrete dynamical system* (X, f) is given by the action of a continuous function $f : X \to X$ on a topological space X, which is usually a metric space (X, d). The (forward) *orbit* of a point $x \in X$ is the sequence $\langle f^n(x) \rangle_{n \geq 0}$. One is interested in the behaviour of orbits of the system. In the interesting cases, the system has one or several indecomposable basic sets in X, on each of which f is invariant and has non-trivial dynamics. An example of such a set is an *attractor*, which attracts all nearby orbits. These can be fixed or periodic points or they can be *strange* or *chaotic* attractors, which have very complex structure. Attractors are observed in physical systems and, therefore, their study is of fundamental importance.

Continuous dynamical systems, e.g. differential equations in $\mathbb{R}^n$, can also be studied by discrete systems. In fact, any *continuous dynamical system*, given by a differentiable vector field on a smooth manifold, gives rise to a continuous flow on the manifold and the *time-one map* of the flow induces a discrete system on the manifold. One can then investigate the behaviour of the continuous system by studying the induced discrete system. Dynamical systems are used to model dynamic behaviour in all branches of science. In fact, it is their distinguished feature that an abstract system can have applications in diverse areas. For an example of this wide ranging application, see [11]. For an introduction to dynamical systems, see for example [9, 22].

In this paper, we consider discrete dynamical systems from a computational point of view. Since the invariant sets, and hence the attractors, of a discrete system (X, f) are closed and, in the interesting cases, compact, it is natural in computing these sets to study the associated dynamical systems (VX, Vf), (UX, Uf) and (LX, Lf) on the the three hyperspaces defined, for a Hausdorff space X, as follows:

- VX, the *Vietoris space*, is the set of all non-empty compact subsets of X with the *convex topology* which has a subbase given by the collections of the form $u_a = \{C \in VX \mid C \subseteq a\}$ and $l_a = \{C \in VX \mid C \cap a \neq \emptyset\}$, where $a \in \Omega X$ is an open set of X. This topology is Hausdorff and, when X is a metric space this, it is equivalent to the one induced by the *Hausdorff metric* d_h defined by $d_h(A, B) = \max(d(A, B), d(B, A))$, where for compact sets C and D, $d(C, D)$ is the infimum of positive numbers δ such that C is contained in the δ-neighbourhood, $\{x \in X \mid \exists y \in D. \, d(x, y) < \delta\}$, of D.

- UX, the *upper space*, is the set of all non-empty compact subsets of X with the base of *upper topology* given by collections $u_a = \{C \in UX \mid C \subseteq a\}$ $(a \in \Omega X)$. This topology is T_0 and, when X is a metric space, is equivalent to the topology induced by the quasi-metric d_u defined by $d_u(A, B) = d(A, B)$. The specialisation ordering $\sqsubseteq_u$ of UX is superset inclusion, i.e.

$$A \sqsubseteq_u B \overset{\text{def}}{\Longleftrightarrow} \forall a \in \Omega X[A \subseteq a \Rightarrow B \subseteq a] \iff A \supseteq B.$$

$(UX, \supseteq)$ is a dcpo, in which the least upper bound (lub) of a directed set of compact subsets is their intersection. When X is locally compact, $(UX, \supseteq)$ is a continuous dcpo, as we will see in the next section.

- LX, the *lower space*, is the set of all closed subsets of X with the subbase of *lower topology* given by the collections $l_a = \{C \in LX \mid C \cap a \neq \emptyset\}$, $(a \in \Omega X)$. This topology is again T_0 and, when X is a compact metric space, is equivalent to the topology induced by the quasi-metric d_l defined by $d_l(A, B) = d(B, A)$. The specialisation ordering $\sqsubseteq_l$ of LX is subset inclusion, i.e.

$$A \sqsubseteq_l B \overset{\text{def}}{\Longleftrightarrow} \forall a \in \Omega X[A \cap a \neq \emptyset \Rightarrow B \cap a \neq \emptyset] \iff A \subseteq B.$$

$(LX, \sqsubseteq_l)$ is a complete lattice, where the lub of a set of closed sets is the closure of their union.

The maps Vf, Uf and Lf are induced by f on the corresponding spaces, i.e. $Vf(A) = f(A)$, $Uf(A) = f(A)$ and $Lf(A) = \overline{f(A)}$, where $f(A)$ is the image of $A \subseteq X$ under $f : X \to X$ and $\overline{B}$ is the closure of B. See for example [20, 21] for the general definition of these spaces.

Barnsley's and Hutchinson's work on *iterated function systems* [13, 2] has already established one important application of dynamical systems on the Vietoris space VX. A nonstandard treatment can also been found in [23]. We briefly review Barnsley's work [2] here. An *iterated function system (IFS)*, $\{X; f_1, f_2, \ldots, f_N\}$, is given by a finite set of continuous maps $f_i : X \to X$ $(i = 1, \ldots, N)$ on a complete metric space X. The IFS is *hyperbolic* if the maps f_i are all contracting. An IFS induces a function $F : VX \to VX$ on the complete space VX, which is defined by $F(A) = f_1(A) \cup f_2(A) \cup \ldots \cup f_N(A)$. If the IFS is hyperbolic, then F will be contracting with contractivity factor $s = \max_i s_i$ where s_i is the contractivity factor of f_i $(1 \le i \le N)$. Therefore, by the contracting mapping theorem, F has a unique fixed point in VX, which is called the *attractor* of the IFS. Barnsley works with $N \ge 2$ contracting affine maps on $\mathbb{R}^n$. Then the attractor is usually a *fractal*, i.e. it has fine, complicated and non-smooth local structure, some form of self-similarity and, usually, a non-integral *Hausdorff dimension*.

Conversely, given any image regarded as a compact set in the plane, one uses a self-tiling of the image and Barnsley's collage theorem to find an IFS with contracting affine transformations, whose attractor approximates the image.

There is also a probabilistic version of the theory that produces coloured images. An IFS with probabilities $\{X; f_1, \ldots, f_N; p_1, \ldots, p_N\}$ is an IFS $\{X; f_1, f_2, \ldots, f_N\}$ such that each f_i $(1 \le i \le N)$ is assigned a weight $0 < p_i < 1$, with

$$\sum_{i=1}^{N} p_i = 1.$$

Then, a map $T : M^1(X) \to M^1(X)$ is induced on the set, $M^1(X)$, of normalised Borel measures of X, which takes a Borel measure $\mu \in M^1(X)$ to a Borel measure $T(\mu) \in M^1(X)$ defined by

$$T(\mu)(B) = \sum_{i=1}^{N} p_i \mu(f_i^{-1}(B))$$

on any Borel subset $B \subseteq X$. When X is compact, Barnsley and Demko [3] define a metric on $M^1(X)$, and, using some Banach space theory, including Alaoglu's theorem, they show that $M^1(X)$ becomes a compact metric space. If the IFS is hyperbolic, T will be a contracting map. The unique fixed point of T then defines a probability distribution on X whose support is the attractor of $\{X; f_1, \ldots, f_N\}$. This distribution gives different point densities in different regions of the attractor, and using a colouring scheme, one can colour the attractor accordingly. These results have found important applications in computer graphics and image compression, and also in learning automata [5, 4, 8].

Our thesis is that in studying any dynamical system (X, f), the induced dynamical systems (VX, Vf) (the *Vietoris dynamical system*), (UX, Uf) (*the upper dynamical system*) and (LX, Lf) (*the lower dynamical system*) on the three hyperspaces are of considerable interest. The invariant sets and in particular the attractors of (X, f) are closed and in the interesting cases compact and are, therefore, fixed points of $Vf : VX \to VX$ and $Uf : UX \to UX$. In this paper, we will in fact only study compact attractors. We also extend the notion of chaos to the case of dynamics on quasi-metric spaces, and show that if (X, f) is chaotic, then (UX, Uf) is also chaotic.

There are two canonical ways of computing the invariant sets and in particular the attractors of a dynamical system. The first, and in fact the more fundamental one, is to find a decreasing sequence of compact sets which shrink down to the invariant set. The smaller the compact set in the sequence, the better it approximates the invariant set. This ordering corresponds to the specialisation ordering of the upper space UX, i.e. for non-empty compact sets A and B we have $A \sqsubseteq_u B$ iff $A \supseteq B$. This method can be used to generate the attractor of an hyperbolic IFS as the unique fixed point of the deterministic map $F : UX \to UX$, where $F(A) = f_1(A) \cup \ldots \cup f_N(A)$. A non-deterministic computation can also be made, whereby the attractor is obtained as the unique fixed point of a continuous map on CUX, where C is the convex (Plotkin) powerdomain functor. Many other invariant sets of dynamical systems, including Julia sets, can be computed by this method.

We propose, in particular, that the upper space construction provides a suitable framework for an effective theory of dynamical systems. Points of X are, in effect, maximal elements of UX. When X is locally compact, $(UX, \sqsubseteq_u)$ is a continuous dcpo, and a point of X, considered as a singleton, can be identified with a shrinking sequence of compact sets. If X is also second countable, i.e. if it has a countable base, then $(UX, \sqsubseteq_u)$ is ω-continuous and an effective theory of dynamical systems can be constructed.

The other canonical method for computing the invariant set is to obtain an increasing sequence of compact sets whose union has the invariant set as its closure. In this case, the bigger the compact set in the sequence, the better the approximation to the invariant set. This ordering corresponds to the specialisation ordering of the lower space LX, i.e. for non-empty compact sets A and B, we have $A \sqsubseteq_l B$ iff $A \subseteq B$. This method can be used for example to generate the attractor of an IFS $\{X; f_1, \ldots, f_N\}$ starting with, say, the set of fixed points of the maps f_i.

Finally, we develop an exciting link between measure theory and domain theory, which can lead to a constructive measure theory. We will use it in this paper to obtain, constructively, Barnsley's invariant measure for an IFS with probabilities.

The link is established by "well-behaved" measures on "well-behaved" topological spaces. Recall [18, page 50] that a positive Borel measure μ on a locally compact Hausdorff space is *regular* if for all Borel subsets B of X we have:

$$\mu(B) = \inf\{\mu(O) \mid B \subseteq O, O \text{ open}\} = \sup\{\mu(K) \mid B \supseteq K, K \text{ compact}\}.$$

When a measure is regular, the measure of any Borel set is determined by the topologically important open sets or alternatively the compact sets. Any measure which is not regular is considered to be pathological. We want to work with spaces on which Borel measures are regular. If X is locally compact and second countable (i.e. countably based), then every open set will be σ-compact [15, page 344], i.e. it is the countable union of compact sets. It then follows from a well-known theorem in measure theory that any measure μ on X which is finite on compact sets is in fact regular [18, page 50]. We conclude that locally compact second countable Hausdorff spaces provide a suitable setting for well-behaved measures.

But we have already seen that a locally compact second countable Hausdorff space has also the interesting property that its upper space is an ω-continuous dcpo. Moreover, Jones' work [14] implies an interesting property of ω-continuous dcpo's. Recall from [19, 14] that a *valuation* on a topological space Y is a map $\nu : \Omega Y \to [0, \infty)$ which satisfies:

(i) $\nu(a) + \nu(b) = \nu(a \cup b) + \nu(a \cap b)$

(ii) $\nu(\emptyset) = 0$

(iii) $a \subseteq b \Rightarrow \nu(a) \leq \nu(b)$

A *continuous* valuation is a valuation such that whenever $A \subseteq \Omega(Y)$ is a directed set (wrt $\subseteq$) of open sets of Y, then

$$\nu(\bigcup_{O \in A} O) = \sup_{O \in A} \nu(O).$$

For any $b \in Y$, the *point valuation* based at b is the valuation $\eta_b : \Omega(Y) \to [0, \infty)$ defined by

$$\eta_b(O) = \begin{cases} 1 & \text{if } b \in O \\ 0 & \text{otherwise.} \end{cases}$$

Any finite linear combination

$$\sum_{i=1}^{n} r_i \eta_{b_i}$$

of point valuations η_{b_i} with constant coefficients $r_i \in [0, \infty)$, $(1 \leq i \leq n)$ is also a valuation on Y.

The *probabilistic power domain*, PY, of a topological space Y consists of the set of continuous valuations ν on Y with $\nu(Y) \leq 1$ and is ordered as follows:

$$\mu \sqsubseteq \nu \text{ iff for all open sets } O, \ \mu(O) \leq \nu(O).$$

PY is a dcpo with bottom in which the lub of a directed set $\langle \mu_i \rangle_{i \in I}$ is given by $\bigsqcup_i \mu_i = \nu$ where for $O \in \Omega(Y)$ we have

$$\nu(O) = \sup_{i \in I} \mu_i(O).$$

Jones shows that if Y is an (ω)-continuous dcpo so is PY, and that any valuation on a continuous dcpo is the directed lub of linear combinations of point valuations, and it extends uniquely to a measure. It follows that on ω-continuous dcpo's, valuations and measures are in fact the same.

Let $M(X)$ be the set of all positive Borel measures μ with $\mu(X) \leq 1$ on the locally compact second countable Hausdorff space X. We will show that $M(X)$ can be embedded in PUX which is an ω-continuous dcpo. This gives us an effective way of obtaining the Borel measures on X.

As an application, we consider any hyperbolic IFS with probabilities $\{X; f_1, \ldots, f_N; p_1, \ldots, p_N\}$. This induces a continuous map on the subdcpo of normalised valuations $P^1 UX$. The unique fixed point of this map has support in X and gives us the invariant measure of the IFS.

2 Chaos and the Vietoris space

Let $f : X \to X$ be a continuous map on a metric space (X, d). We recall some definitions, say from [9]. In this paper, a *neighbourhood* of a point or of a subset of a topological space is any open set containing that point or subset.

Definition 2.1 $f : X \to X$ has *sensitive dependence on initial conditions* if there exists $\delta > 0$ such that, for any $x \in X$ and any neighbourhood N of x, there exists $y \in N$ and $n \geq 0$ such that $d(f^n(x), f^n(y)) > \delta$. $\square$

Therefore, $f : X \to X$ has sensitive dependence on initial conditions if there are points arbitrarily close to any point $x \in X$ which eventually separate from x by at least δ. This condition gives rise to unpredictable dynamics. Small errors in computation due to round-off may become magnified under iteration, so that the result of a numerical computation of an orbit, no matter how accurate, may bear no resemblance to the real orbit.

Definition 2.2 $f : X \to X$ is *topologically transitive* if for any pair of non-empty open sets $a, b \subseteq X$ there exists $n > 0$ such that $f^n(a) \cap b \neq \emptyset$. $\square$

That is to say, a topologically transitive map has points which move under iteration from one arbitrarily small neighbourhood to any other. This means that it is not possible to decompose the dynamical system to two disjoint open sets which are invariant under the map. Note that the above definition does not use the metric and in fact one can make the same definition for any topological space X. Recall that $x \in X$ is a *periodic* point of $f : X \to X$ if $f^n(x) = x$ for some $n \geq 1$. There are many possible definitions of chaos; here we adopt Devaney's definition, which is quite widely accepted.

Definition 2.3 $f : X \to X$ is *chaotic* on X if

(i) f has sensitive dependence on initial conditions.

(ii) f is topologically transitive.

(iii) The periodic points of f are dense in X. $\square$

Intuitively, a map is chaotic if, in Devaney's words, it combines (i) *unpredictability* and (ii) *indecomposability* with an element of (iii) *regularity*.

It has recently been shown that (i) follows from (ii) and (iii) [1]. However, we use the above classical definition, as in the next section, we will extend it to the notion of chaotic dynamics on quasi-metric spaces.

Example 2.4 Let Σ be a finite set. Let Σ^∞ be the set of infinite sequences $a = a_0 a_1 a_2 \ldots$ with $a_i \in \Sigma$ for all $i \geq 0$. We can define a metric d on Σ by

$$d(a, b) = \left\{ \begin{array}{ll} 0 & \text{if } a = b \\ \frac{1}{2^n} & \text{otherwise} \end{array} \right.$$

where $n \geq 0$ is the least integer such that $a_n \neq b_n$. Consider the *shift* map $\sigma : \Sigma^\infty \to \Sigma^\infty$ defined by $\sigma(a_0 a_1 a_2 a_3 \ldots) = a_1 a_2 a_3 \ldots$. Thus, σ removes the first element and shifts all other elements one place to the left: In other words $\sigma(a)$ is the *tail* of the infinite list a. Then it can be shown that σ is chaotic on Σ^∞ (See [9]). $\square$

The shift map has basic importance in dynamical systems as it models many chaotic systems. In computer science, one can view a Turing machine as a dynamical system. In fact, Christopher Moore [16] has showed that Turing machines are equivalent to a class of *generalised shifts*.

Recall that a *relatively compact* subset is one whose closure is compact.

Definition 2.5 Given a dynamical system (X, f), a closed region $C \subseteq X$ is said to be a *trapping region* for f if $f(C)$ is contained in the interior of C. A non-empty subset $\Lambda \subseteq X$ is an *attractor* for f if there is a relatively compact neighbourhood N of Λ for which the closure, $\overline{N}$, of N is a trapping region for f and $\Lambda = \bigcap_{i \geq 0} f^i(\overline{N})$. We say Λ is a *strange attractor* if, furthermore, f is chaotic on Λ. $\square$

Note that with our definition, when X is Hausdorff, attractors are always compact; this is in fact the case in all physical systems.

Example 2.6 Consider the solid two dimensional torus $T = S \times D$, where S is the unit circle and D is the unit disc in the plane. The smooth embedding $f : T \to T$ is defined as follows. T is treated as a rubber ring. It is stretched, twisted and folded to fit inside itself as in the figure below.

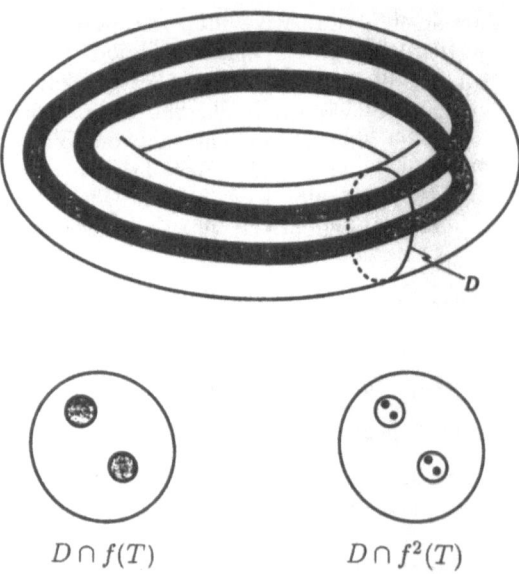

$D \cap f(T)$ $\qquad\qquad$ $D \cap f^2(T)$

Repeated application of f produces longer and longer tori, wrapped around T increasingly many times. It is easy to see that

$$D \cap (\bigcap_{i \geq 0} f^i(T)) = D \cap (\bigcap_{i \geq 0} (Vf)^i(T))$$

is a Cantor set. The attractor $\Lambda = \bigcap_{i \geq 0}(Vf)^i(T) = \lim_{i \to \infty}(Vf)^i(T)$ is called the *solenoid* and is a fixed point of $Vf : VT \to VT$. It can be shown that the dynamics of f on Λ is chaotic (see for example [9]), in particular the periodic points of f are dense in Λ. Note that $(Vf)^i(T)$, $i \geq 0$, is a shrinking sequence of compact neighbourhoods of the attractor Λ, which converges to the latter.$\square$

The strange attractors of the *Hénon* map and the *Plykin* map [9] are obtained in a similar way.

3   The upper space as a computational model

The upper space provides a suitable computational model for dynamical systems. The definition and the examples of attractors in the previous section motivate us to study the dynamics on this space. We first need the following important result for which we have not been able to find a reference in the literature.

Proposition 3.1 Let X be a locally compact Hausdorff space.

(i) $(UX, \sqsubseteq_u)$, where $\sqsubseteq_u$ is superset inclusion, is a bounded complete continuous dcpo, and the Scott topology coincides with the upper topology.

(ii) The way-below relation $A \ll B$ holds if and only if A contains a neighbourhood of B.

(iii) if X is compact, then UX has bottom.$\square$

Clearly, X can be embedded onto the set of maximal points of UX by the singleton map $s : X \to UX$ with $x \mapsto \{x\}$, and for any collection of open sets a_i ($i \in I$) of X, we have

$$s(X) \cap (\bigcup_{i \in I} u_{a_i}) = s(\bigcup_{i \in I} a_i)$$

i.e. the subspace topology induced by UX on the set of maximal elements $s(X)$ is, in effect, the topology of X. Furthermore, any point of X, regarded as the maximal point $\{x\}$ of UX, can be approximated by the closures of its relatively compact neighbourhoods. We can do better if X is second countable.

Proposition 3.2 Let X be a second countable locally compact Hausdorff space. Then,

(i) X has a countable basis of relatively compact neighbourhoods, and UX is ω-continuous with an induced order basis consisting of finite unions of closures of these relatively compact neighbourhoods.

(ii) If X is compact and zero dimensional then UX is ω-algebraic.$\square$

An ω-continuous dcpo can be given an *effective structure* wrt an enumeration of a given order basis, in particular by using the effective theory developed for them in [10], which generalises the corresponding theory for ω-algebraic dcpo's in [17]. This enables us to have the notion of a *computable* element of an effectively given ω-continuous dcpo and that of a *computable* function between two effectively given ω-continuous dcpo's. It then follows that the least fixed point of a computable function on an effectively given dcpo with bottom is computable.

Let X be a second countable locally compact Hausdorff space. We take a countable basis of relatively compact neighbourhoods of X, fix an enumeration e of the induced order basis of UX and assume that UX is effectively given wrt e. All notions of computability, defined below, are understood to be with respect to this fixed enumeration e. We say that a compact set $C \subseteq X$ is *computable* if C is a computable element of UX. We say that a dynamical system (X, f) is *computable* if the continuous function $Uf : UX \to UX$ is computable.

Proposition 3.3 An attractor of a computable dynamical system is computable. $\square$

Recall from the introduction that if X is a metric space, UX is a quasi-metric space. In order to handle chaotic systems in the framework of UX, we need to define sensitive dependence on initial conditions for dynamical systems on quasi-metric spaces. Given a quasi-metric space (Y, d), we say that a continuous map $g : Y \to Y$ has *sensitive dependence on initial conditions* if there exists $\delta > 0$ such that, for any $x \in X$ and any neighbourhood N of x, there exists $y \in N$ and $n \geq 0$ such that $\max(d(f^n(x), f^n(y)), d(f^n(y), f^n(x))) > \delta$. Clearly this definition is consistent with the previous one if d is actually a metric. We say, as before, that $g : Y \to Y$ is *chaotic* if, (i) it has sensitive dependence on initial conditions, (ii) it is topologically transitive, and (iii) its periodic points are dense. We can now show the following.

Theorem 3.4 Let $f : X \to X$ be a continuous map on the metric space X. Then U preserves the three conditions of chaos separately; in particular, if f is chaotic on X then Uf is chaotic on UX. $\square$

Example 3.5 Consider the solenoid again (Example 2.6), now in the context of the upper space. The torus T is the least element, i.e. the bottom, of UT and Λ is the least fixed point of the continuous map $Uf : UT \to UT$ and is obtained as the lub of the chain

$$ T \ll Uf(T) \ll (Uf)^2(T) \ll (Uf)^3(T) \ll \cdots $$

Uf has infinitely many other fixed points as any periodic orbit gives a fixed point of Uf. $\square$

We now study IFSs. We first need a lemma.

Lemma 3.6 Let $(X; f_1, \ldots, f_N)$ be an hyperbolic IFS on a complete and locally compact metric space X. Then, there exists a compact subset $A \subseteq X$ such that $F(A) \subseteq A$, where $F : UX \to UX$ is the induced map on the upper space, i.e. $F(B) = f_1(B) \cup \ldots f_N(B)$. $\square$

In particular, if X is $\mathbb{R}^n$ with the Euclidean metric and s_i, $0 \leq s_i < 1$, is the contractivity factor of f_i $(1 \leq i \leq N)$, then it is easy to check that we have $F(A) \subseteq A$, where A is any closed ball of radius R with $R > \max_i \frac{|f_i(0)|}{1-s_i}$. As a result of the above lemma, we can assume without loss of generality for an hyperbolic IFS that X is compact.

Let $\{X; f_1, \ldots, f_N\}$ be an IFS, with X compact. Then the induced map $F : UX \to UX$ has a least fixed point. We will shortly give a new proof that if the IFS is hyperbolic, this fixed point, i.e. the attractor of the IFS, is unique.

We can obtain the attractor of an hyperbolic IFS as a result of a non-deterministic computation, which gives us the "history" of the points of the attractor. For this, we use the Plotkin power domain CUX of the upper space UX.

Suppose X is a second countable locally compact Hausdorff space. Then CUX is an ω-continuous dcpo and has an order basis consisting of equivalence classes of finite sets, $\{A_1, A_2, \ldots, A_K\}$, of basis elements A_i of UX $(1 \leq i \leq K)$ under the Egli-Milner preorder $\sqsubseteq_{EM}$. We denote this equivalence class by $[\{A_1, A_2, \ldots, A_K\}]$.

Now UX can be embedded in CUX by the singleton map $[.] : UX \to CUX$, defined by $A \mapsto [\{A\}]$. In the other direction, the union map $\bigcup : CUX \to UX$, defined on the above order basis by $[K] \mapsto \bigcup_{A \in K} A$ is the corresponding projection. Note that these maps can also be defined from general categorical considerations.

Given an IFS $\{X; f_1, \ldots, f_N\}$, we define a map $\overline{F} : CUX \to CUX$ which is given on the above order basis by:

$$\overline{F}([\{A_1, A_2, \ldots, A_L\}]) = [\{f_i(A_j) \mid 1 \leq i \leq N, 1 \leq j \leq K\}].$$

Suppose now that X is compact. Then the least fixed point $\bigsqcup_{i \geq 0} \overline{F}^i(X)$ of $\overline{F}$ is (the equivalence class of) the set of lubs of the infinite branches of the finitary branching tree:

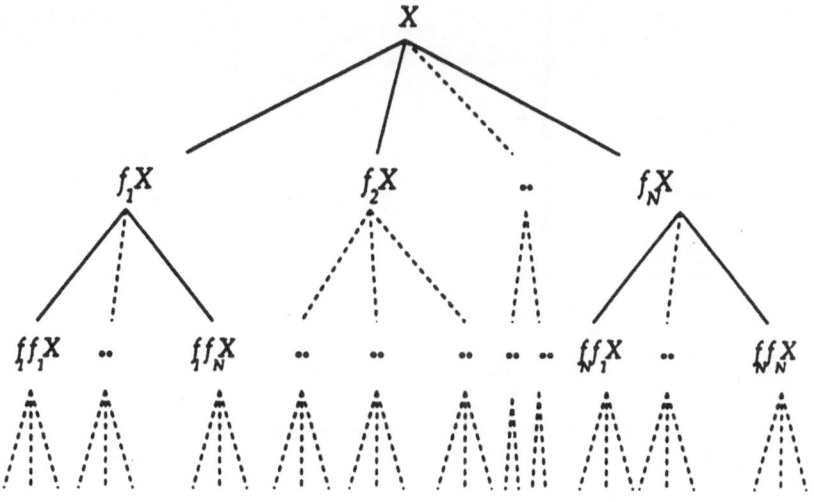

If the IFS is hyperbolic with contractivity s, then the diameter of a compact set A of depth n in any infinite branch of the tree will satisfy $\mathrm{diam}(A) \leq s^n \mathrm{diam}(X)$. Hence the lub of any infinite branch is a singleton set. It then follows easily that the least fixed point of $\overline{F}$ is a maximal element of CUX, and hence it is the unique fixed point of $\overline{F}$.

It is easy to check that the following two diagrams commute:

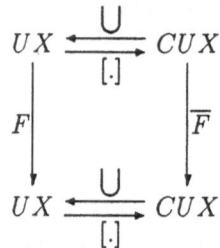

Since the least fixed point operator is a uniform fixed point operator and embeddings and projections are strict maps, we deduce:

Proposition 3.7 Let $\{X; f_1, \ldots, f_N\}$ be an IFS with X compact. Then $F : UX \rightarrow UX$ and $\overline{F} : CUX \rightarrow CUX$ each has a least fixed point, and these fixed points are mapped to each other by the singleton and the union maps. If the IFS is hyperbolic, these fixed points are unique. $\square$

Using $\overline{F}$ to compute the points of the attractor has the advantage that we obtain a neighbourhood basis of any point of the attractor, given by the nodes of the corresponding infinite branch. This can be seen in the generation of the Cantor set below.

Generating the Cantor set with the Plotkin power domain:

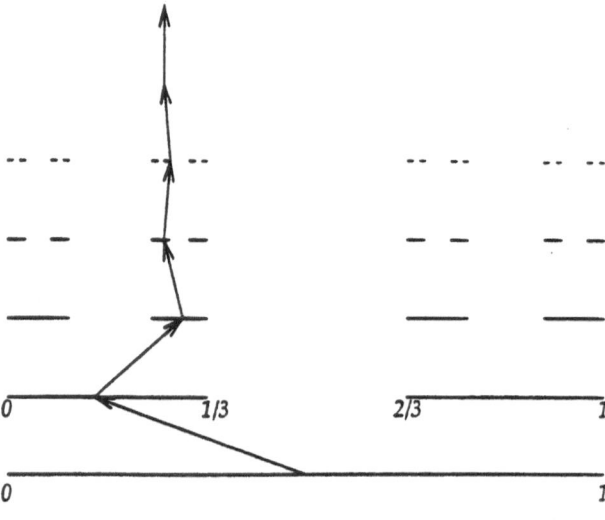

4 Julia sets

Julia sets, together with the Mandelbrot set, have been the object of intensive research in the last decade. See [6] for an overview and an extensive bibliography. Many researchers have investigated the question of computability of these sets. In particular, a team of dynamical system theorists, including Steven Smale, whose work in the 60's opened the ongoing surge of interest in dynamical systems, have developed a theory of computability over real numbers with which they have studied the Julia sets [7].

The upper space provides a framework for investigating the computability of these sets using the usual theory of computability over natural numbers. In this paper, we confine ourselves to the Julia sets of the family of quadratic complex maps of the form $f : \mathbb{C} \to \mathbb{C}$ with $f(z) = z^2 + c$, where $c \in \mathbb{C}$ is a fixed complex number. This family is of fundamental importance as it gives a model for the emergence of chaos in physical systems [12]. The *filled Julia set* is defined to be the set of all points which do not escape to infinity under iteration by f. The *Julia set* itself is the boundary of the filled Julia set. We need the following lemma, whose analogue for the Vietoris space can be found in [2, page 291]:

Proposition 4.1 Let $f : Y \to Y$ be a continuous open map on a Hausdorff space Y. Suppose the compact set $X \subseteq Y$ satisfies $f^{-1}(X) \subseteq X$. Then, the map $f^{-1} : UX \to UX$, which takes any compact set to its pre-image, is well-defined and continuous. $\square$

Suppose now $f : \mathbb{C} \to \mathbb{C}$ is a quadratic complex map with $f(z) = z^2 + c$. Note that f is open as any non-constant analytic map is open. We can choose, say, a large solid rectangle X around the origin, with sides parallel to the axes and with vertices at points with rational coordinates, such that $f^{-1}(X) \subseteq X$. Then we have the map $f^{-1} : UX \to UX$ given by $f^{-1}(A) = \{\sqrt{w - c} \mid w \in A\} \cup \{-\sqrt{w - c} \mid w \in A\}$.

Proposition 4.2 The filled Julia set of the quadratic map $f : \mathbb{C} \to \mathbb{C}$, $f(z) = z^2 + c$, is the least fixed point of $f^{-1} : UX \to UX$. $\square$

By introducing a cut in the complex plane, we can make the two maps $w \mapsto \sqrt{w - c}$ and $w \mapsto -\sqrt{w - c}$ continuous. Then, we have a non-hyperbolic IFS and we can make a non-deterministic computation of Julia sets using the Plotkin power domain. This method works for all cases in which an explicit formula for finding the roots of the polynomial exist, i.e. it works for quadratic, cubic and quartic polynomials and also for special polynomials, for example of the form $z \mapsto z^n + c$ where n is any positive integer.

Since UX is ω-continuous, it can be given an effective structure as explained earlier in this section. A convenient countable order basis for $U\mathbb{C}$ is given by the collection of finite unions of rectangles with sides parallel to the axes and vertices at points with rational coordinates. Since the least fixed point of a computable function is computable, it follows that the filled Julia set is computable if the map $f^{-1} : UX \to UX$ is computable with respect to an enumeration of the above basis. In a future paper we will further investigate this line of research.

Below you can see the first few iterates of f^{-1} for three different quadratic maps, as c decreases from -1 to -3, taken with permission from [2].

Generating Julia sets in the upper space:

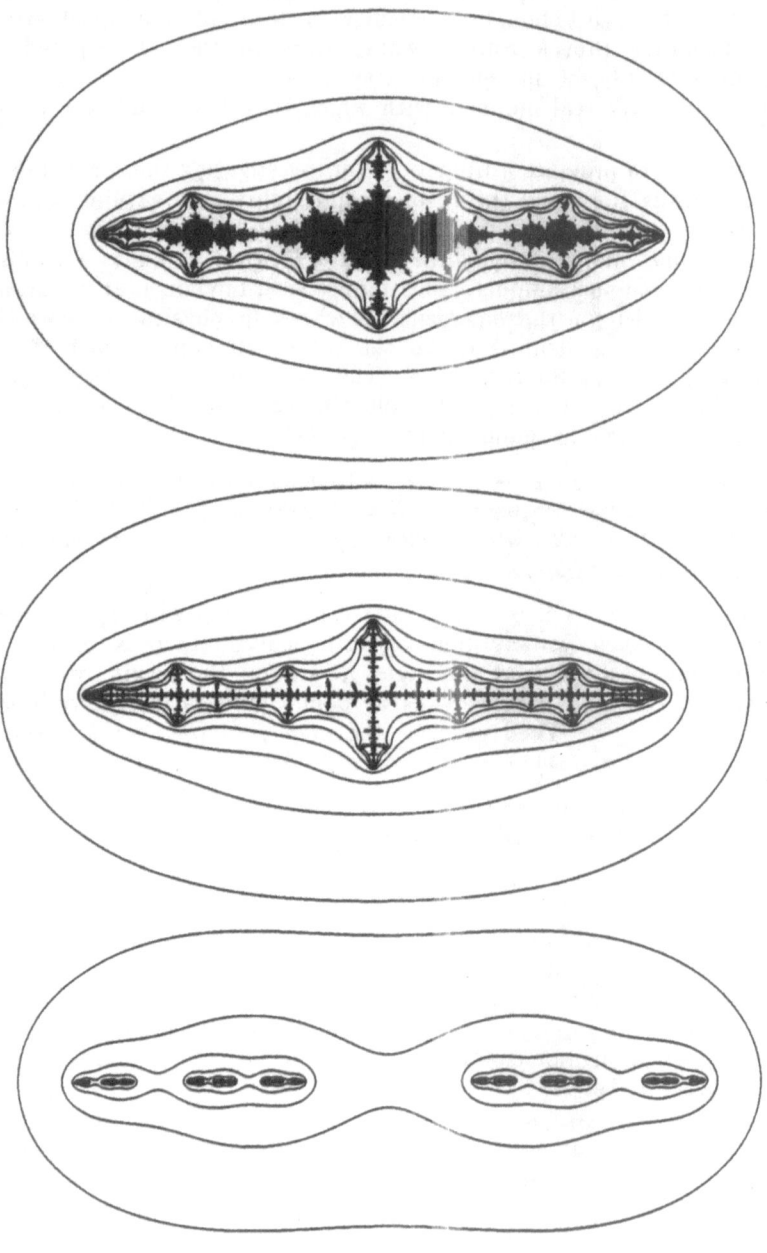

5   The lower space

The lower space can be used in computing the invariant sets, and in particular the attractors of a dynamical system, when it is possible to generate a dense orbit of the invariant set. Hyperbolic IFSs provide a good example. Let $\{X; f_1, \ldots, f_N\}$ be an hyperbolic IFS and let $x_i \in X$ be the unique fixed point of f_i, $1 \leq i \leq N$. Define $F : LX \to LX$ by $F(A) = f_1(A) \cup \ldots \cup f_N(A)$. Suppose $B \subseteq \{x_i \mid 1 \leq i \leq N\}$ is any non-empty subset of the fixed points. Then, we have:

Proposition 5.1 The attractor of the IFS is the unique fixed point of $F : LX \to LX$ and is the lub of the chain

$$B \subseteq F(B) \subseteq F^2(B) \subseteq \ldots \qquad \Box$$

However, the lower space is not in general continuous and, therefore, cannot be given a simple effective structure.

6   Measure theory via domain theory

Let X be a locally compact second countable Hausdorff space. Denote by $M(X)$ the set of all positive Borel measures μ on X with $\mu(X) \leq 1$. Like valuations, these measures can be partially ordered by putting $\mu \sqsubseteq \nu$ iff for all Borel sets $B \subseteq X$ we have $\mu(B) \leq \nu(B)$. Then, as for valuations, $M(X)$ becomes a dcpo.

Consider the upper space UX and its probabilistic power domain PUX (see the introduction for definitions). By using the fact that every open set of X is σ-compact (see the introduction), we can show the following:

Proposition 6.1 For any open set a of X, the subset $s(a) \subseteq UX$ is a G_δ set, i.e. it is the countable intersection of open sets of UX, and is, therefore, a Borel subset of UX. In particular $s(X)$ is a Borel subset of UX. $\Box$

Corollary 6.2 If B is a Borel subset of X, then $s(B)$ is a Borel subset of UX. $\Box$

Conversely, for any Borel subset B of UX, the continuity of s implies that

$$s^{-1}(B) = \bigcup(s(X) \cap B)$$

is a Borel subset of X.

Now consider any continuous valuation μ on UX. Since UX is continuous μ extends uniquely to a Borel measure on UX [14]. We can therefore assume that μ is defined on Borel sets of UX. Conversely, any measure on UX is an ω-continuous valuation. But since UX is ω-continuous, any ω-continuous valuation on UX is in fact continuous. It follows that any measure on UX is a continuous valuation. We conclude that we can identify valuations and measures on UX.

Definition 6.3 A valuation $\mu \in PUX$ is said to be *supported* in X if $\mu(UX - s(X)) = 0$. If μ is supported in X, then the *support* of μ is the set of points $y \in s(X)$ such that $\mu(N) > 0$ for any neighbourhood $N \subseteq UX$ of y. The subset of all valuations which are supported in X is denoted by $S(X)$. $\Box$

Proposition 6.4

(i) A valuation $\mu \in PUX$ is supported in X iff $\mu(\bigcup_i u_{a_i}) = \mu(\bigcup_i s(a_i))$ for all collections of open sets $a_i \in \Omega(X)$, with $i \in I$.

(ii) $S(X)$ is a subdcpo of PUX. $\square$

Definition 6.5 A *normalised* Borel measure on a topological space Y is a Borel measure μ such that $\mu(Y) = 1$. $\square$

We denote by $M^1(X)$, respectively P^1UX and $S^1(X)$, the subset of $M(X)$, respectively PUX and $S(X)$, consisting of normalised measures (valuations). Given any $\mu \in PUX$ with $\mu(UX) = c \neq 0$, we can define $\mu' \in P^1UX$ by $\mu'(O) = \frac{1}{c}\mu(O)$ for any $O \in \Omega(UX)$. Then $\mu \sqsubseteq \mu'$. Therefore, the maximal elements of PUX are precisely the maximal elements of P^1UX. We also have the following:

Proposition 6.6 If $\mu \in S^1(X)$ then μ is a maximal element of PUX. $\square$

We conjecture that the converse of the above result holds as well, i.e. any maximal element of PUX is supported in X.

We will now show that the singleton map $s : X \to UX$ induces an isomorphism between $M(X)$ and $S(X)$. Define the map $e : M(X) \to S(X)$ by $e(\mu)(O) = \mu(s^{-1}(O))$, where $O \in \Omega(UX)$.

Proposition 6.7 The map $e : M(X) \to S(X)$ is well-defined and continuous. $\square$

In the other direction, define $j : S(X) \to M(X)$ by $j(\nu)(B) = \nu(s(B))$, for any Borel subset $B \subseteq X$. It is easy to see that j is continuous and is the inverse of e. Furthermore, e and j restrict to give an isomorphism between $M^1(X)$ and $S^1(X)$.

Recall from the introduction that since UX is ω-continuous, it follows from [14] that PUX is also ω-continuous. Furthermore, any valuation $\mu \in PUX$ is the directed lub of linear combinations of point valuations. In fact, if $B \subseteq UX$ is a countable order basis of UX, then PUX has the following countable order basis:

$$\{\sum_{i=1}^{n} r_i \eta_{b_i} \mid b_i \in B, r_i \text{ rational and } \sum r_i \leq 1\}.$$

We therefore have an effective way of obtaining measures on X as the directed lub of linear combinations of point valuations on UX. This framework can provide a constructive measure theory for locally compact second countable Hausdorff spaces.

We note that the map $j : S(X) \to M(X)$ can in fact be extended to a monotone map $\overline{\jmath} : PUX \to M(X)$ defined by $\overline{\jmath}(\nu)(B) = \nu(s(B))$ for any Borel subset $B \subseteq X$. We then have $\overline{\jmath} \circ e = \mathrm{Id}_{M(X)}$ and $e \circ \overline{\jmath} \sqsubseteq \mathrm{Id}_{PUX}$. However, $\overline{\jmath}$ is not in general continuous. For example, if $X = [0, 1]$ is the unit interval with the Euclidean metric and if $b_i = [0, \frac{1}{i}] \in U([0, 1])$ $(1 \leq i)$, then the ω-chain $\langle b_i \rangle_{i \geq 0}$ in UX has lub $\{0\} \in UX$, and the ω-chain $\langle \eta_{b_i} \rangle_{i \geq 1}$ in PUX has lub $\eta_0 \in PUX$. However, the measure $\overline{\jmath}(\eta_{b_i}) \in M([0, 1])$ is zero everywhere, i.e. it is the bottom of $M([0, 1])$ for all $i \geq 1$, whereas, $\overline{\jmath}(\eta_0) \in M([0, 1])$ is the atomic measure at the point $0 \in [0, 1]$. This means that we cannot dispense with UX to construct the effective theory. In fact, had $\bar{\jmath}$ been continuous, $M(X)$ would have been a continuous retract of the ω-continuous dcpo PUX and would, therefore, have been ω-continuous itself, i.e. $M(X)$ would have been sufficient to construct an effective theory.

7   IFSs with probabilities

We now apply the results of the previous section to IFSs with probabilities. Let X be a compact metric space. Then X is second countable and the results of the previous section hold for X. The upper space UX has now a bottom element, namely X. Furthermore, P^1UX has also a bottom element, namely, the unit point valuation η_X based at $X \in UX$ with

$$\eta_X(O) = \begin{cases} 1 & \text{if } O = UX \\ 0 & \text{otherwise.} \end{cases}$$

Let $\{X; f_1, \ldots, f_N; p_1, \ldots, p_N\}$ be an iterated function system with probabilities. Define

$$T: \quad P^1UX \quad \to \quad P^1UX$$
$$\mu \quad \mapsto \quad T(\mu)$$

by $T(\mu)(O) = \sum_{i=1}^{N} p_i \mu(f_i^{-1}(O))$. Note that

$$T(\mu)(UX) = \sum_{i=1}^{N} p_i \mu(f_i^{-1}(UX)) = \sum_{i=1}^{N} p_i \mu(UX) = \sum_{i=1}^{N} p_i = 1$$

and hence T is well-defined. It is also easy to show that the map $T : P^1UX \to P^1UX$ is continuous and, therefore, has a least fixed point. Furthermore, we have:

Theorem 7.1 Let $\{X; f_1, \ldots, f_N; p_1, \ldots, p_N\}$ be an hyperbolic IFS with probabilities. Then the least fixed point of L is supported in X and its support is the unique attractor of the IFS $\{X; f_1, \ldots, f_N\}$. $\square$

Since by Proposition 6.6, a valuation $\mu \in P^1UX$ is a maximal element if it is supported in X, we immediately deduce:

Corollary 7.2 An hyperbolic IFS with probabilities has a unique fixed point. $\square$

If μ is this unique fixed point, then $j(\mu) \in M^1(X)$, where j is the map defined in the previous section, is the unique invariant measure of the IFS with probabilities as in Barnsley's work. We have therefore obtained a simple and constructive proof of Barnsley's result.

8   Conclusion and further work

We have seen that domain theory can be successfully applied in studying dynamical systems, measure theory, and fractals of IFSs. We have obtained computational models, using the upper space and the probabilistic power domains, which lead to constructive theories in these mainstream branches of mathematics. Furthermore, some of the classic results in these fields, such as the existence and uniqueness of the invariant measure of an hyperbolic IFS with probabilities, can be obtained constructively using these models.

The perspective for development of the subject looks promising. In fact, there are a number of areas for further work; we will briefly mention a few. Using the results on Borel measures in this paper and the theory of integration over valuations in [14], we are led to develop a constructive theory of integration for positive bounded Borel measures on locally compact second countable Hausdorff spaces. This, in turn, can lead into developing a constructive ergodic theory. In another direction, one needs to further investigate, for any dynamical system, the dynamical and ergodic properties of the associated dynamical systems on the Vietoris and the upper spaces. One also has to establish which Julia sets in our theory are computable and how this compares with the results in [7].

Acknowledgement

I am grateful to Reinhold Heckmann for many useful and informative discussions on various power domains during his one year visit at Imperial College. He and Michael Huth kindly reviewed this paper. Thanks also to Samson Abramsky and Siavash Shahshahani for comments on this work. This work has been funded by the SERC "Foundational Structures for Computer Science" at Imperial College.

References

[1] J. Banks, J. Brooks, G. Cairns, G. Davis, and P. Stacey. On Devaney's definition of chaos. *The American mathematical monthly*, 99(4):332–334, 1992.

[2] M. F. Barnsley. *Fractals Everywhere*. Academic Press, 1988.

[3] M. F. Barnsley and S. Demko. Iterated function systems and the global construction of fractals. *The proceedings of the royal society of London*, A399:243–275, 1985.

[4] M. F. Barnsley, A. Jacquin, L. Reuter, and A. D. Sloan. Harnessing chaos for image synthesis. *Computer Graphics*, 1988. SIGGRAPH proceedings.

[5] M. F. Barnsley and A. D. Sloan. A better way to compress images. *Byte magazine*, pages 215–223, January 1988.

[6] P. Blanchard. Complex analytic dynamics on the Riemann sphere. *Bull. A.M.S.*, 11:85–141, 1984.

[7] L. Blum, M. Shub, and S. Smale. On a theory of computation and complexity over the real numbers: NP-completeness, recursive functions and universal machines. *Bull. Amer. Math. Soc. (N.S.)*, 21:1–46, 1989.

[8] P. C. Bressloff and J. Stark. Neural networks, learning automata and iterated function systems. In A. J. Crilly, R. A. Earnshaw, and H. Jones, editors, *Fractal and Chaos*, pages 145–164. Springer-Verlag, 1991.

[9] R. Devaney. *An Introduction to Chaotic Dynamical Systems*. Addison Wesley, second edition, 1989.

[10] A. Edalat. Continuous information categories. Technical Report Doc 91/41, Department of Computing, Imperial College, 1991.

[11] A. Edalat and E. C. Zeeman. The stable classes and the codimension one bifurcations of the planar replicator system. *Nonlinearity*, 5(4):921–939, 1992.

[12] M. J. Feigenbaum. The universal metric prperties of nonlinear transformation. *J. Statistical Physics*, 21:669–709, 1979.

[13] J. E. Hutchinson. Fractals and self-similarity. *Indiana Univ. Math. J.*, 30:713–747, 1981.

[14] C. Jones. *Probabilistic Non-determinism*. PhD thesis, University of Edinburgh, 1989.

[15] S. Lang. *Real Analysis*. Addison-Wesley, 1969.

[16] C. Moore. Generalized shifts: unpredictability and undecidability in dynamical systems. *Nonlinearity*, 4:199–230, 1991.

[17] G. D. Plotkin. Post-graduate lecture notes in advanced domain theory (incorporating the "Pisa Notes"). Dept. of Computer Science, Univ. of Edinburgh, 1981.

[18] W. Rudin. *Real and Complex Analysis*. McGraw-Hill, 1966.

[19] N. Saheb-Djahromi. Cpo's of measures for non-determinism. *Theoretical computing science*, 12(1):19–37, 1980.

[20] M. B. Smyth. Powerdomains and predicate transformers: a topological view. In J. Diaz, editor, *Automata, Languages and Programming*, pages 662–675, Berlin, 1983. Springer-Verlag. Lecture Notes in Computer Science Vol. 154.

[21] M. B. Smyth. Topology. In S. Abramsky, D. Gabbay, and T. Maibaum, editors, *Handbook of Logic in Computer Science*, chapter 5. Oxford University Press, 1992.

[22] W. Szlenk. *An Introduction to the Theory of Smooth Dynamical Systems*. John Wiley & Sons, 1984.

[23] K. R. Wicks. *Fractals and Hyperspaces*, volume 1492 of *Lecture noten in mathematics*. Springer-Verlag, 1991.

Self-duality, Minimal Invariant Objects and Karoubi Invariance in Information Categories

Abbas Edalat

ae@doc.ic.ac.uk
Department of Computing, Imperial College
180 Queen's Gate, London SW7 2BZ, United Kingdom

Abstract

We introduce IP-categories by enriching the notion of I-category (information category) such that every inclusion morphism has a right adjoint or projection. Categories of information systems for various domains in semantics are all examples of IP-categories. We show that a weak notion of substructure relation between two Scott information systems induces general adjunctions between them. An IP-category with a zero object has the self-dual property that its opposite is again an IP-category. In a complete IP-category with a zero object, limits and colimits of chains of projections and inclusions coincide. As a consequence of the self-duality, a simple characterisation of minimal invariant objects of contravariant and mixed functors on IP-categories is obtained. IP-categories are closed under taking the Karoubi envelope. We use the arrow category of an effectively given IP-category to solve domain equations in categories of continuous information systems effectively.

1 Introduction

I-categories, and their concrete instance Information categories, were introduced in [5, 7, 6] as order-enriched categories to generalise the work in [2, 16, 13] on solving domain equations by constructing a cpo of information systems. The class of inclusion morphisms of an I-category induces a partial order $\trianglelefteq$ on objects and, together with the order on homsets, a partial order $\trianglelefteq^m$ on morphisms of the category. In a complete I-category, these partial orders become cpo's. This means, from the point of view of semantics, that the order on objects, representing recursive data types, and the order on morphisms, representing recursive programs, can be combined to obtain a global order on morphisms. It was shown that any ω-chain of inclusions has the least upper bound of the corresponding chain of objects as a colimit. The main new result was that any endofunctor that is standard (i.e. preserves inclusion morphisms) and continuous on the cpo of morphisms of such a category has an initial algebra in the subcategory of strict (i.e. bottom preserving) morphisms and a similar result was obtained in the effective setting. It was also shown that various categories of information systems constructed to represent the basic categories of domains used in semantics and some others like categories of sets and Boolean algebras are concrete examples of I-categories. By reducing all categorical constructions to a simple cpo framework, I-categories therefore provide a powerful yet straightforward machinery and common framework for solving recursive domain equations.

However, I-categories do not yet give us all the results that the more sophisticated categorical methods provide. In particular, we do not get a co-final algebra and the coincidence of the initial and the co-final algebra as in [18]. Furthermore, with the recent ideas of Freyd [9, 10], one can get canonical solutions of domain equations involving contravariant or bi-functors in the more general categorical framework. I-categories are certainly not rich enough to capture these.

In this paper, which is based on [3], we show how to overcome this shortcoming and obtain all the above results in a cpo framework by enriching the notion of I-category to IP-category in which every inclusion morphism $i : A \to B$ has a right adjoint or projection $p : B \to A$ satisfying $i; p \sqsupseteq \text{Id}(A)$ and $p; i \sqsubseteq \text{Id}(B)$. IP-categories, so defined, will be closed under the Karoubi envelope construction. This closure property, which means that we have a common framework for algebraic and continuous information systems, holds because we have allowed an inclusion projection pair to be a general adjunction rather than simply an embedding projection pair with equality in the first equation above.

A new question immediately arises. In all previous work on information systems and logical representations of domains, in particular in [1, 13, 21, 5], the substructure relation $A \trianglelefteq B$ between objects A and B means that B is a conservative extension of A. This relation induces an associated inclusion projection pair between them which is in fact an embedding projection pair and not a general adjunction. What relation between objects then captures this more general notion? The answer is that general adjunctions correspond to logical extensions which are not necessarily conservative. Such an extension is obtained by a "weak" substructure relation between A and B where the entailment predicate on A is a subset, rather than the restriction of, the entailment on B. We can then show that all categories of information systems for domains constructed by various authors are in fact IP-categories with this weak (as well as with the usual) substructure relation and that all the usual constructors on information systems preserve the weak substructure relation.

We prove that any IP-category with a zero object (i.e. an object which is both initial and terminal) has the self-dual property that its opposite is again an IP-category. This self-duality holds for the category as a whole and not just for the subcategory of inclusion-projections like the duality known for O-categories as in [18]. As a consequence of this self duality we immediately get the coincidence of limits and colimits and the coincidence of initial algebra and final coalgebra for complete IP-categories with a zero object and these results can be made effective for ω-algebraic IP-categories. From this, we also obtain the coincidence of the induction and the coinduction principles in the sense that the same data type satisfies both principles [14].

A most useful feature of IP-categories is that the minimal invariant objects of contravariant or bi-functors, which are more generally defined for algebraically compact categories in [9, 10], are characterised by remarkably simple properties in these special categories. These simple features are the consequence of the cpo structure of these self-dual categories which makes them quite convenient to work with in practice. For example, the canonical solution of domain equations involving the function space constructor can be determined in a straightforward way and we no longer need to restrict ourselves to the subcategory of embedding projection pairs as in [18].

The Karoubi invariance of IP-categories enables us to solve domain equations effectively in the categories of continuous information systems, by using the arrow category of the corresponding category of algebraic information systems.

Finally, we note that Smyth [17] has independently developed the notion of "I-category with subsumptions", which is an IP-category whose inclusions are embeddings (and is therefore not closed under the Karoubi construction). He obtains a duality result and the coincidence of initial algebra and final coalgebra for these special IP-categories which are similar to the corresponding results obtained here. Apart from this, the two papers have no bearing on each other.

2 Basics

2.1 I-categories

Recall from [5] that an I-category is a four-tuple $(K, \mathrm{Inc}, \sqsubseteq, \bot)$ where

- K is a category with ordered homsets,
- $\mathrm{Inc} \subseteq \mathrm{Mor}$ is the subclass of *inclusion morphisms* of K such that in each homset, $\mathrm{hom}(A, B)$, there is at most one inclusion morphism which we denote by $\mathrm{in}(A, B)$ or $A \rightarrowtail B$,
- $\sqsubseteq^{A,B}$ is the partial order on $\mathrm{hom}(A, B)$, for all $A, B \in \mathrm{Obj}$,
- $\bot \in \mathrm{Obj}$ is a distinguished object,

which satisfy the following two axioms:

Ax 1 (i) The class of objects Obj and the inclusion morphisms Inc form a partial order represented as a category.

(ii) $\mathrm{in}(\bot, A)$ exists for all $A \in \mathrm{Obj}$, i.e. $\bot$ is a weak initial object, and $\mathrm{in}(\bot, A) \sqsubseteq f$ for all morphisms $f \in \mathrm{hom}(\bot, A)$.

Ax 2 Composition of morphisms is monotone with respect to the partial order on homsets, i.e.

$$f_1 \sqsubseteq f_2 \ \& \ g_1 \sqsubseteq g_2 \ \Rightarrow \ f_1; g_1 \sqsubseteq f_2; g_2$$

whenever the compositions are defined.

An I-category is therefore an order-enriched category, or a 2-category, with some additional structure. The partial orders $\trianglelefteq$ on Obj and $\trianglelefteq^m$ on Mor are defined as follows:

- $A \trianglelefteq B$ if $\mathrm{in}(A, B)$ exists;

♦ $f \trianglelefteq^m g$ if the diagram

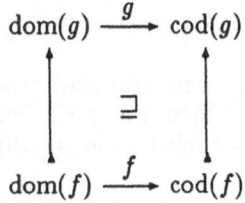

weakly commutes, i.e. if
(i) $\text{dom}(f) \trianglelefteq \text{dom}(g)$,
(ii) $\text{cod}(f) \trianglelefteq \text{cod}(g)$,
(iii) $f; \text{in}(\text{cod}(f), \text{cod}(g)) \sqsubseteq \text{in}(\text{dom}(f), \text{dom}(g)); g$.

A complete I-category further satisfies:

Ax 3 $(\text{Mor}, \trianglelefteq^m)$ is a cpo.

Ax 4 $(\text{Inc}, \trianglelefteq^m)$ is a subcpo of $(\text{Mor}, \trianglelefteq^m)$.

Ax 5 Composition of morphisms is a continuous operation with respect to $\trianglelefteq^m$, i.e. $\bigsqcup_i (f_i; g_i) = (\bigsqcup_i f_i); (\bigsqcup_i g_i)$ whenever $\langle f_i \rangle_{i \geq 0}$ and $\langle g_i \rangle_{i \geq 0}$ are increasing chains in $(\text{Mor}, \trianglelefteq^m)$ with $\text{cod}(f_i) = \text{dom}(f_i)$, for all $i \geq 0$.

Finally, an ω-algebraic I-category is defined by also requiring that:

Ax 6 $(\text{Mor}, \trianglelefteq^m)$ is ω-algebraic.

Ax 7 The (total or partial) maps:

$$\begin{array}{rl} \text{dom}, \text{cod}: & \text{Mor} \rightarrow \text{Obj} \\ \text{in}(-,-): & \text{Obj} \times \text{Obj} \rightarrow \text{Mor} \\ -;-: & \text{Mor} \times \text{Mor} \rightarrow \text{Mor} \end{array}$$

preserve compact points in the corresponding cpo's.

Alternatively an I-category, respectively an (ω-algebraic) complete I-category, can be defined as an internal category to the category of posets with bottom and strict monotone maps, respectively the category of (ω-algebraic) cpo's with strict continuous functions, together with an internal functor inducing the inclusion morphisms. For more details see [4].

2.2 IP-categories

Let K be an I-category and suppose A and B are objects with $A \trianglelefteq B$. We say that the inclusion morphism $\text{in}(A, B)$ has a *right adjoint* or *projection* if there exists a morphism $\text{pr}(B, A): B \rightarrow A$, or simply denoted by $B \twoheadrightarrow A$, such that

$$\text{in}(A, B); \text{pr}(B, A) \sqsupseteq \text{Id}(A) \qquad\qquad \text{pr}(B, A); \text{in}(A, B) \sqsubseteq \text{Id}(B).$$

Note that this is exactly the notion of right adjoint that K gets as a 2-category. The projection morphism, if it exists, is uniquely determined by the inclusion. Furthermore, the inclusion and projection morphisms induce an adjunction (a Galois connection) (e, p) between $\hom(A, A)$ and $\hom(B, B)$ where

$$e: \quad f \longmapsto \quad \mathrm{pr}(B, A); f; \mathrm{in}(A, B) \qquad p: \quad g \longmapsto \quad \mathrm{in}(A, B); g; \mathrm{pr}(B, A).$$

If an inclusion-projection pair satisfies the stronger condition that $\mathrm{in}(A, B); \mathrm{pr}(B, A) = \mathrm{Id}(A)$, then the inclusion becomes a monomorphism and the projection an epimorphism, and, in this case, we call the inclusion an *embedding*.

Definition 2.1 An *IP-category* is an I-category such that every inclusion has a right adjoint and $\bot$ is a terminal object.

We say that an IP-category is *complete* if it is complete as an I-category; it is ω-*algebraic* if it is ω-algebraic as an I-category and also satisfies the following property (which corresponds to **Ax7(ii)**):

♦ $A, B \in (\mathrm{Obj}, \trianglelefteq)$ are compact with $A \trianglelefteq B \Rightarrow \mathrm{pr}(B, A) \in (\mathrm{Mor}, \trianglelefteq^m)$ is compact.

We denote an IP-category by $P = (P, \mathrm{Inc}, \mathrm{Pr}, \sqsubseteq, \bot)$, where Pr is the class of projections. Work in information systems has so far been with embedding-projections rather than the bigger class of proper adjunctions. However, Paul Taylor [19] and Carl Gunter [11] have dealt with adjunctions in the context of domains in their theses.

2.3 Weak substructure of information systems

Consider the category of (Scott) information systems **ISys** as in [13, 16]. Objects are of the form $A = (|A|, \vdash, \mathrm{Con})$, where $|A|$ is a set of tokens, $\mathrm{Con} \subseteq \mathcal{P}_f |A|$ is the set of consistent sets of tokens and $\vdash \subseteq \mathrm{Con} \times \mathrm{Con}$ is an entailment relation. A morphisms $r: A \to B$ is an approximable relation $r \subseteq \mathcal{P}_f(|A|) \times \mathcal{P}_f(|B|)$. The identity morphism on A is the relation $\vdash$. An object A is said to be a substructure of object B, written $A \trianglelefteq B$, if

(i) $|A| \subseteq |B|$.

(ii) $\vdash_A = \vdash_B \cap (|A| \times |A|)$.

(iii) $\mathrm{Con}_A = \mathrm{Con}_B \cap \mathcal{P}_f(A)$.

This is in fact how the substructure relation is defined in [13] and implies that B is a conservative extension of A. If $A \trianglelefteq B$, then we have an inclusion and a projection morphism given by

$$X(\mathrm{in}(A, B))Y \quad \Longleftrightarrow \quad X \vdash_B Y \qquad\qquad Y(\mathrm{pr}(B, A))X \quad \Longleftrightarrow \quad Y \vdash_B X,$$

and we have $\mathrm{in}(A, B); \mathrm{pr}(B, A) = \mathrm{Id}(A)$ and $\mathrm{pr}(B, A); \mathrm{in}(A, B) \sqsubseteq \mathrm{Id}(B)$. **ISys** is then a complete IP-category with embeddings and with distinguished object $(\emptyset, \{(\emptyset, \emptyset)\}, \{\emptyset\})$.

General adjunctions correspond to a weaker notion of substructure relation as follows. We say A is a *weak substructure* of B, if the conditions (i) and (iii) above hold and (ii) is replaced by the weaker condition $\vdash_A \subseteq \vdash_B$. In terms of information, it means that *positive* information is still preserved but, in general, not negative information, i.e. $a \nvdash_A a' \Rightarrow a \nvdash_B a'$ does not hold any more. Defining the inclusions and projections as

before, we can show that they are in fact morphisms which satisfy:
$\mathrm{in}(A,B); \mathrm{pr}(B,A) \supseteq \mathrm{Id}(A)$ and $\mathrm{pr}(B,A); \mathrm{in}(A,B) \subseteq \mathrm{Id}(B)$. The following
proposition shows that all Galois connections between Scott domains
can be captured by the weak substructure relation. Let $F : \mathbf{S\text{-}Dom} \to \mathbf{ISys}$ be
the functor inducing the equivalence between the category of Scott domains
and continuous maps and that of information systems and approximable
maps.

Proposition 2.2 If (e,p) is an adjunction pair between Scott domains D
and E, then there exist information systems A and B with $A \cong F(D)$,
$B \cong F(E)$, such that A is a weak substructure of B and the following
diagrams commutes:

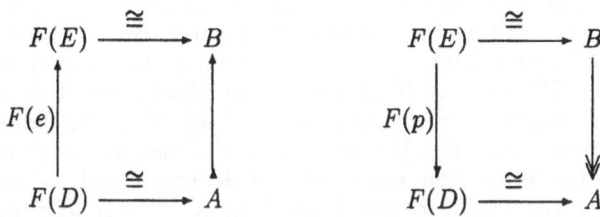

Proof Note that e, being a left adjoint, preserves compact points, but it
is not necessarily one to one. Let $e_0 : \mathcal{K}_D \to \mathcal{K}_E$ denote the restriction
of e to $\mathcal{K}_D$, where $\mathcal{K}_D$ and $\mathcal{K}_E$ are the compact points of D and E
respectively. We represent D as usual by $A = (\mathcal{K}_D, \vdash_D, \mathrm{Con}_D)$, where the
relation $X \vdash_D Y$ holds iff the lub of elements of X is above that of Y,
and Con_D is the set of finite consistent subsets of $\mathcal{K}_D$. Next we consider
$\mathcal{K}_E$ from which we define a new set of tokens $\mathcal{K}_E^+$ representing E. This is
done by replacing every element $a \in \mathcal{K}_E$ which is in the image of e_0 by
all tokens in the set $e_0^{-1}(a)$, i.e. $\mathcal{K}_E^+$ is the smallest set S satisfying:

$$
\begin{cases}
e_0^{-1}(a) \subseteq S & \text{if } a \in \mathrm{Im}(e_0) \\
a \in S & \text{otherwise.}
\end{cases}
$$

The set $\mathcal{K}_E^+$ gives us a representation $B = (\mathcal{K}_E^+, \vdash_E, \mathrm{Con}_E)$ of E in which
all tokens in $e_0^{-1}(a)$ are equivalent for each $a \in \mathrm{Im}(e_0)$. Clearly A and B
satisfy the requirements.$\square$

The category $\mathbf{ISys}$, with the weak substructure relation, is also a
complete IP-category. All the basic constructors on information systems
preserve this weaker notion of substructure relation and the solution of
domain equations remains unchanged. The same construction works for
other information systems; see Section 6 for other examples.

3   Self-dual property of IP-categories.

Recall that a morphism $f : A \to B$ of an I-category is *strict* if the diagram

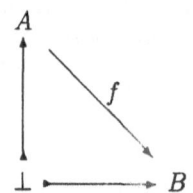

commutes. For an I-category K, we denote the subcategory of strict morphisms by K^s. It then follows that if K is an IP-category, K^s is also an IP-category in which $\bot$ is both initial and terminal, i.e. K^s is a punctuated IP-category. We will now show that the opposite of any punctuated IP-category is itself a punctuated IP-category. Let $K = (K, \text{Inc}, \text{Pr}, \sqsubseteq, \bot)$ be a punctuated IP-category. We know that $\bot$ is both an initial and a final object. By switching inclusions and projections, we can make K^{op} into an IP-category. For clarity, we denote by f_{op} the arrow in K^{op} represented by the arrow f of K. The homsets of K^{op} inherit the order from K. We also let Inc^{op}, the inclusion morphisms of K^{op}, be Pr, the projection morphisms of K considered as arrows in K^{op} and we denote the inclusion morphism from A to B in K^{op} by $\text{in}_{op}(A, B)$, i.e. we define $\text{in}_{op}(A, B) = (\text{pr}(B, A))_{op}$ whenever $A \trianglelefteq B$ in K; similarly we let $\text{Pr}^{op} = \text{Inc}$, i.e. $\text{pr}_{op}(B, A) = (\text{in}(A, B))_{op}$ whenever $A \trianglelefteq B$ in K.

Proposition 3.1 $K^{op} = (K^{op}, \text{Pr}, \text{Inc}, \sqsubseteq, \bot)$ is a punctuated IP-category. If the inclusions of K are embeddings, so are those of K^{op}.

Proof Since $\bot$ is an initial object of K^{op}, **Ax 1**(ii) holds trivially and we only need to check the inclusion-projection equations. If $A \trianglelefteq B$ in K, then

$$
\begin{aligned}
\text{in}_{op}(A, B); \text{pr}_{op}(B, A) &= (\text{pr}(B, A))_{op}; (\text{in}(A, B))_{op} \\
&= (\text{in}(A, B); \text{pr}(B, A))_{op} \\
&\sqsupseteq \text{Id}(A),
\end{aligned}
$$

and if equality holds in K it holds in K^{op} as well. Similarly we have $\text{pr}_{op}(B, A); \text{in}_{op}(A, B) \sqsubseteq \text{Id}(B)$.□

Clearly, we have $A \trianglelefteq B$ in K iff $A \trianglelefteq_{op} B$ in K^{op}. Furthermore:

Proposition 3.2 $f \trianglelefteq^m g$ iff $f_{op} \trianglelefteq^m_{op} g_{op}$.

Proof First we claim that $(f : A \to B) \trianglelefteq^m (g : C \to D)$ iff $A \trianglelefteq C$, $B \trianglelefteq D$, and $\text{pr}(C, A); f \sqsubseteq g; \text{pr}(D, B)$. To see this, suppose first that $f; \text{in}(B, D) \sqsubseteq \text{in}(A, C); g$. Composing both sides with $\text{pr}(C, A)$ from the left and $\text{pr}(D, B)$ from the right and then using the inequalities for inclusion-projections, we get $\text{pr}(C, A); f \sqsubseteq g; \text{pr}(D, B)$. Similarly if $\text{pr}(C, A); f \sqsubseteq g; \text{pr}(D, B)$, we compose both sides with the corresponding inclusions to obtain $f; \text{in}(B, D) \sqsubseteq \text{in}(A, C); g$. This proves the claim. Suppose now that $f \in \text{hom}_K(A, B)$ and $g \in \text{hom}_K(C, D)$, with $A \trianglelefteq C$ and $B \trianglelefteq D$. Then

$$
\begin{aligned}
f; \text{in}(B, D) \sqsubseteq \text{in}(A, C); g &\iff \text{pr}(C, A); f \sqsubseteq g; \text{pr}(D, B) \text{ (by the claim)} \\
&\iff f_{op}; \text{in}_{op}(A, C) \sqsubseteq \text{in}_{op}(B, D); g
\end{aligned}
$$

from which the result follows.□

All this says that the contravariant functor from K to K^{op} which acts as identity on objects and sends $f \in \hom_K(A, B)$ to $f_{op} \in \hom_{K^{op}}(B, A)$ induces an isomorphism between the partial orders $(\mathrm{Obj}_K, \trianglelefteq_K)$ and $(\mathrm{Obj}_{K^{op}}, \trianglelefteq_{K^{op}})$ and one between $(\mathrm{Mor}_K, \trianglelefteq_K^m)$ and $(\mathrm{Mor}_{K^{op}}, \trianglelefteq_{K^{op}})$. We obtain:

Theorem 3.3 If K is a (complete, ω-algebraic) punctuated IP-category, so is K^{op}.

Therefore, for any categorical property true of punctuated IP-categories, the dual property also holds for them. In particular:

Theorem 3.4 The lub of any increasing chain of objects in a complete IP-category K is a bi-limit, i.e. the colimit of the chain of inclusions and also the limit of the corresponding chain of projections in K. It is also a bi-limit of the chain in K^s.

Proof We know from [5] that the lub $D = \bigsqcup D_i$ of the chain

$$D_0 \rightarrowtail D_1 \rightarrowtail D_2 \rightarrowtail \ldots$$

is the colimit of the chain of inclusions in K and also in K^s. The same is true in K^{op}, i.e. D is the colimit of the chain of inclusions

$$D_0 \rightarrowtail_{op} D_1 \rightarrowtail_{op} \rightarrowtail_{op} D_2 \rightarrowtail_{op} \ldots$$

in K^{op} and in K^{op^s}, but this implies that D is the limit of the corresponding chain of projections

$$D_0 \leftarrowtail D_1 \leftarrowtail D_2 \leftarrowtail \ldots$$

in K and in K^s.□

3.1 Coincidence of initial algebras and final co-algebras

Another consequence of self-duality is the coincidence of initial algebra and final coalgebra of endofunctors on punctuated IP-categories. Recall that a functor $F : K \to K'$ between I-categories is *standard* if it preserves the order of homsets and the inclusion morphisms; when K and K' are complete, F is said to be *continuous* on objects (respectively on morphisms) if the induced map on the cpo of objects (respectively the induced map on the cpo of morphisms) is (Scott) continuous. Suppose now that K and K' are IP-categories and F is standard. It then follows from the uniqueness property of projections that F preserves projections as well. Assume now that K is a complete and punctuated IP-category and $F : K \to K$ is a standard endofunctor. Then we have a standard endofunctor $F^{op} : K^{op} \to K^{op}$ defined by $F^{op}(f_{op}) = (F(f))_{op}$, and we get:

Proposition 3.5 F is continuous on objects (morphisms) iff F^{op} is so.

Suppose that K is a complete IP-category and $F : K \to K$ is is standard and continuous on morphisms. We know from [5, page 45] that F has an initial algebra $(D, \mathrm{Id}(D))$ in K^s, which is given by $D = \bigsqcup_{i \geq 0} F^i(\bot)$. This result can be strengthened by only requiring the continuity of the functors on objects. In fact the initial algebra theorem can be stated and proved using the basic lemma in [18, page 765] as follows.

Theorem 3.6 Let K be a complete I-category and F a standard and object-continuous endofunctor. Then F has an initial algebra in K^s.

Proof Recall that $\perp$ is the initial object in K^s. Let T be the chain

$$\perp \rightarrowtail F(\perp) \rightarrowtail F^2(\perp) \rightarrowtail \ldots$$

and put $D = \bigsqcup_i F^i(\perp)$. We know from [5, Lemma 3.6] that $s : T \to D$, with $s_i = \text{in}(F^i(\perp), D)$ is a colimiting cone, and so is $F(s) : F(T) \to F(D)$. Therefore the conditions of the basic lemma in [18, page 765] are satisfied and, hence, the initial F-algebra exists in K^s and is given by (D, α), where $\alpha : F(D) \to D$ is the mediating morphism from $F(T)$ to T. Clearly we have $F(D) = D$ and $\alpha = \text{Id}(D)$.□

By duality we obtain the following.

Theorem 3.7 Let K be a complete IP-category and F a standard and object-continuous functor. Then F has an invariant object $D = F(D)$, such that $(D, \text{Id}(D))$ is an initial algebra and a final co-algebra in K^s.

We use the following categorical generalisation of Tarski's theorem.

Theorem 3.8 Any endofunctor on a small and chain-complete category has an initial algebra.

It follows that if K is a small and chain-complete IP-category with a zero object, then any standard endofunctor on K has an invariant object which is simultaneously an initial algebra and a final co-algebra. In the terminology of Freyd in [9, 10], we can say that punctuated complete IP-categories are *algebraically compact*.

3.2 Effectiveness

We can construct an effective theory for an ω-algebraic IP-category K similar to the case of I-categories in [5] by simply adding the requirement that $f_l = \text{pr}(B_m, A_n)$ is recursive in l, m, n w.r.t. the given enumeration of compact morphisms and compact objects. Then, it follows immediately that if K is effectively given so is K^{op} and we obtain, by self-duality, the effective version of the co-final algebra theorem:

Theorem 3.9 Let F be a computable endofunctor on K with a co-final algebra $D = F(D)$. If (E, k) is a computable F-algebra, the unique morphism $h : E \to D$ satisfying $h = k; F(h)$ is computable and an index for h can be effectively obtained from one for F and one for (E, k).

4 Minimal objects of mixed functors

The self-duality in the previous section enables us to obtain, following Freyd [9], a simple characterisation of the minimal invariant objects of non-covariant functors on IP-categories. W e start by noting that in a category with a zero object, any zero object is characterised by the property that it has only one endomorphism. In particular, given a (covariant) endofunctor F on a punctuated IP-category, the object $D = \bigsqcup F^i(\perp)$ which is both an initial algebra and a final co-algebra is a zero object of the category of invariant objects of F and hence it is characterised by the property that it has only one invariant endomorphism. Let $F : K \to K$ be an object continuous contravariant functor on a complete and punctuated IP-category K. Consider the covariant functor $\hat{F} : K^{op} \times K \to K^{op} \times K$ defined by $\hat{F}(A, B) = (F(B), F(A))$ and $\hat{F}(f, g) = (F(g), F(f))$. Clearly, $K^{op} \times K$ is a complete and punctuated IP-category. Furthermore, the functor $\hat{F}$ is object continuous and has the invariant object (D, D), with $D = \bigsqcup_i F^i(\bot)$, such that $((D, D), (\mathrm{Id}(D), \mathrm{Id}(D)))$ is both an initial algebra and a final co-algebra. Hence, by the above remark, (D, D) has only one invariant endomorphism (k, l), i.e. only one such pair with $F(k) = l$ and $F(l) = k$. Since the same thing can be said about (l, k), we have $l = k$. We have therefore proved the following:

Theorem 4.1 An object continuous contravariant endofunctor F on a complete and punctuated IP-category has an invariant object D which satisfies $F(D) = D$ and is characterised among all invariant objects of F by the property that it has only one invariant endomorphism, i.e. only one morphism $k : D \to D$, namely $\mathrm{Id}(D)$, with $F(k) = k$.

Mixed endofunctors can be treated in a similar way. Suppose $F : K^{op} \times K \to K$ is a bifunctor on a punctuated IP-category contravariant in its first argument and covariant in the second. By considering the covariant functor $\hat{F} : K^{op} \times K \to K^{op} \times K$ with $\hat{F}(A, B) = (F(B, A), F(A, B))$, we obtain the analogue of the above theorem for bi-functors.

Theorem 4.2 An object continuous bi-functor F on a complete and punctuated IP-category has an invariant object D which satisfies $F(D, D) = D$ and is characterised among all invariant objects of F by the property that it has only one invariant endomorphism, i.e. only one morphism $k : D \to D$, namely $\mathrm{Id}(D)$, with $F(k, k) = k$.

The upshot of all this for categories of information systems is that we can, for example, use the function space constructor, which is contravariant in the first argument and covariant in the second, in solving domain equations. Self-duality in punctuated IP-categories allows us to obtain a minimal invariant object in the relevant sense for the function space constructor on the category as a whole. In particular, the solution D of $X \cong A + (X \to X)$ which is inductively defined in [16] is distinguished among all the solutions of the above equation by the property that the identity approximable mapping on D, which is simply the implication $\vdash_D$ is the only invariant approximable mapping on D.

5 Karoubi invariance of IP-categories

Recall that if P is any category, the Karoubi envelope $K(P)$ of P has as objects the pairs (A, r) where A is an object of P and $r : A \to A$ is an idempotent (that is, $r; r = r$), while a morphism from (A, r) to (B, s) is a morphism $f : A \to B$ of P such that $r; f = f; s = f$. Suppose P is an I-category, then the homsets of the Karoubi envelope $K(P)$ of P are ordered by the order induced from P and for idempotents $r : A \to A$ and $s : B \to B$ we define $r \trianglelefteq_{K(P)} s$ iff $r \trianglelefteq_P^m s$, with the inclusion in $K(P)$ given by $\text{in}(r, s) = r; \text{in}(A, B); s$. We furthermore take $\text{Id}(\bot)$ as the distinguished object of $K(P)$ and obtain the following result.

Theorem 5.1 If P is a (complete) I-category, then so is $K(P)$.

Proof It is routine to check that if P is an I-category, so is $K(P)$. To verify that $K(P)$ is complete if P is complete, we show that if $f : (A, r) \to (A', r')$ and $g : (B, s) \to (B', s')$, with $r; f = f; r' = f$ and $s; g = g; s' = g$, are morphisms of $K(P)$, and if $(A, r) \trianglelefteq (B, s)$ and $(A', r') \trianglelefteq (B', s')$, then $f \trianglelefteq^m g$ iff $f \trianglelefteq^m_K g$, where $\trianglelefteq^m_K$ denotes the global partial order in $K(P)$. Putting $e = \text{in}(A, B)$ and $e' = \text{in}(A', B')$, by assumption we have $r; e \sqsubseteq e; s$ and $r'; e' \sqsubseteq e'; s'$. Therefore

$$
\begin{aligned}
f \trianglelefteq^m g &\Rightarrow f; e' \sqsubseteq e; g \\
&\Rightarrow f; r'; e'; s' = r; f; e'; s' \sqsubseteq r; e; g; s' \sqsubseteq r; e; s; g \\
&\Rightarrow f \trianglelefteq^m_K g
\end{aligned}
$$

and on the other hand

$$
\begin{aligned}
f \trianglelefteq^m_K g &\Rightarrow f; r'; e'; s' \sqsubseteq r; e; s; g \\
&\Rightarrow f; e' = f; r'; r'; e' \sqsubseteq f; r'; e'; s' \sqsubseteq r; e; s; g \sqsubseteq e; s; s; g = e; g \\
&\Rightarrow f \trianglelefteq^m g.
\end{aligned}
$$

The proof now follows easily. $\square$

The following result explains the advantage of having inclusion-projections rather than just embedding-projections in the definition of an IP-category.

Theorem 5.2 The Karoubi envelope $K(P)$ of a (complete) IP-category P is a (complete) IP-category. Furthermore, if P has embedding-projections, then the full subcategory of $K(P)$ consisting of projections has also embedding-projections.

Proof Suppose P is an IP-category. If $(A, r) \trianglelefteq (B, s)$, i.e. $A \trianglelefteq B$ and $r \trianglelefteq^m s$, with $e = \text{in}(A, B)$ and $p = \text{pr}(B, A)$, then as before we define the corresponding inclusion and projection in $K(P)$ by $e_K = r; e; s$ and $p_K = s; p; r$ respectively. We check this gives us an inclusion-projection pair:

$$
\begin{aligned}
e_K; p_K &= r; e; s; s; p; r \\
&= r; e; s; p; r \\
&\sqsupseteq r; r; e; p; r \\
&= r; e; p; r \\
&\sqsupseteq r; r \\
&= r \\
&= \text{Id}((A, r));
\end{aligned}
$$

and also

$$
\begin{aligned}
p_K; e_K &= s; p; r; r; e; s \\
&= s; p; r; e; s \\
&\sqsubseteq s; p; e; s; s \\
&= s; p; e; s \\
&\sqsubseteq s; s \\
&= s \\
&= \text{Id}((B, s)).
\end{aligned}
$$

Furthermore if s is a projection, i.e. $s \sqsubseteq \text{Id}(B)$, and $e; p = \text{Id}(A)$, we also get $e_K; p_K = r; e; s; p; r \sqsubseteq r; e; p; r = r = \text{Id}((A, r))$, which together with the first equation above implies that e_K is an embedding. Finally, it is clear that $(\perp, \mathrm{Id}(\perp))$ is a terminal object of $K(P)$.□

In particular, the Karoubi envelope of the ω-algebraic IP-categories of information systems for algebraic posets in the last section will be complete IP-categories. This makes the task of solving domain equations over the categories of continuous information systems which are retracts of algebraic ones particularly simple. However, we need a new effective theory as the Karoubi envelopes are not necessarily ω-algebraic. We proceed as follows. Let P be an effectively given ω-algebraic I-category. We will now show that the *arrow category* of P is an effectively given ω-algebraic I-category, which has $K(P)$ as a subcategory. This will provide us with an effective structure for $K(P)$. The *arrow category* over P, denoted by $P^{\rightarrow}$, is defined as follows. (See [15].) Objects of $P^{\rightarrow}$ are arrows of P. Given two objects f and f' of $P^{\rightarrow}$, a morphism $f \rightarrow f'$ in $P^{\rightarrow}$ is a pair, (a, b), of morphisms of P such that $f; b \sqsubseteq a; f'$. The identity morphism on the object $f : A \rightarrow B$ is given by $(\mathrm{Id}(A), \mathrm{Id}(B))$ and composition of morphisms is done pointwise. It is clear then that $P^{\rightarrow}$ is a category. The homsets of $P^{\rightarrow}$ are ordered by the order induced from P. Given objects $f : A \rightarrow B$ and $f' : A' \rightarrow B'$, we put $f \trianglelefteq_{P^{\rightarrow}} f'$ iff $f \trianglelefteq^m_P f'$ with $\mathrm{in}(f, f') = (\mathrm{in}(A, A'), \mathrm{in}(B, B'))$. We then have:

Theorem 5.3 The arrow category of a (complete, ω-algebraic, effectively given) I-category is another such category.

Proof It is then easy to check that $P^{\rightarrow}$ is an I-category with distinguished object $\mathrm{Id}(\perp)$. Furthermore, $P^{\rightarrow}$ is complete: If $(a_i, b_i) : f_i \rightarrow g_i$, $i \geq 0$, is an increasing chain of morphisms, then its lub is given by $(\bigsqcup a_i, \bigsqcup b_i) : \bigsqcup f_i \rightarrow \bigsqcup g_i$. Clearly an object f of $C^{\rightarrow}$ is compact if f is compact as a morphism of P. Given any morphism $(a, b) : f \rightarrow g$ of $P^{\rightarrow}$, it is not difficult to show that there is an increasing chain of morphisms $(a_i, b_i) : f_i \rightarrow g_i$, $i \geq 0$, whose lub (in $P^{\rightarrow}$) is (a, b), and such that a_i, b_i, f_i and g_i are compact morphisms of $P^{\rightarrow}$ for all $i \geq 0$. From this, it follows that $(a, b) : f \rightarrow g$ is compact in $P^{\rightarrow}$ iff a, b, f and g are compact in P and we easily deduce that $C^{\rightarrow}$ is ω-algebraic. Moreover the enumeration of the basis of P induces an enumeration of the basis of $P^{\rightarrow}$. Then by using the recursive structure of P, i.e. the relations **R1-R5** in [5], we can obtain a recursive structure for $P^{\rightarrow}$ to make it effectively given.□

Suppose now that P is an effectively given IP-category. Since P and P^{op} are both effectively given I-categories, so are their arrow categories. $K(P)$ can clearly be identified with the subcategory of $P^{\rightarrow}$ whose objects are idempotents $f : A \rightarrow A$ and its morphisms are of the form $(a, a) : f \rightarrow g$ with $f; a = a = a; g$. We therefore say an object, respectively a morphism, of $K(P)$ is computable if it is computable as an object, respectively a morphism, of the effectively given ω-algebraic I-category $P^{\rightarrow}$.

Any endofunctor on P induces in the obvious way an endofunctor on $P^{\rightarrow}$. If (A, r) is an object of $K(P)$, then the constant endofunctor on $K(P)$ with value (A, r) can be extended to $P^{\rightarrow}$. All this means that if F is an endofunctor on $K(P)$ obtained by composition of endofunctors induced from P and constant endofunctors, then we can obtain an initial algebra (respectively, co-final algebra) effectively for the domain equation $F(X) \cong X$ in $K(P)$ by solving it effectively in $P^{\rightarrow}$ (respectively, in $P^{op\rightarrow}$), i.e. we have an effective initial algebra (respectively, co-final algebra) theorem for such functors. In particular we can solve domain equations over continuous domains involving disjoint sum, product, function space, the lower, upper and convex power domains and constant endofunctors.

6 Examples

We list some basic examples of concrete IP-categories, which we call *information categories with projections*.

Par. Consider the category of sets and partial maps. The homsets are partially ordered by $f \sqsubseteq g$ if whenever f is defined g is also defined and has the same value. When $A \subseteq B$, we take $in(A, B)$ to be the inclusion map and $pr(B, A)$ to be the partial map which acts as identity on elements of A and is undefined otherwise. This clearly gives us an embedding-projection pair. Furthermore, $\perp = \emptyset$ is the initial and the final object. (**Par**, Inc, Pr, $\sqsubseteq$, $\emptyset$) is a complete IP-category. Any subcategory, whose objects have elements from a countable pool will be ω-algebraic.

Rel. More generally consider the category of sets and relations. The homsets are partially ordered by inclusion of relations. When $A \subseteq B$, we define $in(A, B) \subseteq A \times B$ and $pr(B, A) \subseteq B \times A$ to be the set $\{(a, a) \mid a \in A\}$. This gives a projection-embedding pair and the empty set is initial and terminal. Hence, **Rel** is a complete IP-category, with ω-algebraic subcategories, as in **Par**.

Information systems for domains. We have already seen that **ISys** is an IP-category. Here we list some other examples. In general, any category of information systems for a subcategory of **SFP** is an information category with projections. The following complete information categories, equivalent to the corresponding categories of domains, were constructed in [8]: (i) **BC-ISys**, equivalent to the category of Scott domains and continuous functions, (ii) **SFP-ISys**, equivalent to the category of SFP domains with continuous functions, (iii) **DI-ISys** equivalent to the category of dI-domains with stable maps, (iv) **CS-ISys**, equivalent to the category of continuous Scott domains and continuous functions. In (i), (ii), and (iii) the information systems represent the corresponding domains by the sets of all compact elements, and (iv) is the Karoubi envelope of (i). Most distinguished of all, Abramsky's category of SFP pre-locales, **DPL1**, equivalent to **SFP** [1], which provides the logical representation of SFP objects, is an information category with projections.

All these categories are complete information categories with projections. Moreover, **BC-ISys**, **SFP-ISys** and **DI-ISys** have equivalent ω-algebraic subcategories [8]. These subcategories have objects which are partial orders, rather than simply preorders, with tokens from a countable pool. Consequently, compact objects are precisely the finite objects, i.e. objects with a finite carrier set, and any object then will be the lub of a chain of finite objects.

As for **ISys**, we can weaken the substructure relation in the above categories, except for the case of dI-domains, to obtain general adjunctions rather than simply embedding-projection pairs.

7 Concluding remarks

IP-categories. like I-categories, can be considered as generalised partial orders where the order relation, representing the notion of approximation of objects, is replaced by the inclusion-projection pair. IP-categories provide a very suitable framework for generalizing domains; they are in line with the traditional and successful approach to the problem of comparing domains as objects in a category. Indeed the use of projection-embedding pairs, is at the heart of the categorical solution of domain equations (Smyth/Plotkin), the definition of SFP-objects (Plotkin), and domain-theoretic models of polymorphism (Coquand, Gunter, Winskel).

In the case of I-categories, this generalisation has been studied in [4]. For example, Steve Vickers' *lower bag domain* [20], proposed to model databases, is in fact an example of an I-category. A similar treatment can be carried out for IP-categories. In particular, one can define the notion of *completion* of an IP-category, which will be an algebraic IP-category, and deduce that any algebraic IP-category is the completion of its *base*, i.e. the subcategory of compact objects and morphisms.

We can also obtain other generalisations of categories of domains. For example, if we define an SFP IP-category to be one whose poset of objects is an SFP domain, then the category of Scott information systems and approximable maps can be shown to be an SFP IP-category. One line of research is to determine the cartesian closed categories of small I-categories and of small IP-categories. One can show for example that the category of small directed complete I-categories (with strict morphisms) and standard continuous functors is cartesian closed. The challenge now is to find cartesian closed subcategories consisting of algebraic or continuous I-categories of this category, in much the same way that Jung [12] has classified all cartesian closed subcategories of the category of algebraic and continuous dcpos and continuous functions. A similar job should then be undertaken for IP-categories.

Acknowledgement

I would like to thank Leopoldo Román and Steve Vickers who reviewed this paper and made many useful comments and suggestions. This work has been funded by the SERC "Foundational Structures for Computer Science" at Imperial College.

References

[1] S. Abramsky. Domain theory in logical form. *Annals of Pure and Applied Logic*, 1991.

[2] G. Berry and P.-L. Curien. Sequential algorithms on concrete data structures. Technical report, Report of Ecole Nationale Superieure des Mines de Paris, Centre de Mathematiques Appliquées, Sophia Antipolis, 1981.

[3] A. Edalat. Self duality in information categories. Technical Report Doc 91/42, Department of Computing, Imperial College, 1991.

[4] A. Edalat. Continuous I-categories. In A. Nerode and M. Taitslin, editors, *Logical Foundations of Computer Science*, volume 620 of *Lecture Notes in Computer Science*, pages 127–138. Springer-Verlag, 1992.

[5] A. Edalat and M. B. Smyth. Categories of information systems. In D. H. Pitt, P. L. Curien, S. Abramsky, A. M. Pitts, A. Poigne, and D. E. Rydeheard, editors, *Category theory in computer science*, pages 37–52. Springer-Verlag, 1991.

[6] A. Edalat and M. B. Smyth. Compact metric information systems. In *1992 Rex workshop on semantics of programming languages*. Springer-Verlag, 1993. to appear.

[7] A. Edalat and M. B. Smyth. I-categories as a framework for solving domain equations. *Theoretical Computer Science*, 1993. to appear.

[8] A. Edalat and M. B. Smyth. Information Categories. *Applied Categorical Structures*, 1993. to appear.

[9] P. J. Freyd. Algebraically complete categories. In A. Carboni *et al*, editor, *Proc. 1990 Como Category theory conference*, volume 1488 of *Lec. Notes in Maths*, pages 95–104. Springer Verlag, 1991.

[10] P. J. Freyd. Remarks on algebraically compact categories. In A. M. Pitts M. P. Fourman, P. T. Johnstone, editor, *Applications of categories in computer science*, number 177 in L.M.S. Lecture notes series, pages 95–106. Cambridge University Press, 1992.

[11] C. Gunter. *Profinite Solutions for Recursive Domain Equations*. PhD thesis, University of Wisconsin, Madison, 1985.

[12] A. Jung. *Cartesian Closed Categories of Domains*. PhD thesis, Technische Hochschule Darmstadt, 1988.

[13] K. G. Larsen and G. Winskel. Using information systems to solve recursive domain equations effectively. In D. B. MacQueen G. Kahn and G. Plotkin, editors, *Semantics of Data Types*, pages 109–130, Berlin, 1984. Springer-Verlag. Lecture Notes in Computer Science Vol. 173.

[14] D. J. Lehmann and M. B. Smyth. Algebraic specification of data types: A synthetic approach. *Mathematical Systems Theory*, 14:97–139, 1981.

[15] S. Mac Lane. *Categories for the Working Mathematician*. Springer-Verlag, Berlin, 1971.

[16] D. S. Scott. Domains for denotational semantics. In M. Nielson and E. M. Schmidt, editors, *Automata, Languages and Programming: Proceedings 1982*. Springer-Verlag, Berlin, 1982. Lecture Notes in Computer Science 140.

[17] M. B. Smyth. I-categories and duality. In M. P. Fourman, P. T. Johnstone, and A. M. Pitts, editors, *Application of categories in computer science*, volume 177 of *London Mathematical Society Lecture Note Series*, pages 270–287. Cambrdge University Press, 1992.

[18] M. B. Smyth and G. D. Plotkin. The category-theoretic solution of recursive domain equations. *SIAM J. Computing*, 11:761–783, 1982.

[19] P. Taylor. *Recursive Domains, Indexed category Theory and Polymorphism*. PhD thesis, Cambridge University, 1986.

[20] S. J. Vickers. Geometric theories and databases. In P. Johnstone M. P. Fourman and A. M. Pitts, editors, *Applications of Categories in Computer Science*, pages 288–314. Cambridge University Press, 1991.

[21] G. Q. Zhang. dI-domains as information systems. In G. Ausiello, M. Dezani-Ciancaglini, and S. Ronchi Della Rocca, editors, *Automata, Languages and Programming*, volume 372 of *Lecture Notes in Computer Science*, pages 773–788, Berlin, 1989. Springer Verlag.

Reasoning About Gamma Programs

Lindsay Errington, Chris Hankin and Thomas P. Jensen

{le,clh,tpj}@doc.ic.ac.uk

Department of Computing, Imperial College
180 Queen's Gate, London SW7 2BZ, United Kingdom

Abstract

We describe an axiomatic semantics for the parallel programming language Gamma based on a framework developed by Brookes. This framework is an extension of Floyd-Hoare logic that allows compositional reasoning about the interleaved execution of Gamma programs. We present a proof system for deriving valid assertions about Gamma programs and examine its practical use through an example.

1 Introduction

We present a formal system for reasoning about programs expressed using the Gamma programming formalism [1, 2]. Gamma operates with a single data structure, the multiset, and computation proceeds by rewriting multisets of data. Gamma has proved successful in expressing a variety of algorithms including sorting and graph algorithms. Some of these algorithms can even be derived from their specifications in a semi-formal manner akin to the program derivation technique advocated by Dijkstra and Gries [8].

The basic operation in Gamma is the rewrite operation, written $(R(\overline{x}), A(\overline{x}))$. Here $R(\overline{x})$ is a predicate, called the reaction condition, and $A(\overline{x})$ a function, called the action. A rewrite takes place if there is a vector $\overline{x}$ of elements from the multiset that satisfies the reaction condition. In that case the elements in $\overline{x}$ are removed from the multiset and the elements $A(\overline{x})$ added to the multiset. This process continues until no vector of elements satisfies the reaction condition. Thus, the operation $(x > 1, x - 1)$ would rewrite the multiset $\{5, 0\}$ to $\{1, 0\}$ by the computation

$$\{5, 0\} \xrightarrow{4/5} \{4, 0\} \xrightarrow{3/4} \{3, 0\} \xrightarrow{2/3} \{2, 0\} \xrightarrow{1/2} \{1, 0\}$$

where we have annotated the arrows with the substitution taking place. The computation terminates with $\{1, 0\}$ since neither 1 nor 0 satisfy the reaction condition.

More complex Gamma programs can be built by combining rewrite operations using the operators sequential and parallel composition, denoted by $\circ$ and $+$. The sequential composition $C_2 \circ C_1$ will execute C_1 until it can no longer react in which case C_2 takes over and executes until it no longer can react. The parallel composition $C_1 + C_2$ will continue executing as long as one of C_1 and C_2 can execute. If only C_1, say, can react we let C_1 perform a rewrite and then return to check which of the C_i can react next. If both C_1 and C_2 can react, one is randomly chosen. This non-deterministic aspect of Gamma means that the program

$$(x > 1, 1) + (x > 1, 0)$$

can produce either $\{1\}$ or $\{0\}$ from the multiset $\{5\}$, depending on which of the summands is allowed to react. Notice also how parts of a program can switch between being active and inactive during a computation. The program

$$(\mathsf{even}(x), x - 1) + (\mathsf{odd}(x), x + 1)$$

will not terminate when applied to a non-empty multiset since each summand produces an element that will activate the other.

The interleaving of rewrites in the definition of parallel composition complicates reasoning about Gamma programs to the extent that existing methods for reasoning about sequential programs are inadequate for this task. In this paper we shall use techniques proposed by Brookes [5] to overcome this. Brookes is concerned with axiomatic semantics of programs with shared variables; we shall adapt his developments to the setting of Gamma.

For *sequential* programs it is enough to describe programs by assertions of the form

$$\{P_1\} \xrightarrow{\alpha_1} \{P_2\} \xrightarrow{\alpha_2} \{P_3\} \dots$$

meaning that if we start in a state satisfying P_1 and execute the transition α_1 we reach a state satisfying P_2 where, if we execute α_2, reach a state satisfying P_3 *etc.* When execution of $\alpha_1; \alpha_2$ can be interleaved we might find that even although P_2 holds after α_1 it does not hold before α_2 because an external command has changed the state. We shall therefore be using assertions of the form

$$\{P_1\} \xrightarrow{\alpha_1} \{Q_1\} \{P_2\} \xrightarrow{\alpha_2} \{Q_1\} \{P_3\} \dots$$

saying that if P_i holds before the transition α_i then Q_i holds after α_i has been executed. We accommodate interleaving by *not* requiring any relationship to hold between Q_i and P_{i+1}, allowing the state in which $\alpha_1; \alpha_2$ is executed to be changed from outside. For example, in order to reason about the program $(x = 1, 2) + (x = 1, 3)$ we would need to know about $(x = 1, 2)$ that it satisfies

$$\{M = \{1, 1, 1\}\} \xrightarrow{2/1} \{M = \{1, 1, 2\}\} \{M = \{1, 3, 2\}\} \xrightarrow{2/1} \{M = \{2, 3, 2\}\}.$$

We shall see that with this more complicated type of assertions we will be able to derive assertions about programs from assertions about its constituent parts, *i.e.* we gain compositional reasoning.

The paper is organised as follows. In Section 2 we present the syntax of Gamma and its operational semantics formulated as a labelled transition system. Section 3 defines the transition assertions used to describe Gamma programs together with a relation between programs and assertions defining when a program satisfies an assertion. In Section 4 we give rules for inferring when a Gamma program satisfies a given assertion and show how these rules can be used to reason about programs. Section 5 concludes.

2 The Syntax and Semantics of Gamma

In this paper we consider the version of Gamma defined by Hankin et al. in [9] which includes operators for sequential and parallel composition. Before giving the syntax, we introduce the following classes and associated meta-variables:

$$
\begin{array}{llll}
M & \in \mathbf{M} & = \mathcal{M}\,\mathbf{D} & \textit{non-empty finite multisets over } \mathbf{D} \\
\overline{x} & \in \mathbf{T} & = \sum_{n<\omega} \mathbf{D}^n & \textit{tuples of length } n \geq 0 \\
R & \in \mathbf{R} & = \mathbf{T} \rightarrow \{\mathbf{true}, \mathbf{false}\} & \textit{reaction conditions} \\
A & \in \mathbf{A} & = \mathbf{T} \rightarrow \mathbf{T} & \textit{actions}
\end{array}
$$

The syntax of Gamma programs is defined as follows:

$$
\begin{array}{llll}
\mathbf{C} \ni C & ::= & (R, A) & \textit{rewrite rule} \\
& | & C_1 + C_2 & \textit{parallel composition} \\
& | & C_1 \circ C_2 & \textit{sequential composition}
\end{array}
$$

The underlying domain, $\mathbf{D}$, will be left unspecified. Both reactions and actions are considered to have an arity and we stipulate that in any reaction/action pair (R, A), both R and A must have the same arity. Reactions, nevertheless, are considered to be total functions which yield **false** when applied to a tuple of inappropriate arity. When presenting a Gamma program, we will use the syntax

$$
\overline{x} \rightarrow A(\overline{x}) \Leftarrow R(\overline{x})
$$

as an alternative to (R, A).

Before defining the semantics, we introduce further classes:

$$
\begin{array}{llll}
\alpha & \in \mathbf{Lab} & = (\mathbf{T} \times \mathbf{T}) \cup \{\delta\} & \textit{labels} \\
(C, M) & \in \mathbf{Conf} & = (\mathbf{C} \cup \{\mathbf{nil}\}) \times \mathbf{M} & \textit{configurations}
\end{array}
$$

A label $\overline{y}/\overline{x}$ corresponds to a rewrite on a multiset in which $\overline{y}$ replaces $\overline{x}$ and we will write $M[\overline{y}/\overline{x}]$ for the multiset obtained by replacing $\overline{x}$ with $\overline{y}$ in M ($\overline{x}$ and $\overline{y}$ may have different arities). Note that within the class of configurations, the symbol **nil** is considered a valid program and will be used to indicate termination.

We now give the operational semantics of Gamma using the labelled transition system $(\mathbf{C}, \mathbf{Lab}, \{\overset{\alpha}{\rightarrow} : \alpha \in \mathbf{Lab}\})$ where for each $\alpha \in \mathbf{Lab}$, $\overset{\alpha}{\rightarrow} \subseteq$ $\mathbf{Conf} \times \mathbf{Conf}$ is a transition relation, written $(C_1, M_1)\overset{\alpha}{\rightarrow}(C_2, M_2)$. The family of relations are the least satisfying the rules given in figure 1. Each transition is labelled with a pair $\overline{y}/\overline{x}$ except in those instances where a program rewrites without affecting the multiset whereupon the transition is labelled with δ.

3 Brookes' Assertion Language

Hoare introduced the logic of **while** programs and showed that partial correctness could be proved by structural induction using rules derived from the relational semantics of the language. His logic was *compositional* in the sense that

$$\frac{\overline{x} \subseteq M.R(\overline{x})}{((R,A),M) \xrightarrow{A(\overline{x})/\overline{x}} ((R,A),M[A(\overline{x})/\overline{x}])}$$

$$\frac{\neg \exists \overline{x} \subseteq M.R(\overline{x})}{((R,A),M) \xrightarrow{\delta} (\mathbf{nil},M)}$$

$$\frac{(C_1,M) \xrightarrow{\alpha} (C_1',M')}{(C_1+C_2,M) \xrightarrow{\alpha} (C_1'+C_2,M')} \qquad \frac{(C_2,M) \xrightarrow{\alpha} (C_2',M')}{(C_1+C_2,M) \xrightarrow{\alpha} (C_1+C_2',M')}$$

$$\frac{(C_1,M) \xrightarrow{\delta} (C_1',M) \quad (C_2,M) \xrightarrow{\delta} (C_2',M)}{(C_1+C_2,M) \xrightarrow{\delta} (\mathbf{nil},M)}$$

$$\frac{(C_2,M) \xrightarrow{\alpha} (C_2',M')}{(C_1 \circ C_2,M) \xrightarrow{\alpha} (C_1 \circ C_2',M')} \qquad \frac{(C_2,M) \xrightarrow{\delta} (\mathbf{nil},M) \quad (C_1,M) \xrightarrow{\alpha} (C_1',M')}{(C_1 \circ C_2,M) \xrightarrow{\alpha} (C_1',M')}$$

Figure 1: The operational semantics of Gamma.

the meaning of a syntactic construct was defined in terms of its constituents. See *e.g.* the overview by Patrick Cousot [7] for more on Hoare logics.

Extending Hoare logic to parallel languages has proved difficult and generally requires making compromises such as abandoning compositionality, introducing auxiliary variables, or requiring interference freedom. In contrast, Brookes [5] has defined an axiomatic framework which makes none of the compromises mentioned. Rather than basing the axiomatic definition on the relational semantics, Brookes argues that the transition system defining the operational semantics should be used as basis for reasoning about programs. Instead of asserting pre- and post-conditions of a command, in Brookes' logic one writes pre- and post-conditions for each transition. In the paragraphs which follow we present the variant of Brookes' logic we will need in the next section to give the semantics of Gamma.

3.1 Syntax and Semantics

Transition assertions have the following syntax:

$$\phi \quad ::= \quad P\sum_{i=1}^{n}\alpha_i P_i \phi_i \qquad branching$$

$$| \quad P\bullet \qquad\qquad terminal$$

$$| \quad \theta \qquad\qquad meta\text{-}variable$$

$$| \quad \mu\theta.\phi \qquad\qquad recursion$$

$$| \quad \phi_1 \wedge \phi_2 \qquad\qquad conjunction$$

where P and P_i are conditions on a multiset expressed in ordinary predicate calculus and α_i are atomic actions. We write $M \models P$ if the multiset M satisfies the condition P.

This definition differs only slightly from that used by Brookes. Brookes distinguishes termination from deadlock and for this he requires two forms of terminal assertions. In Gamma, deadlock is not a possibility and we need only one.

When a program C *satisfies* a (closed) assertion ϕ we write

$$C \ \mathbf{sat} \ \phi$$

We now define validity for such formulae. Validity of a branching assertion is defined by appealing to the operational semantics. The formula C **sat** $P\sum_{i=1}^{n}\alpha_i P_i \phi_i$ is valid if, when a multiset satisfies the condition P, then there is a transition, α_i, leading to a new multiset satisfying P_i and such that the modified program, C', satisfies ϕ_i. More formally,

$$\models C \ \mathbf{sat} \ P \sum_{i=1}^{n}\alpha_i P_i \phi_i$$

if and only if the following conditions are satisfied

1. $M \models P \wedge (C,M) \xrightarrow{\alpha} (C',M') \Rightarrow \exists i \leq n \,.\, \alpha = \alpha_i \wedge M' \models P_i \wedge C' \ \mathbf{sat} \ \phi_i$
2. $M \models P \Rightarrow \forall i \leq n \,.\, \exists C_i, M_i \,.\, (C,M) \xrightarrow{\alpha_i} (C_i, M_i)$

A program satisfies a terminal assertion if and only if the program terminates with a multiset satisfying the condition:

$$\models C \ \mathbf{sat} \ P\bullet \iff M \models P \Rightarrow (C,M) \xrightarrow{\delta} (\mathbf{nil}, M)$$

Validity of formulae involving conjoined assertions is defined in the obvious way:

$$\models C \ \mathbf{sat} \ (\phi_1 \wedge \phi_2) \iff \models C \ \mathbf{sat} \ \phi_1 \wedge \models C \ \mathbf{sat} \ \phi_2$$

Validity of a formula involving a recursive assertion requires validity with respect to all finite unfoldings of the assertion. The finite unfoldings are defined as follows:

$$\theta_0 \ = \ \{\mathbf{false}\}\bullet$$
$$\theta_{n+1} \ = \ \phi[\theta_n/\theta] \ \text{for } n \geq 0$$

where $\phi[\psi/\theta]$ denotes the result of substituting ψ for each free occurrence of θ in ϕ, renaming bound variables where necessary to avoid variable capture. Using this, validity of a recursive assertion is defined such that

$$\models C \text{ sat } \mu\theta.\phi \iff \forall n \geq 0.(\models C \text{ sat } \theta_n)$$

3.2 Composing Assertions

We now introduce two "syntactic operations" for composing transition assertions ϕ and ψ. The first, written $\phi\|\psi$, composes ϕ and ψ in parallel. It is defined recursively over the possible combinations of ϕ and ψ. When composing terminal and branching assertions, the terminal condition propagates to the leaves of the assertion tree.

$$
\begin{aligned}
(P\sum_{i=1}^{n}\alpha_i P_i\psi_i)\|Q\bullet &= (P\wedge Q)\sum_{i=1}^{n}\alpha_i P_i(\psi_i\|Q\bullet) \\
P\bullet\|(Q\sum_{j=1}^{m}\beta_j Q_i\psi_j) &= (P\wedge Q)\sum_{j=1}^{m}\beta_j Q_j(P\bullet\|\psi_j) \\
P\bullet\|Q\bullet &= (P\wedge Q)\bullet
\end{aligned}
$$

When both are branching assertions, their parallel composition is obtained by interleaving the respective trees. Let

$$
\begin{aligned}
\phi &= P\sum_{i=1}^{n}\alpha_i P_i\phi_i \\
\psi &= Q\sum_{j=1}^{m}\beta_j Q_j\psi_j
\end{aligned}
$$

Then

$$\phi\|\psi = (P\wedge Q)\left(\begin{array}{c}\sum_{i=1}^{n}\alpha_i P_i(\phi_i\|\psi) \\ +\ \sum_{j=1}^{m}\beta_j Q_j(\phi\|\psi_j)\end{array}\right)$$

Now we consider the parallel composition of recursive and conjunctive formulae. First, when θ is a bound meta-variable, we define $\theta\|\phi = \phi\|\theta = \theta$. Let $\phi = \mu\theta_1.\bigwedge_k \phi_k$ and $\psi = \mu\theta_2.\bigwedge_l \psi_l$ be two general recursive conjunctions. Their parallel composition $\phi\|\psi$ is the recursive conjunction $\mu\theta.\bigwedge_{k,l}\gamma_{k,l}$ where θ is a new meta-variable and each $\gamma_{k,l}$ is derived from ϕ_k and ψ_l. Two rules for deriving $\gamma_{k,l}$ are needed in the discussion which follows.

1. $\phi_k = P\sum_i \alpha_i P_i\delta_i$ and $\psi_l = Q\sum_j \beta_j Q_j\varphi_j$

$$\gamma_{k,l} = (P\wedge Q)\left(\begin{array}{c}\sum_i \alpha_i P_i(\delta_i[\theta/\theta_1]\|\psi) \\ +\ \sum_j \beta_j Q_j(\phi\|\varphi_j[\theta/\theta_2])\end{array}\right)$$

2. $\phi_k = P\sum_i \alpha_i P_i\delta_i$ and $\psi_l = Q\bullet$

$$\gamma_{k,l} = (P\wedge Q)\sum_i \alpha_i P_i(\delta_i[\theta/\theta_1]\|\psi)$$

Note that the rules given earlier are special cases of rules 1 and 2.

We conclude our discussion of the parallel composition operator for transition assertions by relating it to Gamma's parallel composition operator.

Theorem 1 If C_1 sat ϕ and C_2 sat ψ then $C_1 + C_2$ sat $\phi\|\psi$.

Proof (Sketch) The proof is by induction over the structure of transition assertions. We will consider only the case where ϕ and ψ are branching assertions. Let $\phi = P \sum_{i=1}^{n} \alpha_i P_i \phi_i$ and $\psi = Q \sum_{j=1}^{m} \beta_j Q_j \psi_j$. Now suppose there is a multiset M such that $M \models (P \wedge Q)$. Therefore $M \models P$ and since C_1 sat ϕ, by the definition of **sat**, there exists a transition α_i such that $(C, M) \overset{\alpha_i}{\to} (C_i, M_i)$, $M_i \models P_i$ and C_i sat ϕ_i. Note that the same transition is possible in $\phi \| \psi$. What remains to be shown is that C_i sat $(\phi_i \| \psi)$ which we can get by a second induction over paths in assertion trees. ∎

The second operator defined by Brookes is for the sequential composition of transition assertions. Intuitively the sequential composition $\phi; \psi$ replaces the terminal assertions in the assertion tree for ϕ with a copy of ψ. Like the parallel operator, sequential composition is defined recursively over the various combinations of ϕ and ψ which we list below.

$$
\begin{array}{rcl}
P\bullet; (Q \sum_{j=1}^{m} \beta_j Q_i \psi_j) & = & (P \wedge Q)(\sum_{j=1}^{m} \beta_j Q_j \psi_j) \\
(P \sum_{i=1}^{n} \alpha_i P_i \phi_i); \psi & = & P \sum_{i=1}^{n} \alpha_i P_i(\phi_i; \psi) \\
P\bullet; Q\bullet & = & (P \wedge Q)\bullet \\
(\mu\theta.\psi); \phi & = & \mu\theta.(\psi; \phi) \\
P\bullet; (\mu\theta.\psi) & = & P\bullet; \psi[\mu\theta.\psi/\theta] \\
\theta; \phi & = & \theta \qquad \theta \text{ a bound meta-variable}
\end{array}
$$

Sequential composition distributes over conjunction. Let $\phi = \phi_1 \wedge \phi_2$ and $\psi = \psi_1 \wedge \psi_2$. Then

$$
\begin{array}{rcl}
\phi; (\psi_1 \wedge \psi_2) & = & (\phi; \psi_1) \wedge (\phi; \psi_2) \\
(\phi_1 \wedge \phi_2); \psi & = & (\phi_1; \psi) \wedge (\phi_2; \psi)
\end{array}
$$

As with parallel composition, we relate the sequential composition operator for transition assertions with the corresponding Gamma operator.

Theorem 2 If C_1 sat ϕ and C_2 sat ψ then $C_1 \circ C_2$ sat $\psi; \phi$.

3.3 Implication

Finally, still following Brookes, we introduce implication, $\phi \Rightarrow \psi$ for transition assertions. The intuition is that for all programs C, if C sat ϕ then C sat ψ. This permits strengthening pre-conditions and/or weakening post-conditions. It is defined in terms of the other operators and in terms of standard implication in the predicate calculus.

Let $\phi = P \sum_{i=1}^{n} \alpha_i P_i \phi_i$, $\psi = Q \sum_{i=1}^{n} \alpha_i Q_i \psi_i$, then

$$
\begin{array}{rcl}
\phi \Rightarrow \psi & \Longleftrightarrow & (Q \Rightarrow P) \wedge \bigwedge_{i=1}^{n}(P_i \Rightarrow Q_i) \wedge \bigwedge_{i=1}^{n}(\phi_i \Rightarrow \psi_i) \\
P\bullet \Rightarrow Q\bullet & \Longleftrightarrow & Q \Rightarrow P \\
\phi_1 \wedge \phi_2 & \Rightarrow & \phi_1 \\
\phi_1 \wedge \phi_2 & \Rightarrow & \phi_2 \\
\mu\theta.\varphi & \Longleftrightarrow & \varphi[(\mu\theta.\varphi)/\theta]
\end{array}
$$

Finally, we introduce the following inference rule:

$$
\frac{\psi \Rightarrow \theta \vdash \psi \Rightarrow \phi}{\psi \Rightarrow \mu\theta.\phi}
$$

4 The Proof System

The formulation of the proof system for the satisfaction relation **sat** assumes that we are given a formal system for reasoning about multisets and substitutions on multisets. We shall not address the issue of how to construct such a system but just assume that we can prove assertions of the form $\{P\}\, A(\bar{x})/\bar{x}\, \{Q\}$ meaning that if P holds of a multiset M then Q holds of the multiset obtained by substituting $A(\bar{x})$ for $\bar{x}$ in M. Specifically,

$$\{P\}\, A(\bar{x})/\bar{x}\, \{Q\} \iff \forall M.M \models P \land \bar{x} \subseteq M \Rightarrow M[A(\bar{x})/\bar{x}] \models Q$$

This will be used in the rule for reasoning about the basic rewrite construct (R, A).

$$\frac{\{P\}\, A(\bar{x})/\bar{x}\, \{P\}}{(R,A)\ \textbf{sat}\ \mu\theta. \left[\begin{array}{c} \{P \land \exists \bar{y}.\bar{y} = \bar{x} \land R(\bar{x})\} A(\bar{x})/\bar{x} \{P \land \exists \bar{y}.\bar{y} = A(\bar{x})\}\theta \\ \land\ \{P \land \forall \bar{x}.\neg R(\bar{x})\}\bullet \end{array} \right]}$$

$$\frac{C\ \textbf{sat}\ \phi \qquad C\ \textbf{sat}\ \psi}{C\ \textbf{sat}\ \phi \land \psi} \qquad \frac{C\ \textbf{sat}\ \phi \qquad \phi \Rightarrow \psi}{C\ \textbf{sat}\ \psi}$$

$$\frac{C_1\ \textbf{sat}\ \phi \qquad C_2\ \textbf{sat}\ \psi}{C_1 + C_2\ \textbf{sat}\ \phi\|\psi} \qquad \frac{C_1\ \textbf{sat}\ \phi \qquad C_2\ \textbf{sat}\ \psi}{C_1 \circ C_2\ \textbf{sat}\ \psi;\phi}$$

The soundness of the first axiom follows from the operational semantics. Soundness of the rules for parallel and sequential composition follows from theorems 1 and 2 respectively.

Example 1 Consider the following Gamma rules:

$$\begin{aligned} C_1 &= \langle x \rangle \to \langle x-1, x-2 \rangle \Leftarrow x > 1 \\ C_2 &= \langle x \rangle \to \langle 1 \rangle \Leftarrow x = 0 \\ C_3 &= \langle x, y \rangle \to \langle x+y \rangle \end{aligned}$$

The program $C = C_3 \circ (C_2 + C_1)$ applied to a multiset consisting of a single natural number n_0 will halt with a multiset containing a single value which is the n_0'th Fibonacci number (where $f_0 = 1$). To prove this we assert without proof that

1. $P_1 = \{\sum_{m \in M} fib(m) = fib(n_0)\}$ is an invariant for C_1 and C_2.
2. $P_2 = \{\sum_{m \in M} m = fib(n_0)\}$ is an invariant for C_3.

When writing predicates on multisets associated with a program (R, A), we will use the notation $\exists R(\bar{x})$ to mean $\exists \bar{y} . \bar{y} = \bar{x} \land R(\bar{x})$ where $\bar{x}$ is the tuple of variables in (R, A). Using this notation and the axiom in the proof system we assert that C_1 **sat** ϕ_1, C_2 **sat** ϕ_2 and C_3 **sat** ϕ_3 where

$$\phi_1 = \mu\theta_1.\begin{bmatrix} \{P_1 \wedge \exists x > 1\}\langle x-1, x-2\rangle/\langle x\rangle \left\{ \begin{array}{l} P_1 \wedge \exists u, v \ . \\ u = x-1 \\ \wedge \ v = x-2 \end{array} \right\}\theta_1 \\ \wedge \ \{P_1 \wedge \forall x \leq 1\}\bullet \end{bmatrix}$$

$$\phi_2 = \mu\theta_2.\begin{bmatrix} \{P_1 \wedge \exists x = 0\}\langle 1\rangle/\langle 0\rangle\{P_1 \wedge \exists u.u = 1\}\theta_2 \\ \wedge \ \{P_1 \wedge \forall x \neq 0\}\bullet \end{bmatrix}$$

$$\phi_3 = \mu\theta_3.\begin{bmatrix} \{P_2 \wedge \exists\langle x, y\rangle\}\langle x+y\rangle/\langle x, y\rangle\{P_2 \wedge \exists u.u = x+y\}\theta_3 \\ \wedge \ \{P_2 \wedge \neg\exists\langle x, y\rangle\}\bullet \end{bmatrix}$$

From the proof system we have C sat $(\phi_1\|\phi_2); \phi_3$ First we calculate $\phi_1\|\phi_2$ but weaken the post-condition of every transition to include only the respective invariants.

$$\phi_1\|\phi_2 =$$

$$\mu\theta.\begin{bmatrix} \{P_1 \wedge \exists x > 1 \wedge \exists x = 0\} \left(\begin{array}{l} \langle x-1, x-2\rangle/\langle x\rangle\{P_1\}\theta \\ + \ \langle 1\rangle/\langle 0\rangle\{P_1\}\theta \end{array} \right) \\ \wedge \ \{P_1 \wedge \exists x > 1 \wedge \forall x \neq 0\}\langle x-1, x-2\rangle/\langle x\rangle\{P_1\}\theta \\ \wedge \ \{P_1 \wedge \exists x = 0 \wedge \forall x \leq 1\}\langle 1\rangle/\langle 0\rangle\{P_1\}\theta \\ \wedge \ \{P_1 \wedge \forall x \leq 1 \wedge \forall x \neq 0\}\bullet \end{bmatrix}$$

To obtain the transition assertion for the entire program C, we use the fixpoint and conjunction expansion rules defined for sequential composition.

C sat

$$\mu\theta.\begin{bmatrix} \{P_1 \wedge \exists x > 1 \wedge \exists x = 0\} \left(\begin{array}{l} \langle x-1, x-2\rangle/\langle x\rangle\{P_1\}\theta \\ + \ \langle 1\rangle/\langle 0\rangle\{P_1\}\theta \end{array} \right) \\ \wedge \ \{P_1 \wedge \exists x > 1 \wedge \forall x \neq 0\}\langle x-1, x-2\rangle/\langle x\rangle\{P_1\}\theta \\ \wedge \ \{P_1 \wedge \exists x = 0 \wedge \forall x \leq 1\}\langle 1\rangle/\langle 0\rangle\{P_1\}\theta \\ \wedge \ \{P_1 \wedge P_2 \wedge \forall x = 1 \wedge \exists\langle x, y\rangle\}\langle x+y\rangle/\langle x, y\rangle\{P_2\} \\ \mu\theta_3.\begin{bmatrix} \{P_2 \wedge \exists\langle x, y\rangle\}\langle x+y\rangle/\langle x, y\rangle\{P_2\}\theta_3 \\ \wedge \ \{P_2 \wedge \neg\exists\langle x, y\rangle\}\bullet \end{bmatrix} \\ \wedge \ \{P_1 \wedge P_2 \wedge \forall x = 1 \wedge \neg\exists\langle x, y\rangle\}\bullet \end{bmatrix}$$

Inspection of the above assertion shows that for the Fibonnaci program to terminate, the final multiset must satisfy either $\{P_2 \wedge \neg\exists\langle x, y\rangle\}$ or $\{P_1 \wedge P_2 \wedge \forall x = 1 \wedge \neg\exists\langle x, y\rangle\}$. The latter implies the former so on termination we will always have $\{P_2 \wedge \neg\exists\langle x, y\rangle\}$ which means that the final multiset must be a singleton $\{p_0\}$ satisfying $\sum_{m \in M} m = fib(n_0)$ i.e. p_0 is the n_0th Fibonnaci number.

5 Conclusion

In this paper we have taken the first steps towards a formal system for reasoning about Gamma programs. Our approach is based on a language of transition assertions originally conceived by Brookes. This language enables us to reason about interleaving of computations in a compositional manner. The developments presented here suggests that the approach is viable but a number of issues require further examination before a definite conclusion can be reached.

♦ Transition assertions tend to become large and impractical for hand manipulation. This is not surprising since they in a sense characterise all possible executions. Moreover, often we are interested only in some part of the information conveyed by a transition assertion, *e.g.* the input-output behaviour of the program. Some clear-cut principles for extracting particular information must be designed.

♦ Reasoning multiset substitutions must be formalised. This issue raises the question of which properties of multisets are needed in order to get a working logic.

♦ We are still far away from a mechanisation of the Gamma logic. However, initial experiments with the logic seems to indicate that techniques from the abstract interpretation could be applicable here.

♦ Finally, we intend to investigate the relationship between the axiomatic semantics presented here and the denotational semantics for Gamma defined by Sands [11, 10]. Sands' definition is based on *transition-trace sets* which, like transition assertions, are a formalism introduced by Brookes [6]. We suspect that transition-trace sets may provide a model for transition assertions although, as defined by Brookes, they do not provide a satisfactory model for termination.

Acknowledgements

The authors are grateful to Simon Gay and David Sands for their comments on an earlier draft of this paper.

References

[1] Jean-Pierre Banâtre and Daniel Le Métayer. The Gamma model and its discipline of programming. *Science of Computer Programming*, 15:55–77, 1990.

[2] Jean-Pierre Banâtre and Daniel Le Métayer. Programming by multiset transformation. *Communications of the ACM*, 36(1), January 1993.

[3] S.D. Brookes. A fully abstract semantics and proof system for an ALGOL-like language with sharing. In A. Melton, editor, *Prooceedings of the First International Conference on Mathematical Foundations of Programming Semantics*. Springer-Verlag, LNCS 239, 1985.

[4] S.D. Brookes. A semantically based proof system for partial correctness and deadlock in CSP. In *Proceedings of the IEEE Symposium on Logic in Computer Science*, pages 58–65. IEEE Computer Society Press, 1986.

[5] S.D. Brookes. An axiomatic treatment of partial correctness and deadlock in a shared variable parallel language. Technical Report CMU-CS-92-154, School of Computer Science, Carnegie Mellon University, June 1992.

[6] S.D. Brookes. Full abstraction for a shared variable parallel language. In *Logic in Computer Science*, July 1993.

[7] Patrick Cousot. Methods and Logics for Proving Programs. In Jan van Leeuwen, editor, *Handbook of Theoretical Computer Science*. Elsevier Science Publishers, 1990.

[8] David Gries. *The Science of Programming*. Springer Verlag, 1981.

[9] Chris Hankin, Daniel Le Métayer, and David Sands. A calculus of Gamma programs. Technical Report 1758, INRIA, October 1992.

[10] David Sands. Laws of parallel synchronised termination. In this volume.

[11] David Sands. A compositional semantics of combining forms for Gamma programs. In *International Conference on Formal Methods in Programming and Their Applications*. Springer-Verlag, 1993.

Generalising Interpretations Between Theories in the Context of (π-)institutions

José Luis Fiadeiro

llf@inesc.pt

INESC—Logic Engineering Group
Apartado 10105, 1017 Lisboa Codex,
Portugal

Tom Maibaum

tsem@doc.ic.ac.uk

Department of Computing, Imperial College
180 Queen's Gate, London SW7 2BZ, United Kingdom

Abstract

The structural property of π-institutions which requires consequence to be preserved under changes of language is weakened. The proposed weakly structural π-institutions encompass logics in which consequence does depend on the choice of non-logical symbols by associating locality conditions with signatures or signature morphisms. They also enable new logics to be defined by reusing existing ones, extending and adapting them in order to build formalisms that better fit the applications whose specification they are intended to support.

1 Introduction

Logic engineering is an activity in which logics are created and transformed in order to provide the formal framework that best serves specification and verification of a certain class of systems [11]. The theory of institutions [9] is one of the major contributions to this discipline. Together with subsequent work by many authors e.g. [13, 7, 14, 15, 17] it has provided a formal basis for making much of the work carried out in Computer Science independent of the specific logic that happens to be used. Hence, for instance, although ADT specification originated in equational logic, many of the results developed in that particular framework generalise to logics that satisfy some structural conditions.

Institutions characterise logics via a notion of signature (capturing the alphabet of non-logical symbols) and, for every signature, of the language generated for that signature, of the models that are admissible for that signature and of the satisfaction relation between models and formulae of the language for the signature. The basic structural condition of institutions is the satisfaction condition—truth (satisfaction) is invariant under language translation (morphisms). If, instead, we characterise a logic on the basis of its under-lying consequence relation, the corresponding requirement, as formalised in π-institutions [7], is that consequence should be preserved by language trans-lation, i.e. given a language translation σ for formulae over a signature Σ into formulae over a signature Σ', for every Γ and A such that $\Gamma \vdash_\Sigma A$ we should still have $\sigma(\Gamma) \vdash_{\Sigma'} \sigma(A)$. In other words, π-institutions (and institutions) formalise logics in which consequence is independent of any specific choice of non-logical symbols (signature). This property is sometimes called substitutivity in propo-sitional logic.

While experience has shown that many logics of interest in Computing Sci-ence do satisfy this structural property and, hence, constitute (π-)institutions, experience has also shown that many other equally interesting (or, perhaps, even more interesting) logics fail to satisfy it. That is to say, there are log-ics in which the consequence relation does depend on the choice of non-logical symbols. For instance, notions of consequence that rely on the closed world as-sumption or on circumscription mechanisms are not structural in this sense: if through extensions of (non-logical) language we extend the domain over which we are reasoning then these extensions may invalidate inferences that were made on the assumption of a closed domain.

Another example can be given in terms of recent proposals of logics for object-oriented specification [5]: the notion of encapsulation in object-orien-tation provides a mechanism for localising change by fixing the actions that have access to each attribute. Inferences on the properties of an object on the assumption of encapsulation can be invalidated if the language of actions for that object is extended without ensuring that the locality/encapsulation of the attributes is preserved. A similar situation arises in the formalisation of superposition as a mechanism for extending parallel programs [6, 8]: for making sure that an extension of a program preserves all the properties of the original program, we have to prove that the new actions do not interfere with the variables of the original program.

Even many-sorted first-order logic with the notion of interpretation intro-duced in [4] and used in [20] fails to satisfy the structural condition of (π-)institutions: by allowing sorts in a language to be mapped to subsorts of an-other language we have to prove that this mapping satisfies certain properties before we can prove that such translations are theorem preserving. Whereas, because they fail to satisfy these structural properties, these logics do not con-stitute (π-)institutions, they are nonetheless "structural enough" to satisfy some of the properties that have made (π-)institutions so useful in specifica-tion theory, namely the ability to "put theories together to make specifications" [2].

The examples above show that this class of "weakly-structural" logics con-tains at least two examples that have proved to be useful in specification. More generally, we aim at giving further support to one of the most typical tasks of the "logic engineer": to extend and adapt existing logics in order to build a formalism that better fits the nature of the applications whose specification the formalism is intended to support. For instance, this process of adaptation consists, sometimes, in picking up a well known logic (e.g. temporal logic) but restricted to a class of models that are characteristic of the paradigm we wish to support (e.g. encapsulation for object-oriented systems). At other times, we wish to extend the logic with features that it did not have before, e.g. sub-sorts in first-order logic.

The purpose of this paper is to show how the theory of (π-)institutions can be extended in order to encompass a class of logics whose underlying notion of consequence depends on the non-logical language (signatures). In other words, we show how signatures can be given a logical role in localising consequence and thereby provide generalisations to many useful logics of the concept of interpretations between theories. In section 2, we recall the notions of π-institution, institution, and theory and interpretation between theories. In section 3, we motivate the weakening of the structural condition by means of two of the above mentioned examples: first-order logic with sub-sorts and the temporal logic of objects. Finally, in section 4, we define weakly structural π-institutions and show how cocompleteness of the category of theory presentations can be obtained under weak structural conditions.

2 Background

In this section, we recall the basic definitions of π-institutions and institutions. Most of the material is adapted from [7] to which readers should refer for a more detailed account and related material.

2.1 π-institutions

We start by recalling the notion of π-institution adapting from [7][1]:

2.1.1 π-institutions

A π-institution is a triple $(Sig, Gram, \vdash)$ where:

♦ *Sig* is a category (of signatures)

♦ $Gram : Sig \to Set$ (grammar)

♦ $\vdash$ is a $|Sig|$-indexed family of consequence relations, each of which is a relation in $\wp(Gram(\Sigma)) \times Gram(\Sigma)$ such that for every $A \in Gram(\Sigma)$ and $\Gamma, \Delta \in \wp(Gram(\Sigma))$,
  reflexivity $\Gamma \vdash_\Sigma A$ if $A \in \Gamma$
  cut if $\Gamma, \Delta \vdash_\Sigma A$ and $\Gamma \vdash_\Sigma B$ for every $B \in \Delta$, then $\Gamma \vdash_\Sigma A$
  monotonicity if $\Gamma \vdash_\Sigma A$ then $\Gamma, \Delta \vdash_\Sigma A$
  structurality for every $\sigma : \Sigma \to \Sigma'$, if $\Gamma \vdash_\Sigma A$ then $Gram(\sigma)(\Gamma) \vdash_{\Sigma'} Gram(\sigma)(A)$ □

The notion of signature is similar to the notion of *similarity type* that has been used in some definitions of logic e.g. [10]. It formalises the notion of alphabet of the logic, introducing the different categories of non-logical symbols. Morphisms between signatures are just mappings between symbols in the different signatures such that the respective categories are respected (e.g., in first-order logic, a function symbol must be mapped to another function symbol, and not, say, to a predicate symbol). On the other hand, the functor $Gram$ acts as the grammar of the logic: it provides for each signature the set of the well formed formulae that can be built using the symbols given by that signature. The fact

---

[1] The original definition of π-institutions in [7] was based on consequence (closure) operators as in [18].

that $Gram$ is a functor just says that morphisms between signatures are reflected as translations between the languages generated from those signatures.

The properties required on $\vdash$ are typical of consequence relations except, perhaps, for structurality. This property is, sometimes, formulated as "substitutivity" e.g. [16] characterising the fact that consequence is independent of the specific choice of non-logical symbols (signature). Hence, the fact that we substitute (through σ) non-logical symbols by other non-logical symbols should not affect consequence. It is precisely this condition that we shall weaken in the next section.

There are many ways of defining consequence. We can define it via an axiomatic system in the style of Hilbert. Or we might prefer a sequent calculus style of definition. We could also approach it model-theoretically by providing a notion of model for a signature and of truth of a sentence in a model. π-institutions are agnostic with respect to the style of presentation. It is however important to mention that model-theoretic accounts of general definitions of logic have preceded and, indeed, inspired π-institutions. We would thus like to recall the notion of institution as proposed by Goguen and Burstall [9] and which has been at the heart of a wealth of algebraic techniques in specification theory:

2.1.2 Institutions

An institution is a quadruple $(Sig, Gram, Sem, \vDash)$ where:

- Sig is a category (the category of signatures)
- $Gram$ is a functor from Sig into Set (the grammar functor)
- Sem is a functor from Sig into Set^{op} (the semantic functor) [2]
- $\vDash$ is a $|Sig|$-indexed family of relations, such that each $\vDash_\Sigma$ is a subset of $|Sem(\Sigma)| \times Gram(\Sigma)$ (the satisfaction relation for Σ), fulfilling the following condition (known as the satisfaction condition): for every $\sigma : \Sigma \to \Sigma'$ in Sig, A in $Gram(\Sigma)$, m in $|Sem(\Sigma')|$, $m' \vDash_{\Sigma'} Gram(\sigma)(A)$ iff $Sem(\sigma)(m') \vDash_\Sigma A$.

We usually write $m'|_\sigma$ instead of $Sem(\sigma)(m')$. $\qquad\qquad\qquad\square$

We can now define a consequence relation as follows: for every $A \in Gram(\Sigma)$, $\Gamma \in \wp(Gram(\Sigma))$, $\sigma : \Sigma \to \Sigma'$, $\Gamma \vdash_\Sigma A$ iff, for every $m \in Sem(\Sigma)$, $m \vDash_\Sigma A$ if $m \vDash_\Sigma B$ for every $B \in \Gamma$.

It is easy to see that this consequence relation satisfies the required properties including structurality (which is given by the satisfaction condition).

2.1.3 π-institution induced by an institution

Let $(Sig, Gram, Sem, \vDash)$ be an institution. Defining $\vdash$ as above, the induced π-institution is $(Sig, Gram, \vdash)$.

We can also provide proof-theoretic definitions of π-institutions, namely in a Hilbert-style presentation.

---

[2]Institutions use Cat^{op} instead of Set^{op}, i.e. they work with morphisms of models as well. We shall take this simplified view in the paper because we shall not need to deal with morphisms of models.

2.1.4   π-institutions Hilbert-style

A Hilbert-style presentation of a π-institution consists of a triple $(Sig, Gram, \Vdash)$ where :

+ Sig is a category (as before)
+ $Gram : Sig \to Set$ is a functor (as before)
+ $\Vdash$ is a $|Sig|$-indexed family of relations over $2^{Gram(\Sigma)} \times Gram(\Sigma)$ satisfying the following property:

> for every $\sigma : \Sigma \to \Sigma'$ in Sig, $A \in Gram(\Sigma), \Gamma \subseteq Gram(\Sigma)$
> if $\Gamma \Vdash_\Sigma A$ then $Gram(\sigma)(\Gamma) \vdash_{\Sigma'} Gram(\sigma)(A)$

where $\Gamma \vdash_\Sigma A$ iff there is a *proof* of A from Γ, i.e. iff there is a sequence $A_1, \ldots, A_n$ of σ-formulae such that (1) A_n is A, (2) for every $1 \leq i \leq n$, either $A_i \in \Gamma$ or there are $1 \leq i_1 \leq \ldots \leq i_m \leq i-1$ such that $\{A_{i_1}, \ldots, A_{i_m}\} \Vdash_\Sigma A_i$.   □

The relation $\Vdash_\Sigma$ intends to capture the notion of axiom and inference rule for the language defined over Σ. Axioms correspond to the formulae A for which $\varnothing \Vdash_\Sigma A$ holds. The other pairs define the inference rules.

2.1.5   π-institution presented in a Hilbert-style

Given a Hilbert-style presentation $(Sig, Gram, \Vdash)$, the presented π-institution is $(Sig, Gram, \vdash)$ where $\vdash$ is defined as above through the notion of proof.   □

Hence, structurality has an intuitive proof-theoretic interpretation. It means that if in the middle of a proof we need to extend or rename the non-logical symbols that we have been using, we can do so without invalidating any of the previous steps. In other words, there is a canonical way of translating proofs under a signature along a signature morphism which does not require any additional intervention. We shall see that the proposed weakening of structurality will exactly require such an intervention in the form of additional proofs referring to the good behaviour of the morphism.

2.2   Theories and interpretations between theories

The notion of theory is central to specification [21]. Theories and theory morphisms have been defined in π-institutions as follows [7]:

2.2.1   Theories and interpretations between theories

A *theory* is a pair (Σ, Γ) where Γ is a subset of $Gram(\Sigma)$ closed under $\vdash_\Sigma$ (i.e. that contains all its consequences). A *morphism of theories* (interpretation between theories) $\sigma : (\Sigma, \Gamma) \to (\Sigma', \Gamma')$ is a signature morphism (language translation) such that $\sigma(\Gamma) \subseteq \Gamma'$ (i.e., such that every theorem of the source is translated to a theorem of the target theory).   □

From the point of view of establishing building blocks for building complex specifications, theories are not very convenient because they contain too much information: they are closed under consequence. It is much easier to manipulate presentations of theories in which just the (non-logical) axioms of the theory are represented.

2.2.2 Theory presentations

A theory presentation is a pair (Σ, Γ) where Σ is a signature and Γ a set of Σ-formulae. Morphisms of theory presentations $\sigma : (\Sigma, \Gamma) \to (\Sigma', \Gamma')$ are signature morphisms that translate the axioms of the first presentation to theorems of the second, i.e. such that $\Gamma' \vdash_{\Sigma'} \sigma(A)$ for every $A \in \Gamma$. $\qquad\square$

It is easy to prove

2.2.3 Presentation lemma

Morphisms of theory presentations induce interpretations between the presented theories, i.e. every theorem of (Σ, Γ) is translated to a theorem of (Σ', Γ'). $\qquad\square$

That is, we define a presentation functor that maps theory presentations to the presented theories.

One of the major tools for "putting theories together to make specifications" [2] is pushouts of theory presentations. Indeed, the ability to compute amalgamated sums of theory presentations is at the basis of, for instance, simple union of specifications, parameter instantiation, composition of implementation steps, parallel composition of systems, etc. In a π-institution, the category $\mathcal{P}res$ of theory presentations satisfies the following property:

2.2.4 Proposition

If $\mathcal{S}ig$ is finitely co-complete so is $\mathcal{P}res$. The initial theory presentation is (isomorphic to) $(\Sigma^\circ, \varnothing)$ where Σ° is the initial signature.

A pushout of

$$(\Sigma_1, \Gamma_1) \xleftarrow{\ \sigma_1\ } (\Sigma_0, \Gamma_0) \xrightarrow{\ \sigma_2\ } (\Sigma_2, \Gamma_2)$$

is given by

$$
\begin{array}{ccc}
(\Sigma_1, \Gamma_1) & \overset{\mu_1}{\cdots\!\rightarrow} & (\Sigma^\$, \Gamma^\$) \\
\sigma_1 \uparrow & & \uparrow \vdots \; \mu_2 \\
(\Sigma, \Gamma) & \xrightarrow[\sigma_2]{} & (\Sigma_2, \Gamma_2)
\end{array}
$$

where

$$\Sigma_1 \xrightarrow{\ \mu_1\ } \Sigma^\$ \xleftarrow{\ \mu_2\ } \Sigma_2$$

is a pushout of

$$\Sigma_1 \xleftarrow{\ \sigma_1\ } \Sigma_0 \xrightarrow{\ \sigma_2\ } \Sigma_2$$

in $\mathcal{S}ig$ and $\Gamma^\$ = \mu_1(\Gamma_1) \cup \mu_2(\Gamma_2)$. That is, we take the translations of the axioms of the components as axioms of the colimit. $\qquad\square$

3 Localising consequence: motivation

As illustration of the notion of π-institution and motivation for the weakening of structurality we shall analyse two examples.

3.1 Many-sorted first-order logic with sub-sorts

We start with the definition of a many-sorted first-order institution that is structural and then introduce sub-sorts.

3.1.1 Signatures

A many-sorted first-order signature is a triple (S, F, P) where S is a finite set (of sort symbols), F is an $S^* \times S$-indexed family of sets (of function symbols) and P is an S^*-indexed family of sets (of predicate symbols). All these sets are assumed to be finite and mutually disjoint. A signature morphism μ from a signature (S, F, P) to a signature (S', F', P') maps: S to S', F_{us} to $F'_{\mu(u)\mu(s)}$, P_u to $P'_{\mu(u)}$.

3.1.2 Grammar functor

The language generated from a signature is defined as usual. Assuming a fixed set ξ of variables we define, inductively, for each classification $\Xi : \xi \to S$, the S-indexed family of sets $\mathrm{TERM}_\Sigma(\Xi)$:

♦ $\Xi_s \subseteq \mathrm{TERM}(\Xi)_s$

♦ for every $f \in F_{us}$ and $\langle t_1, \ldots, t_n \rangle \in \mathrm{TERM}(\Xi)_u$, $f(t_1, \ldots, t_n) \in \mathrm{TERM}(\Xi)_s$

The language $\mathrm{FORM}_\Sigma(\Xi)$ of formulae over Ξ is also defined inductively as follows:

♦ $\bot, \top \in \mathrm{FORM}_\Sigma(\Xi)$

♦ given $p \in P_u$ and $t_i \in \mathrm{TERM}_\Sigma(\Xi)_{s_i}$ for $u = \langle s_1, \ldots, s_n \rangle$, $p(t_1, \ldots, t_n) \in \mathrm{FORM}_\Sigma(\Xi)$

♦ given $A, B \in \mathrm{FORM}_\Sigma(\Xi)$, $(\neg A), (A \supset B), (A \wedge B), (A \vee B) \in \mathrm{FORM}_\Sigma(\Xi)$

♦ given $A \in \mathrm{FORM}_\Sigma(\Xi)$ and $x \in \Xi_s$, $(\forall x : s)A, (\exists x : s)A \in \mathrm{FORM}_\Sigma(\Xi \setminus \{x : s\})$

The language translation induced by a signature morphism is defined as follows:

♦ every classification Ξ is translated into $\Xi; \sigma$, i.e. the translation of $x : s$ is $x : \sigma(s)$

♦ the translation $\sigma(t)$ of a term t is defined inductively

♦ the translation $\sigma(A)$ of a formula A is defined inductively, with σ 'commuting' with all logical connectives.

3.1.3 Model functor

Given a signature $\Sigma = (S, F, P)$ a Σ-model M maps:

♦ every sort $s \in S$ to a set s_M

♦ every $f : s_1, \ldots, s_n \to s$ to a function $f_M : s_{1_M}, \ldots, s_{n_M} \to s_M$

♦ every $p : s_1, \ldots, s_n$ to a relation p_M in $s_{1_M} \times \ldots \times s_{n_M}$.

Given a signature morphism $\sigma : \Sigma \to \Sigma'$ and a Σ'-model M', the σ-reduct of M', $M' \mid_\sigma$, is the Σ-model defined as follows: $s_{M' \mid_\sigma} = \sigma(s)_{M'}$, $f_{M' \mid_\sigma} = \sigma(f)_{M'}$, $p_{M' \mid_\sigma} = \sigma(p)_{M'}$.

3.1.4 Satisfaction relation

Given a Σ-model M and a classification Ξ, a valuation for Ξ is an S-indexed family of functions $V_s : \Xi_s \to s_M$. Such a valuation has a canonical extension to $\mathrm{TERM}_\Sigma(\Xi)_s$ as follows: $V(f(t_1, \ldots, t_n)) = f_M(V(t_1), \ldots, V(t_n))$. A formula A of $\mathrm{FORM}_\Sigma(\Xi)$ is satisfied in a Σ-model M by a valuation V iff:

♦ $M, V \vDash_\Sigma p(t_1, \ldots, t_n)$ iff $(V(t_1), \ldots, V(t_n)) \in p_M$

♦ first-order connectives: as usual.

Given a Σ-formula A and a Σ-model M, $M \vDash_\Sigma A$ iff $M, V \vDash_\Sigma A$ for every valuation V.

3.1.5 Proposition

The above defines an institution. □

As seen in 2.3, we also obtain a π-institution by taking the consequence relation induced by the satisfaction relation. For this consequence relation we do have the structural property: given a signature morphism $\mu : \Sigma \to \Sigma'$, a Σ-formula A and a collection of Σ-formulae Γ, $\Gamma \vdash_\Sigma A$ implies $\mu(\Gamma) \vdash_{\Sigma'} \mu(A)$.

Let us now consider a generalisation of the notion of signature morphism. As defined above, signature morphisms require us to map sorts of the source signature to sorts of the target signature. However, we would now like, as in [4, 19], to map sorts of the source signature to sub-sorts of the target signature. For instance, we would like to interpret the natural numbers in the integers by mapping the sort *nat* to the subsort of *int* defined by the non-negative integers. For this purpose, we need a way of representing subsorts. We shall do so via predicates. In fact, in order to cater for composition, we shall represent a subsort of a sort s through a finite set of predicates over s. Intuitively, the domain for such a subsort will consist of all the elements of the sort which satisfy each predicate in the set. Hence, first of all, we have to change the notion of signature morphism.

3.1.6 Signature morphisms revisited

A signature morphism μ from a signature (S, F, P) to a signature (S', F', P') maps every sort s to a pair $\mu(s) = (s', \rho)$, where $s \in S'$ and $\rho \subseteq P'_{s'}$, with F_{us} and P_u translated as before.

The predicates in ρ are called the relativisation predicates associated with s. As mentioned above, the reason we work with sets of predicates has to do with composition of morphisms: if $\mu(s) = (s', \rho)$ and $\sigma(s') = (s'', \rho')$ then $(\mu; \sigma)(s) = (s'', \sigma(\rho) \cup \rho')$. The identity morphism maps each sort s to $(s, \varnothing)$.

Clearly, the grammar function also has to be changed. Indeed, properties asserted on a sort have now to be translated into properties over the corresponding subsort. This implies that quantifiers be relativised to the subsorts:

♦ if $\mu(s) = (s', \rho)$ and $\rho \neq \varnothing$, then

$\mu((\forall x : s)A)$ is $(\forall x : s')(\rho(x) \supset \mu(A))$

$\mu((\exists x : s)A)$ is $(\exists x : s')(\rho(x) \wedge \mu(A))$

where $\rho(x)$ denotes the conjunction $p_1(x) \wedge \ldots \wedge p_n(x)$ for $\rho = \{p_1, \ldots, p_n\}$, which we call the *relativisation predicate* for s

♦ if $\mu(s) = (s', \varnothing)$ then $\mu((\forall x : s)A)$ is $(\forall x : s')\mu(A)$, and $\mu((\exists x : s)A)$ is $(\exists x : s')\mu(A)$.

Likewise, the model functor has to be revised: given a signature morphism $\sigma : \Sigma \to \Sigma'$ and a Σ'-model M', if $\sigma(s) = (s', \rho)$ then $s_{M'|_\sigma} = \bigcap_{p \in \rho} p_{M'}$

3.1.7 Weak structurality

It is easy to see why, in this generalised version of first-order logic, we may fail to have structurality. Take a signature Σ that contains a constant c of some sort s and a predicate p of sort s. Let (s', ρ), $c' : s'$ and $p' : s'$ be their images along a signature morphism into a signature Σ'. Then, we have

$$\vdash_\Sigma (\forall x : s)p(x) \supset (\exists x : s)p(x)$$

because the constant c of sort s ensures that the domain associated with s is not empty. However,

$$\vdash_{\Sigma'} (\forall x : s')(\rho(x) \supset p(x)) \supset (\exists x : s')(\rho(x) \wedge p(x))$$

is not valid, i.e. the translation of the axiom above is not an axiom of Σ'. Indeed, we cannot argue in the same way as above because we do not know whether c' satisfies the relativisation predicate. Model-theoretically, it is easy to see why this is so: the modified model functor does not make sure that, for instance, if $c : s$, $c_{M|_\sigma} = \sigma(c)_{M'}$ is an element of the subdomain associated with s. In such cases, the reduct is not even a model for the source signature. Indeed, it is easy to see that only if the domains defined by the relativisation predicates are closed under the operations corresponding to constant and function symbols in the source language, will the reduct of a model of the target signature still be a model for the source signature and the satisfaction condition hold. For instance, we do have in the case above

$$\rho(c') \vdash_{\Sigma'} (\forall x : s')(\rho(x) \supset p(x)) \supset (\exists x : s')(\rho(x) \wedge p(x))$$

That is, the translation of the Σ-theorem holds provided we ensure that the translation of the constant satisfies the relativisation predicate.

More generally, given a signature morphism $\mu : \Sigma \to \Sigma'$, let $loc(\mu)$ be the following set of Σ'-formulae:

♦ for each $c : s$, the sentence $\rho(\mu(c))$ where ρ is the relativisation predicate for s

♦ for each $f : s_1, \ldots s_n \to s$, the sentence

$$(\forall x_1 : s_1') \ldots (\forall x_n : s_n')(\rho_1(x_1) \wedge \ldots \wedge \rho_n(x_n) \supset \rho(\mu(f)(x_1, \ldots, x_n)))$$

where $\mu(s_i) = (s_i', \rho_i)$

with the convention that if $\mu(s) = (s', \varnothing)$, then $\rho(x)$ is the propositional constant $\top$. This set of formulae was adapted from [4, 19]. Those who know these references will see that non-emptiness conditions are missing for the subsorts. The reason is that, herein, we are allowing carrier sorts to be empty.

3.1.8   Proposition

Let $\mu : \Sigma \to \Sigma'$ be a signature morphism and M' a Σ'-model. Then M' satisfies $loc(\mu)$ iff $M'_{|\mu}$ is a Σ-model.

Proof: The satisfaction of the formulae above implies that the domains defined by the relativisation predicates are closed under the operations corresponding to constant and function symbols in the source language.   □

3.1.9   Proposition

Let $\mu : \Sigma \to \Sigma'$ be a signature morphism and M' a Σ'-model. Then, if M' satisfies $loc(\mu)$ the satisfaction condition will hold for M' and any Σ-formula A, i.e. $M' \vDash_{\Sigma'} \mu(A)$ iff $M'_{|\mu} \vDash_{\Sigma} A$.   □

Considering now the consequence relation thus defined:

3.1.10   Proposition

Let $\mu : \Sigma \to \Sigma'$ be a signature morphism, A a Σ-formula and Γ a collection of Σ-formulae. Then $\Gamma \vdash_{\Sigma} A$ implies $\mu(\Gamma), loc(\mu) \vdash_{\Sigma'} \mu(A)$.   □

3.2   Temporal logic of objects

As another example, illustrating another case of weak structurality, we shall use a temporal logic that we have adapted for formalising the notion of object (as in object-oriented specification). This logic is also very close to the temporal logics that have been proposed for reasoning about concurrent systems (e.g. [12]).

We start with a (structural) temporal π-institution.

3.2.1   Temporal signatures

We work with a propositional temporal logic. A temporal signature τ is just a finite set (of propositional symbols). Signature morphisms are total functions. The category of temporal signatures will be denoted by *TempSign*.

3.2.2   Grammar functor

We work with linear temporal logic. Hence, the language TEMP$_\tau$ generated for a signature τ is inductively defined as follows:

♦ $\tau \subseteq$ TEMP$_\tau$

♦ beg $\in$ TEMP$_\tau$

♦ if $A \in$ TEMP$_\tau$ then $(\neg A), (\mathbf{X}A), (\mathbf{G}A) \in$ TEMP$_\tau$

♦ if $A, B \in$ TEMP$_\tau$ then $(A \wedge B), (A \vee B), (A \supset B) \in$ TEMP$_\tau$.

The temporal operators are $\mathbf{X}$ (next) and $\mathbf{G}$ (always in the future). The formula beg denotes the initial state, i.e. it is only satisfied in the initial state. Other operators might have been chosen but these are enough to present our case.

Signature morphisms induce translations as follows:

♦ $\sigma(\text{beg})$ is beg

♦ $\sigma(\neg A)$ is $(\neg\sigma(A))$, $\sigma(\mathbf{X}A)$ is $(\mathbf{X}\sigma(A))$, $\sigma(\mathbf{G}A)$ is $(\mathbf{G}\sigma(A))$

♦ $\sigma(A \wedge B)$ is $(\sigma(A) \wedge \sigma(B))$, $\sigma(A \vee B)$ is $(\sigma(A) \vee \sigma(B))$, $(A \supset B)$ is $(\sigma(A) \supset \sigma(B))$.

We denote by $\mathcal{T}emp\mathcal{G}ram$ the functor defined by this grammar.

3.2.3 Model functor

Models for temporal signatures are linear, discrete, infinite structures with an initial world. A τ-model M is thus a function $\tau \to 2^\omega$ (where ω is the set of natural numbers). That is, $M(p)$ is the set of worlds (instants) in which p holds. The reduct induced by a signature morphism is quite simple: given $\sigma : \tau \to \tau'$ and $M' : \tau' \to 2^\omega$, $M'|_\sigma$ is $(\sigma; M')$. That is, $p \in \tau$ holds exactly at the worlds in which $\sigma(p)$ holds. We denote by $\mathcal{T}emp\mathcal{M}od$ the functor defined in this way.

3.2.4 Satisfaction relation

First, we define satisfaction of a formula at an instant:

♦ $M, i \vDash_\tau p$ iff $i \in M(p)$

♦ $M, i \vDash_\tau$ **beg** iff $i = 0$

♦ $M, i \vDash_\tau \mathbf{X}A$ iff $M, i+1 \vDash_\tau A$

♦ $M, i \vDash_\tau \mathbf{G}A$ iff $M, j \vDash_\tau A$ for every $j \geq i$

♦ propositional connectives: as usual.

A τ-formula A is satisfied by a τ-model M, $M \vDash_\tau A$, iff $M, j \vDash_\tau A$ for every j.

3.2.5 Proposition

Temporal logic as described above constitutes an institution. □

As seen in 2.3, we also obtain a π-institution by taking the consequence relation induced by the satisfaction relation. For this consequence relation we do have the structural property: given a signature morphism $\sigma : \tau \to \tau'$, a τ-formula A and a collection of τ-formulae Γ, $\Gamma \vdash_\tau A$ implies $\sigma(\Gamma) \vdash_{\tau'} \sigma(A)$.

Let us now consider a temporal logic for object-oriented systems. The idea is to have each signature represent the actions and attributes of an object, the models for that signature represent possible behaviours of the object, and the formulae express properties of the behaviour of the object. Because we want to "customise" the logic to this kind of systems, we adapt some of the definitions above in order to make "logical" the underlying principles of object-orientation.

First of all, objects are dynamic entities which have a state that can be changed only through a circumscribed set of actions. Hence, in the signature of an object we shall distinguish between the symbols that account for observations of the state of the object (which we call attribute symbols), and symbols that account for the actions that the object may perform:

3.2.6 Object signatures

An object signature θ is a pair (θ_S, θ_A) of finite and disjoint sets (of attribute and action symbols, respectively). A signature morphism $(\theta_S, \theta_A) \to (\theta'_S, \theta'_A)$ consists of a pair (σ_S, σ_A) of functions $\sigma_S : \theta_S \to \theta'_S, \sigma_A : \theta_A \to \theta'_A$. The category *ObjSign* of object signatures is thus the product category $\mathcal{F}in \times \mathcal{F}in$ where $\mathcal{F}in$ is the category of finite sets.

We also have a forgetful functor $\mathcal{U} : ObjSign \rightarrow TempSign$ that maps each object signature (S, A) to the temporal signature $S \cup A$. Notice that $\sigma_S + \sigma_A$ is well defined for every object signature σ because the sets of attribute and action symbols are disjoint. We define the grammar *ObjGram* and model *ObjMod* functors for objects as the composition of $\mathcal{U}$ with *TempGram* and *TempMod*, respectively.

The difference between attribute and action symbols is needed in order to formalise the encapsulation mechanism: only the actions declared for the object have access to the attributes of the object. This locality principle is made "logical" by restricting the class of models to *loci*.

3.2.7 Loci

A *locus* for an object signature θ is a θ-model M satisfying the following condition. For every i such that, for every $a \in \theta_A$, $i \notin M(a)$, we have for every $s \in \theta_S$ that $i \in M(s)$ iff $(i + 1) \in M(s)$. That is to say, in a locus, whenever none of the actions holds true, i.e. whenever the object remains idle, the attributes remain unchanged. We restrict ourselves to this subclass of models and, thus, the underlying consequence relation becomes $\Gamma \vdash_\tau A$ iff every τ-locus that satisfies all the formulae in Γ also satisfies A.

3.2.8 Weak structurality

It is easy to see why structurality fails. Consider, for instance, the object signature $\theta = (\{s\}, \{a\})$. It is not difficult to prove that

$$(\mathbf{beg} \rightarrow s), (a \wedge s \rightarrow \mathbf{X}s) \vdash_\theta s.$$

Indeed, let M be a θ-locus. The first premiss implies that s holds at $i = 0$. The second implies that whenever a occurs (holds) and s holds, s will hold next. On the other hand, because M is a locus and a is the only action declared in the signature, we know that whenever a does not occur, s stays unchanged. Hence, we can prove by induction that s holds at any i. This is a typical proof for object-based systems. The locality condition is used to circumscribe the actions that may affect the attributes and, thus, we are allowed to infer properties of an object by analysing just the effects of its actions.

Consider now the extension $\theta' = (\{s\}, \{a, b\})$ of θ. That is, assume we extend our object with a new action (a typical situation when using inheritance). Then, we no longer have

$$(\mathbf{beg} \rightarrow s), (a \wedge s \rightarrow \mathbf{X}s) \vdash_{\theta'} s.$$

The reason is that we do not know what b does to s. So, structurality fails for such an extension. However, we are allowed to infer s if we assume that the extension is locality preserving, i.e. if the introduction of the new action does not violate encapsulation by affecting the inherited attributes (this type of extension is called superposition by the parallel and distributed programming community). Indeed, we do have

$$(\mathbf{beg} \rightarrow s), (a \wedge s \rightarrow \mathbf{X}s), (b \rightarrow (a \vee (s \leftrightarrow \mathbf{X}s))) \vdash_{\theta'} s.$$

The third premiss, $(b \rightarrow (a \vee (s \leftrightarrow \mathbf{X}s)))$, requires that either b subsumes a (i.e. b occurs together with a which is plausible in a multiprocessor architecture) or b leaves s unchanged.

More generally, if $\sigma : \theta = (S, A) \rightarrow \theta' = (S', A')$ is an object signature morphism, let

$$loc(\sigma) = \{(b \rightarrow ((\bigvee_{a \in A})\sigma(a)) \vee (\bigwedge_{s \in S} \sigma(s) \leftrightarrow \mathbf{X}\sigma(s)))) \mid b \in A' \setminus \sigma(A)\}$$

3.2.9 Proposition

Let $\sigma : \theta \rightarrow \theta'$ be an object signature morphism, A a θ-formula and Γ a collection of θ-formulae. Then, $\Gamma \vdash_\theta A$ implies $\sigma(\Gamma), loc(\sigma) \vdash_{\theta'} \sigma(A)$. $\qquad$ □

In order to prove this proposition it is worthwhile investigating the reasons for loss of structurality at the model level. As happened with the first-order case, the problem lies with the reduct functor *ObjMod*. More precisely, it may happen that, given an object signature morphism $\sigma : \theta \rightarrow \theta'$, the reduct of a θ'-locus is not a θ-locus. Indeed, this is what was shown above with the extension of $\theta = (\{s\}, \{a\})$ to $\theta' = (\{s\}, \{a, b\})$. The reduct of a θ'-locus in which b, for instance, always sets s to false is not a θ-locus because the θ-object will remain idle during the transitions performed by b and still witness a change on the attributes during these transitions.

However, if a θ'-locus M' does satisfy $loc(\sigma)$, then every transition performed by a θ'-action during which $M'|_\sigma$ is idle, i.e. for which $(\bigvee_{a \in A} \sigma(a))$ is false, will necessarily satisfy $(\bigwedge_{s \in S})\sigma(s) \leftrightarrow \mathbf{X}\sigma(s))$, i.e.$\theta$-attributes will remain invariant as required for a θ-locus.

If $M'|_\sigma$ is a θ-locus then the satisfaction condition holds trivially because it held already for general temporal signatures, thus proving the proposition.

4 Weakly structural π-institutions

4.1 Weakening structurality

The examples given above illustrate how the structural property of π-institutions

for every $\sigma : \Sigma \rightarrow \Sigma'$, if $\Gamma \vdash_\Sigma A$ then $\mathcal{G}ram(\sigma)(\Gamma) \vdash_{\Sigma'} \mathcal{G}ram(\sigma)(A)$

has to be changed to

for every $\sigma : \Sigma \rightarrow \Sigma'$ there is a finite set $loc(\sigma)$ of Σ'-formulae (the *locality axioms for σ*) such that $\Gamma \vdash_\Sigma A$ implies $\mathcal{G}ram(\sigma)(\Gamma), loc(\sigma) \vdash_{\Sigma'} \mathcal{G}ram(\sigma)(A)$

in some logics that are of interest in Computing.

The need for this additional set of formulae reflects the fact that signature morphisms alone are not able to interpret the source signature in the target signature: some properties on the target signature are required which reflect locality conditions associated with the signature morphisms. In other words, signatures are being interpreted in terms of theories (in fact, theory presentations).

We are thus separating two different concerns that, in π-institutions as defined in section 2, are dealt with simultaneously: language translation and implementation of consequence. Indeed, (strong) structurality means that consequence does not need to be catered for under signature morphisms: language translation does it all. Weak structurality shows that, in certain cases, there may be more to the implementation of consequence with respect to one signature than can be conveyed by a simple signature morphism. It shows that consequence implementation may rely on assumptions that are not made logical through a simple language translation. Proof-theoretically, this means that, when in the middle of a proof we want a change of signature, we have some properties to prove before we can proceed without invalidating the previous steps. In other words, we have to prove that we can proceed.

Signatures and signature morphisms are thus given a logical rôle in the sense that they convey some meaning besides structuring the non-logical symbols of the logic into classes. In the case of the temporal object logic, this added value consists of the encapsulation mechanism which gives a logical meaning to the grouping of attribute and action symbols together. In the case of first-order logic with subsorting the use of a theory for interpreting a signature reflects the fact that, as defined, signatures do not accomodate subsorting as a syntactic structure.

Because signature morphisms constitute a monoïd, we have to relate the monoïd operations to the map loc, i.e. we have to say something about $loc(id_\Sigma)$ and $loc(\sigma; \mu)$. Consider first $loc(id_\Sigma)$. Clearly, $\vdash_\Sigma$ should be able to implement itself, i.e. any locality axiom for $loc(id_\Sigma)$ should be logical for Σ: for every $A \in loc(id_\Sigma), \vdash_\Sigma A$.

Consider now $loc(\sigma; \mu)$ for $\sigma : \Sigma \rightarrow \Sigma'$ and $\mu : \Sigma' \rightarrow \Sigma''$. Clearly, locality with respect to $\mu; \sigma$ should be a consequence of locality with respect to σ and to μ. That is, for every $A \in loc(\sigma; \mu), \mu(loc(\sigma)), loc(\mu) \vdash_{\Sigma''} A$.

On the other hand, locality with respect to $\sigma; \mu$ should imply locality with respect to σ: for every $A \in \mu(loc(\sigma))$, $loc(\sigma; \mu) \vdash_{\Sigma''} A$.

Let us prove that both first-order logic with subsorts and the temporal logic of objects satisfy these properties.

4.1.1 First-order logic with subsorts

The identity signature morphisms map each sort s to the pair $(s, \varnothing)$. Hence, the relativisation predicate for each s reduces to $\top$ and each locality axiom is, indeed, a tautology.

Concerning composition, it is easy to prove, first of all, that $\rho_{\sigma;\mu}(t) = \rho_\mu(t) \wedge \mu(\rho_\sigma)(t)$. Consider now a function symbol $f : s \rightarrow s'$. The locality axioms for s that are involved in each set $loc(\sigma; \mu)$, $\mu(loc(\sigma))$ and $loc(\mu)$ are:

$$loc(\sigma; \mu): \quad (\forall x : \mu(\sigma(s)))(\rho_\mu(x) \wedge \mu(\rho_\sigma)(x)$$
$$\supset \rho_\mu(\mu(\sigma(f))(x)) \wedge \mu(\rho_\sigma)(\mu(\sigma(f))(x)))$$

which is equivalent to

$$(\forall x : \mu(\sigma(s)))(\rho_\mu(x) \wedge \mu(\rho_\sigma(x)) \supset \rho_\mu(\mu(\sigma(f))(x)) \wedge \mu(\rho_\sigma(\sigma(f)(x))));$$

$$loc(\mu): \quad (\forall x : \mu(\sigma(s)))(\rho_\mu(x) \supset \rho_\mu(\mu(\sigma(f))(x)))$$

because $\sigma(f) : \sigma(s) \rightarrow \sigma(s')$ in Σ';

$$\mu(loc(\sigma)) : \quad (\forall x : \mu(\sigma(s)))(\rho_\mu(x) \supset (\mu(\rho_\sigma(x)) \supset \mu(\rho_\sigma(\sigma(f)(x)))))$$

which is the translation of $loc(\sigma) : (\forall x : \sigma(s))(\rho_\sigma(x) \supset \rho_\sigma(\sigma(f)(x)))$ and equivalent to

$$(\forall x : \mu(\sigma(s)))(\rho_\mu(x) \wedge \mu(\rho_\sigma(x)) \supset \mu(\rho_\sigma(\sigma(f)(x)))).$$

It is now easy to prove the two properties of the composition.

4.1.2 Temporal logic of objects

There are no locality axioms for the identity morphism which trivially satisfies the requirement. Concerning composition, consider $\sigma : (S, A) \rightarrow (S', A')$, $\mu : (S', A') \rightarrow (S'', A'')$. Each $A \in loc(\sigma; \mu)$ is of the form

$$c \quad \supset \quad ((\bigvee_{a \in A})\mu(\sigma(a))) \vee (\wedge_{s \in S})\mu(\sigma(s)) \leftrightarrow \mathbf{X}\mu(\sigma(s))))$$

for some $c \in A'' \setminus \mu(\sigma(A))$. Assume first that $c \notin \mu(A')$. Then, we have in $loc(\mu)$

$$c \quad \supset \quad ((\bigvee_{b \in A'})\mu(b)) \vee (\bigwedge_{s \in S'})\mu(s) \leftrightarrow \mathbf{X}\mu(s))) \tag{1}$$

Because $\sigma(s) \in S'$ for every $s \in S$, we infer

$$c \quad \supset \quad ((\bigvee_{b \in A'})\mu(b)) \vee \bigwedge_{s \in S})\mu(\sigma(s)) \leftrightarrow \mathbf{X}\mu(\sigma(s))))) \tag{2}$$

Consider now $b \in A'\{\sigma(A)$. Then, from $loc(\mu)$ we have

$$b \quad \supset \quad ((\bigvee_{a \in A})\sigma(a)) \vee (\bigwedge_{s \in S})\sigma(s) \leftrightarrow \mathbf{X}\sigma(s))) \tag{3}$$

which translates to

$$\mu(b) \quad \supset \quad \bigvee_{a \in A})\mu(\sigma(a))) \vee (\bigwedge_{s \in S})\mu(\sigma(s)) \leftrightarrow \mathbf{X}\mu(\sigma(s))))). \tag{4}$$

From (2) and (4) we infer

$$c \quad \supset \quad ((\bigvee_{a \in A})\mu(\sigma(a))) \vee (\bigwedge_{s \in S})\mu(\sigma(s)) \leftrightarrow \mathbf{X}\mu(\sigma(s))))). \tag{5}$$

Consider now the case in which $c = \mu(b)$ for $b \in A' \setminus \sigma(A)$. Then, we are as in (3) above from which we derive (4) and (5). Hence, $\mu(loc(\sigma)), loc(\mu) \vdash_{\theta''} A$ for every $A \in loc(\sigma; \mu)$. The second condition, $loc(\sigma; \mu) \vdash_{\Sigma''} A$ for every $A \in \mu(loc(\sigma))$, is trivial.

4.1.3 Weakly structural π-institutions

A weakly structural π-institution is a triple $(Sig, Gram, loc, \vdash)$ where:

- Sig is a category (of signatures)
- $Gram : Sig \to Set$ (grammar)
- loc maps every $\sigma : \Sigma \to \Sigma'$ to a finite set $loc(\sigma)$ of Σ'-formulae
- $\vdash$ is a $|Sig|$-indexed family of consequence relations, each of which is a relation in $\wp(Gram(\Sigma)) \times Gram(\Sigma)$ such that for every $A \in Gram(\Sigma)$, $\Gamma, \Delta \in \wp(Gram(\Sigma))$,

  reflexivity $\Gamma \vdash_\Sigma A$ if $A \in \Gamma$

  cut if $\Gamma, \Delta \vdash_\Sigma A$ and $\Gamma \vdash_\Sigma B$ for every $B \in \Delta$, then $\Gamma \vdash_\Sigma A$

  monotonicity if $\Gamma \vdash_\Sigma A$ then $\Gamma, \Delta \vdash_\Sigma A$

  structurality for every $\sigma : \Sigma \to \Sigma'$
  - if $\Gamma \vdash_\Sigma A$ then $Gram(\sigma)(\Gamma), loc(\sigma) \vdash_{\Sigma'} Gram(\sigma)(A)$
  - $\vdash_\Sigma A$ for every $A \in loc(id_\Sigma)$
  - $\mu(loc(\sigma)), loc(\mu) \vdash_{\Sigma''} A$ for every $A \in loc(\sigma; \mu)$
  - $loc(\sigma; \mu) \vdash_{\Sigma''} A$ for every $A \in \mu(loc(\sigma))$ □

4.2 Defining weakly structural π-institutions

In the two examples that were chosen in order to illustrate losses of structurality, first-order logic with sub-sorts and a temporal logic of objects, this loss was reflected at the model level in terms of the behaviour of the reduct functor, namely by the fact that taking reducts may not be an operation that is closed for the kind of models we are interested in. There is, however, an important difference between the two cases. In the first-order case, the notion of reduct was not even well defined because it was not defined for all interpretation structures. In the case of the temporal logic of objects, the problem was that we restricted ourselves to a subclass of models for which the reduct functor was not closed. Characterising the subclass through a property which the members of the class have to satisfy, we can place the locality condition itself on the signatures and not on the morphism.

Indeed, it is easy to see that a θ-model is a θ-locus iff it validates $(\bigvee_{a \in A} a) \vee (\bigwedge_{s \in S}(s \leftrightarrow Xs))$. Hence, because temporal logic is a (structural) institution, given a signature morphism $\sigma : \theta \to \theta'$, the reduct of a θ'-model is a θ-locus iff it validates the translation of the formula $(\bigvee_{a \in A} a) \vee (\bigwedge_{s \in S}(s \leftrightarrow Xs))$ i.e., $(\bigvee_{a \in A})\sigma(a)) \vee (\bigwedge_{s \in S}(\sigma(s) \leftrightarrow X\sigma(s)))$.

That is, if we denote the θ-formula $(\bigvee_{a \in A} a) \vee (\bigwedge_{s \in S}(s \leftrightarrow Xs))$ by $loc(\theta)$, we also have that

$$\Gamma \vdash_\theta A \text{ implies } \sigma(\Gamma), \sigma(loc(\theta)) \vdash_{\theta'} \sigma(A).$$

In other words, we might have taken $loc(\sigma)$ to be $\sigma(loc(\theta))$. In fact, $\sigma(loc(\theta))$ and $loc(\sigma)$ are logically equivalent for θ'-loci.

The purpose of this exercise was to illustrate a particular case of weakly structural π-institutions in which we start from a (structural) π-institution and restrict its consequence relation:

4.2.1 Definition by syntactic restriction

Given a π-institution $(Sig, Gram, \vdash)$ and, for each signature Σ, a set $\Phi(\Sigma)$ of Σ-formulae, let $\Vdash_\Sigma$ be defined by $\Gamma \Vdash_\Sigma A$ iff $\Gamma, \Phi(\Sigma) \Vdash_\Sigma A$. Let $loc(id_\Sigma) = \Phi(\Sigma)$ and $loc(\sigma) = \sigma(\Phi(\Sigma))$. Then $(Sig, Gram, loc, \Vdash)$ is a weakly structural π-institution which is said to result from $(Sig, Gram, \vdash)$ by syntactic restriction. *Proof:* The conditions for weak structurality are trivially met because of the equality $loc(\sigma) = \sigma(\Phi(\Sigma))$. $\qquad\square$

4.2.2 Definition by semantic restriction

There is a corresponding semantic way of weakening a π-institution defined by an institution $(Sig, Gram, Sem, \vDash)$, namely by restricting consequence over a signature Σ to a subclass $M(\Sigma)$ of $Sem(\Sigma)$, i.e. by defining $\Gamma \vdash_\Sigma A$ iff every model belonging to $M(\Sigma)$ that satisfies Γ also satisfies A. Indeed, the definition by syntactic restriction that we have just seen corresponds to the case in which $M(\Sigma) = \{m \in Sem(\Sigma) \mid m \vDash \Phi(\Sigma)\}$.

4.2.3 Signature morphisms as formulae

However, in some cases, it may happen that the language is not expressive enough to capture the additional requirements imposed by $M(\Sigma)$ (e.g. restricting ourselves to initial models in the case of equational logic) or, indeed, by the well-definedness of the reduct functor. In this case, it is possible to extend the language of the signature as suggested in [9] by including the signature morphisms themselves as formulae. That is, given signatures Σ and Σ', every morphism $\sigma : \Sigma \to \Sigma'$ becomes itself a Σ'-formula. A Σ'-model m' satisfies σ iff $Sem(\sigma)(m') \in M(\Sigma)$. Translation along a signature morphism is given by composition, i.e. $Gram(\mu)(\sigma)$ is $(\sigma; \mu)$. It is easy to see that this leads us to a weakly structural π-institution in which $loc(\sigma)$ is σ.

There is an example that shows that this technique is not as weird as it seems and that, in fact, it has been used before. Let us define what we call

4.2.4 Substitution Logic

Assume a fixed algebraic signature $\Sigma = (S, \Omega)$ in the sense of [3], i.e. S is a set (of sorts) and Ω is an S-indexed family of finite sets (of operation symbols). Assume also a fixed set ξ of variables. We define a category $Sign(\Sigma)$ as follows: its objects (substitution signatures) are the classifications, i.e. the mappings $\Xi : \xi \to S$. The morphisms $\Xi \to \Psi$ are substitutions $\{t_1/x_1, \ldots, t_n/x_n\}$ where each t_i is a Ψ-term of sort $\Xi(x_i)$. The language over a classification Ξ consists of the equations over Ξ, i.e. pairs (t_1, t_2) of Ξ-terms of the same sort. And, finally, we take the "truth" consequence relation: $A_1, \ldots, A_n \to_\Xi A$ iff every assignment that makes the A_i true also makes A true. Structurality for this π-institution corresponds to a well known inference rule of conditional equational logic: for every substitution $t : \Xi \to \Psi$,

$$(A_1, \ldots, A_n \to_\Xi A) \text{ implies } (A_1(t/x), \ldots, A_n(t/x) \to_\Psi A(t/x)).$$

Assume now that we are working in domains with undefined values so that terms may be partial. In some logics (e.g. [1]) it is usual to restrict the range of variables to defined values. In this case, substitutions are only valid when the terms we are substituting for the variables are defined. Hence,

$$(A_1, \ldots, A_n \rightarrow_\Xi A)$$

no longer necessarily implies $(A_1(t/x), \ldots, A_n(t/x) \rightarrow_\Psi A(t/x))$. Instead, we can only guarantee that

$$(A_1, \ldots, A_n \rightarrow_\Xi A) \text{ implies } (\text{DEF}(t), A_1(t/x), \ldots, A_n(t/x) \rightarrow_\Psi A(t/x))$$

where DEF is a predicate that tests for the definability of terms. Notice how we had to extend the language of the π-institution with a new syntactic category, viz. the predicates DEF, which act as the locality conditions on the morphisms (the terms).

4.3 Theory presentations revisited

We saw in section 2.2 that the presentation lemma, which provides us with a functor from theory presentations to theories, depends on the structurality of the underlying π-institution. Hence, something must change in the definition of morphism of theory presentations for weakly structural π-institutions. Indeed, as defined in 2.2, a morphism of theory presentations assumes that the only thing that has to be "implemented" are the axioms of the source presentation. However, we have seen that in weakly structural π-institutions the signature morphism is not powerful enough to implement the consequence relation: the locality axioms have to be taken into account too. Hence, besides implementing the axioms of the source, a morphism of theory presentations also has to implement the locality axioms:

4.3.1 Presentation morphisms in weakly structural π-institutions

A morphism of presentations $\sigma : (\Sigma, \Gamma) \rightarrow (\Sigma', \Gamma')$ in a weakly structural π-institution is a signature morphism such that

- $\Gamma' \vdash_{\Sigma'} \sigma(A)$ for every $A \in \Gamma$
- $\Gamma' \vdash_{\Sigma'} A$ for every $A \in loc(\sigma)$. $\qquad\square$

We can now prove

4.3.2 Proposition

Let $\sigma : (\Sigma, \Gamma) \rightarrow (\Sigma', \Gamma')$ be a morphism of theory presentations. Then, for every A such that $\Gamma \vdash_\Sigma A$, we have $\Gamma' \vdash_{\Sigma'} \sigma(A)$. That is, morphisms of theory presentations induce interpretations between the presented theories. $\qquad\square$

4.3.3 Co-completeness

Weak structurality also has an impact on colimits of diagrams of theory presentations. Indeed, it is easy to see that it is no longer possible to take just the union of the translations of the component sets of non-logical axioms as axioms of the colimit. In order to make sure that we do obtain locality preserving extensions we also have to take the locality axioms of the components (which are logical for the components to which they belong) as non-logical axioms of the

144

colimit. For instance, a pushout will now be constructed as follows: a pushout of

$$(\Sigma_1, \Gamma_1) \xleftarrow{\sigma_1} (\Sigma_0, \Gamma_0) \xrightarrow{\sigma_2} (\Sigma_2, \Gamma_2)$$

is given by

$$(\Sigma_1, \Gamma_1) \xrightarrow{\mu_1} (\Sigma^\$, \Gamma^\$) \xleftarrow{\mu_2} (\Sigma_2, \Gamma_2)$$

where

$$\Sigma_1 \xrightarrow{\mu_1} \Sigma^\$ \xleftarrow{\mu_2} \Sigma_2$$

is a pushout of

$$\Sigma_1 \xleftarrow{\sigma_1} \Sigma_0 \xrightarrow{\sigma_2} \Sigma_2$$

in *Sign* and $\Gamma^\$ = \mu_1(\Gamma_1) \cup \mu_2(\Gamma_2) \cup loc(\mu_1) \cup loc(\mu_2)$.
Indeed, we have the following result:

4.3.4 Proposition

In a weakly structural π-institution $(Sig, Gram, loc, \vdash)$, if Sig is finitely co-complete then $Pres$ is also finitely co-complete provided the following properties hold:

♦ denoting by Σ^i the initial object of Sig and by $0_\Sigma : \Sigma^i \to \Sigma$ the unique signature morphism from Σ^i to Σ, we require
$$\vdash_\Sigma w \text{ for every } w \in loc(0_\Sigma)$$
That is, the structurality axioms relative to the initial signature must be logical. In the case of first-order logic with sub-sorts and the temporal logic of objects, we have $loc(0_\Sigma) = \emptyset$.

♦ given a pushout diagram

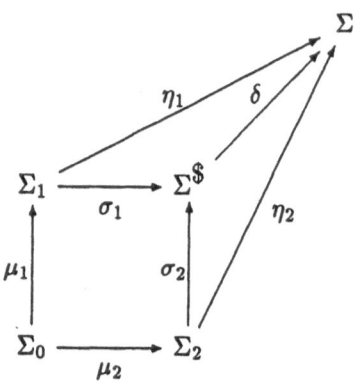

where δ is the unique signature morphism given by the pushout construction, we require

$loc(\eta_1), loc(\eta_2) \vdash_{\Sigma'} w$ for every $w \in loc(\delta)$.

That is, the structural axioms relative to a sum must be derivable from the structural axioms relative to the terms of the sum. In other words, structurality with respect to a sum is a consequence of structurality with respect to the terms of the sum.

In this case, the pushout of

$$(\Sigma_1, \Gamma_1) \xleftarrow{\sigma_1} (\Sigma_0, \Gamma_0) \xrightarrow{\sigma_2} (\Sigma_2, \Gamma_2)$$

is given by

$$(\Sigma_1, \Gamma_1) \xrightarrow{\mu_1} (\Sigma^{\$}, \Gamma^{\$}) \xleftarrow{\mu_2} (\Sigma_2, \Gamma_2)$$

where

$$\Sigma_1 \xrightarrow{\mu_1} \Sigma^{\$} \xleftarrow{\mu_2} \Sigma_2$$

is a pushout of

$$\Sigma_1 \xleftarrow{\sigma_1} \Sigma_0 \xrightarrow{\sigma_2} \Sigma_2$$

in Sig and the resulting set of non-logical axioms is $\Gamma^{\$} = \mu_1(\Gamma_1) \cup \mu_2(\Gamma_2) \cup loc(\mu_1) \cup loc(\mu_2)$. □

It is not difficult to prove that first-order logic with sub-sorts and the temporal logic of objects does satisfy these properties.

4.3.5 Syntactic restriction

In the case of π-institutions weakened by syntactic restriction as defined in 4.2.1 the sufficient condition is to have $\sigma_1(\Phi(\Sigma_1)) \cup \sigma_2(\Phi(\Sigma_2)) \vdash_{\Sigma^{\$}} A$ for every $A \in \Phi(\Sigma^{\$})$. Indeed, we then have

$$
\begin{aligned}
loc(\eta_1) \cup loc(\eta_2) &= \eta_1(\Phi(\Sigma_1)) \cup \eta_2(\Phi(\Sigma_2)) \\
&= \delta(\sigma_1(\Phi(\Sigma_1))) \cup \delta(\sigma_2(\Phi(\Sigma_2)))
\end{aligned}
$$

and

$$\delta(\Phi(\Sigma^{\$})) = loc(\delta).$$

Thus

$$loc(\eta_1) \cup loc(\eta_2) \vdash_{\Sigma^{\$}} loc(\delta).$$

It is easy to see that this is the case for the temporal logic of objects.

4.3.6 Semantic restriction

In the case of π-institutions weakened by semantic restriction as defined in 4.2.2, sufficient conditions are:

♦ $M(\Sigma^i) = Sem(\Sigma^i)$

♦ $M(\Sigma^{\$}) = \{m \in Sem(\Sigma^{\$}) : m \mid_{\sigma_1} \in M(\Sigma_1) em \mid_{\sigma_2} \in M(\Sigma_2)\}$

5 Concluding remarks

In this paper, we extended the theory of (π-)institutions in order to encompass a class of logics which fail to satisfy the structural property that requires consequence to be invariant under language translation, i.e. for which consequence is signature-dependent. The extended notion, which we called weakly structural π-institutions, separates language translation and consequence implementation. The implementation of the consequence relation over a signature along a signature morphism involves a set of non-logical axioms in the language of the target signature that capture locality conditions associated with the source signature. This extension was motivated with two examples: first-order logic with subsorts and a temporal logic of objects.

These two examples illustrate a common activity in "logic engineering": to extend and adapt existing logics in order to build a formalism that better fits the nature of the applications whose specification the formalism is intended to support. For instance, this process of adaptation consists, sometimes, in picking up a well known logic (e.g. temporal logic) but restricted to a class of models that are characteristic of the paradigm we wish to support (e.g. encapsulation for object-oriented systems). Other times, we wish to extend the logic with features that it did not have before, e.g. sub-sorts in first-order logic. The proposed weakly-structural π-institutions support this kind of *reuse* of existing logics.

Theory presentations as building blocks for specification building were also revised under weakning of structurality. The notion of morphism of theory presentations was adapted to the existence of locality conditions that have to be proved in order to obtain interpretations between the presented theories. Sufficient conditions were also given for the category of theory presentations to be finitely cocomplete given the finite cocompleteness of the category of signatures.

References

[1] M. Broy, B. Möller, P. Pepper, and M. Wirsing. Algebraic implementations preserve program correctness. Sci. Comput. Programming 7, 1986.

[2] R. Burstall and J. Goguen, "Putting Theories together to make Specifications", in R. Reddy (ed) *Proc Fifth International Joint Conference on Artificial Intelligence*, 1977, 1045-1058

[3] H. Ehrig and B. Mahr, *Fundamentals of Algebraic Specification 1: Equations and Initial Semantics*, Springer-Verlag 1985

[4] H. B. Enderton, A Mathematical Introduction to Logic, Academic Press 1972

[5] J. Fiadeiro and T. Maibaum, "Temporal Theories as Modularisation Units for Concurrent System Specification", *Formal Aspects of Computing* 4(3), 1992, 239-272

[6] J. Fiadeiro and G. Reichwein, *A Categorial Theory of Superposition*, DMIST/INESC Research Report 1992

[7] J. Fiadeiro and A. Sernadas, "Structuring Theories on Consequence", in D. Sannella and A. Tarlecki (eds)*Recent Trends in Data Type Specification*, LNCS 332, Springer Verlag1988, 44-72

[8] N. Francez and I. Forman, "Superimposition for Interacting Processes", in *CONCUR'90*, LNCS 458, 1990, 230-245

[9] J. Goguen and R. Burstall, "Introducing Institutions", in E. Clarke and D. Kozen (eds) *Proc Logics of Programming Workshop*, LNCS 164, Springer-Verlag 1984, 221-256

[10] W. Hodges, Elementary predicate logic. In D. M. Gabbay and F. Guenthner, editors, *Handbook of Philosophical Logic*, volume 1. Dordrecht: D. Reidel, 1983.

[11] T. Maibaum, "Rôle of Abstraction in Program Development", in H.-J. Kugler (ed) *Information Processing'86*,North-Holland 1986, 135-142

[12] Z. Manna and A. Pnueli, "Verification of Concurrent Programs: The Temporal Framework", in R. Boyer and J. Moore (eds) *The Correctness Problem in Computer Science*, Academic Press 1981, 215-273

[13] B. Mayoh, Galleries and Institutions, Technical report DAIMI PB-191, Aarhus University, 1985.

[14] J. Meseguer, "General Logics", *Proc. Logic Colloquium '87*, eds. H.-D. Ebbinghaus et al, North Holland 1989

[15] A. Poigné, "Foundations are Rich Institutions but Institutions are Poor Foundations", *Proc. Workshop on Categorical Methods in Computer Science*, LNCS 383, Springer-Verlag 1989

[16] M. Ryan and M. Sadler, "Background logic", chapter I.1 of the *Handbook of Logic in Computer Science*, S. Abramsky,D. Gabbay and T. Maibaum (eds), OUP, 1992

[17] D. Sannella and A. Tarlecki, "Building Specifications in an Arbitrary Institution", *Information and Control* 76, 1988, 165-210

[18] A. Tarski, "Fundamentale Begriffe der Methodologie der Deduktiven Wissenschaften", french translation in *Logique,Sémantique, Métamathématique*, vol 1, Armand Colin 1972, 67-116

[19] W. Turski and T. Maibaum, *The Specification of Computer Programs*, Addison-Wesley 1987

[20] P. Veloso and T. Pequeno, "Interpretations between Many-sorted Theories", in *Proc. 2nd Brasilian Colloquium on Logic*, 1978

[21] P. Veloso, T. Maibaum and M. Sadler, "Program Development and Theory Manipulation", *Proc. Third International Workshop on Software Specification and Design*, London, IEEE Computer Society Press

Modelling SIGNAL in Interaction Categories

Simon Gay and Rajagopal Nagarajan

{sjg3,rn4}@doc.ic.ac.uk

Department of Computing, Imperial College
180 Queen's Gate, London SW7 2BZ, United Kingdom

Abstract

Abramsky has recently proposed Interaction Categories as a new paradigm for the semantics of sequential and parallel computation. Working with the category **SProc** of synchronous processes, which is a key example of an Interaction Category, we study synchronous dataflow as part of a programme of gaining experience in the use of Interaction Categories. After making some general points about representing dataflow in **SProc**, we present a detailed model of the synchronous dataflow language SIGNAL. We demonstrate that dataflow is a model of concurrency which can easily be treated in a typed framework, and that the structure of Interaction Categories is appropriate for describing real concurrent languages.

1 Motivation

Abramsky [1] has recently proposed a new paradigm for the semantics of sequential and concurrent computation: Interaction Categories. This term encompasses certain known categories (the category of concrete data structures and sequential algorithms [5], categories of games [2]) as well as a new category **SProc**, with which we will be working in this paper. The distinguishing feature of Interaction Categories is that composition in them is a dynamic process of *interaction*, rather than the static one of function composition found in the familiar categories of traditional mathematics. **SProc** can be read either as "Synchronous Processes" or "Specifications and Processes"; the present work leans towards the first reading. In particular, we are using **SProc** to model SIGNAL [8] - one of a family of synchronous programming languages. Other members of the family include LUSTRE [9], SILAGE [10] and ESTEREL [4]. Synchrony is easier to handle initially; our aim is to deal with asynchrony later. Independently of this, dataflow is a model of concurrency which is well-suited to a typed framework. Thus we choose the synchronous dataflow language SIGNAL as our starting point. LUSTRE has also been modelled; this work is described elsewhere [7]. The purpose of this effort is two-fold: to see how existing programming paradigms are supported in the new framework, and to obtain feedback about how appropriate the categorical structures are.

2 The Interaction Category SProc

We will begin with a brief review of the definition of **SProc**, highlighting those features which are relevant to modelling dataflow. The basic picture is

Objects	Specifications
Morphisms	Processes
Composition	Synchronous composition + restriction.

This category is a model of 2nd-order Linear Logic, and supports polymorphism. It also includes a hierarchy of delay operators (as *monads*) and hence allows asynchrony to be built on top of synchrony *à la* Milner [12]. In addition, specification and verification can be smoothly incorporated via the notion of *specification strutures*, although we are not making use of this as yet. The following definitions relating to **SProc** are based on Abramsky's work.

2.1 Basic Definitions

The objects of **SProc** are pairs $A = (\Sigma_A, S_A)$ where Σ_A is an alphabet of actions (labels) and $S_A \subseteq^{\text{nepref}} \Sigma_A^*$, a non-empty prefix-closed subset of the set of finite sequences over Σ_A, is a safety specification. A *process* of type A, written $p \models A$, is a synchronisation tree with labels from Σ_A, such that $\text{traces}(p) \subseteq S_A$. Following Aczel [3], we will make use of a representation of synchronisation trees as (non-well-founded) sets, in which a process p with transitions $p \xrightarrow{a} q$, $p \xrightarrow{b} r$ becomes $\{(a,q), (b,r)\}$; the synchronisation tree looks like

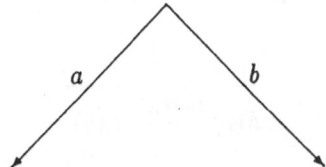

at the top. In order to define the morphisms of **SProc**, we first define a $*$-autonomous structure. Given A and B, the object $A \otimes B$ has

$$\Sigma_{A \otimes B} = \Sigma_A \times \Sigma_B$$
$$S_{A \otimes B} = \{\sigma \in \Sigma_{A \otimes B}^* \mid \text{fst}^*(\sigma) \in S_A \wedge \text{snd}^*(\sigma) \in S_B\}.$$

The duality is trivial on objects: $A^\perp = A$ (this comes from the choice of linear maps). Hence all the multiplicative connectives are the same: $A \bindnasrepma B = A \multimap B = A \otimes B$. Finally, a morphism $p : A \to B$ is a process p such that $p \models A \multimap B$. Since $\otimes$ is self-dual, we have not only a $*$-autonomous category but a *compact-closed* category.

Composition is defined in line with the slogan "relational composition extended in time". If $p : A \to B$ and $q : B \to C$, so that $p \models A \multimap B$ and $q \models B \multimap C$, then the composite $p; q : A \to C$ can be defined by labelled transitions:

$$\frac{p \xrightarrow{(a,b)} p' \qquad q \xrightarrow{(b,c)} q'}{p; q \xrightarrow{(a,c)} p'; q'}$$

in which matching of actions takes place in the common type B (as in relational composition), at each time step. This is the "interaction" of Interaction Categories.

The identity morphisms are synchronous buffers: whatever is received by $\mathsf{id}_A : A \to A$ in the left copy of A is instantaneously transmitted to the right copy. We define the identity proto-morphism $\mathsf{id} = \{((a,a), \mathsf{id}) \mid a \in \Sigma_A\}$ and then obtain id_A by restricting to synchronisation trees whose traces are all in $S_{A \to A}$: $\mathsf{id}_A = \mathsf{id}\restriction_{S_{A \to A}}$.

We extend $\otimes$ and $(\cdot)^\perp$ to functors by defining their action on morphisms as follows. If $p : A \to C$ and $q : B \to D$ then $p \otimes q : A \otimes B \to C \otimes D$ is defined by

$$\frac{p \xrightarrow{(a,c)} p' \qquad q \xrightarrow{(b,d)} q'}{p \otimes q \xrightarrow{((a,b),(c,d))} p' \otimes q'}$$

and $p^\perp : C \to A$ by

$$\frac{p \xrightarrow{(a,c)} p'}{p^\perp \xrightarrow{(c,a)} p'^\perp}.$$

The tensor unit I is defined by $\Sigma_I = \{*\}$, $S_I = \{*^n \mid n < \omega\}$. We also have $\perp = I$. The correct notion of "point" in a $*$-autonomous category is a morphism from I, and indeed we can identify a process of type A with a morphism $p : I \to A$. This will be important for our later work, as will the rest of the $*$-autonomous structure (i.e. closure), which we now define.

If $p : A \otimes B \to C$ then $\Lambda(p) : A \to B \multimap C$ is defined by

$$\frac{p \xrightarrow{((a,b),c)} q}{\Lambda(p) \xrightarrow{(a,(b,c))} \Lambda(q)}.$$

The evaluation morphism

$$\mathsf{Ap}_{A,B} : (A \multimap B) \otimes A \to B$$

is defined via a proto-morphism in the same way as the identities:

$$\mathsf{Ap} = \{(((((a,b),a),b), \mathsf{Ap}) \mid a \in \Sigma_A, b \in \Sigma_B\}$$
$$\mathsf{Ap}_{A,B} = \mathsf{Ap}\restriction_{S_{((A \multimap B) \otimes A) \multimap B}}.$$

We see that the "logical" morphisms giving the closed structure are essentially formed from identities.

We will make essential use of the compact closed structure of **SProc** later, in the following way. If we have a process p of type $A \otimes B$, $p \models A \otimes B$, then we can regard it as a morphism $p : I \to A \otimes B$. Since $(\cdot)^\perp$ is trivial, this is also $p : I \to A^\perp \otimes B$, i.e. $p : I \to A \multimap B$. Hence $p = \Lambda(q)$ where $q : A \to B$. From the definition of $\Lambda(\cdot)$ we can see that q is morally the same process as p; we will abuse notation in the rest of the paper by calling them both p, freely using compact closedness to move types back and forth across arrows.

2.2 Delay

A further part of the structure of **SProc** which we will need when modelling SIGNAL is the delay monads. So far, in the synchronous world to which **SProc** corresponds, any process has to do a genuine action at every time step. We now allow for processes which perform "dummy" or "idle" actions some of the time. There are two delay monads, corresponding to the delay operators in CCS - δ which allows for delay before the first action, and Δ which allows for delay anywhere except before the first action.

Given an object A, δA is defined by

$$\Sigma_{\delta A} = 1 + \Sigma_A$$

where for notational convenience we take $1 = \{*\}$ and assume $* \notin \Sigma_A$, and

$$S_{\delta A} = \{\varepsilon\} \cup \{*^n \sigma \mid (n < \omega) \wedge (\sigma \in S_A)\}.$$

If $p : A \to B$ then

$$\delta p = \{((*, *), \delta p)\} \cup p.$$

Thus δp delays for a while and then behaves as p. ΔA is defined by

$$\Sigma_{\Delta A} = 1 + \Sigma_A$$

and

$$S_{\Delta A} = \{\varepsilon\} \cup \{a_1 *^{n_1} a_2 *^{n_2} a_3 \ldots \mid (n_i < \omega) \wedge (a_1 a_2 a_3 \ldots \in S_A)\}.$$

Δp is like δp with $*$ appearing anywhere except before the first action of p.

It turns out that both of these functors have monad structures. What we will actually be interested in later on is the combined delay functor $\delta \Delta$, which is also a monad by virtue of the fact that there is a distributive law, i.e. a natural transformation $\Delta \delta \to \delta \Delta$.

3 Dataflow in SProc

Having discussed the relevant properties of **SProc**, we can now talk about modelling dataflow in general terms, before moving on to a specific language. **SProc** gives a framework for plugging processes together on typed interfaces, which is what we want as a basis for a typed theory of concurrency. General process calculi such as CCS do not immediately fit into this framework, because of the fact that their parallel composition does not actually corresond to plugging processes together but rather to placing them side-by-side in a way which means that they *may* communicate. What we need to do is work with *restricted* composition, in which two processes in parallel which can communicate with each other are prevented from communicating with anything else. Restricted composition does correspond to connecting processes rigidly together, and this is precisely what happens in a dataflow language as networks are built out of basic nodes. Thus dataflow is a model of concurrency which can very naturally be modelled in **SProc**.

We now describe, in a very general way, how the structure of a compact closed category allows us to construct dataflow networks in a typed framework. Suppose we are working with networks in which all values come from some type A, and we use an object A in our category to model this type. A node

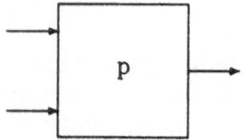

is modelled by a process (morphism) $p : A \otimes A \to A$. Now suppose we have another node q and we wish to connect the two together to form a simple network.

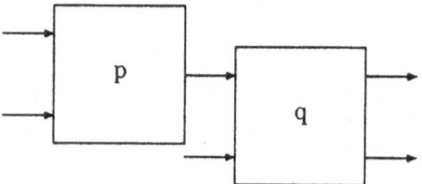

The node q is modelled by a morphism $q : A \otimes A \to A \otimes A$, and to model the network we form

$$(p \otimes \mathrm{id}_A); q : A \otimes A \otimes A \to A \otimes A.$$

Alternatively, we can take the view that to construct our network we first place p and q next to each other without communication to form a network with four inputs and three outputs

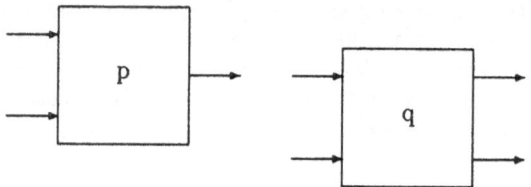

and then add an edge connecting one of the outputs to one of the inputs.

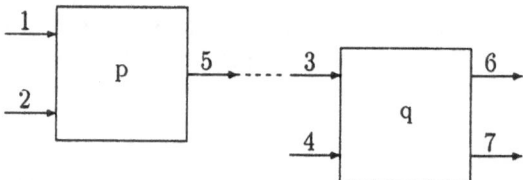

To model this we first form

$$p \otimes q : A_1 \otimes A_2 \otimes A_3 \otimes A_4 \to A_5 \otimes A_6 \otimes A_7,$$

where for clarity we have numbered the occurrences of A. Call this process r. By compact closure we can view this as a morphism

$$r : A_1 \otimes A_2 \otimes A_4 \to A_3^{\perp} \otimes A_5 \otimes A_6 \otimes A_7,$$

where we have retained the $^{\perp}$ on A_3 to indicate that what was previously seen as an input is now being viewed as an output. To get the effect of adding the connection between output 5 and input 3, we apply $\mathsf{Ap}_{A,\perp}$ to $A_3^{\perp}$ and A_5. Recall the general definition of $\mathsf{Ap}_{A,B}$; in the case $B = \perp$ we have

$$\mathsf{Ap}_{A,\perp} : (A \multimap \perp) \otimes A \to \perp,$$

i.e.

$$\mathsf{Ap}_{A,\perp} : A^{\perp} \otimes A \to I$$

since $\perp = I$. This morphism forces the same actions to occur in $A^{\perp}$ and A, which is what we need to say that two ports are connected. This gives

$$r;(\mathsf{Ap}_{A,\perp} \otimes \mathsf{id}_{A_6} \otimes \mathsf{id}_{A_7}) : A_1 \otimes A_2 \otimes A_4 \to I \otimes A_6 \otimes A_7.$$

By composing this with the canonical isomorphism $\lambda : I \otimes A \to A$ to remove the I, we obtain

$$s : A_1 \otimes A_2 \otimes A_4 \to A_6 \otimes A_7,$$

which is a morphism representing the desired network; in fact, $s = (p \otimes \mathsf{id}_A); q$. This procedure is the internalisation of composition in a $*$-autonomous category.

For an acyclic network such as the one above, we can always use composition to build the morphism we want. But if the network contains feedback loops, it is essential to use an Ap morphism to form the final link in each loop. For example, in the network

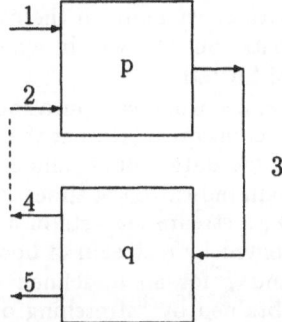

in which the dotted connection forms a cycle, we start with

$$p : A_1 \otimes A_2 \to A_3$$

and

$$q : A_3 \to A_4 \otimes A_5$$

and form

$$\Lambda(p; q);(\mathsf{Ap}_{A,\perp} \otimes \mathsf{id}_A); \lambda : A_1 \to A_5.$$

Note that although compact closure is necessary in order that all the types are formed using $\otimes$ rather than mixtures of $\otimes$ and $\bindnasrepma$, it is not important that $(\cdot)^{\perp}$ is trivial.

Forming a feedback loop in a dataflow network is the way in which a recursive definition is made, and in the usual Kahn-style semantics [11] the behaviour of the resulting network is given by a least fixed point construction. By contrast, our constructions in **SProc** give a process representing the behaviour of a network without explicitly introducing any least fixed points; the resolution of the recursive definitions is distributed among the interactions taking place at each point of connection between input and output. There is therefore some work to be done in order to see that our model gives the expected semantics. This question is dealt with in a forthcoming paper [6].

Another question is how to ensure that a network built from deterministic nodes remains deterministic, in light of the fact that in general, determinism is not preserved by composition in **SProc**. This is also dealt with in [6]; the property which *is* preserved is a combination of determinism and functionality, and we can check that all the nodes used in the modelling of SIGNAL satisfy this property.

4 Overview of the SIGNAL language

SIGNAL is one of a family of synchronous languages, along with ESTEREL, LUSTRE and SILAGE. In this context, *synchronous* means that outputs are produced simultaneously with the inputs which cause them. SIGNAL is a dataflow language and has been widely used in the areas of signal processing and control. A SIGNAL program is an executable specification of constraints expressed in terms of equations. Some of the equations specify that certain outputs are computed from certain inputs according to particular functions; this is familiar from any dataflow language. Other equations specify *relations* between signals. These relations are to do with constraints on the *clocks* of signals. The idea of a clock is shared with LUSTRE, but the way in which clock constraints appear is a characteristic feature of SIGNAL.

The concept of a clock arises when computations of different data streams are allowed to proceed at different rates. Rather than forcing a stream to consist solely of a sequence of genuine data values, undefined elements or delays are allowed. The clock of a stream indicates the times at which the stream contains a defined value. In LUSTRE, a stream consists of a sequence of genuine values and a clock which is represented by a stream of boolean values: t for a defined element of some stream and f for an undefined element. Thus the actual behaviour of a stream is obtained by "stretching out" its data values so that they appear at the times specified by its clock. In SIGNAL, by contrast, there is an "undefined" value $*$ which appears in streams at times when the clock is thought of as f. So the clock (in the LUSTRE sense) of a stream can be extracted from the stream itself.

The relations between clocks which can be expressed in a SIGNAL program are of the form "two streams have the same clock" or "stream A has a slower clock then stream B". Thus rather than completely defining the clock of every stream, as in a LUSTRE program, it is only necessary to express the essential timing constraints. The compiler then calculates the fastest clock on which everything can run.

5 SIGNAL programs as SProc processes

Our model of SIGNAL in **SProc** follows the general plan described previously. In order to represent clocks, a SIGNAL type A is modelled by the **SProc** type

$\delta\Delta A$. The $*$ action coming from the $\delta\Delta$ construction is used as the undefined value. When variables (names of streams) are declared, they are given initial values; this information is used in the construction of the processes modelling certain operators, as we will see later. Clock constraints are expressed by inserting extra processes into the network, which enforce the constraints.

6   SIGNAL operators in SProc

The simplest operators are the *static monochronous operators* which operate only on data and do not affect clocks. If $f : A \to B$ is a function then we have the stream extension $f^\omega : A^\omega \to B^\omega$; a static monochronous operator is a stream function of this form which can also ignore $*$ values. In **SProc** we have $f^\omega : A \to B$ defined by

$$f^\omega = \{((a, f(a)), f^\omega) \mid a \in \Sigma_A\}$$

and then the desired process which takes account of delays is just $\delta\Delta f^\omega$.

SIGNAL has a delay operator denoted by $\$$: the program fragment

$$Y = Z\$k$$

means that the stream Y is obtained by delaying the stream Z by k steps. Thus $y_n = z_{n-k}$ for $n \geq k$; for $n < k$ the values of y_n are taken from the sequence of initial values defined when Z is declared. To model this in **SProc** we use processes $\mathsf{sigdel}_a : \delta\Delta A \to \delta\Delta A$ for each type A and each $a \in \Sigma_{\delta\Delta A}$, where

$$\mathsf{sigdel}_a = \{((x, a), \mathsf{sigdel}_x) : x \in \Sigma_{\delta\Delta A}\}.$$

This deals with the case of a single delay; a longer delay can be built up from a series of single delays.

The remaining operators depend on clocks, and are known as *polychronous*. The when operator takes a signal X and a boolean signal B and outputs X when B is true. For example:

$$
\begin{array}{rccccccc}
X: & 1 & 4 & \bot & 5 & \bot & 6 & \dots \\
B: & t & f & t & t & f & t & \dots \\
X \text{ when } B: & 1 & \bot & \bot & 5 & \bot & 6 & \dots
\end{array}
$$

To model this we introduce a boolean type $\mathbb{B}$ in **SProc** and use

$$\mathsf{when} : \delta\Delta A \otimes \delta\Delta\mathbb{B} \longrightarrow \delta\Delta A$$

where

$$
\begin{aligned}
\mathsf{when} \ = \ & \{((a, t, a), \mathsf{when}) : a \in \Sigma_{\delta\Delta A}\} \\
\cup \ & \{((a, f, *), \mathsf{when}) : a \in \Sigma_{\delta\Delta A}\} \\
\cup \ & \{((a, *, *), \mathsf{when}) : a \in \Sigma_{\delta\Delta A}\}.
\end{aligned}
$$

Next is the deterministic merge operator **default**. U **default** V takes its nth value from U if U is defined there, otherwise from V. This is modelled by

$$\text{default} : \delta\Delta A \otimes \delta\Delta A \longrightarrow \delta\Delta A$$

where

$$
\begin{aligned}
\text{default} \;=\; & \{((a,b,a),\text{default}) : a,b \in \Sigma_{\delta\Delta A}\} \\
\cup \;\; & \{((*,b,b),\text{default}) : b \in \Sigma_{\delta\Delta A}\}.
\end{aligned}
$$

The **event** operator is used to extract the clock of a signal: it produces a boolean signal with value t when its input is defined, f otherwise. Its type is

$$\text{event} : \delta\Delta A \longrightarrow \mathbb{B}$$

and

$$
\begin{aligned}
\text{event} \;=\; & \{((a,t),\text{event}) : a \in \Sigma_A\} \\
\cup \;\; & \{((*,f),\text{event})\}.
\end{aligned}
$$

To deal with clock constraints, first note that it is only necessary to take care of the case in which two signals are made to have the same clock; specifying that one clock is slower than another is a derived case. We use a process

$$\text{synchro} : \delta\Delta A \otimes \delta\Delta B \longrightarrow \delta\Delta A \otimes \delta\Delta B$$

defined by

$$
\begin{aligned}
\text{synchro} \;=\; & \{((*,*,*,*),\text{synchro})\} \\
\cup \;\; & \{((a,b,a,b),\text{synchro}) : a \in \Sigma_A, b \in \Sigma_B\}.
\end{aligned}
$$

The way in which this works is that a process modelling a SIGNAL operator can cope with all possible clocks, so that outputs are non-deterministic to the extent that they contain many possible insertions of *s among the genuine actions. The process synchro passes on its inputs, but with the freedom of their clocks restricted so that both outputs have the same clock.

We now present a small example to illustrate composition and some of the SIGNAL operators. We use Abramsky's "stream of consciousness" tables to show possible traces of processes. The first table is for **when**.

X	B	X when B
1	t	1
4	f	*
*	t	*
5	t	5
*	f	*
6	t	6
$\vdots$	$\vdots$	$\vdots$

We aim to form the composition when ; event. Two possible traces for event are shown below.

Y	event Y
*	f
1	t
2	t
4	t
*	f
5	t
⋮	⋮

Z	event Z
1	t
*	f
*	f
5	t
*	f
6	t
⋮	⋮

To find a possible trace for the composition, we need traces in which the output of when matches the input of event. The second trace of event shown above fits with the trace of when shown, and together these give a trace of

$$\text{when}\,;\,\text{event} : \delta\Delta A \otimes \delta\Delta\mathbb{B} \longrightarrow \delta\Delta\mathbb{B}.$$

The result is a boolean signal which is *not* quite the clock of the signal X.

X	B	X when B	Z	event Z ($Z = X$ when B)
1	t	1	1	t
4	f	*	*	f
*	t	*	*	f
5	t	5	5	t
*	f	*	*	f
6	t	6	6	t
⋮	⋮	⋮	⋮	⋮

7 Conclusions and Future Work

We have shown how to interpret SIGNAL operators and programs in **SProc** in a uniform, typed fashion. The task is made straightforward by the synchronous and relational nature of SIGNAL. Even though it is a simple application, this is a worthwhile task as SIGNAL is already used in large-scale applications in the field of digital signal processing. We have been able to model a SIGNAL program for a digital stopwatch in **SProc**, the details of which do not discuss here due to space restrictions. The use of delay monads to model clocks suggest that we have the right kind of structures in our framework for modelling such languages. This feature is brought out more clearly in modelling LUSTRE [7] where there is a strong interplay between the types and the delays; in SIGNAL this is reflected in the clock calculation. Each SIGNAL fragment can operate on its own clock and the SIGNAL compiler uses the dependencies to construct a hierarchy of clocks. If a single master clock exists (the *coarsest common clock*) it will be derived by the compiler. We aim to show that such a clock derived via our model of a SIGNAL program in the Interaction Category framework is the same as that derived by the compiler.

We also plan to investigate the translation of ESTEREL which is similar in spirit to SIGNAL but has more powerful constructs. There is also work in progress in which we are trying to capture processes directly in **SProc**.

Acknowledgements

We would like to thank Samson Abramsky for being the guiding light. The referees Lindsay Errington and Tom Maibaum provided useful comments. Simon Gay is funded by an SERC Studentship; and Raja Nagarajan by project CONFER (ESPRIT BRA 6454) and ICCF. We gratefully acknowledge their support.

References

[1] S. Abramsky. Interaction categories. In this volume.

[2] S. Abramsky and R. Jagadeesan. Games and full completeness for multiplicative linear logic. Technical Report DoC 92/24, Department of Computing, Imperial College of Science Technology and Medicine, 1992.

[3] P. Aczel. *Non-well-founded sets.* CSLI Lecture Notes 14. Center for the Study of Language and Information, 1988.

[4] G. Berry, P. Couronné, and G. Gonthier. Synchronous programming of reactive systems: An introduction to ESTEREL. Technical Report 647, INRIA, 1986.

[5] G. Berry and P.-L. Curien. Theory and practice of sequential algorithms: the kernel of the applicative language CDS. In J. C. Reynolds and M. Nivat, editors, *Algebraic Semantics*, pages 35–84. Cambridge University Press, 1985.

[6] S. J. Gay. On iteration and interaction. Draft paper, 1993.

[7] S. J. Gay and R. Nagarajan. Modelling LUSTRE in Interaction Categories. Paper in preparation, 1993.

[8] P. le Guernic, T. Gautier, M. le Borgne, and C. le Maire. Programming real-time applications with SIGNAL. *Proceedings of the IEEE*, 79(9):1305–1320, September 1991.

[9] N. Halbwachs, P. Caspi, P. Raymond, and D. Pilaud. The synchronous data flow programming language LUSTRE. *Proceedings of the IEEE*, 79(9):1305–1320, September 1991.

[10] P. N. Hilfinger. Silage, a high-level language and silicon compiler for digital signal processing. In *IEEE Custom Integrated Circuits Conference CICC–85*, pages 213–216. IEEE, May 1985 1993.

[11] G. Kahn. The semantics of a simple language for parallel programming. In *Information Processing 74*, 1974.

[12] R. Milner. *Communication and Concurrency.* Prentice Hall, 1989.

Product Operations in Strong Monads

Reinhold Heckmann

heckmann@cs.uni-sb.de

FB 14 – Informatik, Universität des Saarlandes
Postfach 1150, D-66041 Saarbrücken, Germany

Abstract

If a strong monad M is used to define the denotational semantics of a functional language with computations, a product operation $\bar{\times} : MX \times MY \to M(X \times Y)$ is needed to define the semantics of pairing. Every strong monad is equipped with two standard products, which correspond to left-to-right and right-to-left evaluation. We study the algebraic properties of these standard products in general. Then we define alternative products with similar properties for strict and parallel evaluation in the special case of strong monads in $\mathcal{DCPO}$ which are obtained as free constructions w.r.t. various theories of non-deterministic computation, including both classical and probabilistic theories.

1 Introduction

Following the proposals of Moggi [12, 13], functional languages with various notions of *computations* can be denotationally described by means of (particular kinds of) *monads*. Informally, these monads are constructions mapping domains of values into domains of computations for these values. Computations involving non-deterministic choice, for instance, are handled by *power domain constructions* [14, 15, 1, 7, 8].

In Moggi's work, the semantics of pairing (A, B) is handled in a standard way that corresponds to left-to-right evaluation. Of course, a dual treatment corresponding to right-to-left evaluation is easily available. In this paper, we investigate other kinds of pair evaluation, e.g., non-deterministic choice of the evaluation order, or parallel evaluation of the components. We propose that the monads that Moggi uses in his semantic descriptions be extended by a semantic operation which models the evaluation of pairs. This alternative product will then override the standard product, and thus give rise to alternative kinds of evaluation different from the standard left-to-right evaluation.

The paper is organized as follows: In Section 2, we define *strong monads* in Cartesian closed categories. In Section 3, we study the two standard products '$\bar{\times}$' (left-to-right evaluation) and '$\underline{\times}$' (right-to-left evaluation), which exist for every strong monad. Their algebraic properties should be enjoyed by every alternative product. In Section 4, we concentrate on power domain constructions as special kinds of strong monad. The algebraic properties of their power domains can be described by non-deterministic theories. There are three main examples: the set-like theory S, where choice is commutative, associative, and idempotent; the multiset-like theory M without idempotence; and the probabilistic theory P, where alternatives are chosen with equal probability. In Section 5, we show how strong monads can be obtained as free constructions w.r.t. these algebraic theories. Section 6 is devoted to the specific properties of the standard products in these free power constructions. Then we introduce our first alternative product in Section 7, which non-deterministically chooses the evaluation order. In Section 8, two other alternative products are introduced axiomatically: the strict product and the parallel product. Their main properties are derived from their axiomatic definition. Both are uniquely determined if they exist. In Section 9, we show the existence of parallel products for a large class of theories. The existence of strict products can be shown analogously.

2   Monads and Strong Monads

We define monads according to Definition 1.2 in [12]. There is a different definition in [10], but the two definitions are equivalent as pointed out in [12].

Definition 2.1

A *monad* in a category C is a triple (M, r, E) where

 ♦ M maps objects of C into objects of C,
 ♦ r is a family of arrows $r_X : X \to MX$ for every object X of C,
 ♦ For every arrow $f : X \to MY$, there is an arrow $Ef : MX \to MY$
 such that

(E1) $Ef \circ r_X = f$ for $f : X \to MY$,
(E2) $E r_X = \mathrm{id}_{MX}$,
(E3) $Eg \circ Ef = E(Eg \circ f)$ for $f : X \to MY$ and $g : Y \to MZ$.

We shall often drop the type subscripts of r_X.

According to Moggi's intuitions, the construction M maps domains of values of some type into domains of computations of this type; r maps values v into a trivial computation rv that immediately *results* in v; and E *extends* computation-valued functions defined on values to those defined on computations. An extended function Ef applied to some computation will execute this computation and apply f to the resulting value(s), which in general involves some more computation.

Defining $Mf = E(r_Y \circ f)$ for $f : X \to Y$ makes M into a functor; r then becomes a natural transformation.

An example for a monad in the category $\mathcal{SET}$ is provided by the powerset construction. It has $MX = \{A \mid A \subseteq X\}$, $rx = \{x\}$, and $EfA = \bigcup_{a \in A} fa$ for $f : X \to MY$ and A in MX. The reader is invited to check the validity of the monad axioms. The induced action of M on functions is given by $MfA = E(r \circ f)A = \bigcup_{a \in A} \{fa\} = \{fa \mid a \in A\}$, which is the image of A under f.

In [12], a *strong monad* in a Cartesian category is defined as (M, r, E, t), where $t_{XY} : X \times MY \to M(X \times Y)$ is an additional operation subject to five axioms. This definition suggests some degree of freedom in extending a monad to a strong monad, which actually does not always exist: as shown in [12], t is — once it exists — uniquely determined by its axioms if the underlying category is concrete.

The situation becomes simpler if we restrict ourselves to the case of Cartesian closed categories [10]. As also mentioned in [12], a strong monad is then given by a triple (M, r, E), where E is no longer a (set-theoretic) function between hom-sets, but an arrow $E : [X \to MY] \to [MX \to MY]$ between function objects. The monad axioms have then to be understood as written in the *internal language* [9] of the Cartesian closed category. This internal language is a variant of a simply typed λ-calculus. Axiom (E1) for instance can still — though a bit informally — be written as "$E f \circ r = f$ for $f : X \to MY$", which stands for the equality statement $f : X \to MY \vdash \lambda x^X . E f(rx) = f$. *From now on, all equations actually mean equality statements of the internal language, written slightly informally.*

As we have derived M from E above, we can derive an arrow M from E in case of a strong monad by defining $Mf = E(r \circ f)$. (This definition is to be considered syntactic sugar for the actual definition $M = \lambda f^{X \to Y} . E(\lambda x^X . r_Y(fx))$ in the internal language.)

In the category $\mathcal{SET}$, every set-theoretic function is an arrow, whence every monad is strong. In the category $\mathcal{DCPO}$, a monad (M, r, E) is strong iff the (set-theoretic) function E is Scott continuous.

3 The Two Standard Products of a Strong Monad

Given a strong monad (M, r, E) in a CCC C, one can translate expressions of a typed functional language with computation into the internal language of C, once the base types β of the language have been translated into objects β^* of C. This translation is extended to all types τ in a standard way. The domain of semantic values of type τ is then τ^*, and the domain of computations of type τ is $M\tau^*$.

Every expression $E : \tau$ of the language denotes a computation of type τ. This computation is obtained by a syntactic translation of the expression E into a λ-expression $[\![E]\!] : M\tau^*$. In this paper, we are only interested in one aspect of this: the translation of pairs. Without committing ourselves to anything, we may define $[\![(A, B)]\!] = [\![A]\!] \, \bar{\times} \, [\![B]\!]$, where $\bar{\times}$ is an operation which — according to the typings involved — must have type $MX \times MY \to M(X \times Y)$. (More accurately, $\bar{\times}$ is a family of operations $\bar{\times}_{XY}$, but we drop the type subscripts.) After putting it into our notation, Moggi's choice for '$\bar{\times}$' becomes

$$A \, \vec{\times} \, B = E(\lambda a. \, E(\lambda b. \, r(a, b))B)A,$$

which corresponds to a left-to-right evaluation of pairs. Equally well, one could define

$$A \, \overleftarrow{\times} \, B = E(\lambda b. \, E(\lambda a. \, r(a, b))A)B,$$

which corresponds to right-to-left evaluation.

In the powerset example, we obtain $A \, \vec{\times} \, B = \bigcup_{a \in A} \bigcup_{b \in B} \{(a, b)\}$, which is just the ordinary product set $A \times B$. The dual product $A \overleftarrow{\times} B$ leads to the same result. We call strong monads where $\vec{\times} = \overleftarrow{\times}$ *symmetric*.

We now present the properties of the two standard products.

Theorem 3.1
With every strong monad in a CCC, for both $\bar{\times} = \vec{\times}$ and $\bar{\times} = \overleftarrow{\times}$, the following holds:

(P1) For all a in X and B in MY, $ra \bar{\times} B = M\sigma_a B$, where $\sigma_a b = (a, b)$.
      For all A in MX and b in Y, $A \bar{\times} rb = M\sigma^b A$, where $\sigma^b a = (a, b)$.

(P2) (Naturality)
      For all A in MX, B in MY, $f : X \to X'$, and $g : Y \to Y'$:
      $MfA \bar{\times} MgB = M(f \times g)(A \bar{\times} B)$, where $(f \times g)(a, b) = (fa, gb)$.

(P3) (Associativity)   For A in MX, B in MY, and C in MZ:
      $A \bar{\times} (B \bar{\times} C) = M\alpha((A \bar{\times} B) \bar{\times} C)$, where $\alpha((a, b), c) = (a, (b, c))$.

If the strong monad is symmetric, then $\bar{\times} = \vec{\times} = \bar{\times}$ additionally satisfies

(P4) (Commutativity)   For A in MX and B in MY:
      $B \bar{\times} A = M\gamma(A \bar{\times} B)$, where $\gamma(a, b) = (b, a)$.

Proof: Statements (P1) through (P3) can be shown by equational reasoning in the λ-calculus using the axioms of extension.

For (P4), note that $B \vec{\times} A = M\gamma(A \vec{\times} B)$ holds in general. Thus, '$\vec{\times}$' is commutative iff '$\bar{\times}$' is commutative iff the strong monad is symmetric. $\square$

If we want to augment a given strong monad (M, r, E) with a product operation '$\bar{\times}$' of our choice, then '$\bar{\times}$' should at least satisfy (P1) through (P3) to be as good as the standard products.

4   Power Domain Constructions from Non-Deterministic Theories

We now assume that the functional language with computations, whose semantics shall be described by a strong monad, is a non-deterministic language with a binary choice operator $|$, a special expression fail, and syntactic means for recursion.

The choice operator is open for various different interpretations. We may think that encountering an expression $A \mid B$, the interpreter of the language employs some hidden strategy to choose one of A and B for evaluation, or chooses one of them at random with equal probability, or evaluates both A and B in turn and displays all resulting values (similar to a Prolog interpreter). In any circumstances, we need a semantic function $\oplus : MX \times MX \to MX$ to define $[\![A \mid B]\!] = [\![A]\!] \oplus [\![B]\!]$. (In a typed language, the two branches of a choice should have the same type.)

An evaluation of the expression fail immediately terminates without producing a result. Assuming that this expression can have any type, we need a semantic constant $\diamond : MX$ for every X to define $[\![\text{fail}]\!] = \diamond$.

In order to model recursion, the semantic domains should finally admit some kind of fixed point formation. To do so, we assume that the semantic monad operates within the category $\mathcal{DCPO}$, and that all semantic domains MX actually be cpo's with least element $\bot$. This $\bot$ will then be the semantics of computations that do not yield ordinary results because of non-termination. We do not assume that X itself contains $\bot$; e.g., the domain of integer values is $\{\ldots, -1, 0, 1, \ldots\}$ with the discrete order. We call semantic domains with $\bot$, $\diamond$, and '$\oplus$' *power domains*, and strong monads M which produce power domains MX *power domain constructions*.

Our way to obtain power domain constructions is to set up an algebraic theory with operators $\bot$, $\diamond$, and '$\oplus$' and appropriate axioms of our choice, and then take the free construction in $\mathcal{DCPO}$ w.r.t. this theory. This approach has a long-standing tradition. It was first suggested in [5], then extended in [11], studied more closely in [6] and later [2, 3], and was largely used in [4].

Usually, an algebraic theory consists of a set of operators with given arity and a set of axioms in the form of equations $L = R$ over these operators. Since we want to consider algebraic theories in the category $\mathcal{DCPO}$, we also allow inequations $L \leq R$ as axioms. Also, we allow arities of the form $D \times X^n \to X$, where D is a fixed dcpo, and X is the algebra. In $\mathcal{SET}$, this would give no further generalization, since an operation $f : D \times X^n \to X$ may be replaced by a family $f_d : X^n \to X$ with d in D. In $\mathcal{DCPO}$, this reduction is not possible, because $f : D \times X^n \to X$ stipulates continuity of f in its first argument.

A *non-deterministic theory* or briefly *ND-theory* has two nullary operators $\bot$ and $\diamond$, a binary operator '$\oplus$', and an arbitrary set of axioms, which actually are equations or inequations, or are equivalent to those after introducing some auxiliary operations (an example for the latter case is the probabilistic theory introduced below). An ND-theory should contain the property $\bot \leq x$, as an explicit axiom or as a theorem, to guarantee that $\bot$ will be the least element. The actual choice of the axioms depends on the interpretation of the non-determinism and the number of distinctions we wish to make about the result of computations.

In the remainder of this section, we present some sample ND-theories. First assume that we are interested in the *set* of values a non-deterministic expression may produce. Then we should give '$\oplus$' the properties of set union: associativity $(A \oplus B) \oplus C = A \oplus (B \oplus C)$, commutativity $A \oplus B = B \oplus A$, and idempotence $A \oplus A = A$. A failing expression produces no values at all; thus, $\diamond$ is the neutral element of '$\oplus$': $A \oplus \diamond = A$. A non-terminating expression produces no values, too, whence $\bot = \diamond$. We call this the *lower set-like theory* LS. It is well-known that the free construction for LS is the *lower* or *Hoare power domain* [5].

If we want to retain the information whether a computation is possibly non-terminating, we have to distinguish between $\bot$ and $\diamond$. This is done simply by dropping the axiom $\bot = \diamond$. The element $\diamond$ is still the neutral element of '$\oplus$', since the expressions **fail** | A and A may possibly produce the same values and have the same termination behaviour. We call this theory the *set-like theory* S. Its free construction is none of the classical power constructions. The internal structure of its power domains is studied in [4].

If we want to retain the information, how often a particular value may occur as the result of an expression, then we are interested in the bag or multiset of possible result values, and we have to drop the axiom of idempotence $A \oplus A = A$. According to whether we keep $\bot = \diamond$ or not, the resulting theory is the *lower multiset-like theory* LM or the *multiset-like theory* M. The power domains of LM and M have not been investigated much so far. Although general idempotence does not hold in LM and M, we still have $\diamond \oplus \diamond = \diamond$ by neutrality, and also $\bot \oplus \bot = \bot$, since $\bot \leq \bot \oplus \bot \leq \diamond \oplus \bot = \bot$.

Quite a different theory results from a probabilistic interpretation of non-determinism, where $A \oplus B$ means that A and B are chosen with equal probability $1/2$. Then '$\oplus$' is commutative and idempotent, but not associative, since in $A \oplus (B \oplus C)$, A is chosen with probability $1/2$, whereas in $(A \oplus B) \oplus C$, it has probability $1/4$. On the other hand, there is still something left of associativity: the *rectangle axiom* $(A \oplus B) \oplus (C \oplus D) = (A \oplus C) \oplus (B \oplus D)$, which holds since all four components are chosen with probability $1/4$. The four operands

A, B, C, and D may be thought as arranged at the corners of a rectangle; the axiom then says that they may be combined first horizontally, then vertically, as well as first vertically, then horizontally; hence the name. The rectangle law also holds in the theories S and M as a consequence of commutativity and associativity.

There is another, less obvious axiom for the probabilistic interpretation. In a recursive definition such as $\mathbf{x} = 1 \mid \mathbf{x}$, the result 1 is chosen with probability $1/2$ in the first iteration, with probability $1/4$ in the second, and so on. Altogether, it is chosen with probability 1, and the probability of non-termination is 0. Generalizing, this leads to the axiom that the fixed point iteration for $X = A \oplus X$ yields A, for every A. This fixed-point axiom $\mu X. A \oplus X = A$ is equivalent to $A \oplus A = A$, which is idempotence, together with the conditional axiom $A \oplus B = B \Rightarrow A \leq B$. The fixed-point axiom can be reduced to a set of equations by introducing an auxiliary operation $f : \mathbb{N}_0^\infty \to X$, where $\mathbb{N}_0^\infty$ is the dcpo $\{1 < 2 < \cdots < \infty\}$. With this operation, the fixed point iteration in $\mu X. A \oplus X = A$ can be modelled by the equations $f(0) = \bot$, $f(n+1) = A \oplus f(n)$, and $f(\infty) = A$.

Under the probabilistic interpretation, $\diamond$ is by no means a neutral element. Thus, we obtain as *probabilistic theory* P the theory with commutativity, idempotence, rectangle axiom, and fixed point axiom. The theory with additionally $\bot = \diamond$ is called the *lower probabilistic theory* LP. We conjecture that LP is equivalent to the theory of probabilistic algebras in [7, 8] at least in the case of continuous dcpo's, so that for these dcpo's, the free construction for LP would coincide with the one studied there.

The basic properties that are shared by all theories presented above are the rectangle law, $\diamond \oplus \diamond = \diamond$, and $\bot \oplus \bot = \bot$. ND-theories with these properties will be called *decent*.

5 Free Constructions

Let T be an ND-theory. A *model* of T in the category $\mathcal{DCPO}$, or simply a *T-model*, is a power domain (a dcpo with $\bot$, $\diamond$, and '$\oplus$'), whose operations satisfy the axioms of T.

A T-algebra homomorphism, or shortly *T-morphism*, is a *continuous* function between T-models preserving all operations. T-morphisms are thus continuous, strict ($f\bot = \bot$), $\diamond$-strict ($f\diamond = \diamond$), and additive ($f(A \oplus B) = fA \oplus fB$).

Definition 5.1 (Free constructions)   A *free construction* $(\mathcal{P}, \mathsf{r})$ for an algebraic theory T maps every dcpo X into a T-model $\mathcal{P}X$ with a morphism $\mathsf{r} : X \to \mathcal{P}X$, such that for every T-model A and every morphism $f : X \to A$, there is a unique T-morphism $\bar{f} : \mathcal{P}X \to A$ with $\bar{f} \circ \mathsf{r} = f$.

Categorically speaking, free constructions for T are left adjoint to the forgetful functor from the category of T-models and T-morphisms to $\mathcal{DCPO}$. Free constructions are uniquely determined up to isomorphism. They also exist:

Theorem 5.2   In $\mathcal{DCPO}$, free constructions exist for all algebraic theories.

Proof: The proof idea appears in [6], where the theorem is proved for one particular algebraic theory. This idea is then applied in [2, 3] to a larger class of theories. The same basic idea also applies in generality. $\square$

Free constructions for ND-theories T are power domain constructions: Since $\mathcal{P}Y$ is a T-model, every function $f : X \to \mathcal{P}Y$ has a (unique) extension $Ef = \bar{f}$, which is strict, $\diamond$-strict, and additive, and satisfies (E1) $Ef \circ r = f$. The only properties which remain to be shown are (E2), (E3), and continuity of E. To do so, we collect some facts about free algebras.

Lemma 5.3   Let $(\mathcal{P}, r)$ be a free construction for theory T, and let X be a dcpo. Let B be a subset of $\mathcal{P}X$ that is closed w.r.t. all operations of T and directed joins, and that contains all generators rx. Then B equals $\mathcal{P}X$.

Proof: See [4], Lemma 4.4.   □

From this Lemma, we conclude:

Proposition 5.4   Let $\mathcal{P}$ be the free power construction for an ND-theory T, and X and Y be dcpo's with a binary monotonic operation $\oplus : Y \times Y \to Y$. Let F and G be two morphisms from $\mathcal{P}X$ to Y, which are both additive, and can be compared on generators $(F \circ r \leq G \circ r)$ as well as on empty elements $(F\diamond \leq G\diamond$ and $F\bot \leq G\bot)$. Then $F \leq G$.
The same holds if '$\leq$' is replaced by '$=$' throughout.

Proof: Apply Lemma 5.3 to $B = \{A \in \mathcal{P}X \mid FA \leq GA\}$.   □

Note that in Prop. 5.4, Y need not be a T-model; in particular, it is not required to have $\bot$ and $\diamond$, and its operation '$\oplus$' need not satisfy any axioms; not even continuity of '$\oplus$' is required.

The proposition may be used to prove (E2), (E3), and continuity of E, as shown explicitly in [2]. Later, we need a generalization of the proposition:

Theorem 5.5   Let $\mathcal{P}$ be the free power construction for an ND-theory T, let $X_1, \ldots, X_n$ and Y be dcpo's with a binary monotonic operation $\oplus : Y \times Y \to Y$. Let F and G be two morphisms from $\mathcal{P}X_1 \times \cdots \times \mathcal{P}X_n$ to Y with the following properties:

(1) F and G are both additive in every argument, if the remaining arguments are kept fixed.

(2) If at least one of the A_i is of form ra_i,
    then $F(A_1, \ldots, A_n) \leq G(A_1, \ldots, A_n)$.

(3) If all A_i are empty (i.e., $\diamond$ or $\bot$), then $F(A_1, \ldots, A_n) \leq G(A_1, \ldots, A_n)$.

Then $F \leq G$ can be concluded.
The same holds if '$\leq$' is replaced by '$=$' throughout.

Proof: This is proved by induction on n. For $n = 1$, this is Proposition 5.4. For $n > 1$, we use Proposition 5.4 to show $F' \leq G'$, where $F', G' : \mathcal{P}X_1 \to [\mathcal{P}X_2 \times \cdots \times \mathcal{P}X_n \to Y]$ are curried versions of F and G. By (1), both F' and G' are additive. By (2), $F' \circ r \leq G' \circ r$ holds. The two functions $F'\diamond$ and $G'\diamond$ have $n-1$ arguments, and $F'\diamond \leq G'\diamond$ holds by induction hypothesis. The same is true for $F'\bot$ and $G'\bot$.   □

6   The Standard Products in Free Power Constructions

In this section, we look at the special properties of the standard products in free power constructions. Particularly strong statements are possible in the case of free constructions w.r.t. decent theories. Remember that an ND-theory is decent if it includes the rectangle axiom and the two properties $\diamond \oplus \diamond = \diamond$ and $\perp \oplus \perp = \perp$. The significance of this notion is indicated by the following proposition:

Proposition 6.1   Let T be a decent ND-theory. If X is a power domain and Y a T-model, then the (pointwise defined) sum of additive (strict, $\diamond$-strict) functions from X to Y is additive (strict, $\diamond$-strict) again. The constant functions $\lambda x. \perp$ and $\lambda x. \diamond$ are additive.

Proof: Let f and g be additive, and let $h = f \oplus g = \lambda x. fx \oplus gx$. Then

$$
\begin{aligned}
h(a \oplus b) &= f(a \oplus b) \oplus g(a \oplus b) &= (fa \oplus fb) \oplus (ga \oplus gb) \\
&= (fa \oplus ga) \oplus (fb \oplus gb) &= ha \oplus hb
\end{aligned}
$$

whence h is additive. The remaining statements are simple consequences of $\perp \oplus \perp = \perp$ and $\diamond \oplus \diamond = \diamond$.   □

We now come to the properties of the standard products in free constructions.

Proposition 6.2   Let T be an ND-theory and $\mathcal{P}$ its free construction.

(1) The left product '$\overline{\times}$' is strict, $\diamond$-strict, and additive in its left argument:
$\perp \overline{\times} B = \perp$ $\diamond \overline{\times} B = \diamond$ $(A_1 \oplus A_2) \overline{\times} B = (A_1 \overline{\times} B) \oplus (A_2 \overline{\times} B)$.

(2) The right product '$\overline{\times}$' is strict, $\diamond$-strict, and additive in its right argument.

(3) If T is decent, then both '$\overline{\times}$' and '$\overline{\times}$' are additive in both arguments.

Proof: We concentrate on '$\overline{\times}$'. Remember $A \overline{\times} B = \mathsf{E}(\lambda a. \mathsf{E}(\lambda b. r(a, b))B)A$. Thus (1) follows from the fact that extended functions $\mathsf{E}f$ are always strict, $\diamond$-strict, and additive.

For (3), we compare $FA = A \overline{\times} (B_1 \oplus B_2)$ and $GA = (A \overline{\times} B_1) \oplus (A \overline{\times} B_2)$ by Prop. 5.4. By (1), F is additive, strict, and $\diamond$-strict. By Prop. 6.1, G is additive, strict, and $\diamond$-strict as sum of two such functions. By (P1), $F(ra) = \mathsf{M}\sigma_a(B_1 \oplus B_2)$ and $G(ra) = \mathsf{M}\sigma_a B_1 \oplus \mathsf{M}\sigma_a B_2$ hold. The function $\mathsf{M}\sigma_a = \mathsf{E}(r \circ \sigma_a)$ is additive. Thus, $F(ra)$ equals $G(ra)$.   □

Next, we consider symmetry.

Proposition 6.3   Let T be an ND-theory with free construction $\mathcal{P}$.

(1) If $\mathcal{P}$ is symmetric, then $\perp = \diamond$ holds in all $\mathcal{P}$-powerdomains.

(2) If T is decent with $\perp = \diamond$, then $\mathcal{P}$ is symmetric.

Proof: By Prop. 6.2 (1) and (2), $\perp \overline{\times} \diamond = \perp$ and $\perp \overline{\times} \diamond = \diamond$ hold. If $\mathcal{P}$ is symmetric, then '$\overline{\times}$' and '$\overline{\times}$' coincide, whence $\perp = \diamond$.

For (2), we apply Theorem 5.5 to compare $A \overline{\times} B$ and $A \overline{\times} B$ as functions of two arguments. By Prop. 6.2 (3), both functions are additive in both arguments. By (P1), they yield equal results if $A = ra$ or $B = rb$. By $\perp = \diamond$, they coincide if both A and B are empty.   □

Thus, in particular the power constructions $\mathcal{P}_{LS}$, $\mathcal{P}_{LM}$, and $\mathcal{P}_{LP}$ are symmetric, whereas $\mathcal{P}_S$, $\mathcal{P}_M$, and $\mathcal{P}_P$ are not symmetric. To speak precisely, the non-symmetry statement is only proved after it is shown that the axioms of the respective theories do not imply $\perp = \diamond$. This can be done by presenting models with $\perp \neq \diamond$. The dcpo $\{\perp < \diamond\}$ is an M- and S-model with '$\oplus$' being join, and a P-model with '$\oplus$' being meet.

7   The Choice Product

So far, we have only seen standard products. Now, we try the most obvious non-standard product in a power domain construction: the product $A * B = A \barssen{\times} B \oplus A \barssen{\times} B$, where we choose the evaluation order non-deterministically. To avoid bothering about two different versions of '$*$', we assume that '$\oplus$' is commutative. We shall soon see that idempotence is also important, and finally we assume the rectangle law to make the results of the previous section available. Thus, the following results cover the theories S and P, but not M.

Theorem 7.1   Let T be an ND-theory, where '$\oplus$' is commutative, idempotent, and the rectangular law holds. Then '$*$' has the following properties:
(P1) $ra * B = M\sigma_a B$ and $A * rb = M\sigma^b A$.
(P2) Naturality: $MfA * MgB = M(f \times g)(A * B)$.
(P4) Commutativity: $B * A = M\gamma (A * B)$.
   ♦ Biadditivity: '$*$' is additive in both arguments.
   ♦ $\diamond * \diamond = \diamond$ and $\perp * \perp = \perp$.

Proof: By Prop. 6.1, '$*$' is biadditive as the sum of '$\barssen{\times}$' and '$\barssen{\times}$', which are biadditive by Prop. 6.2. The other statements can be shown by simple equational reasoning.   □

The reader will have noticed that associativity (P3) does not occur in the theorem above. The reason is that it surprisingly does not hold in general. Using biadditivity, $A * (B * C)$ can be expanded into

$$(A \barssen{\times} (B \barssen{\times} C) \oplus A \barssen{\times} (B \barssen{\times} C)) \oplus (A \barssen{\times} (B \barssen{\times} C) \oplus A \barssen{\times} (B \barssen{\times} C)),$$

whereas $(A * B) * C$ becomes

$$((A \barssen{\times} B) \barssen{\times} C \oplus (A \barssen{\times} B) \barssen{\times} C) \oplus ((A \barssen{\times} B) \barssen{\times} C \oplus (A \barssen{\times} B) \barssen{\times} C).$$

It seems as if the two sums could be related after switching the two middle summands by the rectangle law. But this impression is wrong; the first sum contains evaluation orders ABC, ACB, BCA, and CBA, whereas the second sum contains the orders ABC, BAC, CAB, and CBA. Thus, both sums contain a different selection of 4 evaluation orders from the altogether 6 possible evaluation orders for a triple.

Of course, this does not prove that the associativity of '$*$' really fails. Indeed, it *does* hold in the set-like theory S, which will be seen in Section 8, but fails in the probabilistic theory P.

To show non-associativity of '$*$' in P, we need a concrete P-model which can be used to distinguish members of the free P-models $\mathcal{P}X$, which are merely abstractly described by their universal property. Let $\mathbb{I}$ be the dcpo of real numbers from 0 to 1, which becomes a P-model by defining $\perp = 0$, $\diamond = 1$, and $a \oplus b = (a + b)/2$. The operation '$\oplus$' is well-defined and continuous, and obviously commutative, idempotent, and satisfies the rectangular law. The fixed point axiom holds, since equations $x = a \oplus x$ have exactly one solution, namely $x = a$.

Since $\mathbb{I}$ is a P-model, the map $\lambda x. \perp : X \rightarrow \mathbb{I}$ has a (unique) extension $\varphi : \mathcal{P}X \rightarrow \mathbb{I}$ with $\varphi\perp = 0$ and $\varphi\diamond = 1$. Intuitively, φA is the probability that the computation A fails without result.

We compare $L = \bot * (\bot * \diamond)$ and $R = M\alpha((\bot * \bot) * \diamond)$. First, $\bot * \diamond = \bot \, \bar{\times} \diamond \oplus \bot \, \bar{\times} \diamond = \bot \oplus \diamond$ holds. Thus, using additivity, we obtain

$$L = \bot * (\bot \oplus \diamond) = (\bot * \bot) \oplus (\bot * \diamond) = \bot \oplus (\bot \oplus \diamond) \qquad \text{and}$$
$$R = M\alpha(\bot * \diamond) = M\alpha(\bot \oplus \diamond) = \bot \oplus \diamond.$$

Therefore, $\varphi L = 0 \oplus (0 \oplus 1) = 1/4$, whereas $\varphi R = 0 \oplus 1 = 1/2$, whence $L \neq R$ follows.

8 Decent Products

After the attempt to construct an alternative product by an explicit formula has failed to yield an associative product, we try an axiomatic approach. We call a binary operation $\bar{\times} : \mathcal{P}X \times \mathcal{P}Y \to \mathcal{P}(X \times Y)$ a *decent product* iff it is biadditive, satisfies (P1), $\diamond \, \bar{\times} \, \diamond = \diamond$, and $\bot \, \bar{\times} \, \bot = \bot$. From Theorem 5.5, we can conclude immediately:

Proposition 8.1   Let '$\bar{\times}_1$' and '$\bar{\times}_2$' be two decent products. Then $\bar{\times}_1 \leq \bar{\times}_2$ iff $\diamond \, \bar{\times}_1 \, \bot \leq \diamond \, \bar{\times}_2 \, \bot$ and $\bot \, \bar{\times}_1 \, \diamond \leq \bot \, \bar{\times}_2 \, \diamond$. The same holds with '$\leq$' replaced by '$=$'.

Thus, a decent product is uniquely determined by its values on $(\bot, \diamond)$ and $(\diamond, \bot)$. We are particularly interested in the following four possibilities:

- ◆ Left product $\times_L$: $\qquad \bot \times_L \diamond = \bot \qquad \diamond \times_L \bot = \diamond$
- ◆ Right product $\times_R$: $\qquad \bot \times_R \diamond = \diamond \qquad \diamond \times_R \bot = \bot$
- ◆ Strict product $\check{\times}$: $\qquad \bot \, \check{\times} \, \diamond = \bot \qquad \diamond \, \check{\times} \, \bot = \bot$
- ◆ Parallel product $\hat{\times}$: $\qquad \bot \, \hat{\times} \, \diamond = \diamond \qquad \diamond \, \hat{\times} \, \bot = \diamond$

We have already met some of these products:

Proposition 8.2   For a decent theory, the left and right products exist and are given by the standard products '$\bar{\times}$' and '$\bar{\times}$'. For the set-like theory S, the strict product exists and is given by the choice product.

Proof: The standard products satisfy (P1) by Theorem 3.1, and are biadditive and yield the required results for empty arguments by Prop. 6.2. The choice product is decent by Prop. 7.1. In case of theory S, the required behaviour on empty arguments can be easily checked. $\qquad \square$

The properties of left and right product are thus given by the properties of the standard products. The properties of strict and parallel product are as follows:

Theorem 8.3   For every ND-theory T, the strict product $\check{\times}$ and the parallel product $\hat{\times}$ — provided they exist — are biadditive, satisfy (P1), are natural (P2), associative (P3), and commutative (P4).

Proof: Biadditivity is part of the definition (strict and parallel product are decent). To prove (P2), (P3), and (P4), use Theorem 5.5. $\qquad \square$

The strict product is really strict, and the parallel product is $\diamond$-strict:

Proposition 8.4
(1) If $\bot \oplus \bot = \bot$ holds in T and '$\check{\times}$' exists, then $A \, \check{\times} \, \bot = \bot \, \check{\times} \, B = \bot$.
(2) If $\diamond \oplus \diamond = \diamond$ holds in T and '$\hat{\times}$' exists, then $A \, \hat{\times} \, \diamond = \diamond \, \hat{\times} \, B = \diamond$.

Proof: Compare $F = \lambda A. \, A \, \check{\times} \, \bot$ and $G = \lambda A. \, \bot$ by Prop. 5.4. Proceed analogously for '$\hat{\times}$'. $\qquad \square$

9 Existence of Parallel Products

In this section, we show the existence of parallel products for the ND-theories S, M, and P. This is done by a universal construction, which in principle works for all decent ND-theories. The idea is to construct '$\hat{\times}$' by uncurrying a function from $\mathcal{P}X$ to (a sub-dcpo of) $[\mathcal{P}Y \to \mathcal{P}(X \times Y)]$. This function is obtained by extending a suitable function from X. An analogous construction may be used to show the existence of strict products for these theories.

In the sequel, let T be a decent ND-theory, and $\mathcal{P}$ the corresponding free construction. For dcpo's X and Y, let $Z = [\mathcal{P}Y \xrightarrow{\oplus \diamond} \mathcal{P}(X \times Y)]$ be the dcpo of *additive $\diamond$-strict* morphisms from $\mathcal{P}Y$ to $\mathcal{P}(X \times Y)$. We make Z into a T-model by defining '$\oplus$' and $\diamond$ pointwise as $f \oplus g = \lambda B.\, fB \oplus gB$ and $\diamond = \lambda B.\, \diamond$, and additionally $\bot = \lambda B.\, \bot \bar{\times} B$.

The operations are well defined: By Prop. 6.1, $f \oplus g$ is additive and $\diamond$-strict, and the function $\diamond$ is additive. It is obviously $\diamond$-strict. Finally, the function $\bot$ is additive and $\diamond$-strict, since '$\bar{\times}$' is additive and $\diamond$-strict in its right argument.

Next, we have to show that Z is a T-model. We cannot do this in general, because the theory T may contain exotic axioms that do not carry over to the function space. On the other hand, all axioms that occur in this paper do carry over, as is shown in the following discussion.

Equational and inequational axioms with '$\oplus$' as the only operation hold in Z because '$\oplus$' on functions is defined pointwise. This covers commutativity, associativity, idempotence, and the rectangle axiom, and even the fixed point axiom of the theory P, which is equivalent to $A \oplus A = A$ (idempotence) and $A \oplus B = B \Rightarrow A \leq B$.

Similarly, axioms involving $\diamond$ such as $A \oplus \diamond = A$ and $\diamond \oplus \diamond = \diamond$ hold in Z because of the pointwise definition of the function $\diamond$.

The problem is with axioms involving $\bot$, since this function is not defined pointwise. For $\bot \leq A$ for instance, we have to compare $\lambda B.\, \bot \bar{\times} B$ with an arbitrary additive $\diamond$-strict function f by Prop. 5.4. Both functions are additive and $\diamond$-strict. For $\bot$, $\bot \bar{\times} \bot = \bot \leq f\bot$ holds. For generators, we have $\bot \bar{\times} rb = \mathsf{M}\sigma^b \bot = \bot \leq f(rb)$.

For the axiom $\bot = \diamond$, we know from Prop. 6.3 that decent theories with this axiom induce symmetric power constructions, whence $\bot \bar{\times} B = \bot \bar{\times} B = \bot = \diamond$.

Once Z is shown to be a T-model, we introduce the function $p = \lambda a.\, \mathsf{M}\sigma_a$, which maps from X to Z, since $\mathsf{M}\sigma_a = \mathsf{E}(r \circ \sigma_a)$ is additive and $\diamond$-strict as an extended function. Extending p yields $P : \mathcal{P}X \to Z$, which by uncurrying induces a function $\hat{\times} : \mathcal{P}X \times \mathcal{P}Y \to \mathcal{P}(X \times Y)$. We claim that '$\hat{\times}$' is the parallel product for $\mathcal{P}$.

The function '$\hat{\times}$' is additive and $\diamond$-strict in its left argument, since P is the extension of p, extended functions are additive and $\diamond$-strict, and '$\oplus$' and $\diamond$ are defined pointwise in Z. It is additive and $\diamond$-strict in its right argument, since $\lambda B.\, A \hat{\times} B = PA$ is in Z. Considering $\bot$, $\bot \hat{\times} \bot = \bot \bar{\times} \bot = \bot$ holds.

Finally, we show (P1). One part is easy: $ra \hat{\times} B = P(ra)B = paB = \mathsf{M}\sigma_a B$ holds. For the other part, we compare $\lambda A.\, A \hat{\times} rb$ and $\mathsf{M}\sigma^b$ by Prop. 5.4. Both functions are additive and $\diamond$-strict. For generators, $ra \hat{\times} rb = \mathsf{M}\sigma_a(rb) = r(a, b) = \mathsf{M}\sigma^b(ra)$ holds, and for $\bot$, we have $\bot \hat{\times} rb = \bot \bar{\times} rb = \mathsf{M}\sigma^b \bot$ by (P1) of '$\bar{\times}$'.

Summarizing, we have shown the existence of parallel products for the theories S, M, and P. If T is another decent theory, then our method also works if the axioms of T can be proved for the function space Z.

10 Conclusion

To define the semantics of pairing in Moggi's framework, a product operation
$\bar{\times} : MX \times MY \to M(X \times Y)$ for the computational strong monad M is needed.
After having studied the algebraic properties of the two standard products '$\bar{\times}$'
and '$\bar{\times}$', which correspond to left-to-right and right-to-left evaluation, we have
looked for possible alternative products. In the special case, where M is given
by the free construction for a decent non-deterministic theory, we found two
such alternative products: the strict product '$\check{\times}$' and the parallel product '$\hat{\times}$'.

Acknowledgments

This paper was written during my one-year visit at Imperial College, London.
The visit was made possible by a grant of the Deutsche Forschungsgemeinschaft.
I have to thank all the people of the TFM section of Imperial College for their
stimulating environment, and for giving me the opportunity to participate in
their Section Workshop.

References

[1] C.A. Gunter. Relating total and partial correctness interpretations of non-deterministic
programs. In P. Hudak, editor, *Principles of Programming Languages (POPL '90)*, pages
306–319. ACM, 1990.

[2] R. Heckmann. *Power Domain Constructions*. PhD thesis, Universität des Saarlandes,
1990.

[3] R. Heckmann. Power domain constructions. *Science of Computer Programming*, 17:77–
117, 1991.

[4] R. Heckmann. Power domains supporting recursion and failure. In J.-C. Raoult, editor,
CAAP '92, pages 165–181. *Lecture Notes in Comp. Sc. 581*, Springer-Verlag, 1992.

[5] M.C.B Hennessy and G.D. Plotkin. Full abstraction for a simple parallel programming
language. In J. Becvar, editor, *Foundations of Computer Science*, pages 108–120. *Lecture
Notes in Comp. Sc. 74*, Springer-Verlag, 1979.

[6] R. Hoofman. Powerdomains. Technical Report RUU-CS-87-23, Rijksuniversiteit Utrecht,
November 1987.

[7] C.J. Jones. *Probabilistic Non-Determinism*. PhD thesis, University of Edinburgh, 1990.

[8] C.J. Jones and G.D. Plotkin. A probabilistic powerdomain of evaluations. In *LICS '89*,
pages 186–195. IEEE Computer Society Press, 1989.

[9] J. Lambek and P. J. Scott. *Introduction to Higher Order Categorical Logic*, volume 7 of
Cambridge Studies in Advanced Mathematics. Cambridge University Press, 1986.

[10] S. Mac Lane. *Categories for the Working Mathematician*. Springer-Verlag, 1971.

[11] M.G. Main. Free constructions of powerdomains. In A. Melton, editor, *Mathematical
Foundations of Programming Semantics*, pages 162–183. *Lecture Notes in Comp. Sc.
239*, Springer-Verlag, 1985.

[12] E. Moggi. Computational lambda-calculus and monads. In *4th LICS Conference*, pages
14–23. IEEE, 1989.

[13] E. Moggi. Notions of computation and monads. *Information and Computation*, 93:55–92,
1991.

[14] G.D. Plotkin. A powerdomain construction. *SIAM Journal on Computing*, 5(3):452–487,
1976.

[15] M.B. Smyth. Power domains. *Journal of Computer and System Sciences*, 16:23–36,
1978.

On the Equivalence of State-Transition Systems

Michael Huth

mrah@doc.ic.ac.uk

Department of Computing, Imperial College
180 Queen's Gate, London SW7 2BZ, United Kingdom

Abstract

We study frameworks for the equivalence of abstract state-transition systems represented as posets. A basic notion of equivalence is proposed. A least fixpoint operator transforms basic equivalences into strong equivalences (=*Lagois Connections*) which makes Lagois Connections into a category. In the absence of divergence, the two notions of equivalence coincide. We generalize these notions by adding a logical level to express divergence more precisely. Then both generalized notions of equivalence coincide even in the presence of divergence.

1   Introduction

We consider posets as *abstract state-transition systems*. Elements s in a poset $\langle P, \sqsubseteq \rangle$ model *states* and $s \sqsubseteq s'$ expresses the intuition that state s' can be reached by performing a finite sequence of state transitions beginning with state s. The reasons for including the axiom of *antisymmetry* will become apparent in this study. Such an approach excludes an immediate analysis of transition graphs; but it does not constitute a conceptual exclusion, for antisymmetry can be restored by rewriting such systems in form of a *tree of traces*.

What is a reasonable mathematical framework for the equivalence of two such abstract state-transition systems $\langle P, \sqsubseteq \rangle$ and $\langle Q, \sqsubseteq \rangle$? Assuming that P and Q are intuitively equivalent, we should be able to associate to each state s in P a state $f(s)$ in Q and likewise a state $g(t)$ in P for each state $t \in Q$. So we should impose the existence of a pair of set-theoretic functions $f \colon P \to Q$ and $g \colon Q \to P$. Further, *reachability* should be preserved under these state transformations: if $s \sqsubseteq s'$ in P, then $f(s) \sqsubseteq f(s')$ should follow in Q. Therefore, we want f and g to be *monotone maps*. Finally, we expect the state $g(f(s))$ to be reachable from the original state s. Thus, our monotone maps should satisfy the inequalities $\mathrm{id}_P \sqsubseteq gf$ and $\mathrm{id}_Q \sqsubseteq fg$.

Definition 1 Let P and Q be posets. A pair of monotone maps $f \colon P \to Q$ and $g \colon Q \to P$ is called a *poset system* [10]; we denote this by $\langle f, g \rangle \colon P \to Q$. We call a poset system a *basic equivalence* iff $\mathrm{id}_P \sqsubseteq gf$ and $\mathrm{id}_Q \sqsubseteq fg$ hold. □

In [10], another notion of equivalence had been proposed which is a basic equivalence $\langle f, g \rangle \colon P \to Q$ satisfying the equations $fgf = f$ and $gfg = g$; so f and g are additionally *quasi-inverses* of each other. The functions $gf \colon P \to P$ and $fg \colon Q \to Q$ are then *closure operators* with isomorphic image [10]. Such poset systems are called *Lagois Connections* [10]; they are a generalization of the case where one of the abstract state-transition systems sits as a closure inside the other, i.e., where $\mathrm{id}_P = gf$ or $\mathrm{id}_Q = fg$. Lagois Connections have a theory similar to the one of *Galois Connections* [4, 9, 10].

Definition 2 A *poset system* $\langle f, g \rangle \colon P \to Q$ is called a *strong equivalence* iff it is a basic equivalence satisfying the equations $fgf = f$ and $gfg = g$. □

So the terms *strong equivalence* and *Lagois Connection* have the same meaning. We will address three main issues in this piece of work.

- ♦ Are basic and strong equivalences really equivalences in the mathematical sense?
- ♦ If so, are they really different concepts?
- ♦ How do they match with the most common equivalence results in semantics?

2 The Category of Basic Equivalences

There is a natural way of making poset systems into a category [9]; its objects are posets, its morphisms are poset systems $\langle f, g \rangle \colon P \to Q$ and $\langle i, j \rangle \colon Q \to R$, composition is $\langle f, g \rangle \circ \langle i, j \rangle := \langle if, gj \rangle$ and identities are $\langle \mathrm{id}_P, \mathrm{id}_P \rangle \colon P \to P$. Basic equivalences are readily seen to be closed under that composition; so basic equivalences form naturally a category and composition verifies the transitivity of this equivalence notion.

The case of strong equivalences is problematic. Lagois Connections simply are not closed under this composition [10]. But there is an intuitive way of constructing a Lagois Connection out of a basic equivalence $\langle f, g \rangle \colon P \to Q$: if we *feed back* the maps f and g, we obtain for each $n \geq 1$ basic equivalences $\langle (fg)^n f, (gf)^n g \rangle \colon P \to Q$ which form an ascending chain. *If* our posets have limits of ω-chains, then we expect the limit of this chain to be a Lagois Connection. Therefore, we will have to abandon the realm of posets and consider *dcpos*, posets in which every directed set has a supremum [5, 7, 12, 15] (of course, ω-dcpos would suffice).

Definition 3 Let D and E be dcpos. A *dcpo system* $\langle f, g \rangle \colon D \to E$ is a poset system such that f and g are Scott-continuous [5, 7, 12, 15], i.e., they preserve suprema of all directed sets. Define

$$\mathcal{B}(D, E) := \{\langle f, g \rangle \colon D \to E \text{ dcpo system} \mid \mathrm{id}_D \sqsubseteq gf \ \& \ \mathrm{id}_E \sqsubseteq fg\} \quad (1)$$

$$\mathcal{S}(D, E) := \{\langle f, g \rangle \colon D \to E \in \mathcal{B}(D, E) \mid fgf = f \ \& \ gfg = g\} \quad (2)$$

and order $\mathcal{B}(D, E)$ and $\mathcal{S}(D, E)$ by

$$\langle f, g \rangle \sqsubseteq \langle i, j \rangle :\Leftrightarrow f \sqsubseteq i \ \& \ g \sqsubseteq j. \quad (3)$$

□

The letters $\mathcal{B}$ and $\mathcal{S}$ stand for *basic* and *strong* equivalences respectively. If $[D \to E]$ denotes the function space of all Scott-continuous maps $f \colon D \to E$ in the pointwise order, this is a dcpo where directed suprema of sets $\{f_i \mid i \in I\}$ are computed componentwise: $(\bigsqcup_{i \in I} f_i)(d) = \bigsqcup_{i \in I} f_i(d)$ [5, 7, 12, 15]. This makes $\mathcal{B}(D, E)$ and $\mathcal{S}(D, E)$ into dcpos.

Proposition 1 Let D and E be dcpos. Then $\mathcal{B}(D, E)$ is a dcpo and suprema of directed sets are computed componentwise:

$$\bigsqcup_{i \in I} \langle f_i, g_i \rangle = \langle \bigsqcup_{i \in I} f_i, \bigsqcup_{i \in I} g_i \rangle. \tag{4}$$

Moreover, $\mathcal{S}(D, E)$ is a subdcpo of $\mathcal{B}(D, E)$, i.e., the inclusion $\mathcal{S}(D, E) \hookrightarrow \mathcal{B}(D, E)$ is Scott-continuous. $\qquad\qquad\square$

We can recover our poset systems $\langle f, g \rangle \colon P \to Q$ from dcpo systems by identifying the posets P and Q with the algebraic dcpos of their *ideal completions* [4, 7] $\mathrm{Idl}(P)$ and $\mathrm{Idl}(Q)$, and by construing f and g as Scott-continuous maps which *preserve all finite elements*. Recall, that a function $h \colon D \to E$ preserves finite elements iff $h(\mathrm{K}(D)) \subseteq \mathrm{K}(E)$ where $\mathrm{K}(D)$ denotes the poset of *finite*, or *compact elements* [4, 5, 7, 17] of a dcpo D.

Definition 4 For dcpos D and E, define

$$\mathcal{BF}(D, E) := \{\langle f, g \rangle \in \mathcal{B}(D, E) \mid f(\mathrm{K}(D)) \subseteq \mathrm{K}(E), \, g(\mathrm{K}(E)) \subseteq \mathrm{K}(D)\} \tag{5}$$
$$\mathcal{SF}(D, E) := \mathcal{BF}(D, E) \cap \mathcal{S}(D, E) \tag{6}$$

in the order induced by $\mathcal{B}(D, E)$. $\qquad\qquad\square$

The $\mathcal{F}$ in $\mathcal{BF}$ stands for preserving $f$inite elements. Given algebraic dcpos D and E, dcpo systems in $\mathcal{BF}(D, E)$, respectively $\mathcal{SF}(D, E)$, correspond to basic, respectively strong, equivalences between the abstract state-transition systems $\mathrm{K}(D)$ and $\mathrm{K}(E)$. Before we make abstract state-transition systems into a category, we should discuss minimal specifications on posets as representations of abstract state-transition systems. First, such a poset P should satisfy the *descending chain condition* [3]: there do not exist strictly descending chains $a_0 > a_1 > \cdots$ in P; this means that a state of a computation should be reachable by an initial state (a minimal element of P). Second, no strictly ascending chain $b_0 < b_1 < \cdots$ in P should have an upper bound in P. Otherwise, such an upper bound u would be a state with an *infinite previous history* or an *infinite cause*. We do not, however, exclude the possibility of having infinitely many states which can cause a particular state s: the domain in Figure 1 is a representation of such an abstract state-transition system.

Definition 5 Let ASS be the class of all algebraic dcpos D such that $\mathrm{K}(D)$ satisfies the descending chain condition and no strictly ascending chain in $\mathrm{K}(D)$ has an upper bound in $\mathrm{K}(D)$. Define $\mathcal{BF}$ to be the four-sorted structure $(\mathrm{ob}(\mathcal{BF}), \mathrm{morph}(\mathcal{BF}), \circ, \mathrm{id})$ such that $\mathrm{ob}(\mathcal{BF})$ is the class ASS, $\mathrm{morph}(\mathcal{BF})$ is the class of hom-sets $\mathcal{BF}(D, E)$ for D and E in ASS, composition is

$$\langle f, g \rangle \circ \langle i, j \rangle := \langle if, gj \rangle \tag{7}$$

and identities are

$$\langle \mathrm{id}_D, \mathrm{id}_D \rangle \colon D \to D. \tag{8}$$

Define a relation $\sim_t$ on ASS by

$$D \sim_t E \text{ iff } \mathcal{BF}(D, E) \neq \emptyset. \tag{9}$$

$\qquad\qquad\square$

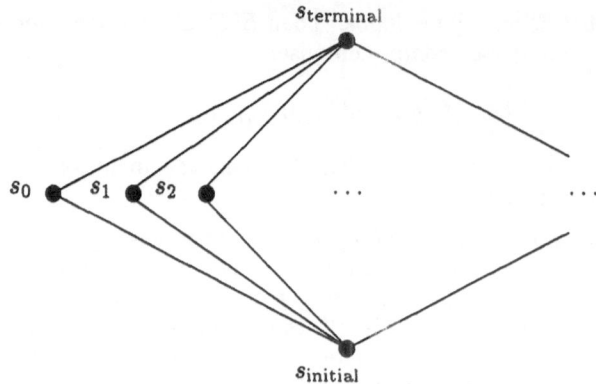

Figure 1: An abstract state-transition system with a state s_{terminal} which can be reached from infinitely many states

We readily note that $\mathcal{BF}$ is a self-dual category, i.e., $\mathcal{BF}$ is equivalent to its dual category [8], and that $\sim_t$ is an equivalence relation on ASS.

Theorem 1 $\mathcal{BF}$ is a self-dual category and $\sim_t$ is an equivalence relation on $\text{ASS} = \text{ob}(\mathcal{BF})$.

   PROOF. *The self-duality follows from the order-isomorphism*

$$\langle f, g \rangle \mapsto \langle g, f \rangle : \mathcal{BF}(D, E) \to \mathcal{BF}(E, D). \tag{10}$$

Composition is clearly well-defined and associative; the pairs $\langle \text{id}_D, \text{id}_D \rangle$ are two-sided identities with respect to this composition. The existence of identities ensures the reflexivity of $\sim_t$, the self-duality of $\mathcal{BF}$ makes $\sim_t$ symmetric and the well-definedness of composition in $\mathcal{BF}$ makes $\sim_t$ transitive. □

Things don't work that smoothly for strong equivalences. At least, we can introduce a least fix-point operator which transforms basic into strong equivalences. This will be the key for obtaining a composition for strong equivalences.

Definition 6 For dcpos D and E and $\langle f, g \rangle \in \mathcal{B}(D, E)$ define

$$\langle f_0, g_0 \rangle \quad := \quad \langle f, g \rangle \tag{11}$$
$$\langle f_{n+1}, g_{n+1} \rangle \quad := \quad \langle (fg)f_n, (gf)g_n \rangle, \qquad n \geq 0 \tag{12}$$
$$\langle f_\omega, g_\omega \rangle \quad := \quad \bigsqcup_{n \geq 0} \langle f_n, g_n \rangle. \tag{13}$$

□

   The pair $\langle f_\omega, g_\omega \rangle$ is well-defined; it is the least Lagois Connection above $\langle f, g \rangle$ in $\mathcal{S}(D, E)$.

Theorem 2 For dcpos D and E, the map

$$\Omega_{\langle D, E \rangle} : \mathcal{B}(D, E) \to \mathcal{B}(D, E), \quad \Omega_{\langle D, E \rangle} := \lambda \langle f, g \rangle.\langle f_\omega, g_\omega \rangle \tag{14}$$

is a Scott-continuous closure operator on $\mathcal{B}(D, E)$ with image $\mathcal{S}(D, E)$. □

This suggests a composition for Lagois Connections. Given dcpo systems $\langle f, g \rangle \in \mathcal{SF}(D, E)$ and $\langle i, j \rangle \in \mathcal{SF}(E, F)$, the dcpo system $\langle f, g \rangle \circ \langle i, j \rangle$ is a morphism in $\mathcal{BF}(D, F)$, so we could define the strong composition of $\langle f, g \rangle \in \mathcal{SF}(D, E)$ and $\langle i, j \rangle \in \mathcal{SF}(E, F)$ to be the least fix point of $\Omega_{\langle D, F \rangle}$ applied to $\langle f, g \rangle \circ \langle i, j \rangle$:

$$\langle f, g \rangle * \langle i, j \rangle := \Omega_{\langle D, F \rangle}\left(\langle f, g \rangle \circ \langle i, j \rangle\right). \tag{15}$$

Of course, it will be vital to know whether this operation will make $\mathcal{SF}$ into a category. Unfortunately, this is not so in the presence of divergence. For example, consider the dcpo $\omega + 1$ where $\mathrm{K}(\omega + 1) = \{0 < 1 < \cdots\}$ is an abstract state-transition system modeling a diverging stream of computation. Define the dcpo systems $\langle f, f \rangle, \langle g, g \rangle \colon (\omega + 1) \to (\omega + 1)$ such that $f(n)$, respectively $g(n)$, is the least odd, respectively even, number above n. Then $\langle f, f \rangle, \langle g, g \rangle \in \mathcal{SF}(\omega + 1, \omega + 1)$ is readily seen, but $\langle f, f \rangle * \langle g, g \rangle = \langle \lambda n.\omega, \lambda n.\omega \rangle$ is not even in $\mathcal{BF}(\omega + 1, \omega + 1)$ as ω is not finite in $\omega + 1$.

However, one might ask why $\langle \lambda n.\omega, \lambda n.\omega \rangle$ does not demonstrate an equivalence on $\omega + 1$? After all, each finite element being mapped to ω leads only to diverging computations.

3 Handling Divergence with a Logical Level

We therefore propose to add a logical level to dcpo systems $\langle f, g \rangle \in \mathcal{B}(D, E)$. If $\mathcal{BD}(D, E)$ denotes those $\langle f, g \rangle \in \mathcal{B}(D, E)$ satisfying the logical level still to be defined, we expect for all D and E in ASS, that

- $\mathcal{BF}(D, E)$ is a subset of $\mathcal{BD}(D, E)$,
- $\mathcal{BD}(D, E)$ is closed under $\circ$ in $\mathcal{B}(D, E)$,
- $\mathcal{BD}(D, E)$ is closed under $\Omega_{\langle D, E \rangle}$ in $\mathcal{B}(D, E)$ and
- the relation $\sim_d$ induced by the sets $\mathcal{BD}(D, E)$ is a computationally meaningful equivalence relation of the class ASS.

Definition 7 For a dcpo D, define

$$D^\infty := D \setminus \mathrm{K}(D) \tag{16}$$

to be the poset of *states of divergence* of D. Given $\langle f, g \rangle \in \mathcal{B}(D, E)$, we call $\langle f, g \rangle$ a *demonstration of equivalence* iff

$$\uparrow(f^{-1}(E^\infty)) \cap \max(D) \subseteq D^\infty \text{ and} \tag{17}$$
$$\uparrow(g^{-1}(D^\infty)) \cap \max(E) \subseteq E^\infty, \tag{18}$$

where $\max(D) := \{d \in D \mid \uparrow(d) = \{d\}\}$. Define

$$\mathcal{BD}(D, E) \quad := \quad \{\langle f, g \rangle \in \mathcal{B}(D, E) \mid \langle f, g \rangle \text{ is demonstr. of equiv.}\} \tag{19}$$
$$\mathcal{SD}(D, E) \quad := \quad \mathcal{BD}(D, E) \cap \mathcal{S}(D, E) \tag{20}$$

in the order induced by $\mathcal{B}(D, E)$. Define the relation $\sim_d$ on ASS by

$$D \sim_d E \text{ iff } \mathcal{BD}(D, E) \neq \emptyset. \tag{21}$$

$\square$

The $\mathcal{D}$ in $\mathcal{BD}$ stands for *divergence*. The conditions on f say the following (the explanation for g is symmetric and we omit it): if f maps $d \in D$ to a state of divergence, this is fine as long as all maximal states in D above d are also states of divergence. For example, $\langle \lambda n.\omega, \lambda n.\omega \rangle : (\omega + 1) \to (\omega + 1)$ is such a demonstration of equivalence. However, there is no demonstration of equivalence between $\omega + 1$ and $\{s\}$ as any equivalence has to map s to $\omega \in (\omega + 1)^{\infty}$, but s is maximal and not a state of divergence. This should suffice to justify the 'soundness' of this equivalence notion. We verify that it satisfies our proposed constraints.

Proposition 2 Let D, E and F be elements in ASS. Then we have the following.

1. Each $\langle f, g \rangle \in \mathcal{B}(D, E)$ induces a bijection between $\max(D)$ and $\max(E)$; if $\langle f, g \rangle \sqsubseteq \langle i, j \rangle$ in $\mathcal{B}(D, E)$, then $\langle f, g \rangle$ and $\langle i, j \rangle$ induce the same bijection,

2. $\mathcal{BD}(D, E)$ is an upper set in $\mathcal{B}(D, E)$,

3. $\mathcal{BD}(D, E)$ contains $\mathcal{BF}(D, E)$ and

4. if $\langle f, g \rangle \in \mathcal{BD}(D, E)$ and $\langle i, j \rangle \in \mathcal{BD}(E, F)$, then $\langle f, g \rangle \circ \langle i, j \rangle := \langle if, gj \rangle$ is in $\mathcal{BD}(D, F)$. $\qquad\square$

Since $\mathcal{BD}(D, E)$ is an upper set in $\mathcal{B}(D, E)$ and since $\circ$ is well-defined on $\mathcal{BD}$, we can draw several conclusions: $\mathcal{BD}$ is a category, $\sim_d$ is an equivalence relation and $*$ is a well-defined operation on the hom-sets in $\mathcal{BD}$.

Theorem 3 $\mathcal{BD}$ is a self-dual category and $\sim_d$ is an equivalence relation on ASS $= \mathrm{ob}(\mathcal{BF})$. Moreover, $\mathcal{BF}$ is a full subcategory of $\mathcal{BD}$ and $\sim_t$ is a subclass of $\sim_d$.

PROOF. *The proof that $\mathcal{BD}$ is a self-dual category is similar to the corresponding proof for $\mathcal{BF}$. Since $\mathcal{BF}(D, E) \subseteq \mathcal{BD}(D, E)$, the rest is clear.* $\qquad\square$

4 The Category of Lagois Connections

We have seen that $*$ is a well-defined operation on the hom-sets in $\mathcal{BD}$. Note that the identities on $\mathcal{BD}$ serve also as two-sided identities for $*$ applied to strong equivalences as $\langle \mathrm{id}_D, \mathrm{id}_D \rangle$ is already a strong equivalence for D in ASS; but how can we prove that $*$ is associative?

The solution follows a general category-theoretical pattern which we have so far not been able to match with standard concepts in category theory [2, 8].

Definition 8 Let $\mathcal{C}$ be a category and Ω a class of set-theoretic functions

$$\Omega_{\langle A,B \rangle} : \mathcal{C}(A, B) \to \mathcal{C}(A, B) \tag{22}$$

for all objects A and B in $\mathcal{C}$. We call Ω *an associative structure over $\mathcal{C}$* iff for all morphisms $f \in \mathcal{C}(B, C)$ and $g \in \mathcal{C}(A, B)$, we have

$$\Omega_{\langle A,C \rangle} \big(f \circ (\Omega_{\langle A,B \rangle} g) \big) \quad = \quad \Omega_{\langle A,C \rangle} (f \circ g) \tag{23}$$

$$= \quad \Omega_{\langle A,C \rangle} \big((\Omega_{\langle B,C \rangle} f) \circ g \big). \tag{24}$$

Define

$$\mathcal{C}[\Omega](A, B) \quad := \quad \mathrm{im}(\Omega_{\langle A,B \rangle}) = \{ \Omega_{\langle A,B \rangle} f \mid f \in \mathcal{C}(A, B) \} \tag{25}$$

$$\mathrm{id}_A^{\Omega} \quad := \quad \Omega_{\langle A,A \rangle} \mathrm{id}_A \text{ and} \tag{26}$$

$$f * g \quad := \quad \Omega_{\langle A,C \rangle} (f \circ g). \qquad\square \tag{27}$$

The four-sorted structure $\big(\mathrm{ob}(\mathcal{C}), \mathcal{C}[\Omega], *, \mathrm{id}^{\Omega}\big)$ is a category and Ω induces a functor $\Omega \colon \mathcal{C} \to \mathcal{C}[\Omega]$.

Theorem 4 Let $\mathcal{C}$ be a category and Ω an associative structure over $\mathcal{C}$. Then we have the following:

1. For all objects A and B in $\mathcal{C}$, the function $\Omega_{\langle A,B\rangle}$ is a retraction on $\mathcal{C}(A,B)$,

2. the four-sorted structure $\big(\mathrm{ob}(\mathcal{C}), \mathcal{C}[\Omega], *, \mathrm{id}^{\Omega}\big)$ is a category and

3. if Ω also denotes the function which leaves objects of $\mathcal{C}$ fixed and maps morphisms $f \in \mathcal{C}(A,B)$ to $\Omega_{\langle A,B\rangle} f$, then Ω is a functor

$$\Omega \colon \mathcal{C} \to \mathcal{C}[\Omega]. \tag{28}$$

□

We will now show that the class of Scott-continuous closure operators of Theorem 2 is an associative structure over the category $\mathcal{BD}$. This will make Lagois Connections into a category. First, we will reduce the complexity of such a proof; note that the operator Ω occurs *nested* in the equations (23)–(24). We can use the concrete poset structure of the category $\mathcal{BD}$ to reduce these equations to equivalent inequalities in which Ω only appears at one level.

Proposition 3 Let $\mathcal{C}$ be a category such that all hom-sets $\mathcal{C}(A,B)$ are posets and composition is monotone. If Ω is a class of closure operators $\Omega_{\langle A,B\rangle}$ on $\mathcal{C}(A,B)$ for all objects A and B in $\mathcal{C}$, then Ω is an associative structure over $\mathcal{C}$ if for all morphisms $f \in \mathcal{C}(B,C)$ and $g \in \mathcal{C}(A,B)$, we have

$$f \circ (\Omega_{\langle A,B\rangle} g) \;\sqsubseteq\; \Omega_{\langle A,C\rangle}(f \circ g) \text{ and} \tag{29}$$

$$(\Omega_{\langle B,C\rangle} f) \circ g \;\sqsubseteq\; \Omega_{\langle A,C\rangle}(f \circ g). \tag{30}$$

In that case, $*$ is monotone. □

Theorem 5 The class of Scott-continuous closure operators Ω of Theorem 2 is an associative structure over the category $\mathcal{BD}$. In particular,

$$\mathcal{SD} := \mathcal{BD}[\Omega] \tag{31}$$

is a category, the *category of Lagois Connections*. The composition in $\mathcal{SD}$ is Scott-continuous and is given by the *feed-back formula*

$$\langle f,g\rangle * \langle i,j\rangle = \bigsqcup_{n \geq 0}\big((ifgj)^n(if), (gjif)^n(gj)\big). \tag{32}$$

PROOF. *The assumptions of Proposition 3 apply, so it suffices to show the inequalities (29)–(30). For $\langle f,g\rangle \in \mathcal{BD}(D,E)$ and $\langle i,j\rangle \in \mathcal{BD}(E,F)$, we compute the first coordinates of expressions occurring in these inequalities. The proof for the second coordinates is similar and we omit it. The first coordinate of $\Omega_{\langle D,F\rangle}\big(\langle f,g\rangle \circ \langle i,j\rangle\big)$ is $\bigsqcup_{n \geq 0}(ifgj)^n(if)$, the first coordinate of $\langle f,g\rangle \circ \big(\Omega_{\langle E,F\rangle}\langle i,j\rangle\big)$ equals $\bigsqcup_{n \geq 0}(ij)^n(if)$ and the first coordinate of $\big(\Omega_{\langle D,E\rangle}\langle f,g\rangle\big) \circ \langle i,j\rangle$ is $\bigsqcup_{n \geq 0}i(fg)^n f$, so we are done if $i(fg)^n f, (ij)^n(if) \sqsubseteq (ifgj)^n(if)$ for all $n \geq 1$; this is an easy induction.* □

One could now define an equivalence relation $\approx_d$ such that $D \approx_d E$ in ASS iff $SD(D, E) \neq \emptyset$. But since $\Omega_{\langle D, E\rangle}(BD(D, E)) = SD(D, E)$, this relation equals $\sim_d$. Thus, these relations render the same concept of equivalence even in the presence of divergence. What can we say in the absence of divergence? If TERM denotes the class of all D in ASS such that $K(D) = D$, then we have the set equalities $BF(D, E) = BD(D, E) = B(D, E)$ as there are no states of divergence for D and E in TERM.

Theorem 6 On the class TERM, the relations $\sim_d$, $\sim_t$ and $\approx_t$ are equal; where we define

$$D \approx_t E \text{ iff } SF(D, E) \neq \emptyset. \tag{33}$$

In particular, $\approx_t$ is an equivalence relation on TERM. □

One might ask whether $\approx_t$ is also transitive on ASS, or whether its transitive closure equals $\sim_t$ or $\sim_d$; we have not investigated this any further.

The feed-back formula intrinsically contains cases of *nilpotency* which had been noted in [10] as instances of a well-defined composition for Lagois Connections.

Proposition 4 For D and E in ASS and $\langle f, g\rangle \in BD(D, E)$, we have

1. $\langle fg, fg\rangle \in BD(E, E)$ and $\langle gf, gf\rangle \in BD(D, D)$,
2. if $fgf = f$, then

$$\Omega_{\langle D, E\rangle}\langle f, g\rangle = \langle f, gfg\rangle, \tag{34}$$

3. if $gfg = g$, then

$$\Omega_{\langle D, E\rangle}\langle f, g\rangle = \langle fgf, g\rangle, \tag{35}$$

4. if fg or gf is idempotent, then

$$\Omega_{\langle D, E\rangle}\langle f, g\rangle = \langle fgf, gfg\rangle, \tag{36}$$
$$\Omega_{\langle E, E\rangle}\langle fg, fg\rangle = \langle fgfg, fgfg\rangle \text{ and} \tag{37}$$
$$\Omega_{\langle D, D\rangle}\langle gf, gf\rangle = \langle gfgf, gfgf\rangle. \tag{38}$$

□

Let us point out the conceptual gain of these results. By acknowledging the logical level as a sound criterion of equivalence, we can prove two objects D and E in ASS to be equivalent by specifying a basic equivalence $\langle f, g\rangle : D \to E$ in $BD(D, E)$. If we prefer to work with a Lagois connection, we can simply take $\langle f, g\rangle$ and compute the least fix point $\Omega_{\langle D, E\rangle}\langle f, g\rangle$ which will be an element of $SD(D, E)$.

There is a larger framework than the categories BD and SD which does not model equivalences of abstract state-transition systems, but which does have a mathematical interest in its own right. If B denotes the four-sorted structure which has all dcpos as objects, dcpo systems as morphisms, ∘ as composition and pairs $\langle \mathrm{id}_D, \mathrm{id}_D\rangle$ as morphisms, then B is a category which contains BD as a non-full subcategory. Likewise, if we consider

$$S := B[\Omega] \tag{39}$$

then we obtain a corresponding version of Theorem 5 for B and S.

5 Basic Equivalences in Semantics

We want to relate the concepts and results of the preceding sections to familiar situations in formal semantics of programming languages. As a first example, let us compare *operational semantics* for a simple deterministic, imperative WHILE-language [5, 12, 15]. The concrete choice of such a language is irrelevant for the purpose of this discussion. We only need to know that states for such a language come in two flavors. A state is either a pair $\langle S, s \rangle$ where S is a statement in the language and s denotes an *environment* which binds free variables in S, or it is a *terminal state* s'. Intuitively, a state s' models the termination of a program's response to an initial environment. Assuming that our programming language does not produce any *stuck* configurations [12], a state $\langle S, s \rangle$ leads to a successor state which is either terminal, i.e., of the from s', or again of the form $\langle S', s' \rangle$.

There are two prominent operational semantics for such WHILE-languages, called *structural operational semantics* and *natural semantics* [12]. The structural operational semantics is defined by a relation $\Rightarrow$ which specifies what the successor states are; then $\Rightarrow^*$ is the transitive closure of $\Rightarrow$. This semantics models a *single-step* computation. The natural semantics models a *big-step* computation. We write $\langle S, s \rangle \rightarrow s'$ iff the computation starting at $\langle S, s \rangle$ ends in state s'. Otherwise, the relation $\rightarrow$ is undefined. Let $\mathcal{NS}$ be the preorder obtained by forming the reflexive closure of $\rightarrow$ on the set of states of our WHILE-language, and let $\mathcal{SOS}$ be the preorder obtained by forming the reflexive closure of $\Rightarrow^*$ on the same set. We have functions $f: \mathcal{NS} \rightarrow \mathcal{SOS}$ and $g: \mathcal{SOS} \rightarrow \mathcal{NS}$ defined by

$$f\langle S, s \rangle \quad := \quad \langle S, s \rangle, \tag{40}$$

$$f s' \quad := \quad s', \tag{41}$$

$$g s' \quad := \quad s' \text{ and} \tag{42}$$

$$g\langle S, s \rangle \quad := \quad \text{if } \langle S, s \rangle \Rightarrow^* s' \text{ then } s' \text{ else } \langle S, s \rangle. \tag{43}$$

We readily check that f is monotone; this means that $\langle S, s \rangle \rightarrow s'$ implies $\langle S, s \rangle \Rightarrow^* s'$, so the big-step deduction is sound with respect to the single-step deduction. We also have $\mathrm{id}_{\mathcal{NS}} \sqsubseteq g f$ because $\langle S, s \rangle \Rightarrow^* s'$ guarantees $\langle S, s \rangle \rightarrow s'$. Further, we obtain $\mathrm{id}_{\mathcal{SOS}} \sqsubseteq f g$ and the equations $f g f = f$ and $g f g = g$. So it looks as if

$$\langle f, g \rangle : \mathcal{NS} \rightarrow \mathcal{SOS} \tag{44}$$

is a Lagois Connection between the preorders $\mathcal{NS}$ and $\mathcal{SOS}$. Yet, we did not prove the *monotonicity* of g; but g simply is not monotone. Consider a transition $\langle S, s \rangle \Rightarrow^* \langle S', s' \rangle$ such that the computation according to $\Rightarrow^*$ is diverging after $\langle S, s \rangle$, and therefore after $\langle S', s' \rangle$ as well. By definition, $g\langle S, s \rangle = \langle S, s \rangle$ and $g\langle S', s' \rangle = \langle S', s' \rangle$, but $\rightarrow$ is a discrete order on the set of states $\langle S, s \rangle$ which give rise to diverging behavior. So our example is really a good *non-example*. The fact that g is not monotone captures the essential difference between these two operational semantics: the one-step ordering on diverging streams has no equivalent in the big-step computation. It is worth pointing out that the mere existence of f and g suffice to prove the usual semantic correspondence theorems [12]; the non-monotone behavior of g does not affect this.

It is possible to state another big-step operational semantics such that we do have a Lagois Connection between it and the structural operational semantics. For that, let D be the ideal completion of $\mathcal{SOS}$; so we just add one limit point for each diverging stream $\langle S_0, s_0 \rangle \Rightarrow \langle S_1, s_1 \rangle \Rightarrow \cdots$. Since our language is assumed to be deterministic, the relation $\Rightarrow$ can be viewed as a Scott-continuous function $h: D \to D$ such that

$$h\langle S, s \rangle \quad := \quad s' \text{ if } \langle S, s \rangle \Rightarrow s', \tag{45}$$

$$h\langle S, s \rangle \quad := \quad \langle S', s' \rangle \text{ if } \langle S, s \rangle \Rightarrow \langle S', s' \rangle \text{ and} \tag{46}$$

$$h s' \quad := \quad s'. \tag{47}$$

Since $\mathrm{id}_D \sqsubseteq h$ is obvious, we conclude $\langle h, h \rangle \in \mathcal{BF}(D, D)$. Therefore, we can define

$$\langle \texttt{bigstep}, \texttt{bigstep} \rangle := \Omega_{\langle D, D \rangle} \langle h, h \rangle \tag{48}$$

which is an element in $\mathcal{SD}(D, D)$. Moreover, $\texttt{bigstep}$ is a Scott-continuous closure operator on D. Its image consists of all elements of D^∞ and all terminal states s'. The n-th approximation $\langle h_n, h_n \rangle$ of the fix point $\langle \texttt{bigstep}, \texttt{bigstep} \rangle$ computes $2n + 1$ steps from a given state $\langle S, s \rangle$ as

$$\langle h_n, h_n \rangle = \langle (hh)^n h, (hh)^n h \rangle = \langle h^{2n+1}, h^{2n+1} \rangle. \tag{49}$$

It would be interesting to relate operational semantics and *abstract machines* [12] using the concepts of basic and strong equivalences. We will not do this here for lack of space. However, let us remark that certain configurations on abstract machines might not correspond to anything meaningful in a given operational semantics. Thus, one should study the mathematical framework proposed in this paper in a setting of *partial* equivalences. We have not yet investigated this any further.

Given an abstract machine for our `WHILE`-language, one usually proves that the semantic function induced by this machine is equivalent to the one induced by the natural semantics. However, one can also prove this using the structural operational semantics [12]. This is being done by introducing a *bisimulation relation* [12]. It seems as if the specification of such a relation is nothing else than the definition of a Lagois Connection between the respective preorders of states, for Lagois Connections $\langle f, g \rangle: P \to Q$ can be characterized as certain equivalence relations on P and Q [10]. This apparent analogy needs further study.

A simple example of a strong equivalence between an abstract machine and an operational semantics can be found in [10]. It relates an operational semantics of *marked infix arithmetic expressions* to a stack machine for evaluating *postfix arithmetic expressions*.

In [6], an abstract semantics for a higher-order functional language with logic variables has been given by *solving simultaneous fix-point equations of closure operators* over Scott-domains. Since constraints are modeled by closure operators [6], one wants to associate a closure operator h with two constraints modeled by f and g. It turns out that this can be viewed as

$$\langle h, h \rangle := \langle f, f \rangle * \langle g, g \rangle. \tag{50}$$

There is an underlying symmetry for the composition $*$ if all participants are closure operators represented as in equation (50). This reflects the permutation

Figure 2: dcpos D_0 and D_1 in ASS with $\max(D_0) \cong \max(D_1)$ such that there is no basic equivalence $\langle f, g \rangle \colon D_0 \to D_1$

symmetry of a finite set of constraints as the composition $*$ is then *commutative*. Our mathematical framework could serve as a 'clean' approach to this kind of constraint semantics.

We saw above that the existence of a Lagois Connection between two operational semantics, where one map was only partially monotone, brought about a correspondence theorem between them: the semantic functions induced by them are extensionally equal. The existence of a basic equivalence is actually stronger than the extensional equality of semantics functions between the respective state-transition systems. For example, let D denote the dcpo in ASS which has one initial state 0 and then two possible successor states a_0 and b_0 which initiate diverging streams of computation $a_0 < a_1 < \cdots$ and $b_0 < b_1 < \cdots$. The semantic function of D equals the one of $\omega + 1$, namely it is $\lambda s.\bot$ as no computation terminates. A basic equivalence $\langle f, g \rangle \colon D \to (\omega + 1)$ would induce bijections between $\max(D)$ and $\max(\omega + 1)$, but the first set has two elements and the second one is a singleton. Therefore, basic equivalences not only control terminating behavior, they also guarantee that the pattern of diverging streams coincide.

Also, having a bijection between $\max(D)$ and $\max(E)$ is not sufficient to conclude $D \sim_d E$. As an example, take the domains D_0 and D_1 in Figure 2 which have each two maximal elements. It is readily seen that there is no basic equivalence $\langle f, g \rangle \colon D_0 \to D_1$.

6 Conclusions

We established a category $\mathcal{BD}$ with abstract state-transition systems as objects and basic equivalences as morphisms. We introduced the concept of an associative structure on a category which lead to the category $\mathcal{SD}$ with abstract state-transition systems as objects and Lagois Connections as morphisms. The categorical structures gave us two equivalence relations; since basic equivalences are transformed into Lagos Connections by a least fix-point operator, these two equivalence relations coincide. We discussed structural operational semantics and natural semantics in light of these results. The supremum of closure operators is the composition in $\mathcal{SD}$. This gives an interactive account of a semantics of constraint programming.

Acknowledgements

Thanks to Austin Melton for sending me a copy of [10] so fast. Samson Abramsky made most valuable comments throughout the progress of this work. Olivier Danvy was a critical and helpful reader of this article. Radha Jagadeesan pointed out to me the relevance of the composition ∗ to his work in [6]. Geoffrey Burn and Abbas Edalat helped shaping this paper as reviewers.

References

[1] S. Abramsky and R. Jagadeesan *New Foundations for the Geometry of Interaction*; in the proceedings of the LICS 1992 conference, pp.211–222

[2] J. Adámek, H. Herrlich and G. Strecker *Abstract And Concrete Categories*, J. Wiley & Sons, Inc., 1990

[3] G. Birkhoff *Lattice Theory*, American Mathematical Society Colloquium Publications, volume 25, third edition, third printing, reprinted with corrections, 1984

[4] G. Gierz, K. H. Hofmann, K. Keimel, J. D. Lawson, M. W. Mislove and D. Scott *A Compendium of Continuous Lattices*, Springer Verlag, New York, 1980

[5] C. A. Gunter *Semantics of Programming Languages*, Foundations in Computing Series, The MIT Press, Cambridge, Massachusetts, 1992

[6] R. Jagadeesan and K. Pingali *Abstract Semantics for a Higher-Order Functional Language with Logic Variables*, in the Conference Record of the Nineteenth Annual ACM SIGPLAN-SIGACT Symposium on Principles of Programming Languages, Albuquerque, New Mexico, January 19–22, 1992, ACM Press, pp. 355–366

[7] A. Jung *Cartesian Closed Categories of Domains*, CWI Tract 66, Amsterdam, 110pp., 1989

[8] S. Mac Lane *Categories for the Working Mathematician*, Springer Verlag, New York, 1971

[9] A. Melton, B. S. W. Schröder and G. E. Strecker *Connections*, in the proceedings of the 7th workshop on the Mathematical Foundations of Programming Semantics, LNCS **598**, Springer Verlag, New York, 1992, pp.492–506

[10] A. Melton, B. S. W. Schröder and G. E. Strecker *Lagois Connections—a Counterpart to Galois Connections*, Technical Report, Department of Information and Computing Sciences, Kansas State University, 1993

[11] R. Milner *Communication and Concurrency*, Prentice Hall International Series In Computer Science, London, 1989

[12] H. R. Nielson and F. Nielson *Semantics With Applications*, Wiley Professional Computing, England, 1992

[13] B. C. Pierce *Basic Category Theory for Computer Scientists*, Foundations of Computing Series, MIT Press 1991

[14] G. Plotkin *The category of complete partial orders: a tool of making meaning*, in: *Proceedings of the Summer School on Foundations of Artificial Intelligence and Computer Science*, Instituto di Scienze dell'Informazione, Universita di Pisa, 1978

[15] D. A. Schmidt *Denotational Semantics*, Allyn and Bacon, Inc., 1986

[16] D. Scott *Domains for Denotational Semantics*, in: *ICALP82*, M. Nielsen and E. M. Schmidt (editors), Springer Verlag, LNCS **140**, 1982

[17] G. Q. Zhang *Logic of Domains*, Birkhäuser, Boston, 1991

Towards a Modal Logic of Durative Actions

Stuart Kent

sjk@doc.ic.ac.uk
Department of Computing, Imperial College
180 Queen's Gate, London SW7 2BZ, United Kingdom

Abstract

This paper proposes an extension of modal action logics, which typically make the assumption that an action is atomic, to include durative actions. These logics have been developed to support the formal specification of information systems: we argue, with particular reference to object oriented systems, that assuming atomicity is too restrictive to express many kinds of temporal constraint. In consequence, we propose that actions be regarded as durative, and encode this by assuming that an action occurs over a sequence of atomic transitions, or interval, rather than a single transition. With this as a pre-requisite, the paper continues to redefine and extend operators of atomic action logics to fit the durative case.

1   Introduction

This paper describes work whose aim is to support the formal specification, characterisation and development of object oriented systems. Specifically, we propose an extension to action logics [16, 18, 7, 15] which have already been used with some success in providing axiomatic semantics to object oriented specification languages [8, 9] and thereby providing a basis for reasoning about object oriented systems and their development. The core of our proposal is a reworking of the semantics of such logics to admit *durative* actions.

An action logic distinguishes between terms denoting actions performed in the system and terms denoting values. The value-denoting terms are used to represent the state of the "abstract machine" being specified. Actions identify transitions to change that state. Typically, the semantics of these logics force actions to be atomic:[1] they are regarded as occurring over single atomic transitions and, with regard to concurrency, it is only possible to express restrictions on their synchronisation. However, when constructing an object oriented model of a system one usually makes the assumption that methods have duration, and, in general, may operate concurrently not just synchronously –ie. one method may start whilst another is in progress, and only parts of a method need to synchronise where conflict avoidance is required. This is reflected in the recent development of OO programming languages, such as DRAGOON [4] and POOL [3], in which concurrent method execution is the norm and language

---

[1]Perhaps an exception to this is [17], which admits compound durative actions (eg. actions constructed using a sequential combinator). However, primitive durative actions (ie. actions whose structure is not determined) are not allowed.

constructs are provided to restrict this concurrency. Furthermore, objects call on the services of other objects by invoking their methods. Such invocations force the invoking method to run concurrently with the invoked method.[2]

In order to specify such systems, it would be desirable to have a specification language in which methods are assumed to be durative, and which has language constructs for imposing restrictions on the concurrency of methods. In providing an axiomatic semantics for such a language, two options present themselves:

♦ Attempt to model methods in terms of atomic actions, and specify concurrency constraints through synchronisation of these atomic actions.

♦ Develop an action logic which admits durative actions and has appropriate language constructs for expressing their concurrent behaviour.

We favour the latter approach, for the same reasons that motivated the use of modal logics for specification in the first place: they are "engineered" to provide a range of operators, which allows the same language to be used both to express behaviour and reason about it.

The paper is organised as follows. Section 2 introduces the time point and interval structures and gives a semantic characterisation of durative actions. This prepares the incremental definition of the logic in Sections 3 – 6, introducing, respectively, the core logic, action combinators for constructing actions from component actions, operators for transforming action terms to formulae and vice-versa (eg. to express when an action is in progress), and a range of temporal operators for relating occurrences of different actions. A summary of results and indication of future work is provided in Section 7.

2 Temporal Structures and Actions

This section introduces the mathematical machinery used in the remainder of the paper. The semantics of action logics, which assume atomicity of actions, may be given in terms of a structure of states or *time points*, and an action is characterised as a collection of atomic transitions (its occurrences) –ie. transitions between neighbouring points.[3] In order to admit durative actions, an occurrence of an action will be regarded as a *sequence* of atomic transitions, alternatively an *interval* comprising at least two time points. To formulate this, we begin by introducing a time-point structure, an interval structure derived from a point structure, and the basic mathematical 'tools' required to manipulate and relate points and intervals. This will be followed by a semantic characterisation of actions along the lines just outlined.

A time point structure and the interval structure derived from it are given by Definition 1.

Definition 1 (point and interval structures)
(a) $\mathcal{T} = \langle T, < \rangle$ is a time point structure, where T is a set of time points and $<$ a discrete, linear ordering with an initial time point t_0.

(b) $\mathcal{I}(\mathcal{T}) = \langle I_{\mathcal{T}}, \lhd_{\mathcal{T}} \rangle$ is the interval structure derived from $\mathcal{T}$ where $I_{\mathcal{T}}$ is the set of intervals and $\lhd_{\mathcal{T}}$ is the precedence ordering on intervals such that:

---

[2]Even in sequential programming languages, such as Smalltalk, the invoked method must be performed within the body of the invoking method.

[3]Note that a transition may observe more than one action.

i. for any $i, j \in I_T, i \vartriangleleft_T j$ if and only if for every $t \in i$ and $t' \in j, t < t'$

ii. $I_T = \left\{ i \,\middle|\, \begin{array}{l} i \in \wp(T) \text{ and for all } t, t' \in i \text{ if there exists} \\ t'' \in T \text{ s.t. } t < t'' < t' \text{ then } t'' \in i \end{array} \right\}$

The point structures used to interpret the action logics referred to earlier have generally been discrete and have an initial time point. To keep things simple, we have also assumed here a linear ordering.[4] From now on, when we write T we will mean the point structure $\langle T, < \rangle$. Similarly, we use the shorthand $\mathcal{I}$ for $\mathcal{I}(T)$, and assume this to be defined as $\langle I, \vartriangleleft \rangle$. Some functions and notation for manipulating points, intervals, sets of points and sets of intervals are given by Definition 2, which assumes a point structure T and associated interval structure $\mathcal{I}$, according to the conventions set out above.

Definition 2 For any $i \in I, s, t \in T, U \subseteq T$ and $J \subseteq I$,

(a) $\mathrm{l}(i)$ and $\mathrm{r}(i)$ represent, respectively, the *left* and *right bounds* of the interval i, where

$$\mathrm{l}(i) = \max\{t' \in T \mid \text{ for every } t'' \in i, t' \le t''\}$$

and

$$\mathrm{r}(i) = \min\{t' \in T \cup \infty \mid \text{ for every } t'' \in i, t' \le t''\}$$

for ∞ s.t. for every $t' \in T, t' < \infty$;

(b) $\mathrm{i}(i) = i - \{\mathrm{l}(i), \mathrm{r}(i)\}$ represents the *interior* of the interval i;

(c) $[s, t], (s, t), [s, t)$ and $(s, t]$ are the intervals defined by,

$$\begin{array}{llll} [s, t] &=& \{t' \mid s \le t' \le t\} & (s, t) &=& \{t' \mid s < t' < t\} \\ [s, t) &=& \{t' \mid s \le t' < t\} & (s, t] &=& \{t' \mid s < t' \le t\} \end{array}$$

(d) $\mathrm{succ}(t) \in T$ is the unique point succeeding t where $\mathrm{succ}(t) > t$ and there exists no $t' \in T$ s.t. $t < t' < \mathrm{succ}(t)$; $\mathrm{pred}(t)$ is the point immediately preceeding t and is defined similarly;

(e) $\mathrm{ev}_t(t) = [t, \mathrm{succ}(t)]$, is the atomic transition or *event* observed from t;

(f) $\mathrm{ev}_U(U) = \{\mathrm{ev}_t(t) \mid t \in U\}$, is the set of events observed from points in the set of points U (note that the set of all events is given by $\mathrm{ev}_U(T)$);

(g) $\mathrm{intvls}(U) = \{i \in I \mid i \subseteq U\}$, is the set of intervals generated from the set of points U;

(h) $\mathrm{max}_{intvls}(J) = \{i \in J \mid \text{ for every } j \in J, i \not\subset j\}$ is the set of maximal intervals in the set of intervals J;

(i) $\mathrm{max}_{ev}(E) = \left\{ i \in I \,\middle|\, \begin{array}{l} \mathrm{ev}_U(i) \subseteq E \text{ and for every } j \in I, \\ \text{if } j \supset i \text{ then } \mathrm{ev}_U(j) \not\subseteq E \end{array} \right\},$

for any $E \subseteq \mathrm{ev}_U(T)$, returning the largest intervals whose events are in E;

(j) $\mathrm{insts}(J) = \{[t] \mid t \in T \text{ and } [t] \in J\}$

As a number of authors have observed [19, 2, 20, 5], there are thirteen primitive relations between intervals: six original relations, their inverses and equality. All relations are disjoint and partition the universal relation. The notation used for the six original relations and their inverses is given by Definition 3, which also assumes an interval structure $\mathcal{I}$.

Definition 3 (interval relations) $\vartriangleleft, \vartriangleright, [-(-]-), (-[-)-],)[,](,$ $([-]-), [(-)-], (-[-]), [-(-)], (-[-]-)$ and $[-(-)-]$ are relations on $I \times I$, such that, for any $i, j \in I$,

---

[4] A possible use of branching time is discussed in the conclusions.

(a) $i \lhd j$ iff $r(i) < l(j)$ iff $j \rhd i$

(b) $i \,[-(-]-)\, j$ iff $l(i) < l(j) < r(i) < r(j)$ iff $j \,(-[-)-]\, i$

(c) $i \,)[\, j$ iff $r(i) = l(j)$ iff $j \,](\, i$

(d) $i \,([-]-)\, j$ iff $l(i) = l(j) < r(i) < r(j)$ iff $j \,[(-)-]\, i$

(e) $i \,(-[-])\, j$ iff $l(j) < l(i) < r(i) = r(j)$ iff $j \,[-(-)]\, i$

(f) $i \,(-[-]-)\, j$ iff $l(j) < l(i) < r(i) < r(j)$ iff $j \,[-(-)-]\, i$

These relations may be compounded in many different ways. For example, the usual set theoretic relations $\subset$ and $\subseteq$ are defined to be $(-[-]-) \cup (-[-]) \cup ([-]-)$ and $\subset \cup =$, respectively. Although we do not define all these compounds explicitly here, when later we refer to an arbitrary relation between intervals, we will mean a primitive or compound relation.

2.1 Actions

As indicated earlier, an occurrence of an action is to be characterised as a sequence of atomic transitions or events. Intuitively, an action must be subject to the condition that one occurrence may not begin either whilst another of its occurrences is in progress or at the same time as another of its occurrences begins.[5] In linear time, this restriction is simply encoded by ensuring that the interiors of occurrences must be disjoint, here assuming that an action is in progress on all interior states of one of its occurrences. This leads to a formulation of the set of actions, as follows:

Definition 4 (actions) For any point structure $\mathcal{T}$,

(a) $Act(\mathcal{T}) = \left\{ a \mid \begin{array}{c} a \in \wp(I), \text{insts}(a) = \emptyset \text{ and} \\ \text{for every } i, j \in a, i(i) \cap i(j) = \emptyset \end{array} \right\}$

(b) $Act_{atom}(\mathcal{T}) = \{a \mid a \subseteq ev_U(\mathcal{T})\}$

The restriction $\text{insts}(a) = \emptyset$ in (a) ensures that the occurrences of an action have at least two time points: ie. one in which it starts, and one in which it either finishes or is in progress.[6] $Act_{atom}(\mathcal{T})$ distinguishes the set of atomic actions, ie. those actions which have only events as occurrences. We will write Act and Act_{atom} as shorthands for $Act(\mathcal{T})$ and $Act_{atom}(\mathcal{T})$, respectively.

Definition 5 provides some functions for constructing various subcomponents of an action. The function ev results in all those events performed during any occurrence of an action a. These include the begin events and the end events, which are given by beg and end, respectively. $prog$ identifies those points in time when an action a is said to be in progress, namely those instants which are contained in the interior of any of its occurrences. The definition assumes a point structure $\mathcal{T}$.

Definition 5 (action subcomponents) For any $a \in Act$,

(a) $ev(a) = \{e \mid e \in ev_U(i - \{r(i)\}), \text{ for some } i \in a\}$

(b) $beg(a) = \{e \mid e \in ev_U(\mathcal{T}) \text{ and there exists } i \in a \text{ s.t. } e \,([-]-)\, i\}$

(c) $end(a) = \{e \mid e \in ev_U(\mathcal{T}) \text{ and there exists } i \in a \text{ s.t. } e \,(-[-])\, i\}$

(d) $prog(a) = \bigcup_{i \in a} i(i)$

---

[5] See [14] for a more detailed discussion on the nature of actions.

[6] Occurrences of an action may have no right bound. Thus an action may be in progress for ever.

3   The Core Logic

Before considering action combinators and temporal operators, we describe the core part of the logic, comprising the first order component and action modalities.

3.1   Syntax

The syntax of the core logic is no different to that used in the action logics mentioned earlier. Our presentation conforms to that of [15]. We begin with the definition of a signature for some arbitrary theory. We distinguish value from action terms, and accordingly distinguish value from action symbols. There are three types of value symbol: logical variables, functions and attributes. Semantically, functions are *rigid*, as their denotation will not change over time, and attributes are *non-rigid*, as their denotation may change with time.

Definition 6 (signature) $\Theta = \langle \Sigma, \Omega, \mathcal{V}, \mathcal{AT}, \mathcal{AC} \rangle$ is a *signature* where:

(a) Σ is a set of sorts

(b) Ω is a $\Sigma^* \times \Sigma$-indexed family of function symbols,[7]

(c) $\mathcal{V}$ is a collection of variables over the sorts,

(d) $\mathcal{AT}$ is a $\Sigma^* \times \Sigma$-indexed family of attribute symbols,

(e) $\mathcal{AC}$ is an Σ^*-indexed family of action symbols.

We will write Θ as a shorthand for the signature $\langle \Sigma, \Omega, \mathcal{V}, \mathcal{AT}, \mathcal{AC} \rangle$. Value terms are variables, or composed from an attribute or function symbol combined with an appropriate number of value term arguments. An action term is either composed from an action symbol combined with an appropriate number of value term arguments, or is formed from an action term or terms in combination with one of a number of combinators. In this section, we only consider uncombinated action terms.

Definition 7 (terms)   The set of terms $Term(\Theta) = VTerm(\Theta) \cup AcTerm(\Theta)$ where:

(a) $VTerm(\Theta) = \bigcup_{S \in \Sigma} VTerm'(\Theta, S)$

(b) for any $x : S \in \mathcal{V}, x \in VTerm'(\Theta, S)$

(c) for any $f : S_1 \times \ldots \times S_n \times S \in \Omega$ and $t_i \in VTerm'(\Theta, S_i)$,
$f(t_1, \ldots, t_n) \in VTerm'(\Theta, S)$

(d) for any $A : S_1 \times \ldots \times S_n \times S \in \mathcal{AT}$ and $t_i \in VTerm'(\Theta, S_i)$,
$A(t_1, \ldots, t_n) \in VTerm'(\Theta, S)$

(e) for any $a : S_1 \times \ldots \times S_n \in \mathcal{AC}$ and $t_i \in VTerm'(\Theta, S_i)$,
$a(t_1, \ldots, t_n) \in AcTerm(\Theta)$

As usual, formulae of the logic are obtained by combining terms with various logical operators in a prescribed way. The formulae of the core logic comprise:

♦ the usual first order formulae, where equalities between value terms are the atomic formulae;

♦ action modalities, [ ]− and [−]−, familiar to modal action logics and used for expressing change.

---

[7]Constants are simply function symbols with zero arity. Predicates are effectively Boolean functions

They are given by Definition 8.

Definition 8 (formulae) For any signature Θ, the set of Θ-formulae is $Form(\Theta)$, where:

$$Form(\Theta) \supset \left\{ \begin{array}{c} (t_1 = t_2), \neg\alpha, (\alpha \wedge \beta), \\ (\alpha \vee \beta), (\alpha \rightarrow \beta), (\alpha \leftrightarrow \beta), \\ \forall x \cdot \alpha, \exists x \cdot \alpha, [\,]\alpha, [at]\alpha \end{array} \left| \begin{array}{c} t_1, t_2 \in VTerm(\Theta), \\ x \in V, at \in AcTerm(\Theta) \\ \text{and } \alpha, \beta \in Form(\Theta) \end{array} \right. \right\}$$

3.2 Semantics

The semantics is given in terms of an interpretation structure and an interpretation function. An interpretation structure for a signature Θ (Definition 9), is a tuple comprising a point structure $\mathcal{T}$, an algebra of sorts for interpreting the sorts and functions of Σ, and a function f assigning appropriate denotations to the actions and attribute symbols. Specifically, f maps an action symbol to a function from the sorts of its arguments to actions, and maps an attribute symbol to a function from the sorts of its arguments to intensions.

Definition 9 (interpretation structure) For any signature Θ, a Θ-*interpretation structure* is a tuple $\Im = \langle \mathcal{T}, \mathcal{U}, f \rangle$, where:

(a) $\mathcal{T}$ is a time point structure,

(b) $\mathcal{U}$ is a tuple $\langle \Sigma_U, \Omega_\mathcal{U} \rangle$ s.t.
$$\Sigma_U = \{S_\mathcal{U} \mid S \in \Sigma\}$$
$$\Omega_\mathcal{U} = \{h_\mathcal{U} : S_{1\mathcal{U}} \times \ldots \times S_{n\mathcal{U}} \rightarrow S_\mathcal{U} \mid h : S_1 \times \ldots \times S_n \times S \in \Omega\}$$

(c) f is a function mapping
$$a : S_1 \times \ldots \times S_n \in \mathcal{AC} \quad \text{to} \quad f(a) : S_{1\mathcal{U}} \times \ldots \times S_{n\mathcal{U}} \rightarrow Act(\mathcal{T})$$
$$A : S_1 \times \ldots \times S_n \times S \in \mathcal{AT} \quad \text{to} \quad f(A) : S_{1\mathcal{U}} \times \ldots \times S_{n\mathcal{U}} \times \mathcal{T} \rightarrow S_\mathcal{U}$$

From now on, we will use $\Im$ as a shorthand for the interpretation structure $\langle \mathcal{T}, \mathcal{U}, f \rangle$.

An interpretation function assigns denotations to terms and formulae at a given point in time.[8] Definition 10 defines the interpretation function over value terms, uncombined action terms, and formulae of the core logic. The definition will be extended to consider other terms and formulae in later sections.

Definition 10 (interpretation function) For any signature Θ, Θ-interpretation structure $\Im$ and Θ-variable assignment A, $[\![\ ]\!]^{\Im, A}$ is a $(\Theta, \Im, A)$-*interpretation function* which maps

$$VTerm(\Theta) \times T \quad \text{to} \quad \bigcup_{S_\mathcal{U} \in S} S_\mathcal{U}$$
$$AcTerm(\Theta) \times T \quad \text{to} \quad Act(\mathcal{T})$$
$$Form(\Theta) \times T \quad \text{to} \quad \{true, false\}$$

such that, for any $t \in T, a : S_1 \times \ldots \times S_n \in \mathcal{AC}, A : S_1 \times \ldots \times S_n \times S \in \mathcal{AT}$, $f : S_1 \times \ldots \times S_n \times S \in \Omega, t_1, \ldots, t_n \in VTerm(\Theta), x \in V, at \in AcTerm(\Theta)$ and $\alpha \in Form(\Theta)$,

---

[8] The alternative is to use intervals of time as the units of evaluation. This point is returned to later.

$$\llbracket x \rrbracket^{\Im,A}(t) = A(x)$$

$$\llbracket f(t_1,\ldots,t_n) \rrbracket^{\Im,A}(t) = f_{\mathcal{U}}(\llbracket t_1 \rrbracket^{\Im,A}(t),\ldots,\llbracket t_n \rrbracket^{\Im,A}(t))$$

$$\llbracket A(t_1,\ldots,t_n) \rrbracket^{\Im,A}(t) = f(A)(\llbracket t_1 \rrbracket^{\Im,A}(t),\ldots,\llbracket t_n \rrbracket^{\Im,A}(t),t)$$

$$\llbracket a(t_1,\ldots,t_n) \rrbracket^{\Im,A}(t) = f(a)(\llbracket t_1 \rrbracket^{\Im,A}(t),\ldots,\llbracket t_n \rrbracket^{\Im,A}(t))$$

$$\llbracket t_1 = t_2 \rrbracket^{\Im,A}(t) = true \text{ iff } \llbracket t_1 \rrbracket^{\Im,A}(t) = \llbracket t_2 \rrbracket^{\Im,A}(t)$$

$$\llbracket [at]\alpha \rrbracket^{\Im,A}(t) = true \text{ iff for every } i \in \llbracket at \rrbracket^{\Im,A}(t),$$
$$\text{if } l(i) = t \text{ then } \llbracket \alpha \rrbracket^{\Im,A}(r(i)) = true$$

$$\llbracket [\ ]\alpha \rrbracket^{\Im,A}(t) = true \text{ iff if } t = t_0 \text{ then } \llbracket \alpha \rrbracket^{\Im,A}(t) = true$$

and where the interpretation of the classical logical connectives is as usual.

Intuitively, an action modality is interpreted as for an atomic action logic, in that the post condition must hold at the end of any occurrence of the action starting in the state in which the formula is true. The difference, of course, is that here occurrences of an action may occur over a sequence of transitions (interval) rather than just a single transition. The usual notions of validity, satisfiability etc. for modal logics apply here.

4 Action Combinators

Action combinators are operators used to construct new actions from component actions. In logics where actions are treated atomically (see eg. [15]), the combinators are parallel $(at \parallel bt)$, choice $(at + bt)$ and complement $(\overline{at})$. The occurrences of a parallel combination of actions is the intersection of the occurrences of the component actions, those of a choice of actions is the union of the occurrences of the components, and the complement of an action comprises all those transitions which do not observe that action.[9] These definitions do not carry over directly to the durative framework, because the result of combining the component actions in the way described may not themselves be actions according to the restrictions defined earlier. In particular, problems arise with the choice combinator, when the interiors of occurrences of the component actions overlap, and with complementation.

In this section we reinterpret the atomic combinators to fit the durative case,[10] and indicate how new 'temporal' combinators could be defined. Looking first at complementation, directly porting the definition from the atomic case would mean that every interval, which is not an occurrence of the component action, would be an occurrence of its complementation. Clearly, such a collection of intervals would not be an action according to the restrictions set out earlier. An alternative interpretation is to use complementation to identify the largest intervals during which the action is not being performed. Formally, extending Definitions 7 and 10:

♦ $AcTerm(\Theta) \supset \{\overline{at} \mid at \in AcTerm(\Theta)\}$

♦ $\llbracket \overline{at} \rrbracket^{\Im,A}(t) = \max_{ev}(ev_U(T) - ev(\llbracket at \rrbracket^{\Im,A}(t)))$

---

[9]That is, performing the complement of an action a means performing any action other than a.

[10]The interpretations given here are similar to those given to operators proposed by [5], who develop an interval algebra in the Z-like specification language GLIDER for the expression of interval constraints. The differences are twofold: firstly, they assume a rational model of time; secondly, they have a difference combinator instead of complementation –this would be defined here as $at_1 \parallel \overline{at_2}$.

We re-interpret the parallel combinator in a similar way to complementation, with the idea that $(at_1 \parallel at_2)$ denotes the action whose occurrences are the maximal periods during which both component actions are being performed. However, here we have to be slightly more careful about what we mean by maximality. Specifically, we would like equivalence between at and $(at \parallel at)$.[11] This will not be the case if $\parallel$ is interpreted as just taking the maximal intervals during which both actions are being performed. The problem arises when two occurrences of at meet. By the definition just suggested, these occurrences will be merged into one maximal occurrence of the action $(at \parallel at)$, thereby blocking the required equivalence. The problem can be avoided by first defining a weaker notion of merging: merge is a function merging a set of intervals into an action, by only merging those intervals whose interiors intersect.

Definition 11 (merge) For any $a \in Act$,

(a) $merge(a) = max_{ev}(ev(a - action(a))) \cup action(a)$

(b) $action(a) = \{i \in a \mid \text{ for all } j \in a, j = i \text{ or } i(j) \cap i(i) = \emptyset\}$

The parallel combinator may now be defined as an extension of Definitions 7 and 10:

♦ $AcTerm(\Theta) \supset \{(at_1 \parallel at_2) \mid at_1, at_2 \in AcTerm(\Theta)\}$

♦ $[\![\, (at_1 \parallel at_2)\,]\!]^{\mathfrak{I},A}(t) = merge([\![\, at_1\,]\!]^{\mathfrak{I},A}(t) \cap [\![\, at_2\,]\!]^{\mathfrak{I},A}(t))$

It is a simple matter to show that this definition yields the desired property of $\parallel$. A similar definition may be given to the choice combinator, and this too ensures that at is equivalent to $(at + at)$.

♦ $AcTerm(\Theta) \supset \{(at_1 + at_2) \mid at_1, at_2 \in AcTerm(\Theta)\}$

♦ $[\![\, (at_1 + at_2)\,]\!]^{\mathfrak{I},A}(t) = merge([\![\, at_1\,]\!]^{\mathfrak{I},A}(t) \cup [\![\, at_2\,]\!]^{\mathfrak{I},A}(t))$

The introduction of durative actions also provides scope for introducing new action combinators:

♦ **beg, end** and **ev**, for identifying atomic component actions, as characterised by the functions beg, end and ev, introduced in Section 2.

♦ *Temporal combinators* such as $at_1 \Leftarrow_R at_2$, for identifying those occurrences of at_1 which are in relation R to an occurrence of at_2, and $at_1 \Uparrow_R at_2$, for "merging" occurrences of at_1 and at_2 which are in relation R to each other.

These are not defined here largely for reasons of space. Nevertheless, it would be wrong to claim that their definitions are obvious. Specifically, it is not entirely clear how $at_1 \Uparrow_R at_2$ should be defined. Consider, for example, a sequential combination of actions, which might be represented as $at_1 \Uparrow_{)(} at_2$. A naive interpretation would result in the action whose occurrences were those intervals exactly containing an occurrence of at_1 meeting an occurrence of at_2. However, this might not be an action, for example, if at_1 and at_2 denoted the same action, which had more than one occurrence in sequence. Apart from finding an alternative interpretation, one possible solution would be to distinguish a type of "underdetermined" actions, where such an action is the union of more than one "determined" action, hence may have occurrences which overlap. As this would lead to at least three types of action (atomic, determined, underdetermined) and possibly more,[12] it would perhaps be better to reconstruct the

---

[11]By the definition we have given, it is not the case that $\overline{\overline{at}}$ is equivalent to at, for the reason that the second complementation will merge any occurrences of at which meet. This, perhaps, is also an undesirable property, but, unfortunately, there seems to be no way of avoiding it.

[12]For example, [14] discusses a number of different types of action expressible in natural language.

logic to include a sort of actions, with different subsorts, which would allow for greater flexibility when defining combinators and other operators. The use of a sort of actions has been suggested before in eg. [17, 9].

5 prog and occ

In the semantic characterisation of actions presented earlier, we introduced the notion of an action in progress. This can be reflected in the logic, by introducing an operator **prog** taking an action as argument and resulting in a formula which is true at those points in time when an action is in progress. Formally, extending Definitions 8 and 10:

- $Form(\Theta) \supset \{prog(at) \mid at \in AcTerm(\Theta)\}$
- $[\![\, prog(at) \,]\!]^{\Im,A}(t) = true$ iff $t \in prog([\![\, at \,]\!]^{\Im,A}(t))$

A natural compliment to this is an operator which takes formulae and returns an action. $occ(\alpha)$ returns the 'action' whose occurrences are the maximal occurrences over which the formula is true, and may be defined as an extension of Definitions 7 and 10:

- $AcTerm(\Theta) \supset \{occ(\alpha) \mid \alpha \in Form(\Theta)\}$
- $[\![\, occ(\alpha) \,]\!]^{\Im,A}(t) = \max_{intvls}(intvls(\{t' \mid [\![\, \alpha \,]\!]^{\Im,A}(t') = true\}))$

Under this interpretation, $prog(occ(\alpha)) \leftrightarrow \alpha$ is not an axiom, because $prog(occ(\alpha))$ is true only on those time points in the *interior* of an occurrence of $occ(\alpha)$. The consequences of this on the logic (eg. whether inverses of these operators will be required to provide a complete deduction calculus) still need to be investigated.

6 Temporal Operators

A number of action logics [16, 18, 7, 15] have deontic operators for prescribing when, in normal circumstances, an action occurs with respect to other actions and with respect to the truth or not of formulae. Deontic operators are used to distinguish between normal and abnormal behaviour,[13] and are of two kinds: *permission* operators, for stipulating when actions may occur, and *obligation* operators for stipulating when actions must occur. Temporal operators can be defined to achieve a similar effect as deontic operators, provided one is willing to lose the normative/non-normative distinction. [6] presents a detailed formal analysis of the relationship between the two views, under the assumption that actions are atomic.

With durative actions, it is possible to define temporal operators which make use of the ability to relate occurrences of actions using interval relations. For example, extending Definitions 8 and 10:[14]

- $Form(\Theta) \supset \{(at_1 \supset_R at_2) \mid at_1, at_2 \in AcTerm(\Theta)\}$, where R is a relation on $I \times I$

---

[13]If a specification does not meet its deontic constraints, then it is viewed as performing abnormally and some form of error recovery will need to be instigated. See eg. [12, 15] for further discussion.

[14]This is an extends the definition of the 'subsumption' operator ($\supset$) of [7], where $at \supset bt$ is true at a point in time provided that if at is observed by the next transition, bt is also.

♦ $[\![\,(at_1 \supset_R at_2)\,]\!]^{\mathfrak{I},A}(t) = true$ iff for every $i \in [\![\,at_1\,]\!]^{\mathfrak{I},A}(t)$, if $\mathrm{l}(i) = t$
then there exists $j \in [\![\,at_2\,]\!]^{\mathfrak{I},A}(t)$ s.t. iRj

This family of operators could be further generalised by specifiying the number of occurrences of at_2 that must be in relation R to at_1, for example as in the formula $(at_1 \supset_{R,n} at_2)$ where n is a term denoting a natural number.

A problem[15] with this definition is that the temporal operators may not be iterated, as they are binary operators on action terms which result in formulae. It is possible that the problem could be circumvented by the introduction and judicious use of 'temporal' action combinators. A more radical approach, would be to interpret formulae over intervals of time, thereby allowing action terms to be treated as formulae, and define interval temporal operators such as those in [20]; however, this moves further away from the action logic style of expressing behaviour. The ideal solution might be to adopt a dual logic approach – an interval logic and a logic with action combinitors and modalities, formally relating theories expressed in the two logics by using the same interpretation structures and signatures.

7 Summary and Further Work

We have considered how a modal action logic might be extended to include durative actions. A logic was developed by reinterpreting existing operators, based on the assumption that actions occur over intervals rather than atomic transitions, and by introducing new 'temporal' operators. Some improvements and possible extensions were also indicated:

♦ A stable set of combinators, in particular 'temporal' combinators, needs to be defined. As discussed in Section 4, this would be related to the introduction of a *sort* of actions.

♦ A dual logic approach – an interval logic and a logic with action combinitors and modalities – could be adopted. In particular, the interval logic would allow temporal operators to be iterated. The two logics could be formally related by using the same interpretation structures and signatures.

♦ A linear time structure has been supposed throughout the paper. Preliminary investigation reveals that a branching time structure could be used to distinguish between the atomic transitions when an action stops and those when it completes as expected (ends).[16]

♦ Deontic operators could be introduced to make the distinction between normal and abnormal behaviour. By combining these with temporal operators, it should then be possible to express mixed temporal/deontic constraints, such as those described in [15].

As well as changes to the logic, there is still much work to be done for the logic to be a useful tool for formal specification. The suitability of the logic in interpreting OO specification languages and for reasoning about specifications and their developments needs to be tested. In this respect, we are considering

---

[15] For example, suppose we want to express a bounded obligation (see [15]), where an action at must be performed during the next future period during which the bounding formula α is true. Without iterating temporal operators, we are only able to express that at must be performed within a period *starting at the current time* during which the formula α is true – ie. by $occ(\alpha) \supset_{\supseteq} at$.

[16] See [14] for a detailed discussion of this distinction.

using the logic to give an axiomatic semantics to an object oriented extension of VDM [1]. In particular, one problem that will need to be addressed is the handling of different granularities of time, both between objects at one level of specification and between different levels of a specification. Finally, we believe it important to develop tools to support the specification process, in particular the substantial proof effort that is involved. To this end, we are in the considering instantiating proof tools, such as the Mural proof assistant [11], with various action logics.

Acknowledgments

Thanks to José Fiadeiro, Stephen Goldsack, Tom Maibaum, Dimitrios Raptis and Mark Ryan for useful comments and discussion. This work was partially supported by ESPRIT Project 6500, Afrodite.

References

[1] Afrodite Language Group. *Language Reference Manual*. Technical Report R.1., ESPRIT Project 6500 Afrodite, CAP Gemini Innovation, Holland, 1993.

[2] J.F. Allen. Towards a General Theory of Action and Time. In *Journal of Artificial Intelligence*, Vol. 23, 1983.

[3] P. America & J. Rutten. A Parallel Object-Oriented Language: Design and Semantic Foundations. PhD thesis, Free University of Amsterdam, 1989.

[4] C. Atkinson, S.J. Goldsack, A. Di Maio & R. Bayan. Object-Oriented Concurrency & Distribution in DRAGOON. In *Journal of Object-oriented Programming*, March 91.

[5] M. Celiktin & A. Lamsweerde. *Specification of Time Constraints with Interval Sequences*. Research Report RR-92-46, Unité d'Informatique, Faculté des Sciences Appliquées, Université Catholique de Louvain, 1992.

[6] J. Fiadeiro & T.S.E. Maibaum. Temporal Reasoning over Deontic Specifications. In *Journal of Logic and Computation 1(3)*, pp357-395, 1991.

[7] J. Fiadeiro & T.S.E. Maibaum. Towards Object Calculi. In *Information Systems Correctness and Reusability (Selected Papers)*, G. Saake & A. Senadas (eds.), IS-CORE 91 Workshop, 1991.

[8] J. Fiadeiro, C. Sernadas, T.S.E. Maibaum & G. Saake. Proof-Theoretic Semantics of Object-Oriented Specification Constructs. In *Object-oriented Databases: Analysis Design and Construction*, R. Meersman & W. Kent (eds), North Holland, 1991.

[9] J. Fiadeiro, C. Sernadas, T.S.E. Maibaum & A. Sernadas. Describing and Structuring Objects for Conceptual Schema Development. In *Conceptual Modelling, Databases and CASE*, P. Loucopoulos & R. Zicari (eds), John Wiley, 1992.

[10] C.B. Jones. *Systematic Software Development using VDM (second edition)*. Prentice Hall, 1990.

[11] C.B. Jones, K.D. Jones, P.A. Lindsay & R. Moore. *Mural: A Formal Development Support System*. Springer-Verlag, 1991.

[12] A. Jones and M. Sergot. On the role of Deontic Logic in the Characterization of Normative Systems. In *Proc. First International Workshop on Deontic Logic in Computer Science - DEON 91*, Springer-Verlag, 1991.

[13] S.J.H. Kent. *A Deduction Calculus for Modal Action Logic with Action Combinators*. FOREST Research Deliverable Report WP3.R2, Imperial College, London, 1991.

[14] S.J.H. Kent. *Modelling Events from Natural Language*. PhD Thesis, Dept. of Computing, Imperial College, London, to be submitted July, 1993.

[15] S.J.H. Kent, T.S.E. Maibaum & W.J. Quirk. Formally Specifying Temporal Constraints and Error Recovery. In Proc. of IEEE First Int. Symposium on Requirements Engineering, San Diego, 1993.

[16] T.S.E. Maibaum. *A Logic for the Formal Requirements Specification of Real-Time, Embedded Systems*. Alvey FOREST Report R3, Imperial College, London, 1986.

[17] J. Meyer & R.J. Wieringa. *Actors, Actions, and Initiative in Normative System Specification*. Technical report no. IR-257, Faculteit der Wiskunde en Informatica, Free University of Amsterdam, 1991.

[18] M. Ryan, J. Fiadeiro & T.S.E. Maibaum. Sharing Actions and Attributes in Modal Action Logic. In *Proceedings of the International Conference on Theoretical Aspects of Computer Science (TACS 91)*, T. Ito & A. Meyer (eds), Springer Verlag, 1991.

[19] J. van Benthem. *The Logic of Time*. Reidel, Dordrecht, 1983.

[20] Y. Venema. Expressiveness and Completeness of an Interval Tense Logic. In *Notre Dame Journal of Formal Logic*, Vol. 31, 1990.

Concurrency, Fairness and Logical Complexity

Marta Kwiatkowska

mzk@mcs.le.ac.uk

Department of Mathematics and Computer Science
University of Leicester, Leicester LE1 7RH, United Kingdom
also visiting
Department of Computing, Imperial College
180 Queen's Gate, London SW7 2BZ, United Kingdom

Abstract

We consider a connection between fairness and Π_3^0 sets of functions made recently by Darondeau, Nolte, Priese and Yoccoz, and extend their work to cater for effective asynchronous transition systems with concurrency structure represented by a Mazurkiewicz independency relation.

1 Introduction

Fairness is usually expressed in terms of logical statements of substantial complexity. A typical notion of (strong process) fairness is defined as follows:

$\forall f \, \forall P. \; P \; infinitely \; often \; enabled \; in \; f \Rightarrow P \; proceeds \; infinitely \; often \; in \; f$

where P denotes a process and f is a computation. Weak (process) fairness is obtained by replacing the premise of the implication with P *almost always enabled in* f (that is, enabled continuously from some point on), giving rise to a weaker statement that each process P proceeds infinitely often unless it terminates or is disabled infinitely often. A variety of fairness notions of different "strength" arises if one replaces the premise with more complex statements such as *there exists infinitely many points in* f *at which all processes are equally often enabled* (probabilistic fairness). One may also wish to take a different notion of a component, such as an action or direction in a non-deterministic guarded command language, instead of the process, thus giving rise to fairness notions of different "granularity". For an overview of fairness issues and various proof systems see *e.g.* [14, 9].

Fairness is known to lead to an increase in the complexity of methods for dealing with it. It is an easy observation that fairness cannot be expressed unless infinite computations are allowed. Moreover, fairness properties (viewed as sets of computations) are not closed with respect to the usual topologies employed in denotational semantics (*i.e.* Scott and metric topologies). Park [21] exhibited the failure of continuity of fairmerge (a relational view of fairness), and proposed monotonicity and transfinite fixpoint induction instead (a similar point was also elaborated on by Manna and Pnueli [15]). Plotkin constructs a powerdomain for countable non-determinism [22]. Apt and Plotkin [3] showed that proving termination under fairness is Π_1^1, and, what is more, it is Π_1^1 complete. Informally, Apt and Plotkin's results are not surprising if they are understood as the statement:

$$\forall f. \; \text{if } f \text{ is fair then it is finite}$$

or, equivalently, *there is no infinite fair computation*. This involves universal quantification over possibly infinite computations, and thus does not belong to the arithmetic hierarchy (Π^0), in which only quantification over numbers is allowed, but to the analytical hierarchy (Π^1), where it is possible to quantify over functions, or, equivalently, over infinite sequences. Thus, on the one hand, fairness is characterized in terms of highly undecidable statements, while, on the other hand, it can be guaranteed by relatively simple algorithms (for instance, a busy waiting mutual exclusion algorithm guarantees weak fairness, while a scheduler with a queueing mechanism will guarantee strong fairness). The intuition (already observed by Abramsky [1]) is that when fairness is considered as a statement of some abstract domain of the computations of *all* programs then it is Π_1^1. However, if it is considered as a statement about the computations of a *particular* program, there may be reasonable assumptions one can make to place it in the arithmetic hierarchy.

We find it useful to follow the intuition originally introduced by Harel in [10], where recursive transformations on trees were considered. The main result showed there was the proof of the existence of a one-one effective transformation between well-founded countably-branching trees (which can be viewed as inductive proofs) and "φ-abiding" finitely-branching infinite trees (which can be viewed as program unfoldings). φ is a formula in an infinitary propositional modal logic, and a tree is said to be φ-abiding iff it has no infinite paths satisfying φ. The claim is that this transformation gives rise to a generic proof system for (quoting Harel [10]) "almost any conceivable notion of fairness".

While Harel's notion of fairness may reach arbitrary levels of the arithmetic hierarchy, in their recent work Darondeau, Nolte, Priese and Yoccoz [7] showed a connection between fairness and Π_3^0 sets of functions. The authors proposed a notion of a recursive (recursively enumerable) transition system, in which (under certain strong assumptions, which we shall explain in the remainder of the paper) every fairness property (viewed extensionally as a set of infinite computations that are fair in some sense) can be identified with a Π_3^0 subset of ω^ω through a reduction to a normal form. Thanks to a well-known recursion theory correspondence, this characterization gives rise to a topological characterization of fairness in terms of Π_3^0 ($F_{\sigma\delta}$ in the Borel hierarchy) sets.

We propose to take the work of [7] one step further by applying it to a non-interleaving semantic model. As exhibited in some earlier papers of the author [12], non-interleaving gives rise to the phenomenon of confusion, which is not present in standard interleaving descriptions of behaviour. We define a notion of a recursive (recursively enumerable) *asynchronous transition system* [25, 12] by enhancing it with concurrency information given in the form of a Mazurkiewicz independency relation [17] (*i.e.* an irreflexive and symmetric relation on transitions), and show that our definition is indeed reasonable since such systems are determined by existing languages (*e.g.* Condition-Event nets, CCS). We then propose a suitable notion of a concurrent computation of such a system, which requires a Π_2^0 preorder on infinite computations. Finally, we characterize the fair sets of infinite computations in terms of an adjustment of the normal form.

2 Fairness, Logical Complexity and Recursion Theory

2.1 Notation

Let A be a set. The set of finite (resp. infinite) sequences over A is denoted by A^* (resp. A^ω); A^∞ is taken to mean $A^* \cup A^\omega$. The prefix order on A^∞ is denoted by $\leq$.

We use ω to denote natural numbers, ω^ω the set of functions on natural numbers, and Ω denotes $\omega \cup \omega^\omega$. It is known that there exists a recursive one-one coding of sequences ω^* of natural numbers to natural numbers ω [23], which gives rise to a bijection between sets ω^∞ and Ω. The function $[k] : \omega^\infty \longrightarrow \omega^*$ which truncates the argument string to the string of length k (or to the length of the argument string if its length is less than k), induces a function $[k]' : \Omega \longrightarrow \omega$, which yields the coding of the truncation. We overload the notation and refer to this function by $[k]$. The application of this function to the argument f is in the postfix notation $f[k]$.

We shall use letters such as x, y to range over ω, f, g over ω^ω, α, β over Ω, and σ, τ over ω^∞.

We say a set (relation) $X \subseteq \omega^m$ is *recursive* iff there is an algorithm for testing its membership, *i.e.* an algorithm which terminates with answer "yes" or "no" depending on whether the element is in the set or not (formally, the characteristic function χ_X is recursive). A set (relation) $X \subseteq \omega^m$ is *recursively enumerable* if there exists an algorithm for enumerating its elements (formally, X is the range of some recursive function).

The *arithmetic* hierarchy (see *e.g.* [23], page 301) of relations on ω^m is defined as follows. Let Δ_1^0 be the recursive relations. Define inductively the family of relations:

$$\begin{aligned}
\Sigma_0^0 = \Pi_0^0 &= \Delta_1^0 \\
\Pi_{n+1}^0 &= \forall \Sigma_n^0 \\
\Sigma_{n+1}^0 &= \exists \Pi_n^0 \\
\Delta_{n+1}^0 &= \Pi_{n+1}^0 \cap \Sigma_{n+1}^0
\end{aligned}$$

where $\forall \Sigma_n^0$ (resp. $\exists \Pi_n^0$) denotes the class of relations S such that for some recursive relation R belonging to Σ_{n-1}^0 (resp. Π_{n-1}^0):

$$< x_1, ..., x_m > \in S \quad \Longleftrightarrow \quad \forall i R(i, x_1, ..., x_m).$$

The family is shown in Figure 1. Note that the recursively enumerable relations are in Σ_1^0. The arithmetic hierarchy is defined similarly for relations in arbitrary products $\omega^m \times (\omega^\omega)^n$.

The arithmetic relations may also be defined (from recursive relations) by logical formulas which include logical connectives, as well as the quantifiers. These formulas may always be transformed into equivalent ones with a single sequence of leading quantifiers (as required by the definition of the hierarchy) by means of the Tarski–Kuratowski algorithm ([23], page 307).

Figure 1: The arithmetic hierarchy

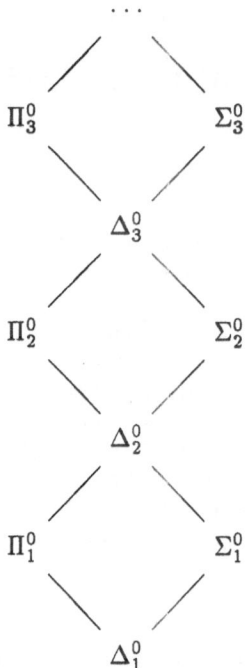

The usual metric on Ω is the ultra-metric δ defined by

$$\delta(\alpha, \beta) \;=\; \begin{cases} 0 & \text{if } \alpha = \beta \\ \frac{1}{1+\alpha \wedge \beta} & \text{otherwise} \end{cases}$$

where $\alpha \wedge \beta = \sup\{k \mid \alpha[k] = \beta[k]\}$, and $\sup\{\} = 0$. As in [7], we call this metric *recursive* (since the relation $\delta(\alpha, \beta) < \frac{1}{n}$ is recursive in (α, β, n)). Π_1^0 metrics are defined similarly. The topology that arises from δ is often called the Baire space; it is zero-dimensional and non-compact. The *derived* set $Der_d(A)$ of the set $A \subseteq X$ in a metric space (X, d) is the set of all $x \in X$ such that for any $n \in \omega$ the open ball with the centre x and radius $\frac{1}{n}$ contains at least one element $a \in A$ distinct from x. In topological terms, $x \in Der_d(A)$ iff $x \in Cl(A \setminus \{x\})$ [11]. It is a straightforward observation that ω^ω is Π_1^0 and is the derived set of ω with respect to the metric δ, since $Der_\delta(\omega) = \{f \mid \forall n \, \exists k . \delta(f, f[k]) < \frac{1}{n}\}$. We shall see later on that each fair set of functions (in some sense) will be characterized as the derived set of ω for a suitable refinement of the usual metric δ.

2.2 Recursive Transition Systems

We find it convenient to work with the notion of an (unlabelled, rooted) transition system $S = (Q, T, s, e, q_0)$, where Q is a set of states, T is a set of transitions, and $s, e : T \longrightarrow Q$ are maps yielding the source and end state of each transition, and $q_0 \in Q$ is the initial state. Given $q \in Q, t \in T$, we shall write $q \xrightarrow{t}$ if $s(t) = q$ and $\xrightarrow{t} q$ if $e(t) = q$. A transition system $S = (Q, T, s, e, q_0)$ is *recursive* (resp. *recursively enumerable*) iff all its components are recursive (resp. Σ_1^0). As a simplification, we shall only consider transition systems which have no sink states, that is, states p such that $\forall t \in T.s(t) \neq p$. A transition system with sink states can easily be transformed to one without by adding "loops" at sink states. This transformation does not have impact on fairness.

A *computation* of a (recursive or recursively enumerable) transition system S is a (finite or infinite) sequence of transitions $(t_i)_{i \in I} \in T^\infty$, $I \subseteq \omega$, such that $s(t_0) = q$ and $s(t_i) = e(t_{i-1})$ for $i > 0$. Clearly, under the assumption of no sink states, a computation of a system S is partial iff it is finite, so we can easily separate the approximations from the "completed" computations. Note that every finite computation can be encoded as an element of ω (this includes T), while every infinite computation can be viewed as a function $f \in \omega^\omega$ (mapping position index to the coding of a transition). We shall abuse the notation by identifying the two representations of computations, *i.e.* an infinite sequence over ω and and a function ω^ω. We use $Fin(S), Inf(S)$ to denote all finite and infinite computations of S respectively. Note that if S is recursive then $Inf(S) = \{f \mid \forall k.f[k] \in Fin(S)\}$ is Π_1^0 (Π_2^0 for r.e. systems [7]). $Inf(S)$ is the derived set of $Fin(S)$ with respect to the Baire metric δ.

2.3 Normal Form for Fairness

A typical notion of (strong) fairness (of a computation f) would be written in the form:

$$\forall P. \, [\exists^\omega k \, \mathrm{E}(f, k, P) \Rightarrow \exists^\omega k \, \mathrm{T}(f, k, P)]$$

where $\exists^\omega k$, $\forall^\omega k$ are defined to be $\forall i \, \exists k \geq i$ (exists infinitely many) and $\exists i \, \forall k \geq i$ (for all but finitely many) respectively, P denotes a process, and E, T are (recursive) predicates which evaluate to true iff the process P is enabled (resp. taken) at the kth stage of the computation f. This can be shown to be Π_3^0 (with a function argument) by means of a calculation using the Tarski-Kuratowski algorithm. In the following we show how the above form may be reduced to a simpler form by putting additional conditions on the transition system.

If we assume that each process is identified with a single transition (an "agent"), then the predicate T reduces to testing for $f(k) = P$. We can simplify further, by requiring that each P "dies" as soon as it is taken in the computation, that is

$$\exists k. \mathrm{T}(f, k, P) \quad \Rightarrow \quad \forall j > k. \neg \mathrm{E}(f, j, P).$$

This in fact imposes an infinite number of agents, and allows us to rewrite the above in the (equivalent under these assumptions) form:

$$\forall P \forall^\omega k. \neg \mathrm{E}(f, k, P)$$

Since we are dealing with computations produced by the reduction process for a particular machine, we can (uniformly) simplify further to:

$$\forall P \forall^\omega k. \neg \mathrm{E}(f[k], P) \tag{1}$$

where we shall treat the derived statement as a *filter* on computations:

$$\{f \mid \forall P \forall^\omega k. \neg E(f[k], P)\}.$$

Now observe that since $E(f[k], P)$ is a recursive relation (and it is in $\omega \times \omega$ if $f[k]$ and P are identified with their codings), we have obtained a Π^0_3 characterization (*i.e.* of the form $\forall i \exists j \forall k. S(f, i, j, k)$ where S is a recursive relation) of the strong (process) fairness we started with, under the simplifying assumptions as outlined above. The predicate E is understood as defining if the agent coded by i is enabled at the truncation of f of length k. The following examples illustrate its meaning.

Example 2.1 Consider the tree unfolding of the process $\text{fix}X.aX + bX$, then the predicate E for the computation a^ω is summarised in the table:

	a_1	b_1	a_2	b_2	a_3	b_3	a_4	b_4	$\cdots$
0	×	×							
1			×	×					
2					×	×			
3							×	×	
4				$\cdots$					

where a_i, b_i symbolically denote the codes of the corresponding transitions and $0, 1, 2, \cdots$ denote stages of the computation.

Example 2.2 Consider the tree unfolding of the process $\text{fix}X.aX \mid \text{fix}X.bX$, then the predicate E for the computation a^ω is summarised in the table:

	a_1	b_1	a_2	b_2	a_3	b_3	a_4	b_4	$\cdots$
0	×	×							
1		×	×						
2		×			×				
3		×					×		
4		×		$\cdots$					

where a_i, b_i symbolically denote the codes of the corresponding transitions and $0, 1, 2, \cdots$ denote stages of the computation. On the other hand, the predicate E for the computation $(ab)^\omega$ is given by:

	a_1	b_1	a_2	b_2	a_3	b_3	a_4	b_4	$\cdots$
0	×	×							
1			×	×					
2					×	×			
3							×	×	
4				$\cdots$					

The interest in the form (1) for fairness is motivated by the fact that it was shown in [7] that *any* Π^0_3 set of functions can be reduced to such form, thus giving (1) the status of a normal form. The claim is that, since extreme fairness [9] is Π^0_3, and extreme fairness implies many known notions of fairness, this normal form is in effect a generic notion of effective fairness. (Strong) extreme fairness [9] can be informally defined as follows. Let $\Gamma = \{\varphi^0, \varphi^1, ...\}$ be any countable collection of state properties (*e.g.* first order definable predicates); then a computation f is *extremely fair* iff for all $\varphi \in \Gamma, i \in \omega$, i infinitely often enabled in states satisfying φ implies i infinitely often taken in states satisfying φ.

The following result links the different concepts introduced so far – recursive transition systems, derived sets in metric spaces, and the normal form for fairness. It shows that there are three equivalent ways of viewing fairness. Recall that the derived set of the finite computations of some recursive or r.e. transition system with respect to the usual (recursive) Baire metric is the set of *all* infinite computations. This includes the fair, as well as the unfair ones. The significance of the result below is that it provides a Π_3^0 method for excluding the unfair infinite sequences from the derived set of the finite computations. More precisely, the set of fair computations coincides with the derived set of the finite computations with respect to a metric, which *refines* the Baire metric.

Proposition 2.3 [7] For any rooted recursively enumerable transition system S the following are equivalent:

1. F is a Π_3^0 subset of $Inf(S)$.
2. F is the derived set of $Fin(S)$ for some Π_1^0 ultra-metric refining the usual Baire metric δ.
3. $F = \{f \mid \forall i \, \forall^\omega k . \neg \mathrm{E}(f[k], i)\}$ for some recursive predicate $E \subseteq \omega \times \omega$.

The refined metric is constructed uniformly from the enabledness predicate E as follows. Firstly, define the predicate completed(i, j), meaning the agent i has finished by stage j of the computation α, by:

$$\text{completed}(i, j) \quad \Longleftrightarrow \quad \forall k \geq j . \neg \mathrm{E}(\alpha[k], i).$$

Then the distance between computations (finite or infinite) is given by:

$$d(\alpha, \beta) = \begin{cases} 0 & \text{if } \alpha = \beta \\ \dfrac{1}{\max\left\{ \frac{1}{1+\eta(\alpha, \alpha \wedge \beta)}, \frac{1}{1+\eta(\beta, \alpha \wedge \beta)} \right\}} & \text{otherwise} \end{cases}$$

where $\eta(\alpha, j) = \max\{i \leq j \mid \forall i' \leq i . \text{completed}(i', j)\}$. Intuitively speaking, the greater the code of the last completed agent, the smaller the distance between the computations, where the "last completed agent" $\eta(\alpha, j)$ of the computation α at stage j is the agent i, all of whose predecessors (*i.e.* with codes below i) are never enabled beyond j, meaning that the computation either terminated before the agents became enabled, or they have been taken. Thus, f is E-fair iff $\lim_{j \to \omega} \eta(f, j) = \omega$.

Note that we have a *different* metric (*i.e.* possibly a different topology!) for each fairness notion.

Example 2.4 In Example 2.2 the computation $(ab)^\omega$ is fair, while a^ω is not fair because $\lim_{j \to \omega} \eta((ab)^\omega, j) = \omega$, while $\lim_{j \to \omega} \eta(a^\omega, j) = a_1$.

3 Recursive Asynchronous Transition Systems

The interesting question arises whether the theory described in the previous sections is capable of handling fairness in a non-interleaving model for concurrency. It has already been observed [20] that since pomsets can be encoded as functions, the results of the previous sections can be applied in any setting which uses a pomset representation of runs. However, we believe that this approach is indirect, because it depends on the coding of a representation of the behaviour, instead of being a direct outcome of a reduction strategy. Therefore, we propose a generalization of effective transition systems with additional concurrency structure. This way, the outcome of a reduction strategy is a sequence, but certain sequences will be rendered "equivalent", in the sense that they only contain inessential differences. Inessential differences are those which arise from permutations of consecutive, concurrent transitions.

We propose to view recursive transition systems as the *outcome of some reduction*, or derivation, following a set of SOS rules. The codes (of states and transitions) are assigned *as the reduction proceeds*, so that the coding is fixed by the reduction strategy. This approach has the advantage of leading to results, which will be preserved through restrictions of transition systems to subsystems accessible from some initial state. For an arbitrary recursive coding, such a restriction does not lead to a recursive coding of a subsystem [6].

To illustrate our idea, consider, for example, CCS [19] with the one-step transition relation $\xrightarrow{a}$, and consider the process $\mathrm{fix}X.aX + bX$. Note that each a-move generates a "new" copy of both a and b by the rule:

$$\frac{P \xrightarrow{a} P'}{P + Q \xrightarrow{a} P'}$$

Since P and Q disappear, so do the codes generated at the previous step of reduction. In contrast, b-moves in the process $\mathrm{fix}X.aX \mid \mathrm{fix}X.bX$ do not give rise to a "new" copy of a because of the rule:

$$\frac{P \xrightarrow{a} P'}{P \mid Q \xrightarrow{a} P' \mid Q}$$

where Q does not disappear, so neither does the code of the a-move.

We now proceed with the definition of an effective asynchronous transition system. Define an *independency* relation [18] to be any irreflexive and symmetric relation $\iota \subseteq T \times T$. The purpose of this relation is to establish the potential for concurrency within the system. Any two transitions that are independent can happen concurrently; for example, they can be executed by separate processors. Note that a transition cannot be concurrent with itself, and concurrency is symmetric. Also note that this defines a *global* relation; when considering languages such as CCS additional labelling on actions has to be used to handle correctly cases such as $a + a$ and $ab(a \mid b)$. This is not a problem for us, since we can assume that these labels would be produced by the reduction process, and hence will be unique.

We shall also require the notion of a *residual* operation (notation $/$) [5] on transitions. As each transition contains information about start and end states, and start and end states of consecutive transitions in a computation must agree, we cannot just permute two independent transitions because we would not necessarily obtain a valid computation. Instead, we require that a transition commutes with the residual of another transition.

As introduced in [25, 12], we define an *asynchronous transition system* (abbrev. ATS) to be the structure $S = (Q, T, \mathsf{s}, \mathsf{e}, \iota, /, q_0)$ such that $S = (Q, T, \mathsf{s}, \mathsf{e}, q_0)$ is a rooted transition system, $\iota \subseteq T \times T$ is an independency relation, $/ : T \times T \longrightarrow T$ is an operation such that t_1 / t_2 is defined whenever $t_1 \iota t_2$, subject to the following axioms being satisfied:

$$(\text{Forw-}\Diamond) \quad \forall q \in Q.(q \xrightarrow{t} p, q \xrightarrow{t'} p', t \iota t' \Rightarrow \exists! q' \in Q.p \xrightarrow{t'/t} q', p' \xrightarrow{t/t'} q')$$
$$(\text{Perm-}\Diamond) \quad \forall q \in Q.(q \xrightarrow{t} p \xrightarrow{t'/t} q', t \iota t' \Rightarrow \exists! p' \in Q.q \xrightarrow{t'} p' \xrightarrow{t/t'} q').$$

The first of the two axioms is a conditional Church-Rosser property. The second axiom ensures that the set of computations of an ATS is closed under permutation of consecutive, independent transitions (both modulo residual). We assume that, just as the codes of transitions are computed as the reduction proceeds, the independency relation will be determined in the same manner. Note that, as soon as the reduction has been performed, the actual labels of moves have been lost, so the independency relation is defined over action occurrences, rather than action labels as is usually the case.

$S = (Q, T, \mathsf{s}, \mathsf{e}, \iota, /, q_0)$ is said to be a *recursive* (resp. *recursively enumerable*) asynchronous transition system iff all its components are recursive (resp. Σ_1^0).

Given an ATS $S = (Q, T, \mathsf{s}, \mathsf{e}, \iota, /, q_0)$ define the relation $\equiv^f$ on finite sequences of transitions as follows. Let $\sigma, \tau \in Fin(S)$. Then

$$\sigma \equiv^f \tau \iff \exists \gamma_1, \cdots, \gamma_n. \quad \sigma = \gamma_1, \gamma_n = \tau,$$
$$\gamma_i = \gamma_i' t_1 (t_2 / t_1) \gamma_i'', t_1 \iota t_2, \gamma_{i+1} = \gamma_i' t_2 (t_1 / t_2) \gamma_i''$$

Thus, two (finite) sequences are equivalent iff they differ in the order of consecutive independent transitions. The case of infinite sequences is a bit more complex, since we need to handle an infinite number of permutations as in $(ab)^\omega$ and $(ba)^\omega$, which clearly should be equivalent if $a \iota b$. We first define a preorder $\preceq^f$ on T^*:

$$\sigma \preceq^f \tau \iff \sigma \leq \gamma \equiv^f \tau.$$

We now extend this preorder to T^∞ by:

$$\sigma \preceq \tau \iff \forall \sigma' \leq \sigma \exists \tau' \leq \tau. \sigma' \preceq^f \tau'.$$

The equivalence relation induced by this preorder (*i.e.* $\equiv \overset{\text{df}}{=} \preceq \cap \succeq$) is called the *trace equivalence* on T^∞. A calculation using the Tarski-Kuratowski algorithm ([23], page 307) shows this equivalence is Π_2^0.

The quotient $Inf(S)/_\equiv$ is the *asynchronous behaviour* of the asynchronous transition system S. An equivalence class $[\sigma]$ of a sequence is called a (Mazurkiewicz) *trace*. That this is a reasonable definition of a behaviour of S (meaning that all the sequences added by the closure under the equivalence relation are actually possible computations of the system) follows from the axiom (Perm-$\Diamond$). Moreover, any two finite equivalent sequences lead to the same state.

Proposition 3.1 For any $\sigma, \tau \in Fin(S)$, $\sigma \equiv \tau$, $q \xrightarrow{\sigma} q'$, $q \xrightarrow{\tau} q''$ implies $q' = q''$.

Proof: By induction from axiom (Forw-◊). □

There exists a strong relationship between asynchronous transition systems and certain classes of trace languages [25, 13].

The discussion in [7] gave examples of effective transition systems, *e.g.* the λ-calculus with β-reduction. What is of interest to us here is whether the notion of an effective *asynchronous* transition system is reasonable, in the sense of whether effective ATS's "occur in nature". It is an easy observation that (finite) Condition-Event nets determine finite asynchronous transition systems, see *e.g.* [12]. CCS with the one-step transition $\xrightarrow{a}$ determines a recursive transition system, while CCS with the $\xRightarrow{a} \stackrel{\mathrm{df}}{=} (\xrightarrow{\tau})^* \xrightarrow{a} (\xrightarrow{\tau})^*$ determines a recursively enumerable transition system. The question of the independency relation being determined is a bit more difficult to settle, because it requires labelling of transitions, but nevertheless Boudol and Castellani [5] showed that CCS determines an ATS. The idea is to label transitions with *proofs* of how to obtain a given transition from a process expression, so, for example, the b-move of $(a \mid b) + c$ is labelled with $+_1(\mid_2(b))$, meaning that it comes from the lefthand-side of the $+$, followed by the righthand-side of the $\mid$ operator. In addition, passing through a guard may be encoded as γ_a, so that the proof of ab is represented by $\gamma_a(b)$. Under these conditions, given a CCS expression, each label uniquely determines the start and end states. For the subcalculus without communication and restriction (see [5] for full definition), the independency relation on such proof terms is the least symmetric relation satisfying:

(i1) $\quad \mid_1 \theta \; \iota \; \mid_2 \theta'$
(i2) $\quad \theta \; \iota \; \theta' \Rightarrow \mid_i \theta \; \iota \; \mid_i \theta'$
(i3) $\quad \theta \; \iota \; \theta' \Rightarrow +_i \theta \; \iota \; +_i \theta'$

The essential rule is (i1), which states that two proof terms are independent iff they appear on either side of the parallel. The remaining rules preserve the relation through the syntax of proof terms.

The intuition for the residual operation is as follows. In the term such as $(a \mid b) + c$, the transitions $+_1(\mid_1(a))$ and $+_1(\mid_2(b))$ are independent, but after $+_1(\mid_1(a))$ has been performed, what remains from $+_1(\mid_2(b))$ is $\mid_2(b)$. Formally, the residual operation, again without communication and restriction, is defined by:

(r1) $\quad (\mid_1 \theta) / (\mid_2 \theta') = \mid_1 \theta$
(r2) $\quad (\mid_2 \theta') / (\mid_1 \theta) = \mid_2 \theta'$
(r3) $\quad \theta \; \iota \; \theta' \Rightarrow (\mid_i \theta) / (\mid_i \theta') = \mid_i (\theta / \theta')$
(r4) $\quad \theta \; \iota \; \theta' \Rightarrow (+_i \theta) / (+_i \theta') = \theta / \theta'$

Observe that both the independency relation and the residual are recursive if the system is. Both diamond properties are proved for an LTS labelled with proofs [5].

4   Fairness for Asynchronous Transition Systems

Let S be a rooted ATS. A phenomenon exhibited by a non-interleaving semantic model, but not considered in the standard interleaving approaches,

Figure 2: Asymmetric confusion $(a \iota b)$

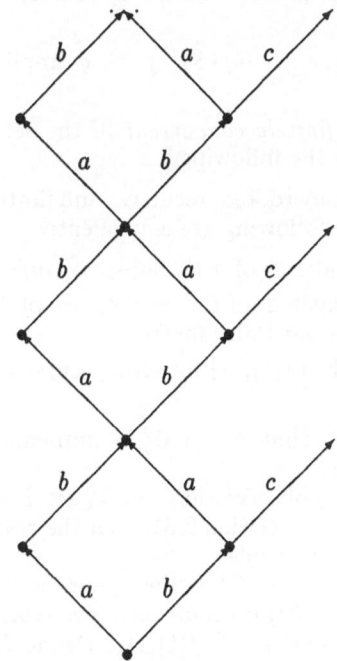

is that of *confusion*. Informally, confusion arises if there is an interference between choice and concurrency. To introduce confusion formally we shall require the notion of a *conflict set* of a transition. For $t \in T$ define $cfl(t)$ to be $\{t' \mid s(t) = s(t') \wedge \neg(t \iota t')\}$. We say a triple (q, t, t') is a confusion if $q \xrightarrow{t}, q \xrightarrow{t'}, t \iota t'$ and $cfl(t) \neq cfl(t/t')$. A triple (q, t, t') is a symmetric confusion iff (q, t', t) is also a confusion, and is asymmetric otherwise.

Figure 2 shows an example of confusion, where $a \iota b$ and for simplicity we have assumed that $a/b = a$, $b/a = b$. Note that $(ab)^\omega$ is fair (since c is never enabled), while $(ba)^\omega$ is *not* fair (since c is infinitely often enabled. Yet, the two sequences are equivalent. This raises the possibility of an undesirable situation, which would make the fairness or unfairness of a computation dependent on the particular choices made by the scheduler. Naturally, we would like to avoid this, and so would propose that fairness properties be closed with respect to equivalence $\equiv$. A similar point has also been made elsewhere, including [2, 12].

We find that we have to impose the following monotonicity condition on the enabledness predicate E. We define the predicate $E \subseteq \omega \times \omega$ to be *monotone* iff

$$\forall f, g. f[k] \iota g[k] \Rightarrow (E(f[k], i) \iff E(g[k], i)).$$

where for finite sequences σ, τ we say $\sigma \iota \tau$ iff they are incomparable under $\preceq$ and there exist $t_1, ..., t_n, t'_1, ..., t'_n, t_i \iota t'_i$ all i, $\gamma \equiv \gamma'$, such that $\sigma = \gamma t_1...t_n$, $\tau = \gamma' t'_1...t'_n$.

The idea of the condition is that the enabledness of a transition is independent of the choice of a sequence within a $\equiv$-equivalence class, as shown by the lemma below.

Lemma 4.1 For all $f, g \in Inf(S)$, $f \equiv g$ implies $\forall i \forall k.(E(f[k], i) \iff E(g[k], i))$.

A recursive ATS is *finitely concurrent* iff the set $C(t) = \{t' \in T \mid t \iota t'\}$ is finite for all t. We have the following.

Proposition 4.2 For any rooted, recursive and finitely concurrent asynchronous transition system S the following are equivalent:

1. F^+ is the closure under $\equiv$ of a Π_3^0 subset of $Inf(S)$.
2. F^+ is the closure under $\equiv$ of the derived set of $Fin(S)$ for some Π_1^0 ultra-metric refining the usual Baire metric δ.
3. $F^+ = \{f \mid \forall i \forall^\omega k. \neg E^+(f[k], i)\}$ for some recursive monotone predicate $E^+ \subseteq \omega \times \omega$.

Proof: $((3) \Rightarrow (1))$ That F^+ is Π_3^0 is immediate. The closure under $\equiv$ follows from Lemma 4.1.

To show $(1) \iff (2)$ observe that if a Π_3^0 set F coincides with the derived set for some metric (by Proposition 2.3), then the respective closures under the trace equivalence $\equiv$ also coincide.

To show $(1) \Rightarrow (3)$ assume F^+ is the closure under $\equiv$ of a Π_3^0 set F. Then $F = \{f \mid \forall i \exists j \forall k. R(f, i, j, k)\}$ for some recursive relation R. By Proposition 2.3 it follows that $F = \{f \mid \forall i \forall^\omega k. \neg E(f[k], i)\}$. Define $E^+(x, i)$ from $E(x, i)$ by:

$$E^+(x, i) \iff E(x, i) \text{ or } \exists y \iota x. E(y, i).$$

The restriction to finite concurrency is essential so that all sequences y independent of x can be enumerated in finite time. Finally, observe that E^+ satisfies the condition of monotonicity and by Lemma 4.1 $F^+ = \{f \mid \forall i \forall^\omega k. \neg E^+(f[k], i)\}$. $\square$

5 Conclusion and Further Work

Several authors have pointed out that fairness and unbounded non-determinism are connected, see *e.g.* [24, 21]. This has led some of them to reject fairness on the grounds that it is not computable. This is in contradiction with the practical knowledge, which provides ample evidence that fairness is an important property of hardware and software systems (such as communication protocols, distributed databases), which can be expressed in logics such as the temporal logic CTL*, mechanically verified by means of a model checker, and guaranteed by an algorithm. What we would like to argue is that there is really no contradiction, because unbounded non-determinism is a proof-theoretic phenomenon (a proof being a well-founded, ω-branching tree), while fairness is a phenomenon of programs (finitely branching trees with possibly infinite paths). Since there exists a one-one effective map between well-founded, ω-branching trees and finitely branching trees with only those infinite paths which satisfy a certain infinitary formula of a modal logic, it follows that fairness is provable, as well as computable in practice.

We have extended a connection between Π_3^0 sets of functions and fairness to cater for effective transition systems with concurrency structure given by an independency of transitions. Since there is a strong correspondence between such sets of functions and the Borel hierarchy – in fact, the following relationship holds ([16], page 799):

$$\Pi_n^0 \;=\; \bigcup_{\epsilon \in \omega^\omega} \Pi_n^0[\epsilon]$$

where boldface Π_n^0 denotes the classical Borel hierarchy of sets of functions, and lightface $\Pi_n^0[\epsilon]$ is a *relativization* of Π_n^0 with an *oracle* ϵ – one might ask whether this work helps to find the right topological conditions that one would like semantic fairness properties (viewed extensionally) to satisfy. Unfortunately, the answer is no because the link with the topology of the semantic domain is lost as soon as the reduction has been performed.

Effective transition graphs have been introduced by de Simone [8], who showed that every r.e. transition graph can be expressed in SCCS or Meije using a certain format of rules. It is an interesting problem if there is any format of rules which can be associated with r.e. asynchronous transition systems, and if similar expressiveness results can be obtained. Also, following the work of Badouel and Darondeau on extracting concurrency from a basic SOS format of rules [4], a generalization to more expressive formats would be desirable.

Acknowledgements

We would like to acknowledge Samson Abramsky, Iain Phillips, Mike Smyth, Philippe Darondeau and Lutz Priese for conversations on the subject. The author is also grateful to the Nuffield Science Foundation grant (SCI/124/528/G) for providing funds to visit the Theory and Formal Methods Section of the Department of Computing, Imperial College.

References

[1] Samson Abramsky. Private communication, 1993.

[2] Krzysztof Apt, Nissim Francez, and Shmuel Katz. Appraising fairness in languages for distributed systems. *Distributed Computing*, 2, 1988.

[3] Krzysztof Apt and Gordon Plotkin. Countable nondeterminism and random assignment. *Journal of the ACM*, 33(4), 1986.

[4] E. Badouel and P. Darondeau. Structural operational semantics and trace automata. In *CONCUR 92*, volume 630 of *Lecture Notes in Computer Science*, pages 302–316. Springer-Verlag, 1992.

[5] Gerard Boudol and Ilaria Castellani. Three equivalent semantics for CCS. In *Semantics of Systems for Concurrent Processes*, volume 469 of *Lecture Notes in Computer Science*. Springer-Verlag, 1990.

[6] P. Darondeau. Private communication., 1993.

[7] P. Darondeau, D. Nolte, L. Priese, and S. Yoccoz. Fairness, distances and degrees. *Theoretical Computer Science*. To appear.

[8] Robert de Simone. Higher-level synchronizing devices in MEIJE-SCCS. *Theoretical Computer Science*, 37:245–267, 1987.

[9] Nissim Francez. *Fairness*. Springer-Verlag, 1986.

[10] D. Harel. Effective transformations on infinite trees with applications to high undecidability, dominoes and fairness. *Journal of the ACM*, 33:224–248, 1986.

[11] K. Kuratowski. *Topology*. Academic Press, 1966.

[12] Marta Z. Kwiatkowska. Event fairness and non-interleaving concurrency. *Formal Aspects of Computing*, 1(3):213–228, 1989.

[13] Marta Z. Kwiatkowska. Fairness for non-interleaving concurrency (PhD Thesis). Technical Report 22, University of Leicester, 1989.

[14] Marta Z. Kwiatkowska. Survey of fairness notions. *Information and Software Technology*, 31(7):371–386, 1989.

[15] Zohar Manna and Amir Pnueli. The anchored version of the temporal framework. In *Linear Time, Branching Time and Partial Order in Logics and Models for Concurrency*, volume 112 of *Lecture Notes in Computer Science*, pages 201–284. Springer-Verlag, 1989.

[16] D. A. Martin. Descriptive set theory. In J. Barwise, editor, *Handbook of Mathamatical Logic*. North-Holland, 1977.

[17] Antoni Mazurkiewicz. Trace theory. In *Petri Nets: Applications and Relationships to Other Models of Concurrency*, volume 255 of *Lecture Notes in Computer Science*, pages 279–324. Springer-Verlag, 1986.

[18] Antoni Mazurkiewicz. Basic notions of trace theory. In *Linear Time, Branching Time and Partial Order in Logics and Models for Concurrency*, volume 354 of *Lecture Notes in Computer Science*, pages 25–34. Springer-Verlag, 1989.

[19] Robin Milner. *Communication and Concurrency*. Prentice-Hall International, 1989.

[20] D. Nolte and L. Priese. Fairness in models with true concurrency. In *CONCUR '91*, Lecture Notes in Computer Science. Springer-Verlag, 1991.

[21] D. Park. On the semantics of fair parallelism. In D. Bjorner, editor, *Abstract Software Specifications*, volume 86 of *Lecture Notes in Computer Science*, pages 504–526. Springer-Verlag, 1980.

[22] Gordon Plotkin. A powerdomain construction. *SIAM Journal of Computing*, 5:452–487, 1976.

[23] H. Rogers. *Theory of recursive functions and effective computability*. McGraw Hill, 1967.

[24] A. W. Roscoe. Two papers on CSP. Technical Report PRG-67, Oxford University, 1988.

[25] M.W. Shields. Deterministic asynchronous automata. In *Formal Methods in Programming*. North Holland, 1985.

Concurrency and Conflict in CSP

Marta Kwiatkowska

mzk@mcs.le.ac.uk

Department of Mathematics and Computer Science
University of Leicester, Leicester LE1 7RH, United Kingdom
also visiting
Department of Computing, Imperial College
180 Queen's Gate, London SW7 2BZ, United Kingdom

Iain Phillips

iccp@doc.ic.ac.uk

Department of Computing, Imperial College
180 Queen's Gate, London SW7 2BZ, United Kingdom

Abstract

As part of an effort to give a "truly concurrent" semantics to process algebra, we refine the failures with divergence model for CSP by adding conflict information. We show that most of the CSP laws are preserved, the exception being the expansion law and the idempotency of choice.

1 Introduction

This paper is part of an effort by many authors to give a "truly concurrent" semantics to process algebra. Many authors have previously contributed in this area, see *e.g.* [16, 15, 9, 12, 4, 2, 14], and the methods have included translation into Petri nets, deriving an event structure, and enhancing the labels in labelled transition systems, often leading to descriptions of low-level character. We propose starting at the high level of abstraction usually associated with process algebras, and define a refinement of the existing failures with divergence model directly from the syntax of CSP terms.

As the touchstone for whether a semantics is truly concurrent, as usual we take the example processes $a \parallel b$ and $a \cdot b + b \cdot a$, where $\parallel$ denotes parallel composition, $\cdot$ denotes sequential composition and $+$ denotes choice. These two are of course equated in the standard interleaving semantics of process algebras such as CCS, CSP, ACP. However, we would expect them to be distinguished by a truly concurrent semantics, since $a \parallel b$ exhibits concurrency (in that actions a and b are causally independent), whereas $a \cdot b + b \cdot a$ does not.

We take the aim of this exercise to be not so much to argue that the two processes are not really behaviourally equivalent, but to express in a precise way our understanding that one is "more concurrent" than the other. The ordering that is thus obtained can be used to inform the process of implementation, since implementation has a direction (from specification to implementation, possibly via various refinements) which frequently involves adding extra concurrency by implementing a "black box" as a collection of connected components. Abramsky has made a similar point [1].

Trace theory [13] provides one solution to the example. The sequences of possible actions are just ε, a, b, ab, ba in each case. In the case of $a \parallel b$, since a, b are independent, denoted $a \iota b$, we say that ab and ba are equivalent, since they are the same except that independent actions are permuted. However, in the case of $a \cdot b + b \cdot a$ the sequences ab, ba are not equivalent, and so we have distinguished the processes.

The disadvantage of trace theory is that it does not handle nondeterminism and deadlock. For instance the processes $a \cdot b$ and $a + a \cdot b$ have the same sequences, namely ε, a, ab, and there is no independence between actions in either case. However, the second process may deadlock after performing a, so that a distinction should be made. It is for this reason that Milner was led to consider a semantics for processes more refined than that used in formal language theory. He proposed observation equivalence (bisimulation), which takes us a long way from traces, and is generally considered the most refined behavioural equivalence. Brookes, Hoare and Roscoe [6] took a different approach, in which they refined the traces[1] model with deadlock information telling us which actions may be refused after some sequence of actions, giving the so-called *failures* model.

The aim of this paper is to make concurrency distinctions within CSP by associating to each process P a *conflict* relation $cf(P)$ on the traces of P. Roughly speaking, the more traces of P are in the relation $cf(P)$, the less concurrent P will be. We define $cf(P)$ in Section 4 by induction on the syntax of CSP and then define the "failures with divergence and conflict" *semantics*. We defer discussion of the *model* to Section 6 as this is not yet fully resolved. We define a partial ordering incorporating conflict, which is a natural refinement of the failures–divergence ordering. We also show that the model forms a complete partial order, and that the operators of CSP are monotonic and continuous with respect to the new ordering. The old model can be embedded into the new one by mapping processes onto those with maximal conflict. In Section 5 we find that many of the usual laws hold, but that equivalences involving choice, such as idempotency and the expansion theorem for unravelling the behaviour of a parallel composition, are now refined into inequalities. Finally, in Section 6, the new model and its properties are discussed.

2　An example

Suppose we wish to build a scheduler to control the activation of n processes. The activation of process i is represented by the action a_i. The processes are to start up essentially in cyclic order:

$$a_1, a_2, \ldots, a_n, a_1, \ldots$$

except that we allow the activations to be at most one ahead of their turn. Thus, if it is i's turn then $i + 1$ is also allowed to go ahead, but, if it does, then

---

[1]Note that in the CSP world "trace" means a sequence of actions performed by a process, whereas for trace theory, it means an equivalence class of such sequences under the equivalence generated by the independence relation.

i must go next before it is $i+2$'s turn. The following CSP program achieves this and corresponds fairly directly to the informal specification:

$$P = P_1 \text{ where } P_i = a_i P_{i+1} \,\Box\, a_{i+1} a_i P_{i+2}.$$

Now suppose we wish to introduce some concurrency into the scheduler. Perhaps the processes are distributed in a ring, and we wish the scheduling to be achieved by passing signals round the ring rather than by the use of a single centralised process. For pure cyclic scheduling it is enough for a_{i+1} to be made dependent on a_i, and the following will achieve the desired result:

$$Q = Q_1 \| \cdots \| Q'_n \text{ where } \begin{aligned} Q_i &= a_i Q'_i \\ Q'_i &= a_{i+1} Q_i. \end{aligned}$$

We adapt this by requiring a_i to be dependent on both a_{i-2} and a_{i-3} (but not a_{i-1}, to allow actions to be one ahead of their turn). We get

$$T = R_1 \| \cdots \| R_{n-2} \| R'_{n-1} \| R'_n \| S_1 \| \cdots \| S'_{n-2} \| S'_{n-1} \| S'_n$$

$$\text{where } \begin{aligned} R_i &= a_i R'_i & R'_i &= a_{i+2} R_i \\ S_i &= a_i S'_i & S'_i &= a_{i+3} S_i. \end{aligned}$$

We have not indicated the alphabets of the processes, which are the obvious ones. Each event a_i requires the participation of four sub-processes.

One can show that T has the same behaviour as P, and indeed they are equated in the standard semantics of CSP (failures semantics - see Section 3). However, there are differences. T has more concurrency, which is reflected in the fact that T has less conflict (it has the same options, of course). In fact, our example illustrates an extreme opposition, in that P has no concurrency, and T has no choice. In general, we can imagine various programs being equivalent in their observed behaviour, but differing in the amount of concurrency they exhibit. And, as this example shows, more concurrency will tend to be reflected in reduced conflict.

If we wish to reflect these differences there are many possibilities. In this paper we investigate an approach which seems to us to be close to the spirit of the standard observational semantics of CSP, while enabling us to make true concurrency distinctions. We refine failures semantics by adding information about which traces (sequences of actions) are in conflict, that is, cannot occur in the same run. In our semantics T will have less conflict than P (in fact T has none), reflecting the greater concurrency in T.

3 Preliminaries

3.1 Notation

We shall use the following notation conventions throughout the paper. Act is a set of action symbols[2]. The set of finite strings (also called $traces$) over the set Act is denoted by Act^*; ε is the empty trace. We use a, b, c to range over Act,

---

[2] We prefer to use the term "action" instead of "event" so as to distinguish between actions and their occurrences; the latter are usually referred to as "events".

and s, t, u to range over $Act^\star$. Given $a \in Act$ and traces $s, t \in Act^\star$, we write as, sa and st for the respective concatenations. String prefix order is denoted by $\leq$. We say s $perm$ t iff the trace s is a permutation of t. $s \subseteq t$ denotes the multiset order; more formally, $s \subseteq t$ iff $\exists s'.s$ $perm$ $s' \leq t$. Given a set L, the set of all finite subsets of L will be denoted by $\mathcal{P}_f(L)$, and the set of all its subsets by $\mathcal{P}(L)$. We use A, B, X, Y to range over $\mathcal{P}_f(Act)$. $s \backslash d$, where $d \in Act$, denotes $hiding$, $i.e.$ the string s with all occurrences of d deleted. Given $A \in \mathcal{P}_f(Act)$, $s \lceil A$ denotes $restriction$, $i.e.$ the string s with all occurrences of actions outside the set A deleted.

We shall also require the following operation of $leftmost$ $difference$ on $Act^\star$. Let $a \in Act, s, t \in Act^\star$. Define

$$
\begin{aligned}
\mathrm{ld}(\varepsilon, s) &= \text{undefined} \\
\mathrm{ld}(as, t) &= \left\{ \begin{array}{ll} \mathrm{ld}(s, t - a) & \text{if } a \in t \\ a & \text{otherwise} \end{array} \right.
\end{aligned}
$$

where $t - a$ denotes the string t with the leftmost occurrence of a deleted.

3.2 The language of CSP

We use a subset of Communicating Sequential Processes (CSP) as described in [7]. This is essentially an alphabet-free version of CSP as introduced in [10]. In this paper only a summary of the language and the model is presented. We refer the reader to [10, 6, 7] for more details.

The syntax of CSP process expressions is as follows:

$$ P ::== 0 \,|\, a{\cdot}P \,|\, P \sqcap Q \,|\, P \,\square\, Q \,|\, P_A \,\|\, Q_B \,|\, P \backslash a \,|\, f(P) \,|\, x \,|\, \mu x.P $$

where P, Q ranges over (syntactic) process expressions, a is an action ranging over the set Act, A, B are (finite) sets of actions, and x is a process variable. 0 represents a deadlocked process (usually denoted STOP). $a{\cdot}P$ denotes prefixing the process P with the action a (usually $a \to P$). We shall often elide $\cdot$ and 0; $e.g.$ the process $a{\cdot}b{\cdot}0$ will simply be denoted by ab. $P \sqcap Q$ is the nondeterministic choice (internal), while $P \,\square\, Q$ the deterministic choice (external). $P_A \,\|\, P_B$ is the mixed parallel operator; here A is the named alphabet for the process P, B the named alphabet for the process Q, and $P_A \,\|\, Q_B$ requires simultaneous participation of P and Q on any actions belonging to $A \cap B$, but the process P may progress independently on actions belonging to $A \setminus B$ (and symmetrically for Q). If it is clear from the context, the alphabets will be omitted. $P \backslash a$ denotes the hiding operator, while $f(P)$ renaming. We assume that $f : Act \longrightarrow Act$ is a 1-1 function. Finally, recursion is handled by terms $\mu x.P$, where μ is a variable binding operator.

We shall denote the set of terms defined by the above syntax by CSP. A term is said to be $closed$ iff it has no free process variables.

4 Semantics

4.1 "Failures with divergence" semantics

The failures semantic model [6] uses a representation of a process as a set of failures, that is pairs (s, X), where $s \in Act^\star$ is a finite sequence of actions and

X is a finite set of actions. The meaning of a failure (s, X) is as follows: the process *may* perform the sequence of actions s, and then *refuse* all the actions in the set X. Formally, a failure set is a subset:

$$F \subseteq Act^\star \times \mathcal{P}_f(Act)$$

satisfying certain axioms which will be discussed in Section 6. For any set F of failures we define

$$tr(F) = \{s \mid \exists X.(s, X) \in F\}.$$

There exists a natural ordering on the failure sets. We say $F_1 \sqsubseteq F_2$ (F_1 is more nondeterministic than F_2) iff $F_1 \supseteq F_2$.

The original failures semantics was not completely satisfactory in that its least element CHAOS was not absorptive. In particular, the law $P \| \text{CHAOS} = \text{CHAOS}$ was not satisfied. The solution introduced in [7] was to consider a more refined semantics which takes account of divergence. A process P is said to *diverge* if it may engage in an unbounded sequence of internal actions, invisible to its environment. An example of such process is $(\mu x.ax)\backslash a$. In order to account for divergence processes are modelled as pairs $\langle F, D \rangle$, where F is a failure set and $D \subseteq Act^\star$ is a divergence set, subject to certain axioms (see Section 6). The set of all such pairs is denoted by $\mathbb{FD}$. Failure–divergence pairs are ordered by:

$$\langle F_1, D_1 \rangle \sqsubseteq \langle F_2, D_2 \rangle \iff F_1 \supseteq F_2 \wedge D_1 \supseteq D_2.$$

This means that the process $\langle F_1, D_1 \rangle$ is more nondeterministic than $\langle F_2, D_2 \rangle$ if it can diverge whenever $\langle F_2, D_2 \rangle$ can diverge and fail whenever $\langle F_2, D_2 \rangle$ can fail. The order gives rise to a complete partial lattice; the least element, denoted $\bot$, has the failure set $Act^\star \times \mathcal{P}_f(Act)$ and the divergence set $Act^\star$. Clearly, the divergence–free processes are isomorphic to the original failures model. We use $div(\cdot)$ and $fail(\cdot)$ to extract the components of the pair $\langle F, D \rangle$.

CSP can be given denotational semantics by means of a compositional mapping from process expressions to the failure–divergence pairs [7]. The closed process expressions can be identified with elements of the domain $\mathbb{FD}$, while process expressions containing free variables create the need for environments. An *environment* ρ ranging over the set Env is a function from process variables to failure–divergence pairs $\mathbb{FD}$. Formally, we have a map

$$\mathcal{FD}[\![\cdot]\!] : \text{CSP} \longrightarrow [Env \longrightarrow \mathbb{FD}].$$

It is often convenient to view $\mathcal{FD}[\![\cdot]\!]$ as a pair of functions such that:

$$\mathcal{FD}[\![P]\!]\rho = \langle fail[\![P]\!]\rho, div[\![P]\!]\rho \rangle$$

for any process expression P and environment ρ.

The maps $fail[\![\cdot]\!]$ and $div[\![\cdot]\!]$ are defined by induction on the syntax of CSP process expressions. For expressions not involving recursion this is summarised in Tables 1 and 2. As the operations thus defined are continuous, the meaning of recursive process terms can be given by:

$$\mathcal{FD}[\![\mu x.P]\!]\rho = \mu(\lambda \langle F, D \rangle.(\mathcal{FD}[\![P]\!])(\rho + [x \mapsto \langle F, D \rangle])).$$

where μ denotes the least fixpoint of the operator on $\mathbb{FD}$ (shown in brackets) which maps the pair $\langle F, D \rangle$ to the meaning of P in the environment which agrees with ρ, except that it maps the variable x to $\langle F, D \rangle$.

Table 1: The failures table. $C(X, Y, Z)$ denotes $X \subseteq A, Y \subseteq B, Z \cap (A \cup B) = \emptyset$.

$$\frac{s \in div(P)}{(st, X) \in fail(P)} \qquad\qquad (\varepsilon, \emptyset) \in fail(0)$$

$$\frac{a \notin X}{(\varepsilon, X) \in fail(aP)} \qquad\qquad \frac{(s, X) \in fail(P)}{(as, X) \in fail(aP)}$$

$$\frac{(s, X) \in fail(P)}{(s, X) \in fail(P \sqcap Q)} \qquad\qquad \frac{(s, X) \in fail(P)}{(s, X) \in fail(Q \sqcap P)}$$

$$\frac{(s, X) \in fail(P)}{(s, X) \in fail(P \square Q)} \; s \neq \varepsilon \qquad\qquad \frac{(s, X) \in fail(P)}{(s, X) \in fail(Q \square P)} \; s \neq \varepsilon$$

$$\frac{(\varepsilon, X) \in fail(P) \quad (\varepsilon, X) \in fail(Q)}{(\varepsilon, X) \in fail(P \square Q)}$$

$$\frac{(s, X \cup \{a\}) \in fail(P)}{(s \backslash a, X) \in fail(P \backslash a)} \qquad\qquad \frac{(s, X) \in fail(P)}{(f(s), f(X)) \in fail(f(P))}$$

$$\frac{(s \restriction A, X) \in fail(P) \quad (s \restriction B, Y) \in fail(Q) \quad C(X, Y, Z)}{(s, X \cup Y \cup Z) \in fail(P_A \parallel Q_B)} \; s \in (A \cup B)^\star$$

Table 2: The divergence table

$$\frac{s \in div(P)}{st \in div(P)} \qquad\qquad \frac{s \in div(P)}{as \in div(aP)}$$

$$\frac{s \in div(P)}{s \backslash a \in div(P \backslash a)} \qquad\qquad \frac{sa^n \in div(P) \;\; \forall n}{s \backslash a \in div(P \backslash a)}$$

$$\frac{s \in div(P)}{f(s) \in div(f(P))}$$

$$\frac{s \restriction A \in div(P) \quad s \restriction B \in tr(Q)}{s \in div(P_A \parallel Q_B)} \; s \in (A \cup B)^\star$$

$$\frac{s \restriction A \in tr(P) \quad s \restriction B \in div(Q)}{s \in div(P_A \parallel Q_B)} \; s \in (A \cup B)^\star$$

$$\frac{s \in div(P)}{s \in div(P \sqcap Q)} \qquad\qquad \frac{s \in div(Q)}{s \in div(P \sqcap Q)}$$

$$\frac{s \in div(P)}{s \in div(P \square Q)} \qquad\qquad \frac{s \in div(Q)}{s \in div(P \square Q)}$$

4.2 The conflict relation

CSP is a specification–oriented language. The point of interest is what can be *guaranteed* of processes in terms of liveness and convergence. As a matter of mathematical convenience, the failures with divergence model records *possible* negative behaviour, *i.e.* failures (deadlocks) and divergence. $P \sqsubseteq Q$ should mean that Q is "better" than P, in the sense that Q makes more guarantees than P. Within the model this becomes $Q \subseteq P$, *i.e.* Q has less "bad" behaviour. As we are interested in refining this model, it is reasonable to assume that the new ordering $P \preceq Q$ should mean that $P \sqsubseteq Q$ and Q guarantees more concurrency. In keeping with the CSP treatment of refusals and divergence, we record *possible* conflicts. The basic idea is that two traces of a process P are in conflict if they *may* belong to different "runs" of P. Clearly, if two traces are not in conflict then they are *guaranteed* to belong to the same run.

To make our notion of possible conflict clearer, consider the following explanation in terms of event structures [17]. Process algebra has been modelled in event structures by various authors. CCS has been treated in [16, 4]. A prime event structure for CSP has been defined in [12].

To each process P we assign a set $E(P)$ of events. Notice that some of these will be labelled with the same action, so that for instance $E(a \,\square\, a)$ will have two events, both labelled with a. We also record whether these events are hidden, so that for instance $E((a \,\square\, b) \backslash b)$ will have two events, one of which is hidden. We have a partial ordering $\leq$ on $E(P)$, and also a conflict relation $\#$ which is symmetric. For example, in $E(ab \,\square\, c)$, $e_1 \leq e_2$ and $e_1 \,\#\, e_3$ where e_1, e_2, e_3 are labelled with a, b, c respectively.

A run r of P is defined to be a lower-closed, conflict-free subset of $E(P)$. In other words, if $e \in r$ and $e' \leq e$ then $e' \in r$, and if $e, e' \in r$ then it is not the case that $e \,\#\, e'$. Let $run(P)$ denote the set of all runs of P. We then define two runs to be compatible if they have a common extension: r_1 is compatible with r_2 iff there exists r such that $r_1, r_2 \subseteq r$. If they are not compatible, we say they conflict: $r_1 \, cf \, r_2$.

Next we suppose an *observation relation* between traces and runs: $obs(t, r)$ means that t is a possible observation of r. In general, there will be several runs corresponding to a given trace because of different events having the same labels, and of hiding. Also, there will be several traces corresponding to a given run (corresponding to different linearizations of the partial order). Finally, we can obtain the conflict relation on traces:

$$s_1 \; cf(P) \; s_2 \quad \Longleftrightarrow \quad \exists r_1, r_2. \; obs(s_1, r_1) \wedge obs(s_2, r_2) \wedge (r_1 \; cf \; r_2).$$

Instead of actually carrying this out, we prefer to define the conflict relation $cf(P) \subseteq (tr(P))^2$ by induction over syntax (see Table 3). We include the rules (div) and (sym) for reasons of convenience, even though they are not strictly over syntax. Both (div) and (sym) could be replaced by a more elaborate version of the other rules. There are two essential rules, (L-R-⊓) and (L-R-□), shown below:

$$\frac{s \in tr(P) \quad s' \in tr(Q)}{s \; cf(P \sqcap Q) \; s'} \qquad \frac{s \in tr(P) \quad s' \in tr(Q)}{s \; cf(P \,\square\, Q) \; s'} \; s, s' \neq \varepsilon$$

The rule (L-R-⊓) ensures that all traces of P, including the empty trace ε, are in conflict with each trace of Q. On the other hand, according to (L-R-□) only

Table 3: The conflict relation

(div)	$\dfrac{s \in div(P)}{s \; cf(P) \; s'}$	(sym)	$\dfrac{s \; cf(P) \; s'}{s' \; cf(P) \; s}$
(pref)	$\dfrac{s \; cf(P) \; s'}{as \; cf(a \cdot P) \; as'}$		
(hide)	$\dfrac{s \; cf(P) \; s'}{s \backslash a \; cf(P) \; s' \backslash a}$	(ren)	$\dfrac{s \; cf(P) \; s'}{f(s) \; cf(f(P)) \; f(s')}$
(L-||)	$\dfrac{s{\restriction}A \; cf(P) \; s'{\restriction}A}{s \; cf(P_A \parallel Q_B) \; s'}$	(R-||)	$\dfrac{s{\restriction}B \; cf(Q) \; s'{\restriction}B}{s \; cf(P_A \parallel Q_B) \; s'}$
(L-$\sqcap$)	$\dfrac{s \; cf(P) \; s'}{s \; cf(P \sqcap Q) \; s'}$	(R-$\sqcap$)	$\dfrac{s \; cf(Q) \; s'}{s \; cf(P \sqcap Q) \; s'}$
(L-R-$\sqcap$)	$\dfrac{s \in tr(P) \; s' \in tr(Q)}{s \; cf(P \sqcap Q) \; s'}$		
(L-$\square$)	$\dfrac{s \; cf(P) \; s'}{s \; cf(P \square Q) \; s'}$	(R-$\square$)	$\dfrac{s \; cf(Q) \; s'}{s \; cf(P \square Q) \; s'}$
(L-R-$\square$)	$\dfrac{s \in tr(P) \; s' \in tr(Q)}{s \; cf(P \square Q) \; s'} \; s, s' \neq \varepsilon$		

those pairs of traces from P and Q are in conflict which are not simultaneously empty. Of the remaining rules, (sym) imposes symmetry, and the rest preserve conflict through the syntactic structure.

Example 4.1 *(Possible conflict)* Note that $a \; cf(a \square b) \; b$, $\varepsilon \; cf(a \sqcap b) \; \varepsilon$, $\varepsilon \; cf(a \sqcap b) \; b$, $a \; cf((a \parallel b) \sqcap a) \; b$.

The complement $(tr(P))^2 \backslash cf(P)$ of the conflict relation will often be referred to as the *compatibility* relation and will be denoted by $\overline{cf}(P)$.

Example 4.2 *(Illustration of compatibility)* Note that $a \; \overline{cf}(ab) \; ab$, $a \; \overline{cf}(a \parallel b) \; ba$.

The next examples illustrate the difficulty caused by the presence of hiding.

Example 4.3 Let $Q = (a \square b) \backslash b$. Then $a \in tr(Q)$, $(\varepsilon, \{a\}) \in fail(Q)$, but $\varepsilon \; \overline{cf}(Q) \; \varepsilon$. Also, $\varepsilon \; cf(Q) \; a$.

Example 4.4 Let Q be the same as in Example 4.3, $R = Q \square a$. Then $\varepsilon \; \overline{cf}(R) \; \varepsilon$, $(\varepsilon, \{a\}) \notin fail(R)$, but $\varepsilon \; cf(R) \; a$. Also, $a \; cf(R) \; a$.

Example 4.5 Let $P = ab \square a$, $s = ab$, $t = \varepsilon$. Note that $s \; \overline{cf}(P) \; t$, $s \; \overline{cf}(P) \; s(t - s)$ but $s \; cf(P) \; a$. A similar case is shown in Example 6.4.

The final two examples exhibit confusion, which is characteristic of an interference between concurrency and choice. These phenomena arise in Petri nets.

Example 4.6 *(Symmetric confusion)* Let $P = (a_{\{a\}} \parallel b_{\{b\}}) \square c$. Then

$$
\begin{aligned}
tr(P) &= \{ab, ba, c, \ldots\} \\
cf(P) &= \{(ab, c), (ba, c), \ldots\}.
\end{aligned}
$$

Observe that either a and b happen, in which case they are independent, or c happens. c is only possible initially, but not after a or b.

Example 4.7 *(Asymmetric confusion)* Let $P = (a \square c)_{\{a,c\}} \parallel bc_{\{b,c\}}$. Then

$$
\begin{aligned}
tr(P) &= \{ab, ba, bc, \ldots\} \\
cf(P) &= \{(a, bc), (ab, bc), (ba, bc)\}.
\end{aligned}
$$

Observe that either a and b happens, in which case they are independent, or b is followed by c, in which case a is prevented from happening.

4.3 "Failures with divergence and conflict" semantics

Formally, the proposed "failures with divergence and conflict" semantics is the set of triples $\langle F, D, C \rangle$ where F is a failure set, D is a divergence set, and $C \subseteq (Act^\star)^2$ is a conflict set, subject to certain axioms to be discussed in Section 6.

The set of all failure–divergence–conflict triples will be denoted $\mathbb{FDC}$. Although the discussion of the precise nature of $\mathbb{FDC}$ is deferred to Section 6, it suffices for our present purposes to postulate that it is a sublattice of the appropriate set ordered by $\supseteq$. It will have directed joins given by set intersection. This will be enough for $\mathbb{FDC}$ to serve as the semantic domain for our new semantics.

We define the order over failure–divergence–conflict triples below.

Definition 4.8 *(Order on failure–divergence–conflict triples)*

$$
\langle F_1, D_1, C_1 \rangle \preceq \langle F_2, D_2, C_2 \rangle \quad \Longleftrightarrow \quad F_1 \supseteq F_2 \wedge D_1 \supseteq D_2 \wedge C_1 \supseteq C_2.
$$

This means that the higher the process in the ordering, the more concurrency (*i.e.* less conflict) it guarantees. This is in agreement with the failures and divergence components, according to which the higher the process in the ordering, the more determinism and the less divergence it guarantees.

As we said earlier, we postulate $(\mathbb{FDC}, \preceq)$ is a dcpo. It may seem that $\mathbb{FDC}$ has arbitrary meets and directed joins. However, in Section 6.2, when we examine the model in detail, we show that meets need not exist — in particular, the meet of a and b.

We overload the notation by using $cf(\cdot)$ to extract the conflict component of the triple $\langle F, D, C \rangle$.

Example 4.9 *(Concurrency vs choice)* Note that $ab \sqcap ba \preceq ab \square ba \preceq a \parallel b$, but the converse inequalities do not hold.

We can now introduce the semantic map

$$\mathcal{FDC}[\![\cdot]\!] : \mathrm{CSP} \longrightarrow [Env \longrightarrow \mathbb{FDC}]$$

which is a suitable extension, compositional in style, of the map mentioned in Section 4.1. For convenience, we view $\mathcal{FDC}[\![\cdot]\!]$ as a triple of functions such that:

$$\mathcal{FDC}[\![P]\!]\rho \;=\; \langle fail[\![P]\!]\rho, \, div[\![P]\!]\rho, \, cf[\![P]\!]\rho \rangle$$

for any process expression P and environment ρ mapping process variables to triples in $\mathbb{FDC}$. The maps $fail[\![\cdot]\!]$ and $div[\![\cdot]\!]$ are as defined in Section 4.1, while the definition of $cf[\![\cdot]\!]$ for finite processes is given inductively in Table 3.

If it is clear from the context, we shall confuse the syntactic and semantic CSP operations.

We can show the following result.

Proposition 4.10 The operations of CSP are monotone and continuous in each argument.

Proof: Monotonicity and continuity of the maps $fail[\![\cdot]\!]$ and $div[\![\cdot]\!]$ is known, see *e.g.* [7]. Continuity of hiding for $cf[\![\cdot]\!]$ follows by an argument similar to that for divergence. The remaining cases are straightforward. □

Proposition 4.10 guarantees the existence of least fixpoint solutions to recursive equations, thus ensuring that process definitions using μ are well defined.

The following relationship between the "old" and the "new" model, reminiscent of the relationship between the failures and failures with divergence model, can be stated. We say that a process P has *maximal* conflict iff $cf(P) = tr(P)^2$. It can be shown that the "old" model is isomorphic to those elements in the "new" model which have maximal conflict. Note that, for any CSP term P, $P \sqcap P$ has maximal conflict. Let $\Psi : \mathbb{FD} \longrightarrow \mathbb{FDC}$ be defined by

$$\Psi(\langle F, D \rangle) \;=\; \langle F, D, tr(P)^2 \rangle.$$

We have the following correspondence.

Lemma 4.11 If $x = \mathcal{FD}[\![P]\!]$ then $\Psi(x) = \mathcal{FDC}[\![P \sqcap P]\!]$.

Proposition 4.12 The elements of $(\mathbb{FDC}, \preceq)$ with maximal conflict are isomorphic to $(\mathbb{FD}, \sqsubseteq)$ via the map Ψ.

Proof:

1. Lift the map Ψ to environments ρ.
2. Show $\mathcal{FDC}[\![P]\!](\Psi\rho) \preceq \Psi(\mathcal{FD}[\![P]\!]\rho)$ for all terms P and environments ρ.
3. Show $\mathcal{FDC}[\![P]\!](\Psi\rho) = \Psi(\mathcal{FD}[\![P]\!]\rho)$ for all terms P and environment ρ such that $cf[\![P]\!](\Psi\rho)$ is maximal.

□

5 The laws

The laws which we have verified as sound (but not complete) are shown in Table 4. As expected, the expansion law is now in the form of an inequality. What was less expected, perhaps, is that the idempotency of choice fails.

Table 4: The laws of CSP with conflict

$$P \square P \preceq P$$
$$P \square Q = Q \square P$$
$$P \square (Q \square R) = (P \square Q) \square R$$
$$P \square (Q \sqcap R) \succeq (P \square Q) \sqcap (P \square R)$$
$$P \square 0 = P$$
$$a(P \sqcap Q) = aP \square aQ$$
$$P \sqcap Q \preceq P$$
$$P \sqcap Q = Q \sqcap P$$
$$P \sqcap (Q \sqcap R) = (P \sqcap Q) \sqcap R$$
$$P \sqcap P \sqcap P = P \sqcap P$$
$$P \sqcap Q \preceq P \square Q$$
$$P_A \parallel Q_B = Q_B \parallel P_A$$
$$P_A \parallel (Q_B \parallel R_C)_{B \cup C} = (P_A \parallel Q_B)_{A \cup B} \parallel R_C$$
$$P_A \parallel 0_B = P_A \qquad \text{if } A \cap B = \emptyset$$
$$P_A \parallel 0_A = 0$$
$$aP_A \parallel bQ_B \succeq a(P_A \parallel bQ_B) \square b(aP_A \parallel Q_B) \qquad \text{where } A \cap B = \emptyset,$$
$$a \in A, b \in B$$
$$(aP)\backslash a = P\backslash a$$
$$(aP)\backslash b = a(P\backslash b) \qquad \text{if } a \neq b$$
$$(P \sqcap Q)\backslash a = (P\backslash a) \sqcap (Q\backslash a)$$

6 Models

The purpose of this section is to discuss the "failures with divergence and conflict model" for CSP. As in the case of the failures–divergence model, which constitutes a sublattice of the set of failure–divergence pairs generated by certain closure conditions (axioms (F1)-(F4) and (D1)-(D2) in Section 6.1), we aim to derive similar axioms for the refined model.

6.1 Failures with divergence model

This section gives an overview of issues pertaining to the failures model, which are syntax independent. Recall that a failure is a pair (s, X) where $s \in Act^*$ is a finite sequence of actions and X is a finite set of actions.

Let F be a failure set, then F must satisfy the following axioms:

(F1) $(\varepsilon, \emptyset) \in F$;
(F2) $(st, \emptyset) \in F \Rightarrow (s, \emptyset) \in F$;
(F3) $(s, X) \in F \wedge Y \subseteq X \Rightarrow (s, Y) \in F$;
(F4) $(s, X) \in F \wedge (sc, \emptyset) \notin F \Rightarrow (s, X \cup \{c\}) \in F$.

Axioms (F1), (F2) and (F3) are closure conditions – they ensure that the set of traces is non-empty and prefix closed, and that the refusals at a given trace are closed under inclusion. Axiom (F4) states that an impossible action can be included in the refusal set.

Recall that $\langle F, D \rangle$ is a failure–divergence pair if F is a failure set and $D \subseteq Act^*$ is a divergence set. The failure–divergence pairs must satisfy:

(D1) $s \in D \Rightarrow st \in D$;
(D2) $s \in D \Rightarrow (st, X) \in F$.

Axiom (D1) ensures that every divergence set is suffix closed, while (D2) states that any divergent trace must be refused.

6.2 The new model

In Section 4.3 we defined a map $\mathcal{FDC}[\![\cdot]\!]$ from the syntax of CSP into the domain $\mathbb{FDC}$. $\mathbb{FDC}$ consists of triples $\langle F, D, C \rangle$, where F is a failure set, D is a divergence set and $C \subseteq (Act^*)^2$ is a conflict set. However, not every such triple deserves to be regarded as a process. We now discuss what additional axioms they should obey to belong to the model.

In the case of the failures with divergence model we can be confident that the axioms (F), (D) are complete, because (assuming Act is finite) any finite failure–divergence pair is in the range of the semantic map $\mathcal{FD}[\![\cdot]\!]$ [8]. We cannot as yet make an analogous statement. However, we have identified certain properties which seem attractive and natural enough that they should be added to the model.

First, we introduce some basic axioms. Let P be $\langle F, D, C \rangle$; then P must satisfy the following axioms:

(C1) $cf(P) \subseteq (tr(P))^2$;
(C2) $s \; cf(P) \; s' \Rightarrow s' \; cf(P) \; s$;
(C3) $s \in div(P) \Rightarrow s \; cf(P) \; t$.

According to the axiom (C1), the conflict relation is defined for valid traces only. Axiom (C2) states that the conflict relation must be symmetric. Axiom (C3) ensures that a divergent trace is in conflict with any trace, thus maintaining the catastrophic character of divergence.

Before we give the remainder of the axioms, we consider two relations which are derived from the conflict relation, or, more precisely, from its complement, the compatibility relation. The relation $co(P)$ is similar to Mazurkiewicz trace equivalence [13], while $pre(P)$ is similar to the trace preorder [11], except that in our model they are not reflexive. Intuitively, Mazurkiewicz trace equivalence equates those traces which are observations of the same run — they may only differ in the order of consecutive independent actions. The trace preorder is a version of string prefix order which ignores the permutations of consecutive independent actions.

Definition 6.1 *(Concurrency)* We say $s \; co(P) \; t$ iff $s \; perm \; t$ and $s \; \overline{cf}(P) \; t$.

Definition 6.2 *(Precedence)* We say $s \; pre(P) \; t$ iff $s \subseteq t$ and $s \; \overline{cf}(P) \; t$.

Note that $s \; co(P) \; t$ iff $s \; pre(P) \; t$ and $t \; pre(P) \; s$.

The following example illustrates $co(P)$.

Example 6.3 Let $P = (a \| b) \square ab$. Then $ab \; perm \; ba$, $ab \; cf(P) \; ab$, $ab \; cf(P) \; ba$, $ba \; co(P) \; ba$.

The relation $co(P)$ equates those traces which are observations of *the same* run, while the relation $pre(P)$ relates an observation of an initial segment of some run with (an observation of) the run itself. It is then reasonable to expect that if $s\ co(P)\ t$ then the behaviour of the system after s should be identical with that after t. We therefore propose the following further axioms:

(C4) $(su, X) \in fail(P), s\ co(P)\ t \Rightarrow (tu, X) \in fail(P)$;
(C5) $u\ cf(P)\ sv, s\ co(P)\ t \Rightarrow u\ cf(P)\ tv$;
(H1) $s\ pre(P)\ t\ pre(P)\ u \Rightarrow s\ pre(P)\ u$;

We expect to see some connection between refusal sets and conflict. For instance, we cannot have both $(sa, \emptyset)$ and $(s, \{a\})$ as observations of a single run. Similarly, if we observe $(s, \{a\})$ and $(s, \{b\})$, and if these are to belong to the same run, then we must also be able to observe $(s, \{a, b\})$. We therefore propose two further axioms. Recall that $\mathrm{ld}(s, t)$ denotes the leftmost difference of traces s and t.

(C6) $(s, \{a\}) \in fail(P),\ t \in tr(P),\ a = \mathrm{ld}(s, t) \Rightarrow s\ cf(P)\ t$;
(C7) $(s, X) \in fail(P), (s, Y) \in fail(P), s\ \overline{cf}(P)\ s \Rightarrow (s, X \cup Y) \in fail(P)$;

If we observe sa and sb, and these do not conflict, then we expect also to observe sab and sba. This is the forward diamond property as seen in asynchronous transition systems [15] and elsewhere. This holds for CSP processes in our model. In fact, if P is constructed from 0, prefixing, $\|$ and $\backslash$ (so that P is conflict-free), then we can also show $sab\ co(P)\ sba$. However, as shown in Example 6.4, the stronger conclusion does not hold in general.

Example 6.4 *(Weak diamond property)* Let $P = Q \backslash d$ where

$$Q = ad(d\ \square\ d)_{\{a,d\}} \| bdd_{\{b,d\}}.$$

Then $a\ \overline{cf}(P)\ b, a\ \overline{cf}(P)\ a, b\ \overline{cf}(P)\ b$. However, $ab\ cf(P)\ ba$.

Unfortunately, when we come to formulate an axiom embodying the forward diamond property, we find the position is more complicated. Suppose that we observe ab and cd, and these do not conflict. Then we should also be able to observe $acbd$, $cabd$ and any other combinations so long as a comes before b and c comes before d. What is happening is that we have inferred a partial ordering on the four events a, b, c, d.

Any trace which is a linearization of the partial ordering should be observable. Unfortunately, this is still not the full picture. If we are given two traces which conflict, we cannot expect to deduce anything further about the process. However, consider this example: a process has traces abc, ba, bda. Suppose also that $abc\ cf(P)\ bda$, but that the other two pairs do not conflict. Then a and b in abc and bda apparently could belong to different runs. However, because neither conflicts with ba we can infer that they are in fact from the same run. It is still the case however that c and d conflict. We therefore deduce the following event structure:

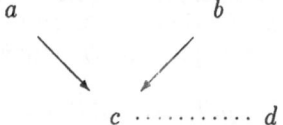

where the dotted line denotes conflict. A possible trace based on this would be abd, which we could not deduce from considering ba, bda on their own.

We are led to the following hypothesis. If T is a set of traces of a process P, then there is an event structure E associated with T (and $cf(P)$ on T). Let $con(T, s)$ hold if s is a possible configuration of E. Then our next axiom states

$$(C8) \quad T \subseteq tr(P), \, con(T, s) \Rightarrow s \in tr(P).$$

We earlier postulated that $\mathbb{FDC}$ should be a dcpo. The following result shows that $\mathbb{FDC}$ does indeed possess arbitrary directed joins given by set intersection, even when all the axioms we have considered are admitted.

Proposition 6.5 Axioms (C1) – (C8) and (H1) are preserved by directed set intersection.

Proof: Omitted. □

The following is a conjecture, which we have proved for all cases except for hiding and axiom (H1).

Conjecture 6.6 The above axioms are preserved by all the CSP operations.

The following example shows that meets do not exist in $\mathbb{FDC}$, unlike in $\mathbb{FD}$, which is a complete semi-lattice with arbitrary meets corresponding to set union.

Example 6.7 (*Non-existence of meets*) Let $P_1 = a \sqcap b, P_2 = (a \,\Box\, b \,\Box\, c) \backslash c$. Their conflict sets are as follows:

$$
\begin{aligned}
cf(P_1) &= \{(\varepsilon, \varepsilon), (\varepsilon, a), (b, \varepsilon), (a, b)\} \\
cf(P_2) &= \{(\varepsilon, a), (b, \varepsilon), (a, b)\}
\end{aligned}
$$

so $cf(P_1) \supseteq cf(P_2)$. However, $fail(P_1) \subseteq fail(P_2)$ since $fail(P_1) = fail(a) \cup fail(b)$, while $fail(P_2) = fail(P_1) \cup \{(\varepsilon, \{a, b\})\}$. Thus, $P_1 \preceq a, b$ and $P_2 \preceq a, b$, but P_1 and P_2 are incomparable. It is easily seen that $cf(P_1)$ and $cf(P_2)$ are least with respect to their respective failure sets. We can now show that the meet of a and b does not exist. Suppose Q is the meet of a and b, then $fail(Q) \subseteq fail(P_1)$, $fail(a), fail(b) \subseteq Q$. Hence, $fail(Q) = fail(P_1)$. Also, $cf(Q) \subseteq cf(P_1)$. But $cf(P_1)$ is least with respect to $fail(P_1)$. Hence, $Q = P_1$. But then $cf(Q) \not\subseteq cf(P_2)$, and $P_2 \preceq a, b$. Therefore, Q is not above P_2 and Q cannot be the required meet.

7 Further work

Obtaining a complete set of axioms for the failures–divergence–conflict triples has proved more difficult than originally thought. One reason for this state

Table 5: The causality relation

(div) $$\frac{s \in div(P)}{s \ cs(P) \ s'}$$

(init) $$\frac{s \in tr(P)}{a \ cs(a \cdot P) \ as} s \neq \varepsilon$$ (pref) $$\frac{s \ cs(P) \ s'}{as \ cs(a \cdot P) \ as'}$$

(hide) $$\frac{s \ cs(P) \ s'}{s \backslash a \ cs(P \backslash a) \ s' \backslash a}$$ (ren) $$\frac{s \ cs(P) \ s'}{f(s) \ cs(f(P)) \ f(s')}$$

(||) $$\frac{s \lceil A \ cs(P) \ s' \lceil A \quad s \lceil B \ cs(Q) \ s' \lceil B}{s \ cs(P_A \, \| \, Q_B) \ s'}$$

(L-⊓) $$\frac{s \ cs(P) \ s'}{s \ cs(P \sqcap Q) \ s'}$$ (R-⊓) $$\frac{s \ cs(Q) \ s'}{s \ cs(P \sqcap Q) \ s'}$$

(L-□) $$\frac{s \ cs(P) \ s'}{s \ cs(P \square Q) \ s'}$$ (R-□) $$\frac{s \ cs(Q) \ s'}{s \ cs(P \square Q) \ s'}$$

of affairs is that, perhaps due to the presence of hiding, the conflict relation on traces, or even failures, is not sufficiently refined to deal with the hidden events. A possible refinement, sufficient to defeat the counter-example to one of the versions of the diamond property (Example 6.4) would be to add causality information. This can be done in terms of syntax-directed rules similar to the conflict relation. A candidate definition has been summarized in Table 5. The essential rules are (init) and (pref), with the remaining rules preserving causality relationships through syntactic structure. Then we could derive a *conflict or causality* relation by putting:

$$cc(P) \ = \ cf(P) \cup cs(P) \cup cs(P)^{-1} \ .$$

The relation $cc(P)$, which is symmetric, would replace the relation $cf(P)$ in the formal triple $\langle F, D, C \rangle$.

Another possibility is to adopt a more discriminating notion of an observation, such as failures, instead of traces. Observations as failures are well motivated, since they can be explained in terms of experiments on machines. A generalization of the conflict relation to work on failures instead of traces is straightforward, and it would lead to finer distinctions. Preliminary analysis shows that processes P_1 and P_2 in Example 6.7 become incomparable, but we cannot yet comment on the importance of this fact.

A third possibility is to develop a two-level framework, which would have some behavioural model with runs at the lower level, and a mapping relating runs to (possibly different) notions of observations. The lower-level could, for example, be an event structure derived from syntax by the rules similar to the construction of Boudol and Castellani for CCS [5]. The behavioural phenomena present at the lower level would then induce the corresponding phenomena on observations. It would appear, however, that this approach might take us further away from our intention to work at an abstract level.

Finally, we would like to derive a complete axiomatization of the failure–divergence–conflict triples, analogous to the axioms (F1)-(F4) and (D1)-(D2). It is relatively well known that any finite CSP process is equivalent to one obtained using 0, prefixing, $\sqcap$ and $\square$ [8]. The interesting point is that the parallel operator $\|$ is not used. We would anticipate that in our model, if there is a satisfactory axiomatization, the parallel operator would play an essential role.

8 Conclusion

We have presented a refinement of the standard failures with divergence model for CSP, the purpose of which was to weaken the expansion law to an inequality. We have shown that the additional information about concurrency, conflict and causality can be derived systematically from the syntax of processes, without the need for additional labelling of actions, as long as the relations are interpreted as representing the possibility (or, dually, a guarantee) of the given phenomenon. We have carried out the construction for a large subset of CSP, which includes hiding. We have found that most equalities hold true in the refined model, the exceptions being the expansion law and the idempotency of choice, which have now taken the form of inequalities. The resulting inequational calculus is only slightly more complex than the original failures with divergence calculus.

We believe we have not yet reached a satisfactory characterization of the elements of the model $(\mathbb{FDC}, \preceq)$. This is probably due to a combination of factors, including the difficulty caused by hiding, the need to axiomatize the possibility of conflict, and the fact that working at the level of observations means that we are in effect working with inexact descriptions of the behaviour, since the runs of the system cannot be known. However, a number of pleasing facts are already clear, such as the correspondence of the "old" model to the elements in the "new" model with maximal conflict.

We believe that this framework is, to a large extent, independent of the choice of the language and model. However, we should point out that it is the semantics of the CSP parallel that makes the construction workable.

Acknowledgements

We would like to acknowledge Samson Abramsky and Mike Shields for discussions on the subject. The first author would like to acknowledge the Nuffield Science Foundation grant (SCI/124/528/G) for providing funds to visit the Theory and Formal Methods Section of the Department of Computing, Imperial College. The second author would like to acknowledge the support of the SERC grant GR/F72475.

References

[1] Samson Abramsky. Causal semantics in process algebra. Draft, 1989.

[2] Luca Aceto and Uffe Engberg. Failure semantics for a simple process language with refinement. In *Foundations of Software Technology and Theoretical Computer Science*, pages 89–108. Springer-Verlag, 1991.

[3] S. Blamey. The soundness and completeness of axioms for CSP processes. In G.M. Reed, A.W. Roscoe, and R.F. Wachter, editors, *Topology and Category Theory in Computer Science*, pages 29–56. Oxford University Press, 1991.

[4] Gerard Boudol and Ilaria Castellani. Permutation of transitions: an event structure semantics for CCS and SCCS. In *Linear Time, Branching Time and Partial Order in Logics and Models for Concurrency*, volume 354 of *Lecture Notes in Computer Science*, pages 411–427. Springer-Verlag, 1989.

[5] Gerard Boudol and Ilaria Castellani. Three equivalent semantics for CCS. In *Semantics of Systems for Concurrent Processes*, volume 469 of *Lecture Notes in Computer Science*. Springer-Verlag, 1990.

[6] S. D. Brookes, C. A. R. Hoare, and A. W. Roscoe. A theory of communicating sequential processes. *Journal of the ACM*, 31(3):560–599, 1984.

[7] S. D. Brookes and A. W. Roscoe. An improved failures model for communicating processes. In *Seminar on Concurrency*, volume 197 of *Lecture Notes in Computer Science*, pages 281–305. Springer-Verlag, 1985.

[8] Stephen Brookes. *A Model for Communicating Sequential Processes*. PhD thesis, 1983.

[9] P. Degano and U. Montanari. Concurrent histories: A basis for observing distributed systems. *Journal of Computer and System Sciences*, 34:422–461, 1987.

[10] C.A.R. Hoare. *Communicating Sequential Processes*. Prentice-Hall International, 1985.

[11] Marta Z. Kwiatkowska. On the domain of traces and sequential composition. In S. Abramsky and T.S.E. Maibaum, editors, *TAPSOFT'91*, volume 493 of *Lecture Notes in Computer Science*, pages 42–56. Springer-Verlag, 1991.

[12] R. Loogen and U. Goltz. A non-interleaving semantics model for nondeterministic concurrent processes. Technical Report 87-15, RWTH Aachen, 1987.

[13] Antoni Mazurkiewicz. Basic notions of trace theory. In *Linear Time, Branching Time and Partial Order in Logics and Models for Concurrency*, volume 354 of *Lecture Notes in Computer Science*, pages 25–34. Springer-Verlag, 1989.

[14] M. Mukund and M. Nielsen. CCS, locations and asynchronous transition systems. In R. Shyamasundar, editor, *Foundations of Software Technology and Theoretical Computer Science*, volume 652 of *Lecture Notes in Computer Science*. Springer-Verlag, 1992.

[15] M.W. Shields. Deterministic asynchronous automata. In *Formal Methods in Programming*. North Holland, 1985.

[16] Glynn Winskel. Event structure semantics for CCS and related languages. In *Automata, Languages and Programming*, volume 140 of *Lecture Notes in Computer Science*, pages 561–567. Springer-Verlag, 1982.

[17] Glynn Winskel. Event structures. In *Advances in Petri Nets*, volume 255 of *Lecture Notes in Computer Science*, pages 325–392. Springer-Verlag, 1987.

A Complete Axiom System for CCS with a Stability Operator

Sarah Liebert

sajl@doc.ic.ac.uk
Department of Computing, Imperial College
180 Queen's Gate, London SW7 2BZ, United Kingdom

Abstract

The language CCS_σ,[7], is obtained by adding an extra operator to CCS to detect stability. One application of this operator is in the testing of equivalence of processes. CCS_σ arose out of a method of testing which records the refusal of some action in a finite time, as well as successes, [6]. Refusal tests record processes refusing actions and then continuing with other actions. This paper discusses refusal testing and other applications of CCS_σ. A complete axiomatization is developed for testing equivalence on CCS_σ processes.

1 Introduction

The calculus in this paper builds upon Milner's CCS, [5] . Several equivalences have been defined upon CCS processes in order to equate processes with similar behaviour. Some of these use direct observation of the possible actions of a process. Another type use the concept of testing. A "test" of some kind is run upon the process being tested and the results of the experiment observed in some way, rather than observing the process alone directly. An external test is one defined in a different language than the process being tested, but which interacts in some way allowing us to observe the behaviour of the process. An internal test is one defined in the tested process's own language and placed in parallel with it. Any resulting sequence of actions performed by the coupled test and process is called a computation. Most tests contain a special action ω to indicate satisfaction of certain conditions, when the tested process has performed the desired actions the test performs ω and then terminates. A computation ending in ω is called a successful computation. Many test systems, e.g. [1], only allow positive results, in the following sense. If a test "asks" a process to perform a certain action, and the process does so, this is a success. If the process is able to refuse the action the test simply deadlocks and no further testing occurs. Phillips [6] proposed a more informative type of testing called refusal testing. Refusal tests can, under some circumstances, deduce that the process which they are testing has refused to perform an action requested of it, and can then continue testing to see how the process will behave after this refusal. This enables more processes to be distinguished than observation of successful action sequences alone.

The original refusal tests [6] were external to the language (CCS) being tested. In original refusal tests, refusal of an action e.g. b, was indicated by the test performing the action $\tilde{b}$, the action of "refusing b", so additional actions in the test language were needed to recognise refusal of each type of action in the tested processes. In order to internalize refusal tests, it turns out that we need only add one extra action to CCS, the new action being called σ. σ is a special action, neither an ordinary visible action nor an invisible action (as there is only one of these – τ). σ actions are enabled only when a process is otherwise stable, i.e. it cannot perform any internal actions or any communications with other processes. Then we can test for "refusal of b" by offering a process $\overline{b}$ and σ, whereupon σ only occurs if no τ $(b\overline{b})$ is possible.

Recall that, in the testing paradigm, [1], a process is tested by being placed in parallel with the test (itself a process) and the ensuing computation (sequence of actions produced) is observed. Tests may contain the special action ω, which represents success. It is said that a process p may pass a test t, p may t, if there is a successful computation possibly resulting from $p|t$. Similarly, p must t if all possible computations are successful. We also say that p mẚy t if p cannot pass test t, and p mẚst t if p is not obliged to pass t.

For example, let $p = a.b + a.c$, and $q = a.(b + c)$. Then p may $\overline{a}(\overline{b} + \sigma.\omega)$, for

$$a.b + a.c|\overline{a}.(\overline{b} + \sigma.\omega) \xrightarrow{\tau} c|\overline{b} + \sigma.\omega \xrightarrow{\sigma} \xrightarrow{\omega}$$

Note that we may also have

$$a.b + a.c|\overline{a}.(\overline{b} + \sigma.\omega) \xrightarrow{\tau} b|\overline{b} + \sigma.\omega$$

which fails. On the other hand, q mẚy $\overline{a}(\overline{b} + \sigma.\omega)$, for

$$a.(b + c)|\overline{a}.(\overline{b} + \sigma.\omega) \xrightarrow{\tau} b + c|\overline{b} + \sigma.\omega \xrightarrow{\tau}$$

which fails.

If we were testing a process with multiple observers there would be a risk of livelock if σ were an ordinary visible action (which observer would synchronise with the process being observed?). To avoid this we make σ a broadcast action: all processes capable of performing σ must synchronise on it.

In [7], Phillips showed that CCS plus the stability operator σ was sufficient to distinguish any processes of CCS which were not refusal-testing equivalent. It turns out, however, that processes which themselves contain σ's may also be tested satisfactorily by other such tests. In this report we therefore consider CCS_σ, the language CCS plus the stability operator σ, as a calculus in which we freely combine "ordinary" CCS processes and those containing σ's, as defined in [7].

As well as testing for the refusal of a specific action, as above, we could use σ to test for stability, as the test process cannot proceed with a σ unless the process being tested is stable [7]. It turns out that there are other uses of CCS_σ; several of these will be discussed here. We may also consider σ as a "tick" action for a simple notion of discrete time, similar to [2, 3]. Here we make use of the fact that σ is a broadcast action; cycles of activity (communication between processes) are punctuated by stabilizing on σ.

The final use which we shall consider for σ is as a priority-lowering prefix, so that a notion of priority may be added to CCS. This usage stems from the idea that offering a process $a + \sigma.b$ is "rather like" offering a with higher priority than b – if the recipient process can perform $\bar{a}$ it must do so, and only if this is not possible will b be offered.

For example, consider a very simple interrupt. Process P engages in repeated c actions until interrupted by process I.

$$P \quad = \quad \text{int}.0 + \sigma.c.P$$
$$I \quad = \quad \overline{\text{int}}.0$$

Now consider another example: a CCS_σ interrupt handler. An interrupt handler I_0 manages two processes P_1 and P_2. P_1 has higher priority than P_2, and I_0 will shut down P_2 for P_1 if necessary. The system is $I_0|P_1|P_2$ where:

$$I_0 \quad = \quad \text{request}_1.\overline{\text{run}}_1.I_1 + \sigma.\text{request}_2.\overline{\text{run}}_2.I_2$$
$$I_1 \quad = \quad \text{leave}_1.I_0$$
$$I_2 \quad = \quad \text{request}_1.\overline{\text{shutdown}_2}.\overline{\text{run}}_1.I_1 + \text{leave}_2.I_0$$
$$P_1 \quad = \quad \overline{\text{request}_1}.\text{run}_1.\overline{\text{leave}}_1.P_1$$
$$P_2 \quad = \quad \overline{\text{request}_2}.\text{run}_2.(\overline{\text{leave}}_2.P_2 + \text{shutdown}_2.P_2)$$

Here σ is used when there are currently no processes running to ensure that any request by P_2 will have lower priority than a simultaneous request by P_1.

To summarize, the special action σ:

♦ occurs only when processes are otherwise stable,

♦ is a broadcast action (processes synchronise on it),

♦ is a test for stability,

♦ and is a priority-lowering prefix.

In the following sections we shall recall the operational semantics of CCS_σ from [7]. We define a testing equivalence (called must testing equivalence) on CCS_σ processes, obtain the corresponding congruence relation between processes, and then introduce a complete axiomatization for the language under this method of testing equivalence.

1.1 Operational Semantics of CCS_σ

We first introduce some definitions which are required to set up the operational semantics, a divergence-free predicate DF and a stability predicate stab:–

Definition 1 $DF(p) \iff p$ has no unguarded occurrence of Ω.

Definition 2 $\text{stab}(p) \iff DF(p) \land p \not\xrightarrow{\tau}$

Let α range over Act, μ range over $Act \cup \{\tau\}$, ν range over $Act \cup \{\tau, \sigma\}$.

The rules for the operational semantics of CCS_σ are explained in the adjacent table. Many of these are similar to the rules for CCS, with invisible actions (τ's) and visible actions occurring under the usual conditions. The summation rules **Sum** and **Sum**$_\sigma$ say that a summation may perform a τ or visible action whenever one of its summands may, but for a σ to occur the summation must also be stable. The first three communication rules are the usual CCS rules, the remaining three pertain to stable processes and state that two stable processes in parallel can execute σ if one of them can, and if both have a possible σ action they must undertake it together, if at all.

$$\text{Act} \; \frac{}{\nu.E \xrightarrow{\nu} E} \qquad\qquad \text{Con} \; \frac{P \xrightarrow{\nu} P'}{A \xrightarrow{\nu} P'} \; A =_{def} P$$

$$\text{Sum} \; \frac{E_j \xrightarrow{\mu} E_j'}{\sum_{i \in I} E_i \xrightarrow{\mu} E_j'} \qquad\qquad \text{Sum}_\sigma \; \frac{E_j \xrightarrow{\sigma} E_j' \; stab(\sum_{i \in I} E_i)}{\sum_{i \in I} E_i \xrightarrow{\sigma} E_j'}$$

$$\text{Res} \; \frac{E \xrightarrow{\alpha} E'}{E \backslash L \xrightarrow{\alpha} E' \backslash L} \; \alpha, \bar{\alpha}, \sigma, \tau \notin L \qquad \text{Rel} \; \frac{E \xrightarrow{\alpha} E'}{E[f] \xrightarrow{\alpha} E'[f]} \; \sigma, \tau \notin dom(f)$$

$$\text{Com}_1 \; \frac{E \xrightarrow{\mu} E'}{E|F \xrightarrow{\mu} E'|F} \qquad\qquad \text{Com}_2 \; \frac{F \xrightarrow{\mu} F'}{E|F \xrightarrow{\mu} E|F'}$$

$$\text{Com}_3 \; \frac{E \xrightarrow{\alpha} E' \; F \xrightarrow{\bar{\alpha}} F'}{E|F \xrightarrow{\tau} E'|F'} \qquad\qquad \text{Com}_4 \; \frac{E \xrightarrow{\sigma} E' \; F \xrightarrow{\sigma} F' \; stab(E|F)}{E|F \xrightarrow{\sigma} E'|F'}$$

$$\text{Com}_5 \; \frac{E \xrightarrow{\sigma} E' \; F \xrightarrow{\sigma}\!\!\!\!\!/ \; stab(E|F)}{E|F \xrightarrow{\sigma} E'|F} \qquad \text{Com}_6 \; \frac{E \xrightarrow{\sigma}\!\!\!\!\!/ \; F \xrightarrow{\sigma} F' \; stab(E|F)}{E|F \xrightarrow{\sigma} E|F'}$$

$$\text{Rec} \; \frac{E(fix(X=E)/X) \xrightarrow{\nu} E'}{fix(X=E) \xrightarrow{\nu} E'}$$

Table 1: Operational Semantics of CCS_σ.

2 The Axiom System

We first give definitions of several terms used informally in the introduction.

Definition 3 A computation of a test t and process p is a sequence of possible actions occurring when they are placed in parallel $p|t$.

Definition 4 A successful computation is a computation whose final action is ω. e.g.

$$p|t \xrightarrow{\tau^*} \xrightarrow{\sigma^*} \xrightarrow{\tau^*} \xrightarrow{\sigma^*} \ldots \xrightarrow{\tau^*} \xrightarrow{\omega}$$

Definition 5 For a process p and test t, p must $t \iff$ all possible computations of $p|t$ are succesful.

Definition 6 For a process p and test t, p may $t \iff$ there exists a successful computation of $p|t$.

In this paper we shall focus on must testing. We define a must testing equivalence as follows.

Definition 7 $p \sqsubseteq q \iff \forall$tests $t.[p$ must $t \Rightarrow q$ must $t]$.

Definition 8 $p =_t q \iff p \sqsubseteq q \land q \sqsubseteq p$.

The relation $=_t$ is not a congruence. We shall write the corresponding congruence, the largest congruence containing $=_t$, simply as $=$ in the axioms for the language.

Definition 9 $p = q \iff p =_t^c q$

The axiom system will be referred to as E. Whilst discussing soundness and completeness of E it is useful to have:-

Definition 10 $p =_E q$ means $p = q$ according to the axioms of E.

Definition 11 $p \sqsubseteq_E q$ means $p \sqsubseteq q$ according to E.

A complete set of axioms for CCS_σ is given in the following table. There are again many similarities with axioms for pure CCS, for example the arithmetic axioms. As in CCS, in CCS_σ we may deconstruct any parallel process to obtain an equivalent process using only summation and prefixing; our expansion theorem has extra terms for parts of the parallel process which may perform σ. The axiom (**M**), using the must testing inequality, embodies an important characteristic of must testing. The process $\tau.X + Y$ may at any time perform a τ, indetectibly, and become X. Hence if $\tau.X + Y$ always passes a test t we know that $\tau.X$ would always pass t, as Y may be discarded in some runs of the process and test $(\tau.X + Y)|t$. The five axioms (**R1**) – (**R5**) are axioms of the original external refusal testing system [6]. They also hold when CCS_σ tests test pure CCS processes, and upon CCS_σ in general, i.e. mixing σ's freely. The σ axioms are of course new to this system. (σ**1**) makes the point that a σ action can never happen in the presence of a possible τ, hence the process $\sigma.X + \tau.Y$ can only perform actions in $\tau.Y$. The laws (τ**1**) – (τ**4**) are derivable from the other axioms. They are included since (τ**1**) – (τ**3**) are the familiar τ-laws of CCS, and (τ**4**) is useful in the proof of completeness of the axiom system.

2.1 Soundness of the Axiom System.

Theorem 2.1 All the axioms of E are sound for CCS_σ must testing.

PROOF. Refer to [4].

3 Characterization of the must congruence.

Two processes are related by the must inequality congruence $\sqsubseteq^c$ if they are related by $\sqsubseteq$ and both or neither have initial τ's, and similarly for σ's.

Theorem 3.1

$$P \sqsubseteq^c Q \iff P \sqsubseteq Q \wedge (Q \xrightarrow{\tau} \Leftrightarrow P \xrightarrow{\tau}) \wedge (Q \xrightarrow{\sigma} \Leftrightarrow P \xrightarrow{\sigma})$$

4 Completeness of E

Theorem 4.1 If P, Q are finite processes and $P \sqsubseteq^c Q$ then $P \sqsubseteq_E Q$.

The proof of completeness proceeds via a definition of normal forms. We prove that any finite process has an equivalent normal form, and that for any P, Q in normal form,

$$P \sqsubseteq^c Q \Rightarrow P \sqsubseteq_E Q$$

For the purposes of this paper we assume that all processes are divergence (Ω) free.

(A1) $X + (Y + Z) = (X + Y) + Z$

(A2) $X + Y = Y + X$

(A3) $X + X = X$

(A4) $X + 0 = X$

(A5) $\mu X[f] = \begin{cases} f(\mu).X[f] & \text{if } f(\mu) \text{ is defined} \\ 0 & \text{otherwise} \end{cases}$

(A6) $(X + Y)[f] = X[f] + Y[f]$

(A7) $0[f] = 0$

(A8) The CCS_σ expansion theorem :

For a process $X = X_1 | \ldots | X_n$,
$$X = \sum \{\alpha.(X_1 | \ldots | X_i' | \ldots | X_n) \setminus L : X_i \xrightarrow{\alpha} X_i', \alpha \notin L \cup L'\}$$
$$+ \sum \{\tau(X_1 | \ldots | X_i' | \ldots | X_j' | \ldots | X_n) \setminus L : X_i \xrightarrow{\alpha} X_i', X_j \xrightarrow{\bar{\alpha}} X_j', i < j\}$$
$$+ \{\sigma(X_1' | \ldots | X_n') \setminus L : stab(X) \wedge (\forall i.X_i \xrightarrow{\sigma} X_i' \vee X_i = X_i' \text{ if } X_i \xrightarrow{\sigma}\!\!\!\!\!/\,)\}$$

(P1) $X|Y = Y|X$

(P2) $X|0 = X$

(REC1) $u[rec\ x{:}u/X] \sqsubseteq rec\ x.u$

(M) $\tau.X + Y \sqsubseteq \tau.X$

(R1) $\mu.X + \mu.Y = \mu.(\tau.X + \tau.Y)$

(R2) $\mu.X + \mu.Y = \mu.X + \mu.Y + \mu.(X + Y)$

(R3) $\tau.(X + \tau.Y) = X + \tau.Y$

(R4) $\tau.(\sum_{i \in I} \mu_i.X_i) + \tau.(\sum_{i \in I} \mu_i.Y_i) = \tau \sum_{i \in I}(\mu_i.X_i + \mu_i.Y_i)$

(R5) $X + \tau.(X + Y) = \tau.(X + Y)$

(σ1) $\sigma.X + \tau.Y = \tau.Y$

(σ2) $\mu(X + \sigma.X) = \mu.X$ if $X \xrightarrow{\sigma}\!\!\!\!\!/\,$

(σ3) $X + \tau(Y + \sigma.Z) \sqsubseteq \tau.(X + Y + \sigma.Z)$ if $X \xrightarrow{\sigma}\!\!\!\!\!/\,$

(τ1) $\alpha.\tau.X = \alpha.X$

(τ2) $X + \tau.X = \tau.X$

(τ3) $\alpha.(X + \tau.Y) = \alpha.(X + \tau.Y) + \alpha.Y$

(τ4) $\tau.x + \tau.y \sqsubseteq \tau.(x + y)$

4.1 Normal Forms

There are three types of normal form:- λnf, τnf and σnf.

Definition 12 p is in λnf iff

$$p = \sum_{a \in A} a p_a$$

where each p_a is in τnf.
  p is in σnf iff

$$p = \sum_{a \in A} a.p_a + \sigma.p_\sigma$$

where each p_a and p_σ is in τnf.
  p is in τnf iff

$$p = \sum_{a \in A} a.p_a + \sum_{i \in I} \tau.p_i$$

where each p_a is a λnf or σnf and each p_i is a λnf or σnf.
  Observe that all subterms of a normal form are themselves normal forms.

We shall also require the notion of a strong normal form:-

Definition 13 A τnf

$$p = \sum_{a \in A} a.p_a + \sum_{I \neq \emptyset} \tau.p_i$$

where each p_i is a λnf

$$p_i = \sum_{B_i} b.p_b^i$$

or a σnf

$$p_i = \sum_{B_i} b.p_b^i + \sigma.p_\sigma^i$$

is a *strong normal form* (or snf.) iff:-

i) $\forall i.B_i \subseteq A$
ii) $\forall a.a \in A \cap B_i \Rightarrow p_a + p_a^i =_E p_a$.

Definition 14 The *depth* of a normal form is the maximum length of any sequence of possible actions including τ's and σ's.

4.2 Normal Form Lemmas

These lemmas constitute a proof that every finite process can be put into normal form, i.e. for any process there is an equivalent process in normal form.

Lemma 4.2 If n is a normal form then there is a normal form n' such that $n' =_E \tau.n$.

Lemma 4.3 If n_1 and n_2 are normal forms then there is a normal form n_3 such that $n_3 =_E \tau.n_1 + \tau.n_2$.

  (Note that n_3 is not necessarily unique).

Lemma 4.4 For normal forms $\{p_a : a \in A\}$ and $\{q_b : b \in B\}$, $A, B \subseteq \text{Act}$; there exist normal forms $r_c : \sum_A a.p_a + \sum_B b.q_b =_E \sum_{A \cup B} c.r_c$, with no increase in depth.

Lemma 4.5 Every finite process p has a normal form $\text{nf}(p)$

Lemma 4.6 *Strong Normal Forms.*

For every τnf

$$d = \sum_{a \in A} a.d_a + \sum_{I \neq \emptyset} \tau.d_i$$

where each d_i is a λnf or σnf, that is, either

$$d_i = \sum_{B_i} b.d_b^i$$

or

$$d_i = \sum_{B_i} b.d_b^i + \sigma.d_\sigma^i,$$

then there exists a strong normal form

$$d' = \sum_{a \in A} a.d_a' + \sum_{I \neq \emptyset} \tau.d_i'$$

with no greater depth than d.

4.3 The Proof of Completeness

If $p \sqsubseteq^c q$ then $p \sqsubseteq_E q$ for finite processes p and q.

PROOF.

This section contains an overview of the proof method, for full details see [4]. The proof owes much to a similar theorem in [3]. The method of proof is by induction. Starting with any two processes p and q such that $p \sqsubseteq^c q$ we find normal forms for p and q, which is possible by the normal form lemmas in the previous section. This cuts down the number of different possible structures for p and q which we have to consider, for example, all parallelism can be removed from the processes. We also make use of a result in [7] restricting the types of must test that need to be considered to produce an adequate testing language, which also applies to "full" CCS_σ, [4]. We require only four types of must test:

$$t ::= \sigma.\omega \mid 0 \mid \sigma.\omega + a.t \mid \sigma.t + \sum_{l \in L} l.$$

The outermost induction is done upon the depth of (the normal forms of) the processes p and q, with three cases for the three types of normal form. For each case it turns out, by the characterization of the congruence, and the normal form lemmas, that p and q must have the same normal form type if $p \sqsubseteq^c q$. By considering the must tests which p and q may pass or fail we aim to "go past" their initial actions (visible, σ or τ) to reach their subprocesses. These subprocesses are themselves normal forms and are also of lesser depth than p (q), and hence we may use the induction hypothesis upon them and only consider applications of axioms at the topmost level of p (q). In the case of

τnf's we make use of the fact that any τnf can be converted to σnf, and find equivalent σnf's for p and q. The advantage of a σnf is that all observable behaviour after the σnf has performed an initial τ action is also obtainable directly (i.e. without τ's). This case is the longest and contains a subinduction on the number of τ-summands of the τnf p, with subcases on the types of subprocesses guarded by τ's, but the method in each is similar to the strategy outlined above.

Acknowledgements

I would like to thank Iain Phillips for his very helpful supervision, Marta Kwiatkowska and Irek Ulidowski for their comments on this paper, and the SERC for funding.

References

[1] R. de Nicola and M.C.B. Hennessy. Testing equivalences for processes. *Theoretical Computer Science*, (34), 1984.

[2] M. Hennessy and T. Regan. A temporal process algebra. Technical report, University of Sussex, 1990.

[3] M. Hennessy and T. Regan. A process algebra for timed systems. Technical report, University of Sussex, 1991.

[4] Sarah Liebert. Ph.d. thesis. forthcoming.

[5] Robin Milner. *Communication and Concurrency*. Prentice Hall, 1989.

[6] Iain Phillips. Refusal testing. *Theoretical Computer Science*, 50, 1987.

[7] Iain Phillips. CCS with broadcast stability. Technical report, Imperial College, 1988.

An Internal Language for Autonomous Categories

Ian Mackie, Leopoldo Román, and Samson Abramsky

{im,lr,sa}@doc.ic.ac.uk

Department of Computing, Imperial College
180 Queen's Gate, London SW7 2BZ, United Kingdom

Abstract

In this extended abstract we present an internal language for symmetric monoidal closed (autonomous) categories analogous to the typed lambda calculus being an internal language for cartesian closed categories. The language we propose is the term assignment to the multiplicative fragment of Intuitionistic Linear Logic, which possesses exactly the right structure for an autonomous theory. We prove that this language is an internal language and show as an application the coherence theorem of Kelly and Mac Lane, which becomes straightforward to state and prove. We then hint at some further applications of this language; a further treatment will be given in the full paper.

1 Introduction

The correspondence between logics and categories is one of the fundamental observations of categorical logic. For example Lambek and Scott [11] show:

- ♦ λ-calculi ~ Cartesian Closed Categories
- ♦ Intuitionistic type theories ~ Toposes

Where the left hand side of the similarity is an *internal language* for the corresponding category on the right. The existence of an internal language for a category brings with it many advantages. Most notably it brings a calculus of diagrams—making geometry into equations.

Since Linear Logic was introduced, the connections made with autonomous categories in [16] and the introduction of a term calculus for proof terms of Linear Logic in [1], there is a natural question of the relationship between the proof terms and the internal language of an autonomous category.

This paper answers this question by adding to the above list:

- ♦ Linear term calculi ~ Autonomous Categories

Several proposals for an internal language for autonomous categories have been suggested by Jay in [8, 9]. The main features of his work are:

1. The objects of the category are the types of the language.

2. The morphisms of the category are the freely generated classes of terms with the basic ingredients of the monoidal structure, taking the congruence which identifies the basic terms. For example if x, y, z are variables of type A, B, C and $\alpha : A \otimes (B \otimes C) \longrightarrow (A \otimes B) \otimes C$ is the basic isomorphism, then the following two terms are equal: $\alpha(x \otimes (y \otimes z)) = (x \otimes y) \otimes z$.

The first point is standard and fixed. However the construction of the morphisms requires that for each additional arrow that we add, we must show that it preserves the congruence. In many cases this is equivalent to showing that a particular diagram commutes, so we need to resort to diagrams again.

Recently, and independently, work has been done by Benton *et al.* [4] on the term assignment for Intuitionistic Linear Logic. In particular they give an equational semantics for the logic in the same spirit as ours, and show that this can be modeled in an autonomous category (with extra structure to handle the exponential). The main additional result that we have is that this language is an internal language, where we have the ability to define the basic ingredients of an autonomous category from the term calculus. We also give a more complete set of reduction rules for the fragment of the logic so that we get the desired properties of Church-Rosser and Strong Normalisation.

We must also mention the work of Richard Blute [6] who proposed using Proof Nets (see *e.g.* [7]), which give very elegant proofs for the coherence theorems of Kelly and Mac Lane. However, proof nets as a language have one major drawback: the handling of the units of the logic. Our language does handle the unit, but we must confess that proof net structures are more elegant and allow us to discard a lot of peripheral syntax that we have; in particular the problematic *commuting conversions* are removed. We will see that the same kind of proof technique he uses applies to our language. The reader is strongly encouraged to compare his results with ours.

The rest of this paper is organised as follows. In Section 2 we give the fragment of Abramsky's linear term calculus and give an equational theory, together with the standard properties of Church-Rosser and Strong Normalisation. In Section 3 we show that the term calculus actually defines an autonomous category, *i.e.* we can *define* the basic ingredients of the category. We also show that our equational theory is *sound* in the model. In Section 4 we give the main result of the paper—we show that the linear term calculus is an internal language of autonomous categories. Section 5 shows the coherence theorems as an application of this language, we also mention some additional applications.

In this extended abstract we will refrain from giving many of the proofs, which can be found in the full paper.

2 Intuitionistic Linear Logic and the Linear Term Calculus

Linear Logic [7] is a resource sensitive logic—resources must be used *exactly* once; the structural rules *weakening* and *contraction* are removed. In the full presentation of Linear Logic the expressive power is regained by re-introducing these structural rules in a controlled manner by adding a type $!A$ (the "exponential"), with the intention that a value of type $!A$ can be used to produce any finite number of copies of a value of type A.

Throughout this paper we consider a particular fragment of Linear Logic: the (exponential-free) Multiplicative Intuitionistic Linear Logic.

We have the following types:

♦ A distinguished type **1**, the unit for the tensor product.

♦ If A and B are types, then $A \otimes B$ is a type, where "$\otimes$" is the *Tensor Product*: both components must be used in the computation.

♦ If A and B are types, then $A \multimap B$ is a type, where "$\multimap$" is *Linear Implication*: functions which use their arguments exactly once.

Our presentation of this fragment will be given as a Natural Deduction system—in sequent form, where the contexts are made explicit.

2.1 Syntax

As with Intuitionistic Logic proofs, it is possible to assign proof terms to Intuitionistic Linear Logic proofs. However, our proof terms must capture the resource constraints of the logic. We therefore define a "Linear λ-calculus" in a careful way to capture the context-sensitiveness of the language. The linear term calculus, as introduced in [1], is the term assignment to Intuitionistic Linear Logic; the theorems of Intuitionistic Linear Logic are the types of the terms with no free variables. Our aim is to use this term calculus to talk about symmetric monoidal closed (autonomous) categories. We show that the term assignment of the $(\otimes, \multimap, \mathbf{1})$ fragment of Intuitionistic Linear Logic is precisely all we need.

Definition 2.1 (Linear Term Calculus) We give the term construction together with their free variables and constraints to capture the linearity.

We adopt a variable convention analogous to that of the λ-calculus given in [2]. All bound variables are chosen to be different from the free variables.

Construction	Constraint	Free Variables (FV)
$\star$	None	$\varnothing$
x	None	$\{x\}$
tu	$FV(t) \cap FV(u) = \varnothing$	$FV(t) \cup FV(u)$
$\lambda x.t$	$x \in FV(t)$	$FV(t) \smallsetminus \{x\}$
$t \otimes u$	$FV(t) \cap FV(u) = \varnothing$	$FV(t) \cup FV(u)$
let t be $\star$ in u	$FV(t) \cap FV(u) = \varnothing$	$FV(t) \cup FV(u)$
let t be $x \otimes y$ in u	$FV(t) \cap FV(u) = \varnothing$ $x, y \in FV(u)$	$FV(t) \cup (FV(u) \smallsetminus \{x, y\})$

We will often write $t \in T_X \iff FV(t) = X$, which is a convenient "infix" notation for stating the free variables of a term.

Definition 2.2 (Free $\star$-sub-terms) We define $\star$ is a free sub-term (*i.e.* not "bound" by a let t be $\star$ in u) of a term as follows:

$$\star \quad \subset \quad \star$$
$$\star \quad \subset \quad \lambda x.t \text{ if } \star \subset t$$
$$\star \quad \subset \quad tu, t \otimes u, \text{let } t \text{ be } x \otimes y \text{ in } u \text{ if } \star \subset t \text{ or } \star \subset u$$

We assign terms to proofs in this fragment of Linear Logic as follows.

Axiom:

$$\frac{}{x : A \vdash x : A} \text{ (Axiom)}$$

Structural Rule:

$$\frac{\Gamma, x : A, y : B, \Delta \vdash t : C}{\Gamma, y : B, x : A, \Delta \vdash t : C} \text{ (Exchange)}$$

Logical Rules:

$$\frac{}{\vdash \star : 1} \text{ (1–intro)}$$

$$\frac{\Gamma \vdash t : 1 \quad \Delta \vdash u : B}{\Gamma, \Delta \vdash \texttt{let } t \texttt{ be } \star \texttt{ in } u : B} \text{ (1–elim)}$$

$$\frac{\Gamma \vdash t : A \quad \Delta \vdash u : B}{\Gamma, \Delta \vdash t \otimes u : A \otimes B} \text{ (}\otimes\text{–intro)}$$

$$\frac{\Gamma \vdash t : A \otimes B \quad x : A, y : B, \Delta \vdash u : C}{\Gamma, \Delta \vdash \texttt{let } t \texttt{ be } x \otimes y \texttt{ in } u : C} \text{ (}\otimes\text{–elim)}$$

$$\frac{\Gamma, x : A \vdash t : B}{\Gamma \vdash \lambda x.t : A \multimap B} \text{ (}\multimap\text{–intro)}$$

$$\frac{\Gamma \vdash t : A \multimap B \quad \Delta \vdash u : A}{\Gamma, \Delta \vdash tu : B} \text{ (}\multimap\text{–elim)}$$

Figure 1: Assignment of linear terms to Linear Logic proofs

2.2 Equational Semantics

We develop an *equational theory* for the calculus. For the sake of clarity, the types of terms will be omitted, but these can be reconstructed (uniquely) from the logical rules given above. (See [14] for the type reconstruction algorithm for the whole of Intuitionistic Linear Logic).

The equations are split into two classes, a structural congruence $\equiv$ and a reduction relation $\longrightarrow$, following the ideas presented in [15]. One sees the structural congruence as a mixing rule that puts redexes into juxtaposition, *cf.* the Chemical Abstract Machine of [5].

♦ Evaluation equations. We write $\longrightarrow_\beta$ for the β-rules and $\longrightarrow_\eta$ for the η-rules.

$$
\begin{array}{lll}
\texttt{let } \star \texttt{ be } \star \texttt{ in } u & \longrightarrow_\beta & u \\
\texttt{let } t \texttt{ be } \star \texttt{ in } \star & \longrightarrow_\eta & t \\
\texttt{let } t \otimes u \texttt{ be } x \otimes y \texttt{ in } v & \longrightarrow_\beta & v[t/x, u/y] \\
\texttt{let } t \texttt{ be } x \otimes y \texttt{ in } x \otimes y & \longrightarrow_\eta & t \\
(\lambda x.t)u & \longrightarrow_\beta & t[u/x] \\
\lambda x.(tx) & \longrightarrow_\eta & t
\end{array}
$$

♦ Commutative conversion rules. Although it is our thesis that the linear term calculus is the right language for our purposes, it has one major drawback in that the syntax allows us to write the "same proof" in different ways. For example, $\text{let } t \text{ be } p \text{ in } \lambda x.u$ and $\lambda x.\text{let } t \text{ be } p \text{ in } u$. These differences are called commuting conversions; the real proofs are those modulo these conversions. We define a syntactic congruence on terms as follows:

To reduce the number of cases we will define *three* kinds of contexts—terms with exactly one hole—as follows:

$$
\begin{array}{rcl}
C_0[\,] & ::= & [\,] \mid C_0[\,]v \mid uC_0[\,] \\
C_1[\,] & ::= & C_0[\,] \mid u \otimes C_1[\,] \mid C_1[\,] \otimes v \\
C_2[\,] & ::= & C_1[\,] \mid \lambda x.C_2[\,]
\end{array}
$$

We will write $\equiv$ for a commutative conversion.

$\text{let } C_0[\text{let } t \text{ be } p \text{ in } v] \text{ be } \star \text{ in } w \equiv$
  $\text{let } t \text{ be } p \text{ in let } C_0[v] \text{ be } \star \text{ in } w$

$\text{let } C_1[\text{let } t \text{ be } p \text{ in } v] \text{ be } x \otimes y \text{ in } w \equiv$
  $\text{let } t \text{ be } p \text{ in let } C_1[v] \text{ be } x \otimes y \text{ in } w$

$\text{let } t \text{ be } \star \text{ in } C_2[u] \equiv$
  $C_2[\text{let } t \text{ be } \star \text{ in } u], \text{ if } \star \not\subset C_2[\,].$

$\text{let } t \text{ be } x \otimes y \text{ in } C_2[u] \equiv$
  $C_2[\text{let } t \text{ be } x \otimes y \text{ in } u], \text{ if } FV(C_2[\,]) \cap \{x, y\} = \varnothing.$

$\text{let } t \text{ be } p \text{ in } (\text{let } u \text{ be } q \text{ in } v) \equiv$
  $\text{let } u \text{ be } q \text{ in } (\text{let } t \text{ be } p \text{ in } v), \text{ if } FV(u) \cap BV(p) = FV(t) \cap BV(q) = \varnothing.$

Notation: We write $\longrightarrow_{\beta\eta}$ for $\longrightarrow_\beta \cup \longrightarrow_\eta$, and $\longrightarrow^*$ for the transitive reflexive closure of a reduction relation. If two terms t and u are equal up to change of bound variables, then we write $t \equiv_\alpha u$.

The one step reduction $\longrightarrow_{\beta\eta}$ can be applied in any context:

$$
\frac{t \longrightarrow_{\beta\eta} u}{C[t] \longrightarrow_{\beta\eta} C[u]}
$$

Moreover we require the reduction relation to be closed under the congruence:

$$
\frac{t \equiv t' \quad t' \longrightarrow_{\beta\eta} u' \quad u' \equiv u}{t \longrightarrow_{\beta\eta} u}
$$

The following proposition states some basic properties of our re-write system. The proofs can be found in the full paper.

Proposition 2.3 1. Subject Reduction: If $\Gamma \vdash t : A$ and $t \longrightarrow_{\beta\eta} t'$, then $\Gamma \vdash t' : A$.

  2. Strong Normalisation: If t is a well typed term, then there are no infinite reduction sequences.

3. Church-Rosser: If $t \longrightarrow_{\beta\eta} u$ and $t \longrightarrow_{\beta\eta} u'$, then for some $v \equiv v'$, $u \longrightarrow_{\beta\eta} v$, $u' \longrightarrow_{\beta\eta} v'$.

4. Uniqueness of Normal Form: A term t, such that $\Gamma \vdash t : A$, has exactly one normal form under the $\longrightarrow_{\beta\eta}$ reduction relation, *i.e.* unique up to structural congruence.

Definition 2.4 (An Autonomous Theory) The extension of the linear term calculus with the following:

♦ a set of base types A; and

♦ a set of basic function symbols $f : A \multimap B$;

   will be called an *autonomous theory*, which we will call **LTC**.

♦ The signature of the theory is defined by the linear term calculus, and the above extensions.

♦ The axioms of the theory are those given by $t = t'$, where equality of terms is the symmetric transitive reflexive closure of the evaluation relation $\longrightarrow_{\beta\eta}$.

♦ The theorems of the theory are those generated by $=$.

3 Interpreting the Deduction System Categorically

We give a model of our language in an autonomous category $\mathcal{C}$. The types will be objects of $\mathcal{C}$ and the terms morphisms. We will show that deductions correspond to morphisms of the category, and that the interpretation is sound with respect to the equational theory given in Section 2.

3.1 Categorical Interpretation

In this section we give a model of the Natural Deduction system (given in Section 2) in an autonomous category. Such a category has exactly the right structure to model this logic "on the nose". We then go on to show that this is a sound model for the logic with respect to the equational theory given in Section 2.

Before giving the interpretation we point out that showing that the interpretation is sound will require some "assumptions" about the commutativity of several diagrams; in particular we will need part of the coherence theorem for *symmetric monoidal* categories. For this extended abstract, we will assume this result; in the full paper we will prove the result from first principles. We will however set up the machinary here for this result.

We give our interpretation of the logical system by defining a function $[\![-]\!]$: **LTC** $\longrightarrow \mathcal{C}$ as follows:

1. an object $[\![A]\!]$ in $\mathcal{C}$ for each base type of the equational theory;

2. a morphism $[\![f]\!] : [\![A]\!] \longrightarrow [\![B]\!]$ for each function symbol $f : A \multimap B$ of the equational theory.

We extend this to all types by:

$$
\begin{aligned}
[\![1]\!] &= 1 \\
[\![A \otimes B]\!] &= [\![A]\!] \otimes [\![B]\!] \\
[\![A \multimap B]\!] &= [\![B]\!]^{[\![A]\!]}
\end{aligned}
$$

i.e. the types are objects of $\mathcal{C}$.

For a context $\Gamma \equiv x_1 : A_1, \ldots, x_n : A_n$, we write:

$$[\Gamma] \equiv (\cdots([A_1] \otimes [A_2]) \otimes \cdots) \otimes [A_n]$$

The meaning of the empty context, which we shall write as "$-$", is interpreted by the tensor unit $\mathbf{1}$, *i.e.* $[-] = \mathbf{1}$.

3.2 Autonomous Categories

We briefly recall the definition of an autonomous category.

Definition 3.1 A *Symmetric Monoidal Closed* (autonomous) category $\mathcal{C}$ is a category equipped with a tensor product, $\otimes$, (Linear) function space, $\multimap$, unit, $\mathbf{1}$, and natural isomorphisms ρ, λ, σ and α, defined by:

1. $\rho_A : A \otimes \mathbf{1} \longrightarrow A$
2. $\lambda_A : \mathbf{1} \otimes A \longrightarrow A$
3. $\sigma_{A,B} : A \otimes B \longrightarrow B \otimes A$
4. $\alpha_{A,B,C} : A \otimes (B \otimes C) \longrightarrow (A \otimes B) \otimes C$

The closedness is given by the bifunctor $- \otimes - : \mathcal{C} \longrightarrow \mathcal{C}$, and for each A, $- \otimes A$ has a right adjoint $A \multimap -$ satisfying the following equations:

(β) $\mathsf{ev} \circ (\Lambda(f) \otimes \mathsf{id}) = f$

(η) $\Lambda(\mathsf{ev} \circ (g \otimes \mathsf{id})) = g$.

Where Λ is *currying*, and ev is *evaluation*.

These data satisfy the coherence *axioms*, *i.e.* certain diagrams commute (see *e.g.* [13]).

3.3 Bookkeeping Morphisms

To preserve the convention on contexts we define several *bookkeeping* morphisms, which can be defined from the basic ingredients of the *symmetric monoidal* category. We develop the following notation : $\mathsf{split}_{\Gamma,\Delta}$ is a morphism between objects in $\mathcal{C}$, where Γ and Δ are just lists of types coming from the context; yielding a specification of how to divide the object representing a context. Similarly for join and exch. We define the morphisms as follows:

♦ $\mathsf{split}_{\Gamma,\Delta} : [\Gamma, \Delta] \longrightarrow [\Gamma] \otimes [\Delta]$.

$$
\begin{aligned}
\mathsf{split}_{-,\Delta} &= \lambda_\Delta^{-1} \\
\mathsf{split}_{\Gamma,-} &= \rho_\Gamma^{-1} \\
\mathsf{split}_{\Gamma,A} &= \mathsf{id}_{\Gamma \otimes A} \\
\mathsf{split}_{\Gamma,(A_1,\ldots,A_n)} &= \alpha_{\Gamma,(A_1,\ldots,A_{n-1}),A_n}^{-1} \circ (\mathsf{split}_{\Gamma,(A_1,\ldots,A_{n-1})} \otimes \mathsf{id}_{A_n})
\end{aligned}
$$

♦ $\mathsf{join}_{\Gamma,\Delta} : [\Gamma] \otimes [\Delta] \longrightarrow [\Gamma, \Delta]$.

$$
\begin{aligned}
\mathsf{join}_{-,\Delta} &= \lambda_\Delta \\
\mathsf{join}_{\Gamma,-} &= \rho_\Gamma \\
\mathsf{join}_{\Gamma,A} &= \mathsf{id}_{\Gamma,A} \\
\mathsf{join}_{\Gamma,(A_1,\ldots,A_n)} &= (\mathsf{join}_{\Gamma,(A_1,\ldots,A_{n-1})} \otimes \mathsf{id}_{A_n}) \circ \alpha_{\Gamma,(A_1,\ldots,A_{n-1}),A_n}
\end{aligned}
$$

$\blacklozenge$ $\text{exch}_{\Gamma,A,B,\Delta} : [\Gamma, A, B, \Delta] \longrightarrow [\Gamma, B, A, \Delta].$

We define this morphism in terms of the above morphisms:

$$\text{join}_{(\Gamma,B,A),\Delta} \circ ((\text{join}_{\Gamma,(B,A)} \circ (\text{id}_\Gamma \otimes \sigma_{A,B}) \circ \text{split}_{\Gamma,(A,B)}) \otimes \text{id}_\Delta) \circ \text{split}_{(\Gamma,A,B),\Delta}$$

3.4 The Interpretation

A judgement $\Gamma \vdash t : A$ will be interpreted as a morphism $[\Gamma \vdash t : A] : [\Gamma] \longrightarrow [A]$ in the category. We define this by induction on the structure of the term t. We will use a shorthand and write $[t]_{\Gamma \to A}$ for $[\Gamma \vdash t : A]$; always omitting the semantic brackets on subscripts, totally omitting the subscript if it is clear from the context.

1. (Axiom) The interpretation of $[x]_{A \to A}$ is given by the identity morphism $\text{id}_A : [A] \longrightarrow [A]$.

2. (Exchange) Assume we have $[t]_{\Gamma,A,B,\Delta \to C}$. Then by pre-composing the exch morphism we have $[t] \circ \text{exch}_{\Gamma,A,B,\Delta} : [\Gamma, B, A, \Delta] \longrightarrow [C]$.

3. (1−intro) The interpretation of $[\star]_{1 \to 1}$ is given by the identity morphism $\text{id}_1 : 1 \longrightarrow 1$.

4. (1−elim) Assume $[t]_{\Gamma \to 1}$ and $[u]_{\Delta \to A}$. Then the interpretation of $[\textbf{let } t \textbf{ be } \star \textbf{ in } u]_{\Gamma,\Delta \to A}$ is given by the morphism $\lambda_A \circ ([t] \otimes [u]) \circ \text{split}_{\Gamma,\Delta} : [\Gamma, \Delta] \longrightarrow [A]$.

5. ($\otimes$−intro) Assume $[t]_{\Gamma \to A}$ and $[u]_{\Delta \to B}$. Then the interpretation of $[t \otimes u]_{\Gamma,\Delta \to A \otimes B}$ is given by the morphism $([t] \otimes [u]) \circ \text{split}_{\Gamma,\Delta} : [\Gamma, \Delta] \longrightarrow [A \otimes B]$.

6. ($\otimes$−elim) Assume $[t]_{\Gamma \to A \otimes B}$ and $[u]_{\Delta,A,B \to C}$. Then the interpretation of $[\textbf{let } t \textbf{ be } x \otimes y \textbf{ in } u]_{\Gamma,\Delta \to C}$ is given by the morphism $[u] \circ \text{join}_{(A,B),\Delta} \circ ([t] \otimes \text{id}_\Delta) \circ \text{split}_{\Gamma,\Delta} : [\Gamma, \Delta] \longrightarrow [C]$.

7. ($\multimap$−intro) Assume $[t]_{\Gamma,A \to B}$. Then the interpretation of $[\lambda x.t]_{\Gamma \to A \multimap B}$ is given by the morphism $\Lambda([t] \circ \text{join}_{\Gamma,A}) : [\Gamma] \longrightarrow [B]^{[A]}$.

8. ($\multimap$−elim) Assume $[t]_{\Gamma \to A \multimap B}$ and $[u]_{\Delta \to A}$. Then the interpretation of $[tu]_{\Gamma,\Delta \to B}$ is given by the morphism $\text{ev} \circ ([t] \otimes [u]) \circ \text{split}_{\Gamma,\Delta} : [\Gamma, \Delta] \longrightarrow [B]$.

3.5 Soundness of the Interpretation

The interpretation of the logical rules is sound, *i.e.* the equations are valid in the model. It can be shown that we can establish the soundness result by appealing only to the coherence *axioms*. The details can be found in the full paper.

Lemma 3.2 (Soundness of the cut rule) If $\Gamma, x : A \vdash t : B$ and $\Delta \vdash u : A$ then one has:

$$[t[u/x]] = [t] \circ \text{join}_{\Gamma,A} \circ (\text{id}_\Gamma \otimes [u]) \circ \text{split}_{\Gamma,\Delta}.$$

Theorem 3.3 (Soundness of the equational theory) If $t \longrightarrow_{\beta\eta} t'$ then $[t] = [t']$.

4 Autonomous Theory to Autonomous Category and Back

In this Section we show how the autonomous theory (**LTC**) given in Section 2 can generate a category $\mathbb{C}(\mathbf{LTC})$. We proceed by showing that $\mathbb{C}(\mathbf{LTC})$ has all the structure of an autonomous aategory. We then define the internal language $\mathcal{L}(\mathcal{C})$ of an arbitrary autonomous category $\mathcal{C}$ which is shown to be an autonomous theory. Hence we proceed to show the categorical logic correspondence which gives the main result of this paper. Given an arbitrary autonomous category $\mathcal{C}$ and the category generated by its internal language $\mathbb{C}(\mathcal{L}(\mathcal{C}))$ then these categories are equivalent. Hence we can use the language to describe morphisms in the category. We essentially follow the recipe given for the relationship between the λ-calculus and cartesian closed categories in [3].

4.1 From Autonomous Theory to Autonomous Category

Proposition 4.1 There is a category $\mathbb{C}(\mathbf{LTC})$ where:

1. The objects are the types of our language.

2. A morphism from A to B, denoted by $f : A \longrightarrow B$, is an equivalence class of pairs, given by $(x : A, t \in T_{\{x\}} : B)$, i.e. the terms have *exactly* one free variable, where equivalence of arrows is:

$$(x : A, t \in T_{\{x\}}) = (y : A, s \in T_{\{y\}}) \text{ iff } t = s[x/y].$$

   i.e. the α-equivalence class of terms of our autonomous theory **LTC**.

3. The identity arrow $\mathrm{id}_A : A \longrightarrow A$ is given by the variable, i.e. the pair $(x : A, x)$.

4. The composition of morphisms $f \equiv (x : A, t \in T_{\{x\}})$ and $g \equiv (y : B, u \in T_{\{y\}})$ written as $g \circ f$ is defined by $(x : A, u[t/y] \in T_{\{x\}})$.

Definition 4.2 We define explicitly the following. Note that ρ_A and ρ_A^{-1} can be defined in terms of the other morphisms.

1. $\lambda_A : 1 \otimes A \longrightarrow A$
   $\lambda_A = (x, \mathtt{let}\ x\ \mathtt{be}\ b \otimes a\ \mathtt{in}\ \mathtt{let}\ b\ \mathtt{be}\ \star\ \mathtt{in}\ a)$
   $\lambda_A^{-1} : A \longrightarrow 1 \otimes A$
   $\lambda_A^{-1} = (x, \star \otimes x)$

2. $\sigma_{A,B} : A \otimes B \longrightarrow B \otimes A$
   $\sigma_{A,B} = (x, \mathtt{let}\ x\ \mathtt{be}\ a \otimes b\ \mathtt{in}\ b \otimes a)$

3. $\alpha_{A,B,C} : A \otimes (B \otimes C) \longrightarrow (A \otimes B) \otimes C$
   $\alpha_{A,B,C} = (x, \mathtt{let}\ x\ \mathtt{be}\ a \otimes u\ \mathtt{in}\ \mathtt{let}\ u\ \mathtt{be}\ b \otimes c\ \mathtt{in}\ (a \otimes b) \otimes c)$

4. The bifunctor $f \otimes g : A \otimes C \longrightarrow B \otimes D$ is given by $(x, \mathtt{let}\ x\ \mathtt{be}\ a \otimes c\ \mathtt{in}\ f(a) \otimes g(c))$, where $f : A \longrightarrow B$, and $g : C \longrightarrow D$.

5. Currying $\Lambda(f) : A \longrightarrow (B \multimap C)$ is given as $(z, \lambda y.t[(z \otimes y)/x])$, where $f : A \otimes B \longrightarrow C \equiv (x, t \in T_{\{x\}})$.

6. Evaluation $\mathrm{ev} : (B \multimap C) \otimes B \longrightarrow C$ is given as $(x, \mathtt{let}\ x\ \mathtt{be}\ f \otimes y\ \mathtt{in}\ f(y))$.

   Then $\otimes : \mathbb{C}(\mathbf{LTC})^2 \longrightarrow \mathbb{C}(\mathbf{LTC})$ is a bifunctor, and for each A, $- \otimes A \dashv A \multimap -$.

Theorem 4.3 The morphisms $\rho, \lambda, \sigma, \alpha, \Lambda$ and **ev** defined above satisfy the definition of a symmetric monoidal category; *i.e.* they satisfy the natural isomorphisms and the coherence axioms [13].

4.2   The Internal Language of an Autonomous Category

Given an autonomous category $\mathcal{C}$, we can construct its *internal language* $\mathcal{L}(\mathcal{C})$ as follows:

* The types of $\mathcal{L}(\mathcal{C})$ are the objects of $\mathcal{C}$.
* For the term construction, we take the tensor and function space structure that we know already exists in $\mathcal{C}$, hence the terms of $\mathcal{L}(\mathcal{C})$ are the terms from **LTC** given in Section 2, together with the following new term formation: if t is a term of type A and $f : A \longrightarrow B$ is an arrow in $\mathcal{C}$, then ft is a new term of type B.
* The equational theory of $\mathcal{L}(\mathcal{C})$ is given by the following equations:

$$\begin{aligned}
\widehat{\mathsf{id}}(t) &= t \\
\widehat{f \circ g}(t) &= \hat{f}(\hat{g}(t)) \\
\widehat{f \otimes g}(t \otimes u) &= \hat{f}(t) \otimes \hat{g}(u) \\
\widehat{\Lambda(f)}(t) &= \Lambda(\hat{f})(t)
\end{aligned}$$

We can now state the main result of this section. From the previous sections and the last construction, given any autonomous category $\mathcal{C}$ we can consider its internal language $\mathcal{L}(\mathcal{C})$ and then generate the autonomous category $\mathbb{C}(\mathcal{L}(\mathcal{C}))$; one natural question is what is the relation between $\mathcal{C}$ and $\mathbb{C}(\mathcal{L}(\mathcal{C}))$.

Theorem 4.4 The categories $\mathcal{C}$ and $\mathbb{C}(\mathcal{L}(\mathcal{C}))$ are equivalent; *i.e.* there are two autonomous functors F and G such that:

$$F : \mathcal{C} \simeq \mathbb{C}(\mathcal{L}(\mathcal{C})) : G$$

5   Coherence

A coherence result for symmetric monoidal and autonomous categories states that every diagram, built up from the basic ingredients given in Section 3, commutes. However the proof of this result is made complicated by the fact that each morphism in the category may be built up from many combinations of these basic ingredients. The technical hiccup is that we can not use induction on diagram pasting. However since we have an internal language with the strong properties of Subject Reduction, Church-Rosser and Strong Normalisation, we have a procedure for working with only normal forms. The technical advantage is that we now have a simple induction principle available which makes these results surprisingly simple.

We begin with a definition and some properties of our deduction system.

Definition 5.1 A type A is *binary* if each atomic formula appears just once positively (to the right of an arrow) and once negatively (to the left of an arrow). This notion extends to judgements in the obvious way.

Lemma 5.2 If $\Gamma \vdash A$ is a binary judgement, then all sub-proofs also are binary judgements.

Lemma 5.3 Given two *cut-free* binary proofs t and u such that $\Gamma \vdash t : A$ and $\Gamma \vdash u : A$, then $t \equiv u$, *i.e.* they are identical upto the syntactic congruence.

We are now in a position to state and prove the coherence theorem for autonomous categories, originally proved by Mac Lane (see [12]) and Kelly and Mac Lane (see [10]). The result drops out trivially since the work has been done once and for all in setting up the internal language. All we need to do is appeal to the properties of this language.

Theorem 5.4 (Coherence) In the free autonomous category two arrows are equal iff they have the same binary type.

PROOF: The result follows from the Strong Normalisation, Church-Rosser and Subject Reduction theorems, and Lemma 5.3. ∎

We remark that since our language is generated by an equational calculus we can always make proofs by induction on the construction of the terms. As demonstrated with the Coherence theorem, this makes proofs very straightforward and direct.

5.1 Other Applications

We close by listing some possible applications of this language. Further details can be found in the full paper.

♦ Adding a Natural Numbers Object (NNO). It is possible to add the type of natural numbers to this languages and use it to reason about NNO's in autonomous categories. A surprising result is that we can get a cartesian structure from the tensor structure; projections and duplications can be made.

♦ It is hoped that a language of this kind can give further insight in to proving some other results. For example: a diagram commutes in the free autonomous category iff it commutes in the category of real vector spaces. This is a well known and used "theorem", but to our knowledge a concrete proof has not materialised.

Acknowledgement

The authors would like to thank Roy Crole, Reinhold Heckmann, Paul Taylor and Steven Vickers for detailed comments on an earlier draft of this paper. This research was supported by grants from the UK SERC and ESPRIT Basic Research Action 6454 "CONFER".

References

[1] S. Abramsky. Computational Interpretation of Linear Logic. *Theoretical Computer Science*, 111:3–57, 1993. Earlier version appeared as Imperial College Technical Report DOC 90/20, October 1990.

[2] H.P. Barendregt. *The Lambda Calculus: Its Syntax and Semantics*. North-Holland, revised edition, 1984.

[3] M. Barr and C. Wells. *Category Theory for Computing Science*. International Series in Computer Science. Prentice Hall, 1990.

[4] N. Benton, G. Bierman, V. de Paiva, and M. Hyland. Term assignment for intuitionistic linear logic. Technical Report No. 262, University of Cambridge, August 1992.

[5] G. Berry and G. Boudol. The Chemical Abstract Machine. In *Conference Record of the Seventeenth Annual ACM Symposium on Principles of Programming Languages*, pages 81–94, 1990.

[6] R. Blute. Linear logic, coherence and dinaturality. Technical report, McGill University, 1992.

[7] J.-Y. Girard. Linear Logic. *Theoretical Computer Science*, 50(1):1–102, 1987.

[8] B. Jay. Languages for monoidal categories. *Journal of Pure and Applied Algebra*, 59:61–85, 1989.

[9] B. Jay. A note on natural numbers objects in monoidal categories. *Studia Logica*, XLVIII:389–393, 1989.

[10] G.M. Kelly and S. Mac Lane. Coherence in closed categories. *Journal of Pure and Applied Algebra*, 1:97–140, 1971.

[11] J. Lambek and P.J. Scott. *Introduction to Higher Order Categorical Logic*. Cambridge Studies in Advanced Mathematics Vol. 7. Cambridge University Press, 1986.

[12] S. Mac Lane. Natural associativity and commutativity. *Rice University Studies*, 49:28–46, 1963.

[13] S. Mac Lane. *Categories for the Working Mathematician*. Springer-Verlag, Berlin, 1971.

[14] I.C. Mackie. Lilac : A functional programming language based on linear logic. Master's thesis, Department of Computing, Imperial College of Science, Technology and Medicine, University of London, September 1991.

[15] R. Milner. Functions as processes. In *Proceedings of ICALP 90*, volume 443 of *Lecture Notes in Computer Science*, pages 167–180. Springer-Verlag, 1990.

[16] R.A.G. Seely. Linear logic, *-autonomous categories and cofree coalgebras. In J.W. Gray and A. Scedrov, editors, *Categories in Computer Science and Logic*, volume 92 of *Contemporary Mathematics*, pages 371–382. American Mathematical Society, 1989.

Continuation Passing Transformation and Abstract Interpretation

Juarez Muylaert Filho and Geoffrey Burn

{jamf,glb}@doc.ic.ac.uk
Department of Computing, Imperial College
180 Queen's Gate, London SW7 2BZ, United Kingdom

Abstract

Compiler writers have found that the continuation passing style (cps) translation exposes various code optimisations. We show that the same is true for
semantically based program analysis techniques: performing a cps-translation on
a program before analysing it may expose more information than can be found
by analysing the original program.

1 Introduction

The problem with any sort of terminating program analysis is that it cannot
always find exact information; the halting problem precludes this. If an analysis
turns out to be less powerful than desired, then there are two things that can
be done:

♦ develop a more powerful program analysis; or

♦ try to transform the program so that more properties are observable by the
program analysis.

In this paper we take the second line of attack; the first is covered in numerous
publications ([4, 8, 10, 17] for example).

As an example, consider the function defined by:

```
f c x = + (if c (x,12) (5,x)).
```

Clearly this function is strict in its second argument, but this cannot be determined using the abstract interpretation given as an example later in the paper.
However, a simple program transformation gives the program

```
f c x = if c (+(x,12)) (+(5,x)).
```

and the same abstract interpretation can determine that this function is strict
in its second argument[1].

Why has this transformation worked? In the original program, the + forces
the evaluation of the condition c, and then + is applied to (x,12) or (5,x)
according to the value of c. In other words, the *continuation* of the evaluation of
c is to apply + to the selected pair; the transformation to get the second version

---

[1]Note that this transformation is not generally valid if + is replaced by an arbitrary function. In fact,
a strictness analysis might first be used to see if the transformation is safe in a particular case, suggesting
that the process of transformation followed by analysis could be iterated.

of the function has effectively moved the continuation to where its argument is produced.

This observation suggests that doing a *continuation passing style (cps)-*translation of a program, which somehow captures its evaluation order, intuitively bringing together an argument and its continuation, may make more properties visible to a program analysis.

The contribution of this paper is to study the relationship between a term and its cps-translation for the *higher-order, typed, lazy functional* language defined in Figure 1[2]. Our two main results show that:

- there is a bijection between the *standard* interpretation of a term and the standard interpretation of its cps-translation; and

- the *abstract interpretation* of the cps-translation of a term may give more information than the abstract interpretation of the original term, and this depends entirely on the abstract interpretation of the language constants.

Similar observations and intuitions have been published by other authors, but these have been less general results, and for different languages. We discuss these in more detail in the next section in order to set our work in context.

Following standard works, we define the notion of an interpretation, and give a correctness theorem for an abstract interpretation, expressed in terms of logical relations, in Section 3. A (call-by-name) cps-translation, slightly different from the one usually appearing in the literature, is given in Section 4. We briefly discuss the advantages of giving a continuation semantics as a two-stage process, firstly doing a cps-translation and then giving a semantics of the result in Section 5. To set the stage for our main results we define some functions to move between direct and cps-semantics in Section 6.1. We then give the bijection between the standard interpretation of a term and the standard interpretation of its cps-translation in Section 6.2, and discuss the relationship for an arbitrary abstract interpretation in Section 6.3. An example abstract interpretation is given in Section 7, where more information is obtained by doing the cps-translation before performing the abstract interpretation. We conclude in Section 8 with a discussion of some open problems.

2 Setting the Work in Context

The proof of the bijection between the standard semantics of a term and its cps-translation can be seen as a reworking of Reynolds' original result in [19], where we use a typed language and he used an untyped one. We have yet to deal with recursive data types.

Prior to our starting the work on comparing the abstract interpretation of a term and the abstract interpretation of its cps-translation, there was considerable evidence that it would be a worthwhile exercise:

- in compiler technology, the sequentialisation of code that comes from cps-translation has made many optimisations more visible to the compiler (see [2, 13, 21] for example).

- Nielson showed that using a continuation semantics for a first-order imperative language in a program analysis gave more information than the direct semantics [16].

---

[2]We will sometimes omit type information to make terms more readable. c_σ is an arbitrary constant.

The set T of types is the least set defined by:

$$\{bool, int\} \subseteq T$$
$$\sigma, \tau \in T \Rightarrow (\sigma \to \tau) \in T$$
$$\sigma, \tau \in T \Rightarrow (\sigma \times \tau) \in T$$

The type system of Λ_T

(1) $x^\sigma : \sigma$ (2) $c_\sigma : \sigma$

(3) $\dfrac{E_1 : \sigma \to \tau, \; E_2 : \sigma}{(E_1 \, E_2) : \tau}$ (4) $\dfrac{E : \tau}{(\lambda x^\sigma.E) : \sigma \to \tau}$

(5) $\dfrac{E_1 : \sigma, \; E_2 : \tau}{(E_1, E_2) : \sigma \times \tau}$ (6) $\dfrac{\lambda x^\sigma.E : \sigma \to \sigma}{\mathbf{fix}_\sigma \, (\lambda x^\sigma.E) : \sigma}$

Abstract Syntax of Λ_T

$\mathbf{true}_{bool}$ $\qquad\qquad$ $\mathbf{false}_{bool}$ $\qquad\qquad$ $\mathbf{if}_{bool \to \sigma \to \sigma \to \sigma}$
$\{0_{int}, 1_{int}, 2_{int}, \ldots\}$ $\quad$ $\mathbf{plus}_{int \times int \to int}$ $\quad$ $\mathbf{fst}_{\sigma \times \tau \to \sigma}$
$\mathbf{snd}_{\sigma \times \tau \to \tau}$

Some example constants

Figure 1: Definition of the Language Λ_T

♦ Consel and Danvy have shown that CPS-translation expresses maximum opportunities for program specialisation (roughly compile-time reduction) for a strict functional language [6].

In this paper we consider a general abstract interpretation (more general than [16, 6]), of a higher-order (more general than [16]), lazy (rather than strict as in [6]) functional (rather than imperative) language.

3 Interpretations of Λ_T

The abstract interpretation framework is from [4], and this section can be skipped by those familiar with it.

In an abstract interpretation, alternative meanings are given to some of the symbols in a language in order to capture some properties of interest. For the purposes of this paper, it is sufficient to consider the case where an interpretation is fixed by giving the interpretation of the base types and the constants in Λ_T. Therefore we can specify a general interpretation, **I**, as in Figure 2. A more general framework is discussed in [4], a review paper contained in this volume.

The *standard* interpretation of Λ_T, its usual denotational semantics, which

$$\mathbf{I}_B \quad = \quad \text{some domain for the base type } B$$
$$\mathbf{I}_{\sigma \to \tau} \quad = \quad \mathbf{I}_\sigma \to \mathbf{I}_\tau$$
$$\mathbf{I}_{\sigma_1 \times \sigma_2} \quad = \quad \mathbf{I}_{\sigma_1} \times \mathbf{I}_{\sigma_2}$$

Interpretation of the Types

$$\mathbf{I} [\![x^\sigma]\!] \rho^\mathbf{I} = \rho^\mathbf{I} \, x^\sigma$$
$$\mathbf{I} [\![c_\sigma]\!] \rho^\mathbf{I} = \mathbf{K}^\mathbf{I} [\![c_\sigma]\!]$$
$$\mathbf{I} [\![E_1 \, E_2]\!] \rho^\mathbf{I} = (\mathbf{I} [\![E_1]\!] \rho^\mathbf{I}) \, (\mathbf{I} [\![E_2]\!] \rho^\mathbf{I})$$
$$\mathbf{I} [\![\lambda x^\sigma . E]\!] \rho^\mathbf{I} = \lambda d \epsilon \mathbf{I}_\sigma . \mathbf{I} [\![E]\!] \rho^\mathbf{I} [d/x^\sigma]$$
$$\mathbf{I} [\![\mathbf{fix}_\sigma \, (\lambda x^\sigma . E)]\!] \rho^\mathbf{I} = \sqcup_{i \geq 0} (\mathbf{I} [\![\lambda x^\sigma . E]\!] \rho^\mathbf{I})^i \perp_{\mathbf{I}_\sigma}$$
$$\mathbf{I} [\![(E_1, E_2)]\!] \rho^\mathbf{I} = (\mathbf{I} [\![E_1]\!] \rho^\mathbf{I}, \mathbf{I} [\![E_2]\!] \rho^\mathbf{I})$$

Interpretation of Language Terms

Figure 2: A General Interpretation of Λ_T

we will denote by $\mathbf{S}$, is obtained by setting $\mathbf{S}_{int}$ and $\mathbf{S}_{bool}$ to be the normal flat domains, and giving the constants their usual interpretation, denoted by $\mathbf{K}^\mathbf{S}$.

Domains in an abstract interpretation are nearly always complete lattices. We will denote an arbitrary abstract interpretation by $\mathbf{A}$. A strictness abstract interpretation is given in Section 7.

The correctness of an abstract interpretation can be stated as a relation between the abstract interpretation and the properties the abstract domain points represent. For the sake of giving an example, we will assume properties are Scott-closed sets, and define a relation $\mathbf{R}_\sigma \subseteq \mathbf{S}_\sigma \times \mathbf{A}_\sigma$ for each type σ. The relation is usually defined for the base types, then extended to constructed types as a logical relation [18]:

$$f \, \mathbf{R}_{\sigma \to \tau} \, g \iff \forall a_1, a_2 . (a_1 \, \mathbf{R}_\sigma \, a_2) \Rightarrow (f \, a_1) \, \mathbf{R}_\tau \, (g \, a_2)$$
$$(a_1, b_1) \, \mathbf{R}_{\sigma_1 \times \sigma_2} \, (a_2, b_2) \iff (a_1 \, \mathbf{R}_{\sigma_1} \, a_2) \wedge (b_1 \, \mathbf{R}_{\sigma_2} \, b_2).$$

If $\mathbf{R}_B \subseteq \mathbf{S}_B \times \mathbf{A}_B$ is

strict: $\perp_{\mathbf{S}_B} \mathbf{R}_B \perp_{\mathbf{A}_B}$,

bottom-reflecting: $s \, \mathbf{R}_B \perp_{\mathbf{A}_B}$ implies $s = \perp_{\mathbf{S}_B}$, and

inductive: for all chains $\{s_n\}$ in $\mathbf{S}_B$ and for all chains $\{a_n\}$ in $\mathbf{A}_B$:

$$[\forall n . s_n \, \mathbf{R}_B \, a_n] \Rightarrow \bigsqcup s_n \, \mathbf{R}_B \bigsqcup a_n,$$

then these properties are inherited at all types, and the following *Correctness Theorem* is standard (c.f. [1, Proposition 3.2]).

Theorem 3.1 If for all constants c_σ, $\mathbf{S} [\![c_\sigma]\!] \, \mathbf{R}_\sigma \, \mathbf{A} [\![c_\sigma]\!]$, then

$$\forall \sigma . \forall E : \sigma . \forall \rho^\mathbf{S}, \rho^\mathbf{A} . \rho^\mathbf{S} \, \mathbf{R} \, \rho^\mathbf{A} \Rightarrow (\mathbf{S} [\![E]\!] \rho^\mathbf{S}) \, \mathbf{R}_\sigma \, (\mathbf{A} [\![E]\!] \rho^\mathbf{A}),$$

where $\rho^\mathbf{S} \, \mathbf{R} \, \rho^\mathbf{A}$ means $\forall x^\sigma . (\rho^\mathbf{S} \, x^\sigma) \, \mathbf{R}_\sigma \, (\rho^\mathbf{A} \, x^\sigma)$. $\qquad\qquad \square$

$$
\begin{array}{rcl}
\mathbf{V}_\gamma[\![\sigma]\!] & = & \mathbf{C}_\gamma[\![\sigma]\!] \to \gamma \\
\mathbf{C}_\gamma[\![\sigma]\!] & = & \mathbf{E}_\gamma[\![\sigma]\!] \to \gamma \\
\mathbf{E}_\gamma[\![B]\!] & = & B \\
\mathbf{E}_\gamma[\![\sigma \times \tau]\!] & = & (\mathbf{V}_\gamma[\![\sigma]\!]) \times (\mathbf{V}_\gamma[\![\tau]\!]) \\
\mathbf{E}_\gamma[\![\sigma \to \tau]\!] & = & (\mathbf{V}_\gamma[\![\sigma]\!]) \to (\mathbf{V}_\gamma[\![\tau]\!])
\end{array}
$$

Figure 3: Translation of Types

We need the statement of this theorem in order to prove that the relationship between the abstract interpretations of a term and its cps-translation is sound.

4 The Call-by-name Cps-Translation

The call-by-name cps-translation used in this paper is given in Figures 3 and 4. A similar translation can be found in [15]. It differs slightly from the more usual scheme, presented in [11] for example, in that the translation functions are parameterised by the "answer type", γ. Moreover, the answer type must be specified, because the abstract interpretation framework of the previous section requires that the only valid types are ones built up from the base types using $\times$ and $\to$.

Using Reynolds' terminology, when γ is the answer type,

$\mathbf{E}_\gamma[\![\sigma]\!]$ is the type of *explicit* values for type σ;

$\mathbf{C}_\gamma[\![\sigma]\!]$ is the type of *continuations* for type σ; and

$\mathbf{V}_\gamma[\![\sigma]\!]$ is the type of *implicit* values (i.e. closures) for type σ.

The following proposition states that the type translation is sound.

Proposition 4.1 If $E : \sigma$ then $\mathbf{T}_\sigma[\![E]\!] : \mathbf{V}_\sigma[\![\sigma]\!]$. ◻

5 Continuation Semantics

In many texts, it is usual to give a continuation semantics in one step. There are two significant advantages in our giving continuation semantics in two stages:

♦ staging means that only two sets of equations are needed in order to define four different semantics: **S** (the standard direct interpretation); **S ∘ T** (the standard continuation interpretation); **A** (the abstract direct interpretation); and **A ∘ T** (the abstract continuation interpretation); and

♦ noting that the translation of constants adds no new constants to the language, although the type instances at which some of the constants are used are different for the constant and its cps-translation, only one abstract interpretation needs to be given and proved correct (as in Theorem 3.1) for each constant. If the semantics were not staged, then separate continuation semantics for both the standard and abstract interpretations would have to be given for each constant, and the latter proved correct against the former.

$$\mathbf{T}_\gamma[\![x^\sigma]\!] \;=\; \lambda k.x\,k$$
$$k : \mathbf{C}_\gamma[\![\sigma]\!]; \; x : \mathbf{V}_\gamma[\![\sigma]\!]$$
$$\mathbf{T}_\gamma[\![c_B]\!] \;=\; \lambda k.k\,c_B$$
$$k : \mathbf{C}_\gamma[\![B]\!]$$
$$\mathbf{T}_\gamma[\![\mathbf{if}_{bool \to \sigma \to \sigma \to \sigma}]\!]$$
$$=\; \lambda k.k\,(\lambda x.\lambda c_1.c_1\,(\lambda y.\lambda c_2.c_2\,(\lambda z.\lambda c_3.x\,(\lambda v.\mathbf{if}\,v\,(y\,c_3)(z\,c_3)))))$$
$$x : \mathbf{V}_\gamma[\![bool]\!]; \; y,z : \mathbf{V}_\gamma[\![\sigma]\!]; \; v : bool;$$
$$k : \mathbf{C}_\gamma[\![bool \to \sigma \to \sigma \to \sigma]\!]; \; \mathbf{if} : bool \to \gamma \to \gamma \to$$
$$c_1 : \mathbf{C}_\gamma[\![\sigma \to \sigma \to \sigma]\!]; \; c_2 : \mathbf{C}_\gamma[\![\sigma \to \sigma]\!]; \; c_3 : \mathbf{C}_\gamma[\![\sigma]\!]$$
$$\mathbf{T}_\gamma[\![\mathbf{plus}_{int \times int \to int}]\!]$$
$$=\; \lambda k.k\,(\lambda d.d\,(\lambda(v_1,v_2).\lambda c.v_1\,(\lambda n_1.v_2\,(\lambda n_2.c\,(\mathbf{plus}(n_1,n_2))))))$$
$$k : \mathbf{C}_\gamma[\![int \times int \to int]\!]; \; c : \mathbf{C}_\gamma[\![int]\!]; \; \mathbf{plus} : int \times int \to int$$
$$d : \mathbf{V}_\gamma[\![int \times int]\!]; \; v_1,v_2 : \mathbf{V}_\gamma[\![int]\!]; \; n_1,n_2 : int$$
$$\mathbf{T}_\gamma[\![\mathbf{fst}_{\sigma \times \tau \to \sigma}]\!] \;=\; \lambda k.k\,(\lambda d.\lambda c.d\,\mathbf{fst}\,c)$$
$$k : \mathbf{C}_\gamma[\![\sigma \times \tau \to \sigma]\!]; \; d : \mathbf{V}_\gamma[\![\sigma \times \tau]\!]; \; c : \mathbf{C}_\gamma[\![\sigma]\!];$$
$$\mathbf{fst} : \mathbf{E}_\gamma[\![\sigma \times \tau \to \sigma]\!]$$
$$\mathbf{T}_\gamma[\![\mathbf{snd}_{\sigma \times \tau \to \tau}]\!] \;=\; \lambda k.k\,(\lambda d.\lambda c.d\,\mathbf{snd}\,c)$$
$$k : \mathbf{C}_\gamma[\![\sigma \times \tau \to \tau]\!]; \; d : \mathbf{V}_\gamma[\![\sigma \times \tau]\!]; \; c : \mathbf{C}_\gamma[\![\tau]\!];$$
$$\mathbf{snd} : \mathbf{E}_\gamma[\![\sigma \times \tau \to \tau]\!]$$
$$\mathbf{T}_\gamma[\![E_1\,E_2]\!] \;=\; \lambda k.\mathbf{T}_\gamma[\![E_1]\!]\,(\lambda f.f\,(\mathbf{T}_\gamma[\![E_2]\!])\,k)$$
$$k : \mathbf{C}_\gamma[\![\tau]\!]; \; f : \mathbf{E}_\gamma[\![\sigma \to \tau]\!]$$
$$\mathbf{T}_\gamma[\![\lambda x^\sigma.e]\!] \;=\; \lambda k.k(\lambda x.\mathbf{T}_\gamma[\![e]\!])$$
$$k : \mathbf{C}_\gamma[\![\sigma \to \tau]\!]; \; x : \mathbf{V}_\gamma[\![\sigma]\!]$$
$$\mathbf{T}_\gamma[\![\mathbf{fix}_\sigma\,(\lambda x^\sigma.e)]\!] \;=\; \lambda k.(\mathbf{fix}_\tau\,(\lambda x.\mathbf{T}_\gamma[\![e]\!]))\,k$$
$$k : \mathbf{C}_\gamma[\![\sigma]\!]; \; x : \mathbf{V}_\gamma[\![\sigma]\!]; \; \tau = \mathbf{V}_\gamma[\![\sigma]\!]$$
$$\mathbf{T}_\gamma[\![(E_1,E_2)]\!] \;=\; \lambda k.k\,(\mathbf{T}_\gamma[\![E_1]\!],\mathbf{T}_\gamma[\![E_2]\!])$$
$$k : \mathbf{C}_\gamma[\![\sigma \times \tau]\!]$$

Figure 4: The Cps-translation $\mathbf{T}_\gamma$

6 Relating a term and its CPS-translation

6.1 General Definitions and Results

The cps-translation results in terms whose semantics have a certain structure which we need to exploit when relating a direct and continuation interpretation for a term. This is captured by the following definition and proposition.

Definition 6.1 Define the predicate $\eta_\sigma : \mathbf{I}_{\mathbf{V}_\gamma[\![\sigma]\!]} \to bool$ by:

$$\eta_B\,(\lambda c.c\,b) = true \quad \forall b \in \mathbf{I}_{\mathbf{E}_\gamma[\![B]\!]}$$
$$\eta_{\sigma \times \tau}\,(\lambda c.c\,(s,t)) \quad \text{if } (\eta_\sigma\,s) \text{ and } (\eta_\tau\,t)$$
$$\eta_{\sigma \to \tau}\,(\lambda c.c\,f) \quad \text{if } \forall s \in \mathbf{I}_{\mathbf{E}_\gamma[\![\sigma]\!]}.\,(\eta_\sigma\,s) \Rightarrow (\eta_\tau\,(f\,s))$$
$$\eta_\sigma(u \sqcup v) \quad \text{if } (\eta_\sigma\,u) \text{ and } (\eta_\sigma\,v)$$
$$\eta_\sigma(u \sqcap v) \quad \text{if } (\eta_\sigma\,u) \text{ and } (\eta_\sigma\,v) \qquad \square$$

$$\phi^I_{\gamma,\sigma} : I_\sigma \to I_{V_\gamma[\sigma]} \qquad\qquad \psi^I_{\gamma,\sigma} : I_{V_\gamma[\sigma]} \to I_\sigma$$
$$\phi^I_{\gamma,\sigma} = J^I_{\gamma,\sigma} \circ \beta^I_{\gamma,\sigma} \qquad\qquad \psi^I_{\gamma,\sigma} = \alpha^I_{\gamma,\sigma} \circ I^I_{\gamma,\sigma}$$

$$\alpha^I_{\gamma,\sigma} : I_{E_\gamma[\sigma]} \to I_\sigma$$
$$\alpha^I_{\gamma,B} = Id_B$$
$$\alpha^I_{\gamma,\sigma_1 \times \sigma_2} = \lambda(d_1, d_2).(\alpha^I_{\gamma,\sigma_1}(I^I_{\gamma,\sigma_1} d_1), \alpha^I_{\gamma,\sigma_2}(I^I_{\gamma,\sigma_2} d_2))$$
$$\alpha^I_{\gamma,\sigma\to\tau} = \lambda f.\alpha^I_{\gamma,\tau} \circ I^I_{\gamma,\tau} \circ f \circ J^I_{\gamma,\sigma} \circ \beta^I_{\gamma,\sigma}$$

$$\beta^I_{\gamma,\sigma} : I_\sigma \to I_{E_\gamma[\sigma]}$$
$$\beta^I_{\gamma,B} = Id_B$$
$$\beta^I_{\gamma,\sigma_1 \times \sigma_2} = \lambda(d_1, d_2).(J^I_{\gamma,\sigma_1}(\beta^I_{\gamma,\sigma_1} d_1), J^I_{\gamma,\sigma_2}(\beta^I_{\gamma,\sigma_2} d_2))$$
$$\beta^I_{\gamma,\sigma\to\tau} = \lambda f.J^I_{\gamma,\tau} \circ \beta^I_{\gamma,\tau} \circ f \circ \alpha^I_{\gamma,\sigma} \circ I^I_{\gamma,\sigma}$$

$$I^I_{\gamma,\sigma} : I_{V_\gamma[\sigma]} \to I_{E_\gamma[\sigma]} \qquad\qquad J^I_{\gamma,\sigma} : I_{E_\gamma[\sigma]} \to I_{V_\gamma[\sigma]}$$
$$I^I_{\gamma,B} = \lambda d.\beta^I_{\gamma,B}(d\,\alpha^I_{\gamma,B}) \qquad\quad J^I_{\gamma,B} = \lambda d.\lambda c.c\,d$$
$$I^I_{\gamma,\sigma_1 \times \sigma_2} = \lambda d.\beta^I_{\gamma,\sigma_1 \times \sigma_2}(d\,\alpha^I_{\gamma,\sigma_1 \times \sigma_2}) \qquad J^I_{\gamma,\sigma_1 \times \sigma_2} = \lambda(d_1, d_2).\lambda c.c\,(d_1, d_2)$$
$$I^I_{\gamma,\sigma\to\tau} = \lambda f.\beta^I_{\gamma,\sigma\to\tau}(f\,\alpha^I_{\gamma,\sigma\to\tau}) \qquad J^I_{\gamma,\sigma\to\tau} = \lambda f.\lambda c.c\,f$$

Figure 5: Maps between direct and continuation values

The last two cases in the definition of the predicate η_σ arise because $\sqcup$ and $\sqcap$ may be used in the abstract interpretation of language constants; they will not appear in values from the standard interpretation. It is important to note that $\sqcup$ and $\sqcap$ are significant in this definition only if they are operating on implicit values, that is, terms in $I_{V_\gamma[\sigma]}$ for some γ and σ.

Proposition 6.2 $\forall\sigma.\forall E : \sigma.\forall\gamma.\forall\rho^{IC}.\ [\forall x^\tau.\eta_\tau(\rho^{IC} x^\tau)] \Rightarrow \eta_\sigma((I \circ T_\gamma)\,[\![E]\!]\,\rho^{IC}).\square$

The key maps in defining the relationship between the direct and continuation interpretation of a term are:

♦ $\phi^I_{\gamma,\sigma} : I_\sigma \to I_{V_\gamma[\sigma]}$; and

♦ $\psi^I_{\gamma,\sigma} : I_{V_\gamma[\sigma]} \to I_\sigma$.

They are defined by induction over the type structure, and their definition can be found in Figure 5. Inspiration for their definition came in part from both [14] and [19]. Notice that these maps have been defined for a general interpretation; they have the same structure for both the standard and an arbitrary abstract interpretation; all that changes is the interpretation of the types.

The following proposition is important for establishing our main results.

Proposition 6.3

1. $\forall E : \sigma.\ \forall\rho^I.\ (\psi^I_{\sigma,\sigma} \circ \phi^I_{\sigma,\sigma})(I\,[\![E]\!]\,\rho^I) = I\,[\![E]\!]\,\rho^I.$

2. $\forall E : \sigma.\forall\rho^S.\ (\phi^S_{\sigma,\sigma} \circ \psi^S_{\sigma,\sigma})((S \circ T_\sigma)\,[\![E]\!]\,(\phi^S \circ \rho^S)) = (S \circ T_\sigma)\,[\![E]\!]\,(\phi^S \circ \rho^S).$

3. If the $\asymp$ is any one of $\sqsubseteq$, $=$ or $\sqsupseteq$, then

$$\forall c_\sigma. (\phi^{\mathbf{A}}_{\sigma,\sigma} \circ \psi^{\mathbf{A}}_{\sigma,\sigma}) (\mathbf{A} \circ \mathbf{T}_\sigma) \, [\![c_\sigma]\!] \asymp (\mathbf{A} \circ \mathbf{T}_\sigma) \, [\![c_\sigma]\!]$$
$$\Rightarrow \forall E : \sigma. \forall \rho^{\mathbf{A}}. (\phi^{\mathbf{A}}_{\sigma,\sigma} \circ \psi^{\mathbf{A}}_{\sigma,\sigma})((\mathbf{A} \circ \mathbf{T}_\sigma) \, [\![E]\!] \, (\phi^{\mathbf{A}} \circ \rho^{\mathbf{A}}))$$
$$\asymp (\mathbf{A} \circ \mathbf{T}_\sigma) \, [\![E]\!] \, (\phi^{\mathbf{A}} \circ \rho^{\mathbf{A}}). \qquad \square$$

As Reynolds pointed out in [19, p.145], we should not expect the second part of Proposition 6.3 to be true for an arbitrary value from the continuation world, because not all such values represent programs in Λ_T, and so the map $\psi^{\mathbf{I}}_{\gamma,\sigma}$ cannot give sensible results in the direct world for such values. The fact that it does hold depends crucially on Proposition 6.2.

The presence of $\sqcup$ and $\sqcap$ at the level of implicit values gives some problems in relating the direct and continuation abstract interpretations. From our experience with various abstract interpretations, we make the following conjecture.

Conjecture 6.4 $\forall c_\sigma. (\phi^{\mathbf{A}}_{\sigma,\sigma} \circ \psi^{\mathbf{A}}_{\sigma,\sigma})((\mathbf{A} \circ \mathbf{T}_\sigma) \, [\![c_\sigma]\!]) \asymp (\mathbf{A} \circ \mathbf{T}_\sigma) \, [\![c_\sigma]\!]$, where $\asymp$ is

* $\sqsupseteq$ if $(\mathbf{A} \circ \mathbf{T}_\sigma) \, [\![c_\sigma]\!]$ contains $\sqcup$ but no $\sqcap$ of implicit values;
* $\sqsubseteq$ if $(\mathbf{A} \circ \mathbf{T}_\sigma) \, [\![c_\sigma]\!]$ contains $\sqcap$ but no $\sqcup$ of implicit values; and
* $=$ if $(\mathbf{A} \circ \mathbf{T}_\sigma) \, [\![c_\sigma]\!]$ contains neither $\sqcup$ nor $\sqcap$ of implicit values. $\qquad \square$

The benefit of this conjecture is that the condition on the constants in the third part of Proposition 6.3 can be done by visual inspection rather than by tedious calculation. We further conjecture that there is equality in the first case of the Conjecture 6.4 if all the constants have additive continuations, and in the second if they all have multiplicative continuations.

6.2 The Standard Interpretation

Using Propositions 6.2 and 6.3, it is a simple structural induction to prove the following theorem, which can be understood as saying that the cps-translation preserves the meanings of programs. Theorem 2 of [19] is similar to the first part of the theorem.

Theorem 6.5

1. $\forall E : \sigma. \forall \rho^{\mathbf{S}}. \mathbf{S} \, [\![E]\!] \, \rho^{\mathbf{S}} = \psi^{\mathbf{S}}_{\sigma,\sigma} ((\mathbf{S} \circ \mathbf{T}_\sigma) \, [\![E]\!](\phi^{\mathbf{S}} \circ \rho^{\mathbf{S}}))$
2. $\forall E : \sigma. \forall \rho^{\mathbf{S}}. (\mathbf{S} \circ \mathbf{T}_\sigma) \, [\![E]\!](\phi^{\mathbf{S}} \circ \rho^{\mathbf{S}}) = \phi^{\mathbf{S}}_{\sigma,\sigma} (\mathbf{S} \, [\![E]\!] \, \rho^{\mathbf{S}}). \qquad \square$

6.3 An Arbitrary Abstract Interpretation

The following theorem states that the relationship between the abstract interpretations of a term and its cps-translation depends entirely on the relationships for the constants. Its proof is a simple structural induction, and relies on Propositions 6.2 and 6.3.

Theorem 6.6 If the $\asymp$ is any one of $\sqsubseteq$, $=$ or $\sqsupseteq$, then

$$\forall c_\sigma. \mathbf{A} \, [\![c_\sigma]\!] \asymp \psi^{\mathbf{A}}_{\sigma,\sigma} ((\mathbf{A} \circ \mathbf{T}_\sigma) \, [\![c_\sigma]\!])$$
$$\Rightarrow \forall E : \sigma. \forall \rho^{\mathbf{A}}. (\mathbf{A} \, [\![E]\!] \, \rho^{\mathbf{A}}) \asymp (\psi^{\mathbf{A}}_{\sigma,\sigma}((\mathbf{A} \circ \mathbf{T}_\sigma) \, [\![E]\!](\phi^{\mathbf{A}} \circ \rho^{\mathbf{A}}))). \qquad \square$$

Interpreting this theorem in terms of whether the right-hand side gives more or less information depends on the meaning of $\asymp$ in a particular abstract

$$\mathbf{K}^{\mathbf{A}} \, [\![\mathbf{true}]\!] = 1 = \mathbf{K}^{\mathbf{A}} \, [\![\mathbf{false}]\!] = \mathbf{K}^{\mathbf{A}} \, [\![\mathbf{0}]\!] = \mathbf{K}^{\mathbf{A}} \, [\![\mathbf{1}]\!] = \ldots$$

$$\mathbf{K}^{\mathbf{A}} \, [\![\mathbf{plus}_{int \times int \to int}]\!] \, (x, y) = x \sqcap y$$

$$\mathbf{K}^{\mathbf{A}} \, [\![\mathbf{if}_{bool \to \sigma \to \sigma \to \sigma}]\!] \, x \, y \, z = \begin{cases} \perp_{\mathbf{A}_\sigma} & \text{if } x = 0 \\ y \sqcup z & \text{otherwise} \end{cases}$$

Figure 6: A Strictness Abstract Interpretation of Some Constants in Λ_T

interpretation. For example, $\asymp$ is $\sqsupseteq$ in the strictness abstract interpretation defined in the next section, so that $(\psi^{\mathbf{A}}_{\sigma,\sigma} \circ \mathbf{A} \circ \mathbf{T}_\sigma)$ gives a value no bigger than that given by $\mathbf{A}$. Moreover, smaller values in a strictness analysis mean more information (i.e. the information ordering is the opposite of the usual definedness ordering), and so Theorem 6.6 means that more information can be found by first doing a cps-translation.

If $\asymp$ is either $\sqsupseteq$ or $\sqsubseteq$, then Theorem 6.6 would be trivially true if we set $\psi^{\mathbf{A}}_{\sigma,\sigma}$ to be respectively the bottom or top function. The following theorem says that $(\psi^{\mathbf{A}}_{\sigma,\sigma} ((\mathbf{A} \circ \mathbf{T}_\sigma) \, [\![E]\!] (\phi^{\mathbf{A}} \circ \rho^{\mathbf{A}})))$ is a valid abstract interpretation of E (c.f. the Correctness Theorem for abstract interpretation — Theorem 3.1).

Theorem 6.7 $\forall E : \sigma. \forall \rho^{\mathbf{S}}. \forall \rho^{\mathbf{A}}.$

$$\rho^{\mathbf{S}} \, \mathbf{R} \, (\phi^{\mathbf{A}} \circ \rho^{\mathbf{A}}) \Rightarrow (\mathbf{S} \, [\![E]\!] \, \rho^{\mathbf{S}}) \, \mathbf{R}_\sigma \, (\psi^{\mathbf{A}}_{\sigma,\sigma} \, ((\mathbf{A} \circ \mathbf{T}_\sigma) \, [\![E]\!] (\phi^{\mathbf{A}} \circ \rho^{\mathbf{A}}))). \qquad \square$$

7 Example: A Strictness Interpretation

In this section we present the canonical strictness abstract interpretation, and show that more information can be obtained by doing a cps-translation before the abstract interpretation.

We use the abstract domain $\mathbf{2} = \{0, 1\}$ with $0 \sqsubseteq 1$ for any base type B. At base types B we define the relation

$$\perp_{\mathbf{S}_B} \mathbf{R}_B \, 0 \text{ and for all } s \in \mathbf{S}_B, \, s \, \mathbf{R}_B \, 1.$$

This relation is strict, bottom-reflecting and inductive (terms defined in Section 3). Strictness interpretations for the constants we will use in our examples are given in Figure 6. Note that $\sqcup$ is given implicit values in interpreting **if**, and that $\sqcap$ is only applied to explicit values. The following results are standard:

Fact 7.1

1. For all constants $\mathbf{c}_\sigma$, $\mathbf{S} \, [\![\mathbf{c}_\sigma]\!] \, \mathbf{R}_\sigma \, \mathbf{A} \, [\![\mathbf{c}_\sigma]\!]$ (e.g. [5, Section A.4]).

2. The strictness abstract interpretation is correct (c.f. Theorem 3.1). $\qquad \square$

In the absence of a proof of Conjecture 6.4, by tedious calculation we can can show that for all constants $\mathbf{c}_\sigma$, $\mathbf{A} \, [\![\mathbf{c}_\sigma]\!] \sqsupseteq \psi^{\mathbf{A}}_{\sigma,\sigma} \, ((\mathbf{A} \circ \mathbf{T}_\sigma) \, [\![\mathbf{c}_\sigma]\!])$, and so Theorem 6.6 allows us to conclude that

$$\forall E : \sigma. \forall \rho^{\mathbf{A}}. (\mathbf{A} \, [\![E]\!] \, \rho^{\mathbf{A}}) \sqsupseteq (\psi^{\mathbf{A}}_{\sigma,\sigma} ((\mathbf{A} \circ \mathbf{T}_\sigma) \, [\![E]\!] (\phi^{\mathbf{A}} \circ \rho^{\mathbf{A}}))).$$

As an example, consider the following term derived from the example in the introduction:

$$F = +G \text{ where } G = \textbf{if } btop\,(bottom, itop)\,(itop, bottom)$$

where $btop$, $itop$ and $bottom$ are terms such that for all $\rho^{\mathbf{A}}$

- $\mathbf{A}\,[\![btop]\!]\,\rho^{\mathbf{A}} = 1$ and $(\mathbf{A}\circ\mathbf{T}_{int})\,[\![btop]\!]\,(\phi^{\mathbf{A}}\circ\rho^{\mathbf{A}}) = \lambda\overline{k}.\overline{k}\,1$;
- $\mathbf{A}\,[\![itop]\!]\,\rho^{\mathbf{A}} = 1$ and $(\mathbf{A}\circ\mathbf{T}_{int})\,[\![itop]\!]\,(\phi^{\mathbf{A}}\circ\rho^{\mathbf{A}}) = \lambda\overline{k}.\overline{k}\,1$; and
- $\mathbf{A}\,[\![bottom]\!]\,\rho^{\mathbf{A}} = 0$ and $(\mathbf{A}\circ\mathbf{T}_{int})\,[\![bottom]\!]\,(\phi^{\mathbf{A}}\circ\rho^{\mathbf{A}}) = \lambda\overline{k}.\overline{k}\,0$.

F has type int, and so its cps-translation is:

$$\mathbf{T}_{int}[\![F]\!] = \lambda k.\mathbf{T}_{int}[\![+]\!]\,(\lambda f.f\,(\mathbf{T}_{int}[\![G]\!])\,k)$$
where
$$\mathbf{T}_{int}[\![+]\!] = \lambda k_1.k_1\,(\lambda d.d\,(\lambda(v,w).\lambda k_2.v\,(\lambda m.w\,(\lambda n.k_2\,(+(m,n))))))$$
$$\mathbf{T}_{int}[\![G]\!] = \lambda k.U\,(\lambda b.\textbf{if } b\,(k\,(W,V))\,(k\,(V,W)))$$
$$\text{where } U = \mathbf{T}_{int}[\![btop]\!],\ V = \mathbf{T}_{int}[\![itop]\!] \text{ and } W = \mathbf{T}_{int}[\![bottom]\!]$$

The abstract interpretation of $\mathbf{T}_{int}[\![F]\!]$ is:

$$(\mathbf{A}\circ\mathbf{T}_{int})\,[\![F]\!] = \lambda\overline{k}.(\mathbf{A}\circ\mathbf{T}_{int})\,[\![+]\!]\,(\lambda\overline{f}.\overline{f}\,((\mathbf{A}\circ\mathbf{T}_{int})\,[\![G]\!])\,\overline{k})$$
where
$$(\mathbf{A}\circ\mathbf{T}_{int})\,[\![+]\!] = \lambda\overline{k}_1.\overline{k}_1(\lambda\overline{d}.\overline{d}\,(\lambda(\overline{v},\overline{w}).\lambda\overline{k}_2.\overline{v}\,(\lambda\overline{m}.\overline{w}\,(\lambda\overline{n}.\overline{k}_2(\overline{m}\sqcap\overline{n})))))$$
$$(\mathbf{A}\circ\mathbf{T}_{int})\,[\![G]\!] = \lambda\overline{k}.\overline{U}\,(\lambda\overline{b}.\mathbf{K}^{\mathbf{A}}\,[\![\textbf{if}]\!]\,\overline{b}\,(\overline{k}\,(\overline{W},\overline{V}))\,(\overline{k}\,(\overline{V},\overline{W})))$$
$$\text{where } \overline{U} = \overline{V} = \lambda\overline{k}.\overline{k}\,1 \text{ and } \overline{W} = \lambda\overline{k}.\overline{k}\,0$$

Reducing this term we get $(\lambda\overline{k}.\overline{k}\,0)$, and $\psi^{\mathbf{A}}_{int,int}\,(\lambda\overline{k}.\overline{k}\,0) = 0$. Compare this with the abstract interpretation of F:

$$\mathbf{A}\,[\![F]\!] = \sqcap\,(\mathbf{K}^{\mathbf{A}}\,[\![\textbf{if}]\!]\,1\,(0,1)\,(1,0))$$
$$= \sqcap\,((0,1)\sqcup(1,0)) = 1,$$

so $\mathbf{A}\,[\![F]\!] \sqsupseteq \psi^{\mathbf{A}}_{int,int}((\mathbf{A}\circ\mathbf{T}_{int})\,[\![F]\!])$ is indeed true.

The information gain in this example arises because the cps-translation essentially pushes the $+$ through the $\textbf{if}$. In fact, if $\mathbf{T}_{int}[\![F]\!]$ is partially reduced before calculating the abstract interpretation, the reductions result in a term which is essentially equivalent to what would have been obtained if we had have started with the following definition of F:

$$F = \textbf{if } btop\,(+(bottom, itop))\,(+(itop, bottom))$$

Sometimes the gain in information comes for a different reason. Consider the following term, which is quite similar to F:

$$M = +\,(\textbf{fix }(\lambda x.\textbf{if } btop\,(\textbf{if } btop\,(bottom, itop)\,(itop, bottom))\,x))$$

Here $+$ cannot be passed through $\textbf{fix}$. Nevertheless, $(\mathbf{A}\circ\mathbf{T}_{int})\,[\![M]\!] = (\lambda\overline{k}.\overline{k}\,0)$. If the calculations are done, then one finds that the term

$$\lambda\overline{k}.[\overline{k}\,(\lambda\overline{k}.\overline{k}\,0, \lambda\overline{k}.\overline{k}\,1)]\sqcup[\overline{k}\,(\lambda\overline{k}.\overline{k}\,1, \lambda\overline{k}.\overline{k}\,0)]$$

occurs in the abstract interpretation of $\textbf{if}$, and this is not the same as

$$\lambda\overline{k}.\overline{k}\,[(\lambda\overline{k}.\overline{k}\,0, \lambda\overline{k}.\overline{k}\,1)\sqcup(\lambda\overline{k}.\overline{k}\,1, \lambda\overline{k}.\overline{k}\,0)] = \lambda\overline{k}.\overline{k}\,(\lambda\overline{k}.\overline{k}\,1, \lambda\overline{k}.\overline{k}\,1)$$

because continuations are not linear in general, and, in particular, a continuation in the translation of $+$ is not.

8 Conclusion and Open Problems

We have shown that doing a cps-translation of a term and then determining its abstract interpretation can give more, less, or the same information as doing the abstract interpretation on the original term, and that this is determined solely by the relationship holding on the programming language constants.

The properties in our example abstract interpretation were Scott-closed sets. We see no problem in generalising this work to where properties are partial equivalence relations (pers), which were introduced into abstract interpretation by Hunt [12]. All that needs to be changed is the definition of the relation defining the correctness of an abstract interpretation, and the restatement and proof of Theorem 6.7.

There remain a number of open questions about this approach.

♦ Can the gain in power be characterised?

♦ There are other ways of getting more power in an abstract interpretation (e.g. adding disjunctive properties into the set of properties used in an abstract interpretation; see [4, Section2.2] and [7, 8] for example). How does the increase in power obtained from these compare with the approach of this paper? Often properties are added to an abstract interpretation by using different interpretations of the type constructors. What happens when the direct and continuation abstract interpretations have different interpretations of the type constructors?

♦ Can the power gained by the cps-translation be encoded in a number of local transformations which leave the structure of the program essentially unchanged? We are aware from personal communication that Sabry and Felleisen are working on this problem for strict languages, building on their work reported in [20].

♦ Related to the previous point, Bondorf has shown that improvement in program specialisation when a cps-translation is done first in a strict language, reported by Consel and Danvy in [6], can be obtained by writing the specialiser in cps-style instead (and running it on the original program) [3]. The key to this improvement appears to be a transformation made on the cps-style specialiser, which seems like our example of pushing the + through an **if**. We have yet to understand this work fully.

♦ Finally, the abstract interpretation of a term is essentially parameterised by the answer type γ given to a program when translating it with $\mathbf{T}_\gamma$. How does varying γ affect the abstract interpretation of a term?

One problem with the approach for which we see no immediate solution is that the cps-translation results in a very higher-order program. This increases the complexity of the abstract interpretation process because abstract domains are much bigger (see [4, Sections 2.4 and 2.5] for a discussion of this problem). However, it is clear that not all points in the continuation world represent values which are the abstract interpretation of something (c.f. Proposition 6.2), and so maybe there is some way to filter the abstract domains to a more manageable size when doing an abstract interpretation, or perhaps to define a suitable widening operator [9]. We plan to investigate this problem further.

Acknowledgements

We thank David Sands for suggesting the problem to us, and he and Sebastian Hunt for their helpful discussions about this work at various times. We thank Chris Hankin and Ian Mackie for their helpful comments about drafts of this paper.

Juarez Muylaert-Filho is sponsored by the Brazilian agency CAPES under contract 889/90-5. Geoffrey Burn is partially funded by ESPRIT Working Group 6809 (Semantique) and SERC grant GR/H 17381 ("Using the Evaluation Transformer Model to make Lazy Functional Languages more Efficient").

References

[1] S. Abramsky. Abstract interpretation, logical relations and Kan extensions. *Journal of Logic and Computation*, 1(1):5–39, 1990.

[2] A. W. Appel. *Compiling with Continuations*. Cambridge University Press, 1992.

[3] A. Bondorf. Improving binding times without explicit CPS-conversion. In *Proceedings of the 1992 ACM Conference on LISP and Functional Programming*, pages 1–10, San Fransisco, California, 22–24 June 1992.

[4] G.L. Burn. The abstract interpretation of functional languages. In this volume.

[5] G.L. Burn. *Lazy Functional Languages: Abstract Interpretation and Compilation*. Research Monographs in Parallel and Distributed Computing. Pitman in association with MIT Press, 1991. 238pp.

[6] C. Consel and O. Danvy. For a better support of static data flow. In J. Hughes, editor, *Proceedings of the Conference on Functional Programming and Computer Architecture*, pages 496–519, Cambridge, Massachussets, USA, 26–28 August 1991. Springer-Verlag LNCS523.

[7] P. Cousot and R. Cousot. Systematic design of program analysis frameworks. In *Proceedings of the Sixth Annual Symposium on Principles of Programming Languages*, pages 269–282. ACM, January 1979.

[8] P. Cousot and R. Cousot. Abstract interpretation and application to logic programs. *Journal of Logic Programming*, 13(2–3):103–179, 1992.

[9] P. Cousot and R. Cousot. Comparing the Galois connection and widening/narrowing approaches to abstract interpretation. In M. Bruynooghe and M. Wirsing, editors, *Programming Language Implementation and Logic Programming, Proceedings of the Fourth International Symposium*, pages 269–295. Springer-Verlag LNCS631, Leuven, Belgium, August 1992.

[10] P. Granger. Combinations of semantic analyses. In INRIA, editor, *Proceedings of Informatika 88 (French-Soviet Workshop)*, pages 71–88, Nice, February 1988.

[11] R. Haper and M. Lillibridge. Polymorphic type assignment and CPS conversion. In O. Danvy and C. Talcott, editors, *Proceedings of the ACM SIPLAN Workshop on Continuations CW92*, pages 13–22, San Fransisco, USA, 21st June 1992. Stanford University Report number STAN-CS-92-1426.

[12] L.S. Hunt and D. Sands. Binding time analysis: A new PERspective. In *Proceedings of the Symposium on Partial Evaluation and Semantics-Based Program Manipulation (PEPM'91)*, pages 154–165, Yale University, USA, 11–19 June 1991. ACM.

[13] D.A. Kranz, R. Kelsey, J.A. Rees, P. Hudak, J. Philbin, and N.I. Adams. Orbit: An optimising compiler for scheme. In *Proceedings of the SIGPLAN '86 Symposium on Compiler Construction*, pages 219–233. ACM, June 1986.

[14] A. Meyer and M. Wand. Continuation semantics in the typed lambda-calculus. In *Proceedings of Logics of Programs*, pages 219–224, Berlin, 1985. Springer-Verlag LNCS 193.

[15] C.R. Murthy. Control operators, hierarchies, and pseudo-classical type systems: A-translation at work. In O. Danvy and C. Talcott, editors, *Proceedings of the ACM SIPLAN Workshop on Continuations CW92*, pages 49–71, San Fransisco, USA, 21st June 1992. Stanford University Report number STAN-CS-92-1426.

[16] F. Nielson. A denotational framework for data flow analysis. *Acta Informatica*, 18:265–287, 1982.

[17] F. Nielson. Two-level semantics and abstract interpretation. *Theoretical Computer Science*, 69:117–242, 1989.

[18] G.D. Plotkin. Lambda definability and logical relations. Technical report, Department of AI, University of Edinburgh, 1973.

[19] J.C. Reynolds. On the relation between direct and continuation semantics. In *Proceedings of the Second Colloquium on Automata, Languages and Programming*, pages 141–156, Saarbrucken, 1974. Springer-Verlag.

[20] A. Sabry and M. Felleisen. Reasoning about programs in continuation-passing style. In *Proceedings of the 1992 ACM Conference on Lisp and Functional Programming*, pages 288–298, San Fransisco, California, 22–24 June 1992. Full version in Rice University Technical Report Rice TR 92-180.

[21] G.L. Steele Jr. Rabbit: A compiler for scheme. Technical Report AI Tech. Rep. 474, MIT, Cambridge, Mass., 1978.

A Note on Expressiveness of Process Algebra

Iain Phillips

iccp@doc.ic.ac.uk
Department of Computing, Imperial College
180 Queen's Gate, London SW7 2BZ, United Kingdom

Abstract

We extend the work of Baeten, Bergstra & Klop by showing that every recursively enumerable transition system can be expressed in process algebra up to weak bisimulation.

The various forms of process algebra (CCS [5], CSP [4], ACP [2]) are known to have universal computing power, in the sense that they can compute any recursive function on e.g. the natural numbers (see for instance [5], page 135). It is common to give them an operational semantics in terms of (labelled) transition systems. We can then ask to what extent process algebra can express transition systems. To make the question more precise, given an equivalence $\sim$ on transition systems we can ask:

For any transition system T within a certain class, is there a process algebra term p such that $O(p) \sim T$?

Here $O(p)$ is the operational semantics of p. Not every transition system can arise as the semantics of a process. A necessary condition is that it should be a *transition graph*, viz. it should have a starting state (the root), and every state must be reachable from the root.

The question first received attention from de Simone [3]. He showed the positive result that any recursively enumerable (r.e.) transition graph can be expressed by a (finite) MEIJE-SCCS term up to isomorphism (Theorem 3.2). Baeten, Bergstra & Klop [1] showed two expressiveness results, one positive and one negative:

♦ Every computable transition graph (with a finite set of labels) is expressible by a finite guarded specification in ACP_τ, but in this case up to weak bisimulation (Theorem 6.11).

♦ There is a computable transition graph which cannot be expressed by any finite guarded specification in ACP up to strong bisimulation (Theorem 8.2).

Vaandrager [6] points out that de Simone allows unguarded recursion. Vaandrager proves a strengthened version of Baeten, Bergstra & Klop's second result, namely, for any r.e. language L with an effective operational semantics there is a computable transition graph which cannot be expressed by L up to trace equivalence. It follows, of course, that de Simone's language does not have an effective operational semantics in Vaandrager's sense.

Baeten, Bergstra & Klop's first result leaves open the question of whether finite guarded process algebra can express r.e. transition graphs up to weak bisimulation. This note answers this in the affirmative. Our method is simply to show that any r.e. transition graph can be converted to a computable transition graph which is equivalent under weak bisimulation.

We start by giving precise definitions of the terms we have used already:

Definition 1 A *labelled transition system* is a triple $(P, A, \rightarrow)$, where P is a set of states, A is a set of labels and $\rightarrow$ is a relation on $P \times A \times P$. A *transition graph* (TG) is a transition system together with a root $r \in P$ such that every $p \in P$ is reachable from r. We let g range over TGs. A TG is *r.e.* if there is a coding of P, A into the natural numbers such that P, A are r.e. and $\rightarrow$ is r.e. A TG is *computable* if it is finite branching, and given any $p \in P$ the set of immediate derivatives $\{(a, q)|p \xrightarrow{a} q\}$ can be computed effectively in p.

Notice that with a computable TG, given any n we can compute its unfolding to depth n. Clearly any finite TG is computable. To clarify the distinction between the two types of TG, note the following: it might be that in an r.e. TG the set of derivatives of a given p was finite. We could effectively enumerate the whole of this set in a finite time. However we would not then know that we had finished the enumeration. With a computable TG we have this further information. We give an example of an r.e. TG which is finite branching and has a finite label set, but is not computable:

Example 2 Let K be an r.e. set which is not recursive. For instance, K might be the set of all n such that the nth Turing machine halts when given input n. Our TG will have states p_n, q_n $(n \in \mathbb{N})$, root p_0, labels a, b, and transitions $p_n \xrightarrow{a} p_{n+1}$ (all n), and

$$p_n \xrightarrow{b} q_n \text{ iff } n \in K.$$

See Figure 1. For purposes of illustration we have taken $0 \notin K$, $1 \in K$, $2 \notin K$, $3 \in K$.

We refer the reader to [5] for the definitions of weak and strong bisimulation.

Theorem 3 Let g be an r.e. TG. Then there exists a computable TG g' such that g, g' are weakly bisimilar.

We use the following lemma in the proof:

Lemma 4 Let $X \subseteq \mathbb{N}$ be r.e. Then there exists a total recursive function $f : \mathbb{N} \rightarrow \mathbb{N} \cup \{\uparrow\}$ such that

♦ $rge(f) \cap \mathbb{N} = X$

♦ if $n \in X$ then there exist infinitely many $i \in \mathbb{N}$ such that $f(i) = n$.

PROOF OF LEMMA. We proceed informally. Let some machine M be given which enumerates X. This machine computes by stages. Define $f(i) = \uparrow$ for any stage i at which M has output nothing. If and when a stage i_0 is reached at which M first outputs a number n_0, let $f(i_0) = n_0$. Values of f for $i > i_0$ are then obtained by enumerating the values output by M in rotation following the plan

$$0, 1, 0, 1, 2, 0, 1, 2, 3, \ldots$$

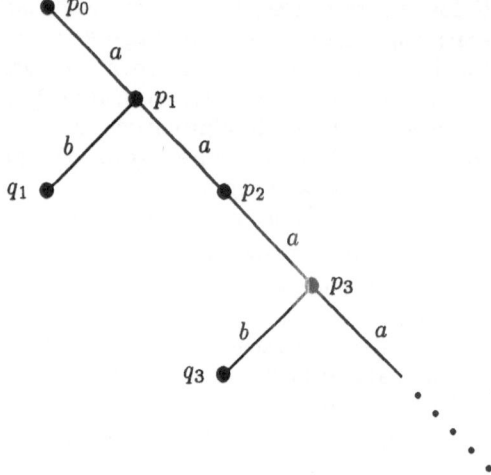

Figure 1

and marking time by further rotation if the output from M fails to keep up (and in particular, of course, if X is in fact finite). $\square$

REMARK. f has the further property that if $f(i) = \uparrow$ then $f(j) = \uparrow$ for all $j < i$. We do not need this in what follows.

PROOF OF THEOREM. Let g be an r.e. TG $(P, A, \rightarrow, r)$. We define a new TG g' with states $P \times \mathbb{N}$. We write (p, n) as $p.n$. The new root will be $r.0$ and the new set of labels will be $A \cup \{\tau\}$. We may or may not have $\tau \in A$. It remains to define the new $\rightarrow$. Consider any state p of g. Let $p.i \xrightarrow{\tau} p.(i+1)$ for each i, so that we create an infinite chain of τ's in g', starting at $p.0$. Let $(a_0, p_0), (a_1, p_1), \ldots$ be an effective enumeration of the derivatives of p. Let f be the corresponding function given by the lemma. At the ith node $p.i$ of the chain we create an extra branch $p.i \xrightarrow{a} q.0$ if $f(i) = (a, q)$. If $f(i) = \uparrow$ then we do not branch at that node. See Figure 2.

In the example shown, $f(0) = \uparrow$, $f(1) = (a, q)$, $f(2) = (a', q')$, $f(3) = (a, q)$, etc.

Carry out this process uniformly for all $p \in P$. We now have a new TG g' which is weakly bisimilar to g, with weak bisimulation $\{(p, p.n) | p \in P, n \in \mathbb{N}\}$. It is plainly computable. $\square$

REMARKS. The new TG is not only finitely branching; each node has out-degree either 1 or 2. Notice that it is everywhere divergent in the sense that from every state there is an infinite sequence of τ's. However, it may be argued that we have only really introduced divergence in the case where p has no derivatives (which, of course, we cannot in general discover in finite time). In the other cases the divergence can be eliminated by an assumption of fairness of choice. The above proof was inspired by Lemma 6.10 of [1] which states that a computable TG is weakly bisimilar to a TG with branching at most 2, and where τ-cycles are introduced.

Corollary 5 Every r.e. TG $(P, A, \rightarrow, r)$ where A is finite can be expressed by a finite guarded ACP_τ specification up to weak bisimulation. $\square$

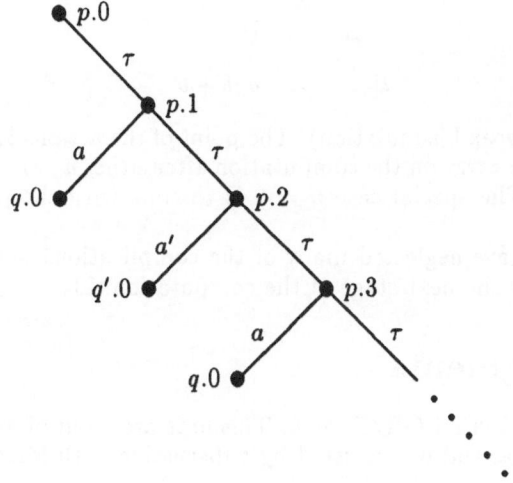

$p.0$

τ

$p.1$

a

$q.0$

τ

$p.2$

a'

$q'.0$

τ

$p.3$

a

$q.0$

τ

Figure 2

REMARK. Baeten, Bergstra & Klop restrict themselves to finite A in their first result. This may not be necessary, in view of the following:

Proposition 6 (cf [1] Theorem 6.8, Corollary 6.9) Let g be a computable TG where

♦ each state has one or two successors
♦ a τ is always immediately possible

Then there is a process S such that $O(S)$ and g are weakly bisimilar.

IDEA OF PROOF. Apart from using techniques such as in [1] to express in process algebra both the storage of numbers in counter processes and the computable functions which modify these counters, we need to deal with a possibly infinite A. Let A be enumerated as $a_0, a_1, \ldots$ with $\tau = a_0$. To correspond to a given state of g, we need S to offer either τ alone, or τ together with a_n, some n. Let us assume that we have calculated n and stored it in a counter. We actually store $n + 1$, so that $n = 0$ corresponds to the case of τ alone. We now indicate how S can produce the required choice of actions. We use CCS-style notation. The counter is specified by

$$C(n) = d^n e$$

Define the relabelling R by

$$R(a_i) = a_{i+1}$$

(all $i \in \mathbb{N}$). Let a process B be given by

$$B = eb' + dB'$$
$$B' = e(a_0 b + b') + dB'[R]$$

Let

$$B_n = (B|C(n)) \backslash \{d, e\}$$

Then

$$B_0 \approx b'$$
$$B_{n+1} \approx a_n b + b'$$

(where $\approx$ denotes weak bisimulation). The point of the actions b, b' is to trigger the processes which carry on the computation after either a_n or τ (respectively) has taken place. The special case $n = 0$ is to cope with the possibility that only a τ is offered.

Of course, we have neglected many of the complications, such as the need to regenerate B for the next stage of the computation. $\square$

Acknowledgments

Supported by SERC grant GR/F72475. This note arose out of discussions with Marta Kwiatkowska, and was assisted by a discussion with Mike Smyth.

References

[1] J.C.M. Baeten, J. Bergstra, and J.-W. Klop. On the consistency of Koomen's fair abstraction rule. *Theoretical Computer Science*, 51:129–176, 1987.

[2] J.C.M. Baeten and J.-W. Klop. Process algebra for synchronous communication. *Information and Computation*, 60:109–137, 1984.

[3] R. de Simone. Higher-level synchronising devices in MEIJE-SCCS. *Theoretical Computer Science*, 37:245–267, 1985.

[4] C.A.R. Hoare. *Communicating Sequential Processes*. Prentice-Hall, 1985.

[5] R. Milner. *Communication and Concurrency*. Prentice-Hall, 1989.

[6] F.W. Vaandrager. Expressiveness results for process algebras. In J. de Bakker, W.P. de Roever, and G. Rozenberg, editors, *Semantics: foundations and applications*, 1993. Lecture Notes in Computer Science Vol. 666.

Prioritising Preference Relations

Mark Ryan

mdr@doc.ic.ac.uk
Department of Computing, Imperial College
180 Queen's Gate, London SW7 2BZ, United Kingdom

Abstract

We describe some ideas and results about the following problem: Given a set, a family of "preference relations" on the set, and a "priority" among those preference relations, which elements of the set are best? That is, which elements are most preferred by a consensus of the preference relations which takes account of their relative priority? The problem is posed in a deliberately general way, to capture a wide variety of examples.

Our main result gives sufficient conditions for the existence of 'best' elements for an important instance of the problem: preference relations are pre-orders, the priority among them is a partial order, and the definition of best elements uses a generalisation of lexicographic ordering.

1 Introduction

A popular framework for the logical semantics for defaults is *model preference relations*. In that semantics, a default denotes a relation on language interpretations (or models) which measures how nearly interpretations satisfy the default. This view was started, in essence, by McCarthy's circumscription [6], where a default is a wish to minimise the extension of a predicate, and the preference relation on interpretations prefers those interpretations having a smaller extension of the predicate. The view has been generalised many times, notably by D. Makinson [5], in which an overview may be found. The idea of model preference is also the basis of the framework of ordered theory presentations [7, 9] and is used by P.-Y. Schobbens [12], B. Grosof [3], and others.

In this paper, we show how to extend the semantics to a *prioritised* set of defaults. A prioritised set of defaults is a set of defaults equipped with a priority, i.e. a partial order on the defaults, and thus denotes a prioritised set of preference relations. How should these preference relations be put together to make one single 'global' preference relation, representing the prioritised defaults? We answer this question in the next section, and discuss the consequences of our answer throughout the paper.

The idea of priority among defaults is not new; for example, Lifschitz defines prioritised circumscription [4] in which the notion of priority is a total order among predicates to be minimised. The model preference relation he gives to such a totally prioritised defaults is the lexicographic combination of the individual preference orderings. In this paper, we prove a general result about the generalisation of this lexicographic ordering to partial order priorities. The generalisation was first given in [7]; a similar definition given by Grosof [3] is equivalent under natural conditions.

An important property of the preference relations which are denoted by defaults is that it be possible to find *maximal elements*. Makinson [5] defines that a model preference relation is *stoppered* if for every interpretation there is an interpretation which is as or more preferred and is, indeed, maximally preferred. Maximally preferred interpretations are intuitively those which are closest to fully modelling the defaults, subject to other constraints. (Some authors let the ordering go the other way, and are therefore interested in minimal interpretations.) We ask the question: what are sufficient conditions on the individual preference relations so that the global preference relation is stoppered?

We take the view (as do most authors) that a model preference relation is a pre-order, i.e. a reflexive and transitive order. The global relation is the lexicographic combination of the individual preferences; it too is a pre-order. (In [11] we take the more general view that a preference relation is an arbitrary binary relation, and consider which properties are preserved by the lexicographic combination.)

In the next section, and for the remainder of the paper, we abstract slightly and consider prioritised preference over an arbitrary set, not just a set of models. We assume that preferences between elements of the set are expressed as preorders, and that the priority among them is a partial order.

2 Prioritised preference

Recall that a pre-order is a reflexive and transitive relation. A partial order is a reflexive, anti-symmetric and transitive relation. Let $(X, \sqsubseteq)$ be a pre-order or a partial order. We write $x \sqsubset y$ if $x \sqsubseteq y$ and $y \not\sqsubseteq x$; and $x \equiv y$ if $x \sqsubseteq y$ and $y \sqsubseteq x$.

Definition 1 Let X be a set. A *prioritised family of preferences* on X is a triple $(I, \leqslant, \{\sqsubseteq_i\}_{i \in I})$, where

♦ $(I, \leqslant)$ is a finite, partially ordered set, and

♦ for each $i \in I$, $\sqsubseteq_i$ is a pre-order on X.

Example 2 I like vegetarian food; I like nuts; I like tomatoes, especially with chili. My first preference is to take priority over the other two, which are incomparable in priority. Available are lamb casserole; nut roast with tomato sauce; and pasta with tomato chili sauce. Thus, there is no dish satisfying all of my preferences, but some are better at doing so than others.

The food preferences of example 2 may be represented as a family of prioritised preferences over the set of dishes $X = \{\ell, n, p\}$. In this case, $I = \{V, N, T\}$ (each letter representing a preference) with $< = \{(V, N), (V, T)\}$ and the orderings $\sqsubseteq_V$, $\sqsubseteq_N$, $\sqsubseteq_T$ are respectively the first three of

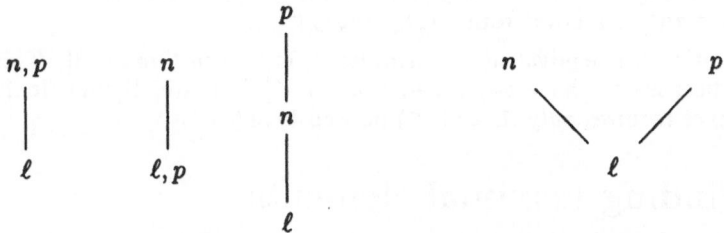

The fourth ordering represents the consensus of the prioritised preferences, which we will shortly define.

Notice that $i < j$ means that $\sqsubseteq_i$ has a *higher* priority than $\sqsubseteq_j$. But $x \sqsubseteq_i y$ means that y is preferred to x by i.

Definition 3 Let $(I, \leqslant, \{\sqsubseteq_i\}_{i \in I})$ be a prioritised family of preferences on a set X. The *globalisation* or *consensus* of $\{\sqsubseteq_i\}_{i \in I}$ is the relation $\sqsubseteq$ on X defined by

$$x \sqsubseteq y \quad \text{if} \quad \forall i \in I. \, (x \sqsubseteq_i y \text{ or } \exists j \in I. \, (j < i \text{ and } x \sqsubset_j y)).$$

That is, y is as preferred as x overall if it is as preferred according to each of the relations except possibly those for which there is a relation of greater priority, at which y is strictly preferred to x.

The remainder of this section is devoted to theorems and remarks which further motivate and explain this definition.

Lemma 4 $x \sqsubseteq y$ iff $\forall i \in I. \, (x \sqsubseteq_i y \text{ or } (\exists j < i. \, x \sqsubset_j y \text{ and } \forall k < j. \, x \sqsubseteq_k y))$.

Proof $\Leftarrow$ immediate. $\Rightarrow$ Find j minimal with $x \sqsubset_j y$. $\qquad\square$

The definition of globalisation is a generalisation to partial orders of the usual lexicographic ordering. That is to say, if $(I, \leqslant)$ is a total ordering, say $\{1 < 2 < \cdots < n\}$ then the globalisation is the following:

$$
\begin{aligned}
x \sqsubseteq y \quad &\text{if} \quad x \sqsubset_1 y \\
&\text{or} \quad x \sqsubseteq_1 y \text{ and } x \sqsubset_2 y \\
&\text{or} \quad x \sqsubseteq_1 y, \, x \sqsubseteq_2 y \text{ and } x \sqsubset_3 y \\
&\text{or} \quad \cdots \\
&\text{or} \quad x \sqsubseteq_1 y, \, x \sqsubseteq_2 y \ldots \text{ and } x \sqsubseteq_n y
\end{aligned}
$$

Our convention that $i < j$ implies $\sqsubseteq_i$ has greater priority than $\sqsubseteq_j$ matches with the lexicographic ordering.

Proposition 5 The globalisation $\sqsubseteq$ of a prioritised family of preference relations is a pre-order.

Proof Reflexivity is obvious. For transitivity, suppose $x \sqsubseteq y \sqsubseteq z$, and let $i \in I$. We shall show $x \sqsubseteq_i z$ or $x \sqsubset_j z$ for some $j < i$.

Suppose $x \sqsubseteq_i y$. If $y \sqsubseteq_i z$ then $x \sqsubseteq_i z$. Otherwise, $y \not\sqsubseteq_i z$, so let $j_1 < i$ be such that $y \sqsubset_{j_1} z$ and $y \sqsubseteq_k z$ for $k < j_1$ (lemma 4). If $x \not\sqsubseteq_{j_1} y$, then let $j < j_1$ be such that $x \sqsubset_j y$. Then $j < i$ and $x \sqsubset_j z$ follows from $x \sqsubset_j y$ and $y \sqsubseteq_j z$. If $x \sqsubseteq_{j_1} y$, set $j = j_1$. Then $j < i$, and $x \sqsubset_j z$ follows from $x \sqsubseteq_j y$ and $y \sqsubset_j z$.

On the other hand, suppose $x \not\sqsubseteq_i y$ and let $j_2 < i$ be such that $x \sqsubset_{j_2} y$ and $x \sqsubseteq_k y$ for all $k < j_2$ (lemma 4). Again, consider separately the two cases

$y \sqsubseteq_{j_2} z$ and $y \not\sqsubseteq_{j_2} z$. If $y \sqsubseteq_{j_2} z$, set $j = j_2$; then $j < i$, and $x \sqsubseteq_j z$ follows from $x \sqsubseteq_j y$ and $y \sqsubseteq_j z$. Otherwise, $y \not\sqsubseteq_{j_2} z$ so let $j < j_2$ be such that $y \sqsubset_j z$; then $j < i$, and $x \sqsubseteq_j z$ follows from $x \sqsubseteq_j y$ and $y \sqsubset_j z$. □

Definition 3 is equivalent to a similar definition in Grosof [3]. This proof follows because we have stipulated that $(I, \leqslant)$ is finite, though in fact the equivalence requires only that $(I, \leqslant)$ be well-founded.

3 Finding maximal elements

We are interested in finding elements which are 'best' according to the consensus of the prioritised preference relations; that is, we are interested in finding $\sqsubseteq$-maximal elements. In the terminology of default reasoning, we want to show that $\sqsubseteq$ is *stoppered*. As is well-known, **Zorn's lemma** [1] can be used to prove that maximal elements of an ordering exist. Zorn's lemma says that a pre-order has a maximal element if every chain in the pre-order has an upper bound.

Definition 6

1. Let $(X, \sqsubseteq)$ be a pre-order. A subset Y of X is a $\sqsubseteq$-*chain* if Y is totally ordered by $\sqsubseteq$; that is, $\forall y, z \in Y. \ y \sqsubseteq z$ or $z \sqsubseteq y$.

2. A chain Y in $(X, \sqsubseteq)$ has an *upper bound* $a \in X$ if $\forall y \in Y. \ y \sqsubseteq a$.

Proposition 7 (Zorn's Lemma) A pre-order $(X, \sqsubseteq)$ has a maximal element if every chain in X has an upper bound.

Before we apply Zorn's lemma, we establish the existence of certain key preferences which will enable us to reduce $\sqsubseteq$-chains to $\sqsubseteq_i$-chains. We do this in the first of the following two lemmas. Then, in the second of the two, we compose the $\sqsubseteq_i$ chains to give another chain. We show that this chain has an upper bound, and that its upper bound serves as an upper bound of the $\sqsubseteq$ chain we started with.

The next few definitions and lemmas are technical lemmas whose real purpose is to assist in the proof of theorem 13.

Definition 8 Let $(I, \leqslant, \{\sqsubseteq_i\}_{i \in I})$ be a prioritised family of preferences on a set X, and let $x, y \in X$. The x, y-*frontier*, written $\mathrm{fr}(x, y)$, is the set of $\leqslant$-minimal elements of the set $\{i \in I \mid x \not\equiv_i y\}$.

Note that if $\{i \in I \mid x \not\equiv_i y\} = \varnothing$ then $\mathrm{fr}(x, y) = \varnothing$.

Lemma 9 Suppose $x \sqsubseteq y$. Then $i \in \mathrm{fr}(x, y)$ iff $x \sqsubset_i y$ and $\forall j < i. \ x \equiv_j y$.

Proof (If) Immediate. (Only if) Let $x \sqsubseteq y$ and $i \in \mathrm{fr}(x, y)$. (1) We prove $x \sqsubset_i y$; for if not, by definition 3 $\exists j < i. \ x \sqsubset_j y$, i.e. $x \not\equiv_j y$, contradicting i's minimality. (2) Since $i \in \mathrm{fr}(x, y)$, $x \not\equiv_i y$. Thus $x \sqsubset_i y$.

Now suppose $j < i$. Since i is minimal in $\{i \in I \mid x \not\equiv_i y\}$, we have $x \equiv_j y$. □

Definition 10 Let $J \subseteq I$. We write $x \sqsubseteq_J y$ if $\forall j \in J. \ x \sqsubseteq_j y$. We also write $\downarrow J$ for $\{i \in I \mid \exists j \in J. \ i \leqslant j\}$.

Lemma 11 Let $Y \subseteq X$ be a $\sqsubseteq$-chain with no maximal element. Then there exists $J \subseteq I$ and $a \in Y$ such that

1. $\forall j \in J. \ \forall i \in I. \ \forall x, y \in Y. \ (a \sqsubseteq x \sqsubseteq y$ and $i \leqslant j)$ implies $x \sqsubseteq_i y$ — that is, $\{y \in Y \mid a \sqsubseteq y\}$ forms a $\sqsubseteq_{\downarrow J}$-chain.

2. $\forall j \in J. \forall x \in Y. a \sqsubseteq x$ implies $\exists z \in Y. (x \sqsubset z$ and $x \sqsubset_j z)$ — that is, the same set also forms a $\sqsubseteq_J$-chain with no maximal element.

3. $\forall i \in I. \forall x, y \in Y. a \sqsubseteq x \sqsubseteq y$ implies $(x \sqsubseteq_i y$ or $\exists j \in J. j < i)$.

Proof The idea of the proof is the following. First, we obtain a set $I' \subseteq I$ which contains those i which participate in frontiers all the way up the chain Y. Then find an element a of Y above which *all* the frontiers are in I'. J is defined as the minimal elements of I'. Then it is possible to prove property 1. Property 2 follows because we have stipulated that Y have no maximal element; that is, for each $y \in Y$ there is a $y' \in Y$ with $y \sqsubset y'$. Property 3 follows because J is the set of minimal elements of I'.

Let $I' = \{i \in I \mid \forall x \in Y. \exists y, z \in Y. x \sqsubseteq y \sqsubseteq z$ and $i \in \mathrm{fr}(y, z)\}$.

♦ If $I' = I$ then let a be an arbitrary element of Y.

♦ Otherwise, for each $i \in I - I'$ let $x_i \in Y$ be such that $\forall y, z \in Y$, if $x_i \sqsubseteq y \sqsubseteq z$ then $i \notin \mathrm{fr}(y, z)$, and let $a = \max_{\sqsubseteq}\{x_i \mid i \in I - I'\}$. That each x_i can be found follows from the definition of I', and that their maximum can be found is guaranteed by the facts that Y is a chain and I is finite.

Now we show that I' is non-empty. Let $x, y \in Y$ be such that $a \sqsubseteq x \sqsubseteq y$. The fact that Y has no maximal element guarantees that these can be found. Since $x \sqsubset y$, $\mathrm{fr}(x, y) \neq \varnothing$, and since $a \sqsubseteq x, y$, we have $\mathrm{fr}(x, y) \subseteq I'$.

1. Let $j \in J$, $i \in I$ and $x, y \in Y$ be such that $i \leqslant j$ and $a \sqsubseteq x \sqsubseteq y$. If $i \in \mathrm{fr}(x, y)$ then $x \sqsubset_i y$ (lemma 9); otherwise, if $i \notin \mathrm{fr}(x, y)$ and $x \not\sqsubseteq_i y$ then $\exists j' < i. x \sqsubset_{j'} y$, contradicting the minimality of j in J.

2. Let $j \in J$ and $x \in Y$ with $a \sqsubseteq x$. Since $j \in I'$, we can pick $y, z \in Y$ with $x \sqsubseteq y \sqsubseteq z$ and $j \in \mathrm{fr}(y, z)$. By part 1, $x \sqsubseteq_j y \sqsubseteq_j z$; and since $j \in \mathrm{fr}(y, z)$ we have $y \sqsubset_j z$. By transitivity, $x \sqsubset_j z$.

3. If $x \not\sqsubseteq_i y$ then $\exists j' \in \mathrm{fr}(x, y) \subseteq I'. j' < i$ (lemma 4), and since J consists of the minimal elements of I' (and I is finite!), $\exists j \in J. j < j'$. $\qquad\square$

Now we show, subject to a certain condition, that it is possible to find an upper bound for any $\sqsubseteq$-chain. The condition says that upper bounds can be found for intersections (i.e. conjunctions) of the $\sqsubseteq_i$ relations.

Lemma 12 Suppose for every $J \subseteq I$, every $\sqsubseteq_J$-chain has an upper bound. Then every $\sqsubseteq$-chain has an upper bound.

Proof Let Y be a $\sqsubseteq$-chain. If Y has a maximal element, then that serves as its upper bound. Suppose, then, that Y has no maximal element. Let $J \subseteq I$ and $a \in Y$ be as defined in lemma 11. Let $K = J \cup \{k \in I \mid \forall j \in J. j \not\leqslant k\}$. We now show that the set $\{x \in Y \mid a \sqsubseteq x\}$ forms a $\sqsubseteq_{\downarrow K}$ chain. Without loss of generality, let $x, y \in Y$ be such that $a \sqsubseteq x \sqsubseteq y$, and $i \in I$ and $k \in K$ be such that $i \leqslant k$. We need to show that $x \sqsubseteq_i y$. If $k \in J$ then $x \sqsubseteq_i y$ by lemma 11(1). Otherwise, $\forall j \in J. j \not\leqslant k$ (definition of K). Therefore, $j \not\leqslant i$. Suppose $x \not\sqsubseteq_i y$. Then by 11(3), $\exists j \in J. j < i$, a contradiction. So $x \sqsubseteq_i y$.

Now let b be a $\sqsubseteq_{\downarrow K}$ upper bound for $\{x \in Y \mid a \sqsubseteq x\}$. We show that it is also a $\sqsubseteq$ upper bound for that set, and hence for Y. Let $x \in Y$ with $a \sqsubseteq x$; we show that $x \sqsubseteq b$, using definition 3.

First note that (i) $j \in \downarrow K$ implies $x \sqsubseteq_j b$ (by definition of b). Also, (ii) $j \in J$ implies $x \sqsubset_j b$. To see this, take y such that $x \sqsubset_j y$ by lemma 11(2); but then $y \sqsubseteq_j b$, so $x \sqsubset_j b$.

Now let $i \in I$. We show that either $x \sqsubseteq_i b$ or $\exists j < i.\ x \sqsubseteq_j b$. If $i \in \downarrow K$, $x \sqsubseteq_i b$ by (i). If $i \notin \downarrow K$, then $i \notin K$. By definition of K, $\exists j \in J.\ j < i$; by (ii), $x \sqsubseteq_j b$. $\qquad\square$

Thus, we are in a position to provide sufficient conditions for being able to find maximal elements.

Theorem 13 Let $(I, \leqslant, \{\sqsubseteq_i\}_{i \in I})$ be a prioritised family of preferences on a set X with globalisation $\sqsubseteq$, such that for every $J \subseteq I$, every $\sqsubseteq_J$-chain has an upper bound. Then $\sqsubseteq$ has maximal elements.

Proof By Zorn's lemma and lemma 12. $\qquad\square$

The sufficient conditions for finding maximal elements may feel a bit unsatisfactory, and one might ask whether they can be weakened. For example, maybe being able to find upper bounds on all $\sqsubseteq_i$-chains (but not necessarily their intersections) is sufficient. However, the following example shows that this is not so.

Example 14 Let $X = (\mathbb{N} \times \mathbb{N}) \cup \{(0, \omega), (\omega, 0)\}$. Let $I = \{1, 2\}$ with $\leqslant$ the discrete ordering (i.e. $< = \varnothing$) and

$$(x, y) \sqsubseteq_1 (x', y') \quad \text{if} \quad x \leqslant x' \quad \text{according to the numerical ordering}$$
$$(x, y) \sqsubseteq_2 (x', y') \quad \text{if} \quad y \leqslant y' \quad \text{ditto}$$

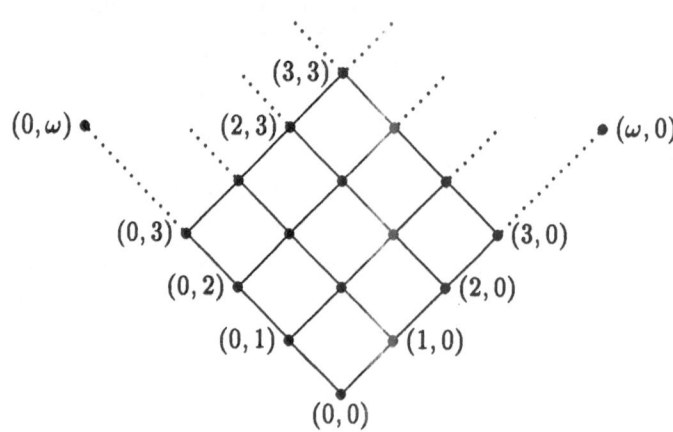

Notice that although the premise of lemma 12 fails, all $\sqsubseteq_1$-chains and $\sqsubseteq_2$-chains have upper bounds. The globalisation is defined as $(x, y) \sqsubseteq (x', y')$ if $x \leqslant x'$ and $y \leqslant y'$. It has no maximal element. The chain $(0, 0) \sqsubseteq (1, 1) \sqsubseteq (2, 2) \sqsubseteq \cdots$ has no upper bound according to this relation. So this example shows that upper bounds on the $\sqsubseteq_i$ orderings is not enough.

4 Are these really the best elements?

The contribution of the preceding two sections is as follows: in the first section, we gave the definition of the 'globalising' or 'consensus' relation for a prioritised family of preferences, and examined its properties. In the second section, we showed that (under certain conditions) it is possible to find 'best' elements according to those preferences – namely, those maximal in the globalising relation.

Are these really the best elements? There is a particular case of prioritised preference relations in which one may have conflicting intuitions. In this section we examine those intuitions and propose an alternative definition.

4.1 Totally prioritised families of preferences

An order $\leqslant$ is *total* if for each $i, j \in I$, we have $i \leqslant j$ or $j \leqslant i$.

Suppose our $(I, \leqslant)$ is a total order $\{1 < 2 < \cdots < n\}$. We will write this *totally prioritised family of preferences* as $\{\sqsubseteq_i\}_{i \leqslant n}$. Note that the preference orderings $\sqsubseteq_i$ need not be total; it is the priority relation $\leqslant$ which is total.

This notation is convenient because in this case we can characterise the globalising relation inductively. We write the globalisation of $\{\sqsubseteq_i\}_{i \leqslant n}$ as $\sqsubseteq^n$.

Proposition 15

1. $x \sqsubseteq^0 y$ always; and
2. $x \sqsubseteq^i y$ if $x \sqsubseteq_i y$ or ($x \equiv_i y$ and $x \sqsubseteq^{i-1} y$).

The proof is straightforward. In this case we may expect that the maximal elements in the globalisation relation $\sqsubseteq^n$ can be found in the following way.

Procedure 16 (incorrect) Start with the set X. Take the maximal elements according to the relation $\sqsubseteq_1$ (it has the highest priority). Then, from the resulting set, choose those which are maximal in $\sqsubseteq_2$. From that set, take those which are maximal according to $\sqsubseteq_3$. Continue in this way until each of the relations has been considered.

Any element found in this way is indeed $\sqsubseteq^n$-maximal, but it turns out that this does not yield *all* of the $\sqsubseteq^n$ maximal elements. To find all the maximal elements, proceed as follows.

Procedure 17 (correct) Start, as before, with the set X. Take the $\sqsubseteq_1$-maximal equivalence classes. This is a set of sets; each element inside the sets is $\sqsubseteq_1$-maximal, and each set is a $\equiv_1$ equivalence class. Now for each such equivalence class, take the $\sqsubseteq_2$-maximal equivalence classes. This gives another set of sets, several of them resulting from each one of the previous set of sets. Continue in this way until all the relations have been considered.

To formalise this procedure and state the necessary theorem, we need the following notation.

Definition 18 Let $(X, \sqsubseteq)$ be a pre-order, and $\equiv$ the corresponding equivalence relation. If $Y \subseteq X$, then $\mathrm{Max}_{\sqsubseteq}(Y)$ is the set of $\equiv|_Y$-equivalence classes which are $\sqsubseteq$-maximal. That is,

$$\mathrm{Max}_{\sqsubseteq}(Y) = \{Z \subseteq Y \mid \forall z \in Z. \ (z \text{ is } \sqsubseteq\text{-maximal in } Y, \text{ and} \\ \forall x \in X. \ x \in Z \text{ iff } x \equiv z)\}.$$

Notice that this is not the set of maximal elements of Y; rather, it is a set of sets whose union is the set of maximal elements. It is, in fact, the set of maximal elements of Y partitioned by $\equiv|_Y$.

Proposition 19 Let $\{\sqsubseteq_i\}_{i \leqslant n}$ be a totally prioritised family of preferences on X. Define the sets $\mathbf{X}_0, \mathbf{X}_1, \ldots, \mathbf{X}_n \subseteq \mathcal{P}(X)$ as follows.

1. $\mathbf{X}_0 = \{X\}$, and
2. $\mathbf{X}_j = \{Y \subseteq X \mid \exists Z \in \mathbf{X}_{j-1}. Y \in \mathrm{Max}_{\sqsubseteq_j}(Z)\}$ $(1 \leqslant j \leqslant n)$.
   (Equivalently, $\mathbf{X}_j = \bigcup_{Z \in \mathbf{X}_{j-1}} \mathrm{Max}_{\sqsubseteq_j}(Z)$.)

Then: x is $\sqsubseteq^n$-maximal iff $\exists Y \in \mathbf{X}_n. x \in Y$.

In spite of this rather awkward notation, the difference between the two procedures is easy to see.

Example 20 Suppose $X = \{a, b\}$, $\sqsubseteq_1 = \{(a, a), (b, b)\}$, and $\sqsubseteq_2 = \{(a, a), (b, b), (a, b)\}$. That is, $\sqsubseteq_1$ and $\sqsubseteq_2$ are

Procedures 16 and 17 yield $\{b\}$ and $\{a, b\}$ respectively as the set of $\sqsubseteq^2$-maximal elements.

Procedure 16 takes the view that as $\sqsubseteq_1$ has not decided the matter between a and b, then it should be up to $\sqsubseteq_2$ to determine that b is superior to a and thus that b is overall maximal. On the other hand, procedure 17 takes the view that $\sqsubseteq_1$ has decided the matter between a and b; it says that they are incomparable. Since $\sqsubseteq_2$ is of less priority, it gets no say.

Example 21 Suppose $X = \{a, b\}$, $\sqsubseteq_1 = \{(a, a), (b, b), (a, b), (b, a)\}$, and $\sqsubseteq_2 = \{(a, a), (b, b), (a, b)\}$. That is, $\sqsubseteq_1$ and $\sqsubseteq_2$ are

Both procedures yield $\{b\}$ as the set of $\sqsubseteq^2$-maximal elements.

Moral of story: there is a difference between saying that two elements are incomparable and saying that they are equivalent!

4.2 Squashing pre-orders into total orders

Our final question is this: is there a way of defining the globalisation of a family of prioritised relations in such a way that, in the totally prioritised case, procedure 16 yields the right results? The answer is 'yes', in certain conditions which we will state; but the definition is rather unnatural. We take this to be evidence of the unnaturalness of that procedure.

The essence of the definition is to squash the pre-orders $\sqsubseteq_i$ into total pre-orders $\sqsubseteq_i^*$ in such a way as to preserve maximal elements. Then we use the definition of globalisation (definition 3).

If $\sqsubseteq$ is a pre-order, $\sqsubseteq^*$ is the squashed version.

Definition 22 Let $(X, \sqsubseteq)$ be a pre-order. The pre-order $\sqsubseteq^*$ on X is defined as follows.

$$x \sqsubseteq^* y \quad \text{if} \quad |{\uparrow}x| \geqslant |{\uparrow}y|$$

where

♦ ${\uparrow}x = \{y \in X \mid x \sqsubset y\}$, and

♦ $|Y|$ is the cardinality of Y, and $\geqslant$ compares cardinalities.

Example 23 Here are some examples of $\sqsubseteq$ with the squashed version $\sqsubseteq^*$

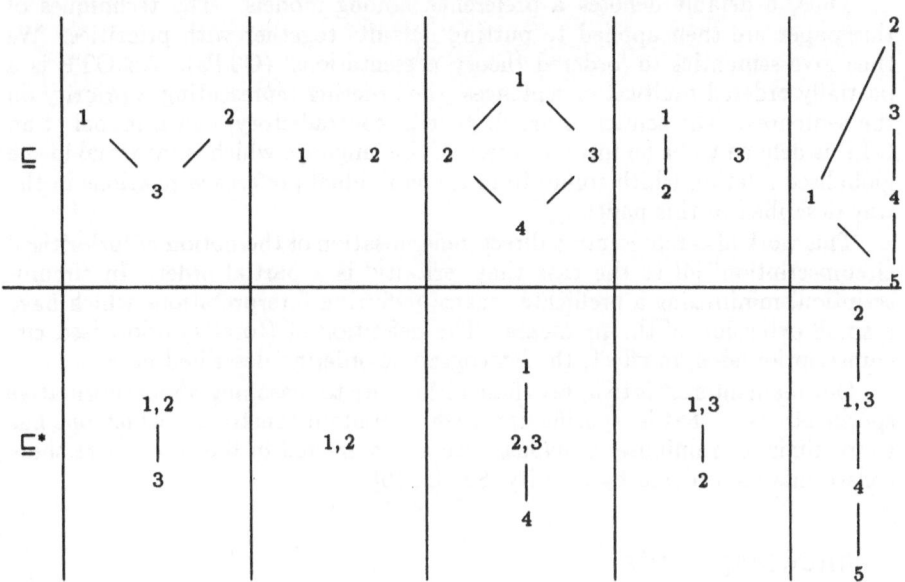

Proposition 24

1. $\sqsubseteq^*$ is total.

2. If x is $\sqsubseteq$-maximal then x is $\sqsubseteq^*$-maximal.

3. If $\sqsubseteq$ has maximal elements then: if x is $\sqsubseteq^*$-maximal then x is $\sqsubseteq$-maximal.

Proof 2. x is $\sqsubseteq$-maximal implies $|{\uparrow}x| = 0$ implies x is $\sqsubseteq^*$-maximal.

3. Let y be any maximal element. Then $|{\uparrow}y| = 0$. Now suppose x is $\sqsubseteq^*$-maximal; then $|{\uparrow}x| = 0$, so x is $\sqsubseteq$-maximal. □

Proposition 25 Let $\{\sqsubseteq_i\}_{i \leqslant n}$ be a totally prioritised family of *total* preferences on X. (That is to say, each $\sqsubseteq_i$ is also total; $\forall x, y.\ x \sqsubseteq_i y$ or $y \sqsubseteq_i x$.) Then the globalisation $\sqsubseteq$ is also total.

Proof Suppose $y \not\sqsubseteq x$. We show that $x \sqsubseteq y$. Since $y \not\sqsubseteq x$, there is i such that $y \not\sqsubseteq_i x$ and $\forall k < i.\ y \not\sqsubseteq_k x$. But since these are total orders, this implies $x \sqsubseteq_i y$ and $\forall k < i.\ x \sqsubseteq_k y$. Therefore, $x \sqsubseteq y$. □

Thus, $*$ is an operation which conflates procedures 16 and 17.

5 Applications

The motivation for studying this problem is to establish the foundations of *default reasoning*. In the framework we propose (which is the subject of [8]), defaults are represented by sentences in the language. The idea of default reasoning is that it is in general not possible to satisfy the defaults, but nevertheless we want models of our theory which are as close to satisfying the defaults as possible. To that end, we define orderings which measure how well an interpretation of a logical language satisfies a given sentence in the language. Thus, we write $M \sqsubseteq_\phi N$ to mean that N satisfies ϕ at least as well as M does. This definition and examples can be found in [8] and [7]. Clearly, we will be interested in interpretations which are $\sqsubseteq_\phi$-maximal.

Thus, a default denotes a preference among models. The techniques of this paper are then applied to putting defaults together with priorities. We thus give semantics to 'ordered theory presentations' (OTPs). An OTP is a partially ordered multiset of sentences, the ordering representing a priority on the sentences. The sentences are in general contradictory, and a model of an OTP is defined to be an interpretation of the language which is maximal in the globalised relation which comes from the individual preference relations in the way described in this paper.

This work also represents a direct generalisation of the notion of 'prioritised circumscription' [4] to the case that 'priority' is a partial order. In circumscription, minimizing a predicate means preferring interpretations which have a small extension of the predicate. The definition of (totally) prioritised circumscription uses, in effect, the lexicographic ordering described here.

Our main interest is to apply these techniques to reasoning about 'normative specifications' – that is, specifications which contain constraints which one has to maximise or minimise. Obviously, we are interested in the case where these constraints are ordered by priority. See [2, 10].

Acknowledgments

Many thanks to David Makinson and Pierre-Yves Schobbens for useful correspondence and discussion on early versions of these results. Thanks to the referees Reinhold Heckman, Roy Crole and Abbas Edalat for useful comments on a draft of this paper.

References

[1] B. A. Davey and H. A. Priestley. *Introduction to Lattices and Order.* Cambridge Mathematical Textbooks. Cambridge University Press, 1990.

[2] J. Fiadeiro and T. Maibaum. Temporal reasoning over deontic specifications. *Journal of Logic and Computation*, 1(3):357–395, 1991.

[3] B. N. Grosof. Generalising prioritization. In J. Allen, R. Fikes, and E. Sandewall, editors, *Proc. Second International Conference on Principles of Knowledge Representation and Reasoning (KR'91)*, pages 289–300. Morgan Kaufmann, 1991.

[4] V. Lifschitz. Pointwise circumscription. In M. L. Ginsberg, editor, *Readings in Non-monotonic Logic*. Morgan Kaufmann, 1987.

[5] D. Makinson. General theory of cumulative inference. In M. Reinfrank, J. de Kleer, and M. L. Ginsberg, editors, *Non-monotonic Reasoning*. Lecture Notes in Artificial Intelligence 346, Springer-Verlag, 1988.

[6] J. McCarthy. Circumscription—a form of non-monotonic reasoning. *Artificial Intelligence*, 13:27–39, 1980.

[7] M. D. Ryan. Defaults and revision in structured theories. In *Proc. Sixth IEEE Symposium on Logic in Computer Science (LICS)*, pages 362–373, 1991.

[8] M. D. Ryan. *Ordered Presentations of Theories: Default Reasoning and Belief Revision.* PhD thesis, Department of Computing, Imperial College, 1992.

[9] M. D. Ryan. Representing defaults as sentences with reduced priority. In B. Nebel and W. Swartout, editors, *Proc. Third International Conference on Principles of Knowledge Representation and Reasoning (KR'92)*. Morgan Kaufmann, 1992.

[10] M. D. Ryan. Towards specifying norms. *Annals of Mathematics and Artificial Intelligence*, 1993. In print.

[11] M. D. Ryan and P.-Y. Schobbens. Laws of generalised prioritisation. In preparation.

[12] P.-Y. Schobbens. *Exceptions in Algebraic Specifications.* PhD thesis, Unité d'Informatique, Université Catholique de Louvain, Belgium, 1992.

Laws of Parallel Synchronised Termination

David Sands

dave@diku.dk
DIKU, University of Copenhagen
Universitetsparken 1
DK-2100 København Ø, Denmark

Abstract

The salient feature of the composition operators for Gamma programs is that for termination, the parallel composition operator demands that its operands must terminate synchronously. This paper studies the inequational partial correctness properties of the combination of sequential and parallel composition operators for Gamma programs, provable from a particular compositional semantics (Brookes-style transition traces) and shows that the "residual program" input-output laws originally described by Hankin *et al.* are also verified by the model.

1 Introduction

The Gamma Model   The Gamma formalism was proposed by Banâtre and Le Métayer [3] as a means for the high level description of parallel programs with a minimum of explicit control. Gamma is a minimal language based on local rewriting of a finite multiset (or *bag*), with an appealing analogy with the chemical reaction process. As an example, a program that sorts an array $a_0, \ldots, a_n$ (of integers, say) could be defined as follows. Represent the array as a multiset of pairs $\{(0, a_0), \ldots, (n, a_n)\}$, then just specify a single rule: "exchange ill-ordered values"

$$sort_A : ((i, x), (j, y) \rightarrow (i, y), (j, x) \Leftarrow i < j \ \& \ x > y).$$

$i < j \ \& \ x > y$ specifies a property (a *reaction condition*) to be satisfied by the selected elements (i, x) and (j, y); these elements are replaced in the multiset (the *chemical solution*) by the elements $(i, y), (j, x)$ (the product of the reaction). Nothing is said in this definition about the order of evaluation of the comparisons; if several disjoint pairs of elements satisfy the reaction condition the comparisons and replacements can even be performed in parallel.

The computation terminates when a stable state is reached, that is to say when no elements of the multiset satisfy the reaction condition (or in general, any of a number of reaction conditions). The interested reader may find a long series of examples illustrating the Gamma style of programming in [3]. The benefit of using Gamma in systematic program construction in the Dijkstra-Gries style are illustrated in [2].

A Calculus of Gamma Programs   For the sake of modularity it is desirable that a language offers a rich set of operators for combining programs. It is also fundamental that these operators enjoy a useful collection of algebraic laws in order to make it possible to reason about composed programs. Hankin, Le Métayer and Sands [6] defined two composition operators for the construction of Gamma programs from basic reactions, namely sequential composition $P_1 \circ P_2$ and parallel composition $P_1 + P_2$. The intuition behind $P_1 \circ P_2$ is that the stable multiset reached after the execution of P_2 is given as argument to P_1. On the other hand, the result of $P_1 + P_2$ is obtained (roughly speaking) by executing the reactions of P_1 and P_2 (in any order, possibly in parallel), terminating only when neither can proceed further—in the spirit of the original Gamma programs.

As a further simple example, consider the following program which sorts a multiset of integers:

$$sort_B : match \circ init$$
$$\textbf{where} \quad init : \quad (x \to (0, x) \Leftarrow integer(x))$$
$$match : \quad ((i, x), (i, y) \to (i, x), (i + 1, y) \Leftarrow x \le y)$$

The reaction *init* gives each integer an initial rank of zero. When this has been completed, *match* takes any two elements of the same rank and increases the rank of the larger.

In fact we get a sort program for a multiset of integers by placing $sort_A$ in parallel with $sort_B$ as $sort_A + sort_B$.

Hankin *et al.* [6] derived a number of program refinement and equivalence laws for parallel and sequential composition, by considering the input-output behaviour induced by an operational semantics. So, for example, the program $sort_A + sort_B$ which is by definition $sort_A + (match \circ init)$ is refined by the program

$$(sort_A + match) \circ init.$$

This refinement is an instance of a general refinement law:

$$P + (Q \circ R) \ge (P + Q) \circ R,$$

and is one of a number of laws relating parallel and sequential composition. The main shortcoming of such refinement laws from [6] is that there is no guarantee that the refinement and equivalences described are compositional, so that a refinement of a sub-program does not necessarily imply a refinement of the program.

In [10] the author directly addresses this problem by defining a compositional (denotational) semantics for Gamma. A few of the laws from [6] are shown to hold also in this model, and questions of abstractness, and alternative combining forms are studied. In this paper we continue this study of the properties of this language in particular addressing the laws concerning the so-called *residual program*— a synactic characterisation of the program part of the state just before its termination.

In **Section 2** we summarise the operational semantics of Gamma programs, and in **Section 3** we sketch the denotational semantics given in [10] which adapts a method of Brookes [4] for giving a (fully abstract) denotational semantics for a parallel shared variable *while* language. The key technique is to give the meaning of a program as a set of *transition traces* which represent both the computation steps that the program can perform, and the ways that the program can interact with its environment. In **Section 4** we show how the model can verify a number of typical and some not so typical laws of parallel and sequential compositions. In **Section 5** we consider the residual program properties from [6], and show that the residual program notion arises naturally from the laws.

2 Operational Semantics

In this section we consider the operational semantics of programs consisting of basic reactions (written $(A \Leftarrow R)$), where R is the reaction condition, and A is the associated action, both assumed to have the same arity), together with two *combining forms*: sequential composition, $P_1 \circ P_2$, and parallel combination, $P_1 + P_2$ as introduced in [6].

$$P \in \mathbf{P} ::= (A \Leftarrow R) \mid P \circ P \mid P + P$$

To define the semantics for these programs we define a single step transition relation between *configurations*. The *terminal* configurations are just multisets, and the *intermediate* configurations are program, multiset pairs written $\langle P, M \rangle$, where $M \in \mathbf{M}$ is the set of finite multisets of elements. The domain of the elements is left unspecified, but is expected to include integers, booleans and tuples.

We define the single step transitions first for the individual reactions ($A \Leftarrow R$). A reaction terminates on some multiset exactly when there is no sub-multiset of elements which (when viewed as a tuple) satisfy the reaction condition. We will not specify the details of the reaction conditions and actions, but assume, as previously, that they are total functions over tuples of integers, truth values, tuples etc.

$$\langle (A \Leftarrow R), M \rangle \to M \quad \text{if } \neg \exists \vec{a} \subseteq M . R\vec{a}$$

Otherwise, if we can form a tuple from elements of the multiset, and this tuple satisfies the reaction condition, the selected elements can be replaced by the elements produced by the associated action function:

$$\langle (A \Leftarrow R), M \uplus \vec{a} \rangle \to \langle (A \Leftarrow R), M \uplus A\vec{a} \rangle \quad \text{if } R\vec{a}$$

The *terminal transitions* have the form $\langle P, M \rangle \to M$, and are only defined for programs not containing sequential composition, so the remaining *terminal* transitions are defined by the following synchronised-termination rule:

$$\frac{\langle P, M \rangle \to M \quad \langle Q, M \rangle \to M}{\langle P + Q, M \rangle \to M}$$

The remaining intermediate transitions are given by first defining what we will call *active contexts*.

Definition 1 An *active context*, $\mathbf{A}$ is a term containing a single hole [ ]:

$$\mathbf{A} ::= [\,] \mid P + \mathbf{A} \mid \mathbf{A} + P \mid P \circ \mathbf{A}$$

Let $\mathbf{A}[P]$ denote active context $\mathbf{A}$ with program P in place of the hole.

The idea of active contexts is that they isolate parts of a program that can affect the next transition, so that for example, the left-hand side of a sequential composition is not active (but it can become active once the right-hand side has terminated). The remaining transitions are defined by the following two rules:

$$\frac{\langle P, M \rangle \to \langle P', M' \rangle}{\langle \mathbf{A}[P], M \rangle \to \langle \mathbf{A}[P'], M' \rangle} \qquad \frac{\langle Q, M \rangle \to M}{\langle \mathbf{A}[P \circ Q], M \rangle \to \langle \mathbf{A}[P], M \rangle}$$

The first says that if there is a possible reaction in an active context then it can proceed, while the second says that if the right hand side of a sequential composition can terminate, then it can be erased.

In [6] an equivalent definition is given in terms of the more traditional SOS style, and active contexts are given as a derived construction to facilitate proofs of certain properties.

3 Transition Trace Model

In this study we only consider the simplest of the input-output orderings, that of *partial correctness* (the $\leq_L$ order of [6]).

We define $P_1 \leq P_2$ whenever, for each possible input M, if P_1 can terminate producing some multiset N then so can P_2.

This partial correctness preorder, and associated equivalence $\sim$ was was shown to satisfy a number of properties in [6] (in fact they are stated for a stronger ordering which also treats nontermination as a possible "result").

Because of the lack of a general substitutivity property, the use of the partial correctness laws in reasoning about programs is limited. As is standard, we are therefore interested in the largest contextual (pre)congruence relation contained in $\leq$. Let $\mathbf{C}$ range over general program contexts, then we define *operational approximation* and *operational congruence* respectively by:

$$P_1 \sqsubseteq_o P_2 \iff \forall \mathbf{C}. \, \mathbf{C}[P_1] \leq \mathbf{C}[P_2]$$
$$P_1 \equiv_o P_2 \iff P_1 \sqsubseteq_o P_2 \,\&\, P_2 \sqsubseteq_o P_1$$

We will now describe a semantics for programs which is suitable for reasoning about operational approximation and equivalence. It is clear that we must consider intermediate behaviour of programs to obtain a substitutive equivalence. However, it is not enough to consider just the sequences of intermediate states in a program's execution, because they do not take into account the possible *interference* (from the program's surrounding context) that can occur during execution. The solution we adopt is an adaptation of a technique for giving denotational semantics to shared-variable *while* languages proposed by Brookes [4]; related tequniques include Hennessy and Plotkin's *resumptions* [7] and Abrahamson's *move* sequences [1].

Transition Traces We adapt Brooke's transition trace model for our language. We define the meaning of a command as a set of transition traces, and show that the definition can be given compositionally.

Definition 2 The transition trace function $\mathsf{T}[\![\_]\!] : \mathbf{P} \to \wp((\mathbf{M} \times \mathbf{M})^+)$ is given by

$$
\begin{aligned}
\mathsf{T}[\![P]\!] = \ &\{(M_0, N_0)(M_1, N_1)\ldots(M_k, N_k)| \\
&\langle P, M_0 \rangle \to^* \langle P_1, N_0 \rangle \ \& \\
&\langle P_1, M_1 \rangle \to^* \langle P_2, N_1 \rangle \ \& \ldots \& \ \langle P_k, M_k \rangle \to^* N_k\}
\end{aligned}
$$

The intuition behind the use of transition traces to give meaning to a program is that each transition trace

$$(M_0, N_0)(M_1, N_1)\ldots(M_k, N_k) \in \mathsf{T}[\![P]\!]$$

represents a terminating execution of program P in some context starting with multiset M_0, and in which each of the pairs (M_i, N_i) represents computation steps performed by (derivatives of) P and the adjacent multisets N_{i-1}, M_i represent possible interfering computation steps performed by the context. The partial correctness ordering is recoverable from the transition traces by considering the transition traces of length one:

$$P_1 \leq P_2 \iff \{(M, N) \mid (M, N) \in \mathsf{T}[\![P_1]\!]\} \subseteq \{(M, N) \mid (M, N) \in \mathsf{T}[\![P_2]\!]\}.$$

A key feature of the definition of transition traces (in comparison with related approaches) is that they use the reflexive-transitive closure of the one-step evaluation relation, $\to^*$. An important consequence of this reflexivity and transitivity is that they are closed under certain "stuttering" and "absorption" properties described below. In the following, let ϵ denote the empty sequence. Let α and β range over elements of $(\mathbf{M} \times \mathbf{M})^*$.

Definition 3 A set $T \subseteq \wp((\mathbf{M} \times \mathbf{M})^+)$ is closed under left-stuttering and absorption if it satisfies the following two conditions

$$\text{left-stuttering} \ \frac{\alpha\beta \in T, \beta \neq \epsilon}{\alpha(M, M)\beta \in T} \qquad \text{absorption} \ \frac{\alpha(M, N)(N, M')\beta \in T}{\alpha(M, M')\beta \in T}$$

Let $\ddagger T$ denote the left-stuttering and absorption closure (henceforth just closure) of a set T. "Stuttering" represents the fact that we can have an arbitrary interference by the context without any visible steps performed by the program. The concept is well known from Lamport's work on temporal logics for concurrent systems [9]. Notice that we say *left*-stuttering to reflect that the context is not permitted to change the state after the termination of the program. In this way each transition trace of a program charts an interaction with its context, until the point of its termination. The *absorption* property is important because prevents "idle" computation steps from becoming semantically significant, which is a problem with the resumption approach [7].

A Compositional Definition of Transition Traces

We now show that the transition traces of a command can be given a denotational definition, which shows that transition trace semantics can be used to prove operational equivalence.

For the basic reaction-action pairs $(A \Leftarrow R)$, we build transition traces by simply considering all sequences of mediating transitions, followed by a terminal transition. Define the following sets:

$$\text{mediators}_{(A \Leftarrow R)} = \{(M,N) \mid \langle (A \Leftarrow R), M \rangle \rightarrow^* \langle (A \Leftarrow R), N \rangle\}$$
$$\text{terminals}_{(A \Leftarrow R)} = \{(M,N) \mid \langle (A \Leftarrow R), M \rangle \rightarrow^* N\}.$$

Sequential composition has an easy definition. We just concatenate the transition traces from the transition traces of the components, and take their closure. Define the following sequencing operation for transition trace sets:

$$T_1 \, ; T_2 = \{\alpha\beta \mid \alpha \in T_1, \beta \in T_2\}.$$

Not surprisingly parallel composition is built with the use of an interleaving combinator. First we define interleaving on single traces: for α and β in $(\mathbf{M}, \mathbf{M})^*$ let $\alpha \natural \beta$ be the set of all their interleavings, given inductively by

$$\epsilon \natural \beta = \beta \natural \epsilon = \{\beta\}$$
$$(M,M')\alpha \natural (N,N')\beta = \{(M,M')\gamma \mid \gamma \in \alpha \natural (N,N')\beta\}$$
$$\cup \{(N,N')\gamma \mid \gamma \in (M,M')\alpha \natural \beta\}.$$

Now to define the transition traces of $P_1 + P_2$ we must ensure that the traces of P_1 and P_2 are interleaved, but not arbitrarily. The termination step of a parallel composition requires an agreement at the point of their termination. For this purpose, we define the following interleaving operation on transition traces:

$$T_1 \oplus T_2 = \{\alpha(M,M) \mid \alpha_1(M,M) \in T_1, \alpha_2(M,M) \in T_2, \alpha \in \alpha_1 \natural \alpha_2\}$$

Proposition 4 ([10]) The transition traces of a program are characterised by the following denotational definition:

$$\mathsf{T}[\![(A \Leftarrow R)]\!] = (\text{mediators}_{(A \Leftarrow R)})^* \, ; \text{terminals}_{(A \Leftarrow R)}$$

$$\mathsf{T}[\![P_1 \circ P_2]\!] = \natural(\mathsf{T}[\![P_2]\!] \, ; \mathsf{T}[\![P_1]\!])$$

$$\mathsf{T}[\![P_1 + P_2]\!] = \natural(\mathsf{T}[\![P_1]\!] \oplus \mathsf{T}[\![P_2]\!]).$$

Define the transition trace ordering on programs $\sqsubseteq_t$ as

$$P_1 \sqsubseteq_t P_2 \iff \mathsf{T}[\![P_1]\!] \subseteq \mathsf{T}[\![P_2]\!].$$

The operations used to build the compositional definition are all monotone with respect to subset inclusion, and so a simple induction on contexts is sufficient to give

$$P_1 \sqsubseteq_t P_2 \Rightarrow \forall \mathsf{C}. \, \mathsf{C}[P_1] \sqsubseteq_t \mathsf{C}[P_2]$$

and since $P \sqsubseteq_t Q$ implies $P \leq Q$, we have the desired characterisation of operational approximation:

$$P_1 \sqsubseteq_t P_2 \Rightarrow P_1 \sqsubseteq_o P_2.$$

However, as we showed in [10] we cannot reverse the implication—the transition trace semantics is not (inequationally) *fully abstract*.

4   Basic Laws

In this section we present a number of the basic laws of synchronised termination.

Transition Trace Properties   Certain structural laws follow directly from the properties of the transition trace combinators, which we state without proof.

Proposition 5   Let S_1, S_2, T_1, T_2, etc. range over sets of transition traces not including ϵ (but not necessarily closed). Then we have the following:

$$
\begin{array}{rcl}
T_1 \oplus T_2 & = & T_2 \oplus T_1 \\
T_1 \oplus (T_2 \oplus T_3) & = & (T_1 \oplus T_2) \oplus T_3 \\
\ddagger(\ddagger T_1 \oplus \ddagger T_2) & = & \ddagger(T_1 \ominus T_2)
\end{array}
$$

$$
\begin{array}{rcl}
T_1 \,;\, (T_2 \,;\, T_3) & = & (T_1 \,;\, T_2) \,;\, T_3 \\
\ddagger(\ddagger T_1 \,;\, \ddagger T_2) & = & \ddagger(T_1 \,;\, T_2) \\
\ddagger(T_1 \,;\, T_2) & = & (\ddagger T_1 \,;\, \ddagger T_2) \cup (\ddagger T_1 \bowtie \ddagger T_2)
\end{array}
$$

where $A \bowtie B = \{\alpha(M, N)\beta \mid \alpha(M, N') \in A, \ (N', N)\beta \in B\}$

The "skip" laws   The program which "does nothing"—one which can never perform any reactions and therefore can only terminate—will be represented by a single reaction-action pair $(A \Leftarrow False)$. Since the reaction condition is false, the action A, and arity are irrelevant.

In terms of the basic input-ouput partial correctness ordering it is clear that $(A \Leftarrow False)$ obeys the usual "skip" laws of being an identity for sequential and parallel composition. However, in terms of operational approximation one of these identities fails. Namely,

$$(A \Leftarrow False) \circ P \not\equiv_o P$$

The intuition for this is that $(A \Leftarrow False)$ acts as a de-synchroniser for parallel composition: P must synchronise with its context in order to terminate, but with $(A \Leftarrow False) \circ P$, P is allowed to terminate autonomously, leaving $(A \Leftarrow False)$ to synchronise with its context—which it is trivially always able to do. As an example consider the following two atomic programs:

$$P_1 : x \to 0 \Leftarrow x = 1 \qquad P_2 : x \to 1 \Leftarrow x = 0.$$

Notice that, for example, $\langle P_1 + P_2, \{1\}\rangle$ can never terminate, but $\langle((A \Leftarrow False) \circ P_1) + P_2, \{1\}\rangle \to^* \{1\}$, and so $((A \Leftarrow False) \circ P_1) + P_2 \not\sqsubseteq_o P_1 + P_2$.

Note that we cannot prove any inequalities by appealing to the transition traces, because we lack full abstraction. However, the positive statement

$$P_1 + P_2 \sqsubseteq_o ((A \Leftarrow False) \circ P_1) + P_2$$

can be proved via the transition traces. It should be clear that $\mathsf{T}[\![(A \Leftarrow False)]\!] = \ddagger\{(M, M) \mid M \in \mathbf{M}\}$. Now consider a transition trace $\alpha \in \mathsf{T}[\![P]\!]$. Suppose that the last transition in α is (N', N). Since $(N, N) \in \mathsf{T}[\![(A \Leftarrow False)]\!]$ we know that

$$\alpha(N, N) \in (\mathsf{T}[\![P]\!] \,;\, \mathsf{T}[\![(A \Leftarrow False)]\!]).$$

By absorbtion it follows that

$$\alpha \in \ddagger(\mathsf{T}[\![P]\!] \, ; \, \mathsf{T}[\![(A \Leftarrow False)]\!]) = \mathsf{T}[\![(A \Leftarrow False) \circ P]\!].$$

The remaining compositions with the "skip" program are identities, and are provable by simple applications of the closure properties. Many of the following laws involve the "de-synchroniser", $(A \Leftarrow False)$.

The "chaos" laws There are programs that always diverge. Consider any nullary reaction $Chaos = (() \rightarrow A \Leftarrow True)$ which says: if the empty set is a subset of the multiset, replace that subset by A (some arbitrary multiset). Clearly such a reaction is always applicable, and as a consequence for all contexts $\mathbf{C}$ and programs P,

$$Chaos \equiv_t \mathbf{C}[Chaos] \sqsubseteq_t P.$$

More interestingly, the "near-chaos" program consisting of a *unary* reaction $Await_\theta = (x \rightarrow x \Leftarrow True)$ terminates only on the empty set, since for any other multiset the unary reaction condition is applicable. This program was used in [10] to show that the transition trace semantics is not fully abstract, by showing that for all programs P, $P \circ Await_\theta \sqsubseteq_o Await_\theta$, but that $P \circ Await_\theta \not\sqsubseteq_t Await_\theta$.

Proposition 6 (The sequential laws)

1. $P \circ (Q \circ R) \equiv_t (P \circ Q) \circ R$
2. $P \circ (A \Leftarrow False) \equiv_t P$
3. $P \sqsubseteq_t (A \Leftarrow False) \circ P$
4. $(A \Leftarrow R) \equiv_t (A \Leftarrow R) \circ (A \Leftarrow R)$

The first two laws follow directly from properties of the transition trace combinators. The last of the sequential laws is an instance of a more general law involving residual programs which we consider in the next section.

Proposition 7 (The parallel laws)

1. $P + (Q + R) \equiv_t (P + Q) + R$
2. $P + Q \equiv_t Q + P$
3. $P \equiv_t (A \Leftarrow False) + P$
4. $P \sqsubseteq_t P + P$
5. $(A \Leftarrow R) \equiv_t (A \Leftarrow R) + (A \Leftarrow R)$

PROOF   The fourth law has the least straightforward proof, which is given in essentially the same way as the proof for the corresponding input-output property in [6].

It is sufficient to show that the *strict traces*, $ST[\![P]\!]$ of a program P, defined to be

$$\begin{aligned}
ST[\![P]\!] = \quad & \{(M_0, N_0)(M_1, N_1) \ldots (M_k, N_k)| \\
& \langle P, M_0 \rangle \rightarrow \langle P_1, N_0 \rangle \ \& \\
& \langle P_1, M_1 \rangle \rightarrow \langle P_2, N_1 \rangle \ \& \ldots \& \ \langle P_k, M_k \rangle \rightarrow N_k\}
\end{aligned}$$

is contained in $\mathsf{T}[\![P + P]\!]$, since the closure of the strict traces yields the transition traces. The proof of this follows from an induction on the length of each strict transition trace. This uses the obsevation that every non-terminal transition of a program can be expressed by a proof whose last inference has one of two possible forms:

$$\text{active}\;\frac{\langle (A \Leftarrow R), M \rangle \rightarrow \langle (A \Leftarrow R), M' \rangle}{\langle \mathbf{A}[(A \Leftarrow R)], M \rangle \rightarrow \langle \mathbf{A}[(A \Leftarrow R)], M' \rangle}$$

and

$$\text{passive}\;\frac{\langle Q', M \rangle \rightarrow M}{\langle \mathbf{A}[Q \circ Q'], M \rangle \rightarrow \langle \mathbf{A}[Q], M \rangle}$$

Now it easily follows from the definition of active contexts that every *active* step $\langle R, N \rangle \rightarrow \langle R, N' \rangle$ can be matched (in a single step) by $R + R$, and every *passive* step $\langle R, N \rangle \rightarrow \langle R', N \rangle$ can be matched by two steps by $R + R$, *viz.*

$$\langle R + R, N \rangle \rightarrow \langle R' + R, N \rangle \rightarrow \langle R' + R', N \rangle.$$

The details of the induction are then straightforward. (We also have a slightly simpler proof by structural induction, using the second law of the next proposition) □

Proposition 8 (The Parallel-Sequential Laws)

1. $(P + Q) \circ R \sqsubseteq_t P + (Q \circ R)$
2. $(P_1 + P_2) \circ (Q_1 + Q_2) \sqsubseteq_t (P_1 \circ Q_1) + (P_2 \circ Q_2)$
3. $P \circ (Q + R) \sqsubseteq_t (P \circ Q) + (P \circ R)$

PROOF

1. $(P + Q) \circ R \equiv_t\;(P + Q) \circ ((A \Leftarrow False) + R)\quad [7(3)]$
   $\sqsubseteq_t\;(P \circ (A \Leftarrow False)) + (Q \circ R)\quad [8(2)]$
   $\equiv_t\;P + (Q \circ R)\quad [6(2)]$

2. Let $p_1 = \mathsf{T}[P_1], q_1 = \mathsf{T}[Q_1]$, etc. From the compositional definition, is necessary to show that

$$\ddagger(\ddagger(q_1 \oplus q_2) \,;\, \ddagger(p_1 \oplus p_2)) \subseteq \ddagger(\ddagger(q_1 \,;\, p_1) \oplus \ddagger(q_2 \,;\, p_2)).$$

By the properties of the closure operation, it is sufficient to show that

$$(q_1 \oplus q_2) \,;\, (p_1 \oplus p_2) \subseteq \ddagger((q_1 \,;\, p_1) \oplus (q_2 \,;\, p_2)).$$

The details are omitted.

3. $P \circ (Q + R) \sqsubseteq_t\;(P + P) \circ (Q + R)\quad [7(4)]$
   $\sqsubseteq_t\;(P \circ Q) + (P \circ R)\quad [8(2)]$

□

5 Residual Program Laws

In [6] a notion of "residual program" was introduced as a particularly simple syntactic characterisation of the program component of any configuration that is an immediate predecessor of a terminal configuration (multiset).

Definition 9 (Residual Program) The *residual part* of a program P, written $\underline{P}$, is defined by induction on the syntax:

$$\underline{(A \Leftarrow R)} = (A \Leftarrow R) \qquad \underline{P_1 \circ P_2} = \underline{P_1} \qquad \underline{P_1 + P_2} = \underline{P_1} + \underline{P_2}$$

This provides us with a simple (ie. weak) postcondition for programs via the following property:

$$\langle P, M \rangle \rightarrow^* N \iff \langle P, M \rangle \rightarrow^* \langle \underline{P}, N \rangle \rightarrow N$$

As a notational convinience, we define the predicate Φ on a program and a multiset to be true if and only if the residual part of the program is terminated with respect to the multiset:

$$\Phi(P, M) \Leftrightarrow \langle \underline{P}, M \rangle \rightarrow M.$$

Intuitively, $\Phi(P, M)$ holds if M is a possible result for the program P. The significance of this is that the predicate $\Phi(P, \_)$ can be constructed syntactically by considering (the negations of) the reaction conditions in $\underline{P}$.

A number of operational laws involving residual programs where presented in [6]. Here we show that these laws (and some additional ones) can be verified in our compositional model. The intuition behind the fact that laws also hold in the compositional model is that the residual part of a program expresses concisely the termination synchronisation requirement of the program with its context.

The following key result from [6] establishes when sequential composition correctly implements parallel combination:

$$(\forall M.(\Phi(Q, M) \wedge \langle P, M \rangle \rightarrow^* N) \Rightarrow \Phi(Q, N)) \Rightarrow P \circ Q \leq P + Q.$$

This does not hold for operational approximation because in the premise, it is assumed that P takes over from the execution of Q without interruption. An obvious strengthening of this premise gives

Proposition 10

$$(\forall M.\Phi(P, M) \Rightarrow \Phi(Q, M)) \Rightarrow P \circ Q \sqsubseteq_t P + Q$$

PROOF   Assuming $(\forall M.\Phi(P, M) \Rightarrow \Phi(Q, M))$, it is sufficient to prove that

$$\mathsf{T}[\![Q]\!] \, ; \mathsf{T}[\![P]\!] \subseteq \ddagger(\mathsf{T}[\![P]\!] \oplus \mathsf{T}[\![Q]\!])$$

The details are omitted.   □

Proposition 11 (Residual-Program Laws)

1. $P \equiv_t \underline{P} \circ P$
2. $(P + \underline{R}) \circ (Q + R) \sqsubseteq_t (P \circ Q) + R$
3. $(P \equiv_t \underline{P}) \Rightarrow (P \equiv_t P + P)$

PROOF   The first part is easily proved by noting the following operational property (see [6]):

$$\langle P, M \rangle \rightarrow^* \langle P', M' \rangle \Rightarrow \underline{P} = \underline{P'}.$$

The details are then straightforward from the operational definition of transition traces.

The second law is a consequence of the first, since

$$(P + \underline{R}) \circ (Q + R) \sqsubseteq_t \quad (P \circ Q) + (\underline{R} \circ R) \quad [8(2)]$$
$$\equiv_t \quad (P \circ Q) + R$$

The last part is a generalisation of 7(5), and hinges on the fact that residual programs cannot contain sequential compositions, so the result follows by a simple induction on the structure of residual programs.   □

The following proposition shows that residual programs arise naturally from the laws, by showing that every program is refined by (ie, approximated by) a "product of sums" of basic reactions.

Define $\sum_{i=1}^{n} P_i$ as $P_1 + \cdots + P_n$, and $\prod_{i=1}^{n} P_i$ as $P_1 \circ \cdots \circ P_n$.

Proposition 12 For all programs P, there exists a set of basic reactions

$$\{(A_{ij} \Leftarrow R_{ij}) \mid i \in \{1 \ldots n\}, j \in \{1 \ldots m_i\}\}$$

such that $\prod_i \sum_{j=1}^{m_i} (A_{ij} \Leftarrow R_{ij}) \sqsubseteq_t P$.

PROOF   We give a normalising rewrite system which constructs such a product-of-sums.

Consider the law 8(1) $(P+Q) \circ R \sqsubseteq_t P+(Q \circ R)$. Orienting this inequality from right to left gives the rewrite rule

$$P + (Q \circ R) \longrightarrow (P + Q) \circ R$$

from which we form an associative-commutative rewriting system $\longrightarrow_{ac}$ (see eg. [5]), with + as an associative-commutative operator and ∘ as a commutative operator. It should be clear that if $Q \longrightarrow_{ac} R$, then

1. $R \sqsubseteq_t Q$, and
2. if $R \not\longrightarrow_{ac}$ then R is a product-of-sums.

For termination we just use a simple polynomial interpretation of terms: interpret parallel composition as multiplication, sequential composition as sum, and the basic reactions as the integer 2. This interpretation respects the ac-equivalence, and it is simple to check that the rewrite strictly reduces the size of the corresponding interpretation (which is always positive).   □

Now we also have an interesting property of the above rewrite system with respect to residual programs, namely that the leftmost of the products is equal (modulo ac) to the residual of the original program. This can be seen as follows. The rewriting process obtains a program $(\prod_i P_i) \sqsubseteq_t P$ such that each of the P_i is of the form $\sum_j (A_j \Leftarrow R_j)$. Now we make use of the following:

$$\forall C. \underline{Q_1} = \underline{Q_2} \Rightarrow \underline{C[Q_1]} = \underline{C[Q_2]}$$

which is proved by a simple induction on contexts.

Now note that the rewrite rule preserves residual programs, and so by the above property, $\prod P_i$ is equivalent to $\underline{P}$ up to associativity and commutativity of $+$. Since each $\overline{P_i}$ contains no sequential compositions, then $\underline{P} = \prod P_i = P_1$.

More "parallel" sums of products can be produced by using law $8(2)$ as a rewrite rule. One possible interest of this result is that programs in the form of a product of sums are relatively easy to reason about in the manner of [2], and is likely to simplify the application of the compositional logic of [8], since it localises the parallel compositions.

6 Conclusions

We have presented the (in)equational partial correctness properties of the combination of sequential and parallel composition operators for Gamma programs, provable from the compositional semantics first presented in [10]. We have shown that almost all of the laws of the (non-monotonic) input-output ordering considered in earlier work [6], including the "residual program" laws, also hold in this model. The equational reasoning provided by the compositional semantics simplifies a number of the earlier proofs, and has revealed an interesting factorisation law which says that every program is refined by a product-of-sums.

Acknowlegements

Thanks to Simon Gay for comments on an earlier draft, and to Fritz Henglein for some useful technical suggestions. This work was supported by the Danish Research Council, DART Project (5.21.08.03).

References

[1] K. Abrahamson. Modal logic of concurrent nondeterministic programs. In *Proceedings of the International Symposium on Semantics of Concurrent Computation*, volume 70, pages 21–33. Springer-Verlag, 1979.

[2] J.-P. Banâtre and D. Le Métayer. The Gamma model and its discipline of programming. *Science of Computer Programming*, 15:55–77, 1990.

[3] J.-P. Banâtre and D. Le Métayer. Programming by multiset transformation. *CACM*, January 1993. (INRIA research report 1205, April 1990).

[4] S. Brookes. Full abstraction for a shared variable parallel language. In *Logic In Computer Science*, 1993. (to appear).

[5] N. Dershowitz and J-P. Jouannaud. *Rewrite Systems*, volume B, chapter 15. North-Holland, 1989.

[6] C. Hankin, D. Le Métayer, and D. Sands. A calculus of Gamma programs. Research Report DOC 92/22 (28 pages), Department of Computing, Imperial College, 1992. (short version to appear in the Proceedings of the Fifth Annual Workshop on Languages and Compilers for Parallelism, Aug 1992, Springer-Verlag).

[7] M. Hennessy and G. D. Plotkin. Full abstraction for a simple parallel programming lanuage. In *Mathematical Foundations of Computer Science*, volume 74 of *LNCS*, pages 108–120. Springer-Verlag, 1979.

[8] C. Hankin L. Errington and T. Jensen. Reasoning about Gamma programs. In this volume.

[9] L. Lamport. The Temporal Logic of Actions. Technical Report 79, DEC Systems Research Center, Palo Alto, CA, 1991.

[10] D. Sands. A compositional semantics of combining forms for Gamma programs. In *International Conference on Formal Methods in Programming and Their Applications*. Springer-Verlag, 1993.

Implementing Process Calculi in C

Zvi Schreiber

mzs@doc.ic.ac.uk

Department of Computing, Imperial College
180 Queen's Gate, London SW7 2BZ, United Kingdom

Abstract

Process calculi are commonly used to specify and verify communication protocols. Once verified, it is desirable to be able to implement a protocol or other concurrent design using automatic assistance and in a provably correct way. Previously, the author has introduced a representation for a process calculus program in the form of a graph with parameters. A formally proved mapping from CCS programs to this representation has also been presented. Here we present a translation from the representation to a subset of C which has a formal semantics. The translation is formally defined and proved correct (the proof is not included here but is presented in [14]). While other work has already been done on such translations, this is the first translation with a correctness proof, therefore being more in the spirit of formal methods. Further, we introduce a flexible approach to resolving non-determinism which gives this translation a practical advantage.

Introduction

Process calculi offer a formal framework for the specification and verification of concurrent systems such as communication protocols. The paper assumes some familiarity with process calculi. Examples of process calculi are LOTOS [2], CCS [10], CSP [5] and ACP [1].

In most cases some of the components will be implemented in software. C [8] is a popular choice of programming language for reasons of performance and portability. Automatic translation is clearly both quicker and safer than manual coding. Further, the author has found that translation offers an easy way of making formal specifications accessible to non-experts as well as providing rapid prototyping.

Of course, process calculus specifications have abstractions which leave some choices to be made at implementation time. We start by outlining our approach to these.

Data types While different process calculi have broadly similar constructors, the data types used for the values seem to have little in common. For example, LOTOS uses algebraic data types based on ACT ONE while CCS is usually used with concrete types [3]. This paper, which is not intended to be specific to a particular calculus, does not address the issue of data types and assumes that a mapping for implementing the expressions of the process calculus is provided.

External actions For every external channel, the C code assumes that two *interface routines* are provided by the user, one implementing output and one implementing input on the channel. These routines may return a bad return code if the communication is not available.

Non-determinism Non-determinism in process calculi has two distinct roles:

♦ leaving open more than one choice of implementation

♦ allowing a choice of actions to be resolved by the environment at run time.

In the translation presented in this paper, each state is implemented as a loop which repeatedly calls the interface routines for the transitions available in that state. If the routine returns a negative return code, the loop will try some other action and may eventually retry this unavailable action. The user can achieve the above aims (respectively) by the following means.

♦ At translation time, the user may influence the translation and choose the order in which the actions of a particular state are tried by the code.

♦ The user programs the interface routines which control the strategy of how long particular actions are tried for, allowing the actual behaviour to be determined at run time.

The looping does not imply a *busy waiting* scheme. The user is free to use blocking I/O calls in the interface routines or to cause execution to be suspended for some time when an action is unavailable.

Parallelism Parallelism is also used in different ways. When verifying a system, we usually have a composite agent $A_1 | A_2 | \cdots$ representing the entire system. Here, some of the A_i may model hardware components and others software components. At this high level we would simply expect to pick out the components to be implemented by software and translate those.

Within a particular component, parallelism is used as an architectural mechanism. Here, the user must choose whether to implement these in a distributed way or to "cross product" the different agents to obtain a single sequential program which is large and fast. Our method allows the latter approach. The user can still revert to the former by translating different components separately (and writing interface routines which use inter-process communication to achieve synchronisation).

We do not assume any multi-tasking ability on the target system so any dynamic parallelism (where an agent has a transition leading to a composite agent) must be implemented sequentially.

Outline

In [13, §1], a representation was introduced for process calculus programs as well as a verified mapping from CCS programs to the representation. This representation is described in Section 1 and is the starting point for our translation. Section 2 introduces a subset of C which is sufficient for our translation and defines an operational semantics for this subset. In Section 3, the translation is presented.

1 Representation

1.1 Restrictions

We are interested in agents that lend themselves to verification and to implementation without dynamic allocation of resources. The following restrictions on the process calculus agents are therefore imposed.

♦ No agent may have infinitely many different transitions (different instances of $a?(\underline{x})$ are counted as one). In value-passing CCS this can be guaranteed by banning unguarded recursion and infinite $\sum$s.

♦ No agent may be able to evolve into infinitely many other agents (different instances of $A(\underline{x})$ counting as one). In value-passing CCS this can be guaranteed by banning any parallel operator | from occurring within a recursion.

Note that many systems, particularly low level protocols, obey these restrictions.

1.2 The need for representation

Consider the CCS-like specification of a buffer *Buff* which reads values on *in* and outputs even integers on channel *even*! and odd integers on channel *odd*!.

$$Buff \quad := \quad in?(x).Buff'(x)$$
$$Buff'(x) \quad := \quad \textbf{if } even(x) \textbf{ then } even!(x).Buff \textbf{ else } odd!(x).Buff$$

Starting from *Buff*, notice that under the standard operational semantics of CCS the only reachable states are *Buff* and $Buff'(v)$ for different values of v. In general, given the above restrictions, all the reachable states will be instantiations of finitely many value-passing agents. This leads to the idea of representing an agent by a finite directed graph in which each node corresponds to one such value-passing agent and is associated with parameters and each edge is decorated with details of the transition it represents.

Such a representation makes further work independent of the underlying process calculus and free of the burden of interpreting the process calculus syntax. Most importantly, the parallel operators are "cross producted" in generating the representation so the representation is purely sequential.

The *parameterised graph* (*p.g.*) construct has been introduced by the author for this purpose and is now presented. In [13, §1], compositional operators are given to transform a CCS agent definition into a *p.g.*. The transformation is proved correct. Taken together with the present paper, a fully verified translation from CCS to C is achieved.

1.3 Parameterised graphs

Assume that the values in the process calculus language are all taken from a set V (ranged over by v, w) and that sorts are taken from U (ranged over by u). Each element $u \in U$ is a subset of V. Whenever S is a set we will write $\underline{S}$ for $\bigcup_{n \in \mathbb{N}} S^n$.

Description of parameterised graphs Firstly, every graph has a set Act of channels (consisting of the names of all channels declared in the underlying program) and a function Γ_A with domain Act associating each channel with a sort[1]. Let Act be ranged over by a.

The set (ranged over by α) of actions possible in a $p.g.$ $\mathcal{P}$ is given by:

$$act(\mathcal{P}) = \{\tau\} \cup \{a?(\underline{v}) : a \in Act, \underline{v} \in \Gamma_A(a)\} \cup \{a!(\underline{v}) : a \in Act, \underline{v} \in \Gamma_A(a)\}.$$

τ is an internal action; $a!(\underline{v})$ represents the output of value $\underline{v}$ on channel a and $a?(\underline{v})$ represents the input of value $\underline{v}$ on channel a.

A $p.g.$ has a set of nodes $\wp$ (ranged over by p, q) and a map Γ_N associating each node with a sort. There is a distinguished initial node $\iota \in \wp$.

The set of states of a parameterised graph $\mathcal{P}$ is given by:

$$state(\mathcal{P}) = \{p(\underline{v}) : p \in \wp, \underline{v} \in \Gamma_N(p)\}.$$

We now need to describe the transitions. Suppose node p has an internal (τ) transition. We need to know which node q the transition leads to. We also need to know for what values of p's parameters this transition is possible (since this could be restricted by an **if**). This is given by a function γ from $\Gamma_N(p)$ to $\{\mathbf{true}, \mathbf{false}\}$. Finally, we need a function f which, given the value of the parameters of p, gives the values of the parameters of q after the transition. So we mark an internal transition by a tuple $tau(q, \gamma, f)$.

A send transition is marked by a tuple $send(a, q, \gamma, f, g)$ where a is the channel name, q, γ, f are as before, and g is a function mapping the values of the parameters of p to the values of the output. A receive transition is marked by $rcv(a, q, \gamma, f)$ where f's domain is now the product of the sort of p and the sort of a. Given the values of p's parameters *and* the values of the input, f gives the values of the parameters of q following the transition.

Definition 1.1 A parameterised graph is a tuple $(Act, \Gamma_A, \wp, \iota, \Gamma_N, T)$ where:

♦ Act and $\wp$ are finite disjoint sets   ♦ $\Gamma_A : Act \to \underline{U}$, $\Gamma_N : \wp \to \underline{U}$ ♦ $\iota \in \wp$

♦ $\Gamma_N(\iota)$ is the singleton set[2] $\{()\}$

♦ for each $p \in \wp$, $T(p)$ is a finite set of elements of type $tau(q, \gamma, f)$, $rcv(a, q, \gamma, f)$ or $send(a, q, \gamma, f, g)$ where $q \in \wp$; $a \in Act$; $\gamma : \Gamma_N(p) \to bool$; $f : \Gamma_N(p) \to \Gamma_N(q)$, or, in a rcv, $f : \Gamma_N(p) \times \Gamma_A(a) \to \Gamma_N(q)$; and, finally, $g : \Gamma_N(p) \to \Gamma_A(a)$.

We call the domain of all parameterised graphs[3] PG, ranged over by $\mathcal{P}$.

---

[1]In fact we allow the sort to be a product $u_1 \times \cdots \times u_n$ so that channels can pass tuples $\underline{v}$. This is standard in LOTOS but unusual for other calculi.

[2]This condition is not strictly necessary. We introduce it to save us worrying about what the initial parameters mean in the context of a C program. If we give this some meaning — for example having the program read these values from the command line — we can drop this restriction.

[3]Strictly, we define two graphs to be isomorphic if one is obtained from the other by relabelling $\wp$ and take PG to be the set of equivalence classes.

Example The parameterised graph $\mathcal{P} = (Act, \Gamma_A, \wp, \iota, \Gamma_N, T)$ is a representation of *Buff* if we let:

$$
\begin{aligned}
Act &= \{in, even, odd\} & \Gamma_A &= \{(in, \mathbb{N}), (even, \mathbb{N}), (odd, \mathbb{N})\} \\
\wp &= \{Empty, Full\} & \iota &= Empty \\
\Gamma_N &= \{(Empty, \{()\}), (Full, \mathbb{N})\} \\
T &= \{(Empty, \{rcv(in, Full, \lambda v \in \{()\}.\mathbf{true}, \lambda v \in \{()\}.v)\}) \\
&\quad\quad (Full, \{send(even, Empty, \lambda v \in \mathbb{N}.e(v), \lambda v \in \mathbb{N}.(), \lambda v \in \mathbb{N}.v), \\
&\quad\quad\quad\quad send(odd, Empty, \lambda v \in \mathbb{N}.o(v), \lambda v \in \mathbb{N}.(), \lambda v \in \mathbb{N}.v)\})\}
\end{aligned}
$$

where we have represented functions by their graphs and where e and o are predicates which respectively hold when their arguments are even and odd. □

1.4 Operational Semantics

We give a parameterised graph $\mathcal{P} = (Act, \Gamma_A, \wp, \iota, \Gamma_N, T)$ an operational semantics in the form of a *labelled transition system* (*l.t.s.*) $(state(\mathcal{P}), act(\mathcal{P}), \rightarrow)$.

The transition relation $\rightarrow \subseteq state(\mathcal{P}) \times act(\mathcal{P}) \times state(\mathcal{P})$ is defined to be the least relation such that:

$$
\begin{aligned}
send(a, q, \gamma, f, g) \in T(p) \wedge \underline{v} \in \Gamma_N(p) \wedge \gamma(\underline{v}) &\Rightarrow p(\underline{v}) \xrightarrow{a!(g(\underline{v}))} q(f(\underline{v})) \\
rcv(a, q, \gamma, f) \in T(p) \wedge \underline{v} \in \Gamma_N(p) \wedge \underline{w} \in \Gamma_A(a) \wedge \gamma(\underline{v}) &\Rightarrow p(\underline{v}) \xrightarrow{a?(\underline{w})} q(f(\underline{v}, \underline{w})) \\
tau(q, \gamma, f) \in T(p) \wedge \underline{v} \in \Gamma_N(p) \wedge \gamma(\underline{v}) &\Rightarrow p(\underline{v}) \xrightarrow{\tau} q(f(\underline{v})).
\end{aligned}
$$

In the above example we would derive transitions such as:

$$
\begin{aligned}
Empty() &\xrightarrow{in?(0)} Full(0), & Empty() &\xrightarrow{in?(1)} Full(1), \cdots \\
Full(0) &\xrightarrow{even!(0)} Empty(), & Full(1) &\xrightarrow{odd!(1)} Empty(), \cdots.
\end{aligned}
$$

1.5 Extensions for LOTOS

The LOTOS model of communications is somewhat different to that of CCS, CSP and ACP. A modified version of a *p.g.* is therefore needed to represent LOTOS agents and different interface routines are needed to implement LOTOS agents. This is discussed in [14].

2 The target language

2.1 Interface routines

The choice of subset of C is very much based upon our use of interface routines so these are described first.

We assume that, for each channel, the programmer will write two routines which will be linked in with the code we generate. For the channel *in*, for example, we may take the *base name* of these routines to be **in**. We then assume that there will be two routines provided, **in_s()** and **in_r()**.

The first of these is passed some values and it waits for a certain amount of time to see if it can send these values synchronously on the channel modelled by *in*. It returns a boolean indicating whether a communication took place. The second of these waits for a while to see if values can be received synchronously and, if so, passes back the values and a return code of **true**. The values are passed back in variables supplied by the calling code using a call-by-name mechanism. If there are internal transitions, the programmer must also write a routine **tau()** which returns a boolean indicating whether an internal transition should occur.

The programmer must prove that these routines will always return; that they give a **true** return code *iff* the relevant transition has occurred; and that a receive routine modifies the variables passed to it to give the received value, but does not modify the variables if a transitions does not occur.

2.2 The syntax of C′

We only need a subset of C's commands and structures to implement parameterised graphs. We now introduce a convenient subset of C and call it C′. Our intention, of course, is that the semantics we give to a C′ program I is equivalent to the semantics of I viewed as a C program. This cannot be proved, however, since C does not have a formal semantics.

Basic syntactic categories Let *ident* be the set of variable identifiers consisting of a letter followed by alphanumerics and underscores and ranged over by x, y, z. Let *name* be the set of possible base names for external functions, defined as for *ident* and ranged over by F.

Let *expr* consist of C expressions ranged over by e with the subcategory of boolean valued expressions ranged over by b. *expr* must include each identifier x in *ident* as an expression giving the value associated with x. Let *sexpr* consist of C sort expressions ranged over by s including the distinguished sort **bool** (which is not standard C but may easily be defined). We do not specify *expr* and *sexpr*. We assume that they express precisely the same values as their counterparts in the values language of the underlying process calculus.

Function declarations The program must start by declaring all (externally defined) functions called. The declaration consists of the type of the return code, the name of the function, a list of the types of the parameters enclosed in parentheses and a semi-colon. The type of the parameter may be followed by a * to indicate a call-by-name convention. In this case the function is called with **&x** (where x is an identifier of appropriate type) instead of an expression and the function may modify the value associated with x. In C′ we need only allow declarations of the interface routines. The allowed declarations are therefore **bool tau();** or pairs of declarations:

   bool $F\_s(s_1, \ldots, s_n)$;   **bool** $F\_r(s_1*, \ldots, s_n*)$;.

These functions are respectively called using **tau()**, $F\_s(e_1, \ldots, e_n)$ and, for a receive, $F\_r(\&x_1, \ldots, \&x_n)$. We will use $\bar{b}$ to range over such function calls.

Variable definitions Global variables are defined after the function declarations and may be assigned an initial value (we will make use of this to assign an initial value to the state variable). We have no need for local variables in our translation so these are excluded from C′. A variable x of type s is defined by $s \ x;$, or is defined and initialised to the value of expression e by $s \ x=e$.

The statements We use d to range over statements and D to range over sequences of statements. The main body of the program consists of the string `main()` followed by a compound statement — a sequence of statements enclosed in braces, $\{D\}$.

The simplest statement is an assignment `x=e;`. Infinite repeating of the statement d is performed by `for (;;)` d. Conditionals have the form:

`if` (b') `then` d_1 [`else` d_2].

Here b' may be a boolean expression, b, or a call to an interface routine, $\bar{b}$ (as specified above). It may also be a conjunction b `&&` $\bar{b}$. In C, the second conjunct is not evaluated if the first is false.

Any statement d may be labelled `case` $e:d$. The `switch` (e') $\{D\}$ statement causes execution to jump to the first labelled statement in D with expression e equal in value to e'. `break;` causes a jump to the end of the switch statement.

A more formal definition of the syntax of C' is presented in [14].

2.3 Operational Semantics

We now introduce a set of states and an operational semantics for C', so that we will be able to prove the correctness of our translation. The semantics is a *Structural Operational Semantics* (or small-step semantics, [12, 11]). *Natural semantics* (or big-step semantics, [11]) are inappropriate as we are not interested in termination.

Assume that the set of possible values of C expressions is V just as for the process calculus values language. Similarly, assume that the set of possible sorts is again U. (In fact, we could allow the set of values to be any set $V_{c'}$ provided there were a surjective partial map $\theta : V_{c'} \hookrightarrow V$. However this extra generality complicates the notation and is not particularly profound.)

We assume that we are equipped with a function:

$$\mathcal{V}[\![\ ]\!] : expr \to (ident \to V_\perp) \to V_\perp$$

which is overloaded to evaluate elements of $expr$ and $sexpr$ (given a mapping from variables to values).

Let $I \in C'$ be a program. Define the states of I:

$$state_{c'}(I) = \{(\{D\}, \sigma) : valid(\{D\}, I), \sigma \in store(I)\}.$$

The idea is that in state (d, σ) the program has compound statement d left to execute and store σ. In this definition $valid(d, I)$ means that all identifiers and external functions referenced within statement d are declared or defined in I and $store(I) \subseteq (ident \to V_\perp)$ consists of all functions σ with no type errors[4] with respect to the variable definitions in I.

We must now define the possible transitions on the set of states. Most transitions would be performed internally by the interpreter or CPU in a deterministic manner and these will be written $\longrightarrow$. The exception is when a call is made to an external routine (always in an `if`). The routine may return **false**

---

[4]This means that for $x \in ident$, either $\sigma(x) = \perp$ or I includes a definition "$s\ x$;" or "$s\ x = e$;" for some s, and $\sigma(x) \in \mathcal{V}[\![s]\!](\lambda x'.\perp)$.

case	$(\{\texttt{case } e:\quad d\}, \sigma) \twoheadrightarrow (\{d\}, \sigma)$
assgn	$(\{x\texttt{=}e;\}, \sigma) \twoheadrightarrow (\{\}, \sigma[x \mapsto v]) \quad \mathcal{V}[\![e]\!]\sigma = v$
cmpnd	$(\{\{D\}\}, \sigma) \twoheadrightarrow (\{D\}, \sigma)$
comp	$(\{D_1\}, \sigma) \xrightarrow{\alpha} (\{D_1'\}, \sigma') \Rightarrow (\{D_1 D_2\}, \sigma) \xrightarrow{\alpha} (\{D_1' D_2\}, \sigma')$
for	$(\{\texttt{for}(;;)\ d\}, \sigma) \twoheadrightarrow (\{d\ \texttt{for}(;;)\ d\}, \sigma)$
switch$_1$	$(\{\texttt{switch } (e_1)\ \{\texttt{case } e_2 : d_1\ \dots d_n\}\}, \sigma) \twoheadrightarrow (\{d_1 \dots d_r\}, \sigma)$ $\qquad \begin{cases} \mathcal{V}[\![e_1]\!]\sigma = \mathcal{V}[\![e_2]\!]\sigma \\ r = n \text{ or } d_{r+1} = \texttt{break} \\ \forall i \leq r : d_i \neq \texttt{break}; \end{cases}$
switch$_2$	$(\{\texttt{switch } (e_1)\ \{\texttt{case } e_2 : d_1\ \dots d_n\}\}, \sigma) \twoheadrightarrow (\{\texttt{switch } (e_1)\ \{d_1 \dots d_n\}\}, \sigma) \qquad \mathcal{V}[\![e_1]\!]\sigma \neq \mathcal{V}[\![e_2]\!]\sigma$
switch$_3$	$(\{\texttt{switch } (e_1)\ \{d_1\ \dots d_n\}\}, \sigma) \twoheadrightarrow (\{\texttt{switch } (e_1)\ \{d_2 \dots d_n\}\}, \sigma) \qquad d_1 \text{ not labelled}$
switch$_4$	$(\{\texttt{switch } (e_1)\ \{\}\}, \sigma) \twoheadrightarrow (\{\}, \sigma)$
if	$(\{\texttt{if } (b)\ d\}, \sigma) \twoheadrightarrow (\{\texttt{if } (b)\ d\ \texttt{else } \{\}\}, \sigma)$
if$_t$	$(\{\texttt{if } (b)\ d_1\ \texttt{else } d_2\}, \sigma) \twoheadrightarrow (\{d_1\}, \sigma) \quad \mathcal{V}[\![b]\!]\sigma = \textbf{true}$
if$_f$	$(\{\texttt{if } (b)\ d_1\ \texttt{else } d_2\}, \sigma) \twoheadrightarrow (\{d_2\}, \sigma) \quad \mathcal{V}[\![b]\!]\sigma = \textbf{false}$
if$_t^{\&\&}$	$(\{\texttt{if } (b\ \&\&\ \bar{b})\ d_1\ \texttt{else } d_2\}, \sigma) \twoheadrightarrow (\{\texttt{if } (\bar{b})\ d_1\ \texttt{else } d_2\}, \sigma) \quad \mathcal{V}[\![b]\!]\sigma = \textbf{true}$
if$_f^{\&\&}$	$(\{\texttt{if } (b\ \&\&\ \bar{b})\ d_1\ \texttt{else } d_2\}, \sigma) \twoheadrightarrow (\{d_2\}, \sigma) \quad \mathcal{V}[\![b]\!]\sigma = \textbf{false}$
if$_t^{\tau}$	$(\{\texttt{if } (\texttt{tau}())\ d_1\ \texttt{else } d_2\}, \sigma) \xrightarrow{\tau} (\{d_1\}, \sigma)$
if$_t^!$	$(\{\texttt{if } (F\_\texttt{s}(e_1, \dots, e_n))\ d_1\ \texttt{else } d_2\}, \sigma) \xrightarrow{F!(\underline{v})} (\{d_1\}, \sigma)\ \mathcal{V}[\![e]\!]\sigma = \underline{v}$
if$_t^?$	$(\{\texttt{if } (F\_\texttt{r}(\&x_1, \dots, \&x_n))\ d_1\ \texttt{else } d_2\}, \sigma) \xrightarrow{F?(\underline{v})} (\{d_1\}, \sigma') \qquad \begin{cases} \underline{v} \in sort_{c'}(F) \\ \sigma' = \sigma[x_i \mapsto v_i] \end{cases}$
if$_f^{\tau!?}$	$(\{\texttt{if } (\bar{b})\ d_1\ \texttt{else } d_2\}, \sigma) \twoheadrightarrow (\{d_2\}, \sigma)$

Figure 1: The semantics of a program $I \in C'$

at run time and we will skip the following statement. It may also return **true** (causing us to execute the statement), but this will only happen if an outside interaction has occurred. A transition which relies on an external interaction (that is, relies on an interface routine returning **true**) is marked $\xrightarrow{\alpha}$ where α is an element of the set of external actions over I which we now define by:

$$act_{c'}(I) = \{F!(\underline{v}) : \underline{v} \in sort_{c'}(F)\} \cup \{F?(\underline{v}) : \underline{v} \in sort_{c'}(F)\} \cup \{\tau\}.$$

Here $sort_{c'}(F)$ represents the value $\mathcal{V}[\![s_1]\!](\lambda x.\bot) \times \cdots \times \mathcal{V}[\![s_n]\!](\lambda x.\bot)$ where I contains the declaration **bool** $F\_s(s_1,\ldots,s_n)$; **bool** $F\_r(s_1*,\ldots,s_n*)$;.

$\xrightarrow{}$ will therefore be non-deterministic, with the transition corresponding to a return code of **true** labelled by the relevant action and the transition corresponding to **false** unlabelled.

Formally, we define the relation $\longrightarrow \subseteq state_{c'}(I) \times (\{\varepsilon\} \cup act_{c'}(I)) \times state_{c'}(I)$ to be the smallest satisfying the rules of Figure 1 (ε indicating an unlabelled transition).

In looking at transitions from one program state to another, we will mostly be interested in what external routines have returned **true** at some point in between. We therefore write $(I',\sigma) \xrightarrow{\alpha_1}\cdots\xrightarrow{\alpha_n} (I'',\sigma')$ where $\alpha_i \in act_{c'}(I)$ whenever:

$$(I',\sigma)\,(\longrightarrow)^*\xrightarrow{\alpha_1}(\longrightarrow)^*\cdots(\longrightarrow)^*\xrightarrow{\alpha_n}(\longrightarrow)^*\,(I'',\sigma').$$

Read this *there is an execution path from (I',σ) to (I'',σ') assuming the transitions $\alpha_1,\ldots,\alpha_n$ occur.* We will write $\Longrightarrow$ when $n = 0$. We will also write $(I',\sigma) \Longrightarrow_1 (I'',\sigma')$ when there is precisely one labelled transition.

The *initial state* of any program I is $(main(I),\sigma)$. Here σ is such that for each definition "s $x = e$;" appearing in I, $\sigma(x) = \mathcal{V}[\![e]\!](\lambda x'.\bot)$ and σ maps all other variables to $\bot$. $main(I)$ is the compound statement introduced by **main()**.

3 The PG to C′ translation

Let $\mathcal{P} = (Act, \Gamma_A, \wp, \iota, \Gamma_N, T)$ be a *p.g.* fixed throughout this section and the next. Let $\alpha(p) = |\Gamma_N(p)|$ give the number of parameters of node p and $\alpha(a) = |\Gamma_A(a)|$ give the number of parameters of channel a.

3.1 Preliminaries

Suppose we are equipped with the following C′ expressions, base names for external functions and identifiers where all the base names are distinct and all the identifiers are distinct and not equal to **state**.

♦ For each $p \in \wp$ and $1 \le i \le \alpha(p)$, let e_i^p be an expression implementing the sort u_i where $\Gamma_N(p) = u_1 \times \cdots \times u_n$. This means that $\mathcal{V}[\![e_i^p]\!](\lambda x.\bot) = u_i$. Write $\underline{e}^p$ for $e_1^p,\cdots,e_n^p$. Similarly for $a \in Act$ and $1 \le i \le \alpha(a)$ let e_i^a implement the sort of channel a's i-th parameter.

♦ For each channel $a \in Act$, let the interface routines implementing communications on that channel be F^a_s, F^a_r.

♦ We will use a state variable to keep track of the state we are in. For each $p \in \wp$ let K^p be a unique integer which will be assigned to the state variable when we are in state p.

♦ In the code for state $p \in \wp$ we need variables to store the values of p's parameters. (The values of these variables will be irrelevant when the state variable is not equal to K^p.) For each $p \in \wp$ and $1 \leq i \leq \alpha(p)$, let $x_i^p \in ident$ be the variable which will store the value of p's i-th parameter. We will use the notation $\sigma(\underline{x}^p)$ for $(\sigma(x_1^p), \ldots, \sigma(x_{\alpha(p)}^p))$.

♦ When undergoing a transition from node p to node q we must assign values to the x_i^q by evaluating expressions involving the x_i^p. This causes problems when $p = q$ since we might modify x_1^p only to find that its old value is needed in the calculation of x_2^p. For each p and i we therefore need an additional variable y_i^p for temporary storage.

♦ When a routine F^a_r is called to check for input on channel $a \in Act$, it needs a mechanism for passing back the values of the input. For each $a \in Act$ and $1 \leq i \leq \alpha(a)$, let $z_i^a \in ident$ be the temporary variable in which the i-th parameter of the input on a will be passed back.

We also assume that we are equipped with a general mapping providing expressions which implement functions in the $p.g..$ Let $\| \ \|_{C'}^{fn} : (V \hookrightarrow V) \times \underline{ident} \to expr$ where $\|f, \underline{x}\|_{C'}^{fn}$ gives a tuple of expressions implementing f in terms of the variables $\underline{x}$. This means that $\forall \sigma : V[\![\|f, \underline{x}\|_{C'}^{fn}]\!]\sigma = f(\sigma(\underline{x}))$.

Example Continuing the buffer example of §1.3 we will let $F^{in} = \mathbf{in}$, $F^{even} = \mathbf{even}$ and $F^{odd} = \mathbf{odd}$. We therefore assume that the there will be routines $\mathbf{in\_r}$, $\mathbf{in\_s}$ etc. available to the program we generate for $Buff$. We further let $K^{Empty} = 0$, $K^{Full} = 1$, $x_1^{Full} = \mathbf{value}$, $y_1^{Full} = \mathbf{value\_tmp}$, and finally $z_1^{in} = \mathbf{in\_1}$.

A real translator would automatically generate these names using the names from the process calculus specification. □

3.2 The declarations and definitions

We can give the function declaration and variable definition parts of the program in terms of $\mathcal{P}$ by:

$$\|\mathcal{P}\|_{C'}^{fdecl} = \left\{ \begin{array}{l} \mathtt{bool\ tau();} \\[4pt] \mathtt{bool\ } F^{a_1}\_\mathtt{s}(e_1^{a_1}, \ldots, e_{\alpha(a_1)}^{a_1}); \quad \mathtt{bool\ } F^{a_1}\_\mathtt{r}(e_1^{a_1}*, \ldots, e_{\alpha(a_1)}^{a_1}*); \\ \qquad\qquad \vdots \qquad\qquad\qquad\qquad\qquad \vdots \\ \mathtt{bool\ } F^{a_j}\_\mathtt{s}(e_1^{a_j}, \ldots, e_{\alpha(a_j)}^{a_j}); \quad \mathtt{bool\ } F^{a_j}\_\mathtt{r}(e_1^{a_j}*, \ldots, e_{\alpha(a_j)}^{a_j}*); \end{array} \right.$$

$$\|\mathcal{P}\|_{C'}^{vdefn} = \left\{ \begin{array}{llll} e_1^{p_1}\ x_1^{p_1}; \ \ldots\ e_{\alpha(p_1)}^{p_1}\ x_{\alpha(p_1)}^{p_1}; & \cdots & e_1^{p_k}\ x_1^{p_k}; \ \ldots\ e_{\alpha(p_k)}^{p_k}\ x_{\alpha(p_k)}^{p_k}; \\ e_1^{p_1}\ y_1^{p_1}; \ \ldots\ e_{\alpha(p_1)}^{p_1}\ y_{\alpha(p_1)}^{p_1}; & \cdots & e_1^{p_k}\ y_1^{p_k}; \ \ldots\ e_{\alpha(p_k)}^{p_k}\ y_{\alpha(p_k)}^{p_k}; \\ e_1^{a_1}\ z_1^{a_1}; \ \ldots\ e_{\alpha(a_1)}^{a_1}\ z_{\alpha(a_1)}^{a_1}; & \cdots & e_1^{a_j}\ z_1^{a_j}; \ \ldots\ e_{\alpha(a_j)}^{a_j}\ z_{\alpha(a_j)}^{a_j}; \\ \mathtt{int\ state\ =\ } K^{\iota}; \end{array} \right.$$

where $p_1, \ldots, p_k$ is an enumeration of $\wp$, and $a_1, \ldots, a_j$ is an enumeration of Act.

3.3 The main body of the program

A single transition When we make a transition from node p to node q we need a way to set up parameters for q. Suppose the function f expresses the relationship between the parameters. In terms of the parameters of p, the i-th parameter of q may be assigned the expression $\|(f)_i, \underline{x}^p\|_{C'}^{\text{fn}}$. If e_i is a shorthand for this expression then one way of doing this is:

$$\|p, q, f\|_{C'}^{\text{assgn}} \;=\; y_1^q = e_1; \;\cdots\; y_n^q = e_n; \qquad x_1^q = y_1^q; \;\cdots\; x_n^q = y_n^q;$$

Now recall that in the case of a *rcv* action, the values of the parameters of q must be calculated in terms of the parameters of p *and* the input values (stored in the z_i^a). In this case, f takes more parameters so, if the input is on channel a, we will let e_i be a shorthand for $\|(f)_i, \underline{x}^p \underline{z}^a\|_{C'}^{\text{fn}}$ and define $\|p, q, a, f\|_{C'}^{\text{assgn}'}$ by the same expression as $\| \;\|_{C'}^{\text{assgn}}$.

A single transition $t \in T(p)$ of node p is implemented by a test for the preconditions (given by γ) followed, if successful, by a call to the interface routine and a test of the return code. If the return code is **true** then the variables are adjusted to the new state. Let:

♦ $e^\gamma = \|\gamma, \underline{x}^p\|_{C'}^{\text{fn}}$ and $(e_1^g, \ldots, e_{\alpha(a)}^g) = \|g, \underline{x}^p\|_{C'}^{\text{fn}}$

♦ $\bar{b}$ be the C function call $\begin{cases} F^a\_\text{s}(e_1^g, \ldots, e_{\alpha(a)}^g) & \text{if } t = send(a, q, \gamma, f, g) \\ F^a\_\text{r}(\&z_1^a, \ldots, \&z_{\alpha(a)}^a) & \text{if } t = rcv(a, q, \gamma, f) \\ \text{tau}() & \text{if } t = tau(q, \gamma, f) \end{cases}$

♦ d_t be the statements $\|p, q, f\|_{C'}^{\text{assgn}}$ or $\|p, q, a, f\|_{C'}^{\text{assgn}'}$ as appropriate

and define $\|p, t\|_{C'}^{\text{act}} \;=\;$ **if** $(e^\gamma$ **&&** $\bar{b})$ $\{d_t$ **state** $= K^q;\}$

Sets of transitions We define $\|p, T\|_{C'}^{\text{acts}}$ for T a set of transitions to be the result of concatenating the code $\|p, t\|_{C'}^{\text{act}}$ for each transition $t \in T$, in any order with an **else** inserted after all but the last block of code. This is where the user may be allowed to influence the choice without compromising correctness, by choosing to put the transition which is most important first.

A node A node $p \in \mathcal{P}$ is implemented as a **case** label followed by the code for that node's transitions[5] and a **break**:

$$\|\mathcal{P}, p\|_{C'}^{\text{node}} \;=\; \textbf{case } K^p : \|p, T(p)\|_{C'}^{\text{acts}} \textbf{ break};.$$

All the nodes The code for all the nodes is given by:

$$\|\mathcal{P}\|_{C'}^{\text{nodes}} = \textbf{switch (state) } \{D\}$$

where D is the concatenation of $\|\mathcal{P}, p\|_{C'}^{\text{node}}$ for each $p \in \wp$ in any order.

The entire program Finally, the code for the whole program is given by:

$$\|\mathcal{P}\|_{C'} = \|\mathcal{P}\|_{C'}^{\text{fdecl}} \; \|\mathcal{P}\|_{C'}^{\text{vdefn}} \; \text{main}()\{\textbf{for } (;;) \; \|\mathcal{P}\|_{C'}^{\text{nodes}}\}.$$

Example The implementation of *Buff* is given in Figure 2. □

---

[5]This implies that if a state of nil is reached then the program will loop endlessly. This definition could be modified to insert termination code where $T(p)$ is empty.

```
bool tau();
bool in_s(int);  bool in_r(int*);        bool even_s(int);  bool even_r(int*);
bool odd_s(int);  bool odd_r(int*);
int  value;       int  value_tmp;        int  in_1;         int  state = 0;

main()
{ for(;;)
    switch (state)
    { case 0:
        if (true && in_r(&in_1))
        { value_tmp = in_1;  value = value_tmp;  state = 1; }
        break;
      case 1:
        if (!(value & 1) && even_s(value))
        { state = 0; }
        else if ((value & 1) && odd_s(value))
        { state = 0; }
        break;
    }
}
```

Figure 2: $\|\mathcal{P}\|_{C'}$ for *Buff* with *even*(n) implemented as $!(n\&1)$, *odd*(n) as $(n\&1)$.

3.4 Correctness

Each *p.g.* is associated with an *l.t.s.* $(state(\mathcal{P}), act(\mathcal{P}), \rightarrow)$ which has initial state $\iota()$. Each C' program is associated with an *l.t.s.* $(state_{C'}(I), act_{C'}(I), \Rightarrow \Rightarrow_1)$ which has initial state $(main(I), \sigma)$. We can define the correctness of the translation by requiring that whenever a program is generated from a *p.g.* by the above scheme, the two *l.t.s.*s be related by some equivalence.

The following theorem is proved in [14].

Theorem 3.1 If $\mathcal{P} = (Act, \Gamma_A, \wp, \iota, \Gamma_N, T)$ is a *p.g.* and $I = \|\mathcal{P}\|_{C'}$ and if we identify

$$a!(\underline{v}) \in act(\mathcal{P}) \quad \text{with} \quad F^a!(\underline{v}) \in act_{C'}(I)$$
$$a?(\underline{v}) \in act(\mathcal{P}) \quad \text{with} \quad F^a?(\underline{v}) \in act_{C'}(I)$$
$$\tau \in act(\mathcal{P}) \quad \text{with} \quad \tau \in act_{C'}(I)$$

then

$$((state(\mathcal{P}), act(\mathcal{P}), \rightarrow), \iota()) \sim ((state_{C'}(I), act_{C'}(I), \Rightarrow_1), (main(I), \sigma))$$

($\sim$ being strong bisimulation) where $\sigma(\textbf{state}) = K^\iota$ and $\sigma(x)$ is undefined for all other variables (the initial store of I).

Comparison with other work

Representation [7] presents a *state machine* construct similar to that of a *p.g.* and semantic functions for obtaining the representation from LOTOS; this is extended in [6]. One difference is that the state machines have global parameters. They may be executed by a C interpreter.

Translation A translation of *Squeak* (based on CSP and CCS) into C is described in [4] and a translation of LOTOS into C is described in [15]. Both are aimed at specific environments so do not tackle the idea of interface routines.

TOPO [9] is a LOTOS to C translator which does allow arbitrary interfaces using interface routines and has an approach to parallelism similar to ours. An important difference is that it resolves non-determinism randomly at translation time.

None of these representations and translations has a correctness proof.

References

[1] J. A. Bergstra and J. W. Klop. Process algebra for synchronous communication. *Information and Computation*, 60:109–137, 1984.

[2] T. Bolognesi and E. Brinksma. Introduction to the ISO specification language LOTOS. *Computer Networks and ISDN Systems*, 14:22–59, 1987.

[3] G. Bruns. A language for value-passing CCS. Technical Report ECS-LFCS-91-175, LFCS, Dept of Computer Science, University of Edinburgh, The King's Buildings, Edinburgh EH9 3JZ, August 1991.

[4] L. Cardelli and R. Pike. Squeak: a language for communicating with mice. In *ACM SIGRAHP*, volume 19, number 3, pages 199–204, July 1985.

[5] C. A. R. Hoare. *Communicating Sequential Processes*. Prentice-Hall, 1985.

[6] G. Karjoth. XFSM: A formal model of communicating state machines for implementing specifications. Technical Report RZ 2209 (#75693), IBM Research Division, 09/12/91.

[7] G. Karjoth. Implementing process algebra specifications by state machines. In *Protocol Specification, Testing, and Verification, VIII*, pages 47–62. IFIP, 1988.

[8] B. W. Kernighan and D. M. Ritchie. *The C Programming Language*. Prentice-Hall, Englewood Cliffs, New Jersey 07632, 2nd edition, 1988.

[9] J. A. Mañas and T. de Miguel. From LOTOS to C. In K. Turner, editor, *Formal Description Techniques I*, pages 79–84. North-Holland, 1988.

[10] R. Milner. *Communication and Concurrency*. Prentice-Hall, 1989.

[11] H. R. Nielson and F. Nielson. *Semantics with Applications*. John Wiley & Sons Ltd., Baffins Lane, Chichester, West Sussex PO19 1UD, England, 1992.

[12] G. D. Plotkin. *A Structural Approach to Operational Semantics*. Computer Science Dept, Aarhus University, September 1981.

[13] Z. Schreiber. Verification and analysis of value-passing CCS programs with infinite sorts. Technical Report DoC 92/9, Department of Computing, Imperial College, 180 Queen's Gate, London SW7 2BZ, June 1992.

[14] Z. Schreiber. Implementing process algebra in C. Technical Report DoC 93/5, Department of Computing, Imperial College, 180 Queen's Gate, London SW7 2BZ, June 1993.

[15] P. van Eijk, H. Kremer, and M. van Sinderen. On the use of specification styles for automated protocol implementation from LOTOS to C. In *Protocol Specification, Testing and Verification, X*, pages 157–168. IFIP, 1990.

An Exact Interpretation of while

Paul Taylor

pt@doc.ic.ac.uk
Department of Computing, Imperial College
180 Queen's Gate, London SW7 2BZ, United Kingdom

Abstract

The behaviour and interaction of finite limits (products, pullbacks and equalisers) and colimits (coproducts and coequalisers) in the category of sets is illustrated in a "hands on" way by giving the interpretation of a simple imperative language in terms of partial functions between sets of states. We show that the interpretation is a least fixed point and satisfies the usual proof rule for loop invariants.

1 The language

We shall interpret a language with the following ⟨command⟩s in a category:

>   **skip**
> | ⟨command⟩ ; ⟨command⟩
> | **let** ⟨variable⟩ = ⟨expression⟩ : ⟨type⟩
> | **discard** ⟨variable⟩
> | ⟨variable⟩ := ⟨expression⟩
> | **if** ⟨Boolean expression⟩ **then** ⟨command⟩ **else** ⟨command⟩ **fi**
> | **while** ⟨Boolean expression⟩ **do** ⟨command⟩ **od**

Clearly **skip** and sequencing (;) correspond to identity and composition, so each command is a *morphism*, but what are the *objects* which serve as its source and target?

Each command of a program has a "compile-time" as well as its run-time effect: here just the declaration (**let**) and un-declaration (**discard**) of variables. Before the command (in the text) there is a certain collection Γ of variables which are **in scope**, so in particular they may be used in forming expressions. At the end the scope, Δ, consists of Γ, *plus* the newly declared variable(s), *minus* those which have been discarded. Γ and Δ are the source and target respectively of the morphism representing the command; by construction the source of one command is the target of the previous one, as it must be for composition to be defined.

We do not require scopes to be nested, instead adopting the rule that if a variable name is in scope then it may not be the subject of a definition. This apparently weak convention is convenient because it allows assignment to be defined in terms of the other commands:

$x := a$ is the same as   **let** $x' = a$; **discard** x ; **let** $x = x'$; **discard** x'

where x' is a new variable, *i.e.* not in scope. In programming **discard** is, apart from this, redundant (provably so in a certain sense in our formal language) but it has been added for an exact match with the categorical concept (products) which is being used to interpret the language.

Abstractly we have already said enough about the objects: they are lists of variables. (Similarly we have also given the morphisms as programs, but we shall see that we must impose an equivalence relation on them.) Variables are **typed**: we need the **Boolean type 2** (with its elements **yes** and **no**), but shall not introduce any (other) type constructors.

Concretely, a type is the **set** of values which may be taken by a variable to which it is attributed. The **state** of the machine is determined by the **tuple** of current values of the variables in scope, and so the object $[\![\Gamma]\!]$ representing the scope Γ is the **product** of (the sets interpreting) the types. In particular,

[**discard** x] is the **product projection** which omits $[\![x : X]\!]$.

and we write $\hat{x} : [\![\Gamma]\!] \times X \longrightarrow [\![\Gamma]\!]$ for it.

To say what **expressions** are, we need a language of algebraic operations.

$$\langle\text{expression}\rangle \quad ::= \quad \langle\text{variable}\rangle$$
$$| \quad \langle\text{constant}\rangle$$
$$| \quad \langle\text{operator}\rangle(\langle\text{expression}\rangle, ..., \langle\text{expression}\rangle)$$

The categorical interpretation of algebra is very well known. Each $\langle$operator$\rangle$ f and $\langle$constant$\rangle$ c has an intended meaning as a morphism $f : Y_1 \times \cdots \times Y_m \to Z$ or $c : 1 \to Z$ in the category, $\vec{Y}$ and Z being the argument and result types.

In the scope $\Gamma \equiv [x_1 : X_1, \ldots, x_n : X_n]$, expressions are interpreted as

$$[\![x_i]\!] \qquad\qquad : [\![\Gamma]\!] = X_1 \times \cdots \times X_n \xrightarrow{\pi_i} X_i$$

$$[\![c]\!] \qquad\qquad : [\![\Gamma]\!] \xrightarrow{\;!\;} 1 \xrightarrow{\;c\;} Y$$

$$[\![f(e_1, \ldots, e_m)]\!] : [\![\Gamma]\!] \xrightarrow{\langle [\![e_1]\!], \ldots, [\![e_m]\!]\rangle} Y_1 \times \cdots \times Y_m \xrightarrow{\;f\;} Y$$

by structural induction, where the $[\![e_i]\!] : [\![\Gamma]\!] \to Y_i$ interpret the subexpressions.

$$[\![\textbf{let } y = e : Y]\!] : [\![\Gamma]\!] \xrightarrow{\langle id, [\![e]\!]\rangle} [\![\Gamma]\!] \times Y$$

$$[\![\textbf{discard } x_i]\!] \quad : [\![\Gamma]\!] \xrightarrow{\widehat{x_i}} X_1 \times \cdots \times X_{i-1} \times X_{i+1} \times \cdots \times X_n$$

$$[\![x_i := e]\!] \qquad : [\![\Gamma]\!] \xrightarrow{\langle \pi_1, \ldots, \pi_{i-1}, [\![e]\!], \pi_{i+1}, \ldots \pi_n\rangle} [\![\Gamma]\!]$$

similarly interpret the declaration and un-declaration commands.

The following equations may be proved by structural induction

$$[\![\textbf{let } x = a \, ; \textbf{discard } x]\!] \quad = \quad id$$
$$[\![\textbf{let } x = a \, ; \textbf{let } y = c]\!] \quad = \quad [\![\textbf{let } y = c^{[x := a]} \, ; \textbf{let } x = a]\!]$$
$$[\![\textbf{discard } x \, ; \textbf{let } y = b]\!] \quad = \quad [\![\textbf{let } y = b \, ; \textbf{discard } x]\!]$$
$$[\![\textbf{discard } x \, ; \textbf{discard } y]\!] \quad = \quad [\![\textbf{discard } y \, ; \textbf{discard } x]\!]$$

where x does not occur in b (it may in c), nor y in a.

The meta-notation $c^{[x:=a]}$ means the substitution of a for x in c. It is defined in the usual way, but is in fact much simpler than in the λ-calculus because there is no variable binding or renaming. The equation which uses this may be read in either direction: from left to right, to give the fully substituted version or closed form, or from right to left, to reduce each expression to a sequence of single operations or subroutine calls.

The foregoing description may be read directly as an interpretation of the language in a category (such as **Set**) with products. However it may also be taken as an *abstract* definition of a category out of the language: the objects are lists of typed variables and the morphisms are programs subject to the equations given. This category itself has products, and the interpretation is a product-preserving functor from it to the desired semantic category.

2 Interpretation on subsets

So far we have only allowed the objects in the semantic category to be *products* of sets, but it is convenient to extend the interpretation to subsets. In an imperative understanding the notation

$$\{\phi\}\, P\, \{\psi\}$$

means "if the program P is run from an initial state satisfying ϕ then when (if) it terminates ψ will hold." In the case of the whole program, ϕ and ψ constitute the **specification**. Of course we may always take $\phi = \bot$ and $\psi = \top$, but this vacuous specification says that the program is good for nothing.

The predicates ϕ and ψ do not need to be computable: even when they are it would often be more complicated to compute them than the program itself, and sometimes they involve universal quantification over infinite sets.

We can express the property categorically by saying that in the square

$$
\begin{array}{ccc}
\{\vec{x} : \phi(\vec{x})\} & \cdots\cdots\blacktriangleright & \{\vec{y} : \psi(\vec{y})\} \\
\Big\downarrow & & \Big\downarrow \\
[\![\vec{x} : \vec{X}]\!] & \xrightarrow{\ [\![P]\!]\ } & [\![\vec{y} : \vec{Y}]\!]
\end{array}
$$

there is some map at the top making it commute; it is unique since the right hand map is an inclusion.

There are corresponding logical rules:

$$\{\phi(\vec{x})\}\,\mathbf{discard}\ y\,\{\phi(\vec{x})\} \qquad \{\psi\}\,\mathbf{skip}\,\{\psi\} \qquad \{\psi(\vec{x}, a)\}\,\mathbf{let}\ y = a\,\{\psi(\vec{x}, y)\}$$

where y does not occur (freely) in ϕ, and

$$\frac{\{\phi\}\, P\, \{\psi\} \qquad \{\psi\}\, Q\, \{\chi\}}{\{\phi\}\, P\,;\, Q\, \{\chi\}} \qquad\qquad \frac{\phi' \vdash \phi \qquad \{\phi\}\, P\, \{\psi\} \qquad \psi \vdash \psi'}{\{\phi'\}\, P\, \{\psi'\}}$$

It is more idiomatic to prove a program by inserting **mid-conditions** between the lines than by this repetitive sequent-style notation. It is then a **natural deduction** with definitions but no temporary hypotheses.

Each command P and post-condition ψ have a **weakest precondition** $P^*\psi$ for which the property is valid, indeed we have given $\{P^*\psi\}\,P\,\{\psi\}$ above. Categorically, the square is then a **pullback**, satisfying a universal property similar to that for a product. We shall only need this special case, called an **inverse image**, in which two of the sides are inclusions.

3   Conditionals

Now we shall add the **if then else fi** construction to the language. The use of the word "**if**" is misleading: The test is not of a general predicate as in the last section, but a computable function with two possible terminating values, called **yes** and **no** to make the distinction from logic clear. Nor does **if** mean implication: in fact it is related to disjunction.

For correct scoping, the two branches must end up with the same variables; in particular any that only one declares must be discarded.

To interpret the conditional we first evaluate the test, and restrict the interpretations of the two branches to the subsets on which it succeeds and fails.

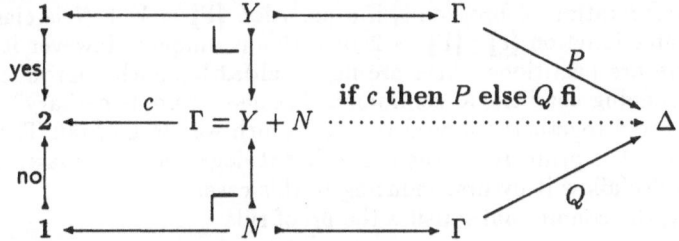

First consider Γ, c, Y and N fixed, the rest variable. The dotted map always exists and is to be determined uniquely by the pair $Y \to \Delta \leftarrow N$, so Γ is the **coproduct** $Y + N$. By definition this satisfies the universal property we have just given: the same as that for the product but with the arrows reversed.

The **boolean type** $\mathbf{2} = \mathbf{1} + \mathbf{1}$ is, as we shall see, the primitive case. The two structural maps from the terminal object are the constants **yes** and **no**.

However many categories have coproducts which are quite unsuitable for interpreting conditionals. For example, they coincide with products in the category of finite dimensional vector spaces, where a cancellation law also holds; this means that the **distributive law**

$$A \times (Y + N) \cong (A \times Y) + (A \times N)$$

is valid only when one of the summands on the right vanishes. This equation is needed so that the interpretation of a conditional using $Y + N$ is unaffected by the presence of "passive" variables A. In fact we require a stronger property.

The condition c gives a partition $\Gamma = Y + N$, but it may be recovered from it by considering the command

> **if** c **then let** $x = $ **yes else let** $x = $ **no fi** ; **discard** Γ

Hence the commutation of the two squares on the left must define a bijection

- ♦ between morphisms $X \to \mathbf{2}$, where $\mathbf{2}$ is the coproduct $\mathbf{1} + \mathbf{1}$
- ♦ and coproduct diagrams $Y \to X \leftarrow N$.

More precisely, these provide the objects of two categories (whose morphisms are appropriate commutative triangles) which are to be equivalent [3].

By choosing appropriate collections of squares it is not difficult to show that

- the two squares are pullbacks, indeed inverse images,
- the structure maps $Y \to Y + N$ and $N \to Y + N$ are (regular) monos,
- (stable) the pullback of any coproduct diagram is another such,
- in particular the distributive law holds,
- there is a **strict initial object 0** (the empty set): *i.e.* any map $X \to 0$ is an isomorphism; equivalently $X \times 0 \cong 0$ for any object X, and
- the components of the coproduct are **disjoint**, *i.e.* the pullback (intersection) of the structure maps is **0**.

Specifying **stable disjoint coproducts** and the strict initial object is usual; they imply our (more useful) form of the definition, but this is trickier to show.

Set enjoys these properties by of the **tag** construction of the disjoint union:

$$Y + N \cong (Y \times \{\text{yes}\}) \cup (N \times \{\text{no}\})$$

In the interpretation of programs, if a partition $[\![\Gamma]\!] = Y + N$ is classified by a computable function $[\![c]\!] : [\![\Gamma]\!] \to \mathbf{2}$ then this is unique. However it may not exist: there are partitions which are not **decidable**. Such coproducts are no good for defining conditional commands, because "complementary" programs can't be pasted together: we need to know which way to go *first*. The Boolean type $\mathbf{2} = \mathbf{1} + \mathbf{1}$ is primitive in the sense that it does allow this pasting, and its pullbacks also allow it by first reducing to this case.

Finally, the conditional satisfies the proof rule

$$\frac{\{\phi \wedge c\}\, P\, \{\psi\} \qquad \{\phi \wedge \neg c\}\, Q\, \{\psi\}}{\{\phi\}\, \text{if } b \text{ then } P \text{ else } Q \text{ fi } \{\psi\}}$$

because of stability: $\{\phi\} = \{\phi \wedge c\} + \{\phi \wedge \neg c\}$.

4 Partial functions

Programs in the fragment of the language which we have defined so far always terminate, and so can be interpreted as total functions between sets. This is no longer possible when we add loops: since the Halting Problem is insoluble there is no restriction which we can place on programs in order to guarantee termination without destroying the expressive power of the language.

A **partial function** with **source** X, **target** Y and **support** U in a category S is a diagram of the form

$$
\begin{array}{ccc}
U & \xrightarrow{\ f\ } & Y \\
{\scriptstyle i}\big\downarrow & & \\
X & &
\end{array}
$$

where $U \hookrightarrow X$ is mono — a subset. If there is an isomorphism $e : V \cong U$ we regard the pair $\langle e;i,\ e;f \rangle$ as the same partial function as $\langle i, f \rangle$. More generally the existence of any map (necessarily a unique mono) making the two triangles commute is taken as an instance of an order relation between partial maps.

Every **total** function (in particular the identity) is also partial: we just put $i = \mathsf{id}_X : X = U \hookrightarrow X$.

Composition is defined by pullback (inverse image):

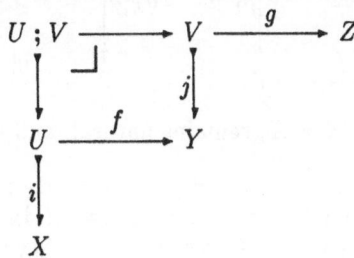

and is easily shown to be associative.

In the interpretation using *total* functions, discarding a variable immediately after it is declared with a value has no effect. Now

$$\mathsf{supp}(e) = [\![\mathbf{let}\ x = e\ ;\ \mathbf{discard}\ x]\!].$$

is a partial endofunction $\langle i, i \rangle : [\![\Gamma]\!] \rightharpoonup [\![\Gamma]\!]$ where $\langle i, f \rangle = [\![e]\!]$. It is sometimes convenient to regard this as a subset of $[\![\Gamma]\!]$ instead.

Instead of allowing *all* monos to be the supports of partial maps, one may restrict to a class $\mathcal{M}$ of them, satisfying the following conditions:

- ♦ $\mathcal{M}$ contains all isomorphisms,
- ♦ $\mathcal{M}$ is closed under pullback against arbitrary maps, and
- ♦ $\mathcal{M}$ is closed under composition.

Write $\mathsf{P}(\mathcal{S}, \mathcal{M})$ for the category of partial maps whose supports belong to $\mathcal{M}$ in the category $\mathcal{S}$.

Given partial maps $\langle i, f \rangle : Z \rightharpoonup X$ and $\langle j, g \rangle : Z \rightharpoonup Y$, we must take the intersection of their supports in order to define a partial map into a **product**:

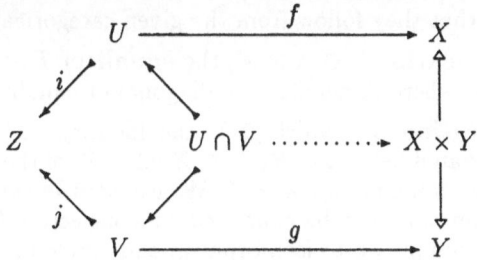

This means that the pairing is **strict**, *i.e.* only defined when both components are. In general, therefore, composition with the projections does not recover the components, so this is not the product in the category of partial functions.

It nevertheless defines a **tensor product**: a functor of two arguments which is coherently associative and commutative. The behaviour of the projections is less natural here than amongst total functions:

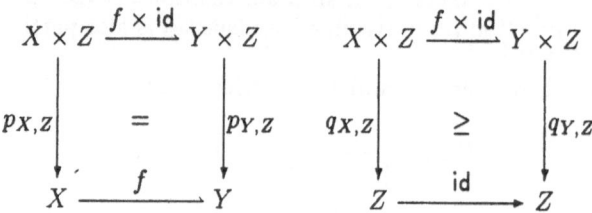

The diagonal, $d_X : X \to X \times X$, remains natural, and they all satisfy

$$
\begin{array}{ccccc}
d_X \, ; p_{X,X} & = & \mathsf{id}_X & = & d_X \, ; q_{X,X} \\
(\mathsf{id}_X \times p_{Y,Z}) \, ; p_{X,Y} & = & p_{X,Y \times Z} & = & (\mathsf{id}_X \times q_{Y,Z}) \, ; p_{X,Z} \\
(p_{X,Y} \times \mathsf{id}_Z) \, ; q_{X,Z} & = & q_{X \times Y, Z} & = & (q_{X,Y} \times \mathsf{id}_Z) \, ; q_{Y,Z} \\
d_{X \times Y} \, ; (p_{X,Y} \times q_{X,Y}) & = & \mathsf{id}_{X \times Y} & &
\end{array}
$$

Abstractly, a category $\mathcal{P}$ together with a functor $\otimes : \mathcal{P} \times \mathcal{P} \to \mathcal{P}$ and natural transformations $d : \mathsf{id} \to (- \times -)$, $p_{-,X} : - \times X \to \mathsf{id}$ and $q_{X,-} : X \times - \to \mathsf{id}$ satisfying these equations is called a **p-category**. Giuseppe Rosolini [6, 7] showed that any p-category $(\mathcal{P}, \otimes)$ has a full embedding $\mathcal{P} \hookrightarrow \mathsf{P}(\mathcal{S}, \mathcal{M})$ such that $\otimes$ restricts to the categorical product in $\mathcal{S}$.

We do not have an equivalence, because the supports of $\mathcal{P}$-maps may be missing. For example $\mathcal{P}$ may be defined from a programming language which has only the type $\mathbb{N}$ of natural numbers but is adequate for arithmetic; then $\mathcal{S}$ and $\mathcal{M}$ consist of the **recursively enumerable** sets of numbers.

The coproduct in $\mathcal{S}$ also extends to a functor on $\mathsf{P}(\mathcal{S}, \mathcal{M})$, where it remains the coproduct. It is not stable disjoint there, but we do not want it to be.

5   Relational algebra

Partial functions are a special case of **binary relations**, $R \hookrightarrow X \times Y$, in a category, which we shall use as a tool to study **while** in the next section. The following results are familiar for **Set**, but it would be instructive to show by diagram chasing that they follow from the given categorical definitions.

♦ For an **endo-relation** $U \subset X \times X$, the **equaliser** $E \hookrightarrow U \rightrightarrows X$ is isomorphic to $U \cap \Delta$, where Δ denotes the diagonal or equality relation on X.

Consider **composition**, for which Δ is the identity. The pullback gives a subobject, abbreviated below as $xRySz \subset X \times Y \times Z$, of the three-fold product, but not necessarily a mono into $X \times Z$. We use **stable image factorisation** to get one: any function may be expressed as a surjection followed by a mono in a way which is unique up to isomorphism and stable under pullback.

The logical form of relational composition uses an **existential quantifier**, which obeys **Frobenius' law**

$$
\exists x. \phi \wedge \psi(x) \iff \phi \wedge \exists x. \psi(x)
$$

where x does not occur in ϕ. The quantifier is represented categorically by

$$wQxRySz \longrightarrow \exists y.wQxRySz \longmapsto wQx \wedge \exists y.xRySz \longmapsto Q \times Z$$

$$xRySz \longrightarrow \exists y.xRySz \longmapsto X \times Z$$

factorisation. To say that this is *stable* means that the mono in the middle of the top row is invertible, *i.e.* Frobenius' law holds, whence

♦ relational composition is associative.

Although the coproduct of algebras is not stable disjoint, their homomorphisms *do* have stable image factorisation: they form **regular categories**.

A relation R is **diamond** (or **confluent**, or satisfies the **Church-Rosser** property) if $R^{op} ; R \subset R ; R^{op}$. Then

♦ powers of a diamond relation are diamond;

♦ if T is transitive and diamond then $T ; T^{op}$ is transitive;

♦ if T is also reflexive then $T ; T^{op}$ is its equivalence closure.

To make full use of relational algebra we need unions: it will come as no surprise to the reader now that these must also be stable under pullback. With just finite stable unions we can now interpret disjunction as well as conjunction and existential quantification; this fragment is known as **coherent logic**.

♦ Relational composition distributes over stable unions.

♦ If U is a partial function then $R = U \cup \Delta$, its reflexive closure, is diamond.

Extending to stable **countable unions**,

♦ the **transitive closure** of U is $T = \bigcup_{n \in \mathbb{N}} U^n = \bigcup^{\uparrow}_{n \in \mathbb{N}} R^n$,

from which one can show by brute force that

♦ $T = \Delta \cup (U ; T)$,

♦ $E ; T = E$,

♦ if the relation A satisfies $A ; U \subset U ; A$ then $A ; T \subset T ; A$, and

♦ for any partial function $V : X \rightharpoonup Z$, if $V = U ; V$ then $V = T ; V$.

Alternatively, if all unions exist and are preserved by the monotone functions $(-) ; A$ and $A ; (-)$ then these have right adjoints, $(-)/A$ and $A \backslash (-)$, which both reduce to **Heyting implication** when $A \subset \Delta$. The foregoing results may then be proved in a finitary way using the universal properties. We show that

$$E \backslash E \qquad \Delta \cup (U ; T) \qquad A \backslash T ; A \qquad V \backslash V$$

are transitive whenever T is, and hence contain the transitive closure.

By putting first R and then R^{op} for A we have

♦ if R is diamond then so is T

We now have quite a lot of information about the **equivalence closure** of a relation, especially if it is a partial function. Only in the case of equivalence relations do we have a direct construction of the **coequaliser** in **Set**: it is the set of equivalence classes. Here and in categories of algebras every equivalence relation (**congruence**) is the kernel pair (pullback) of its **quotient** (coequaliser);

Michael Barr called such a (regular) category **exact**, though the word has also been used in other senses. An exact category with stable disjoint sums is called a **pretopos**; stable binary unions may be constructed as the quotient of the coproduct by the equivalence relation induced by the intersection.

For a general parallel pair we have first to take its image as a relation, and then the equivalence closure. This involves stable directed unions, which are a feature of finitary algebraic theories but not part of the definition of a pretopos.

6   Loop programs

We are now ready to interpret the program

while c **do** U **od**

which, without loss of generality, satisfies the following simplifying properties:

- The condition c is guaranteed to terminate without side-effect. This can be ensured by inserting **let** $x = c$ before the loop and $x := c$ at the end of its body. The test is then just that of a (Boolean) *variable*.
- If the body U were executed in a state where $c = $ no, then it would terminate with no effect. Replacing U by **if** c **then** U **else skip fi** achieves this.

Now we write

- $X = [\Gamma]$ for the type (set of states) at the beginning and end of the loop.
- $Y, N \subset X$ for the subsets on which the condition c succeeds and fails, respectively; then $X = Y + N$ by the first assumption.
- $i, f : U \rightrightarrows X$, with i injective, for the two maps which describe the partial endomorphism of X interpreting the body U of the loop.
- $E \hookrightarrow U \rightrightarrows X$ for their equaliser, so $E \cong U \cap \Delta$. By the second assumption, $N \subset E$, and it is convenient to regard these as binary subrelations of Δ.
- $R = U \cup \Delta$, T and K for the reflexive, transitive-reflexive and equivalence closures of U.
- Q for the coequaliser of $i, f : U \rightrightarrows X$.

The loop will be interpreted as the relation $W = K \,;\, N \subset X \times X$: we must show that this is functional. For any functional relation, *i.e.* for a parallel pair one of which is mono,

$$E \longmapsto U \overset{i}{\underset{f}{\rightrightarrows}} X \longrightarrow Q$$

I claim that the composite from the equaliser to the coequaliser is also mono. The reflexive closure R is diamond, as then is the transitive-reflexive closure T, so $K = T \,;\, T^{\mathrm{op}}$ is the equivalence closure. Two elements $x, y \in E$ of the equaliser become identified in the coequaliser $Q \cong X/K$ iff $\langle x, y \rangle \in K$, by exactness. Then

$$\langle x, y \rangle \in E \,;\, K \,;\, E^{\mathrm{op}} = E \,;\, T \,;\, T^{\mathrm{op}} \,;\, E^{\mathrm{op}} = E \,;\, E^{\mathrm{op}} = E \subset \Delta$$

since $E = E \,;\, T$, but then $x = y$ as claimed. This result depends on stability of unions: it fails in the category of groups.

Now consider the kernel pair of the composite $N \hookrightarrow Q$.

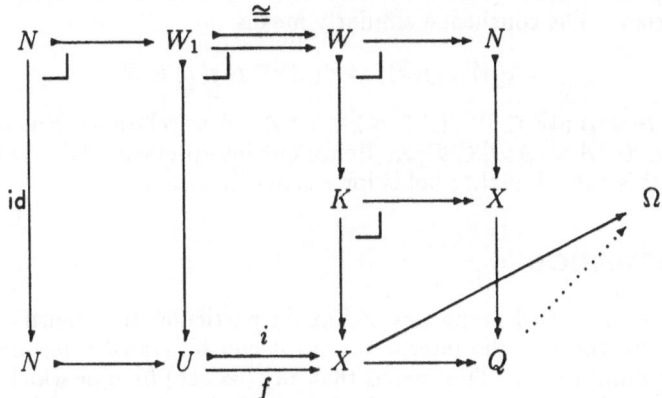

We showed that the vertical map $W \hookrightarrow K \twoheadrightarrow X$ is mono. This is the support of the interpretation of the loop, and $W \twoheadrightarrow N \hookrightarrow X$ is the effect.

The partial endofunction W satisfies the equation

$$W \equiv \textbf{if } c \textbf{ then } U \text{ ; } W \textbf{ else skip fi}$$

and the condition is no on exit. Since $N = N^{\text{op}} \subset E = E \text{ ; } T$,

$$W = K \text{ ; } N = T \text{ ; } T^{\text{op}} \text{ ; } N = T \text{ ; } N$$

By construction $N \subset E \subset U \subset T$, so $N = N^3 \subset U \text{ ; } T \text{ ; } N$. Then

$$W = T \text{ ; } N = (\Delta \cup U \text{ ; } T) \text{ ; } N = N \cup U \text{ ; } T \text{ ; } N = U \text{ ; } T \text{ ; } N = U \text{ ; } W$$

Also $N \subset W_1 = W$ and $W = K \text{ ; } N = K \text{ ; } N \text{ ; } N = W \text{ ; } N$. In terms of the program equation, these mean respectively that W behaves like $U \text{ ; } W$ when $c = \textbf{yes}$ and like **skip** when $c = \textbf{no}$, and that afterwards $c = \textbf{no}$.

This is not yet enough to show that the interpretation is correct: we want to show that it is the *least* fixed point. We must show that $W \subset V$ for any functional relation V satisfying $N \subset V = U \text{ ; } V$. But the two cases for c give $N \subset V$ and $V = U \text{ ; } V$. Then $V = T \text{ ; } V$, so $W = T \text{ ; } N \subset T \text{ ; } V = V$.

Any map $\phi : X \to Z$ with $i \text{ ; } \phi = f \text{ ; } \phi$ is *invariant* in the strict sense that its value is restored after each iteration, so it is the same when the loop terminates (if it does) as at the beginning. Such a map factors through the coequaliser. However, according to standard usage, a **loop invariant** is a predicate (so $Z = \Omega$) which, *if* it holds before execution of the body *then* it holds afterwards. In other words ϕ may *become* valid when it had not been before, and the converse implication is not relevant. The correctness of **while** loops is always shown by finding an appropriate invariant, using the following proof rule:

$$\frac{\{c \wedge \phi\} \, U \, \{\phi\}}{\{\phi\} \textbf{ while } c \textbf{ do } U \textbf{ od } \{\neg c \wedge \phi\}}$$

for any predicate ϕ. The premise of the rule means

$$\forall u \in U. \; i(u) \in Y \wedge \phi(i(u)) \Rightarrow \phi(f(u))$$

but the second assumption makes the proviso $i(u) \in Y$ unnecessary. Putting $A = \{\langle x, y \rangle : (x = y) \wedge \phi(x)\}$, it becomes $A \, ; U \subset U \, ; A$ with equality iff it is a strict invariant. The conclusion similarly means

$$\forall x \in W.\phi(j(x)) \Rightarrow \phi(g(x)) \wedge g(x) \in N$$

i.e. $A \, ; T \, ; N \equiv A \, ; W \subset W \, ; (A \cap N) \equiv T \, ; A \, ; N$ as relations. But we showed that $A \, ; U \subset U \, ; A \Rightarrow A \, ; T \subset T \, ; A$. Hence our interpretation W is correct with respect to this rule. Equality holds for a strict invariant.

7   Discussion

Although we have used properties of **Set**, in particular the transitive closure, to *prove* correctness of the interpretation, it can be *stated* using finite limits and finite colimits alone. This means that any (**exact**) functor which preserves finite limits and colimits preserves the interpretation.

Moreover correctness is *reflected* if the functor $F : \mathcal{C} \hookrightarrow \mathcal{S}$ is also full and faithful. For suppose that both categories have the limits and colimits needed to draw the diagrams in the previous section (so F makes these agree) and that in $\mathcal{S}$ we have shown that $FW \rightrightarrows FX$ is a functional relation satisfying

♦ $FN \subset FW = FU \, ; FW$,

♦ $\forall V. \ FN \subset V = FU \, ; V \Rightarrow FW \subset V$, and

♦ $\forall A. \ A \, ; FU \subset FU \, ; A \Rightarrow A \, ; FW \subset FW \, ; (A \cap FN)$.

Then F preserves composition and intersection of relations, and reflects their containment, so these properties restrict to $\mathcal{C}$.

When can a category without infinite unions be embedded in one with them, thereby generalising the interpretation?

Stability of the coequaliser is clearly necessary, but unfortunately seems not to be sufficient. If the coequaliser of U and its kernel K exist then K is always the union of powers of U and U^{op}, even though we have not asked for a general infinitary union operation. Then a pretopos $\mathcal{C}$ can be embedded in a topos of sheaves on $\mathcal{C}$ preserving (finite limits, coproducts, quotients of equivalence relations and) the coequaliser of U iff *this union is stable under pullbacks in* $\mathcal{C}$.

Using this condition there is a simpler way to extend the proof: we only need unions of relations, not the extra objects in this sheaf topos. Define an **ideal relation** $\mathfrak{A} : X \to Y$ to be a *set* of relations $A \subset X \times Y$ which is closed downwards and under whatever *stable* unions already exist. For example

$$(A) = \{B : B \subset A\} \quad \{B : B \, ; E \subset E\} \quad \{B : V \, ; B \subset V\}$$

Composition and the lattice operations extend to ideal relations, indeed we have an example of an **allegory**. The last two examples are transitive, as is

$$\{B : (A \, ; B) \subset \mathfrak{T} \, ; A\}$$

for any transitive ideal relation $\mathfrak{T}$. The same argument goes through as before, the crucial point being

$$(K) = \mathfrak{T} \, ; \mathfrak{T}^{\text{op}}$$

where we return from the ideal transitive closure $\mathfrak{T}$ to the real equivalence closure K. For this we need that the latter be a *stable* union. To sum up,

The language is correctly interpreted in any pretopos such that each functional relation has an equivalence closure which is stably the union of powers. Any function which preserves finite limits and colimits also preserves the interpretation.

Consider the following special case, with $x : \mathbb{N}$, which always terminates:

$$\textbf{while } x > 0 \textbf{ do } x := x - 1 \textbf{ od}$$

On exit $x = 0$, so the coequaliser is $Q \cong N = \{0\}$, whilst $Y = \{n : n \geq 1\}$, so succ $: \mathbb{N} \cong Y$. The condition $X = Y + N$ and the interpretation of the program then reduce to the coproduct and coequaliser diagrams

$$1 \xrightarrow{\;0\;} \mathbb{N} \xleftarrow{\;\text{succ}\;} \mathbb{N} \qquad \mathbb{N} \underset{\text{id}}{\overset{\text{succ}}{\rightrightarrows}} \mathbb{N} \longrightarrow 1$$

This characterisation of $\mathbb{N}$ shows [4] that exact functors (in particular inverse images of geometric morphisms) between toposes preserve $\mathbb{N}$.

The word "exact" in the title refers to the properties of **Set** relating limits and colimits which are technically known as exactness. The pun which suggests logical **completeness** is a cheat, because the full power of the coequaliser is not exploited. Analogously to the distinctions between non-normalising terms in the untyped λ-calculus, it makes a subtle identification amongst non-terminating states. For further research it would be interesting to ask whether by varying the loop condition c a **full abstraction** result can be proved.

I was a Ph.D. student [8] when I found the interpretation of **while** as a coequaliser; I wrote [9], discussing p-categories, when I was a Research Assistant on *Foundational Structures in Computer Science*, and now I am an Advanced Research Fellow, all funded by the Science and Engineering Research Council.

I would like to thank Samson Abramsky, Peter Freyd, Martin Hyland, Barry Jay, Leopoldo Román, Giuseppe Rosolini, Mark Ryan, Art Stone and Bob Walters for their comments.

References

[1] Michael Barr and Charles Wells. *Toposes, Triples and Theories.* Springer Verlag, 1984.

[2] Michael Barr and Charles Wells. *Category Theory for Computing Science.* Prentice-Hall International Series in Computer Science. Prentice-Hall, 1990.

[3] Aurelio Carboni, Stephen Lack, and Bob Walters. Introduction to extensive and distributive categories. *Journal of Pure and Applied Algebra*, 84:145–158, 1993.

[4] Peter Freyd. Aspects of topoi. *Bull. Austral. Math. Soc.*, 7:1–76, 1972.

[5] Peter Freyd and André Scedrov. *Categories, Allegories.* North-Holland, 1990.

[6] Edmund Robinson and Guiseppe Rosolini. Categories of partial maps. *Inform. and Comput.*, 79:95–130, 1988.

[7] Guiseppe Rosolini. *Continuity and Effectiveness in Topoi.* PhD thesis, Carnegie-Mellon University, 1986.

[8] Paul Taylor. *Iterated partial maps in a regular category.* Manuscript, DPMMS, Cambridge, 1984.

[9] Paul Taylor. *An exact interpretation of while, I and II.* Dept. of Computing, Imperial College, 1987. Available by anonymous FTP from theory.doc.ic.ac.uk in the directory /theory/papers/Taylor; also appeared in the draft version of these proceedings.

[10] Bob Walters. *Categories and Computer Science.* Carslaw Publications (1991), and Cambridge University Press (1992).

Congruences for τ-respecting Formats of Rules

Irek Ulidowski

ex13ulidowi@clstr.unl.ac.uk and iu@doc.ic.ac.uk
School of Computing
University of North London
Eden Grove
London N7 8DB

Abstract

The aim in the paper is to investigate four *implementable* formats of rules in the setting of Transition System Specifications (TSS) and in the presence of silent actions and divergence. For each of the formats the coarsest equivalence is proposed such that it refines trace equivalence and it is a congruence for the format.

1 Introduction

In Milner's CCS [10], as in a number of other process calculi, the operational meaning of processes is given in terms of a labelled transition system. The states of the system are the CCS ground terms called processes. The transitions between the processes are defined inductively by a set of transition rules. Each transition rule determines the transitions of a composite process in terms of the transitions of its component processes. For example, for the CCS ground term $a0 + b0$, the transition $a0 + b0 \xrightarrow{a} 0$ can be inferred from the transition $a0 \xrightarrow{a} 0$ using a general transition rule

$$\frac{X \xrightarrow{a} X'}{X + Y \xrightarrow{a} X'}$$

for the choice operator $+$. A set of rules associated with each operator can be thought of as giving the operational meaning of that operator.

Milner defined in [10] a number of operational equivalences on processes. The main interest in the paper is in the so-called *weak* equivalences. These are defined over transition systems with silent transitions 'hidden'. An example of such equivalences is weak bisimulation [10]. It is considered to be the finest extensional behavioral equivalence: two processes are weak bisimular if they have the same externally observable behaviour.

An important property each equivalence should have is *substitutivity* or *congruence* for some process calculus: two equivalent processes p and q are congruent if for all contexts $C[\cdot]$ over the calculus the processes $C[p]$ and $C[q]$ are equivalent. But weak bisimulation is not a congruence for CCS since $a0$ and $\tau a0$ are weak bisimular but $a0 + b0$ and $\tau a0 + b0$ are not. There are two ways in which this particular problem can be dealt with. If one wishes to keep the CCS + then *observation* congruence must be used instead of weak bisimulation [10]. On the other hand one may retain weak bisimulation as well motivated and canonical equivalence and consider using operators for which weak bisimulation is a congruence. In particular one may consider other than + choice operators: for example the external and internal choice operators of CSP [9]. In this paper we follow the later approach.

Imagine that one wishes to extend a particular calculus with extra operators. It would involve extending the syntax with the names of new operators and adding a set of transition rules for these operators. If the extended calculus is to be of any interest it must satisfy at least the following conditions:

♦ the extended calculus induces a transition relation;

♦ all operators preserve silent and independent of the observer character of τ-transitions;

♦ weak bisimulation remains a congruence for the extended calculus.

One of the aims in the paper is to establish what operators can be added to calculi like CCS (without +), CSP and ACP such that the extended calculi satisfy the above three conditions. Examples of operators one may like to consider are as follows:

1. The sequential composition operator ;. Process $p; q$ behaves like p until p stops, then it behaves like q. It can be defined as in CSP, but in [3] it is introduced by the following transition rules with *negative* premises

$$\frac{X \xrightarrow{a} X'}{X;Y \xrightarrow{a} X';Y} \qquad \frac{X \xnrightarrow{a} \text{all } a, \quad Y \xrightarrow{b} Y'}{X;Y \xrightarrow{b} Y.}$$

Unlike transition rules of CCS the second rule defines the transitions of $X;Y$ in terms of the absence of the transitions of X and in terms of transitions of Y. Other process operators which have associated rules with negative premises are the priority operator [7], the stability operator [14] and the refusal testing operators [1, 16].

2. Sometimes, especially when modelling the testing of processes, there is a need for *copying* operators like the ones used in [1, 16, 4]. Consider the *a-if-b* operator [4] with the defining rule

$$\frac{X \xrightarrow{a} X' \qquad X \xrightarrow{b} X''}{a\text{-}if\text{-}b(X) \xrightarrow{a} a\text{-}if\text{-}b(X')}$$

and the binary operator *twice* with the rule [15]

$$\frac{T \xrightarrow{copy} T'}{twice(T, P) \xrightarrow{\tau} (T' \, after \, l \parallel P) \parallel (T' \, after \, r \parallel P).}$$

Process $a\text{-}if\text{-}b(p)$ will repeatedly perform an action a as long as its subprocess p can perform both actions a and b at each step. Process $twice(t, p)$, induced by a *copy* move of the testing process t, produces two copies of the tested process p and runs them in interleaved parallel with the two subtests of t: $t' after \, l$ and $t' after \, r$. The *a-if-b* and *twice* operators as well as many other copying operators cannot be defined in CCS [6].

We think that it is more productive to consider families of calculi where operators have meaning defined by transition rules in some format rather than to consider extensions of calculi with particular operators. This general approach to process calculi is called Transition System Specification (TSS) [8, 7] and it is used in the paper.

The aim in the paper is to investigate four families of process calculi each defined by TSS's in one of the four formats of *implementable* rules. These calculi satisfy the conditions stated above. For each of the formats we propose a natural equivalence and argue that it is the coarsest equivalence which refines trace equivalence and which is a congruence for the format. In other words the proposed equivalence relates exactly those processes which can not be distinguished by the format's contexts (via traces).

Remark. Since we consider possibly diverging processes all main results concern appropriate preorders. The results for the corresponding equivalences can be obtained in a standard way. The proofs of 'coarseness' rely on the following results: (a) refusal simulation and simulation preorders can be characterised, for image-finite processes, by copy+refusal respectively copy testing preorders [16, 15] and (b) refusal trace preorder can be characterised by refusal testing preorder [13, 16].

2 Basic Definitions

These are standard definitions [8, 7, 17] leading to the introduction of Transition System Specifications and labelled transition systems.

Definition 2.1 Let V be an infinite set of variables ranged by $X, X_i, Y, Y_i, \ldots$. A signature Σ is a set of pairs (f, n) where $f \notin V$ and $n \in \mathbb{N}$ is an arity of f. An element $(c, 0)$ of Σ is called a constant symbol. The set of open terms over Σ with variables from V is denoted by $\mathbb{T}(\Sigma, V)$. The set of closed terms is written as $\mathrm{T}(\Sigma)$. $var(t)$ denotes a set of variables appearing in a term t.

Definition 2.2 Let Σ be a signature. A Σ context with n holes $C[X_1, \ldots, X_n]$ is a member of $\mathbb{T}(\Sigma, \{X_1, \ldots, X_n\})$ in which X_i, $1 \leq i \leq n$, occurs only once. If $t_1, \ldots, t_n$ are Σ terms then $C[t_1, \ldots, t_n]$ is a term obtained by substituting X_i by t_i, $1 \leq i \leq n$. A preorder $\sqsubseteq$ on $\mathrm{T}(\Sigma)$ is a precongruence (or substitutive) if for all Σ contexts $C[X]$ we have $t \sqsubseteq t'$ implies $C[t] \sqsubseteq C[t']$.

Definition 2.3 Let Σ be a signature and A be a set of action labels. Expressions of the form $t \xrightarrow{a} t'$ are called transitions and expressions $t \xrightarrow{a}\!\!\!\!\!/\;$ are called notransitions, for $t, t' \in \mathbb{T}(\Sigma, V)$ and $a \in A$. The set of rules over Σ and A consists of all expressions

$$\frac{\phi_1 \ \cdots \ \phi_n \ \psi_1 \ \cdots \ \psi_m}{\phi}$$

where $\phi, \phi_1, \ldots \phi_n$ are transitions and $\psi_1, \ldots, \psi_m$ are notransitions, and $n, m \in \mathbb{N}$. $\phi_1 \ldots \phi_n$ are called the *positive* premises and $\psi_1 \ldots \psi_m$ are the *negative* premises. ϕ is the conclusion. A Transition System Specification or a *calculus* is a triple $P = (\Sigma, A, R)$ with Σ and A as above and R a set of rules over Σ and A.

The purpose of a TSS $P = (\Sigma, A, R)$ is to define a transition relation $\rightarrow_P \subseteq$ $T(\Sigma) \times A \times T(\Sigma)$. The transition relation describes how closed terms over Σ evolve, under actions in A, to other closed terms. Due to the presence of notransitions in the premises it is not obvious whether or not a given TSS P determines a transition relation. An example of P which does not determine a transition relation can be found in [3]. A thorough discussion on the existence of a transition relation *associated* with P, its uniqueness and whether or not it *agrees* with P can be found in [3, 8, 7].

In the rest of the paper we shall only consider those TSS P for which a transition relation associated with P exists and it is the unique transition relation that agrees with P. Hence such TSS P determines a labelled transition system $(T(\Sigma), A, \rightarrow_P)$, where $T(\Sigma)$ is a set of states or processes and $\rightarrow_P \subseteq$ $T(\Sigma) \times A \times T(\Sigma)$ is a transition relation associated with P (henceforth we omit the subscript P). Elements (s, a, s') of $\rightarrow$ are written as $s \xrightarrow{a} s'$.

3 Formats of Rules

At present there is a number of different formats of rules used to define an operational semantics in Plotkin style.

The oldest is the De Simone format [6] which allows rules of the form

$$\frac{\{ X_i \xrightarrow{a_i} X_i' \}_{i \in I}}{f(X_1, \ldots, X_n) \xrightarrow{a} t}$$

where $a_i, a \in A$; $(f, n) \in \Sigma$; $X_1, \ldots, X_n, X_i'$ are distinct variables in V; $I \subseteq \{1, \ldots, n\}$; and t is a Σ open term with variables in $\{Y_1, \ldots, Y_n\}$ defined by $Y_i = X_i'$ if $i \in I$ and $Y_i = X_i$ otherwise.

The GSOS format, due to Bloom, Istrail & Meyer [3], extends the De Simone format. It allows both positive and negative premises as well as multiple use of term variables (called *copying*) in the premises and in the term t in the conclusion. The form is as follows

$$\frac{\{ X_i \xrightarrow{a_{ik}} X_{ik} \}_{i \in I, k \in K_i} \quad \{ X_j \xrightarrow{b_{jl}} \}_{j \in J, l \in L_j}}{f(X_1, \ldots, X_n) \xrightarrow{a} t}$$

where $a_{ik}, b_{jl}, a \in A$; X_i, X_{ik} are all different variables; $I, J \subseteq \{1, \ldots, n\}$; $K_i, L_j \subseteq \mathbb{N}$, for suitable i, j, k, l. The open term t contains at most the variables $X_1, \ldots, X_n, X_{ik}$, for suitable i, k. The use of multiple copies of X_i, $i \in I$, in the premises and in the term t is called *implicit* copying. The use of multiple copies of X_i, $i \notin I$, and X_{ik} in the term t is called *explicit* copying.

Any TSS P in the GSOS format has a number of pleasant properties [3]:

- there exists a transition relation associated with P which agrees with P and which is unique;
- this transition relation is finitely branching;
- bisimulation is a congruence for GSOS calculi.

There are two other formats of rules due to Groote and Vaandrager [8, 7] which are more general than the GSOS format: the pure *tyft/tyxt* and pure *ntyft/ntyxt* formats. The rules in the *tyft/tyxt* format have open terms on the right hand side of transitions in the premises (as opposed to variables as in the GSOS and De Simone formats). The *tyxt* rules have the conclusion of the form $X \xrightarrow{a} t$. The *ntyft/ntyxt* rules are the same as the *tyft/tyxt* rules but also allow notransitions with open terms in the premises. In general it is not obvious whether or not a TSS in the pure *tyft/tyxt* or pure *ntyft/ntyxt* format induces a transition relation. A number of complex conditions, stated in [8, 7, 5], resolve this problem. However, it is not guaranteed that the transition relation, if it exists, is finitely branching, but bisimulation is a congruence for pure *tyft/tyxt* and *ntyft/ntyxt* contexts.

It is no surprise that the testing power of the above formats differs. This is because the rules of different formats use different information about the sub-terms behaviour in order to establish the behaviour of the term on the left in the conclusion. The premises of De Simone rules refer only to the sequential and 'positive' behaviour of terms ($X \xrightarrow{a} X'$). The GSOS rules refer also to the 'negative' behaviour of terms in the premises ($X \xrightarrow{a}\!\!\!\!\!/\,$) and to some local branching behaviour through copying. The *tyft/tyxt* rules, although unable to directly refer to the information about the negative behaviour, can refer to the complete positive, sequential behaviour by using open terms (instead of variables) in the premises. These rules can even refer to some aspects of global behaviour via the *lookahead* facility as described in [8]. Finally, the *ntyft/ntyxt* format refers to both the positive and the negative sequential behaviour and, thanks to lookahead and copying, to the local and global behaviour of terms.

In order to exhibit the different testing power of the above formats the relevant trace congruences induced by these formats are shown below [7]:

format of rules	trace congruence
De Simone format	trace equivalence
GSOS format	ready simulation equivalence
tyft/tyxt format	simulation equivalence
ntyft/ntyxt format	bisimulation

4 Silent Actions and the ISOS Format

Silent actions play an important role in major concurrent calculi like CCS and CSP. In CCS they are used to model the unobservable interaction between concurrent components of processes. In CSP the silent actions are the result of abstraction from the internal behaviour of processes. The formats described in the previous section treat all the actions as essentially visible[1]. Recently a more intuitive and, we think, a more appropriate treatment of silent actions in the rules has been proposed by Bloom [2] and Vaandrager [17]. In order to guarantee that τ keeps its independence of the environment and its internal character they imposed a number of properties concerning the use of τ in the rules of the De Simone and the GSOS formats.

---

[1] However there are special rules provided by the *tyft/tyxt* and *ntyft/ntyxt* formats to give the silent action τ its intended meaning, but the equivalences considered are strong versions of simulation and bisimulation. More seriously as a result of using the rules for τ, the notion of stability, which is central to refusal testing, loses its meaning.

The aim of this section is to find a number of mild restrictions on the GSOS format so that silent actions keep their traditional meaning and weak bisimulation *is* a congruence for the resulting format. Firstly the properties of Bloom and Vaandrager are presented.

Let $P = (\Sigma, A \cup \{\tau\}, R)$ be a GSOS calculus, where $\tau \notin A$, and let $(f, n) \in \Sigma$ and $1 \leq i \leq n$. A function f is said to test its i-th argument if there is a rule in R with the conclusion $f(X_1, \ldots, X_i, \ldots, X_n) \xrightarrow{a} t$ and $X_i \xrightarrow{a_{ik}} X_{ik}$ or $X_j \xrightarrow{c_{jl}}$ in the premises, where $i, j \in \{1, \ldots, n\}$ and $a_{ik}, c_{jl} \in A$.

The parallel operators of CCS and CSP test both their arguments. Also the CCS + and the external choice operator of CSP test both arguments. But the unary prefixing operators $a\cdot$ do not test their arguments because the rules for $a\cdot$ are axioms. For the same reason the internal choice operator of CSP does not test either of its two arguments.

The first property on P, called *non-blocking* in [17], was introduced by Bloom [2]:

♦ *Non-blocking*: for all $(f, n) \in \Sigma$ and each argument i tested by f the set R contains a τ-*rule* (also called a *clearing* rule in [17]), i.e. a rule of the form

$$\frac{X_i \xrightarrow{\tau} X_i'}{f(X_1, \ldots, X_i, \ldots, X_n) \xrightarrow{\tau} f(X_1, \ldots, X_i', \ldots, X_n).}$$

Example 4.1 CCS does not posses the non-blocking property: there are no τ-rules for the operator $+$. If the τ-rules were added to CCS then $+$ would becomes the CSP external choice operator. Other CCS operators, all CSP and TCCS (Testing CCS) [11] operators which test their arguments have the associated τ-rules among their defining rules.

Even when the above defined P is non-blocking one may find other GSOS operators which can distinguish between weak bisimular processes.

Example 4.2 Assume that the non-blocking P contains a unary operator *see-τ* defined by a single GSOS rule:

$$\frac{X \xrightarrow{\tau} X'}{see\text{-}\tau(X) \xrightarrow{a} see\text{-}\tau(X')}$$

It is clear that, for the CCS-like weak bisimular processes $\tau\tau 0$ and $\tau 0$, the processes $see\text{-}\tau(\tau\tau 0)$ and $see\text{-}\tau(\tau 0)$ are not weak bisimular.

As the result Vaandrager proposed in [17] a second property called *redundancy*. Redundancy together with non-blocking deals with the above problems.

The property is defined for the De Simone format extended with the single *stuttering* axiom $X \xrightarrow{*} X$, where $* \notin A \cup \{\tau\}$ is a special action denoting stuttering or idling.

♦ *Redundancy*: for each rule in R which is not a clearing rule, but has $X_i \xrightarrow{\tau} X_i'$ as the premises, there is another rule in R which is exactly the same except that it has $X_i \xrightarrow{*} X_i$ as premises.

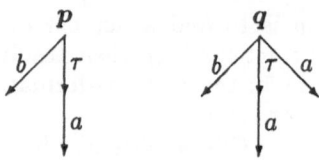

Figure 1.

If P, as described in example 4.1, also satisfies redundancy then apart from the rule for *see-τ* there is also the following rule

$$\frac{X \xrightarrow{*} X}{\textit{see-}\tau(X) \xrightarrow{a} \textit{see-}\tau(X).}$$

Now, since $\tau 0 \xrightarrow{*} \tau 0$, the term $\tau 0$ can perform as many a action as $\tau\tau 0$ can. Hence $\tau 0$ and $\tau\tau 0$ cannot be distinguished by the contexts of such P.

We conjecture that weak bisimulation is a congruence for De Simone calculi satisfying non-blocking and redundancy. However, weak bisimulation is not a congruence for TSS's in the GSOS format satisfying the non-blocking and redundancy properties. The following example describes two operators which are defined by the rules which use two types of implicit copying. These operators can be used to distinguish between weak bisimular processes.

Example 4.3 Let P be a GSOS calculus which satisfies non-blocking and redundancy. Let an unary operator *a-and-b* be in P. *a-and-b* shows, by its trace, whether or not its argument can perform a and b. The rule for *a-and-b* is

$$\frac{X \xrightarrow{a} X' \quad X \xrightarrow{b} X''}{\textit{a-and-b}(X) \xrightarrow{c} 0.}$$

It is easy to check that the context *a-and-b*(X) distinguishes between weak bisimular processes p and q shown in Figure 1. Next consider an unary operators *a-then-b*, *then-b* of P and their defining rules (τ-rules are not shown):

$$\frac{X \xrightarrow{a} X'}{\textit{a-then-b}'(X) \xrightarrow{\tau} \textit{then-b}(X)} \qquad \frac{X \xrightarrow{b} X'}{\textit{then-b}(X) \xrightarrow{c} 0}$$

The right hand side of the conclusion of the rule for *a-then-b* uses X although it evolved to X' as it produced the behaviour of *a-then-b*(X). This implicit copying facility allows *a-then-b* to distinguish between weak bisimular processes p and q in Figure 1.

It is clear from the above example that some forms of implicit copying must be excluded from the GSOS format if weak bisimulation is to be a congruence for GSOS contexts. In [15, 16] we proposed the *Implementable* SOS format (ISOS) for which weak bisimulation is a congruence. The ISOS format is essentially the non-blocking GSOS format which does not allow implicit copying and, instead of the redundancy property, does not allow rules with τ transitions in the premises other than the τ-rules.

Definition 4.4 Let $P = (\Sigma, A \cup \{\tau\}, R)$ be a TSS. A rule in R is called a cr-rule if it has the following form

$$\frac{\{ X_i \xrightarrow{a_i} X_i'\}_{i \in I} \quad \{ X_j \overset{\tau}{\nrightarrow} \overset{b_{jk}}{\nrightarrow}\}_{j \in J, k \in K_j}}{f(X_1, \ldots, X_n) \xrightarrow{a} t}$$

where $a_i, b_{jk} \in A$, $a \in A \cup \{\tau\}$; $(f, n) \in \Sigma$, $X_1, \ldots, X_n, X_i'$ are distinct process variables; $I, J \subseteq \{1, \ldots, n\}$; $K_j \subseteq \mathbb{N}$ for all j. The term t is in $\mathbb{T}(\Sigma, \{Y_1, \ldots, Y_r\})$ where Y_i are defined as in the De Simone format. P is in the ISOS format if R consists of cr-rules and P is non-blocking.

The ISOS format enjoys some useful properties:

♦ weak bisimulation is a congruence for ISOS calculi [15];

♦ intuitive (non-blocking property), natural and simple (no need for redundancy property) treatment of silent action τ;

♦ ISOS rules specify realistically implementable operators: for n subprocesses $X_1, \ldots, X_n$ the cr-rule for f specifies the behaviour of $f(X_1, \ldots, X_n)$ solely in terms of the *observable* behaviour of $X_1, \ldots, X_n$ (X_i performs a_i or X_j refuses b_{jk}); and if copying takes place it is explicit.

There is a slightly more general format of rules than the ISOS format which enjoys also these properties. This more general format is like the ISOS format but also allows some forms of implicit copying. Its rules can have multiple occurrences of process variables on the left in the transitions in the premises, provided that the variables appear in some notransitions in the premises. Moreover, process variables which appear on the left in both transitions and notransitions in the premises can appear in the term t of the conclusion. However, since the effect of the operators of this more general format can be achieved by suitable ISOS contexts [15] the more general format is not considered here.

5 Other Implementable Formats

One easily notices that cr-rules without (explicit) copying and without negative premises are simply De Simone rules. This suggests that apart from the ISOS format and the De Simone format there are two other formats worth considering: ISOS without copying and ISOS without refusals. The following definition makes this precise.

Definition 5.1 Let $P = (\Sigma, A \cup \{\tau\}, R)$ be a TSS. A rule in R is a r-rule if it is a cr-rule without a multiple use of process variables (i.e. without copying). A rule in R is a c-rule if it is a cr-rule without notransitions in the premises (i.e. without refusals). P is in the *Refusal* SOS (RSOS) respectively *Copy* SOS format (CSOS) if P is non-blocking and R consists of r-rules respectively c-rules. The calculus P is an ISOS (CSOS, RSOS or De Simone) calculus if P is in the ISOS (CSOS, RSOS or De Simone) format.

Since the ISOS format is a sub-format of the GSOS format an ISOS calculus induces a labelled transition system in a standard way. However weak equivalences are usually defined over a derived transition system where τ transitions are hidden. Since the premises of ISOS rules refer to both the positive and the negative behaviour it is technically useful to 'label' the derived transition relation with both actions and refusals of actions ($\tilde{a}$). In order to make the results as general as possible a notion of divergence is considered. For example, a constant operator Ω defined by $\Omega \xrightarrow{\tau} \tau\Omega$ has clearly a divergent behaviour. Hence a divergence predicate is incorporated into a derived transition system.

Definition 5.2 Let $(T(\Sigma), A \cup \{\tau\}, \rightarrow)$ be a labelled transition system induced by $P = (\Sigma, A \cup \{\tau\}, R)$. The *observational* transition system with divergence is a structure $(T(\Sigma), \mathsf{RAct}, \Rightarrow, \Uparrow)$ where

- $\mathsf{RAct} \equiv \mathsf{Act} \cup \tilde{A}$, for $\mathsf{Act} \equiv A \cup \{\varepsilon\}$ and $\tilde{A} \equiv \{\tilde{a} \mid a \in A\}$;
- $\Rightarrow \subseteq T(\Sigma) \times \mathsf{RAct} \times T(\Sigma)$ is a *derived* transition relation defined as follows:

  $p \xRightarrow{a} q \equiv p \xrightarrow{\tau^*} \xrightarrow{a} q$

  $p \xRightarrow{\tilde{a}} q \equiv p \xrightarrow{\tau^*} q \xnrightarrow{\tau} \ \& \ q \xnrightarrow{a}$

  $p \xRightarrow{\varepsilon} q \equiv p \xrightarrow{\tau^*} q$;

- $p \Uparrow \equiv p \xrightarrow{\tau^\omega}$.

6 Results

The main purpose of the paper and the aim of this section is to find, for each of the implementable formats defined above, the coarsest preorder which refines trace preorder and which is a congruence for the format. The appropriate equivalences are obtained for these preorders in a standard way.

Given a calculus $P = (\Sigma, A \cup \{\tau\}, R)$ we shall define four process preorders over the observational transition system $(T(\Sigma), \mathsf{RAct}, \Rightarrow, \Uparrow)$.

Definition 6.1 Let $p, q \in T(\Sigma)$ and $\mathsf{L} \in \{\mathsf{Act}, \mathsf{RAct}\}$. Traces, Partial Traces and Generalised Traces are defined as follows

$$
\begin{aligned}
Traces(p, \mathsf{L}) &\equiv \{t \mid t \in \mathsf{L}^* \ \& \ \exists q. \ p \xRightarrow{t} q\} \\
PTraces(p, \mathsf{L}) &\equiv \{t \cdot \mid t \in \mathsf{L}^* \ \& \ \exists q. \ p \xRightarrow{t} q \ \& \ q \Uparrow\} \\
GTraces(p, \mathsf{L}) &\equiv Traces(p, \mathsf{L}) \ \cup \ PTraces(p, \mathsf{L}).
\end{aligned}
$$

An ordering $\leq$ on generalised traces is defined as follows: $t \leq t$ always; $s \cdot \ \leq t$ and $s \cdot \ \leq t \cdot$ if s is a prefix of t.

It is clear that $\leq$ is a partial ordering.

Definition 6.2 Trace preorder $\preccurlyeq_T$ and refusal trace preorder $\preccurlyeq_{RT}$ are defined as follows, where $\sqsubseteq_C$ is the convex ordering:

$$
\begin{aligned}
p \preccurlyeq_T q &\equiv GTraces(p, \mathsf{Act}) \sqsubseteq_C GTraces(q, \mathsf{Act}) \\
p \preccurlyeq_{RT} q &\equiv GTraces(p, \mathsf{RAct}) \sqsubseteq_C GTraces(q, \mathsf{RAct})
\end{aligned}
$$

Next, simulation preorder $\sqsubseteq_S$ and refusal simulation preorder $\sqsubseteq_{RS}$ [16] are introduced in terms of two families of binary relations $\sqsubseteq_L^{n,\mathsf{L}}$, $\sqsubseteq_U^{n,\mathsf{L}}$ where $n \in \mathbb{N}$ and L is as before.

Definition 6.3

$$
p \sqsubseteq_L^{0,\mathsf{L}} q, \ p \sqsubseteq_U^{0,\mathsf{L}} q \quad \text{always} \quad (\text{i.e. } \sqsubseteq_L^{0,\mathsf{L}}, \sqsubseteq_U^{0,\mathsf{L}} = T(\Sigma) \times T(\Sigma))
$$

$$p \mathrel{\underset{L}{\subseteq}}^{n+1,L} q \;\; \equiv \;\; \forall \mu \in L.$$
$$\forall p'. \; p \overset{\mu}{\Rightarrow} p' \text{ implies } \exists q'. \; q \overset{\mu}{\Rightarrow} q' \; \& \; p' \mathrel{\underset{L}{\subseteq}}^{n,L} q'$$

$$p \mathrel{\underset{U}{\subseteq}}^{n+1,L} q \;\; \equiv \;\; \forall \mu \in L. \; p{\Downarrow} \text{ implies}$$
$$q{\Downarrow} \; \&$$
$$\forall q'. \; q \overset{\mu}{\Rightarrow} q' \text{ implies } \exists p'. \; p \overset{\mu}{\Rightarrow} p' \; \& \; p' \mathrel{\underset{U}{\subseteq}}^{n,L} q'$$

$$p \mathrel{\underset{S}{\subseteq}} q \;\; \equiv \;\; \forall n. \; p \mathrel{\underset{L}{\subseteq}}^{n,\text{Act}} q \;\; \& \;\; \forall n. \; p \mathrel{\underset{U}{\subseteq}}^{n,\text{Act}} q$$

$$p \mathrel{\underset{RS}{\subseteq}} q \;\; \equiv \;\; \forall n. \; p \mathrel{\underset{L}{\subseteq}}^{n,\text{RAct}} q \;\; \& \;\; \forall n. \; p \mathrel{\underset{U}{\subseteq}}^{n,\text{RAct}} q$$

It is easy to show that the defined preorders make up the following lattice under a set inclusion, where arrows represent $\subset$

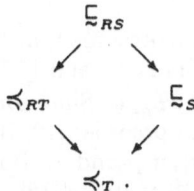

The following is proved in [15].

Theorem 6.4 Refusal simulation preorder $\mathrel{\underset{RS}{\subseteq}}$ is substitutive for any ISOS calculus.

But simulation preorder and refusal trace preorder (and thus trace preorder) are *not* substitutive for ISOS calculi, as can be seen below.

Example 6.5 Consider processes p, q, r, s in Figure 2. Clearly p and q are simulation equivalent. But an ISOS operator *ref-b* (which is also a RSOS operator), defined by the rules

$$\frac{X \overset{\tau}{\nrightarrow} \overset{b}{\nrightarrow}}{\textit{ref-b}(X) \overset{a}{\rightarrow} 0} \qquad \frac{X \overset{\tau}{\rightarrow} X'}{\textit{ref-b}(X) \overset{\tau}{\rightarrow} \textit{ref-b}(X')}$$

distinguishes between p and q: $\textit{ref-b}(p) \overset{a}{\Rightarrow}$ but $\textit{ref-b}(q) \overset{a}{\nRightarrow}$. Processes r and s are refusal trace equivalent. Process s has the following property: it can perform a after which it can perform bc and bd. On the other hand r does not have this property. Since the property can be encoded by an ISOS context $\pi(X)$ (also a CSOS context) defined below it is clear that refusal trace preorder is not substitutive for ISOS calculi.

$$\frac{X \overset{a}{\rightarrow} X'}{\pi(X) \overset{\tau}{\rightarrow} \pi'(X', X')} \qquad \frac{X \overset{b}{\rightarrow} X' \; Y \overset{b}{\rightarrow} Y'}{\pi'(X, Y) \overset{\tau}{\rightarrow} \pi''(X', Y')} \qquad \frac{X \overset{c}{\rightarrow} X' \; Y \overset{d}{\rightarrow} Y'}{\pi'(X, Y) \overset{e}{\rightarrow} 0}$$

Theorem 6.6 Let P be an ISOS calculus such that the observational transition system for P is image-finite. Then refusal simulation preorder is the coarsest substitutive preorder which refines trace preorder.

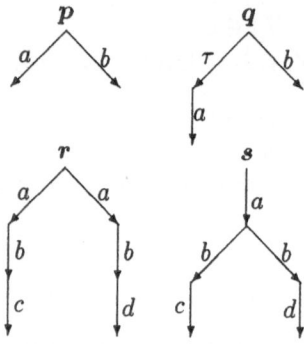

Figure 2.

Proof. A proof by contradiction. Assume that there exists a preorder $\sqsubseteq$ which is ISOS substitutive and it refines $\preccurlyeq_T$ and $\sqsubseteq \not\sqsubseteq \sqsubseteq_{RS}$. Hence there are terms $p, q \in T(\Sigma)$ such that $p \sqsubseteq q$ and $p \not\sqsubseteq_{RS} q$. Since for image-finite processes $\sqsubseteq_{RS}$ coincides with copy+refusal testing preorder [12, 16], then there is a copy+refusal test t which distinguishes between p and q. But copy+refusal testing can be mimicked, via traces, by the ISOS contexts [16]. So there is a particular context $test(t^*, X)$ such that $test(t^*, p) \not\preccurlyeq_T test(t^*, q)$. Hence $test(t^*, p) \not\sqsubseteq test(t^*, q)$ which contradicts the assumption that $\sqsubseteq$ is ISOS substitutive.

Next we shall consider the CSOS format. The CSOS rules, c-rules, are cr-rules but without refusals. Due to the presence of copying, which allows to capture the local branching behaviour, the CSOS congruence has a character of simulation.

Theorem 6.7 Simulation preorder $\sqsubseteq_S$ is substitutive for any CSOS calculus.

The proof is very similar to the proof of Theorem 6.4. Firstly we define a binary relation $S \subseteq T(\Sigma) \times T(\Sigma)$ as the smallest relation which contains $\sqsubseteq_S$ and which is substitutive for CSOS contexts. Then we show that S is a simulation.

Theorem 6.8 Let P be an CSOS calculus such that the observational transition system for P is image-finite. Then simulation preorder is the coarsest substitutive preorder which refines trace preorder.

The proof is similar to that of Theorem 6.6.

r-rules of the RSOS format are essentially cr-rules but without copying. Another way of describing r-rules is that they are De Simone rules with extra refusals in the premises. The results for the De Simone format in [17] suggest that the coarsest equivalence for the RSOS format which refines trace equivalence is among trace-like equivalences. It is not the trace equivalence generated by $\preccurlyeq_T$: processes p and q in Figure 2 are trace equivalent but not RSOS congruent.

Theorem 6.9 Refusal trace preorder $\preccurlyeq_{RT}$ is substitutive for any RSOS calculus.

The proof involves defining two simulation-like relations which are shown to coincide with the lower and upper parts of refusal trace preorder. Using these relations one proceeds as in the proof of Theorem 6.4. The details can be found in [16].

Theorem 6.10 Let P be an RSOS calculus. Then refusal trace preorder is the coarsest substitutive preorder which refines trace preorder.

The proof is similar to that of Theorem 6.6. Lastly we have a restricted version of Theorem 6.9.

Theorem 6.11 Trace preorder $\preccurlyeq_T$ is substitutive for any De Simone calculi.

Acknowledgements

I would like to thank Iain Phillips for many discussions on the subject. Many thanks to Sarah Liebert, Mark Harman and Zvi Shreiber for comments and suggestions. The work reported here was strongly influenced by the work of Bard Bloom and Frits Vaandrager. Thanks to my former colleagues at Imperial College for inviting me to the Workshop.

References

[1] S. Abramsky. Observation equivalence as a testing equivalence. *Theoretical Computer Science*, 53, 1987.

[2] B. Bloom. Strong process equivalence in the presence of hidden moves. Preliminary report, MIT, 1990.

[3] B. Bloom, S. Istrail, and A.R. Meyer. Bisimulation can't be traced: preliminary report. In *Conference Record of the 15th ACM Symposium on Principles of Programming Languages*, San Diego, California, 1988.

[4] B. Bloom, S. Istrail, and A.R. Meyer. Bisimulation can't be traced. Technical report, MIT, 1992.

[5] R.N. Bol and J.F. Groote. The meaning of negative premises in transition system specifications. Technical Report CS-9054, CWI, 1990.

[6] R. de Simone. Higher-level synchronising devices in MEIJE-SCCS. *Theoretical Computer Science*, 37, 1985.

[7] J.F. Groote. Transition system specifications with negative premises. Technical Report CS-8950, CWI, 1989. An extended abstract appeared in J.C.M. Baeten and J.W. Klop, editors, *Proceedings of Concur90*, Amsterdam, LNCS 458, pages 332-341. Springer-Verlag, 1990.

[8] J.F. Groote and F. Vaandrager. Structured operational semantics and bisimulation as a congruence. Technical Report CS-8845, CWI, 1988. An extended abstract appeared in G. Ausiello and M. Dezani-Ciancaglini, and S. Ronchi Della Rocca, editors, *Proceedings ICALP, 89*, Stresa, LNCS 372, pages 423-438. Springer-Verlag, 1989.

[9] C.A.R. Hoare. *Communicating Sequential Processes*. Prentice Hall International, 1985.

[10] R. Milner. *Communication and Concurrency*. Prentice Hall International, 1989.

[11] R. De Nicola and M. Hennessy. CCS without τ's. In H. Ehrig, R. Kowalski, G. Levi, and U. Montanari, editors, *TAPSOFT '87*, Berlin, 1987. Springer-Verlag. LNCS 250.

[12] I. Phillips. Copy testing. Unpublished manuscript, 1985.

[13] I. Phillips. Refusal testing. *Theoretical Computer Science*, 50, 1987.

[14] I. Phillips. CCS with broadcast stability. Technical report, Imperial College, 1988.

[15] I. Ulidowski. *Local Testing and Implementable Concurrent Processes*. Forthcoming PhD thesis, Imperial College, University of London.

[16] I. Ulidowski. Equivalences on observable processes. In *Proceedings of 7th Annual IEEE Symposium on Logic in Computer Science*, Santa Cruz, California, 1992.

[17] F.W. Vaandrager. On the relationship between process algebra and input/output automata. In *Proceedings of 6th Annual IEEE Symposium on Logic in Computer Science*, Amsterdam, The Netherlands, 1991.

Author Index

Published in 1990–92

AI and Cognitive Science '89, Dublin City
University, Eire, 14–15 September 1989
A. F. Smeaton and G. McDermott (Eds.)

**Specification and Verification of Concurrent
Systems,** University of Stirling, Scotland,
6–8 July 1988
C. Rattray (Ed.)

Semantics for Concurrency, Proceedings of the
International BCS-FACS Workshop, Sponsored
by Logic for IT (S.E.R.C.), University of
Leicester, UK, 23–25 July 1990
M. Z. Kwiatkowska, M. W. Shields and
R. M. Thomas (Eds.)

Functional Programming, Glasgow 1989
Proceedings of the 1989 Glasgow Workshop,
Fraserburgh, Scotland, 21–23 August 1989
K. Davis and J. Hughes (Eds.)

Persistent Object Systems, Proceedings of the
Third International Workshop, Newcastle,
Australia, 10–13 January 1989
J. Rosenberg and D. Koch (Eds.)

Z User Workshop, Oxford 1989, Proceedings of
the Fourth Annual Z User Meeting, Oxford,
15 December 1989
J. E. Nicholls (Ed.)

**Formal Methods for Trustworthy Computer
Systems (FM89),** Halifax, Canada,
23–27 July 1989
Dan Craigen (Editor) and Karen Summerskill
(Assistant Editor)

Security and Persistence, Proceedings of the
International Workshop on Computer
Architecture to Support Security and Persistence
of Information, Bremen, West Germany,
8–11 May 1990
John Rosenberg and J. Leslie Keedy (Eds.)

**Women into Computing: Selected Papers
1988–1990**
Gillian Lovegrove and Barbara Segal (Eds.)

3rd Refinement Workshop (organised by
BCS-FACS, and sponsored by IBM UK
Laboratories, Hursley Park and the Programming
Research Group, University of Oxford),
Hursley Park, 9–11 January 1990
Carroll Morgan and J. C. P. Woodcock (Eds.)

Designing Correct Circuits, Workshop jointly
organised by the Universities of Oxford and
Glasgow, Oxford, 26–28 September 1990
Geraint Jones and Mary Sheeran (Eds.)

Functional Programming, Glasgow 1990
Proceedings of the 1990 Glasgow Workshop on
Functional Programming, Ullapool, Scotland,
13–15 August 1990
Simon L. Peyton Jones, Graham Hutton and
Carsten Kehler Holst (Eds.)

4th Refinement Workshop, Proceedings of the
4th Refinement Workshop, organised by BCS-
FACS, Cambridge, 9–11 January 1991
Joseph M. Morris and Roger C. Shaw (Eds.)

AI and Cognitive Science '90, University of
Ulster at Jordanstown, 20–21 September 1990
Michael F. McTear and Norman Creaney (Eds.)

Software Re-use, Utrecht 1989, Proceedings of
the Software Re-use Workshop, Utrecht,
The Netherlands, 23–24 November 1989
Liesbeth Dusink and Patrick Hall (Eds.)

Z User Workshop, 1990, Proceedings of the Fifth
Annual Z User Meeting, Oxford,
17–18 December 1990
J.E. Nicholls (Ed.)

IV Higher Order Workshop, Banff 1990
Proceedings of the IV Higher Order Workshop,
Banff, Alberta, Canada, 10–14 September 1990
Graham Birtwistle (Ed.)

ALPUK91, Proceedings of the 3rd UK
Annual Conference on Logic Programming,
Edinburgh, 10–12 April 1991
Geraint A. Wiggins, Chris Mellish and
Tim Duncan (Eds.)

Specifications of Database Systems
International Workshop on Specifications of
Database Systems, Glasgow, 3–5 July 1991
David J. Harper and Moira C. Norrie (Eds.)

**7th UK Computer and Telecommunications
Performance Engineering Workshop**
Edinburgh, 22–23 July 1991
J. Hillston, P.J.B. King and R.J. Pooley (Eds.)

Logic Program Synthesis and Transformation
Proceedings of LOPSTR 91, International
Workshop on Logic Program Synthesis and
Transformation, University of Manchester,
4–5 July 1991
T.P. Clement and K.-K. Lau (Eds.)

Declarative Programming, Sasbachwalden 1991
PHOENIX Seminar and Workshop on Declarative
Programming, Sasbachwalden, Black Forest,
Germany, 18–22 November 1991
John Darlington and Roland Dietrich (Eds.)